Six Screenplays
by
Robert Riskin

Six Screenplays by Robert Riskin

Edited and Introduced by

Pat McGilligan

UNIVERSITY OF CALIFORNIA PRESS

Berkeley Los Angeles London

University of California Press
Berkeley and Los Angeles, California

University of California Press
London, England

Library of Congress Cataloging-in-Publication Data

Riskin, Robert.
Six screenplays / by Robert Riskin ; edited and introduced by Pat McGilligan.
p. cm.
Includes bibliographical references.
ISBN 0–520–20305–4 (c : alk. paper). — ISBN 0–520–20525–1 (p : alk. paper)
1. Motion picture plays. I. McGilligan, Patrick. II. Title.
PN1997.A1R52 1997
791.43′75—dc20 96–34595
CIP

Printed in the United States of America

1 2 3 4 5 6 7 8 9

The paper used in this publication meets the minimum requirements of American National Standard for Information Sciences—Permanence of Paper for Printed Library Materials, ANSI Z39.48-1984

for Fay Wray

Contents

A Note on Sources

Only one of the six scripts in this volume has been previously published according to the screenwriter's specifications. The other five have been painstakingly reconstructed by comparing Robert Riskin's script drafts available from the Fay Wray collection in the Cinema-Television Library at the University of Southern California, the Frank Capra collection in the Cinema Archives at Wesleyan University, dialogue transcripts originally provided for censorship review as maintained by the New York State Archives, and all extant and obtainable theatrical and video versions of the films.

Riskin himself carefully reviewed and polished the script of *It Happened One Night* that was published in *Twenty Best Film Plays* (ed. John Gassner, Crown, 1943), and it can be observed, from reading that authorized version, that Riskin customarily made changes from the final draft of the script into what might be called the final shooting script. He tended to minimize camera instructions, clarify transitions, and include last-minute changes that arose on the set, while preserving favorite snippets of scenes later left on the cutting-room floor. Interestingly, Riskin divided the authorized version of the *It Happened One Night* script into "parts" or what might otherwise be termed "acts."

Riskin never had the same occasion or opportunity to publish the scripts of *Platinum Blonde, American Madness, Mr. Deeds Goes to Town, Lost Horizon,* or *Meet John Doe,* so we have tried to do our best, taking the example of *It Happened One Night* as a guide to his intentions.

Platinum Blonde and *American Madness* were both "reconstructed" from undated script drafts. It is apparent from these drafts that Riskin worked less and less in terms of camera movement and angles as his career progressed (obviously after having discussed many of the scenes with Frank Capra beforehand and trusting him as director). As much as possible, we have retained the original language of these scripts—including camera movement, descriptions of characters and settings, blocking and atmospheric touches—without overly straying from the film as it exists today. At times we made a decision as Riskin might have, to keep pieces of scenes that fell, inadvertently or by necessity, by the wayside. Other times, for the sake of authenticity, we have preserved camera directions that Capra obviously overruled, if they do not conflict too greatly with the finished result.

Mr. Deeds Goes to Town and *Lost Horizon* were both "reconstructed" from dated final drafts. The final draft of *Mr. Deeds Goes to Town* is marked 10 December 1935, and *Lost Horizon* is dated 23 March 1936. Most of the emendations for these two scripts (many more in the case of *Lost Horizon* than *Mr. Deeds*) came with respect to dialogue, but where the staging turned out to be somewhat different, again we made a decision whether it was a difference that made a difference—and whether to reflect these changes in the script. In some, mostly minor instances, going back to the example of *It Happened One Night,* we chose to stick with Riskin's original language even if what transpired in his script diverged slightly from the action or dialogue in the finished film.

Meet John Doe presented the trickiest problem. Two versions of this script have already been published since the film is in public domain. One, in *Best American Screenplays* (ed. Sam Thomas, Crown, 1986), which has a foreword by Frank Capra, is approximately identical to the final draft deposited among Riskin's and Capra's papers. In his book devoted to the script and analysis of *Meet John Doe* (Rutgers University Press, 1989), editor Charles Wolfe "reconstructs" the script otherwise—with more meticulous descriptions of the images and itemizing the shots with an attention to individual camera moves that would have made Riskin wince. Speaking of the final draft version, Wolfe wrote, "Students and scholars should keep in mind that it [the 1986 script version] is neither an accurate shooting script *nor* an accurate continuity script."

Despite its value as an educational resource, Wolfe's book stints on Riskin's contribution. (Capra's name is emblazoned on the cover; Riskin's is not mentioned.) Our version of *Meet John Doe* upholds as much of Riskin's language as possible while adhering to the dialogue transcript in order to accurately convey a final form that the screenwriter himself might have approved.—P. M.

ACKNOWLEDGMENTS

Platinum Blonde is published with cooperation of Peter Swerling on behalf of the Jo Swerling Estate.

It Happened One Night is published with kind permission of the Samuel Hopkins Adams Estate.

Mr. Deeds Goes to Town is published with kind permission of the Clarence Budington Kelland Estate.

Lost Horizon is published with kind permission of the James Hilton Estate.

Special thanks to Michael Hodgson, Nat Segaloff, Ned Comstock at USC, Leith G. Johnson at Wesleyan, Su Lesser and Tracy Fabrick in Licensing at Columbia/Sony, J. D. Brown, for diligent editing, and Ernest Callenbach of the UC Press, who gave the green light.

Photographs are courtesy of the Academy of Motion Picture Arts and Sciences, the University of Southern California Cinema-Television Archives (the Fay Wray/Robert Riskin collection), and the Cinema Archives, Wesleyan University (the Frank Capra collection).

Continuity transcripts were furnished through the gracious cooperation of William A. Evans, New York State Archives, Cultural Education Center.

Authorized permission to publish this collection of screenplays was granted by Fay Wray, Frank Capra, and Columbia Pictures (Sony Pictures Entertainment).

Introduction

Pat McGilligan

Robert Riskin, a towering figure among screenwriters, has cast a long shadow. One of the exemplars of the early sound era, Riskin produced, in a career interrupted by patriotic duty and abbreviated by tragedy, as consistent, entertaining, thoughtful, and enduring a body of work as anyone writing under contract in Hollywood during the 1930s and 1940s.

Details about his life are difficult to obtain. A reticent man, he did not enjoy interviews for press purposes ("he doesn't talk about himself without considerable prodding"),[1] and the handful he gave were noticeably brief and pointed, or kidding. For the most part Riskin let his films speak for him. Today, sixty years after they were made and forty years after his death, these films continue to speak for him, always in an enjoyable way, and sometimes with eloquence. This book collects for the first time six of the best vintage Riskin scripts: *Platinum Blonde* (1931), *American Madness* (1932), *It Happened One Night* (1934), *Mr. Deeds Goes to Town* (1936), *Lost Horizon* (1937), and *Meet John Doe* (1941).

These six films were directed by Frank Capra. Riskin worked with other directors on some appealing films, and on some merely intriguing ones, but he spent most of his career teamed with Capra. He is listed, in one way or another, in the credits of thirteen Capra films. Capra was certainly "the name above the title," but Riskin was the man who provided the story or the script, without which there would have been nothing *but* a title. These six scripts represent the heyday of Riskin's and Capra's remarkable collaboration.

*   *   *

1. "Variations on a Theme," *New York American,* April 4, 1937.

The small number of articles and publicity handouts about Riskin show how much his life resembled one of his scripts.[2] Riskin, like one of his cocky lead characters, was a self-made man, and his magical transformation was finalized, in Cinderella-man fashion, in Hollywood. He didn't spring from an Ivy League network, wasn't weaned in the big city newsrooms that spawned so many film writers (although he hung around newsrooms, and picked up pointers). His theater experience included some writing and was important to his development, but he was first known more as a producer of modest, even forgettable, plays. Although his show business background prior to his coming to Hollywood was diverse and unusual, no one could have predicted that he would blossom as a scriptwriter and become, almost directly upon entering the industry in 1930, one of the paragons of the profession.

Riskin was born in the Jewish ghetto of the Lower East Side in New York City on March 30, 1897—the same year, as it happens, that Capra was born in Sicily, Italy. He was one of five children of immigrant parents, Bessie and Jakob, who had left Russia to escape conscription in the czar's army. He and his two brothers (Everett and Murray) and two sisters (Essie and Rose) grew up speaking Yiddish. Articles recounting his boyhood depict a precocious child fond of making up stories and telling jokes, who moved with his family as his parents shuttled between jobs in Baltimore and Philadelphia, eventually landing in Brooklyn.

Actress Fay Wray, known best for her role as the beautiful lady held squirming and screaming in King Kong's paw, was married to Riskin between 1942 and 1955, and she has described his upbringing in an unpublished biographical essay:

> The father and grandfather spent much time discussing philosophy; the mother treated life with a touch of humor. These influences enriched the lives of the young Riskins and compensated for the very modest financial circumstances of their early years.
>
> Even as a youngster, writing appeared to be a natural expression for him. On one occasion, when he and some friends amassed, collectively, the

2. My principal source for Riskin's story in the years leading up to his arrival in Hollywood is "Biography of Robert Riskin as Screen Writer" by Fay Wray, dated September 5, 1979. The manuscript is held in the Fay Wray collection, which includes the Riskin papers, at the University of Southern California. In addition, I have cited material from Fay Wray's autobiography, *On the Other Hand: A Life Story* (St. Martin's Press, 1989), which contains loving passages about Riskin, and I have also relied heavily on my own interview with her.

amount of $1.93 to take a trip to Coney Island, he returned home to compose a poem entitled, significantly, 'A Dollar Ninety-Three.'"[3]

In *Frank Capra: The Catastrophe of Success,* his provocative biography of Frank Capra, Joseph McBride wrote that Riskin was "short and streetwise," wielding his "satirical tongue as a self-defense against the Irish boys who tormented him and against the equally combative Italians who lived in the adjoining neighborhood."[4] As a youth Riskin snuck into neighborhood theaters in Flatbush and copied down the jokes of vaudevillians. Like his older brother Everett, he earned pocket money selling the *Saturday Evening Post* on streetcars.

He could not afford even to dream of college and, in fact, dropped out of school after eighth grade to work as an office boy in a textile firm. At fifteen, he was secretary to the boss, a certain Joe Golden. Golden noticed Riskin's furtive attempts at writing short stories and rhyme (Riskin was a lifelong dabbler at short fiction and poetry) and asked the young man to ghost a love letter. When the love letter failed its desired objective, Riskin was summarily fired.

His next job was as office boy and secretary for two shirt makers named Heidenheim and Levy, Jewish immigrants who spoke mangled English. Heidenheim and Levy had invested in silent comedy shorts that were being produced on a flea-sized budget in Florida; they hoped the short films would be distributed by Famous Players–Lasky. Because Riskin was always cracking jokes, the shirt manufacturers asked his opinion of the one- and two-reel comedies. Riskin's brash verdict was that they "stank." "A moron could write better, a blind man could direct better, and as far as the acting is concerned, I could be funnier," he is alleged to have declared.[5]

When Famous Players–Lasky rejected the films, Riskin's extreme opinion was suddenly validated, and the shirt makers decided to form a new production unit with Riskin as executive producer. They sent the office boy—who had shown himself to be bright and capable, yet who had as much con artist in his blood as, say, Peter Warne in *It Happened One Night*—to Jacksonville, Florida. There he headed up a small company of people and organized a studio operation while supervising production of a series of family comedies dubbed "Klever Komedies."

3. Wray, "Biography of Robert Riskin as Screen Writer."
4. Joseph McBride, *Frank Capra: The Catastrophe of Success* (Simon & Schuster, 1992), p. 234. McBride's heavily researched book provides an indispensable counterpoint to Frank Capra's autobiography.
5. Jerry D. Lewis, "Top Story Man," *Collier's,* March 29, 1941.

Riskin's immersion into the motion picture field came earlier than Frank Capra's, who roughly at the same time that Riskin was producing "Klever Komedies" was majoring in chemical engineering at Throop College of Technology in Pasadena. Riskin had no prior experience. He was only seventeen years old. "He knew that he would have to look older than he did in order to command respect," one article recounted, "so he grew a moustache. But there was one spot on his lips where the moustache wouldn't grow, so he darkened it with mascara."[6]

His small motion picture production company was reportedly successful enough at the box office. "Soon they were able to afford for their star Victor Moore [and his wife, Erma Littlefield] of the New York theatre," wrote Fay Wray, "whose particular comedy style, the worried wonderment of the 'little man,' presaged qualities that would be found in Riskin's later film characters."[7]

There is no way of telling how much these early films overlapped Riskin's later work or how good they were. Riskin sometimes wrote, sometimes directed the "Klever Komedies." The stories, according to Fay Wray, were created "off the cuff," progressing as circumstances and opportunity allowed.[8] Riskin showed talent at living life off the cuff, and in time there were approximately 104 of the Riskin-produced comedies, filmed in various locales on the eastern seaboard.

When America entered World War I, Riskin enlisted in the navy. After the Armistice was signed, he returned to New York City, where he had trouble acquiring a fresh toehold. According to published accounts, he took jobs selling linoleum, spark plugs, and teething rings. Some claim that he squeezed in courses at Columbia University. He lived for a time at a poor-man's Friar's Club, the Green Room, a four-story building at 47th and Broadway that catered to theater people. Here he met new friends and wrote some revue material for such up-and-coming performers as Louis Wolhiem, Frank McHugh, and Spencer Tracy.

He and his brother Everett, the only other Riskin family member to be bitten by the show business bug, formed a partnership. The Riskin brothers produced a string of short subjects, called "Facts and Follies," which promoted muscle-building as a way of meeting and marrying the prettiest girls; they also filmed an animated series dubbed "Riskinettes," for which they created puppets made of rubber and activated with air channeled through tubes which were hooked up to a large typewriter with keys.

6. Lewis, "Top Story Man."
7. Wray, "Biography of Robert Riskin as Screen Writer."
8. Wray, "Biography of Robert Riskin as Screen Writer."

These activities passed the time and attracted some attention, but being New Yorkers the Riskins set their eyes on the main prize: Broadway. In 1924 they put up a shingle as theatrical producers. Interestingly, their first plays were written by people other than Riskin himself; his own emergence as a playwright came almost as an afterthought, several years later.

The first Riskin-Riskin production to achieve the status of a *New York Times* review was not a comedy but an agrarian drama with a solemn tyranny-of-the-soil theme. *The Mud Turtle,* written by Elliot Lester, lasted fifty-two performances in 1925. *She Couldn't Say No,* mounted by the Riskins the next year, was an all-out farce featuring seasoned comedienne Florence Moore as a lawyer with falsified credentials. Written by B. M. Kaye, it was destined to prove their longest-running show—seventy-two performances. Also in 1926 came *A Lady in Love,* about a young damsel who must marry a choleric old boor in order to rescue her father from the clutches of a bailiff. The mock-Restoration comedy, written by Dorrance Davis and starring Peggy Wood, limped through seventeen performances. The Riskins produced several other shows that had varying degrees of success, including a revival of *The Bells,* a melodrama that had been made famous by Henry Irving.

One of the plays Riskin and his brother optioned and planned to produce in the mid-1920s was written by John Meehan, the actor, writer, and occasional director, who was affiliated with David Belasco, Florenz Ziegfeld, and George White productions. This play was in the rewriting stage when Meehan and Riskin attended the Dempsey-Sharkey boxing match in the summer of 1927. Going home afterwards, they spotted the tent, uptown, where Uldine Utley, a well-known female evangelist, was preaching. Riskin had a brainstorm, which he revealed to Meehan in the subway: they ought to write a topical play about religious fakery, capitalizing on people like Utley (or the better-known Aimee Semple McPherson). Coincidentally, both had been reading Sinclair Lewis's new novel *Elmer Gantry,* about an ex-football player who shamelessly promotes himself into celebrity evangelist status.

Meehan's play was set aside while they teamed up to work on the idea. The Broadway columnist for the *New York Times,* who knew of Riskin primarily in his capacity as a producer, was skeptical about the novice writing team. "The play, according to gossip," reported the newspaper, "was the notion of R. R. Riskin, one of the two Riskin brothers who have been producing plays hereabouts for several seasons. The job of writing, or most of it, he turned over to John Meehan, an all-around theatrical man who has been playwright, actor and director in his day. More recently [writer-director] George Abbott has been lending a hand."[9] Riskin's first

9. "Woman Evangelist in 'Bless You, Sister,'" *New York Times,* December 27, 1927.

credit as coauthor appeared on the drama that resulted, *Bless You, Sister,* a theme play, decidedly more drama than comedy, about a minister's daughter whose disgust for the pious ways of organized religion leads her into a soul-saving racket. Jointly staged by Meehan and Abbott, *Bless You, Sister* opened in December 1927, starring Alice Brady. It survived twenty-four performances.

The gap in prominent credits between 1927 and 1930 indicates that Riskin had found his niche and was devoting more time to his writing. He was comfortable with collaboration from the beginning, a trait that was to serve him well in Hollywood. In 1928–1929, he teamed up with Edith Fitzgerald, his companion of the time (sometimes erroneously reported in contemporary accounts as his wife). Their first play was optioned but not produced, but their next, *Many a Slip,* proved to be their springboard.

Many a Slip, Riskin's first genuine comedy, is about a newspaperman tricked into marriage by a girlfriend who fakes a pregnancy. Sylvia Sidney played the lead. Riskin not only co-wrote (Edith Fitzgerald's name appeared first in the alphabetical billing) and co-produced (with brother Everett) but also made his debut as a stage director. Although *Many a Slip* ran only twenty-four performances in early 1930, the nascent Riskin touch was noted by reviewers such as J. Brooks Atkinson, who observed in the *New York Times* that although the humor was "labored and obviously manufactured to snare easy laughs," the play did have "moments when an amusing and observant bit of dialogue causes you to sit up and wonder if what is about to follow will redeem parts of what has gone before."[10]

Riskin turned 33 in 1930, newly established as a playwright and director. No longer a "boy prodigy," he found he was a recognized name—and a hot commodity. Hollywood needed fresh talent, particularly dialogue specialists, to sate the demand generated by the frenzied production of talking pictures. Since the October 6, 1927, premiere of Warner Brothers' first talkie, *The Jazz Singer,* the studios had been frantically switching to sound and scooping up new personnel—especially East Coast actors, directors, and writers—to help the movies learn to speak.

If Riskin needed a nudge, he got one with the sale to Hollywood of two of his plays. *Many a Slip* was purchased by Warner Brothers and adapted by Harvey Thew, sans Riskin's involvement, into *Illicit,* directed by Archie Mayo and starring Barbara Stanwyck, in 1931. *Bless You, Sister* was snapped up by Columbia Pictures. If Riskin needed further impetus, he received it from the stock market crash of October 29, 1929. Riskin was always loose with money, generous with friends, and adventurous at cards, the racetrack, and investments. After losing a

10. "Many A Slip," *New York Times,* February 4, 1930.

good deal of money in the crash, he realized that Broadway was in temporary eclipse. Motion pictures presented an opportunity to steady his income.

Riskin and Fitzgerald were both invited to Hollywood in 1930. (Meehan was another who wound up in Hollywood as a scriptwriter.) Here their paths and devotion to each other diverged. Fitzgerald stayed around for a time, accumulating minor credits, before she went back to New York and resumed her career as a playwright.

When Riskin went west, his older brother Everett tagged along. Both signed on at Columbia Pictures. One brother settled down to scriptwriting, the other became a staff producer. Everett Riskin eventually specialized in tasteful, top-of-the-line comedies for Columbia including *She Married Her Boss* (1935), *Theodora Goes Wild* (1936), *The Awful Truth* (1937), *Holiday* (1938), and *Here Comes Mr. Jordan* (1941). Later he worked as a producer at MGM, producing such memorable films as *A Guy Named Joe* (1943) and *Kismet* (1944), and one of his brother's few wartime credits, *The Thin Man Goes Home* (1944).

* * *

The story is told—like some other stories about Riskin, it may be too good to be true—that shortly after the writer arrived at Columbia he and other writers still in their novitiate were ushered into a story conference. People in the room were discussing a screen property already well along in the stages of preproduction. Riskin barely noticed a short, swarthy man wearing a dark sweater sitting quietly in a corner until the man got up and began to wax effusive over the film's scenario. With a start, Riskin realized it was *Bless You, Sister* that the short, swarthy man—who turned out to be Frank Capra—was extolling.

Riskin's first impression of Capra was that "he looked like a mug" and told a story "badly."[11] When called upon for his assessment of the script, Riskin went into his well-worn "It stinks!" routine. He wondered aloud why anyone would be so foolhardy as to make a film based on his flop play, which could never hope to turn much of a profit and would only serve to generate unwelcome controversy. "My brother and I were stupid enough to produce it on Broadway," Riskin (allegedly) declared. "It cost us almost every cent we had. If you intend to make a picture out of it, it proves only one thing: You're even more stupid than we were."[12]

By 1930 Frank Capra was already a figure with some prestige in Hollywood. After a long apprenticeship as a gag writer with Hal Roach and Mack Sennett, he had moved on to become the director of noteworthy Harold Lloyd features for First

11. McBride, *Frank Capra,* p. 227.
12 Lewis, "Top Story Man."

National (including *Tramp, Tramp, Tramp, The Strong Man,* and *Long Pants*). Capra had been at Columbia since 1928 and had already put together the superb technical unit (notably, cameraman Joseph Walker and editor Gene Havlik) that would help shape even greater successes to come.

Columbia was known at this time as a "Poverty Row" studio—its specialties included short subjects, low-budget serials, and "B" programmers (short films that filled out a program)—but its poverty has always been exaggerated. The man who ran Columbia, Harry Cohn, liked to talk poor, yet he had an "eagerness to win respectability" and he habitually "committed the studio to expensive projects which, in turn, meant higher salaries for everyone involved."[13] Capra, Columbia's most respected director, was one of the expensive jewels in Cohn's crown, though the director had not yet connected with audiences to the point where each and every one of his motion pictures was guaranteed to be a hit.

His themes and subject matter, and the quality of his films, varied markedly. People passionately argue the genealogy of Capra's thematic ideas (for example, did the public "confession" of his film's heroes originate with Capra or Riskin?), but there can be no question that, in 1930, Capra had not yet found his stride; the word "Capraesque" had not yet been coined.

Riskin's glib prophecy about *Bless You, Sister* was correct. Retitled *The Miracle Woman,* Riskin's play was intelligently adapted by Jo Swerling, who kept the original writer's "terse, colloquial, witty dialogue largely intact" while "closely following his briskly paced story construction."[14] But when the film was released in the summer of 1931, it turned out to be one of Capra's less memorable efforts, one of the flops and setbacks of his early career.

The self-deprecating writer had made an impression on Harry Cohn and on Frank Capra. "Perhaps the audacity and integrity of Riskin declaiming against his own work was what interested Capra," Fay Wray noted. "More than likely, it was also a personal quality. Riskin had the easy assurance of self-respect. His sense of humor was subtle and sure. Wit and timing enhanced his style of speaking as well as his writing."[15]

Riskin also made an impression on a colleague: Jo Swerling. Swerling was a slightly more experienced writer among the newly arrived droves from the East, "a squat, heavy-set, seething young man, furiously chain-smoking strong White

13. Bernard F. Dick, *The Merchant Prince of Poverty Row* (University Press of Kentucky, 1993), p. 52.

14. McBride, *Frank Capra,* p. 228.

15. Wray, "Biography of Robert Riskin as Screen Writer."

Owl cigars—which he carried loose in his pockets," according to Capra. "His thick glasses so enlarged his watery blue eyes he looked like a mad white owl himself. One got the odd impression the cigar was smoking the man."[16]

A onetime comic-strip artist, an ex-newspaperman, and a former playwright, Swerling was a kindred spirit. He and Riskin had similar personalities and political leanings (like Riskin's, Swerling's Jewish family had fled czarist Russia). During his career Swerling would write for Capra almost as often as did Riskin; Swerling was one of the principal architects of the Christmas classic, *It's a Wonderful Life* (1946). Under the Columbia umbrella, Riskin and Swerling became best of friends, shared credit on several films, and unofficially consulted with each other about whatever the other was working on.

* * *

One of Riskin's first jobs, in early 1931, was to concoct some flavorful dialogue for Capra's film *Platinum Blonde,* one of the earliest of the scoundrels-of-the-press cycle of which Hecht-MacArthur's *The Front Page* was the archetype.

The script was a product of the studio assembly line. The original story was formulated by New York City newspaperman Douglas W. Churchill and Columbia contract writer Harry Chandlee (a journeyman scenarist who went on to win an Academy Award nomination for his contribution to *Sergeant York* in 1941). Dorothy Howell drafted an adaptation,[17] and Swerling inherited the main scriptwriting chores.

It is unclear whether Capra had anything to do with Riskin's assignment. Probably it was Swerling who recommended his self-assured new friend as the right person to work over the dialogue scenes. McBride made it clear that the shooting script of *Platinum Blonde* was completed before the director put in a single day of work (even then, according to McBride, Capra made only "a few minor pencil changes").[18]

16. Frank Capra, *Frank Capra: The Name Above the Title* (Macmillan, 1971), p. 114.

17. Columbia story editor Dorothy Howell was a regular scenarist for Capra and Columbia beginning with the 1928 silent *Say It With Sables* and including credits on the Capra-directed *Submarine* (1928), *The Donovan Affair* (1929), *Rain or Shine* (1930), and *Dirigible* (1931), and as Jo Swerling's collaborator on *The Miracle Woman. Platinum Blonde* was, in a sense, a passing-of-the-torch: thereafter Howell disappeared from the credits of Capra's films, and Riskin emerged as his main collaborator.

18. McBride, *Frank Capra,* p. 232.

In any case, the project was right for Riskin, and Riskin was right for Capra. The newsroom setting, with the hard-boiled male reporter and plucky female reporter, was pervasive in the literature of that era and, especially, in Hollywood, where it served as a respectable blind for sex, violence, and vernacular. Riskin had already shown with *Many a Slip* that he was familiar with the swaggering reporter as a hollow hero. The writer had no practical newspaper background, but he showed a special familiarity and fondness for that world in his scripts, and he often went to lengths to incorporate newspaper types. (In *Mr. Deeds Goes to Town* he gave the press agent played by Lionel Stander, whose character is a lowlife thug in the original published story, a checkered past as a reporter.)

The cynical reporter of *Platinum Blonde,* Stew Smith, is also a frustrated playwright who carries a Joseph Conrad novel around for inspiration—and who doesn't take adequate notice of a patient, heart-of-gold "sob sister" named Gallagher, who is hopelessly in love with him. He is too busy being smitten by a rich and snobby socialite, Anne Schuyler. The reporter's job is to write up the family's most recent scandal; the snob's mission is to reform the wise-cracking reporter, to make a gentleman out of a tramp.

When Stew Smith marries Anne Schuyler, he becomes a "cinderella man," in Riskin parlance, a common man anointed by wealth and fame who doesn't feel quite at ease in his fairy-tale surroundings—and that is when the fun begins. This theme became the subtext of other Riskin scripts, and considering the writer's own humble beginnings, it may have been a deeply felt subtext. Fay Wray remarked when interviewed that Stew Smith seemed to be modeled after Riskin himself, to the point where, watching the film years later, she recognized some of the slang and breezy mannerisms as Riskin's own.

Columbia cast a relative newcomer from Broadway, Robert Williams, as Stew Smith. He played the "rich wife's magnolia" with a winning blend of rough edges and suavity and tenderness. An enormously likable and promising young actor receiving the star buildup, Williams would have had a major career, on the evidence of *Platinum Blonde,* if he had not died abruptly from an emergency operation following appendicitis shortly after the release of the film.

The lovestruck newspaper gal was played by Loretta Young and the socialite by Jean Harlow, in one of the early "blonde bombshell" roles that helped boost her to stardom. But it is really Robert Williams's showcase; the female characters seem bland in comparison with Stew Smith, and the love angle between the reporter and the socialite is not entirely convincing. One romantic scene is especially overlong and dully scripted, and it is not helped by Capra, who photographed it from a discreet distance, gauzily, through a fountain spray.

Although there are gaps in the script, they can be diagnosed from the distance of elapsed time as the patchwork of several drafts and the awkwardness of writers who were in the process of getting to know each other as well as learning the ropes of Hollywood. The dialogue is nevertheless exceedingly clever, and at its best brims with the kind of wise-cracking banter that became Riskin's stock-in-trade. There is wordplay and nonsensical asides, the first of his musicalized scenes (a "garter's duet" between Williams and Harlow), and sudden moments of overwhelming sweetness.

Stew Smith's delayed reaction to Gallagher is worth waiting for—and doesn't come until the fadeout. He has left Anne Schuyler and is rewriting his play with Gallagher's help. As they brainstorm, he realizes she is the character his dumb hero should have fallen for all along. When he finally says as much, she collapses in his arms, sobbing with happiness and relief. He strokes her hair, murmuring, "Aw, what's the matter, Gallagher?"—a beautifully affecting moment.

It is hard to identify each writer's contribution, and Swerling could be just as funny and just as socially alert as Riskin. One of the funniest scenes, however, is a long conversation about "puttering" that was precisely Riskin's sort of thing. This duel of small talk takes place between Stew Smith and a butler (played by Halliwell Hobbes) whose name is a hoity-toity version of Smith: Smythe. Adding to the impression that the scene was Riskin's contribution, the Smith-Smythe pages, like several other sparkling scenes in *Platinum Blonde,* were absent from early drafts and appear only in the shooting script.

```
                    STEW
Smythe, what do you do with yourself - I mean,
when you're not carrying those double-strength -
what do you do with yourself?

                    SMYTHE
Well, sir, I putter.

                    STEW
Smythe! I mean - when you're alone and want to
amuse yourself, then what?

                    SMYTHE
I just putter.

                    STEW
Hmm, you just putter. Do you have to have a put-
ter to putter?

                    SMYTHE
Oh no, sir. I putter with me hands.
```

STEW
Well, isn't that nice? You just go right ahead with your hands. That's all right. How do you do it?

SMYTHE
Well sir, I'll show you.

He demonstrates, touching objects on a table and blowing dust off a lampshade.

SMYTHE
That's puttering, sir.

STEW
No! Well, well, well! That's all right, if you like it. Can anybody do that?

SMYTHE
Oh no, sir. Some people are natural putterers. Others can never master it.

STEW
Oh my. You mean, some people are born and never will become putterers?

SMYTHE
Yes sir.

STEW
Oh my, wouldn't that be tragic? To know that you could never be a putterer.

SMYTHE
Yes sir.

STEW
How about me? Do you think if I concentrated and put my whole soul into it, that some day I might be a putterer?

SMYTHE
You sir? Uh-uh. You could never be a putterer. Not a good putterer, sir.

STEW
Well, if I couldn't be a good putterer, I wouldn't want to putter. But why? What makes you think I couldn't be a good putterer?

SMYTHE
Well sir, to be a putterer, one's mind must be at ease. A person with a problem could never be

```
a putterer. For instance, sir, a fish can putter
in water but not on land because he'd be out of
place. An eagle can putter around a rugged moun-
taintop but not in a cage, because he'd be rest-
less and unhappy. Now sir, if you'll pardon me,
with all respect, as a Smythe to a Smith, you
are an eagle in a cage.

                    STEW
A bird in a gilded cage?

                    SMYTHE
Yes.

                    STEW
That's all I wanted to know!
```

Exquisite minor characters abounded in a Riskin script. Sometimes they were awarded the best lines. With Smith and Smythe, Riskin had fun with a sideshow while, in a nutshell, the scene points out the moral of the film: Stew Smith is a bird in a gilded cage.

Riskin's first assignment proved a tremendous success in 1931, and today *Platinum Blonde* holds up as "a first-rate film, probably the most under-rated of Capra's career."[19]

*   *   *

Riskin was not yet permanently bracketed with Capra. *Platinum Blonde* was part of an early grind of hard work at Columbia that included *Men Are Like That* (adaptation and dialogue, 1931), *Men In Her Life* (adaptation and dialogue, 1931), *The Big Timer* (co-script, 1932, based on a Riskin story), *Shopworn* (co-dialogue with Swerling, 1932), *Night Club Lady* (script, 1932), *Virtue* (script, 1932), and *Ann Carver's Profession* (script from his story, 1933). All these were programmers. In addition, Riskin was credited on *The Ex-Lady* (1933), a Warner Brothers film that was a quick remake of *Illicit.*

Writing so much, and at such a frenetic pace, made Riskin an early convert to the struggle to unionize screenwriters in Hollywood. He was present at the first meetings of the organization in 1933 and was on the initial committee that developed the proposed code of working rules. At first Riskin was identified with the moderate faction, who were low-key in their demands and remained loyal to the

19. McBride, *Frank Capra,* p. 233.

producers; the more assertive scriptwriters wanted to affiliate with the Authors League of America, the established New York–based group that aggressively represented playwrights. When, in 1936, the conservative opposition split off into a hard-line group, the Screen Playwrights, Riskin aligned himself with the liberal majority and threw his energies into the emerging Screen Writers Guild. Thereafter, into the 1940s, he tended to side with the progressive bloc led by writers such as Philip Dunne and Julius Epstein.

No doubt the salad days of the early 1930s were a learning crucible, and Riskin did have things to learn. His first screenplay ran nearly 300 pages and because of its unmanageable length it was rejected by the Columbia story editor. (Length was often a problem for Riskin, and he found whittling down his own long scripts a headache.)

Between studio assignments Riskin labored on an original screenplay, which he was thinking of calling "Faith." Like *Bless You Sister,* "Faith" was inspired by current events, this time the nationwide banking crisis. The American economy was stressed to the breaking point by widespread inflation, unemployment, and poverty. Banks were failing across the country. The studios were suffering unprecedented financial losses, and Hollywood was watching the economic disaster "with great apprehension," as Andrew Bergman noted in his study of the link between Depression America and its films.[20] Some studios responded with hard-hitting "social problem" films. Warner Brothers led the way with desperate hoboes, ruthless gangsters, crusading reporters, even socially themed musicals. Columbia lagged behind.

Riskin's script for "Faith" was an up-to-date national parable, with explicit references to Depression breadlines. It was intentionally stark, not in the least comedic, yet distinctly upbeat, expressing "faith" in the American people's ultimate good character and judgment. The story centers on a heroic bank president, Thomas Dickson (played by Walter Huston), who Riskin based on a composite of banker "Doc" Giannini and his brother A. P. Giannini, the financial wizards of the Bank of America.[21] The Gianninis had a stated policy of granting loans based on character, not equity, a policy not unlike George Bailey's credo in *It's a Wonderful Life.* Indeed, the entire script might be seen as a first draft of that later masterpiece—a Capra film that Riskin did *not* write—from its populist hero who believes

20. Andrew Bergman, We're In the Money: Depression America and Its Films (New York University Press, 1971), p. xx, introduction.

21. It may or may not have been coincidental that the Bank of America was also Columbia's bank, and Giannini a longtime studio board member. The bank was in a precarious state and in need of a public pat on the back.

in the people against corporate interests, right down to the near suicide and the last-minute reprieve from the public.

It was a complicated script with a surfeit of plot threads—a rebellious board, a shaky marriage, a bank robbery, and investor paranoia—all coming together within twenty-four hours on a single set, as in a stage play. Short on Riskin's trademark humor, the script was also short on another of his strengths, romantic scenes, with most of the latter going to two vanilla supporting characters: an assistant bank teller (played by Pat O'Brien) and Dickson's secretary (Constance Cummings). Riskin focused on the main character and the central theme: a bank president who believes so fiercely in people's honesty and goodwill that he refuses to cave in during a bank run.

It was a bold idea, and the bank run builds to a superbly orchestrated montage, a mob scene of terrified investors that was the first of its type in a Capra-Riskin film ("You can't reason with a mob," mutters Thomas Dickson, enunciating one of the motifs of the Capra-Riskin canon). As the investors outside mill in terror, Dickson, alone inside his office, ponders a gun resting in his desk drawer. Abject and broken, his pale face is silhouetted. Dickson feels betrayed. But the real source of his despair is not "the people," because he understands and forgives their fickleness. He has lost faith in his wife, whom he suspects of infidelity. Fortunately, Mrs. Dickson arrives in the nick of time to explain a misunderstanding, small savers flood the bank to shore up the institution, and the ending becomes one of the most moving affirmations of faith depicted in American cinema.

Nobody handled crowd scenes better than Capra, and Walter Huston was not the first or last of his leading men who the director guided to a tour-de-force performance. Not often revived, *American Madness* was important and admired in its time. It was the first of the Capra-Riskin rabble-rousers, the first of their collaborations to venture into political issues and depict a world where "populist heroes fight social wrongs, demonstrating that folksy common sense and immediate action are the only possible cures for an American society groping its way out of the Depression."[22]

Did *American Madness* amount to a populist creed? (Dickson sounds pretty much like a New Dealer—FDR crossed with John Doe—as he spouts monologues extolling the honest Joneses of the world.) Was it somehow a veiled Communist tract? (Dickson is scornful not only of the muckamucks on his board, but of the credibility of police. When the Inspector tells Dickson that his bank teller has a

22. Sam Frank, "Robert Riskin," *Dictionary of Literary Biography,* vol. 26, ed. Robert E. Morsberger, Stephen O. Lesser, and Randall Clark (Gale Research Co., 1984), p. 251.

bank record, Dickson mutters, "What difference does that make? We all have records." It's as subversive a line as any Riskin ever wrote.) Were there fascist instincts at work? (McBride asserted that Capra, who never voted for FDR, was a closet Mussolini admirer.) Or was it, more mysteriously, a product of the Capra-Riskin teamwork, combining two people's ideologies, and their disparate, blended—sometimes even contradictory—tendencies?

* * *

People have fixated on the differences between Capra and Riskin, and Capra usually gets credit for the idealistic politics.

The kind of faith expressed in *American Madness* was "typical of Capra," wrote Andrew Bergman.[23] Raymond Carney felt certain that Capra provided the "heart, sentiment and soaring idealism," while Riskin supplied the "worldly wise smartness and wit [that] counterbalanced Capra's operatic idealism."[24] Leland A. Poague in his book echoed the opinion that in the Capra-Riskin partnership it was the director's populist philosophy that predominated, while "Riskin provided Capra with the extra verbal snap that made their collaborative efforts the great hits that they were."[25]

But Andrew Bergman assigned even the film's inspirational title of "Faith" to the director, whereas, as McBride established, the script was completed by Riskin before Capra put in a single day of work. ("Faith" was retitled *American Madness* after shooting began.) In fact, initial scenes were filmed by the first director Allan Dwan, who was replaced by a second director, Roy William Neil, before Capra was brought in. "Capra followed Riskin's story and dialogue almost to the letter, and he also adhered closely to the screenplay's unusually detailed visual plan," wrote McBride. "Many of what usually are described as directorial 'touches' in *American Madness* actually were the screenwriters'." These included the famous scene of the bank run, which, although generally attributed to Capra, is "fully developed in the script."[26]

Riskin was every bit the soaring idealist, and it is a mistake to underestimate his importance. And it would also be a mistake to underestimate Capra's. They

23. Bergman, *We're In the Money,* p. 135.
24. Raymond Carney, *American Vision: The Films of Frank Capra* (Cambridge University Press, 1986), pp. 299–300.
25. Leland A. Poague, *The Cinema of Frank Capra* (A. S. Barnes/Tantivy Press, 1975), pp. 96–97.
26. McBride, *Frank Capra,* p. 252.

were symbiotic on every level, including that of politics. Their friendship was real, their collaboration close, mysteriously kindred, and complexly interwoven. In private they functioned as each other's best audience. In a word—borrowing from one of the characters of *Platinum Blonde*—they "vibrated" well together. As Wray noted, "Both these men had come from modest beginnings. Both knew what it was to be an 'average man.' Each, respectively, had the optimism and character to rise above circumstances. Character here is a key word for character is the element, they knew, that motivates plot rather than the other way around."[27]

For people who make a point of tracking down *American Madness* today, the second Capra-Riskin collaboration holds up as a "social document" as well as "an important work of the imagination."[28] This, we are proud to say, is the first publication of its screenplay.

* * *

Surprisingly, *American Madness* was the only original script that Riskin ever crafted for Capra. Hollywood studios preferred in general to purchase and assign already published material. Harry Cohn was not eager to employ someone to sit around for an indefinite period of time, cogitating an original idea with which Cohn was not familiar and, equally important, which had no track record with the public. Also, in this Golden Age not only of motion pictures but also of newspapers and magazines, there was an industry-wide paranoia about uncopyrighted work: it was considered safer to purchase and adapt a work than to start from scratch and expose oneself to possible charges of plagiarism.

Although *American Madness* was a bold leap forward for both Capra and Riskin, the writer and director were not yet strictly thought of as a team. Their partnership was "still a flirtation, not yet a marriage."[29] The film that cemented their bond was *Lady For A Day,* made in 1933.

This film was not about a populist doer of good deeds, although it did provide some sharp-edged commentary on the Depression. Nor was it any kind of love story. It was a loose adaptation of Damon Runyon's 1929 short story "Madame La Gimp," in which a street corner vendor, a poor aging woman down on her luck, pretends to be living a life of luxury as a high society personage in order to not disappoint her daughter. When the daughter pays an unexpected visit, accompanied

27. Wray, "Biography of Robert Riskin as Screen Writer."

28. John Raeburn, "*American Madness* and American Values," in *Frank Capra: The Man and His Films,* ed. Richard Glatzer and John Raeburn (University of Michigan Press, 1975), p. 67.

29. McBride, *Frank Capra,* p. 263.

by a blue-blood fiancé, the old lady enlists the help of some "dese-dem-and-dose" gangsters to shore up her well-meaning lie.

Most Riskin scripts are known for their common-man heroes. Richard Corliss, in *Talking Pictures,* his influential book about Hollywood screenwriters, made the observation that "the closer the male lead to Riskin's own personality, the more successful the film."[30] But Riskin also did well in the heroine department: think of Ellie Andrews in *It Happened One Night,* Babe Bennett of *Mr. Deeds Goes to Town,* and Ann Mitchell of *Meet John Doe.* These are three of the all-time spunky, resourceful, and richly nuanced female characters of 1930s screen comedy. The grandmotherly lead character of *Lady For A Day* is added proof that Corliss's observation is useful but not always true.

Indeed, it was Riskin who championed the property to Capra, insisting he could adapt the offbeat story. He wrote it superbly. His fourth draft was filmed "virtually intact," according to McBride. "Capra's working script contains the fewest number of pencil changes of any working scripts in his files, except for the silent scripts. Riskin's was a masterful job of screenplay construction and dialogue which Capra transferred faithfully to the screen in just twenty-four days of shooting."[31]

This most unlikely project with its picturesque Times Square characters proved one of the surprises of 1933, "a stunning artistic and financial success that sealed the thirty-six-year-old Capra's status as one of Hollywood's master directors."[32] It brought Academy Award nominations, the first, for writer and director both, as well as for seventy-five-year-old May Robson, whose character had been changed by Riskin from a flower-seller in Runyon's short story to the apple-seller "Apple Annie." These major-category Oscar nominations were the first ever for lowly Columbia Pictures and a proud honor for Harry Cohn.

Lady For A Day was important not only for all these reasons but also because it was the first script on which Riskin and Capra worked together from start to finish. Once the pattern was set, their working method always remained the same. They met daily and talked—a phase that sometimes lasted for weeks. Riskin then wrote a draft and met with Capra again. They talked some more, and more drafts followed. Sometimes they were still talking right up through the filming, with Riskin doing versions of scenes and the photography delayed while they worked out nagging differences.

There is little evidence that Capra acted as a hands-on writer, per se, and plenty of evidence that he functioned with writers more as a magnificent story editor.

30. Richard Corliss, *Talking Pictures* (Overlook Press, 1974), p. 218.
31. McBride, *Frank Capra,* p. 295.
32. McBride, *Frank Capra,* p. 289.

Indeed, Capra was more of a would-be writer; on more than one occasion the director found himself claiming and losing screen credit before the Writers Guild grievance committee. Even Capra's own memoir, McBride reported, needed the assistance of several uncredited helpers.

As has been mentioned, Riskin himself had unusual sensitivity toward collaborators, and when adapting works he tried to consult and please the original authors. He tried to stay true to the spirit of the source material. Like many of the authors Riskin adapted, Damon Runyon was impressed by the screenwriter's ability to capture the essence of "Madame La Gimp" while departing liberally in particulars. Runyon was so pleased that in his newspaper column he publicly diverted all praise to Riskin; privately he telegraphed the screenwriter, thanking Riskin for what he had wrought from "my feeble story . . . your understanding of the characters amazed and delighted me . . . you made the yarn a hundred times better than the original."[33]

It was the first of Riskin's scripts to be published, and we regret that space in this volume is limited, or we would have included *Lady For A Day*.[34]

* * *

No less pleased was Samuel Hopkins Adams, whose "Night Bus" serial—which like "Madame La Gimp" first appeared in *Cosmopolitan* magazine—was immortalized by Riskin as the 1934 film *It Happened One Night*.

Adams was a prolific and not inconsiderable author of short stories, serials, homespun as well as crusading novels, and serious biographies. He had a track record of selling stories to Hollywood. His "Night Bus" serial was solid and appealing. But nothing about the story in its original form would suggest that as a motion picture it would become a model of screwball comedy, one that other people in Hollywood would strive to imitate and emulate for decades to come.

Riskin first made strategic modifications in the two lead characters. In "Night Bus" the male protagonist, Peter Warne, is a college-educated chemist. In the film script he is a ruthless reporter, a familiar Riskin type in the familiar situation—the same as *Platinum Blonde*—"of a reporter falling for a spoiled society dame."[35] More important, Warne is sincere and good-hearted (if a tad bland) in

33. Telegram from Damon Runyon to Robert Riskin, dated September 8, 1933, held among Riskin's papers at USC.

34. *Lady For A Day* was published in *Four-Star Scripts,* ed. Lorraine Noble (Doubleday, Doran & Company, 1936).

35. McBride, *Frank Capra,* p. 305.

Adams's story, while Riskin from the outset depicts the character in more hard-boiled terms.

When we first meet Peter Warne (Clark Gable) in the film, he is inebriated and surrounded by other drunken reporters clustered around a phone booth. Warne is putting on the big show of telling off his editor while he is actually in the act of being fired. Boarding a cross-country bus, he meets a pretty young lady, Ellie (Claudette Colbert), whom the audience knows to be a runaway heiress. Although not immune to her good looks, Warne takes a visceral dislike to her. When he learns her true identity, Warne cannot help but expound, to the point of obnoxiousness, on the faults of rich people. Meanwhile, Warne proves himself an opportunist, scheming behind Ellie's back to get his old newspaper job back by promoting her plight to make headlines.

Riskin altered fewer aspects of the heiress character. He made a practical name change—from Elspeth to Ellie—and small details were added that enriched her characterization. Riskin's hurdle was how to develop this spoiled heiress into a sympathetic person for his Depression era audience. He added a crucial speech for Ellie in which she reveals that she has never had any independence because she has always been smothered by her overprotective father and told what and what not to do. More subtly, Riskin fashioned a series of reversals (climaxing in the hitchhiking scene and the ensuing scene in which Warne shouts at her out of hurt male pride) that equalized the humanity of the two characters. Gradually, the audience finds itself in Ellie's corner."[36]

Adams opened his story on the bus. Riskin started his script off with a bang: an argument on a pleasure yacht, with the young heiress and her father disputing the wisdom of her forthcoming marriage to a playboy, ending with the heiress jumping, fully clothed, into the water. This, plus Warne's drunk scene on the telephone, serves to introduce the two main characters in their own, not entirely congenial, environments. After that, once the principals "meet cute" on the night bus, a sur-

36. Capra claims in his autobiography that one of his friends, Myles Connolly, suggested the "big story change" of making the characters sympathetic, but this statement should be taken with a grain of salt. According to Capra, Connolly told him, "It's *The Taming of the Shrew.* But the shrew must be worth taming, and the guy that tames her must be one of *us.*" Connolly was a great "story editor," wrote Capra. After hearing Connolly's critique, Riskin exclaimed, "What chumps we are!" according to Capra, and "we rewrote the whole story in a week" (Capra, *The Name Above the Title,* p. 164).

Note the "we." Connolly, a former newspaperman who had written a religious novel that was a bestseller among Catholics, did pal around with Capra and toss out ideas good and bad. But this was also one of Riskin's crucial strengths, knowing when to take—or leave—suggestions, and as McBride established, Capra's book occasionally distorts and diminishes Riskin's achievements.

prising amount of Adams's original plotline was sequentially expropriated and intelligently reworked by the scenarist.

Adam's original story line contains the purse-snatching incident, the nosy traveling salesman and relentless masher named Shapley, even the Walls of Jericho, the blanket strung up as a divider between their beds in a roadside motel: "While she was gone, he extracted a utility kit from his bag, tacked two nails to the end walls, fastened a cord to them, and hung a spare blanket, curtainwise, upon it. " 'The walls of Jericho,' was his explanation, as she came in. 'Solid porphyry and marble. Proof against any assault.' "[37]

Oh, what Riskin did with this brief notion! First he put Ellie Andrews in the room during the elaborate scaffolding, palpably uneasy as Peter Warne elaborately explains what he is going to do and tries to coax her into some cooperation. Her response is stony. He talks on, dragging in Joshua and the Israelites while segueing into that fabled moment in screen history when Gable-as-Warne delivers a lesson in male striptease:

PETER
(indicating her bed with a wave of his hand)
Do you mind joining the Israelites?

Ellie doesn't answer or budge.

PETER
You don't want to join the Israelites? All right, don't. Perhaps you're interested in how a man undresses. You know, it's a funny thing about that; quite a study in psychology.

He is getting out his pajamas.

PETER
No two men do it alike.

He is shedding coat and vest.

PETER
You know I once knew a man who kept his hat on until he was completely undressed. Yes. Now he made a picture. Years later his secret came out. He wore a toupee. You know I have a method all my own. If you noticed, the coat came first. Now the tie—
(he tugs it off)
—next the shirt.
(peeling off shirt)
Now, according to Hoyle, after that the pants should be next. There's where I'm different.

He sits on edge of bed and unties shoes.

37. Samuel Hopkins Adams, *Night Bus* (Dell, 1933), p. 15.

```
                    PETER
       I go for the shoes next. First the right, then
       the left. After that, it's every man for him-
       self.
               (stands up and starts unfastening trousers)
CLOSE-UP ELLIE as she dashes into the corner by her bed, safe be-
hind the Walls of Jericho.
```

This delightful scene runs several minutes from beginning to end, just the way Riskin (and Capra) liked a scene to run on. It begins on a note of high comedy and ends in a moment of double entendre and intense, sublimated eroticism:

```
A close view shows Ellie glancing over at the blanket. Despite her-
self, the suggestion of a smile flits across her face.

                    ELLIE
       You haven't got a trumpet by any chance, have
       you?

Peter gets the idea and smiles broadly.

                    PETER
       No. Not even a mouth organ.
```

The clothesline blanket keeps them apart, and Warne (as well as the audience) has to imagine Ellie as she is undressing on the other side, throwing her clothes over the blanket. "I wish you'd take those things off the Wall of Jericho," he grumbles, eyeing her lingerie as he lays back in bed, smoking a cigarette. Brooding, he smokes his cigarette, making small talk that ends, finally, in their formal introduction of each other. It is a scene made all the more perfect by the fact that the Walls of Jericho are brought back and the situation reversed toward the end of the film. Then it is Ellie smoking a cigarette and brooding as she finds herself separated from Warne—the man she has grown to love—not only by the Walls of Jericho but by the gulf of class distinctions.

The famous hitchhiking scene was similarly enhanced by Riskin. There is hitchhiking in Adams's version, but no female-male one-upmanship, only Warne's demonstration of the proper "digital gesture" and a line of advice: "The first rule of thumb is to look as neat and decent as you can. It inspires confidence in the passing motorist's breast." The hitchhiking scene in the film reveals Warne's arrogance but also Ellie's insouciance. Warne boasts he is going to write a book called "The Hitchhiker's Hail" and brags that he knows several different methods of successful hitchhiking. All lead to failure, as the camera illustrates. Then Colbert-as-Ellie gives Warne his comeuppance. She hitches her skirt, bares her legs, and stops traffic.

The man who picks them up, a rapscallion of the road, is also from Adams's story. In Riskin's script his part is humorously embroidered; among other things he is turned into one of the frustrated, full-throated singers in Capra-Riskin films, launching, while driving his car, into impromptu arias on hitchhiking and tonsils and finally, a catchy ditty that is echoed later in the script: "Young people in love are very seldom hungry!"

*   *   *

It appears that Capra and Riskin settled on "Night Bus" almost out of desperation, searching for a project they could bring to fruition quickly and relatively inexpensively after *Lady For A Day.* Capra first read the story in a Palm Springs barbershop while waiting for a haircut. Capra told the story to Riskin, who thought it sounded cute but insubstantial. When it came time to sell the story on its merits to Columbia production executives, Riskin insisted on doing the verbal salesmanship, feeling that Capra, with his hammy instincts, would bungle the pitch. In a sense this was the first thing that Riskin always brought to a script, something that is absent from a casual perusal of "Night Bus": a tone that reflected nothing so much as his own charming personality.

In person or on the page, Riskin could put across his characters. But the major accomplishment of *It Happened One Night,* which is underrated by people who are unfamiliar with "Night Bus" or who focus too exclusively on Capra, was in the realm of construction. While Riskin often received kudos for his witty dialogue, he was a master adapter.

It is one thing to read an appealing play, novel, or short story, and quite another to organize it properly as a screenplay, opening it up and lengthening it (or shortening it), making the myriad choices of keeping a character here and deleting one there, adding a scene, incident, or crucial detail, writing appropriate dialogue where dialogue is necessary, and ending up with something that is whole and organic and also cinematic. Unfortunately, Hollywood history is full of examples of great works—short stories, novels, and prize-winning plays—ruined by clumsy adaptation, or faithfully transcribed unto tedium.

Riskin's experience as a Broadway producer and playwright shaped his theory of the well-made screenplay. (Indeed, he preferred the terminology as two unconnected words, *screen play,* and that is how his credit appeared on the screen for *It Happened One Night.*) He sought to minimize parallel action and the intercutting of scenes (flashbacks, and cutting back and forth in time or space). "Parallel action (if, in the use of it, we can be guided by a rule) should scarcely be used except in instances where the two actions are related to each other—story-wise," he wrote once, "or where some social observation is being made via action."[38]

38. Robert Riskin, "The Theme's The Thing," undated, unattributed clipping in the Riskin papers at USC.

Nor did he like to disturb scenes with camera angles; he wanted scenes to play on, uninterrupted, as they might on the stage. "I have had scenes run for minutes at a time," wrote Riskin, "and remained on a 'two-shot' until its conclusion—having found that it was more impressive this way. To disturb it with 'close-up' and 'different angles' would rob the scene of its intended purpose."[39]

He liked to say in interviews that he divided his screenplays into two or three acts, guiding the story toward an invisible curtain separating the acts. At the same time, he would divide each act into scenes, then each scene of each act into mini-scenes, until the structure was multisegmented, infinitely connected, and melded, as he stated on one occasion:

> There are no set rules for writing a scenario. Each person works differently. My own method is to begin by staring at the walls for a considerable time. Then I sharpen my pencils—and again stare at the walls.
>
> The usual length of a scenario is 100 pages. The first I wrote was 250 pages long with 550 scenes. It was thrown out.
>
> It is necessary to have two or three characters in mind, with possibly three climaxes for each act. The rest usually writes itself.
>
> Every scene must have a beginning, middle, and end, no matter how small. Each little scene has a climax of its own, which may be at the end of the first act. This, in turn, builds up to the end of the film in cumulative fashion. In all, a picture should have about ten small climaxes, each one completed by a laugh, a tear, or any other emotional period.[40]

* * *

In the more didactic Capra-Riskin films, such as *Mr. Deeds Goes to Town,* one can almost forget that there is a swell romance taking place, but *It Happened One Night* contains a bare minimum of editorializing. Although Peter Warne's ability to stretch a dollar may have struck a chord with Depression audiences—harking back, as McBride has pointed out, to Riskin's boyhood short story "$1.93"[41]—the love story was uppermost. Even Ellie Andrews's tycoon father is made to serve cupid, his sympathetic treatment contrasting with the characterization of the rich money-grubbers in most Capra-Riskin films (his character is straight out of "Night

39. Riskin, "The Theme's The Thing."

40. Riskin writing as guest columnist for Sheila Graham, *Cincinnati Times-Star,* July 31, 1936.

41. McBride, *Frank Capra,* p. 306.

Bus"). This is another thing overlooked by people anxious to focus on other issues: above all else, romantic comedy was this screenwriter's forte.

For Riskin, romance came naturally. This writer knew what it was like to be a ladies' man—he was well suited to write those clever love scenes that light up Capra films like fireworks. Riskin was a notorious Hollywood bon vivant, never as shy or tongue-tied with the ladies as he could be with newspaper interviewers. Hollywood gossip columns of the 1930s reported that he nightclubbed with Ginger Rogers, Loretta Young, Glenda Farrell, Elizabeth Allen, Carole Lombard, and other lovely first ladies of the screen. (Whereas Capra, according to McBride's portrait, rarely if ever indulged in affairs, and was married to the same woman for fifty years.)

Sidney Buchman described Riskin as "the exact opposite of Capra: imagine a very cultivated, nonchalant playboy, and you will have an idea of their rapport."[42] Newspaper accounts invariably described him as short and slender with dark eyes, strikingly handsome, a natty dresser. He was known to refer to himself, jokingly, as "a dissipated George Raft,"[43] and like one of his most famous film characters he was quite capable of losing his temper while on the town. On one occasion, while at a celebrity-filled Hollywood nightclub, Riskin became involved in a well-publicized fracas with Harry Ruskin, another screenwriter whose name was sometimes confused with his. After heated words were exchanged, Riskin decked Ruskin, according to contemporary accounts, with "a single, well aimed blow to the jaw."[44]

Riskin had definite ideas about screen romance. The love scenes should be comedic, the wooing between lovers a verbal donnybrook or a musical duet. In Riskin's eyes, a courtship ought to be offhand. He detested obvious sentimentality and felt the emotional subtext of a scene should be subtle. When Riskin was wooing Fay Wray, he sent her one dozen roses with a card that read: "One dozen roses." She knew what he was doing: underplaying his feelings by quoting from a popular song ("Give me one dozen roses/Put my heart in beside them/And send them to the one I love").

The female characters might have masculine jobs and names (such as Gallagher); their affection might be confused with professional friendship ("You're my pal, aren't you?" Stew Smith asks Gallagher. "Don't turn female on me"). Women were expected to be smart and tough as well as sexy and adorable. They

42. McBride, *Frank Capra,* p. 236.

43. Cecilia Ager, "Mr. Riskin Spells Significance With A Capital $," *PM,* January 27, 1941.

44. The Riskin-Ruskin fracas is amusingly detailed in "Arline's Smash Hit Put Jack on the Floor," *New York Journal,* May 16, 1936.

could be stubborn bachelorettes (Babe Bennett in *Mr. Deeds Goes to Town*), or a struggling eldest daughter responsible for the family upkeep (Ann Mitchell in *Meet John Doe*).

The men were supposed to have old-fashioned, chivalric instincts (like Longfellow Deeds, dreaming of rescuing "a lady in distress"). But they could also voice feminist concerns (when his press agent tries to fix him up with a date, Deeds complains to his valet, "He talks about women as if they were cattle"). They showed unusual vulnerability. They could actually experience an emotional breakdown over a woman. A long time before George Bailey came along, Riskin wrote characters for Capra—in *American Madness* and *Mr. Deeds Goes to Town*—who could fail in a big way and be tempted by suicide.

It Happened One Night has no suicide, minimal social preachment, no angry crowd scenes. What it has is a crowd of happy people singing "The Man on the Flying Trapeze" while riding on a bus—one of the highwater scenes of 1930s screen comedy, entirely invented by Capra and Riskin. (There is no group singalong in "Night Bus.") Scenes like that one made the film Riskin's and Capra's most deceptive triumph. "There was something, indeed, about *It Happened One Night* that defied description or analysis," wrote Joseph McBride, "even after Capra made the film." Despite "all the merits of its story and screenplay, and Capra's masterful direction," McBride added, what turned this project into an everlasting lark of a film was in the end elusive and mysterious.[45]

Until, McBride theorized, one factored in the fortuitous casting of Clark Gable and Claudette Colbert. The script was originally tailored for Robert Montgomery, but Columbia thrust Gable, who was on loan from MGM partly as punishment for extravagant contract demands, into the role. Colbert was not enthusiastic about *It Happened One Night* either, and according to Capra and McBride behaved rebelliously on the set. These two stars who gave so much pizzazz to their parts were in fact unwilling conscripts.

Capra's work was not just faithful, it was as equally masterful as the script. The director kept everything blithe and amusing, the scenes moving along at a clip, entertaining and involving and ultimately memorable. It was deceptively simple direction, which elevated Riskin's script into one of the all-time great motion pictures.

It Happened One Night captured an unprecedented five major Academy Awards in 1934: Best Picture, Best Director, Best Script, Best Actor, Best Actress. Apart from earning his first and only Oscar, Clark Gable could take satisfaction in having set off a panic in the undershirt business, courtesy of the roadside motel scene in which Peter Warne strips for bed and reveals that he is not wearing an under-

45. McBride, *Frank Capra,* p. 303.

shirt. Perhaps this was sweet revenge for Riskin, who had marked time in the garment industry.

* * *

In four short years Riskin had become one of the most celebrated writers in the motion picture industry. According to newspaper accounts, he was making $2,000 weekly. Scribes newly arrived in Hollywood, people like novelist James M. Cain or European emigré Billy Wilder, stopped by to meet him, ask for tips, and talk over whatever script they were working on. He loved interruptions, odd hours, and late nights; he received journalists late in the mornings, wearing circles under his eyes and a kimono ("I'm never conversational before I coffee," as the Edward Everett Horton character, Alexander P. Lovett, says in *Lost Horizon*).

He and Capra extracted unusual freedoms at Columbia. Unlike most of the studio's contract employees, they were allowed to work off the lot, usually at Riskin's place or Capra's house. After *It Happened One Night*, they made a habit of convening at their lucky place, where they had brainstormed 1934's Oscar-winning Best Picture, the La Quinta Hotel, in the desert some twenty miles from Palm Springs.

Riskin wrote with notorious ease wherever he was, the words seeming to appear on the page as effortlessly as one of those long, cockeyed speeches might trip from the tongue of a Riskin character. Bob Thomas, Maurice Zolotow, and Richard Corliss have all reported the identical vignette of "a casual, amiable man sitting on the porch of his Columbia back-lot bungalow, and writing his dialogue in longhand on a yellow pad, as if he were composing a letter to his friends back East."[46]

For a long time Riskin kept quarters at the Beverly Wilshire Hotel. Eventually he bought a house in Beverly Hills. He liked to stay in bed most mornings, wearing his silk pajamas while writing, and, as he worked, stroking the head of his little dachshund whom he had named "Mr. Deeds." After he had finished his daily allotment of pages, Riskin would dispatch Mr. Deeds downstairs to alert the cook that he was ready for lunch. A secretary took the pages covered in longhand for transcription. The afternoon was set aside for tennis and horse racing, the evenings for stud poker and a tour of nightclubs.

He was gentlemanly in person—like one of his characters—with impeccable manners, impeccable dress. Irene Selznick said that Riskin possessed "the quality of nobility."[47] He always seemed merry, and he was an enjoyable person to be

46. Corliss, *Talking Pictures*, p. 218. See also Bob Thomas, *King Cohn* (Putnam, 1967), and Maurice Zolotow, *Billy Wilder in Hollywood* (Putnam, 1977).

47. Irene Selznick was cited in my interview with Fay Wray.

around. His seriousness could be sudden, and his eloquence surprising, emerging suddenly out of a stream of amiable, matter-of-fact conversation. This too was like one of his characters.

For Columbia, Riskin squeezed in *Carnival,* directed by Walter Lang (story and script, 1934), and probably his best-known credit independent of Capra, *The Whole Town's Talking* (co-script with Jo Swerling, 1935), a diverting, if thoroughly atypical John Ford film from a W. R. Burnett novel about a gangster posing as his double, a meek clerk.

Next, for Capra and Columbia, Riskin went to work on *Broadway Bill.* It was based on an unpublished story by *New York Daily Mirror* columnist Mark Hellinger about a broken-down racehorse and the small-time owner who believes in him as a long shot for the big race.

Riskin had a soft spot for racehorses. He owned and raced horses with his brother and was a regular better. He applied himself admirably to the material, even if it was reputedly Capra (with the help of writer Sidney Buchman) who tacked on the film's ending, when the horse, Broadway Bill, expires of a heart attack at the finish line.

Starring Warner Baxter and Myrna Loy, *Broadway Bill* was well regarded in its day, although it seems a little rickety by today's standards. Like Damon Runyon, Hellinger was more than satisfied with the adaptation. In his newspaper column he wrote that his story had been so much improved by Hollywood that Capra and Riskin "unquestionably deserve most of the credit. So I am very careful to limit myself in the bows I take."[48]

Broadway Bill was a lightweight transition film for Capra and Riskin, but to what were they transitioning? Up to this point, they had shown alertness to headlines and populist ideas, and they had demonstrated a flair for romantic and screwball comedy. Nobody could have guessed they would bring these elements together so resoundingly in their next film, their undying masterpiece, *Mr. Deeds Goes to Town.*

* * *

Clarence Budington Kelland was a short-story writer and novelist of some standing. His Scattergood Baines stories about a fat Yankee peddler, which promoted old-fashioned American values, appeared in the *Saturday Evening Post* and other

48. Mark Hellinger, "All In A Day," *New York Daily Mirror,* 1934 clipping, in Riskin's papers at USC.

magazines. "Opera Hat," which first appeared in *American Magazine,* was a Kelland serial with a greeting-card poet named Longfellow Deeds as its protagonist.

It must go down as a mystery how "Opera Hat" came into Capra's possession. According to the director in his autobiography, Clarence Budington Kelland's magazine serial was in a valiseful of available stories that he took home to read one night. (Some unsung story editor would therefore deserve the credit for channeling the material to his attention.) Like "Night Bus," "Opera Hat" was solid and appealing, but not a story that cried out to be filmed. What did interest Capra was the central character: a man who wakes up one day to find himself heir to twenty million dollars.

Capra was also intrigued by the premise "country boy out-slicks city slickers," Kelland's usual theme line.[49] Kelland went off on a tangent, however, with Deeds inheriting a New York City opera company and being sidetracked into a backstage crime of passion. Kelland's serial devolved into a "tediously protracted murder mystery."[50]

Capra and Riskin wanted Longfellow Deeds to represent the common man, someone whose innate decency and folksiness would mandate the casting of Gary Cooper. So Riskin went to work with his knack for story line, his talent for whimsy and romance, and his political feelings. The story was extensively revamped. The murder mystery disappeared, and the opera angle was played down. (In Kelland's serial, the inheritance comes to Deeds after his uncle, Victor Semple, is killed in a motor accident in Italy, "during his annual hunt for tenors.")[51] Riskin focused on the inheritance, which is the jumping-off point, and the characterization of Deeds. The inheritance evolved into a symbol of economic disparity, while Deeds was fleshed out, made colorful and sympathetic—at once a rube and almost a saint—and his idiosyncratic behavior given logic and motivation.

In both Kelland's and Riskin's versions, Longfellow Deeds is a fish out of water in the big city, flummoxed by valets and manipulated by high-powered attorneys. The film script would underscore Deeds's ambivalence about inherited wealth. But the master stroke was the invented character of the shady newspaper lady, Babe Bennett, a female variant of Peter Warne. This gave Deeds a lady love to conquer, and his association with Babe Bennett leads to his being treated shabbily by the press—especially by Bennett.

49. Capra, *The Name Above the Title,* p. 179.
50. McBride, *Frank Capra,* p. 328.
51. Clarence Budington Kelland, "Opera Hat," *American Magazine,* April-August 1935, pp. 86–88.

In anyone else but Riskin's hands, a character like Deeds might have verged on caricature. The screenwriter, who believed in Deeds, made him as true and vivid and unforgettable a figure as has ever been put on film. Kelland invented the character, certainly, but Riskin borrowed selectively from Kelland, adding his own subtle touches and empathetic shading.

In Kelland's serial Deeds's greeting-card poetry verges on corniness. In Riskin's version the poetry is just as corny, and it becomes a running gag (Deeds never does find his rhyme for Budington), but it also leads to a cathartic scene in which the shady Babe Bennett (played by Jean Arthur), already weighed down by guilt, must read aloud a simple but moving poem that Deeds has dedicated to her. The screenwriter, who was himself a closet poet, must have savored that moment, just as he must have relished the scene where the postcard poet confronts the haughty literati at a Manhattan nightclub (a burlesque of the Algonquin Round Table). The poet meets the literati in Kelland's story too, but Riskin cleverly edited Kelland, and, with Babe Bennett at the table watching Deeds squirm, he ratcheted the scene up into a higher emotional level.[52]

Deeds was a tuba player in Kelland's serial, but Riskin made more of the tuba, including it in Deeds's first scene and then incorporating it into the rest of the story. It is a sure laugh-getter in several scenes, including Deeds's train trip to New York. The tuba-playing impulse figures into one of the best Capra-Riskin musicalized scenes: Jean Arthur, with two sticks, drumming "Swanee River" on a Central Park bench while Gary Cooper mimicks his tuba, performing a basso "Humoresque" in counterpoint. In the courtroom, finally, Deeds's tuba is offered as a symbol of his lunatic behavior, but Deeds makes a long speech defending it as a quirk of behavior indicating, beneath the surface, a thoughtful man.

Riskin not only embraced the "country boy outslicks city slickers" theme but also explored and deepened it. He gave Deeds deep Mandrake Falls roots by mentioning his father, a doctor, who delivered many of the town babies, and he made Deeds the co-owner of a local tallow factory with a recalcitrant employee (another one of the running gags). Deeds's country-hick demeanor is a central element of the sight-seeing scene at Grant's Tomb ("I see a small Ohio farmboy becoming a great soldier. . . . Things like that can only happen in America"). It crops up when Deeds embarks on a madcap night on the town (he ends up doffing his clothes and marching through the streets shouting "Back to nature!") and ap-

52. The binging poet who befriends Deeds in the literati scene is played by Walter Catlett who, in one of those reverberations that make Capra-Riskin films so richly layered, also portrays Bingy, Stew Smith's newspaper reporter rival, in *Platinum Blonde.*

proaches eloquence in a later, bittersweet scene, when he muses aloud to Babe Bennett as they walk the city streets:

```
                    DEEDS
People here are funny. They work so hard at liv-
ing, they forget how to live. Last night after I
left you I was walking along and I was looking
at the tall buildings. And I got to thinking
about what Thoreau said. They created a lot of
tall palaces here but they forgot to create the
noblemen to put in them. I'd rather have Man-
drake Falls!
```

The country-hick theme spurred the most controversial aspect of the *Mr. Deeds* script: the deeding away of acreage and seed money to poor people and downtrodden farmers. Once again, Riskin had astutely diagnosed the national political mood—he was well aware that Depression era proposals like the Townsend Plan and popular politicians such as Huey Long were stirring widespread debate on sharing the wealth. Purely on a structural level, Deeds's giveaway was a unique idea, taking the story in a direction where no one could have predicted it would go. On a thematic level it was inspired.

The thematic seeds are sown early in the script when Longfellow Deeds states a vague notion to help people with his unwelcome inheritance. But Deeds appears to forget about all that as he is distracted by—falls in love with—Babe Bennett. He later is confronted by a desperately poor farmer who accuses Deeds of profligacy and raises a gun, bent on shooting him. This prompts Deeds's decision to donate a portion of his unwanted wealth to ordinary people in need. When Deeds tries to launch his giveaway program he is arrested, institutionalized, and eventually "crucified" in court, in the parlance of the script, by devious lawyers trying to gain control of the estate.

The Christ analogy is plain, with Deeds as one of Capra-Riskin's most compelling "messianic innocents," in Joseph McBride's words. The crucified hero may be a staple of all drama and literature harking back to the Bible; it may have embryonic antecedents in earlier Capra films; it was certainly carried forward expertly in Capra pictures *not* written by Riskin—most notably in *Mr. Smith Goes to Washington* (1939) and *It's a Wonderful Life*. But there can be no question that Riskin advanced the hero-as-public-martyr in *American Madness* and that, in Capra's work, the concept came to its first thematic maturity in *Mr. Deeds Goes to Town*.

The courtroom scenes in the third act are absent from Kelland's serial. They are entirely Riskin's contribution. The crucifixion of Deeds is as thoroughly blueprinted in the script as the bank run of *American Madness*. A series of witnesses and experts attest to Deeds's insanity. The suspenseful atmosphere builds to a pitch with nary a word from the defendant, who refuses to speak in his own behalf until, finally, a distraught (and reformed) Babe Bennett rushes to the front of the courtroom (she had been manipulated as a witness earlier) and makes an emotional plea in his defense. Over and over again, the crooked lawyer Cedar, who is leading the attack on Deeds, demands of her, "You are in love with him, aren't you?" until Babe Bennett, her face streaked with tears, shouts back, "Yes!" (This is a tidy variation on the scene in *It Happened One Night* where Ellie's father, on the day of her wedding to King Westley, presses the same question on Peter Warne; he finally snaps back, "Yes! But don't hold that against me. I'm a little screwy myself").

Bending legal decorum, Riskin then turns the courtroom climax into a romp in which the crucifixion is bungled and Christ climbs down from the cross, preaching a hilarious sermon. The enemy volleys, the hooting and rooting from the sidelines, and the last-minute turnaround by Babe Bennett are nicely modulated. The denouement is neither predictable nor pedantic. The spinster aunts who think everyone in the whole world is "pixillated" except themselves are a wonderful touch, and they have the film's ideal last line.

Of course the giveaway program wasn't in Kelland's serial, and it was that element of the plot, coming in the midst of an ongoing political debate over the future of a nation mired in trouble and turmoil, that resembled another plank in a Capra-Riskin populist platform. Critics and audiences had only the highest acclaim for the luminous performances by Gary Cooper and Jean Arthur, the first-rate contributions from the usual gallery of Capra-Riskin supporting players, and the overall entertainment value of *Mr. Deeds.* All the debate centered on the film's (and, by extension, Capra's and Riskin's) politics.

Variety registered a complaint that the rant of the desperate farmer (played by John Wray), who denounces the headline antics of Longfellow Deeds ("I just wanted to see what a man looked like that could spend thousands of dollars on a party when people around him were hungry!"), amounted to "quasi-Communistic" propaganda. Some thought *Mr. Deeds* was not so much a Communistic statement as a Capra-Riskin endorsement of the New Deal. Others thought it merely a feel-good escapist movie that was even faintly Republican in its simple solutionism.

The debate has never really waned. Capra's films tended to "break political 'rules' and splice ideologies together," wrote Donald C. Willis in *The Films of Frank Capra.* "Depending on one's political point-of-view and on what Capra film or films or parts of Capra films one is talking about, Frank Capra is an advocate of Communism, fascism, Marxism, populism, conservatism, McCarthyism, New-Dealism, anti-Hooverism, jingoism, socialism, capitalism, middle-of-theroadism, democracy or individualism. It's no accident that there are so many interpretations of his films."[53]

Riskin's populism (he hated that word) was from the heart. Over and over again his scripts affirmed their "faith" (a word that recurs in *Mr. Deeds*) in "the people," an optimism often founded upon lead characters who were strangers or nobodies. Critics still prefer to call that formula "Capraesque," although some think it should be known, at least equally, as "Riskinesque."

Clarence Budington Kelland seems to have been one of the people who did not like what *Mr. Deeds* appeared to advocate with its potshots at high-priced lawyers, rich people, and inequities of the system. Kelland was a vocal conservative and an opponent of FDR (in 1942, he became an executive and the publicity director of the Republican National Committee). His "Opera Hat" had been transformed, his conservative politics vitiated. Kelland became one of the rare authors to take some umbrage at a Riskin adaptation, and he refused to give his permission for the script, which was nominated for Best Screenplay of 1936, to be anthologized in *Twenty Best Film Plays*.[54]

This, almost sixty years later, is the first authorized publication of Riskin's script. Apart from some gag work, tightening, and changing the locales of a few scenes, Capra did very little tinkering with the shooting script.[55] Riskin might have balked at calling it his best script, but *Mr. Deeds* was and always remained his favorite film.

* * *

Mr. Deeds led to a big budget, and bigger expectations, for Capra's planned film of James Hilton's best-seller *Lost Horizon*.

It was Jo Swerling who got Capra interested in the 1933 novel about a Far Eastern mountain utopia where people lived in harmony with nature and devoted themselves to spiritual fulfillment. Then, as Capra and Riskin went to work, Swerling played devil's advocate, arguing with Riskin that Hilton's tale couldn't possibly make a good picture unless Shangri-La could be made utterly credible. There was too little action, too much philosophic content. The trick would have to be credibility.

53. Donald C. Willis, *The Films of Frank Capra* (Scarecrow Press, 1974), p. 9. See also McBride, *Frank Capra*, p. 259.

54. *Twenty Best Film Plays* was published by Crown in 1943. The collection was assembled by John Gassner and included an introduction by Dudley Nichols. See also Lewis Gannett, "Books And Things," *New York Herald Tribune*, November 30, 1943.

55. McBride, *Frank Capra*, p. 346.

Riskin had mentioned Thoreau in *Mr. Deeds,* and Walden Pond-type places were on his mind during publicity sessions for *Lost Horizon.* "After a night of doing the town and a steadying noontime breakfast," wrote a reporter for *Variety* who met with Riskin, "ponderings upon Thoreau slunk into his conversation, and he wondered fleetingly if Thoreau's simple life was so fantastic and fairyland after all, or is it the real thing; and is the fantasy, actually, the mad life we live today."[56]

The screenwriter was once again at one with his audience, tapping into a public mood of weariness with international affairs and a cyclical clamor for isolationism. Dictators ruled in foreign lands; World War II was on the horizon. There was a fervent identification with Hilton's tempting idea of, somewhere, an idyllic and humane Utopia.

Hilton's well-known novel began to undergo alteration once Riskin launched into the scriptwriting. While speculation mounted in the press, the author stayed open-minded. As an occasional scenarist for Hollywood projects himself, Hilton knew there were difficult obstacles to making a legitimate screen version of his novel, and he also knew the rules of the game. Hilton gave several interviews saying he was conferring frequently with the scenarist and director and liked what Riskin was proposing to do with his novel.

"It was really amazing to see how Robert Riskin has kept the feeling, the spirit of the book," Hilton was quoted as saying. "He did a most remarkable piece of work really. Of course, he had to change several things; he asked me about them all. They were none of them important. If you wrote them all down I suppose it would sound as though they'd made a lot of changes. That wouldn't be fair. None of the changes are structural. They don't affect the theme or the central story."[57]

Hilton had started his novel with a frame-flashback in which two adventurers ("celibate Englishmen in a foreign capital") ponder the unknown fate of the British attaché Robert Conway, last glimpsed dodging police and natives, questing the mysterious Shangri-La in the remote Far East. Riskin didn't like frame-flashback structures, but he incorporated it anyway (it was cut back in the final film). His script really got going when the action shifted to the present with a terrific scene in which Conway fights off a mob and puts refugees on planes in the midst of a revolution. Conway is among a handful that, because of fortunate circumstances, are able to escape on the last flight out. It is some time before this group realizes that their plane has been inexplicably shanghaied.

56. "Bob Riskin Muses on 'Lost Horizon' And Wisecracking to a B'way Chorine," *Variety,* April 7, 1937.

57. See Hilton's comments in Eileen Creelman, "Picture Plays and Players," *New York Sun,* July 24, 1936.

Their fate is to be stranded in Shangri-La. Among the small band, only Conway (played by Ronald Colman) and the business profiteer Henry Barnard (Thomas Mitchell) retained Hilton's characterizations. The others experienced major changes: Hilton's bigoted female missionary became Riskin's tubercular ex-prostitute Gloria (Isabel Jewell). (Gloria becomes healthier as the story unwinds and develops a conveniently warm relationship with the profiteer.) Hilton's aggressive young vice-consul Mallison was tied more closely to the plot by making him into George (John Howard), the younger brother of Conway, a character who basks in reflected glory and obviously is not made of the same stuff as Conway. This was a cunning stroke: Conway's abandonment of Shangri-La makes more sense in Riskin's screenplay than in Hilton's book—Conway needed the extra motivation provided by the foolish brother.

A paleontologist was added for balance and welcome comedy relief. He was played by the reliable Edward Everett Horton. Hilton's novel was bereft of humor, and the film could have used more of it, as Horton's chirrupy scenes serve to underline.

One can almost hear the raised voice of Harry Cohn insisting on a part for a lovely leading lady. The only such figure in the novel is Lo-Tsen, a royal Manchu who plays the harp and proves alluring to both Conway and Mallison. In the film, there is no Lo-Tsen, but there is Maria (Margot), a pianist, who becomes the younger brother's romantic partner. Her desire to escape Shangri-La helps propel the third act.

The love interest Riskin created for Conway is Sondra, played by Jane Wyatt. Sondra is an expert horsewoman, tutors schoolchildren, speaks to squirrels (and they to her), swims in the nude at the fuzzy end of a long lens. Nothing is wrong with the actress's performance, but the character of Sondra remains one of the film's hurdles. She is distinctly "American" and is too obviously included as the obligatory sweetheart for handsome Ronald Colman. Riskin even contrived for the two to "meet cute": arriving in Shangri-La, Conway stumbles as he gazes up at her on a portico; Sondra covers her mouth to hide her laughter.

In all, the characters are not as motley or eccentric as, say, the Vanderhof-Sycamore family of Capra and Riskin's later *You Can't Take It With You* (1938). Once the excitement of Act One is over and the travelers have arrived at their surprise destination, the audience must be content with them—and with Shangri-La. Any suspense there might be as to their dilemma is undercut by Robert Conway, who is instantly swept away and convinced of the eternal merits of Shangri-La. Act Two is surprisingly low-key and protracted.

Conway is Riskin's most disenchanted hero, troubled by the outside world. The heart and soul of *Lost Horizon,* Conway was drawn faultlessly, and Ronald

Colman shouldered the role admirably. He has one of Riskin's most lyrical soliloquies, describing an airplane chasing its shadow as he muses about a love that is fated. Conway's disillusioned mutterings make more sense than do Chang's homilies (Chang's "a little courtesy all around" bromide for society rings particularly hollow). Indeed, Chang (H. B. Warner), the emissary of the High Lama, overstays his welcome on the screen, and there are one too many of the long expository scenes between Chang and Conway. Portions were excised from the final version of the film.

Capra made some arguable decisions that undercut aspects of Riskin's script. Conway's summit meetings with the High Lama became one issue that Riskin and Capra couldn't resolve. While the director vacillated over the casting of the role,[58] the dialogue was written and rewritten to vary the tone. Riskin and Capra had an unusual disagreement that was conveyed in public interviews: Riskin wanted "a kindly Franciscan sort of fellow, gently and indulgently appreciating the wayward world," according to one contemporary account.[59] The writer wanted Walter Connolly, the jovial tycoon of *It Happened One Night,* to play the part. Capra preferred "a sterner sort, a little more positive in his concern about the way of the world, a Paul of the Himalayas."[60]

Finally, the director settled on character actor Sam Jaffe. But Jaffe's initial scenes left Capra dissatisfied, so they were rewritten and refilmed with Walter Connolly. After viewing Connolly's footage, Capra changed his mind, and Jaffe was recalled from the New York stage and refilmed with different makeup. McBride pointed out that Sidney Buchman—another Columbia star writer and Capra's eventual collaborator on *Mr. Smith Goes to Washington*—polished up the final version of the High Lama scenes.[61] These scenes—Buchman pretty much worked from Riskin's draft—proved atmospheric, but somehow the moment to which the script builds, the scene between the two brothers where George convinces Conway to leave, is an inadequate climax.

Jo Swerling was right: Conway may have been an utterly credible character, but the setting was a problem that was never quite solved. Shangri-La looked unfortunately like an overdone Beverly Hills mansion with modern-style pavilions, and the costumes were a mishmash of styles, with traditional Tibetan clothing alongside Jane Wyatt's fashionable riding breeches. (Riskin can hardly be blamed.)

58. The first two veteran actors Capra sought to cast in the part were A. E. Anson and Henry B. Walthall; both died before filming.

59. John T. McManus, "Sunny Spain for Mr. Riskin," *New York Times,* April 11, 1937.

60. McBride, *Frank Capra,* p. 358.

61. McBride, *Frank Capra,* pp. 359–360.

Both writer and director wavered over the ending. At least three were filmed. The first reverted to Hilton's original frame-flashback strategy and ended with Gainsford's toast to Conway; the second had Conway climbing the mountains in endless search of Shangri-La; the third, the version used in the film's initial release, showed Conway struggling over a windblown pass to Sondra, who is "beckoning him onward to the accompaniment of a montage of ringing bells," in McBride's words.[62] This ending undermined Hilton's spiritualism, and an audience might easily assume that Conway was thinking of Sondra as much as the wisdom of the ages:

> Riskin argued against such a soppy fade-out, and he and Capra prevailed on Columbia to let them recut [the ending] after the film had been playing for several weeks. The final ending dropped Wyatt and simply showed Conway gazing off toward Shangri-La, concluding with a shot of the lamasery and the orgasmic bell montage (a ringing bell would become Capra's trademark, ending several of his later pictures).[63]

Lost Horizon was the first of the Capra-Riskin films to be plagued by second-guessing in regard not only to the script but also the budget and other production issues. The film went over schedule and budget, eventually costing close to two million dollars, an unprecedented outlay for Columbia. The first edited version of the film ran more than three hours. The final cut had to be severely trimmed, partly over Capra's objections, to slightly over two hours. On top of everything else, Capra's editing jettisoned "some of the more thoughtful overtones of [Riskin's] *Lost Horizon* script."[64]

Much of the behind-the-scenes toil and trouble leaked out to Hollywood columnists and was common knowledge well before the film was released. Each new Capra-Riskin film was by now surrounded by an expected air of controversy—in this case, controversy combined with "dire predictions."[65] The release of the film in the spring of 1937 was accompanied by unusually bruising criticism, with some viewers bemoaning the departures from Hilton's beloved book and others lamenting the film's talky idealism, slow stretches, and occasional incongruities. The *New*

62. McBride, *Frank Capra,* p. 364.

63. McBride, *Frank Capra,* p. 364.

64. McBride, *Frank Capra,* pp. 355, 427. The lost twenty-two minutes, lopped off after initial previews, were painstakingly tracked down and reinserted by film historian Robert Gitt for a "restored" version in the late 1970s, so that today most video versions run near to the original release length of 132 minutes.

65. "See Elizabeth Yeaman, "Lost Horizon Movie of Dream-Life Escape Marvel of Production," *Hollywood Citizen-News,* February 20, 1937.

York Times summed up the pros and cons by declaring that *Lost Horizon* had provoked "more violent debate than any picture ever made in Hollywood."[66]

The film also had appreciative audiences and ardent defenders, among them Frank Nugent, the film critic for the *New York Times,* who hailed the latest Capra-Riskin as a "great picture . . . [with] relatively minor faults."[67] The lavish screen adaptation of Hilton's novel may have been predestined to be a disappointment at the box office, but it was widely admired in Hollywood. *Lost Horizon* was honored with several Academy Award nominations in craft categories, as well as receiving a nomination as Best Picture of 1936.

Any postmortem on the film nowadays tends to focus on the well-documented problems while missing the obvious point that over time *Lost Horizon* has become one of the best-loved pictures of its era. Visually beautiful, impeccably acted, haunting in its philosophical certitude, it has cast a subtle spell over audiences in release and revival for sixty years. Time has been generous to the film, and if one measure of greatness is risk, then *Lost Horizon,* certainly one of the most courageous Capra-Riskin films, is also one of their greatest.

* * *

It may not be irrelevant that Capra and Riskin took a trip to Russia together after *Lost Horizon* was released in 1937—perhaps they hoped to find a budding Shangri-La. They visited Moscow and Leningrad, met illustrious film personnel, and were interviewed by *Izvestia.* They returned, disappointed by "socialism's vaunted Utopia," in Fay Wray's words.

Lost Horizon and its tensions had taken a toll. For five years Capra and Riskin had flourished at a studio where others had foundered. Harry Cohn gave them extraordinary freedoms at Columbia, but he was also difficult to please, inflexible on some subjects, and crude in his methods. He knew how to play people against each other and his temper could be insufferable.

Cohn "had a touch of sentiment within him which he worked fiercely at concealing," wrote Fay Wray, who worked as an actress at Columbia on more than one film.

> Most would say with absolute success. What he also had was a sensitivity to and recognition of talent. He was more likely to express this recognition behind the back of the appreciated one than to his face. His rough, unpolished

66. McManus, "Sunny Spain for Mr. Riskin."
67. Frank Nugent, "Scanning Lost Horizons," *New York Times,* March 7, 1937.

style, his challenging, goading attitude was reeled out like a fishing line to make his listeners rise to the bait.

Most who were associated with him would resent his style, some of his producers would say he was at his best when he left them absolutely alone. Capra and Riskin disliked his manner, were sometimes stimulated by his energy, but knew they had his admiration and regard even if it was delivered in adversarial adjectives.[68]

During the 1930s Capra had emerged as a Columbia mainstay, as Lewis Jacobs noted in *The Rise of the American Film,* with Riskin "as much Capra's backbone as Capra is Columbia's."[69] But the honeymoon was over between Capra and Cohn. Partly because of the inflated expense and grandiose expectations for *Lost Horizon,* partly because of personality differences, the director and studio boss were at swords' points by the beginning of 1937. Cohn then further aggravated Capra by advertising a Columbia "B" picture as a Frank Capra film although Capra had nothing to do with it; the film director and studio boss went to court, filing breach-of-contract lawsuits against each other.

Capra and Riskin were already estranged, according to McBride's book, which alleges that disagreements over the High Lama casting led Riskin to insist that Cohn honor a clause in his contract and give him an opportunity to direct.[70] A contemporary report in the *New York Times* reported alternatively that Riskin had been "assigned" to direct.[71] Either way, it was true he had been warming up to the idea of directing a motion picture. Now, with Capra in enforced idleness, it made sense, and Riskin took the plunge, preceding by several years the wave of more celebrated Hollywood writer-directors such as Preston Sturges, John Huston, and Billy Wilder.

When You're In Love (1937) was about a European opera star who "hires" a husband to keep up appearances during her United States tour. The story by Ethel Hill and Cedric Worth, taken from Columbia script files, was decidedly piffle. But Cary Grant and Grace Moore would be the stars, Riskin's brother Everett was on the job as producer—and Riskin himself, Cohn argued, could polish the script.

Riskin was essentially conned into wearing two hats. He wasn't very enthusiastic about writing *and* directing. He accepted the assignment with "misgivings," reported the *New York Times,* "because he doesn't profess to understand the

68. Wray, "Biography of Robert Riskin as Screen Writer."
69. Lewis Jacobs, *The Rise of the American Film* (Harcourt, Brace & Co., 1939), p. 476.
70. McBride, *Frank Capra,* p. 359.
71. McManus, "Sunny Spain for Mr. Riskin."

technique of the musical cinema."[72] As the directing deadline approached, the inadequacies of the script he had written became apparent:

> After a few futile days of scrutiny of it, he marched into Harry Cohn's office and tossed the tattered script on the desk.
>
> "This is terrible," he announced, just like a seasoned director. "You'll have to get me a new writer."
>
> Mr. Cohn just grinned maliciously, and went on reading his mail.[73]

Riskin said candidly in interviews that he missed Capra's expert input and editing of his ideas. "Every scene I wrote seemed unsatisfactory," he said in one interview. "I'd rewrite every night and then I'd rewrite again on the set. Director Riskin kept saying to writer Riskin, 'For the love of Pete, why didn't you get me a real writer?'

"I discovered, for instance, that you simply can't have too great an economy of dialogue. Frequently when we were working together on a script Capra has said to me, 'We don't need that; we've said it before.' And when it came to directing my own script, I found that I'd overwritten, time and time again."[74]

When You're In Love proved a pleasant film, but Riskin had found the double assignment to be a chore. It is worth a reminder here that the writer's and director's chairs are not interchangeable. A director's responsibility is different and requires a different energy, commitment, and exercise of the imagination. In those long-ago days, not many screenwriters enjoyed or succeeded at directing. Riskin would not repeat the experience.

* * *

In the meantime Capra had ironed out his disagreements with Cohn, and the director and Riskin were able to reunite on a high-energy adaptation of George S. Kauffman and Moss Hart's play *You Can't Take It With You.*

The Pulitzer Prize–winning stage comedy presents the unorthodox Vanderhof-Sycamore family of Syracuse, New York. Poor but blissfully happy, members of the family experiment with fireworks in the cellar, write avant-garde plays, and practice

72. McManus, "Sunny Spain for Mr. Riskin."
73. McManus, "Sunny Spain for Mr. Riskin."
74. Rose Pelswick, "Famous Writer, Europe Bound, Bares Woes in Making Film," *New York Journal,* April 1, 1937. See also Eileen Creelman, "Picture Plays and Players," *New York Sun,* April 22, 1937.

ballet in the living room. What plot there is revolves around the "normal" daughter who wants to marry a scion of a stuffy old-line New York family, the Kirbys.

The lead characters and main setting (the living room of Grandpa Vanderhof) stayed the same in Riskin's adaptation, but the screenwriter opened up the play, dropped the Grand Duchess, added minor characters, and fortified the plotline (while making it more socially conscious) by tying the capitalistic Mr. Kirby into an underhanded attempt to purchase city blocks, including the Vanderhof residence, to situate his expanding munitions complex. "With few exceptions, the mad goings-on in the Sycamore household are intact," wrote Douglas W. Churchill in the *New York Times,* "but the theme of the useless struggle for money is brought forward."[75]

By now people were alert to the pattern of Capra-Riskin films and newspaper columnists were quick to anticipate and carp about alterations from the source material that seemed to be aimed at consciousness-raising. In this instance, public complaint was lodged also by Hart, who worried that his play was being turned into one of those "message pictures."[76]

Riskin always claimed that he didn't write message pictures ("he hates the word," according to one article). He was also a pragmatic man who knew what it meant to sell a stage play to Hollywood without looking backward. He met with Hart, according to one contemporary account, and listened as the writer "beat his breast in horror after reading what Mr. Riskin had done," encumbering his "innocent screwball comedy" with "social significance" ("another phrase Mr. Riskin hates"). Riskin "listened attentively, then thanked Mr. Hart for giving him out of his eloquent anguish a couple of good ideas for making it even more socially significant."[77]

Audiences did not seem to mind, and they flocked to the hilarious film. Moss Hart went public again, this time with his revised opinion—an endorsement of the motion picture's script. *You Can't Take It With You* proved extremely successful in 1938, and Riskin logged another Academy Award nomination for Best Adapted Script, the writer's fourth. Riskin lost the award to the MGM adaptation of George Bernard Shaw's *Pygmalion,* but Capra and the film did better, taking Best Director and Best Picture of 1938.

75. Douglas W. Churchill, "Wood Turned to Gold in Hollywood," *New York Times,* February 13, 1938. This is the same Douglas W. Churchill who co-wrote the story used for *Platinum Blonde.*

76. Ager, "Mr. Riskin Spells Significance With A Capital $."

77. Ager, "Mr. Riskin Spells Significance With A Capital $." The Hart-Riskin brouhaha is mentioned in other undated, unsourced clippings in the Riskin files at USC.

* * *

Now it was Riskin who abandoned Capra, quitting Columbia and signing on as a producer for Sam Goldwyn. Meanwhile Capra went to work with Sidney Buchman on *Mr. Smith Goes to Washington.*

It may have been the monetary aspects of the deal as much as terminal disenchantment with Harry Cohn that took Riskin to Goldwyn as a producer. It may have been the challenge of doing something new and different. On paper, Riskin seemed a natural as producer: all accounts praised his executive skills, his good judgment and salesmanship, his congenial ability to work with disparate persons, his grasp of complex schedule and budget dynamics.

Riskin's producing stint was short-lived, however, yielding only two pictures: Henry Hathaway's *The Real Glory* (1939), about a heroic army medic in the aftermath of the Spanish-American War, and *They Shall Have Music* (1939), Goldwyn's sincere attempt to make a movie star out of Jascha Heifetz. Producing turned out to be no more gratifying than directing, and Capra, who had finished *Mr. Smith Goes to Washington* and broken away from Columbia, had no trouble luring Riskin back.

Capra and Riskin came together for the final time, incorporating themselves as an independent production entity, Frank Capra Productions, Inc. They were installed in the old headquarters of Hearst's Cosmopolitan Pictures at Warner Brothers, where they were given stage space, physical equipment, and some operating cash. Capra and Riskin made up the difference themselves with bank loans; Capra mortgaged his house and farm, while Riskin put up stocks and bonds as collateral.

This time there was no doubt as to their intentions. Riskin and Capra deliberately set out to serve as "lighthouses in a foggy world," as Connell, the newspaper editor in *Meet John Doe,* puts it. They would make a film that would "astonish the critics with contemporary realities," in the director's words: "The ugly face of hate; the power of uniformed bigots in red, white and blue shirts; the agony of disillusionment, and the wild dark passions of mobs. We would give them a brutal story that would make Ben Hecht sound like Edgar Guest."[78]

The story they chose had a long work-up. It began as "A Reputation," a short story by Richard Connell first published in *Century Magazine* in 1922. In the magazine version, a Manhattan clerk crashes a Park Avenue party to announce that he is going to protest the dismal state of the world by jumping to his death off the Central Park reservoir.

78. Capra, *The Name Above the Title,* p. 297.

Connell was a familiar figure around Hollywood by the 1930s, a hardworking writer best known in a long career for contributing the screen stories for such films as *Brother Orchid* (1940), *Two Girls and a Sailor* (1944), and *The Kid From Brooklyn* (1946). Swerling knew Connell, and with Connell's permission tried for a while in the mid-1930s to develop a stage version of "A Reputation," then abandoned the idea. Next Connell and another Hollywood writer, Robert Presnell, wrote a screen treatment of "A Reputation," which they titled "The Life and Death of John Doe." Connell and Presnell had been trying to peddle it to various producers for a long time when it was shown, inevitably, to Riskin.

Riskin presented it to Capra, who liked it instantly. "The Life and Death of John Doe" was slated as the first endeavor of Frank Capra Productions, Inc. Connell and Presnell were taken off the script but were honored on the screen, with their names prominently displayed on the main title card. (Connell is also the name of a crucial character, the hardbitten newspaper editor, played by James Gleason. Riskin liked sneaking in author's names, such as Budington in *Mr. Deeds,* as a kind of homage.)

The John Doe story became the premise for Capra and Riskin's most wrenching Christ parable. Riskin made radical changes in the original story. First and foremost, the suicide became an elaborate hoax, dreamed up as a newspaper circulation stunt by Ann Mitchell (played by Barbara Stanwyck), another of Riskin's shady newspaper ladies. When the public takes the hoax to heart and a John Doe movement is launched spontaneously, a John Doe stand-in must be found and exploited. Riskin brought him to life as John ("Long John") Willoughby (played by Gary Cooper), a homeless drifter and ex-baseball pitcher who shows up at the newspaper office, not claiming, unlike a long line of other unfortunates, to have written the suicide note, but hoping for some work.

Willoughby is proclaimed a "typical American," down on his luck, outraged by the state of the world (actually, his "outraged" photograph is staged by Ann Mitchell; he is acting out how he would react to an umpire's bad call at the plate). Willoughby's sidekick is one of Riskin's most irascible characters, an unsociable, completely incorruptible hobo dubbed Colonel (played by Walter Brennan). Their inexplicable rapport is summarized in their musical affinity: both play "doohickies." One of Capra and Riskin's most elegiac musical scenes takes place on a freight train when Willoughby plays the happy-go-lucky "Hi Diddle Dee Dee" (from Walt Disney's *Pinocchio*) on the harmonica while the Colonel hoists his spindly legs in a sprightly tap dance.

The Colonel serves as a bracing antidote for the cloying sentiment enunciated by other characters. He is against all bourgeois comforts and platitudes, denouncing everybody within earshot as "heelots" ("a lot of heels"), one of Riskin's made-up words. Yet Riskin never wrote more persuasive platitudes. Never were the heartfelt sentiments as simply and beautifully expressed. Other screenwriters would gladly jump off the Central Park reservoir just to write one speech of the sort that seems to proliferate in *Meet John Doe,* sometimes emerging from the mouths of fringe characters (such as the small-town soda jerk, Bert).

The apotheosis of Riskin's humanism is represented in speeches like the one Willoughby delivers on national radio, the words "ghosted" by Ann Mitchell, who cribs from her father's diary:

```
                    JOHN
I'm gonna talk about us, the average guys, the
John Does. If anybody should ask you what the
average John Doe is like, you couldn't tell him,
because he's a million and one things. He's Mr.
Big and Mr. Small. He's simple and he's wise.
He's inherently honest, but he's got a streak of
larceny in his heart. He seldom walks up to a
public telephone without shoving his finger into
the slot to see if somebody left a nickel there.
  He's the man the ads are written for. He's the
fella everybody sells things to. He's Joe
Doakes, the world's greatest stooge and the
world's greatest strength.
  Yes, sir. Yessir, we're a great family, the
John Does. We're the meek who are supposed to
inherit the earth. You'll find us everywhere. We
raise the crops, we dig the mines, work the fac-
tories, keep the books, fly the planes and drive
the busses! And when a cop yells, "Stand back
there, you!" he means us, the John Does!
  We've existed since time began. We built the
pyramids, we saw Christ crucified, pulled the
oars for Roman emperors, sailed the boats for
Columbus, retreated from Moscow with Napoleon
and froze with Washington at Valley Forge!
  Yes, sir. We've been in there dodging left
hooks since before history began to walk! In our
struggle for freedom we've hit the canvas many a
time, but we always bounced back!
  Because we're the people - and we're tough!
```

As Willoughby, Cooper gives a mesmerizing performance, capturing all the levels of a man who, while a failure and fake, grows to believe in an idea—the John Doe movement of ordinary people—that is bigger than himself. His performance is matched by Stanwyck's portrayal of Ann Mitchell, a convert to her own hoax. Riskin needed a villain worthy of his hero, and he created one in D. B. Norton, played by Edward Arnold—the first of the truly despicable villains to show up in Capra's canon.

Norton, an industrialist, is also a paramilitarist with his own private corps of storm troopers. He has Napoleonic ambitions, and manipulates the John Doe movement to attain his own sinister ends. Here was another instance where Riskin was brave and prescient about what was going on in America. The pro-Nazi Bund and fascist sympathizers were a genuine movement in the United States, and in Hollywood as well there were those who performed military drills in the Hollywood Hills while secretly supporting foreign tyrants. Audiences of the time understood the shorthand when Norton was characterized by the script as fifth-columnist who desired an "iron hand" to build a "new order."[79]

Willoughby sees the light in a quietly impressive Riskin scene. Sick at heart over what is going on, the newspaper editor, Connell, gets thoroughly plastered, pulls Willoughby aside, and makes an emotional confession about fighting for democracy in World War I and seeing his own father shot down alongside him in battle. "I'm a sucker for this country," Connell says, telling Willoughby the truth about D. B. Norton's chicanery. (More than once in a Riskin script, the crusty newspaper editor turns out to be a softie at heart.) Willoughby is outraged to learn how he has been duped. He makes a beeline for Norton's mansion, where Norton and other muckamucks are celebrating their plans for a national takeover. Ann Mitchell is there, too, and Willoughby rises to the occasion, denouncing her and the others. Then, in the midst of an apocalyptic rainstorm, he heads to a mass meeting of John Doe followers to publicly denounce the charade.

This climatic scene is a tour de force of Capra-Riskin images: Willoughby, rain drenched, his face lined with hurt . . . thousands of umbrellas sheltering thousands of ordinary John Does . . . a silent prayer for "the homeless and hungry." D. B. Norton's goons and cops arrive in haste; newsboys shout headlines and hand out "extras" proclaiming John Doe a fraud. The camera captures shocked, frozen, upturned faces. Willoughby attempts to speak in his own defense and his words are strangled as Norton grabs the loudspeaker to condemn him vociferously. Organized boos and catcalls break out, tomatoes are thrown, and Willoughby is abjectly humiliated.

In case audiences miss the analogy, Ann Mitchell and Connell, sequestered by police, make the point crystal clear. "They're crucifying him!" sobs Ann Mitchell, as she listens to the radio. "Well boys," mutters Connell, "you can chalk up another one to the Pontius Pilates."

79. This may have been a case of borrowing from Sinclair Lewis, whose 1935 novel *It Can't Happen Here* fancied a New England fascist elected to the presidency. In any case, Capra and Riskin were not coy about the cautionary politique of *Meet John Doe,* and publicity articles such as "*Meet John Doe* Pictures a Fascist Putsch in the U.S.A.," by John T. McManus in *PM,* March 7, 1941, spelled out the "message."

After that, John Doe—Willoughby—disappears, becoming a public joke. But Ann Mitchell, Connell, the Colonel, and some diehard John Doe followers suspect that Willoughby's conscience tortures him, and that he will try to follow through on his vow to kill himself in order to redeem his reputation. The story ends in a tableau on the roof of one of New York's tallest buildings on Christmas Eve.

How ought the story to end? Once again Riskin and Capra were indecisive. They considered letting Willoughby jump to his death. Reportedly, Riskin argued for the last shot to be one of the Colonel cradling Willoughby in his arms, carrying the body down a moonlit street. They devised one ending where Norton actually apologizes and volunteers to publish the letter Willoughby has written, admitting publicly to the whole story in the newspaper he owns. Norton ends up murmuring "Merry Christmas," but the last line belongs to the Colonel, who also undergoes a change of heart, exclaiming, "Well, looks like I gotta give the Heelots one more chance!"[80]

Ultimately, Capra and Riskin chose the only solution upon which they could agree. Willoughby is on the roof, about to jump, when out of the shadows step Norton and his cohorts, trailed by the Colonel and a few John Does. Norton taunts Willoughby with the threat that his suicide will be kept out of the newspapers. Willoughby, who has taken the precaution of writing a confessional letter and posting it to Connell, hesitates. A feverish Ann Mitchell dashes forward, clings to Willoughby, and declares her love for him before collapsing in his arms. The John Does chorus their faith in him. Dazed and speechless, without a single further line of dialogue, Willoughby lifts Ann Mitchell in his arms and carries her toward the elevator. "There they are, Norton," Connell barks over his shoulder to Norton, left behind on the rooftop, "the *people*—try and lick that!"

Filming for *Meet John Doe* was more than usually secretive (a lesson from the experience of *Last Horizon*), and anticipation ran high for the reunion of Capra and Riskin. The reaction from critics was mixed. Opening on the cusp of World War II, the love-thy-neighbor idealism seemed outdated and the speeches wordy. Even *Time* magazine, which featured Gary Cooper on its cover, gave the film a backhanded compliment. "Super-schmalz," the magazine sniffed.[81] Hollywood awarded *Meet John Doe* precisely one Academy Award nomination, to Connell and Presnell for Best Story.

Especially because of the last reel—the "false ending," in Parker Tyler's words, of John Doe deciding against suicide— *Meet John Doe* has the modern-day reputa-

80. The several "revised endings" are published and discussed in *Meet John Doe,* ed. Charles Wolfe (Rutgers University Press, 1989).

81. *Time,* March 3, 1941.

tion among critics of "an ambitious but troubled work."[82] "It is astonishing, but true," wrote Capra, "*Meet John Doe* missed becoming a lasting film classic because we couldn't end it!"[83]

Yet, who among us would vote for Willoughby to take the jump? Although the ending represented a genuine dilemma for Capra and Riskin, its significance has been overrated. Capra was wrong—*Meet John Doe* did become a lasting classic. Fans of the film treasure its wealth of memorable characters, situations, and set-pieces executed by a director at the height of his powers. Lovers of film literature will treasure the script for some of Riskin's most daring writing: his most ambivalent hero, his fascist villain, and the intricately woven story that holds a mirror up to dark America.

Frank Capra Productions, Inc., was short-lived. Budget overruns had pushed the costs past one million dollars, and special tax laws limited the profits. According to a contemporary account, despite "heavy grosses being rolled up," the company had no choice but to dissolve: "Behind this decision, it is understood, is the effect of the excess profits tax which Congress has imposed on all industry, which, so far as independent picture-making is concerned, will take so much of these profits away there will not be enough left to make the effort and risk involved worthwhile."[84] (In fact, *Meet John Doe* eventually went into public domain, and nowadays it is hard to find a decent print of it; many television and video versions show the effects of age.)

That once again Riskin and Capra were forced to break up was partly circumstantial, and at the time it was neither seen nor intended as permanent. The relative failure of *Meet John Doe* was a factor, but World War II also intervened, a momentous event that threw more than one Hollywood career off stride.

Sadly, and unsuspected at the time, *Meet John Doe* was the peak of Riskin's career.

* * *

Riskin, stated McBride uncategorically, was Frank Capra's social conscience in regard to filmmaking. Capra was someone who always voted Republican and someone whose views tended toward the political Right, although at times he was influenced by the liberal viewpoints of Riskin, Swerling, Buchman, and others.[85]

82. Parker Tyler is quoted in *Meet John Doe,* ed. Charles Wolfe, in his introduction.
83. Capra, *The Name Above the Title,* p. 304.
84. "Capra-Riskin Dissolving Corp.," *Hollywood Reporter,* April 23, 1941.
85. McBride, *Frank Capra,* pp. 251–263, 334–342.

Riskin was solidly a Democrat and one of the more public-spirited screenwriters. Perhaps his Jewish heritage was a factor in his political views and in his actions once World War II began. Even before America entered the war Riskin left Hollywood to work in London at the request of the British government, to advise on the production of propaganda films. After the bombing of Pearl Harbor, Riskin swiftly returned to the United States to join the government's Office of War Information as chief of its overseas Motion Picture Bureau, in charge of producing films for informational purposes and psychological warfare. He held this important post, spending months at a time in the European theater, until May 1945.

His letters to Fay Wray from London during the blitz were uncommonly reflective and revealing:

LONDON, 1944

Actually, a great many people enjoyed the raids. Certainly the danger was there . . . the ever present imminence of your own destruction . . . but something else was there . . . *company.* It is difficult to be lonely when you are sharing a common danger with people all about you. I found, after the first few days, that I was disappointed when the alert failed to sound. I was alone in my room . . . removed from the world around me when nothing happened. But the moment the siren started, I was no longer alone . . . thousands . . . millions of other hearts stirred simultaneously . . . skipped a beat just as mine skipped. At that moment, they were in the room with me . . . and I was with them . . . in a million homes . . . in a million cellars. At times like that, no matter how impoverished you might feel . . . in worldly goods or in the spirit . . . you are lifted to a level of equality with the most blessed of human beings. Envy of another's riches . . . fear through insecurity . . . a floundering ego . . . all vanish. For one moment, you are the equal of the most courageous . . . for one moment, the brains, the genius, the gifts, the accumulated wealth, the high positions of the mightiest disappear . . . and all are one . . . of which you are an equal part.

LONDON, 1944

True, deep-rooted convictions are rare. People see wisdom in many ideas . . . conflicting ideas . . . their hearts and their minds leap from one concept to another. In an era of chaos . . . when all the social forms and changes . . . when every concept of economic and spiritual existence is dusted off and paraded before the hard-ridden masses of the world . . . it is no wonder that John Q. Public is straddling the fence. It is no wonder that he is punch-drunk and unable to assert himself. Where is *that idea*? Where is that big, unchallengeable, fundamentally unshakeable idea which snaps John Doe out of his binge and about which he says, "Now that's what I mean. That's what I've waited for . . . that's what *I* stand for . . . and the rest is bilge."

Will that idea come in time to save us? I, personally, believe it will. Perhaps not in this generation . . . or even in the next . . . but come it must. Because, I still contend, despite all their larceny, people are good. Most of larcenous behavior is acquired . . . and the extent to which the individual practices it is dictated by necessity. Create a society of abundance for all and the need for larceny is reduced to a minimum. Of course it will never be perfect unless that green snow falls and changes the nature of man . . . but our jungle existence *can* be eradicated to some extent . . . and eventually to a great extent.

I tried to say something of this sort in *Meet John Doe.* And it is interesting to note (as you and I have noted before) the number of books on religion which are successful in wartime. You see, people need goodness to lean on in times of wickedness and evil. They need to remind themselves that the human race . . . of which they are a part . . . is not all evil . . . that its impulses are virtuous and charitable and unselfish. They need this, for they cannot look upon *themselves* as wicked. No person, except for rare pathological cases, thinks of himself as anything but a good, honest human being.[86]

With fellow screenwriters Philip Dunne and Joseph Krumgold, Riskin supervised roughly forty short films for the Office of War Information intended to advertise America in a friendly light. The films were dubbed in some twenty-two languages, then sent overseas, along with newsreels, for weekly showings.

These short films included:

- *The Autobiography of a Jeep,* a witty memoir of a Jeep that proudly explains its origins, functions, and rise to reknown as the American soldier's general purpose vehicle.
- *The Valley of the Tennessee,* a portrait of how a ruined land was revived through cooperative effort, "superbly filmed in a style reminiscent of the powerful Farm Security Administration photographs of the mid '30s."[87]

86. Quoted with permission from Wray, *On the Other Hand,* pp. 228, 253.
87. Jonathan Starr, printed program for the Robert Riskin Film Retrospective, University of Southern California, March 22, 1987.

- *Swedes in America,* a tour, with Ingrid Bergman as guide, of the customs and traditions of Swedish-Americans, emphasizing the democratic spirit of American Swedes in Minnesota.
- *Library of Congress,* an introduction to the great library which affirmed the conviction that democracy must build on an enlightened citizenry.
- *Pipeline,* a record of the construction of the world's largest pipeline across seven states, a tribute to American know-how.
- *The Town,* directed by Joseph von Sternberg, a portrait of a small Indiana town that celebrates America as a melting pot.
- *People to People,* a populist piece about an exchange visit, which follows four British trade unionists as they journey through the United States.
- *Arturo Toscanini/Hymn of the Nations,* "an intimate, emotional study of the great maestro . . . a magnificent piece of work,"[88] in which Toscanini conducts his rousing arrangement of Verdi's "Hymn of the Nations," with Jan Peerce and the Westminster Choir.[89]

In his Capra biography, McBride chronicled the director's initial disappointment at being made a "desk man" in Washington, D.C., and how Capra pushed to go overseas to get closer to the action in order to direct his inspirational *Why We Fight* series. Some Hollywood figures felt they had to distinguish themselves with battleground documentaries. It was characteristic of Riskin, who held as high and important a government position as anyone from the motion picture industry, that his war work consisted of a variety of unassuming and edifying morale-building documentaries that emphasized musical inspiration, decent values, ordinary achievement, and America's rally-round-the-flag spirit.

* * *

Wartime was important for other reasons. In August 1942, Riskin married Fay Wray. It was her second marriage. (Her first husband, John Monk Saunders, was a screenwriter, a former journalist, and an Air Corps lieutenant who had specialized

88. Bosley Crowther, "Speaking Up for America," *New York Times,* undated clipping in Riskin's files at USC.

89. Riskin's World War II informational films are covered by Jonathan Starr in his enlightening program notes for the USC–Robert Riskin Retrospective, and additional details were drawn from Bosley Crowther's "Speaking Up for America" and also his "Destination Abroad," *New York Times,* August 29, 1943.

in aviation stories.) On the day of their wedding, Riskin, sensitive to the feelings of Fay Wray's daughter Susan, presented Susan, as well as her mother, with a ceremonial ring. In time he and Fay Wray had two children, Robert Jr. and Victoria.

After resigning from government service in April 1945, Riskin returned to Hollywood and formed Robert Riskin Productions. It was announced that he would write and direct a series of features for RKO. The trade papers listed the titles slated for production: "The Girl From Bogardus," "Impact," "Now It Can Be Told," "Johnny Appleseed," "You Belong to Me," and "Magic Town."

Although Capra was still in service—he would not be formally discharged for another two months—there was no public hint that Capra and Riskin were permanently estranged. When Capra formed Liberty Films, with Sam Briskin, William Wyler, and George Stevens, there was speculation that Riskin would work on another project with the director sooner or later. After all, Riskin and Capra were still the best of friends, as well as the best of collaborators.

McBride argued in his book that bad feelings were simmering between them over authorship of their films, with Capra, the frustrated writer, feeling resentful of Riskin's ability. McBride defined *Meet John Doe* as a parable of pseudonymous authorship whose plot mirrored these underlying tensions. "The irreconcilable irony of the [*Meet John Doe*] situation is that without a writer, John Doe is (as Capra would be) helpless: when John Doe rebels and tries to speak for himself, Norton does not allow him to do so, and at the end all he can write for himself is a genuine suicide letter."[90]

But Riskin and Capra still liked to spend time with each other, even when they were not working together. They had stimulating conversations. They listened to each other, made each other laugh. When together at a dinner party, the two of them would perform hijinks, much like the characters in a goofball scene from one of their movies. They would sing nonsense songs or juggle balls. Or they would take hold of each other's ankles, make a ball of themselves, and roll around the living room, upending furniture. Their time together was always a kind of workshop production.

Capra and his wife continued to come to the Riskin house for dinner and other occasions. At one dinner party in the late 1940s, Capra cast aspersions on the son of a mutual friend, declaring he was a Communist. Riskin was nominally anti-Communist, although he would never stoop to red-baiting, and Capra's comment bothered him. McBride's book asserted that Capra eventually shamed himself by turning his back on his politically progressive friends and associates—people who had been loyal colleagues. If Riskin had not become ill, it is possible he too would have

90. McBride, *Frank Capra,* p. 433.

been vulnerable when the House Committee on Un-American Activities invaded Hollywood, swooping down on Sidney Buchman and other Capra collaborators.[91]

There is no question that Riskin was wounded further when Capra sought credit for his writing contribution to *Riding High* (1950), the remake of *Broadway Bill.* According to Capra, Riskin had declined his offer to work on the remake. According to McBride, quoting Fay Wray, Riskin's offer to work on the remake in fact had been rejected by Capra. In any case, the *Riding High* script was patched together by five writers apart from Capra, who sought to share the main screenplay credit equally with Riskin. Riskin made a formal protest to the Screen Writers Guild, which awarded him a co-script credit along with writers Melville Shavelson and Jack Rose. Capra was denied a credit.[92]

Despite the resulting tensions, had Riskin continued to write and flourish in Hollywood, he and Capra probably would have teamed up again because they were twice as good in collaboration—and because Riskin was such an easygoing and self-effacing person. He and Capra never had a spectacular "divorce." Fay Wray said in an interview that she was the most surprised person in the world to read the implication in Capra's statements, later on in his life, that they had any kind of falling-out.

*   *   *

Riskin was still writing with famous, relaxed ease. He liked to take a bridge table and set it out on the lawn. He loved to sit in the sun while working on a script. The children might be making a lot of noise and running around him, playing games, but it didn't seem to bother him. Jo Swerling might drop by (they spent hours discussing the play Swerling was working on, *Guys and Dolls*), but Riskin welcomed diversions and gave of himself freely, without self-interest, to others.

The ease was deceptive. Sometimes Riskin was preoccupied with a script problem the way a mathematician might be stuck on an especially tangled equation. Driving back from Palm Springs one day, he drifted off the road and crossed over to the other side of the dividing line, driving for several hair-raising moments on

91. Riskin stuck his neck out against Hollywood's vocal right-wing element. In 1945, Riskin debated Donald Crisp and James K. McGuinness, two leaders of the film industry conservatives, on an ABC Radio "Town Meeting." They argued that social and political ideas in motion pictures amounted to propaganda. Riskin countered that motion pictures couldn't escape from and indeed depended on the infusion of controversial ideas.

92. McBride, *Frank Capra,* p. 550.

the wrong side of the highway until he was elbowed back to reality by Fay Wray. He explained that he had been distracted by thinking about a scene in the script on which he was working.

When Fay Wray told him she was thinking of trying her hand at writing either a play or a book, he encouraged her, as he encouraged everybody, to go ahead and give it her best. But he also warned her that writing amounted to a lonely profession and, apart from everything else, it was hard, terribly hard, work.

Riskin Productions was not a success. The only project on the program that came to fruition was *Magic Town* (1947), which Riskin co-wrote with Joseph Krumgold. The film is about a middle-American town that is invaded by a pollster because it is the perfect barometer of national opinion. With James Stewart as the pollster, the film had a distinct Capra-Riskin tone. It is not as momentous as the film Capra made with James Stewart around the same time, *It's a Wonderful Life*. Nor is it as dark and disturbing, indicating that Riskin had come out of World War II with his idealism resilient. For all its faults it holds up as a whimsical slice of Americana. William Wellman's direction was somewhat heavy-handed, and Wellman always insisted that Capra should have taken on the job. With Capra and some tinkering, *Magic Town* might have been something grand.

Instead, Riskin's only independent film was a box-office failure and a disappointment to many critics who were wishing for another achievement like *Mr. Deeds Goes to Town*. He was forced to fold his operation in 1949 and liquidate the assets, among which was a story he had written called "You Belong to Me," also originally intended for James Stewart. Riskin sold the rights to Paramount, which alerted Frank Capra, who snatched it up. This story, about a newspaperman who takes war orphans under his wing in order to win over his girlfriend, went through six writers before becoming Capra's 1951 musical film *Here Comes the Groom*.

In the meantime Riskin had signed a contract with 20th Century-Fox, for whom he quickly wrote two films: *Mister 880* (1950), based on *New Yorker* articles by St. Clair McKelway about an elderly counterfeiter, and *Half-Angel* (1951), based on the true case of a multiple personality who was a nighttime sleepwalker and a daytime amnesiac. When eventually produced, both were not half bad, although they needed a rewrite and polish (and would have had them had Riskin not become ill).

In December 1950, Riskin delivered the first draft of "Belvedere," which was planned for Clifton Webb, to Darryl Zanuck, head of production at Fox. Riskin enclosed the following memo: "Dear Darryl: Season's Greetings. All I can give you for Christmas is the script for 'Belvedere.' I hope it is just what you wanted from Santa."[93]

Those were some of the last words he would write. For a few weeks Riskin had shown signs of "approaching vascular problems," according to contemporary newspaper accounts. In late December he was hospitalized at Cedars of Lebanon hospital; on December 27, while in the hospital, he suffered a major stroke. Removal of a blood clot probably saved his life, but he was left paralyzed on the left side, dysfunctional on the cerebral side of the brain, and confined to his bed or wheelchair.

Riskin was not without lucidity, but neither was he in complete command of his faculties. He became a person stuck in time, under constant medication and the supervision of nurses around the clock. He continued to toy with a script idea, a story about a man who was a ship's captain with one family on an island and another family on the mainland, but the stroke had compromised his ability to write. He would dictate snatches of the script to Fay Wray, maybe achieve a polished sentence or two, then start over again on the same sentence. Ironically, his stroke took place during the filming of *Here Comes the Groom,* for which, ultimately, he and co-writer Liam O'Brien would receive an Oscar nomination for Best Story.

Riskin's tragedy was well known and widely reported in Hollywood, and many people, friends and associates, visited him. The astonishing thing is that Capra never did—he telephoned only once in five years—and, in fact, skipped Riskin's funeral. (In his autobiography Capra never mentions Riskin's illness or death.) It was as if a curtain had fallen between them. It was maddening and mysterious.

For a long, long time Fay Wray did not know how to make sense of Capra's behavior. She tried to rationalize it as Capra caring too much about Riskin to see him in such a sorry state. But she grew to believe that, as Capra's career began to lull, it became vital for him to usurp Riskin. Riskin's illness relieved Capra of the responsibility of sharing the credit for their joint ventures. After Riskin's death, Capra made only two films. One, *A Pocketful of Miracles* (1961), was a remake of Riskin's 1933 script for *Lady For A Day.*

Riskin was unable to be present when, in February 1955, the Writer's Guild of America honored him with its highest award, the Laurel Award for a lifetime of "distinguished contribution to the film medium." Fay Wray accepted in her husband's absence. When finances dwindled, Riskin was transferred to the Motion Picture Hospital, where he died on September 20, 1955, after having suffered for nearly five years. The Los Angeles newspapers hailed Riskin as "one of Hollywood's greatest screenwriters." At Riskin's funeral, his good friend Jo Swerling

93. Wray, "Biography of Robert Riskin as Screen Writer."

was among the pallbearers, and George Jessel gave the eulogy. "The story of Robert Riskin is in three acts," Jessel said, "You can write the first two on a joyful note; you will have to write the last with a tear."[94]

* * *

As Peter Warne's editor laments in *It Happened One Night,* "You think you've got a swell yarn, then something comes along, messes up the finish, and there you are."

After Riskin's death, Capra, in his autobiography and in public pronouncements, began to promote his importance as "the name above the title" to Riskin's detriment: "Yes, Robert Riskin was a giant among scriptwriters—at least when he worked with me."[95] Capra besmirched himself as much as Riskin with these statements, and their partnership, nearly perfect in its time, was given a taint from which it may never quite recover.

In truth, the trend of film criticism in the United States has been toward auteurist glorification, and Capra was not the only one extolling his own accomplishments. From Graham Greene's astonishing statement, after seeing *Mr. Smith Goes to Washington,* that "now it is difficult to believe that Riskin's part was ever very important"[96] to Leland A. Poague's more recent verdict that "if anything, Riskin was too much of an alter ego for Capra," their rapport producing "lazy masterpieces" from "artistic in-breeding,"[97] most opinion has favored Capra. McBride's book, coming after Capra's death in 1991, went to extreme lengths in the opposite direction, upholding Riskin to the point of denigrating Capra.

This collection of Riskin's work is not intended to launch fresh debate over who did what, who dominated the teamwork, who provided what ingredient in the chemistry, or who wrote this crucial scene or devised that memorable moment—that would not be in the spirit of Riskin. For motion picture lovers, this collection will provide hours of purely pleasurable distraction. For students of script form, this is a long-overdue opportunity to become acquainted with a writer's writer and learn from one whose films brought joy to people and whose clarion voice made a difference in our lives.

94. "Rites for Robt. Riskin Draw Film Notables," *Los Angeles Times,* September 24, 1955.

95. See Frank Capra, "'One Man, One Film'—the Capra Contention," *The Los Angeles Times,* Sunday Calendar, June 26, 1977, and the response, "'Someone Else's Guts'—the Rintels Rebuttals," by David W. Rintels, in the same issue. The article that fueled their debate, "Someone's Been Sitting in His Chair," by David W. Rintels, had appeared earlier that month, in the *Los Angeles Times,* Sunday Calendar, June 5, 1977.

96. Graham Greene, "A Director of Genius: Four Reviews," *Frank Capra: The Man and His Films,* pp. 110–116.

97. Poague, *The Cinema of Frank Capra,* p. 97.

Anne Schuyler (Jean Harlow) and Stew Smith (Robert Williams) in the "garter duet" from *Platinum Blonde*.

Platinum Blonde

Columbia Pictures, 1931, 88 minutes

Produced by Harry Cohn

Directed by Frank Capra

Story by Harry E. Chandlee and Douglas W. Churchill

Adaptation by Jo Swerling

Continuity by Dorothy Howell

Dialogue by Robert Riskin

Cast: Loretta Young (*Gallagher*), Robert Williams (*Stew Smith*), Jean Harlow (*Anne Schuyler*), Louise Closser Hale (*Mrs. Schuyler*), Donald Dillaway (*Michael Schuyler*), Reginald Owen (*Dexter Grayson*), Walter Catlett (*Bingy Baker*), Edmund Breese (*Conroy, the Editor*), Halliwell Hobbes (*Smythe, the Butler*), Claude Allister (*Dawson, the Violinist*), Bill Elliott (*Dinner Guest*), Harry Semels (*Waiter*), Olaf Hytten (*Radcliffe*), Tom London, Hal Price, Eddy Chandler, Charles Jordan (*Reporters*), Dick Cramer (*Speakeasy Proprietor*), Wilson Benge (*Butler*), Dick Prichard.

PLATINUM BLONDE

FADE IN

1. INT. CITY ROOM OF NEWSPAPER OFFICE - DAY - FULL SHOT
General atmosphere, typical of a busy newspaper office. Copy boys running about, shirtsleeved reporters and rewrite men pounding away on typewriters. Little wire baskets containing cylinders of copy whizzing back and forth, such as are used in some department stores, etc.

SOUND
(Morkrum machines,[1] typewriters, telephone bells and all other sounds relative to a newspaper office)

When shot has been fully established:

CAMERA STARTS TRUCKING DOWN MAIN AISLE
It takes in the battery of Morkrum machines clattering away; the crescent-shaped copy desk; the desk of the sporting editor, with a big cauliflower-eared pugilist and his manager standing by the side of the sporting editor, a hefty guy in his shirtsleeves, smoking a big cigar and wearing a green eye-shade; the desk of the society editor, a prissy old lady, who takes down a worn copy of the Blue Book as the camera passes her and starts looking up some data; and any other interesting or typical bits that can be thought out. At the far end of the room is the desk of Conroy, the City Editor.

Everything shows evidence of feverish activity and great haste.

2. CLOSE SHOT
On Conroy, the City Editor at his desk, speaking on the telephone.

CONROY
Yeah, that's all I ever get from you guys - a lot of hard luck stories. You come back here and I'll give you an assignment. It will be a last interview - with the cashier!

He hangs up, looks around with a scowl.

Stew! Stew Smith!

REPORTER
Oh Mr. Conroy, give me a crack at that Schuyler story, will you?

CONROY
You? If you ever got your foot into a drawing room, you'd step on a sliding rug! Stew is the only man that's got brains enough to handle this. Scram!

A Copy Boy rushes by on an errand.

Say Spud, did you find Stew?

COPY BOY
Not yet.

CONROY
Well, did you look in the--

COPY BOY
First place I looked.

CONROY
Not there, eh? For cryin' out loud, where is that--? Go and dig him up! Stew! Stew Smith!

CAMERA TRUCKS ON:
Until it takes in a sort of make-shift screen, concealing a corner of the room.

LAP DISSOLVE TO:

3. CLOSE SHOT
On the other side of the screen. Stew Smith is holding something in his hand. His hat tilted back on his head, and he is regarding this plaything intently. Gallagher is sitting close to him, also gazing intently at the plaything. Gallagher is a girl, one of the sob sisters[2] on the newspaper, dressed in a trim but inexpensive little tailored suit.

STEW
Here it is. Pray for me, Gallagher. Pray for me. Hold everything ...

4. CLOSE SHOT
On the object in his hand, one of those hand-puzzles where you have to land jumping beans in the holes.

5. DOUBLE SHOT

GALLAGHER
Stew, your hands are shaking. You've been drinking again.

STEW
Come on, come on. Here they come, Gallagher! Here they come!

Conroy's shouts are heard in the background.

GALLAGHER
(conspiratorially)
The boss is getting hoarse.

STEW
There's the third one. If I don't get the last one, there's a certain sob sister I know that's going to get a kick right in the ... oh! Whoops, almost had that.

6. MED. CLOSE SHOT
Conroy, the City Editor at his desk, looking about with a scowl for Stew.

CONROY
(bellowing)
Stew! Stew Smith!

The Copy Boy races over to whisper something to Conroy.

CONROY
What? The screen?

7. CLOSE SHOT
On Stew Smith

STEW
Gallagher! I made it!

8. MEDIUM SHOT (FROM CONROY'S ANGLE)
The screen, concealing the washbasin corner.

CONTINUATION, SCENE 6
A wrathy Conroy, his eyes centering suspiciously on something. With his eyes on the screen, Conroy reaches out and grasps a heavy telephone book on the corner of his desk. Still looking off, he heaves it forcefully.

9. MED. CLOSE SHOT
Showing the screen. The telephone book crashes into it, overturning it and revealing Stew and Gallagher on the other side. They both look up, startled. The newsroom erupts in laughter.

CONTINUATION, SCENE 6
Conroy, glaring off fiercely.

CONROY
Come over here!

10. MEDIUM SHOT
Conroy at his desk. Stew saunters into the scene.

STEW
Look, I quit!

CONROY
Yeah?

STEW
Yeah.

CONROY
Yeah?

STEW
You're always picking on me. It took me three hours to get those little gadgets in those holes, and you screw it up in a minute. Hey, look!

He gives the hand-puzzle to Conroy, who is immediately captivated by the fascinating object in his hand.

11. CLOSE DOUBLE SHOT

STEW
(superior)
Mmm, not as easy as it looks, is it?

Conroy puts it down with a disgusted look.

CONROY
Aagh! No wonder you're batty. Would it be imposing too much upon you if I asked you to do a little work today? Just to sort of break the monotony?

STEW
With me you can always do business.

CONROY
Do you know what to do in a drawing-room?

STEW
It isn't a question of knowing what to do, it's knowing how to get in one that counts.

The telephone rings, Conroy answers it.

CONROY
(speaking on the phone)
Yeah, yeah. Okay, okay.

He hangs up, turns back to Stew.

Now listen, we've got a tip that the Schuyler family has finally made a deal with that chorus dame.

STEW
Gloria Golden?

CONROY
Yeah, little Gloria.

STEW
The human cash register. Got her hooks into the Schuyler kid, eh?

CONROY
Right - for the first time this year.

STEW
(modestly)
Well - it's only April.

CONROY
Come on, get going, get going!

STEW
(loftily)
Get going where? I can write that yarn without stepping out of the office.

CONROY
Yeah - and get us into a million dollar libel suit. It wouldn't be the first time. Now, you get over there and get a statement out of the old lady, the sister, or the kid. Any of them - but get it.

STEW
(resigned)
All right. Give me a voucher for expenses.

12. CLOSE DOUBLE SHOT (ANOTHER ANGLE)

CONROY
What expenses? All you need is carfare to Long Island. You'd better get a shave and a shine, because you, you're going to have a tough time getting in there as it is.

STEW
I know those bluenoses. Their ancestors refused to come over on the Mayflower because they didn't want to rub elbows with the tourists. So they swam over.

He turns away and exits.

FADE OUT:

FADE IN

13. EXT. THE SCHUYLER HOUSE - DAY - MEDIUM SHOT
Someone pacing outside the mansion gates.

14. EXT. THE SCHUYLER HOUSE (ANOTHER ANGLE) DAY - CLOSE SHOT
A guard dog pacing inside the gates.

15. INT. INSIDE THE MANSION - DAY - CLOSE SHOT
A parrot on its perch, hopping from foot to foot.

16. INT. SCHUYLER DRAWING ROOM - DAY - CLOSE SHOT
Michael Schuyler, a callow youth with the usual dissipated, spoiled look. His fingers are nipping out little chunks of a folded piece of paper, dropping the bits on the floor. This is indicative of a habit of the individual in question when undergoing nervous stress. He is very fidgety and apprehensive, as he glances around.

CAMERA PANS OVER TO SHOW
Anne Schuyler, a beautiful and aristocratic, though slightly hard girl, a few years older than Michael.

CAMERA PANS OVER TO SHOW
Mrs. Stuyvesand Van Alstyne Schuyler, mother of Anne and Michael. A grande dame, stern and glowering. Her attitude indicates suppressed nervousness and anger. She glares over in the direction of Michael. Then she turns and looks in another direction.

MRS. SCHUYLER
(viciously)
Dexter Grayson, if you were any kind of a lawyer, you'd get those letters back!

CAMERA PANS OVER TO SHOW
Dexter Grayson, the family lawyer standing, his hands clasped behind his back, just completing the pacing of a few short steps in his best courtroom manner, his head bowed in an attitude of deepest thought. He is dressed in striped afternoon trousers and black coat. He turns to regard Mrs. Schuyler.

GRAYSON
But I keep telling you how difficult it is, Mrs. Schuyler. The last time I asked her for those letters, she made very uncouth noises with her mouth.

CAMERA PANS OVER TO SHOW
Anne Schuyler, trying desperately to keep from laughing.

CAMERA DRAWS BACK
To reveal a full shot of the room and group. They are in the magnificent drawing room of the Schuyler home, resembling the Union Depot and furnished with almost imperial splendor and magnificence. They very much resemble a jury in session. As they continue:

MICHAEL
I don't know why you're making all this fuss. I only sent her six of them.

MRS. SCHUYLER
(sarcastic)
If you had to make a fool of yourself, why didn't you tell it to her instead of writing?

MICHAEL
Because I couldn't get her on the phone.

MRS. SCHUYLER
Imbecile!

ANNE
You should have known better than to write, Romeo. I found that out a long time ago.

MRS. SCHUYLER
I should say you had. At the rate you two are going, we'll have to leave the country to save our faces.

ANNE
Splendid, Mother. Let's hop over to Monte Carlo. It's a great place to save a face.

MRS. SCHUYLER
Oh, shut up!

A butler appears in the doorway. He is about to say something, but he stammers and turns.

MRS. SCHUYLER
(stopping him)
What is it, Smythe?

SMYTHE
Pardon me, madam - but what am I to say to the newspapermen?

Mrs. Schuyler looks distractedly at Grayson.

17. CLOSER SHOT
Mrs. Schuyler and Grayson. She rises and speaks imperiously:

MRS. SCHUYLER
Dexter, go out and tell those ruffians I have nothing to say.

Grayson faces her placatingly.

GRAYSON
You can't do that. Leave it to me. I know how to handle reporters.

MRS. SCHUYLER
(with a shudder)
All right, then - get it over with.

18. MEDIUM FULL SHOT
Grayson turns officiously toward the waiting butler.

GRAYSON
We've decided to see the reporters. Send in the man from the Tribune first.

SMYTHE
Very good, sir.

MRS. SCHUYLER
Oh, Smythe, some bicarbonate of soda, quick - double strength. I know those news mongrels[3] will upset me.

SMYTHE
I've anticipated it, madame. The bicarbonate is ready.

The butler exits.

19. INT. SCHUYLER LIBRARY - DAY - FULL SHOT
This room resembles the Grand Central Station. It is lined with bookcases filled with gorgeous first editions and special bindings, and is furnished in the extreme of magnificence and luxury.

Present are Stew and Bingy, reporter from the Tribune. Stew is seated, idly leafing through a first edition.

Bingy, still with his hat on, spots an expensive music box on a nearby table, opens it and does a little jig to the tune that is emitted.

20. CLOSER SHOT
Bingy, as he lingers at the table. He is a lazy, sloppy-looking guy. His face needs a shave and his pants need pressing. There is a spot of dried ketchup on his tie. On the table is a humidor. Bingy opens it and lifts out a handful of cigars.

21. CLOSE SHOT - STEW
As he looks up from the book, he suggests:

STEW
Hey Bingy, you'll find the silverware in the dining room.

CONTINUATION, SCENE 20
Bingy turns, putting the cigars in his pocket.

BINGY
Much obliged.

22. MEDIUM FULL SHOT
Smythe enters.

SMYTHE
(frigidly)
Mr. Grayson has decided to see you.

Both Stew and Bingy start forward eagerly. Smythe continues:

SMYTHE
The gentleman from the Tribune, first.

23. CLOSER THREE SHOT
Bingy beams broadly and Stew is disappointed.

STEW
There are no gentlemen on the Tribune.

SMYTHE
I understand, sir.

Smythe leads the way out. As Bingy passes by, Stew trips him.

BINGY
Say, take it easy! Take it easy! Listen, my boy. No use you hanging around here. Just buy the Tribune tonight and read all about it. You can rewrite it for your last edition.

STEW
Couldn't make the last edition. It'd take me four hours to translate your story into English.

BINGY
Oh, is that so?

STEW
I'm afraid.

Bingy turns to leave.

Take off your hat. You might make an impression.

Bingy dutifully doffs his hat.

Impossible. Put it on again.

BINGY
Hey, make up your mind, will you?

Bingy hurriedly puts his hat back on as he disappears.

24. INT. SCHUYLER DRAWING ROOM - DAY - MEDIUM CLOSE SHOT
By the door which leads out into the hall. The butler enters and stops, standing stiffly. Bingy enters behind him, shambling awkwardly. He stops in some consternation as he sees:

25. MEDIUM SHOT (FROM HIS ANGLE)
The Schuyler jury. Grayson, Mrs. Schuyler, Anne and Michael, all surveying him in varying degrees of unfriendliness.

CONTINUATION, SCENE 24
Bingy hesitates uneasily as he regards this impressive assemblage. Quickly, he takes his hat back off. Then he smiles nervously and starts forward.

BINGY
Hi, folks!

CONTINUATION, SCENE 25
Grayson comes forward to meet him, attempting to be very cordial. Bingy is seized by a sudden impulse to sneeze. He does so, violently. There is awkward silence. Mrs. Schuyler throws off a visible shudder.

BINGY
What's the matter? Isn't there a 'bless you' in the crowd?

GRAYSON
You're the Tribune man?

BINGY
Yeah, hello. How are you?

Bingy extends his hand. Grayson pointedly ignores it.

GRAYSON
(cordially)
Fine. Have a seat.

BINGY
Thanks, I will.

Bingy crosses the room, taking note of the beauteous Anne.

GRAYSON
This way.

BINGY
Oh, man!

Bingy sits gingerly on the edge of a handsome chair.

BINGY
Oh, boy!

26. MEDIUM CLOSE SHOT
Bingy and Grayson. Grayson picks up a very flossy and expensive cigarette box from the small end table beside the chair. It is made of gold and semi-precious stones are inset in the cover. Grayson opens the lid and takes out a cigarette, but pointedly does not offer one to Bingy.

Grayson remains standing before the reporter, who is very uncomfortable and ill at ease.

GRAYSON
Fine newspaper the Tribune.

BINGY
Well, I should say!

GRAYSON
I knew your managing editor very well.

BINGY
Is that so?

GRAYSON
Yale '21, I believe.

BINGY
(uncomprehending)
Huh?

GRAYSON
We were classmates.

27. CLOSE SHOT - MRS. SCHUYLER
She clears her throat menacingly, as she looks sternly at Grayson.

MRS. SCHUYLER
Ahem!

BINGY
What's the matter? She got a cold?

CONTINUATION, SCENE 26
Bingy and Grayson. Both look over. Grayson gives her a quick reassuring glance, as though to say "leave it to me now." He continues his conversation with the reporter.

GRAYSON
I got him his job on the paper. I'm a stockholder, you know.

BINGY
Is that so?

GRAYSON
As one Tribune man to another--

He laughs.

BINGY
(laughs)
Yeah!

GRAYSON
But right now I'm acting in the capacity of Mrs. Schuyler's attorney.

BINGY
Oh, that's all right with me. I won't hold it against you. But you see, I'm here to find out about--

GRAYSON
I know, I know. But there's no truth in the story whatsoever.

BINGY
Oh yeah?

28. MEDIUM SHOT
Grayson and Bingy. He takes Bingy by the arm and leads him over to a corner of the room, assuming a confidential pose.

GRAYSON
(speaking as they walk)
However, I've taken the trouble to prepare a little statement. Here it is. Here.

29. CLOSER TWO SHOT
Grayson and Bingy. Grayson takes an envelope out of his pocket and hands it to Bingy. Bingy opens the flap and sees the contents.

INSERT: ENVELOPE
The corner of a fifty dollar bill protrudes.

BACK TO SCENE:
Bingy quickly shuts the envelope up. Grayson is watching him closely.

GRAYSON
So, you see how silly that rumor is?

BINGY
Why, sure. It's a lotta hooey.

GRAYSON
That's what I wanted to say, but I couldn't think of it.

Grayson starts leading him toward the door. CAMERA PANS WITH THEM as Grayson leads him toward the door, talking as they walk.

GRAYSON
Thank you very much.

BINGY
All right, all right, don't mention it.

GRAYSON
Give my regards to your managing editor.

BINGY
I certainly will.

They stop at the door. Bingy extends a handshake, which is again refused. He stops and looks back at the jury.

30. MEDIUM SHOT FROM HIS ANGLE
The Schuylers all sitting silently and contemplating him.

BINGY
Well, so long folks!

He flutters his eyes at Anne.

BINGY
Thanks!

He takes one last look at Mrs. Schuyler and is again gripped by a violent sneeze.

MRS. SCHUYLER
(rising to the occasion)
Uh, bless you!

ALL
Bless you!

BINGY
Thanks.

The butler appears in the doorway behind him. Bingy exits past him, beaming.

BINGY
(waving to butler)
So long!

Grayson nods to the butler.

GRAYSON
Smythe, bring in the other reporter.

SMYTHE
Yes, sir.

31. INT. SCHUYLER DRAWING ROOM - MEDIUM FULL SHOT
The group awaiting the advent of the Post reporter. Stew is shown in by the butler, still carrying the Conrad book in his hand. They give him the once-over. Mrs. Schuyler raises her lorgnette with a magnificent gesture. Stew eyes them with animation, not in the slightest discouraged by this supercilious scrutiny. He starts toward them.

32. MEDIUM SHOT
As Stew approaches them.

STEW
Schuyler's the name, I presume? Yes, thank you, thank you. My name's Smith - Stewart Smith. No relation to John, Joe, Trade or Mark. Of course you can't have everything.

He smiles engagingly on them. Stew addresses Mrs. Schuyler ingratiatingly, disregarding her expression of obvious distaste.

STEW
Nice set of Conrads you have out there, Mrs. Schuyler. I was just glancing through this one.
(indicates the book in his hand)
What's Michael tearing the paper about?

GRAYSON
Just a habit. Mr. Schuyler is a bit put out by all the rumors going around.

33. CLOSER SHOT - STEW AND GRAYSON

STEW
Rumors? Rumors? Since when is a breach-of-promise case a rumor?

GRAYSON
No breach-of-promise case has been filed. The matter has been settled out of court.

STEW
(very cagey)
Oh I see, but Gloria doesn't seem to be satisfied with the twenty thousand dollars.

34. A MEDIUM SHOT OF GROUP
At this, Mrs. Schuyler rises wrathfully.

MRS. SCHUYLER
(furiously to Grayson)
Dexter Grayson, you told me it was only ten thousand--and you didn't even get those letters from that Jezebel!

STEW
Oh, so you did give her ten thousand dollars, eh? and there <u>are</u> letters ...

Behind Stew's back, Grayson makes violent gestures for her to shut up.

STEW
Well, well. That takes it out of the rumor class, doesn't it?

GRAYSON
We admit nothing. However, I have a little statement all prepared.

He takes Stew's arm and walks him off toward a corner much in the same manner as he handled Bingy, and lowers his voice confidentially.

35. CLOSER SHOT - STEW AND GRAYSON
Apart from the others.

STEW
A statement? Good.

GRAYSON
I have it here.

STEW
Good.

Grayson takes an envelope out of his pocket and hands it to Stew. Stew puts the book under his arm, takes the envelope and extracts the contents. It is another greenback.

STEW
(with interest)
Fifty bucks, eh?

He regards it a moment, then replaces the bill in the envelope. His voice is matter-of-fact, and almost casual.

STEW
Don't you know you should never offer a newspaper man more than two dollars? If you do, he'll think it's counterfeit. I don't need fifty dollars. As a matter of fact, I've got fifty dollars.

Grayson is considerably disconcerted. He tries again.

GRAYSON
The man from the Tribune seemed perfectly satisfied.

STEW
Who, Bingy? Yeah, Bingy would. He never saw fifty dollars before. You could have bought him for six bits. Funny thing about Bingy. The more he gets - the more he prints. He looks stupid, doesn't he? But oh how smart he gets when he bends over a typewriter.

He hands the envelope back to Grayson and turns away.

36. MEDIUM SHOT
Schuyler group - taking his action with dismay. Stew starts walking back toward them, talking as he walks, Grayson beside him, considerably distracted.

STEW
So ten grand was the amount you gave the girl? Any other statement you folks would like to make?

There is an explosive chorus from the group.

GROUP
(ad-lib talking at the same time)
That's not so!
We have nothing more to say!
We'll make no statements.

He turns to them, holding up his hand and speaking plaintively.

STEW
Wait a minute. Don't get excited. I wouldn't worry about it. A little publicity never hurt anybody.

37. CLOSE SHOT - MRS. SCHUYLER
She is on the point of an apopletic stroke. She advances menacingly toward Stew. She calls to Grayson.

MRS. SCHUYLER
(shrieking at him)
Dexter, have this person leave immediately.

38. MEDIUM SHOT - THE GROUP
Stew is not at all perturbed. Dexter takes him by the arm and starts to lead him out.

GRAYSON
I think you'd better go.

STEW
Go?! Wait a minute - that's a great story! Newspaper reporter was forcibly ejected from Schuyler Mansion, and--

Anne comes up to him.

ANNE
Wait a minute--

He faces her and cannot help but register an appreciation of her beauty.

ANNE
Don't mind Mother.

STEW
(cheerfully)
I don't mind her if you don't.

CONTINUATION SCENE 37
Mrs. Schuyler, almost choking in her wrath at this outrageous stranger.

MRS. SCHUYLER

Anne!

39. CLOSE SHOT - ANNE AND STEW
Anne stifles a smile at this cheerful insolence.

ANNE

I'm sure you're quite willing to be decent about this.

STEW

Decent? Why Miss Schuyler, I want to be noble.

Anne continues in her most devastating manner.

ANNE

You're not going to print this silly thing, are you?

STEW

(noncomittally)

No? Why not?

She puts her hand lightly on his arm.

ANNE

Because my name's Schuyler too. And I haven't done a thing, but I'll suffer with Michael. And so will Mother.

40. CLOSEUP - STEW
He has been listening to this and enjoying it immensely. He looks over at Mrs. Schuyler.

41. REVERSE ANGLE ON MRS. SCHUYLER
Who is making a show of holding back a flood of tears.

CONTINUATION SCENE 40

STEW

Mother's suffering already!

CONTINUATION SCENE 39
Anne, not wanting to lose her point, looks up at Stew pleadingly.

ANNE

As a special favor to me, you won't print that story, will you?

CONTINUATION SCENE 40
Stew, looking down at her in frank approval and admiration.

ANNE

(pleading)

Please--

Stew hesitates still.

42. MEDIUM SHOT
Mrs. Schuyler, Michael, and Grayson. All watching the couple intently, hanging on the next words--wondering if Anne is going to succeed. They are tense and expectant.

43. CLOSE SHOT - ANNE AND STEW
He is looking down into her soft, melting eyes. Then he smiles.

STEW
You know something, lady, if you sold life insurance, I'd go for a policy in sixty seconds.

ANNE
Oh, thank you, I knew you'd understand.

CONTINUATION SCENE 42
The three. They relax and exchange relieved and triumphant glances. Apparently Anne has won.

44. MEDIUM SHOT - ENTIRE GROUP
Stew turns aside.

STEW
May I use your telephone?

ANNE
(eagerly)
Certainly. Right over there.

STEW
You're all right.

She indicates. Stew starts for the telephone. Anne walks to her mother's side. Stew gets to the telephone and picks up the receiver.

STEW
Hello, Beekman 1300?
(he turns to wink at the group)
That's an unlucky number. You know that, don't you?

45. CLOSE SHOT - STEW
At the telephone. He turns back to the instrument as he gets his connection.

STEW
(into phone)
Hello, Toots? Is Conroy there? Give me Conroy.
(pause)
He isn't? Try the washroom, will you?

While he waits for the connection, he turns and addresses the group expansively.

STEW
Say, I interviewed a swell guy the other day Einstein. Swell guy, a little eccentric, but swell. Doesn't wear any garters. Neither do I as a matter of fact. What good are garters anyway--?
(he turns back to the phone)
Hello, Conroy? This is Smith talking. I'm up at the Schuylers. No, I'm not having tea - that is, not yet.
(again, he winks expansively at the group--then returns to Conroy)
Is she beautiful? Oh boss, her pictures don't do her justice. If I was that guy Ziegfield - what?

46. CLOSE SHOT - ANNE AND MRS. SCHUYLER
Anne smiles in spite of herself at this flattery. Stew's voice goes on.

STEW'S VOICE
Yes, it's easy to see where her beauty comes from. From her mother.

For the first time, Mrs. Schuyler unbends to the extent of giving forth a smile. She cannot help but be pleased at this compliment. The atmosphere is now very friendly. Everybody feels that everything is all right.

CONTINUATION SCENE 45
Stew at the phone

STEW
Now wait a minute. Just hold on. Keep your shirt on. I'm coming to that. The Schuylers admit the story is true. Right. They gave the gal ten thousand bucks. But she's got some letters - and she's holding out for more dough - and it looks to me like she's going to get it.

47. MEDIUM SHOT - SCHUYLER GROUP
Horrified and shocked at this betrayal and double-crossing.

STEW
(on the phone--breezily)
Right boss. I'll be right over. Right - no, I don't think I can get any pictures now. Right.

He casually hangs up and turns from the phone.

MRS. SCHUYLER
(involuntary gasp)
Oh-h-h . . .!

Anne confronts him as if he were a reptile of the lowest order.

ANNE
(voice cold as ice)
I've met some rotters in my time, but without a doubt, you're the lowest excuse for a man I've ever had the misfortune to meet--

Stew starts walking toward the door, still holding his book. The family is tremendously indignant and agitated.

Stew stops, turns, looks at them. He is met by icy glares. He indignantly takes a nickel out of his pocket and hands it to Grayson.

STEW
(with dignity)
Well, if you feel that way about it, here's a nickel for the phone call.

He glares at them--turns and walks out.

They watch him walk out, stunned and open-mouthed.

FADE OUT:

FADE IN: DAY

INSERT: Dingy board sign outside a building.

JOE'S

LAP DISSOLVE TO:

INSERT: Three column heading in newspaper:

SCHUYLER HEIR SETTLES
BREACH OF PROMISE
SUIT FOR $10,000.
Gloria Golden, Follies Beauty,
Retains Love Letters.

LAP DISSOLVE TO:

INT. JOE'S SPEAKEASY - DAY

48. MEDIUM FULL SHOT
A reasonably respectable speakeasy, smoke-filled. Quite a number of men and a few women are leaning on the bar and seated around at the tables. Stew and Gallagher are seated at one of the rude round tables, smoking, drinks before them. Gallagher is reading the newspaper story.

49. CLOSE SHOT - STEW AND GALLAGHER
She is grinning at the story.

STEW
--and she walked up to me and put her hand on my shoulder and said,
(mimicking Anne)
'Mr. Smith, You wouldn't print that story, would you?' Oh no, I wouldn't print it - read it!

50. CLOSE SHOT - GALLAGHER
Over Stew's shoulder. She laughs at his attempted imitation.

GALLAGHER
You're sure going to be poison to that Junior Leaguer[4] from now on!

STEW
I hope not ... I've got to call on her this morning!

Gallagher looks up in astonishment.

GALLAGHER
You what?

STEW
Sure, I must drop in on the mad wench. Her wounds need soothing.

GALLAGHER
For heaven's sake, Stew, are you completely bats? What for? I thought the story was cold. You can't go back there.

STEW
Sure, the story is cold, but I'm not. I'm sizzling - look! Psst!

He moistens a finger, touches it to his wrist, and makes a sizzle noise.

Gallagher looks over quizzically--a little suspicious--a little jealous.

GALLAGHER
(a drawn-out knowing utterance)
O-o-oh! Came the dawn, came the dawn!

51. CLOSE SHOT - STEW
Over Gallagher's shoulder.

STEW
And with it came love! Oh Gallagher, you've got to meet her. She's it--

GALLAGHER
--and that--

STEW
(enthusing)
--and those and them.

Gallagher takes a sip of her drink before answering.

GALLAGHER
Well, I've seen her pictures, and I don't think she's so hot.

STEW
(disparaging gesture)
Oh, you don't appreciate it. Her pictures don't do her justice. Why, Gallagher, she's queenly - she is queenly - and I know queens!
(continues in exaltation)
And oh, has she got herself a nose - and I know noses too. That little snozzle of hers is the berries, I tell you. And is she cute when she throws that little snozzle to the high heavens!

52. DOUBLE SHOT

GALLAGHER
Of course I haven't got a nose.

Stew gives her a hurt look.

STEW
(shaking his head)
Sure, sure. You've got a nose, Gallagher. You've got a nose. But there's different women, Gallagher. You know, like brewery horses and thoroughbreds.

GALLAGHER
(deliberately misunderstanding)
On now, Stew, don't be too hard on her. I wouldn't call her a brewery horse.

STEW
Gallagher! She's the real McCoy!

GALLAGHER
And the rest of us are truck horses?

STEW
(reproachfully)
There you go, talking like a woman!

GALLAGHER
(a trifle resentfully)
Well!

STEW
Well, you're my pal, aren't you? Then don't turn female on me.

During these last few speeches, Gallagher has been regarding him with a curious expression. She loves being his pal, but wishes he would realize she is also a woman.

53. MEDIUM SHOT
Stew seems a little resentful of her attitude. He rises.

STEW
Pay that check, will you Gallagher? I'll give it back to you some time. Maybe.

He flourishes the book of Conrad, which has been lying on the table in front of him, and makes a grand gesture.

STEW
I go now - I go with Conrad in quest of my youth! Fry those tomatoes, will you, Gallagher?

He strikes a pose--and exits.

Gallagher, sits, looking after him, considerably disturbed.

54. CLOSER SHOT - GALLAGHER
Sitting, looking dismally after Stew.

She opens her bag and takes out a mirror, surveying herself with frank disapproval. She pulls out a curl of hair before each ear, tries to soften the severe brim of the hat. She puts a finger to the tip of her nose and tilts it up, studying the effect. Then, with a sigh of disgust, she throws mirror and bag onto the table.

LAP DISSOLVE TO:

55. INT. SCHUYLER ENTRANCE HALL - DAY - LONG SHOT
Smythe, the butler, previously introduced, comes from the direction of the rear of the house, and proceeds down the long, vast hallway towards the front door. The bell keeps ringing steadily.

The butler reaches the wide front door.

56. CLOSER SHOT
As the butler opens the door and reveals Stew standing outside, hatless, a book in his hand, a spring overcoat slightly askew, the pockets bulging with contents. The butler quickly tries to slam the door in Stew's face, but Stew's right foot comes forward with a practiced newspaperman's gesture and he forces his way into the room.

STEW
(reproachfully)
Now, now Jeeves.[5] Was that nice? Was that being a gentleman, Jeeves? Was it, Jeeves? Your name is Jeeves, isn't it?

SMYTHE
(stiffly)
The name is Smythe.

STEW
Smythe! Well, well, well! With a Y, huh?
(wags his head)
Congratulations! What a small world. Brothers under livery. Shake!
(he grabs the butler's hand)
Now, as a Smith to a Smythe--

SMYTHE
(glacially)
Mrs. Schuyler is not at home.

57. TWO SHOT - ANOTHER ANGLE

STEW
I know, I know. I waited outside till she went out. She's a very nice lady, but we don't vibrate well together.

58. MEDIUM SHOT
Anne, dressed in smart sports clothes, starts to cross thru the hall. She stops as she sees the butler engaged in conversation with Stew.

SMYTHE
(hollowly)
No one's at home, sir.

Anne starts walking toward them. Stew spots her.

STEW
Now Jeeves, what would you call this - 'no one'?

Anne comes up to them.

59. CLOSER THREE SHOT
Anne looks up and sees that the butler is frowning and uncomfortable and addresses him.

ANNE
What's wrong?

SMYTHE
Mrs. Schuyler left orders, Miss, that if this person came here again, I was to call the police.

STEW
That's a good idea - telephone the police. The number is Spring 3100. Get a couple of cops over and we can have a rubber of bridge.

ANNE
You may go, Smythe.

SMYTHE
But I--

STEW
Now the lady said you may go--

The butler bows stiffly and exits.

ANNE
(to Stew--directly)
What do you want?

STEW
Well, I tell you, yesterday when I was here, I had one of your books in my hand, and when I got outside, I realized I still had your book in my hand. So as long as I had your book in my hand, I thought I might as well take it home and read it. This morning, I got up and put your book in my hand, and here's your book in your hand.

He extends the Conrad book, and Anne, making no effort to take it, he throws it on the table.

ANNE
(haughty)
That's considerate of you.

STEW
Yeah, that was considerate of me. I recommend you read it.

60. CLOSER TWO SHOT

ANNE
(stiffly)
I'm not interested in your literary recommendations.

STEW
Well, maybe it's a bit heavy for you. Perhaps if you'd like something lighter - something with a touch of romance--

He takes a package of letters out of his overcoat pocket held together by a rubber band. He extracts one of them and opens it.

STEW
Just listen to this--
(reading)
Adorable Babykins--
Does her miss her Baby? Him sends his booful li'l sweetums a billion oceans full of kisses.
Bobo is so lonely--!

ANNE
(interrupting coldly)
Just a moment. I don't see how that <u>trash</u> could possibly concern me.

Stew advances a little closer, putting up a finger.

STEW
(mysteriously)
Ah! But you don't know who Bobo is. And you don't know who Babykins is.

ANNE
I'm not interested. Smythe will open the door.

She begins to walk away.

STEW
(brightly)
But Bobo is your brother, Michael. And of course nobody would ever guess who Babykins is.

Anne turns and stares at him, incredulously, for a moment.

ANNE
Where did you get those letters?

STEW
I stole them when I was interviewing Babykins about Bobo.

Anne looks up coldly.

ANNE
I suppose you're going to print them?

STEW
No - give you another guess.

61. MEDIUM CLOSE SHOT (TRUCK SHOT)
The two.

Anne surveys him with frank scorn and dislike.

ANNE
(scornfully)
Oh, I don't need another guess. It's quite obvious.

STEW
So, it's obvious, huh?

She turns toward the library.

ANNE
Will you step into the library?

STEW
(with alacrity)
Sure, I'll take a chance.

Anne walks majestically with head held high--thru the hall--thru the living room and to the library. CAMERA TRUCKING AHEAD OF THEM. This is a very long walk with Anne walking ahead, Stew trailing.

STEW
(while walking with Anne single file)
You know, the Indians used to walk like this.
(pause)
Except the squaw always walked in the back--

(pause)
You know why that was? That was in case of attack from the front.
(pause)
Of course, if the attack was from the rear, she had to depend upon her papoose.
(pause)
Oh yes, the papooses always had bows and arrows.
(pause)
Of course, if she wasn't married--then she'd have to protect her own - er, er--
(indicates rear with thumb over shoulder)
(still walking)
What country is this library in?
(pause)
Miss Schuyler, how about carfare back to the front door, huh?

62. INT. SCHUYLER LIBRARY - MEDIUM SHOT
Anne sweeps in, followed by Stew. She walks directly to a desk, opens a drawer and takes out a large check book. She draws up a chair and seats herself.

63. CLOSE SHOT

Anne at the desk, starting to fill in the date on a blank check.

ANNE
What are your initials - Mr. - er--

64. CLOSE SHOT - STEW
Who has remained standing. He is watching her with a peculiar expression.

STEW
Smith. Stewart Smith. My friends call me Stew. It's an injustice too because I hold my liquor all right.

CONTINUATION SCENE 63
Anne writes on the check. Then she looks up.

ANNE
Will - uh - five thousand be enough?

65. DOUBLE SHOT

STEW
For what?

ANNE
For the letters, of course.

66. MEDIUM CLOSE SHOT
As Stew walks closer and addreses her.

STEW
Gee, you shouldn't do that, Miss Schuyler. That's all right for your lawyer friend, but you shouldn't go around thinking you can buy people.
(hands her the letters)
They're yours.

Anne has been listening to him with a puzzled expression, impressed by his obvious sincerity.

ANNE
I don't know how to thank you. Mother'll be so grateful - she'll probably want to kiss you.

STEW
Your mother will want to kiss me? Give me back my letters.
(grabs the letters)
That's the breaks I get. It's the mothers that are always grateful to me.
(with a smile, he hands the letters back)
Here.

ANNE
You're a peculiar person. Why the other day I pleaded with you not to send in that story and --
(gestures with letters)

67. CLOSE TWO SHOT

STEW
(patiently again)
I know but that was news. This is blackmail and I don't like blackmail.

Anne is regarding him with searching scrutiny. She smiles. Her icy, belligerent attitude has vanished.

ANNE
I won't even pretend it isn't a very great favor. I wish there was something I could do for you--

STEW
Well, you could make this table a little - uh - a little less wide.
(he leans over closer to her)
There is something you can do for me, Miss Schuyler.

The smile goes out of Anne's eyes--the suspicion returns--she is saying to herself--"I was right the first time!"

STEW
(engagingly)
I haven't had any lunch yet. Have you got anything in the icebox?

The hard, disdainful look leaves Anne's face as she stares at this incredible guy with his incredible request. With a twinkle in her eyes, she responds:

ANNE
Oh, you fool!

LAP DISSOLVE TO:

INT. SCHUYLER DINING ROOM
68. MED. FULL SHOT
A lovely, sunny room, cretonne drapes and colorful painted furniture. Stew and Anne are sitting at the table. Anne looks amused and

definitely speculative. Stew has the manner of having lived in this house all his life. He draws the cup of tea to him and puts in a lump or two of sugar.

Between him and Anne on the corner of the table is a modernistic, squatty little tea-pot.

STEW
After years of research, I finally discovered that I was the only guy in the world who hadn't written a play, so believe it or not, in my spare time I'm now writing a play.

69. CLOSE TWO SHOT
Anne is casually amused.

ANNE
Really?

STEW
Yeah, I haven't figured out the plot yet, but it's laid in a Siberian village.

ANNE
You're a bit eccentric, aren't you?

STEW
Me? No - most ordinary guy in the world, me. Only one thing wrong with me--

ANNE
You don't wear garters!

Stew helps himself to another lump of sugar.

STEW
Naw, that's just a symbol of my independence.

He leans closer, looking directly into her face.

STEW
I'm color blind. That's what's wrong - I'm color blind. I've been sitting here for a half hour looking at you and I don't know yet whether your eyes are blue or violet.

Anne smiles at this unexpected statement, and stares at him very critically.

ANNE
I'm just beginning to believe that something could be done with you.

STEW
Say, you could do anything with me you wanted to. Putty - just putty, that's me.

STEW
(leaning closer)
Now getting back to those eyes of yours - would you mind if I kind of got closer so I could see them?

ANNE
Not if you're going to lose any sleep about it.

70. CLOSE SHOT
He gets closer, takes her chin in his hand and gets an eyeful.

ANNE
Now, how would you like them--open like this?

She smiles radiantly.

STEW
Close them both.
(getting warm)
Something tells me I'd better leave.

During the last speech Mrs. Schuyler enters and stops in the doorway, surveying this astonishing scene with stupefied indignation and rage.

Anne gets quickly to her feet as Mrs. Schuyler sails forward.

MRS. SCHUYLER
That's an excellent idea.

ANNE
Oh, hello Mother!

STEW
(easily)
Hello - hello, Mrs. Schuyler. Come right in.
Will you have a slug of tea?

He hospitably indicates the table. Mrs. Schuyler is speechless with fury. She does not immediately reply. Then:

MRS. SCHUYLER
What is this person doing here?

ANNE
Why--

Stew goes on.

STEW
As a matter of fact, I was just trying to decide the color of Anne's eyes. I can't tell whether they're blue, or whether they're violet. What would you say, Mrs. Schuyler?

MRS. SCHUYLER
(bursting)
Why--

ANNE
(quickly)
Don't say it, Mother, please. Mr. Smith came here today to do us a great favor.

71. CLOSER SHOT
Anne, Mrs. Schuyler and Stew. Mrs. Schuyler, with an effort, restraining her impulse to yank Stew out by the collar, speaks:

MRS. SCHUYLER
(bursting with wrath)
Indeed? Perhaps he will do me a great favor.

STEW
(elaborate bow)
With pleasure, Madame!

MRS. SCHUYLER
Get out of here.

ANNE
(distressed)
Oh, Mother!

STEW
(with dignity)
It's all right. It's all right, Anne. I can take a hint. A bit subtle, but I get it. It's all right.

ANNE
Please go. I'll explain to Mother.

He steps close to Mrs. Schuyler's side.

STEW
The caviar was lovely, Madam.

72. WIDER SHOT
Stew starts to the door, smiles at Anne, and remarks to Mrs. Schuyler as he passes her:

STEW
You must come over and see <u>us</u> sometime.

Mrs. Schuyler freezes in inarticulate anger, as Stew gives a courtly bow and exits.

FADE OUT

FADE IN

<u>INT. SCHUYLER DRAWING ROOM - NIGHT</u>

73. MEDIUM SHOT
Anne in a stunning evening dress is seated, a cocktail in one hand, cigarette in the other. Dexter Grayson, in evening clothes, is standing before her.

GRAYSON
Where were you yesterday?

74. CLOSE SHOT - ANNE
She has a far-away, speculative look in her eyes.

ANNE
Oh, Stew and I went for a long ride.
(dreamily)
Dexter, is there any finishing school we can send him to?

75. CLOSE SHOT - GRAYSON

GRAYSON
(witheringly)
Yes - Sing Sing.

CONTINUATION SCENE 74
Anne. She ignores this crack.

ANNE
Just the same, he's going to be a different person when I get through with him.

CONTINUATION SCENE 75
Grayson. He is looking at her, deeply disturbed.

GRAYSON
When <u>you</u> get through with him?

76. DOUBLE SHOT

ANNE
Yes, it'll be a very interesting experiment.

GRAYSON
(sneering)
To make a gentleman out of a tramp?

ANNE
Exactly.

GRAYSON
Now, Anne, you remember how much it cost to get rid of that baseball player?

ANNE
You don't seem to understand that this one's different. He has brains.

77. MED. CLOSE SHOT
Grayson seats himself beside her on the divan.

GRAYSON
(fervently)
But what about me, Anne?

She looks at him coldly with almost an expression of dislike.

ANNE
You? Oh, don't go serious on me, Dexter.

LAP DISSOLVE TO:

<u>INT. PENTHOUSE APT. - NIGHT</u>

78. MED. SHOT TRUCKING
An elaborate, modernistic roof apartment, thronged with people all in evening dress. Stew and Anne are walking down among them. Anne is radiant, and Stew is happily guiding her among the stuffed shirts. Anne stops before a group. There is the sound of conversation, laughter, clink of glasses, music from stringed invisible orchestra, etc.

ANNE
Hello, Natalie. Mr. Stewart Smith ... Miss Montgomery, Mrs. Eames, Mrs. Radcliff, Mr. Radcliff--

STEW
How-di-do.

GROUP
(ad-lib acknowledgements)

79. MED. CLOSE SHOT - DEXTER GRAYSON
Standing, helping himself to a cocktail, which a footman is passing about. Dexter looks off with a frown of disapproval.

80. CLOSE SHOT - GROUP OF WOMEN
They are looking off in Anne's direction.

FIRST WOMAN
Say, who's Anne's new boyfriend?

SECOND WOMAN
Well, if these old ears don't deceive me, I believe his name is Smith.

FIRST WOMAN
Smith! Can't be one of the brothers - he hasn't a beard on.[6]

SECOND WOMAN
Well, he must have something if Anne has got her clutches on him.

There is the sound of a piano chord being struck.

81. MED. FULL SHOT
Mrs. Baxter, the hostess, is standing importantly by the grand piano at which is seated an anaemic-looking young man. Beside her stands a stout, swarthy Italian with bristling mustachios. Mrs. Baxter bows toward the swarthy one, who bends almost double in acknowledgement. There is a polite scattering of applause, and some of the guests seat themselves.

Martini starts to sing.

Unnoticed by the rest, Stew and Anne slip out of the door into the roof garden.

EXT. ROOF GARDEN
82. MED. FULL SHOT
A most beautiful, romantic spot. Rose trees in blossom, a vine-covered pergola, a splashing fountain, a few choice marble statues, low, deep chairs placed to make a gorgeous spot. Stew and Anne enter from the direction of the house. The garden is dark except for the lights from the interior of the house. From within, comes the voice of the singer rendering an extremely romantic, sentimental Italian love song. This will continue to the FADE OUT of the scene.

Stew and Anne walk, still hand in hand, toward the edge of the pergola where the shadows are deeper and where a couple of glorified steamer chairs are placed. There is a full moon overhead.

She leads him toward a waterfall effect, a glass partition down which water trickles. They go behind the dimly lit fountain and sit in a low, deep divan. We see them in silhouette as they go into a passionate embrace. All we hear is the faint voice of Martini--and the uninterrupted splashing of the fountain.

CUT TO:

83. CLOSEUP - ANNE & STEW
On divan, arms around each other.

STEW
Anne, pinch me, will you? Throw me out of here. Give me the air. Throw me out of this joint, will you?

Anne smiles happily and pinches his nose.

ANNE
Why should I? We're happy, aren't we, darling?

STEW
Throw me out - because I'm beginning to get goofy ideas, and they concern you, Anne.

ANNE
(passionately)
None of your ideas can be goofy, Stew, if they concern me.

STEW
(struggling)
My name is Smith well, that you seem to have been able to stand for the last month. I'm white, male and over twenty one. I've never been in jail - that is, not often. And I prefer Scotch to Bourbon. I hate carrots. I hate peas. I like black coffee and I hate garters. I make seventy-five bucks a week and I've got eight hundred and forty-seven bucks in the bank - and - I don't know yet whether your eyes are blue or violet.

ANNE
(although he is very close to her)
That's because you're too far away, Stew.

Throughout his speech, Anne never takes her eyes off him. As he fumbles now, he turns. Their eyes meet. His overwhelming desire for Anne overcomes him.

He dismisses as futile his effort to be practical, sweeps her into his arms and kisses her passionately.

FADE OUT:

FADE IN

<u>INT. CITY ROOM OF MORNING POST - DAY</u>

84. MEDIUM FULL SHOT
Typical atmosphere, as before.

LAP DISSOLVE TO:

85. MEDIUM SHOT
Featuring Stew at his desk, which is directly in front of the battery of Morkrums whose clatter comes into the sound track.

Stew finishes up a phone call. He sits at his desk, staring pensively at his typewriter. He is smoking a pipe and is in his shirtsleeves. His hair is rumpled, and strewn over the desk is a bunch of crumpled up pieces of paper, indicating that he has made numerous unsuccessful starts at writing something. A fresh blank sheet of paper is now in the typewriter.

Nearby, at another desk, asleep in a swivel chair, with his feet elevated to the desk, the low snoring of another reporter blends with the sounds of the Morkrums and other noises of the City Room. At the reporter's elbow is a telephone.

86. MEDIUM SHOT
Desk of Conroy, the City Editor. A small upright plate on his desk indicates his position. This is near the copy desk. Characteristic activities are background for any action that may take place. Reporters come up to throw their stories on Conroy's desk; the phone rings, etc.

A boy comes in with a large number of newspapers under his arm which he throws on Conroy's desk. There are several copies of each of the rival newspapers in town. Conroy spreads them out and begins to examine them.

87. CLOSE SHOT - STEW
It is evident that he is nervous and jumpy about something. Finally he starts to pound the typewriter.

INSERT: Sheet of paper in typewriter on which is being typed.

ACT 1
SCENE 1
A STREET IN ARABY

88. CLOSE SHOT - GALLAGHER
As she talks on the phone to one of her girlfriends

GALLAGHER
(sotto voce)
Sure I got a new dress. A new hat too. (listens) Well, I'll try to get Stew to come with me. (she glances in his direction) Yeah - he's all right. You know, he thinks he's stuck on some society gal. (listens) Naw, it won't last. It better not last!

89. CLOSER SHOT - CONROY
Hastily glancing over the headlines of the papers. The phone rings. Without looking at it, Conroy answers:

CONROY
What? Oh, I'll be surprised, eh? Listen if there's any news in that sheet that I haven't thrown in the wastepaper basket, I'll eat it.

He is looking down at the papers and suddenly his eyes focus on something which causes the cigar to drop from his mouth and an expression of mingled amazement and rage comes into his face. We do not see at this point what it is he has read, but we know it must be something sensational. Abruptly he hangs up the phone.

CUT TO:

CONTINUATION SCENE 87
Stew, as he studies his typewriter. Over his CLOSEUP comes the excited outraged voice of Conroy.

CONROY'S VOICE
Hey Stew! Stew Smith!

A look of infinite weariness and disgust comes over Stew's face and he grits his teeth.

STEW
Me?

His general expression registers "Good god, there he goes again." With one finger he pounds out four letters:

INSERT: Sheet in typewriter: Next to

A STREET IN ARABY

Stew has typed:

NUTS

He yanks the sheet out of the typewriter.

CONTINUATION SCENE 89
Conroy. He looks over and bellows furiously.

CONROY
You double-crossing hound! Come over here!

CONTINUATION SCENE 87
Stew gets up from his machine, crumples the sheet of paper into a wad and flings it at the sleeping reporter. The wad strikes him in the face; he wakes abruptly and automatically reaches for the phone. He picks up the receiver and in a voice fogged with sleep calls a number. Stew exits.

90. MEDIUM SHOT
At Conroy's desk. Conroy's expression is one of bitter reproach as he leans back in his swivel chair as Stew approaches and stands by the desk.

STEW
Now listen boss, if you're going to kick about that expense account--

CONROY
(interrupting fiercely)
Do you call yourself a reporter?

91. MEDIUM SHOT
Of other reporters, the older man at the copy desk, and perhaps a sob sister or two nearby, who look up with expectant interest, expecting to hear Stew get a bawling out.

92. CLOSE SHOT - GALLAGHER
At her desk. She looks up worried and apprehensive.

CONTINUATION SCENE 90
Stew and Conroy.

STEW
It has been alleged - yes--

CONROY
You wouldn't know news if you fell into a mess of it, nose first. So you're the bright lad that's never been scooped!

STEW
(defensively)
Not on my own beat, no.

CONROY
(howling so that he can be heard all over the room)
No? Well, where were you when <u>that</u> happened?

He slaps the copy of the Tribune furiously and shoves it into Stew's face.

93. CLOSE SHOT - STEW
Not knowing what it is all about, Stew, with an injured expression, takes the paper and looks at it.

INSERT: Front page of Tribune

ANN SCHUYLER ELOPES WITH REPORTER
(with subheads giving more explicit information)

94. MEDIUM SHOT
The other reporters, copy readers, sob sisters, etc., seeing the unusual commotion and Stew's bewildered reaction, get out of their chairs and cross over to the City Desk, where they take up other copies of the same paper to look at. There are amazed and excited exclamations.

95. CLOSER SHOT - STEW AND CONROY
Stew, still staring dumbly down at the paper. A few others are crowding around, glancing over his shoulder, etc.

CONROY
I've heard of people being scooped on their own funerals, but this! Holy mackerel! Why, it's news when Anne Schuyler gets her fingernails manicured, but this! She gets married to one of our own reporters and the Tribune beat us to it!
(he notices other reporters milling around)
Well! What do you guys want? Go on, get back to your desks. Go back to your work.
(returning his attention to Stew)
Now don't tell me you were drunk at the time and don't remember! Or is this one of Bingy's snow-storms?

STEW
No, no - it's true, all right, only we didn't want to get it in print yet, that's all.

CONROY
Why not?

STEW
Well, you see, I've acquired one of those new mother-in-laws, and we were afraid she wouldn't understand the whole idea. So we were going to wait till she went to Europe.

CONROY
What do I care about your mother-in-law! You're still working for this paper, aren't you! Or are you?

STEW
Yes, sir.

CONROY
Well, it's your business to get news! And here you had a story right in your own lap and you let the Tribune scoop us on it. Making a first class Grade A monkey out of me. If it ever hap pens again - just don't bother about coming back. That's all.

He dismisses Stew with a wave of his hand.

STEW
Thanks for your congratulations.

96. MEDIUM SHOT
Stew turns away from Conroy's desk, and a group of his confreres come up, surrounding him in a series of ad-lib congratulations. (Some slightly profane, pounding him on the back, whooping, and in general manifesting great surprise and glee.) This group is in- creased by copy readers, office boys and everybody jabbering and shouting at him.

GROUP
(ad-lib congratulations)

Stew manages to break thru them and exits from scene.

97. MEDIUM SHOT
Gallagher--to intercut with above scene. She gets up and goes over, CAMERA PANNING WITH HER and picks up another copy of the paper and reads the headlines.

98. CLOSER SHOT - GALLAGHER
Her face stricken and sick as she reads about Stew's marriage. Abruptly she turns away, out of scene.

99. MEDIUM SHOT
At Gallagher's empty desk. Stew comes in trying to stave off the mob. He turns on the congratulators, pushing them off.

STEW
What's the matter with you mugs? Can't a guy get married without all this?
(looks around)
Where's Gallagher? Anybody seen Gallagher?

He forcibly breaks away from them and walks back toward the door, the last of the wisecracks and goodnatured jeers being flung after him.

LAP DISSOLVE TO:

INT. JOE'S SPEAKEASY

100. MED.CLOSE SHOT
Gallagher is seated alone at a table, looking very forlorn. Her life is suddenly empty. A drink is in front of her, untouched. She is fighting hard to keep her emotions under control.

Stew enters the speakeasy and mingles with patrons, who offer congratulations. He comes to a stop by the table. She looks up, forcing a smile.

STEW
Well, well, well! Gallagher, old pal! There you are. What did you run away for?

GALLAGHER
I didn't run away.

Stew draws out the other chair at the table and sits down.

101. CLOSER SHOT OF THE TWO
He looks across at her, grinning boyishly, utterly unaware that what he has done has hurt her deeply.

STEW
Sure, you ran away. Aren't you going to congratulate a guy?

GALLAGHER
(with sincerity)
Sure. I wish you all the luck in the world, pal.

She puts her hand tenderly on his.

STEW
Thanks, thanks.

GALLAGHER
I hope you'll be very happy.

Stew expands under the comradeship of Gallagher. He wants to talk.

STEW
Oh sure, we'll be happy. What's the matter with your eyes?

GALLAGHER
It's the smoke.

STEW
(calling to bartender)
Joe! A little snifter.
(returning his attention to Gallagher)
Say, wasn't I a lucky guy to fall into a girl like that, huh?
(he notices the newspaper, which Gallagher has been reading)
Look at that! I don't know how I rate that, Gallagher. Gosh, there's a swell girl. I want you to meet her.

GALLAGHER
Who me? She wouldn't want to meet me. I'm just an old load of hay.

102. CLOSE SHOT - STEW
As his drink is served.

STEW
Ah! Thank you, Joe.
(returning his attention to Gallagher)
Tell you what - we'll have one of those parties down at your house - one of those spaghetti parties, you know. Gee, we haven't had one of those in a long time, have we Gallagher?

103. CLOSE SHOT OF THE TWO

GALLAGHER
(quietly)
Not since you broke into society.

STEW
(waxing reminiscent)
Remember the time we had a spaghetti party, and while I was serving the spaghetti I dropped it on the floor, and while those mugs weren't looking, I picked it up and served it to them anyway! Remember that? Yes, Anne would love that.

104. CLOSE SHOT - GALLAGHER
Looking across at him.

GALLAGHER
Do you think your wife would walk up three flights of stairs just to eat out of paper plates?

105. DOUBLE SHOT

STEW
Who - Anne? Sure, Anne would love that.

GALLAGHER
Remember, she's a Schuyler.

STEW
Now get this, Gallagher - Smith. That's the name.

GALLAGHER
(murmurs)
My error.

STEW
Well, if she doesn't want to come, I'll come down alone.

GALLAGHER
(shaking her head)
Oh no, you won't, Mr. Smith. You're a married man now. Mother always warned me never to run around with married men.

STEW
(resentfully)
Say, what kind of a pal are you? You're not going to leave me flat?

Gallagher tries to be elaborately casual.

GALLAGHER
Oh, I'll call you up some time. And if your social duties permit - why -

STEW
Cut that out. Just because I'm married - there's no reason for that.

Gallagher looks up and off, seeing something that startles her.

106. MED. SHOT
Conroy, the City Editor, entering the speakeasy.

CONTINUATION SCENE 105
Stew and Gallagher.

GALLAGHER
(interrupting in a whisper)
Hey, ixnay - here's the ossbay.[7]

Stew looks around, also startled.

107. MED. SHOT
Stew buries his head in the newspaper, in pretense of looking for something. Conroy appears at the table and stops. He indicates Stew.

CONROY
What's the Benedict[8] looking for in the newspaper - his lost freedom?

Stew slowly sticks his head up over the top of the table, looking up.

STEW
(grinning sheepishly)
Well, if it isn't old Fagin[9] himself.

Conroy sits down at the table.

STEW
Gallagher and myself just came over here to do a little work on a story -

CONROY
(disgustedly)
Baloney!
(calls off)
Joe! Bring me a special!

108. CLOSER THREE SHOT
Gallagher tries to be very bright and smiling.

GALLAGHER
(to Conroy)
Isn't it swell about Stew's marriage?

CONROY
(looking straight at her)
Is it?

Gallagher, self-conscious, realizes this tough old buzzard is on to her. She looks back at him for a moment - then drops her head. Stew is oblivious to this by-play. Conroy turns to Stew.

CONROY
Well, when are you quitting?

STEW
Quitting? I'm not thinking about quitting.

Joe comes in with a drink for Conroy.

CONROY
I take it you don't have to work for a living any more--

He takes a sip of his drink and looks over meaningfully.

CONROY
--Mr. Schuyler.

STEW
(in a flash of anger)
Now get this, Conroy. My name is Smith. Always was Smith - and always gonna be Smith

CONROY
Is that so?

STEW
That's so.

109. CLOSEUP - CONROY
He shows that he is genuinely interested in Stew and his problems, but can't help being a little sarcastic.

CONROY
Anne Schuyler's in the Blue Book - you're not even in the phone book. Think that one over, sucker.

CAMERA PANS to CLOSEUP of GALLAGHER.

GALLAGHER
(quickly in Stew's defense)
That doesn't make any difference--
(quietly)
--if they love each other.

CAMERA PANS BACK to CLOSEUP of CONROY.

CONROY
Blah! It's like a giraffe marrying a monkey.
(looking off at Stew)
Listen - you'll never be anything but just the reporter that married the Schuyler's millions. Stew Smith is dead and buried. From now on, you'll be just Anne Schuyler's husband. A rich

wife's magnolia. If you can smoke that without getting sick, you're welcome to it.

CAMERA PANS to CLOSEUP of STEW:

GALLAGHER'S VOICE
But that's perfectly ridiculous.

STEW
(defensively)
Wait a minute. Now, Gallagher, let me do the talking. Get this, Conroy - Anne Schuyler has got a lot of dough, all right - and I married her, all right - but her dough and me? No connection.

110. MED. CLOSE THREE SHOT
Gallagher is looking fixedly at Stew - very much worried about Conroy's dismal prophecies. Conroy shakes his head in sorrowful gloom.

CONROY
(as if he had not heard Stew)
Just a boid in a gilded cage -[10]

STEW
A what?

CONROY
You heard me. A bird in a gilded cage.

STEW
Aw, you've been reading a lot of cheap tabloids. Anne and myself are going to move downtown in a nice little flat, we're gonna forget all about this social stuff, and we're gonna be known as Mr. and Mrs. Stew Smith. How do you like that?

CONROY
(sarcasm)
And live on your salary, I suppose?

STEW
Yeah, live on my salary - that is, until I finish writing my play.

CONROY
(snorts)
What play?

STEW
My play.

CONROY
The one about the Siberian bloodhound?

STEW
Siberian bloodhound? No. That's been all rewritten. It's laid in Araby now.

CONROY
Araby?

STEW
Sure.

CONROY
Araby, my eye--!

111. WIDER SHOT
Conroy, having finished his drink, pushes back his chair and rises. He puts an affectionate hand on Stew's shoulder.

CONROY
Well, I'm sorry to see a good reporter go blooey--
(starts away)
Let me know when you're quitting.

STEW
I'm not quitting!

CONROY
No?

STEW
No!

CONROY
(singing)
'For he's only a bird in a gilded cage, a beautiful sight to see--'
(he waves his hand)
Tweet, tweet - ha, ha--

He laughs loud and raucously and exits.

112. CLOSE SHOT - STEW AND GALLAGHER
Stew glares after Conroy.

STEW
(under his breath)
Laugh laugh, you hyena!

Gallagher realizes that Conroy has hit home with the truth and is sorry for Stew. She puts her hand over his sympathetically.

GALLAGHER
Don't pay attention to him, Stew. He doesn't know what he's talking about.

STEW
Pay attention? I'm not paying any attention to him. You think that guy could get me upset? Hah! Not that mug. He's a tough mug - hard, cynical. He doesn't know the fine things in life - that guy.
(he swirls his drink, thinking)
A bird in a gilded cage, huh? It's getting so a guy can't step out without being called a magnolia. Stew Smith, a magnolia! Not me. Say, I'm not going to hang around and be a speakeasy rat all my life! I'll tell you that. Not me, not me. I'm going to step out and mean something in this world. You watch me.
(he swirls his drink, clearly bothered, lost in his own thoughts)
Say, am I a lucky guy to be near Anne Schuyler? I've been hit with a carload of horseshoes, and believe me I know it. Lucky, I'll say I'm lucky!

(pause)
Don't you think I'm lucky, Gallagher?

GALLAGHER
Sure - I think so, Stew.

STEW
I knew you would, pal.
(clearly bothered)
A bird in a gilded cage, eh?

GALLAGHER
How is her family going to feel about it?

STEW
Her family? Oh, they'll be all right. I'll bring them around.
(swirling his drink)
Gilded cage?! Besides, I'm not marrying her family. Stew Smith in a gilded cage! Stew Smith? Ha!
(clearly bothered)
That mug. What does he know?

LAP DISSOLVE TO:

INT. SCHUYLER DRAWING ROOM - DAY

113. MED. FULL SHOT
Another jury scene. This time it is Anne who's on the carpet. Grayson, in correct afternoon attire, his hands behind his back and his head sunk, is pacing back and forth in a very depressed and gloomy fashion.

Anne is seated, her demeanor betokening sullen defiance.

Michael is pacing, nervously smoking a cigarette.

MICHAEL
I don't know what you need me here for - it isn't my funeral.

Mrs. Schuyler stands by a table, staring at a spreadout newspaper which is laid out on the table. She flings the newspaper aside.

MRS. SCHUYLER
You stay right here, Michael. Some day you'll be head of this family, but thank heaven I shan't be here when it happens. And I hope you never have a daughter who gives you gastritis as Anne has me!

She pulls the bell rope for the butler.

ANNE
Now Mother, calm yourself. There's no use in getting so excited.

114. MEDIUM SHOT
Mrs. Schuyler is vastly agitated.

MRS. SCHUYLER
Oh, isn't there?

(as Anne starts to get up)
Sit down!
(looking off)
Smythe!

The butler appears in the doorway.

MRS. SCHUYLER
(in a weak, agonized voice)
Some bicarbonate - quick!

SMYTHE
Double strength!

The butler bows and exits. She passes a nervous hand over her eyes. Anne comes up to her

ANNE
Mother, if you keep this up, you'll have a nervous breakdown before you go to Europe.

115. CLOSER SHOT
Anne, Grayson and Mrs. Schuyler.

MRS. SCHUYLER
It's a good thing your father passed away before he saw insanity ravage the family. I can't imagine what made you do such a thing. A reporter! Of all things, a reporter! A barbarian who lets his socks come down!

ANNE
Mother, I promise you that he won't be a reporter much longer. Once I get him away from that atmosphere and get him away from a man named Gallagher--

MRS. SCHUYLER
(as Anne starts to get up again)
Sit down!

116. WIDER SHOT
The butler enters with a tray on which is a glass of bicarbonate of soda and brings it to Mrs. Schuyler. Walking immediately behind the butler is Stew, airily debonair. The butler glances somewhat uneasily at Mrs. Schuyler as he presents the tray. She glares blackly at Stew without a word of greeting, and taking the foaming glass from the tray, starts to lift it to her lips.

STEW
(airily)
Drink hearty, Mother.

Once more, Anne starts to rise out of her seat.

MRS. SCHUYLER
Anne!

Mrs. Schuyler pauses - glowering at Stew. Stew nods perfunctorily to each member of the jury, the total innocent.

STEW
Hello, Anne. Mr. Grayson.

(to Michael)
And you.
(to Mrs. Schuyler)
Mrs. Schuyler!

Grayson does not acknowledge the greeting. Mrs. Schuyler, having drained the glass, dismisses the butler with a wave of the hand, and directs her attention again to the matter at hand.

MRS. SCHUYLER
(in command)
Well, what's to be done? He's here now.

They are all silent - reluctant to speak in front of Stew. Stew looks at them all - a little puzzled - then he walks over toward Mrs. Schuyler.

117. MEDIUM CLOSE SHOT
Mrs. Schuyler and Stew.

STEW
Nobody seems to want to do anything--
(to Mrs. Schuyler, brightly)
Why not ask me? Perhaps I can offer a suggestion. Do what about what?

MRS. SCHUYLER
(witheringly)
About what? Your marriage to Anne!

STEW
(with a tone of dismissal)
Oh, my marriage to Anne. Now Mrs. Schuyler, we don't want you to go to any trouble about that. We just want the usual blessings, that's all.

118. MEDIUM SHOT
Mrs. Schuyler's eyes flash. She draws herself up with haughty dignity.

MRS. SCHUYLER
Young man, I want you to know that I object violently to this whole affair!

This finally brings Anne out of her seat. She rises and crosses to Stew, making a show of embracing him.

ANNE
Now Mother, your attitude is perfectly ridiculous. It's done now. Stewart and I are married.

STEW
(to Mrs. Schuyler)
I'm afraid she's right, Mrs. Schuyler. I'm really very sorry, Mrs. Schuyler, that you feel this way. I was in hopes that you would like me. I'm not the burglar that you think I am. After all, we're married. I think the thing to do is to kiss and make up - Mother.

MRS. SCHUYLER
(furiously)
Stop calling me Mother!

STEW
(easily)
All right, Grandma--

MRS. SCHUYLER
(glaring)
This man's impossible! I can't talk to him.
Grayson, let's go where we can talk - hic!
(she emits a burp, then fixes a glacial look at Anne)
See what you've done to me!?

Without another word, she turns and flounces angrily out of the room. Grayson follows her. At the doorway he pauses, starts to say something. They all look at him expectantly - but no words come out.

STEW
Got it too, huh?

Grayson gives a harrumph and exits.

119. CLOSER MEDIUM SHOT
Anne, Michael and Stew. Michael grins at Stew.

MICHAEL
Who won that round?

Michael starts moving toward the door.

STEW
(ruefully)
I'm afraid your mother won that round - that is, she got in the last blow.

MICHAEL
I don't feel the way they do. You're really not as bad as everybody thinks.

STEW
(effusively - shaking his hand)
You're beginning to appreciate me, eh? Thanks!

MICHAEL
Don't worry too much about Mother - she's enjoying this. Come on upstairs, I'll give you a little -

He indicates a snifter, grins and exits. Anne crosses to Stew and puts her arm around his shoulder.

STEW
(to Michael)
A little--? Sure, I'll be right up.
(to Anne)
He's all right. I like him.

ANNE
I'm glad.

He sees two figures pass above in a proscenium alcove, first Mrs. Schuyler, then Grayson. He makes an elaborate bow to each, and is impressed by Grayson's return bow.

STEW
He can bend!

120. CLOSER SHOT
Anne takes a step backwards and sits down with him on one of the divans. CAMERA TILTING DOWN WITH THEM. He puts an arm about her.

ANNE
Come here baby!

Anne starts fussing abstractedly at Stew's tie. They kiss.

ANNE
I haven't seen you for three hours. You're neglecting me already--

During her speech she has been picking away at a stain on his tie. Stew looks down and notices it.

STEW
What's the matter? Something I et, no doubt. Egg marks the spot--

ANNE
You ought to get some new ties, Stewart.

STEW
I don't need any new ties. I've got another tie - I've got another one besides this one. And it's a pip, too. There's only one thing wrong with it. You know what that is? It has a little weakness for gravy, and once in a while it leans a little toward ketchup. Of course that's only in its weaker moments. When you move down to my place, I'll show it to you.

Anne is somewhat taken aback at the suggestion that she's to move into his place.

ANNE
Your place?

121. TWO SHOT - ANOTHER ANGLE

STEW
Yeah. Oh, it's great. Of course it doesn't compare with this coliseum of yours here, but 'twill serve m'lady, 'twill serve.
(elaborate)
The architecture has a little feeling of Missouri Gothic - and the furniture sort of leans toward Oklahoma Renaissance - with a tiny touch of Grand Rapids.

ANNE
(gently insistent)
Don't you think it's silly of us to think of living there when we have this whole big house--

STEW
When 'we' ...? You mean, you'd like to have <u>me</u> live <u>here</u> in <u>your</u> house?

Anne cuddles closer into his collar.

ANNE
Sure. We can have the whole left wing and be all by ourselves all the time.

Stew is slightly dazed.

122. CLOSEUP - STEW
He is slightly dazed.

STEW
(cynically)
We could have the whole left wing? Wouldn't that be nice! Would that be room enough for us?

123. TWO SHOT

ANNE
(seriously - missing his sarcasm)
Oh darling, of course it would. If it isn't - there are six rooms and two baths - but if that isn't enough, Mother will give us the blue room too, I think.

STEW
Oh, Mother will give us the blue room. You haven't a red room, have you? Well, bless her heart. Wouldn't that be nice! My, oh my - six rooms and two baths and a blue room. I guess she would let us have the right wing if we needed it, wouldn't she?

ANNE
But we don't need it, I'm sure.

STEW
I see, we won't need that. Plenty of room, plenty of room.

124. WIDER SHOT
He gets up and paces the floor. He looks at Anne and sees that she is taking him seriously. He drops down beside her.

STEW
(dropping his kidding)
Look Anne, you're not serious about this, are you?

ANNE
Of course I am Stewart.

125. CLOSER TWO SHOT

STEW
Now let's get this settled--

She cuddles closer, tweaking his nose.

ANNE
You have the cutest nose I've--

STEW

Never mind my nose. What kind of a chump do you think I am? You think I'm going to live here in <u>your</u> house - on <u>your</u> dough? What do you think my friends would all say? Don't be silly. I'd get the razzing of my life for that. 'A bird in a gilded cage' - that's what I'd be. Not me. Oh no, not me!

ANNE

What do you think my friends would say if they found me in a little cheap flat?

STEW

It isn't cheap. It's nice.

ANNE

(cuddling closer)

Listen Stew baby, let's not talk about things like that now--

STEW

Wait a minute. I'll do anything you ask me, Anne, but I will not live--

ANNE

(cuddling closer - and stroking his nose)

Oh, I love that nose. It's such a sweet nose.

They kiss.

STEW

Nevertheless, whether the nose is sweet or not, I'm not going to live in your house. You may as well get that straight.

They kiss again, longer.

STEW

You do want me to be happy, don't you? Then I'm not going to live in your house ...

They continue to kiss as ...

LAP DISSOLVE TO:

INT. STEW'S BEDROOM - MORNING

126. CLOSE SHOT - STEW

In bed, asleep, all curled up, his head on his arm. CAMERA TRUCKS BACK showing the magnificent bedroom, with carved wooden panellings, a raised, canopied bed. The clothes that Stew has taken off the night before are draped haphazardly about the room. When the Camera gets to a point that takes in a LONG SHOT of the room, the door to the hall opens and a correctly attired valet appears. He closes the door noiselessly, goes over to the windows, and draws the brocaded drapes aside. Then he crosses to a covered object and with a small flourish removes the cover - revealing a birdcage. He approaches the bed.

127. CLOSER SHOT

As Dawson the valet stops beside the bed. The valet leans over and speaks distinctly.

DAWSON

Mr. Smith, sir--

There is no movement from the form on the bed.

DAWSON
Mr. Smith, sir!

Still no response. The valet taps the bedclothes-shrouded shoulder gently.

DAWSON
Mr. Smith, sir--

Sleepily, Stew turns, his eyes heavy with sleep.

128. MEDIUM SHOT

DAWSON
How do you like your bath, sir?

STEW
I like my bath all right. How do you like your bath?

Stew peers up, puzzled.

STEW
Who are you?

DAWSON
(surprised)
I'm your valet, sir. Dawson is the name, sir.

STEW
You're my what?

DAWSON
Your valet, sir.

Stew still stares at him. Then he nods to himself - thinks he gets the idea. Stew kicks back the covers and sits on the edge of the bed in his pajamas. Still sitting on the edge of the bed, he starts to slip his feet into a pair of slippers. The valet bends on one knee to help him.

STEW
Thank you, thank you, thank you! I'll do that for you some time. That's very sweet. Say listen, what did you say your name was?

DAWSON
Dawson, sir.

STEW
Dawson, huh? Was I very drunk last night?

DAWSON
Drunk, sir?

Stew rises and starts to reach for a dressing gown, but again the valet beats him to it - holding it for him and helping him slip into it.

STEW
Yes. I must have been pretty much plastered if I hired a valet.

DAWSON
Oh, but _you_ didn't engage me, sir.

Stew, surprised, turns on him quickly.

STEW
Who did engage you then, if I didn't engage you? What are you doing with my pants--

The valet picks up his pants.

STEW
Did you take anything out of those pants?

DAWSON
Oh no, sir!

STEW
What are you doing fooling around in here?

DAWSON
Miss Schuyler - I mean, Mrs. Smith - she engaged me this morning, sir.

Stew pulls out a cigarette. The valet, without missing a beat, leans over and offers a light. A wary Stew accepts.

STEW
Hmmm. So Mrs. Smith engaged me a valley, huh? That's very nice of Mrs. Smith - to engage me a valley.

129. WIDER SHOT
Stew walks over and gets a cigarette out of a box on a small table, waving his hand in a gesture of dismissal. The valet is right behind him, holding up his bathrobe for Stew to step into.

STEW
(putting on the bathrobe)
Say, you <u>are</u> nice. You're all right. You'd make a good wife.

DAWSON
Thank you, sir.

STEW
But not for me! Though I like you well enough. You're a nice fellow. You're all right. But I'm sorry I don't need any valleys today.

The valet pays no attention to him, but walks around the room, picking up the clothes that Stew has flung about.

DAWSON
Oh, but indeed you do, sir, if you don't mind my saying so. A gentleman's gentleman, as it were. Someone to draw your bath, lay out your clothes, help to dress you - it's really most essential, sir.

Stew, with his cigarette between his lips, stands watching the valet as he retrieves the various articles of cast-off clothing. The valet's manner is somewhat patronizing. He walks over to a chifferobe and starts opening the drawers, preparatory to laying out fresh things for Stew. Suddenly, Stew stalks over to him, takes him by the shoulder, and yanks him around to face him.

130. CLOSER SHOT - STEW AND DAWSON
The valet is astonished and somewhat alarmed at the belligerent expression on Stew's face.

STEW
(over-sweetly)
Are you trying to tell me that I need someone to help me put on my pants and button them up?

DAWSON
Quite so. Quite.

STEW
Now I'm sorry. I appreciate your efforts. But I don't need anybody to help me button my pants - I've been buttoning my pants for thirty years all right, and I can button 'em with one hand as a matter of fact.

DAWSON
Now Mr. Smith, now please--

Stew is rapidly losing his temper.

STEW
You've got a nice face, Dawson, you wouldn't want anything to happen to your face, would you?

The valet puts a bewildered hand to his face.

DAWSON
Oh no, sir--

Stew releases him with a definite motion toward the door.

STEW
All right, outside!

DAWSON
(bewildered)
I beg your pardon, sir?

STEW
(gesturing violently)
Outside!

The valet gazes at Stew as if he thinks the man is insane. He is considerably alarmed.

DAWSON
I think I understand, sir. You mean you want me to go?

STEW
(smiling admiringly)
There you are. You caught on. You see, you're nice and you're smart too. You caught on right away. Outside! Go on! Outside! And don't come back!

131. MEDIUM SHOT
The valet starts edging toward the door.

DAWSON
No, sir. No!

Stew's eyes bulge as he notices the birdcage for the first time.

STEW
Wait a minute, what's this?

INSERT: Birdcage.

BACK TO SCENE:

DAWSON
That's a canary, sir.

STEW
That's a canary! Who brought that in here? Canary, huh? Go on, get that out of here. Get that out of here!

DAWSON
(frightened)
Yes, sir. Very good, sir.

STEW
(ranting)
A bird! A bird in a gilded cage! Get that thing out of here!

DAWSON
Yes sir!

The valet hurries off, carrying the birdcage. As he nears the door, there is a light tap on the door connecting Stew's room and Anne's. The door opens and Anne comes in, wearing a ravishing and revealing negligee. She carries a small jeweler's box in her hand. She crosses the room toward Stew.

ANNE
Good morning, darling.

She looks over and sees Dawson at the hall door.

ANNE
Oh, Dawson, see that all Mr. Smith's clothes go to the cleaners this morning, please, will you?

The valet bows. Stew looks at her blankly.

DAWSON
Very good, madame.

He closes the door discreetly and goes out.

132. CLOSER SHOT - ANNE AND STEW
As they hug.

STEW
Say, who is this mug?

Anne sits down on the rumpled bed.

ANNE
I've got a present. Shut your eyes. Keep 'em closed. I know you're going to love them.

STEW
(eyes closed, feeling the package)
Little - couldn't be an automobile, could it?
(he opens the package)
Well, well! Ain't that nice!

He holds them up - expensive garters.

ANNE
Do you like them?

STEW
Got my initials on them too. They're cute. They're nice little things - what do you do with them?

ANNE
You wear them of course, silly.

STEW
Oh no. No, no. Not me. I haven't worn these things for years.

ANNE
I know that.

STEW
Besides I'd look foolish. I couldn't look Gallagher in the face.

ANNE
Darling, I don't care whether you can look Gallagher in the face or not, but you're gonna be a good boy and wear garters.

STEW
Honey, I love you. I'll eat spinach for you. I'll go to the dentist twice a year for you. I'll wash behind my ears for you. But I will <u>never</u> wear garters!

His arms go about Anne. Under the force of his embrace Anne sinks back on the pillows. Stew leans forward looking down at her.

133. CLOSE TWO SHOT - STEW AND ANNE
Nose to nose.

ANNE
(adopting a sing-song)
Oh, yes you will my dear - oh, yes you will my dear - you'll wear garters and you'll like it too!

STEW
(picking up her sing-song)
Oh, no I won't my dear - oh, no I won't my dear -
I'll wash behind my ears, but no I won't my dear!

He bends to kiss her again, but she gently resists, and continues the sing-song.

ANNE
Oh, yes you will my dear - oh, yes you will my dear - you'll eat spinach but you'll wear garters too!

STEW
Oh, you can't carry a tune - you can't carry a tune - all you are good for is to sit and spoon, spoon. Oh no, I won't wear garters--

ANNE
Oh yes you will wear garters--

They melt into each other's arms.

LAP DISSOLVE TO:

INT. CITY ROOM OF NEWSPAPER OFFICE - DAY

134. MEDIUM FULL SHOT
General activity, as before.

CAMERA TRUCKS DOWN THE MAIN AISLE until it centers on Stew at his desk, sitting low in his chair, his feet cocked up on the corner of his desk, reading a newspaper

CAMERA TRUCKS UP CLOSER centering on his feet on the desk. One trouser leg is pulled slightly up and reveals a garter.

135. MEDIUM CLOSE SHOT
Stew, reading the newspaper. It is opened up before his face.

INSERT: Headlines - about a three-column article:

ANNE SCHUYLER AND CINDERELLA HUBBY TO OCCUPY SCHUYLER MANSION

As Stew reads this, he looks very glum and depressed.

136. MEDIUM SHOT
A reporter, the one Stew had socked with a wad of paper in an earlier sequence, shambles past and stops abruptly, staring at Stew's feet.

INSERT: Of what he sees. Stew's feet. The socks are strangely taut.

BACK TO SCENE:
The reporter glances up and sees that Stew cannot see him, and then carefully lifts Stew's trouser leg a few inches.

INSERT: Stew's feet and legs. As the reporter's hand lifts the trouser leg, the fancy solid-gold garters are on full display.

BACK TO SCENE:
The reporter stares at them goggle-eyed. He can hardly contain himself at the sight of the garters. He looks off:

REPORTER
(cautiously)
Psst!

137. WIDER SHOT
One or two other reporters hear him and look over curiously. The reporter looks very mysterious and important and makes a motion for silence and caution. They get up and cross on tip-toe to join him.

138. MEDIUM SHOT
The men around Stew. They quietly gather around his feet and the reporter who made the discovery proudly displays his find. One or two more step by and all stare. Stew still has the paper up in front of his face.

FIRST REPORTER
Is it real?

2ND REPORTER
Of course it's real!

3RD REPORTER
Any diamonds on them?

REPORTER
Musta set him back at least six bits.[11]

139. MEDIUM CLOSE SHOT
Stew. (Camera behind him and shooting over his head.) He is suddenly attracted by this unusual conversation and lowers his paper, revealing the group of six or seven men in a huddle round his feet.

2ND REPORTER
One just can't wear those and be decent.

3RD REPORTER
Yes you can, if you belong to the Four Hundred.[12]

2ND REPORTER
I wonder what number he is.

Stew flares in anger. Several of them are bending low to get a close peek. With a violent gesture, Stew kicks his foot forward and sends a couple of them sprawling. Stew gets to his feet.

STEW
Go on, get out of there! What's the matter with you mugs? Didn't you ever see a guy with a pair of garters on before?

140. MEDIUM SHOT
The two reporters who have done most of the talking scramble to their feet. The second reporter speaks in mock perplexity.

REPORTER
What do you suppose he wears them for?

2ND REPORTER
Can it be possible to hold his socks up?

3RD REPORTER
Yeah, exactly.
(effeminately)
You know, one's hose look horribly untidy when they hang loose-like, don't you think so, Percifield?

Stew gets up as his phone rings. He pays no attention to it. Hank, another reporter, answers.

4TH REPORTER
(same effeminacy)
Yes, my dear chap - they look ghastly - they look ghastly!

STEW
Go on! Screw! Get out of here!

He starts out when Hank calls to him:

HANK
Hey, Stew!

Stew turns.

HANK
(indicating phone)
Your policeman!

Stew comes back and, frowning, picks up the phone.

141. CLOSE SHOT
Stew at phone.

STEW
Hello? Oh hello dear. Wait just a minute--
(to reporters, hovering around)
Come on! Beat it, will you? Screw! Screw! This is my wife! In your respective chapeaux and over your cauliflower ears.

REPORTERS
(ad-lib teasing comments as they exit scene)

INT. ANNE'S BEDROOM
142. CLOSEUP - ANNE
She is lying on her stomach on a rubbing table, as used by a masseuse. We see a considerable part of her back, on which a middle-aged Swedish masseuse is industriously working. Anne has the telephone in her hand. Throughout her scene, we hear very telling whacks:

ANNE
(into phone)
But it's nearly six o'clock darling, and you know how long it takes you to dress.
(pause)
But the Ambassador is coming at eight, and you've got to be ready by the time he gets here.

LAP DISSOLVE TO:

EXT. SCHUYLER LONG ISLAND ESTATE
143. LONG SHOT OF ESTATE

DISSOLVE INTO:

144. EXT. FRONT ENTRANCE GATE
Two footmen stand at either side of a huge iron gate. Cars and limousines are arriving, dropping off guests in evening wear.

INT. CORRIDOR SCHUYLER HOME
145. Gallagher is just entering. Smythe holds door open for her.

GALLAGHER
I'd like to see Miss Wilson, please.

SMYTHE
Who shall I say, madam?

GALLAGHER
Miss Gallagher of the Post.

SMYTHE
Yes, miss.

He leaves.

146. INT. SCHUYLER RECEPTION HALL
MOSS AND FONTANA are doing a beautiful tango. Guests scattered around the room, watching interestedly.

CUT BACK TO:

147. INT. CORRIDOR SCHUYLER HOME
Gallagher is still waiting. Smythe enters, leading Miss Wilson, a refined-looking girl of 26 or so, her hand extended.

SMYTHE
Miss Gallagher of the Post.

MISS WILSON
Oh yes - of course. Miss Gallagher?

GALLAGHER
Yes.

MISS WILSON
I'm Miss Wilson - Mrs. Schuyler's social secretary.

GALLAGHER
I was sent from the Post in place of our social editor.

MISS WILSON
Yes, of course. Miss Ramsey telephoned me. Well, what would you like to have?

GALLAGHER
Why, a list of the guests. That's the usual thing, isn't it?

MISS WILSON
Yes, of course. I'll get it for you--
(smiling)
In the meantime, would you like to take a look around?

GALLAGHER
Yes, thank you.

The CAMERA MOVES WITH THEM as they start for the Reception Room.

MISS WILSON
That's a lovely dress.

GALLAGHER
Thank you.
(pause)
Where is Mr. Smith?

MISS WILSON
Mr. Smith? Oh, you mean Ann Schuyler's husband?

GALLAGHER
Yes.

MISS WILSON
He's probably very tired. You see, he's had to meet all these people personally tonight.

GALLAGHER
I bet.

MISS WILSON
You newspaper people have a lot of fun with him, don't you? What is it you call him - the Cinderella Man?

CUT TO:

148. INT. ENTRANCE OF BALLROOM
Moss and Fontana are just finishing their dance. Gallagher stands in doorway with Miss Wilson, watching them. Excited voices comment on the dance. Miss Wilson beckons to Gallagher to follow her.

CAMERA TRUCKS with them as they weave in and out of crowd. Miss Wilson points out celebrated guests to her.

MISS WILSON
There's the Spanish Ambassador.

Gallagher steals a glance at the celebrated gentleman.

GALLAGHER
You know, he looks like one.

Miss Wilson laughs delightedly. At this point they are interrupted by a butler.

149. MEDIUM SHOT

BUTLER
Miss Wilson--

MISS WILSON
Yes?

BUTLER
Mrs. Smith would like to see you.

MISS WILSON
(to Gallagher)
Will you excuse me? Make yourself at home for just a moment, please.

GALLAGHER
Thanks.

Miss Wilson follows butler out of scene. Gallagher is left alone. She wanders about the huge ballroom, peering here and there, searching for Stew. Finally she comes to a large open French door and steps out.

150. INT. TERRACE LEADING OFF SCHUYLER BALLROOM
Several groups of men and women are seated at tables. Gallagher enters from ballroom, glances quickly at all the men. Disappointed at not finding Stew, she crosses terrace and descends broad stone steps and advances into garden.

151. INT. SECLUDED SPOT IN GARDEN
Stew, his head cupped in his hands, is seated on a stone bench. Gallagher wanders into scene. She sees Stew and stops. Stew does not move. Gallagher, with a happy smile on her lips, moves closer to him. Stew suddenly becomes conscious of someone near him and looks suddenly up. He sees Gallagher; his face breaks into a happy grin.

GALLAGHER
Mr. Smith, I've read some of your plays and I'd like an autograph.

STEW
Well, well! If it isn't my old friend! Turn around, gal! Let's get a look at you.

GALLAGHER
There you are--!

152. CLOSER SHOT OF THE TWO

STEW
Well, daughter of the slums - how did you get out of the ghetto?

GALLAGHER
I'm pinch-hitting for our society editor tonight. I wanted to see some life in the raw.

STEW
Aw, you wanted to see some life in the raw, huh? Well gal, I'm afraid we ain't got no raw life up here.

GALLAGHER
Well, I'll have to look someplace else.

STEW
No, no! Maybe we could interest you in some well done butterflies, or perhaps some slightly fried pansies, or better still, some stuffed shirts. And guaranteed every one of them will give you a good stiff pain in the neck.

GALLAGHER
(fixing his tie)
Say, who's been tying your ties lately? It looks rotten.

He suddenly realizes there's something different about Gallagher. He takes a step back so as to look her over carefully - blinks his eyes.

STEW
Gee Gallagher, do you look good! What are you doing to yourself?

GALLAGHER
Nothing.

STEW
What did you do to that hair? And where did you get that dress?

GALLAGHER
I dyed one and washed the other.

STEW
(enthusiastically)
Oh, you dyed one and washed the other. Well! You certainly look good.

153. ANOTHER PART OF THE GARDEN
Anne is walking in direction of Stew and Gallagher. She stops suddenly when she sees them. Her body stiffens.

CUT BACK TO:

ANOTHER SHOT - STEW AND GALLAGHER
From Anne's angle. Gallagher is facing in the direction of Anne.

GALLAGHER
Don't turn around now - but there's a very beautiful girl up there who seems to be staring at us.

STEW
Staring at us?

GALLAGHER
My mistake - she's glaring.

STEW
Must be my wife.

He turns - sees Anne.

STEW
It <u>is</u> my wife. Hi Anne. Don't go away. Stay right there, because I'm going to bring a friend up I want you to meet.

They exit.

154. MED. CLOSE SHOT - ANNE
Standing as before. She is looking off with slightly narrowed eyes. Stew and Gallagher come up to her.

STEW
Anne, prepare yourself for the treat of your life. This is Gallagher.

ANNE
(astounded)
<u>Gallagher!</u>

STEW
Sure - my pal on the paper. She's subbing for the society editor tonight.

Anne turns an acid smile on the uncomfortable Gallagher.

155. CLOSER THREE SHOT

ANNE
Oh, yes, of course. How do you do?

STEW
Gallagher, this is Mrs. Smith.

Anne winces slightly at this name.

GALLAGHER
How do you do?

There is a short, awkward pause.

ANNE
(bitter-sweet)
You know, Stewart, you failed to mention that Miss Gallagher was a very beautiful young girl.

STEW
Gallagher?

Gallagher flashes a look at Stew - seeing that he fails to get the dynamite behind Anne's casually pleasant phrases. Anne plunges ahead. Her tone is unmistakable now.

ANNE
Yes. As a matter of fact, you failed to mention that Gallagher was a girl.

STEW
(surprised)
Didn't I? That's funny. Isn't it funny?

ANNE
(with a world of meaning)
Yes isn't it?

156. CLOSE SHOT - STEW AND ANNE
Stew is beginning to realize that all is not well as it could be.

STEW
You see, we never look at Gallagher as a girl--

He breaks off.

ANNE
(with her eyes on Gallagher)
No? What do you look upon her as?

STEW
(fumbling for words)
Why, down at the office, we always look at Gallagher as - eh - just Gallagher, that's all.

CAMERA PANS QUICKLY TO CLOSE SHOT of GALLAGHER. She tries to back Stew up.

GALLAGHER
(not so comfortable herself)
They all consider me just as one of the boys.

STEW
Right!

157. MED. SHOT OF THE THREE

ANNE
(a deadly acid smile)
Indeed? How interesting.

GALLAGHER
(same kind of smile)
Yes - isn't it.

Anne takes Stew's arm, drawing him away from Gallagher.

ANNE
Miss Wilson will give you the guest list and any other details you may need, Miss Gallagher.

GALLAGHER
(resenting the tone of dismissal)
Thank you. I'll go and look for her at once. Goodbye, Mrs. Smith.

ANNE
Goodbye, Miss Gallagher.

GALLAGHER
Goodbye, Stew--

She leaves scene.

158. MED. CLOSE SHOT - STEW AND ANNE
Stew turns and faces her.

STEW
That was kind of a rotten thing to do, Anne. After all, Gallagher is my friend. The least you can do is be courteous to her.

ANNE
I thought I was very charming, Stewart.

STEW
You did? That's a lot of hooey! I'll go and apologize.

He promptly walks away from her in Gallagher's direction.

ANNE
(furious)
Stewart, please!

She glares angrily at the departing Stew.

<u>EXT. TERRACE</u>
159. CLOSE SHOT
Gallagher has just reached the ballroom when Stew catches up to her.

STEW
I'm sorry, Gallagher - really, I am sorry.

GALLAGHER
(reassuringly)
Oh, that's all right, Stew. Forget it. As far as she's concerned, I'm just part of the hired help.

STEW
No, no. Strange, I've never seen Anne act that way before. (pause) It's funny I never thought to tell her you were a girl, isn't it?

GALLAGHER
Yes.

INT. SCHUYLER ENTRANCE HALL
160. MED. CLOSE SHOT
The butler is just opening the door. Bingy, looking more disreputable than usual, steps inside.

BINGY
Hello, there, Meadows![13]

SMYTHE
(disapproving once-over)
Who is it you wish to see, sir?

BINGY
I want to see Stew Smith. Oh excuse me - I mean Mr. Smith.

SMYTHE
Pardon me, Mr. Smith is engaged. We are having a reception here this evening--

BINGY
Oh, a party! Great, great! Jolly times and merry pranks. That's me. I'm a guy who loves parties. You know--

He is distracted by two elegantly-dressed ladies strolling by.

BINGY
--a beautiful pair of shoulders! But listen now, as a favor, will you please make it snappy, Laughing Waters,[14] and tell Stew Smith I gotta see him because if you don't my whole family's going to die.

SMYTHE
I'll tell Mr. Smith at once, sir. Have a seat.

BINGY
Well, I got a seat, but I have no place to put it.

The butler turns to leave, then turns back, his face expressing distinct disapproval.

SMYTHE
Pardon me, sir, but I've heard that one before.

INT. SCHUYLER BALLROOM

161. CLOSE SHOT

Stew and Gallagher standing together. The butler is seen leaving the scene, having just informed Stew of Bingy's presence at the reception.

STEW
(to Gallagher)
Excuse me. I just want to make sure and see he doesn't take away any of the vases.
(starts to leave, then turns back)
Well, well, well! My little pal, Gallagher, a girl, huh?
(unexpectedly, he bends to kiss her hand)
(tenderly)
That's just to give you an idea that I know how to treat a gal. Get fresh with me and I'll sock you in that little nose of yours. Excuse me. I'll be right back.

He exits. Gallagher is left staring at her hand wonderingly.

INT. SCHUYLER ENTRANCE HALL

162. MED. SHOT

Bingy gets up from his throne chair, and crosses into the doorway of the library opposite him. He stops by a carved low-boy, and curiously examines a large antique vase. Stew comes in and stops with a smile as he sees him.

Bingy, his hand on the vase, looks up. Stew walks over to him.

STEW
(referring to vase)
What's the matter, Bingy, a little clumsy to get in your pocket?

Bingy sets down the vase and surveys him.

BINGY
No. I was just looking at it. Pretty, ain't it? I was just looking for the price tag.

INT. SCHUYLER LIBRARY

163. CLOSER SHOT OF THE TWO

Bingy looks him up and down in silent, insolent scrutiny. Stew begins to burn.

STEW
What do you want?

BINGY
Oh, nothing. I just blew over - I wanted to see how the old newshound looked made up for a gentleman.

STEW
(sore)
Would you like to have me turn around for you, Bingy?

BINGY
Oh boy, I'd love it.

Stew makes a complete turn and faces Bingy again.

STEW
How's that?

BINGY
(appraisingly)
Not bad - not good - but not bad. You ought to be able to fool about almost anybody.

STEW
Is that so? Well, have you seen enough - or would you like a photograph?

BINGY
A photograph? What's the matter? Hasn't mama had you done in oils yet?
(singing)
"Just A Gigolo ... "[15]

STEW
Now get this mug. You've got the kind of chin I just love to touch. And if you don't get out of here, I'm going to hang one right on it.

Bingy assumes a conciliatory attitude.

BINGY
Take it easy! Take it easy, Dempsey.[16] Just relax, my boy, relax and open your pores.

164. CLOSER TWO SHOT
Stew glares at him. Bingy goes on.

BINGY
I bring a message from Garcia.

STEW
Yeah?

BINGY
Yeah. The boss sent me over to offer you a job. He wants you to write a daily column on the Tribune.

STEW
(skeptically)
Yeah - go on.

BINGY
It's all right. You can write your own ticket. A hundred and fifty bucks a week.

STEW
(thinks a bit - quietly)
I'll bite. What's the catch?

BINGY
There's no catch. This is on the up and up. Of course all you have to do is just sign the article - by Anne Schuyler's Husband.

165. MED. SHOT
Taking in the doorway. The butler starts to pass by. Stew's eyes are blazing.

BINGY
Well, how does the old Cinderella man feel about that?

With a quick motion, Stew clips Bingy on the jaw. Bingy, caught unawares, reels backward.

166. CLOSER SHOT IN DOORWAY
Bingy describes a backward arc, just as Smythe, the butler, seeing he can be of service, steps forward and catches him.

SMYTHE
Well done, sir. Very neat.

STEW
(through his teeth)
<u>That's</u> what I think of it, Bingy!

Bingy sags in the butler's arms. The butler looks at Stew inquiringly. Stew nods.

STEW
(to butler)
Smythe, the - er - gentleman is leaving.

SMYTHE
Yes, sir.

Bingy is carried out. Stew stands glaring after them.

FADE OUT:

FADE IN

<u>INT. SCHUYLER HOME</u>
167. MEDIUM CLOSE SHOT
Anne and her mother at the breakfast table.

ANNE
Good morning, Mother. Didn't I tell you that he'd be marvelous. Everybody thought he was so charming last night.

MRS. SCHUYLER
I was so worried for fear he'd knock over a vase or something. I must have acted like an idiot.
(notices the morning paper in Anne's hands)
What does it say about the reception last night?

ANNE
Oh, the usual thing. Blah, blah, blah attended the blah, blah reception and wore the same blah, blah things.

MRS. SCHUYLER
(reproachfully)
Stop it. Anne. You're behaving like the person you're married to.

ANNE
You don't have anything to complain about, Mother. He was all right last night, wasn't he? I told you not to worry about him.

MRS. SCHUYLER
It was a miracle. The man was ill or something.

She suddenly notices front page of paper Anne is reading. Her face freezes in horror. She screams.

MRS. SCHUYLER
(screaming)
Ah-ah-ah!

ANNE
Mother!

MRS. SCHUYLER
(frantically gesturing at paper)
Look! Look! The front page!

Anne turns paper and reads the article.

CUT TO:

INSERT: NEWSPAPER
CINDERELLA MAN GROWS HAIR ON CHEST
ATTACKS REPORTER IN SCHUYLER HOME.
"I wear the pants," says Anne Schuyler's husband.
"It's Okay with me," says Anne.

168. MEDIUM SHOT
Mrs. Schuyler gets up. Paces wildly about room. In a frenzy.

MRS. SCHUYLER
I knew it! I knew it! I felt it in my bones!

She is interrupted by the entrance of Grayson, who dashes into the room, his eyes ablaze. In his hand he has a copy of the morning paper.

GRAYSON
(tapping paper in hand)
Did you see the papers? "Cinderella Man Grows Hair On Chest!" This is the most terrible kind of publicity that could possibly--

MRS. SCHUYLER
(interrupting)
Don't you think I know it, Grayson?
(as Smythe the butler enters with tray)
Smith - send for Mr. Smythe! Er - Smythe, send for Mr. Smith!

SMYTHE
(as he turns to go)
Double-strength!

MRS. SCHUYLER
(muttering, as she exits scene)
"Cinderella Man Grows Hair On Chest!"

GRAYSON
(close behind, contemptuously)
"I wear the pants," says Anne Schuyler's husband!

INT. SCHUYLER ENTRANCE HALL - DAY

169. MEDIUM SHOT

Stew, now dressed in a business suit, comes from the direction of the stairs and stops just before he gets to the door of the drawing room. From within there is an ominous silence. Stew looks longingly in the direction of the front door - then back at the drawing room, squares his shoulders and goes in.

INT. SCHUYLER DRAWING ROOM

170. CLOSE SHOT

As Stew stops just inside the doorway. He had been prepared for this, but it strikes terror into his soul, just the same.

171. MEDIUM FULL SHOT

From his angle in the doorway. The jury - Dexter Grayson, hands behind his back - is standing, gazing at Stew with a fishy eye. Mrs. Schuyler stares haughtily. Anne is crying softly.

CONTINUATION SCENE 170

Stew - looking around at the gallery of faces. Then he forces a jaunty smile to his face as he starts to enter, whistling as he goes.

STEW

Good morning, everybody--

(he gets a cold, frigid, silent reception)

Well, maybe it isn't a good morning, huh?

(to Anne)

Anne, did you ever get the feeling that there was someone else in the room with you?

172. MEDIUM SHOT

MRS. SCHUYLER

Have you seen this?

(shows him newspaper)

STEW

Yes - the worm!

MRS. SCHUYLER

I beg your pardon?

STEW

He's a worm - and I'm gonna step on him!

MRS. SCHUYLER

To engage in a brawl! A cheap, common brawl, in my own home! "I wear the pants!" The pants! Not even the trousers!

GRAYSON

I've tried to stop the evening papers, but it's useless.

173. CLOSER SHOT - STEW AND GRAYSON

STEW

You quit trying to stop anybody--

GRAYSON

Well, at best you might deny it.

STEW
Why deny it? The more you deny, the more they print. Let them alone! The thing to do is to sit still and keep our traps shut.

GRAYSON
Traps shut!

STEW
Certainly! I'll take care of this guy Bingy myself, personally.
(sees Anne crying)
Now what are you crying about?

174. MEDIUM SHOT

ANNE
Is this true, Stewart? Did you really say it?

STEW
Yes, I said it. Sure, I said it. I didn't say it for publication, however.

MRS. SCHUYLER
And you struck him right here in our house--?

STEW
Yes, I'm sorry, I struck him right here in your house. And I'll strike anybody in anybody's house that calls me a Cinderella Man.

GRAYSON
Well, what else do you expect them to call you?

ANNE
Dexter.

175. CLOSEUP - STEW

STEW
(burning)
That's the fourteenth crack you've made to me. I'm keeping count. When you get to twenty, I'm gonna sock you right on the nose. As a matter of fact, I ought to sock you right now.

176. MEDIUM FULL SHOT

MRS. SCHUYLER
Anne Schuyler, are you going to sit there and watch this man insult us? Haven't you any decency left?

ANNE
(defending him)
Why doesn't Dexter show some decency? And you might show some too, Mother. What do you expect a man to do when he's called such names?
(to Stew)
I'm glad you hit that reporter, Stewart. He deserved it.

MRS. SCHUYLER
(rising)
All right, all right! It's your funeral, Anne Schuyler!

She flounces out. Grayson remains behind.

STEW
(to Grayson)
Go on, beat it, shadow.

Grayson turns to go, then braves the last word.

GRAYSON
Cinderella Man! That's fifteen.

He leaves in a huff. Stew puts his arms around the crying Anne.

FADE OUT:

FADE IN

INT. SCHUYLER DRAWING ROOM

177. FULL SHOT
Six or eight people of distinction scattered around the room. All dressed in full evening clothes. Among them is Grayson, Anne, her mother, and one man in aviator's uniform. The men have their coats and hats in their hands, the women have their evening wraps on. Apparently they are ready to leave for someplace and are being detained. An indistinct murmur of ad-lib conversation is heard.

178. CLOSE SHOT
On Smythe, the butler, as he approaches Mrs. Schuyler.

SMYTHE
Pardon me, madam. They phoned through from the Mayor's committee to remind you it's past the hour for the reception.

MRS. SCHUYLER
Are the cars ready?

SMYTHE
They've been ready for the last half hour.

179. MED. CLOSE SHOT - GROUP
Including Captain White, a young, handsome aviator.

AVIATOR
(modestly)
I hope I don't have to make any speeches tonight, Anne.

ANNE
Oh, you can't disappoint all the women. After all it isn't every day they get to see a famous round-the-world flier.

AVIATOR
Yes, I know, but they scare me to death. This is the fourth dinner you've taken me to this week. I'm running out of material.

ANNE
Are you complaining?

AVIATOR
Yes, there are always too many other people around.

LADY
Anne, it's getting late. What are we waiting for?

ANNE
We're waiting for my husband--
(lightly, concealing her irritation)
If you'll excuse me, I'll run up and see what the slowpoke's doing.
(to aviator)
I'll be right back--

She starts out, climbing stairs to Stew's room.

INT. STEW'S BEDROOM
180. MEDIUM SHOT
Stew stands in front of a mirror, fumbling with his dress tie. He pauses, his hands still on his tie.

ANNE
(reproachfully)
Stewart! We're all waiting for you. Where's your valet?

STEW
I poisoned him.

ANNE
Stop trying to be funny, and get ready, will you?

As he struggles with his collar, it springs off.

STEW
I'm not going!

ANNE
What are you talking about?

STEW
I'm talking about - I'm not going out.

181. CLOSEUP - ANNE

ANNE
(controlling her anger)
What am I going downstairs and tell those people?

STEW
Go downstairs, and tell them - anything. Tell them I'm not going. Tell them I'm not home.

ANNE
(getting angrier by the minute)
Stewart, would you mind telling me why you're not going?

182. CLOSEUP - STEW

STEW
Yes, I'll tell you - for the same reason I've never wanted to go out with those social parasites, those sweet-smelling fashion plates. I don't like them. They bore me. They give me the jitters.

ANNE'S VOICE
Do you know you're talking about my friends?

STEW
Yes, I'm talking about your friends, and they still give me the jitters.

183. DOUBLE SHOT

ANNE
Well, are you going - or aren't you?

Stew makes a move to embrace her.

STEW
Anne, come here. Listen--

ANNE
(sternly - slipping away from him)
Look out for my lipstick, Stewart.

STEW
I'll tell you what. Let's you and me sneak out all by ourselves--

ANNE
(interrupting)
Are you crazy?

STEW
Think of the fun we can have - we'll sneak down the back stairs and get in the valet's Ford. How's that?

ANNE
Will you stop being silly, Stewart?

STEW
(trying hard)
I'll tell you what let's do - I'll take you and introduce you to all my gang. Would you like that?

ANNE
(hard)
But I don't want to meet your gang.

STEW
I don't mean the newspaper fellows that you don't like. Another gang I know - you'd love them. They're writers and musicians and artists - a great crowd of people - people who do great things. People who are worthwhile.

ANNE
Meaning, my friends aren't worthwhile, I suppose?

STEW
Oh, they're all right, Anne. But I--

ANNE
(interrupting belligerently)
That's exactly what you mean. Heaven knows you've made that clear to me often enough. Well, I'm sick and tired of it. I've given you party after party - I've taken you to some of the best houses in this town - and introduced you to people of importance - and are you grateful? No! You insult them and act like a bore. I'm sick and tired of having to make excuses for you and the things that you've done. Perhaps it's just as well you're not coming tonight. Maybe I can enjoy myself for once without having to worry about you, and what you're going to do.

With which violent declaration, she flounces out of the room, leaving Stew staring after her, angry and hurt. Impulsively, he follows her to the door - a retort on his lips. When he gets there, however, she has vanished. He returns to the room, wanders about thoughtfully, extracts cigarette from box, fumbles it - walks to window - stares out - turns back to room - heaves a lonely sigh.

He notices his reflection in the mirror, and gestures toward it.

STEW
And that, my friends, is what is known as the society belle telling ex-star-newspaper-reporter to go to - how-have-you-been, Mr. Smith!

184. CLOSE SHOT
As Stew sits in a typewriter chair. He rolls up the sheet in the machine so that he can read what is already written.

INSERT: TYPEWRITTEN SHEET, IN TYPEWRITER

ACT 1
SCENE 1
AN HACIENDA IN MEXICO
Strumming of guitars are dimly heard.

BACK TO SCENE:
He studies it for a moment, frowning in dissatisfaction. He's stuck. He leans back in the chair and looks up for inspiration.

INSERT: A BIG CLOCK, TICKING AWAY THE TIME.

INT. SCHUYLER GRAND FOYER
185. LONG SHOT
Of Stew Smith pacing the grand foyer. Seen from overhead, he is dwarfed by the surroundings. He tries hopscotching on the pattern of the floor. That wears thin quickly. Supremely bored, Stew gives a shout and is rewarded with a cavernous echo. Smythe the butler then appears, nervously crouched behind some grillwork.

186. MEDIUM SHOT - STEW AND SMYTHE

SMYTHE
Did you call, sir?

STEW
Smythe, come here. I want to talk to you.
(Smythe looks unenthusiastic.)
Come on, Smythe, talk to me. Smythe, I'm going nuts. I'm going nuts in this house! This big ...come on, I'm not going to hurt you. Come on, what's the matter with you?

Stew gives another shout and is rewarded with another loud echo. This coaxes Smythe out from behind the grillwork.

STEW
Shhh! Do you hear something?

SMYTHE
Yes, sir.

STEW
You try it.

SMYTHE
(reluctant)
Me, sir?

STEW
Yeah.

Smythe gives it a timid try.

STEW
No, no. Give it more volume.

Smythe gives a more satisfactory yell. Stew nods approval. Smythe begins yelling and shouting in earnest.

STEW
No, that's enough. I just wanted you to get the idea. Now you know. This house is haunted.

SMYTHE
(incredulous)
No, sir!

STEW
Yes. Have you looked in the closets all over ...?

SMYTHE
Yes, sir.

STEW
Found no skeletons?

SMYTHE
No, sir.

STEW
It's haunted just the same.

SMYTHE

Yes, sir.

Smythe has heard enough. He turns to leave, but Stew grabs him.

STEW

Smythe, what do you do with yourself - I mean, when you're not carrying those double-strength - what do you do with yourself?

SMYTHE

Well, sir, I putter.

STEW

Smythe! I mean - when you're alone and want to amuse yourself, then what?

SMYTHE

I just putter.

STEW

Hmmm, you just putter. Do you have to have a putter to putter?

SMYTHE

Oh no, sir. I putter with me hands.

STEW

Well, isn't that nice? You just go right ahead and putter with your hands. That's all right. How do you do it?

SMYTHE

Well sir, I'll show you.

He demonstrates, touching objects on a table and blowing dust off a lampshade.

SMYTHE

That's puttering, sir.

STEW

No! Well, well, well! That's all right, if you like it. Can anybody do that?

SMYTHE

Oh no, sir. Some people are natural putterers. Others can never master it.

STEW

Oh my. You mean, some people are born and never will become putterers?

SMYTHE

Yes sir.

STEW

Oh my, wouldn't that be tragic? To know that you could never be a putterer.

SMYTHE

Yes sir.

STEW
How about me? Do you think if I concentrated and put my whole soul into it, that some day I might be a putterer?

SMYTHE
You sir? Uh-uh. You could never be a putterer. Not a good putterer, sir.

STEW
Well, if I couldn't be a good putterer, I wouldn't want to putter. But why? What makes you think I couldn't be a good putterer?

SMYTHE
Well sir, to be a putterer, one's mind must be at ease. A person with a problem could never be a putterer. For instance, sir, a fish can putter in water but not on land because he'd be out of place. An eagle can putter around a rugged mountaintop but not in a cage, because he'd be restless and unhappy. Now sir, if you will pardon me, with all due respect, sir, as a Smythe to a Smith, you are an eagle in a cage.

STEW
A bird in a gilded cage?

SMYTHE
Yes.

STEW
That's all I wanted to know!

Stew rushes off upstairs. Smythe gives the echo one last try.

FADE OUT:

INT. STEW'S ROOM
187. MEDIUM SHOT
As Stew makes a telephone call.

STEW
Hello, Gallagher old pal. How are you, old pal?

INT. GALLAGHER'S ROOM - NIGHT
188. MEDIUM SHOT
A simple room, probably in a boarding house or cheap hotel. Gallagher is on the phone. A typewriter stands nearby.

GALLAGHER
Oh, hello Stew. I'm pretty good, can't complain. How's our gentleman of leisure?

CONTINUATION SCENE 187
Stew at phone.

STEW
I'm on the coast of Norway and I can't get out - will you come and get me out of the coast of Norway?

CONTINUATION SCENE 188
Gallagher at phone.

GALLAGHER
Oh, your play. Hmmm, Act One, Scene One: Coast of Norway - and then a lot of blank. Is that it?

CONTINUATION SCENE 187
Stew at phone.

STEW
Yeah. Come on, don't be silly.
(pause)
All right, if you feel like you need a chaperone, call up Hank. Yeah. You'll find him at Joe's, no doubt. Yeah. Hank would be my idea of a perfect bodyguard.
(pause)
Sure you would. I knew I could depend on you, old pal. Snap it up, will you, Gallagher?

CONTINUATION SCENE 188
Gallagher at phone.

GALLAGHER
Okay.

She hangs up, joyful at the prospect of seeing Stew. She hums softly to herself as she picks up the receiver again.

INT. SCHUYLER ENTRANCE HALL - NIGHT
189. MED. SHOT

SOUND
(bell ringing)

Stew comes out of the library. Smythe is going down the hall. Stew intercepts him.

STEW
Smythe, I'll get this. I'm expecting some friends.

SMYTHE
Very good, sir.

190. MED. CLOSE SHOT
At entrance door. Stew enters and opens it. Gallagher and Hank enter.

STEW
Well, Gallagher! Glad to see you.

GALLAGHER
Hello, Stew.

STEW
Hello, Hank. How are you?

HANK
Fine, but kinda thirsty.

STEW
Come right in - I'll get you a drink.

HANK
Okay - you remember Joe--

STEW
Sure.

HANK
I sort of invited him along to bend an elbow. You don't mind, do you?

STEW
It's all right. Bring him in.

Joe appears in the open doorway. Stew sees him.

HANK
Come in, Joe. It's all right.

STEW
Hello, Joe.

JOE
Hello kid, how are you? Glad to see you.

Stew starts to close the door.

JOE
Just a minute - Johnson's outside. You don't mind if he comes in and dips a beak[17] do you?

STEW
No, no, bring him in. The more the merrier.

JOE
Come on in!

Johnson appears in the open doorway. Stew sees him.

STEW
Hello, Johnson.

JOHNSON
Hello, Stew, old pal. How are you?

STEW
Glad to see you. Come in, kid.

Stew starts to close the door.

JOHNSON
Wait a minute. I got two of the boys I brought along - they were cruising around with nothing to do. You don't mind if I bring them in?

STEW
You brought two of the boys? That's all right. Bring them in. What's the difference?

The two enter, followed in a single file by 12-14 men and women, all of whom greet Stew as they enter, ad-libbing hello's and handshakes. Stew stares at them dumbfoundedly.

191. MEDIUM FULL SHOT
They swarm into the hallway and overflow into the rooms on either side. The butler stands aghast at this invasion. Stew starts to close the door when three or four more troop in, shouting cheery greetings. Stew regards them in amazement.

192. CLOSER SHOT - STEW
As he watches them file past.

STEW
I'm sorry nobody could come.

HANK
The rest of the gang had to get out the morning edition - but they'll be down later.

STEW
Now Hank, are you sure they're coming? It will be lonesome without them.
(to Smythe)
Smythe, take this crowd in there and give them a drink. And find out what the boys in the back room want!

Smythe gulps nervously, as he is dragged off by the revellers.

INT. SCHUYLER DRAWING ROOM
193. FULL SHOT
The gang have taken seriously Stew's suggestion that they make themselves at home. They have draped themselves about the place - a couple are strumming on the piano and others are inspecting the room in awe-struck attitudes. Smythe is being propelled around the room by the revellers.

SMYTHE
It isn't done, gentlemen! It isn't done, I say! It isn't done!

INT. SCHUYLER ENTRANCE HALL
194. MEDIUM SHOT - GALLAGHER AND STEW

STEW
Well, Gallagher, you certainly took no chances, did you?

GALLAGHER
I'm sorry, Stew. I asked Hank, and Hank did the rest.

STEW
I see. Hank brought them all. That's all right. We'll give them a drink and throw 'em out. How's that?

GALLAGHER
Okay.

STEW
(as Smythe passes by, being propelled by revellers)
Smythe! Give them one drink and throw 'em out!

SMYTHE
(dazed)
Yes, sir.

Bingy pokes his head in the door, wearing a false beard.

STEW
(spotting him)
Is there a green elephant standing beside that bwana?

BINGY
No, it's just little Bingy Baker.

Stew rolls up his sleeves, preparatory to launching a punch.

BINGY
(warningly)
Uh-uh.

Bingy dons a pair of glasses, and points to them meaningfully. He enters, cautiously, watching Stew warily.

BINGY
(striking a pose)
Big Chief Bingy come to white man's tepee to make friends. Big Chief very sorry. To show how sorry - will bend over and let white man kick Big Chief where sun never shines.

STEW
Excuse me, Gallagher. I wouldn't miss this one for the world.

He bends over, and Stew winds up and delivers a hard kick to his backside. Bingy straightens stiffly, then removes a bottle of alcohol from the target area.

BINGY
Fire water all right.
(he takes a drink)

Both start laughing.

BINGY
Well, Stew, that's all thrashed out. By golly, I'm surely glad to see that you're not really sore. You know our racket - after all, news is news.

STEW
Sure, sure. That's all right. That was a great story, Bingy. A great story - wish I'd printed it.

BINGY
I gave you the breaks, didn't I? That hairy chest story!

STEW
(indicating Bingy's false beard)
You've raised it up to the chin, I see.
(laughs)
Go on in the other room and get yourself a drink.

Bingy emits a war-whoop and proceeds into the drawing room, where Smythe is still being held hostage by the party.

195. CLOSER SHOT
Gallagher and Stew.

STEW
You know what I should do with you? I should sock you right in that funny little nose.

GALLAGHER
Yes - and I'd love it.

SMYTHE
Sure, you'd love it.

He draws her out of the entrance hall, and the CAMERA MOVES WITH THEM as they head upstairs, the party around them going in full force.

INT. STEW'S SITTING ROOM
196. MEDIUM SHOT
Stew and Gallagher enter. Apparently they have been talking about Stew's play on the way upstairs.

GALLAGHER
How far have you gotten?

STEW
Well, I've just been able to get off that Norway coast - so far.

Stew gestures toward the typewriter from which a sheet of paper is protruding. Gallagher crosses to it. She rolls up the sheet so she can read what is typed on it.

GALLAGHER
(reading)
'Act One - Scene One - A Street in Old Madrid--'

She turns as Stew walks over to her.

GALLAGHER
(smiling)
Well, you're not getting your play done, but you're certainly covering a lot of territory.

STEW
(grins)
Haven't I covered some territory? It feels like I've been on a Cook's Tour[18] some place.

197. CLOSER TWO SHOT
Stew, standing before her.

GALLAGHER
(seriously)
Stewart, have you ever been to Old Madrid?

STEW
(grinning in spite of himself)
Been where?

Gallagher
To Old Madrid.

STEW
Never even been to New Madrid.

GALLAGHER
Then how do you expect to write about it?

STEW
Oh - draw on my imagination, I suppose.

GALLAGHER
Did Conrad draw on his imagination?

Stew is brought up with a start.

STEW
Did who?

GALLAGHER
Conrad.

STEW
What do you know about Conrad?

GALLAGHER
I don't know a thing about him, but isn't he the one you're always yelling about?

Stew is noticeably impressed with this point of view.

STEW
Gosh, you look cute.

Gallagher warms up to her subject.

GALLAGHER
Isn't he the one that always writes about things - only the things he knows about?

STEW
Right.

GALLAGHER
Didn't he go to sea before he wrote about it?

STEW
Right.

198. MEDIUM SHOT

GALLAGHER
Then why don't you write about something you know? Write about yourself and Anne. The poor boy who marries a rich girl - now there's a swell theme.

STEW
Gee, that's an idea, Gallagher. That's an idea there. I wonder now ...

GALLAGHER
Oh, sure. She'd make a beautiful heroine ...

STEW
(warming up -
he puts arm around Gallagher's shoulder)
And there's her mother - and what a character that old dame would make with her double-strength - and that lawyer friend of theirs - he'd make a great villain - and there's you!

GALLAGHER
(smiling)
What could I be?

STEW
You could be something.
(inspiration striking, he dashes to the typewriter)
I've got an idea, Gallagher. Let's get this set That's a great idea for a play. Pal, get me a cigarette, will you?

GALLAGHER
Here you are.

STEW
All right, thanks. Now, let's see. How will I start? Hey pal, how would you start?

LAP DISSOLVE TO:

INT. SCHUYLER ENTRANCE HALL
199. MED. FULL SHOT
Shooting through into the drawing room. It is many hours later. The members of the party, including Smythe, are pretty well lit. On the floor of the entrance hall a dice game is in progress. In the drawing room four or five are hanging over the piano singing "The Grasshopper Jumped Over Another Grasshopper's Back."

In general, a large time is being had. As the scene opens a door-bell is ringing. A key is heard in the lock.

200. CLOSER SHOT - GROUP - IN ENTRANCE HALL
The outer door starts to swing open. One of the party guests, very wall-eyed now, and carrying a whiskey bottle in his hand, staggers toward the door. It opens wider, and Anne and Mrs. Schuyler and Dexter Grayson stand gasping in the opening. The guest comes up to them.

GUEST
(starting to close door)
Say, you can't come in here - this is a private party.

Anne pushes the door violently, which sends the guest sprawling. He stays where he lands, holding the bottle in both arms across his chest. Anne and her mother advance into a CLOSE SHOT and look off with incredulous horror and amazement.

201. MEDIUM SHOT
On a drunk Bingy as he peers at them from an alcove above.

BINGY
(recognizing Grayson)
Hey, my old classmate from Harvard! Whoopee! Harvard, '98!
(spotting Mrs. Schuyler)
Hello, mama!

202. MEDIUM SHOT
Most are too cock-eyed or too engrossed in the ongoing crap game to notice them.

DEXTER
I know who's the cause of it all!

ANNE
Oh, Dexter!

One of the men wanders in from the drawing room in time to hear this conversation. He assumes an attitude of exaggerated courtesy and gallantry as he bows before them.

Anne and her mother are almost bursting with fury. They spot Smythe, across the room, thoroughly in his cups.

MRS. SCHUYLER
(to butler)
Smythe! Smythe - who are these people?

Smythe comes stumbling up, a grin plastered on his face.

SMYTHE
(thoroughly plastered)
Friends of mine. Very lit-lit-literary people.

GRAYSON
(confidentially, to Mrs. Schuyler)
He's drunk.

MRS. SCHUYLER
(aghast)
Smythe, you've been drinking.

SMYTHE
(proudly)
I have. Double-strength!

GRAYSON
(confidentially)
Very drunk.

MRS. SCHUYLER
(indignant)
Where is Mr. Smith?

SMYTHE
Well, for crying out loud, I don't know. And I don't care. Whoopee!

He jubilantly exits scene.

GRAYSON
(confidentially)
Very, very drunk.

INT. STEW'S SITTING ROOM
203. MEDIUM SHOT
Stew gets to his feet as an idea strikes him.

STEW
Now Gallagher, if we could only get a great scene - a tremendously emotional scene - some-

thing that would just wring the hearts out
of the public - to bring the curtain down in the
second act - that would be okay. Couldn't dig
one out of your hat some place, could you?

GALLAGHER
Nope - afraid I'm all out of tricks tonight.

STEW
Now, we've got it right up to where the boy's
wearing his white spats and going to teas and
the frau enters how's that?

GALLAGHER
Very good.

204. MED. CLOSE SHOT
At the partially opened door into the hall. It opens wider, and
Anne looks in. She stares in horrified amazement.

205. MEDIUM SHOT (FROM HER ANGLE)
Gallagher, her shoes off, sprawled out on the chaise longue,
stretches luxuriously and yawns. CAMERA PANS TO Stew at the typewriter, hair mussed, coffee pot and cups prominent, the dressing
gown over the back of his chair. Neither of them has seen Anne.

CONTINUATION SCENE 204
Anne. She gasps as she quietly steps further into the room.

206. CLOSE SHOT - GALLAGHER
Gallagher, caught in the midst of a grand stretch, sits up
abruptly, startled. She stares uncomfortably off at Anne.

207. CLOSE SHOT - STEW
At the typewriter. He glances up momentarily and very absently, and
goes right on typing.

STEW
(absently)
Oh hello, Anne—

He types furiously.

ANNE
(tight-lipped)
Good morning. What does this mean?

Stewart looks up surprised at the tone of her voice.

STEW
What does what mean?

208. MEDIUM SHOT - THE THREE
Gallagher, sensing scene, starts hastily looking for her shoes. One
of them has been shoved under the chaise longue and she has to get
down on her hands and knees to retrieve it. Anne comes in and confronts them, her hands on her hips.

STEW
Oh, that mob downstairs. I guess I got so interested in the play I forgot all about them.

ANNE
I see.

STEW
Have we got a play, Anne? Oh, have we got a play! Of course most of it is Gallagher's. She did most of it. That brain of hers just snaps like that all the time.

He indicates by snapping his fingers. Gallagher quietly gathers up her things, apprehensive of the storm about to break.

ANNE
(coldly)
I'm not interested in the way her brain snaps.

Stew stares at Anne as Gallagher, her hat in her hand, her coat over her arm, starts for the door.

GALLAGHER
I think I better go, Stew.

ANNE
I think you should, Miss Gallagher.

STEW
Wait a minute, Gallagher.

Gallagher stops, transfixed by the new tone in his voice. He comes over to Anne.

209. CLOSE TWO SHOT - ANNE AND STEW

STEW
What's the idea, Anne?

ANNE
The idea is simply this - that I want those people to leave here immediately.

STEW
Now wait a minute. Aren't you being a little unreasonable?

ANNE
Unreasonable! Have you any idea what the place looks like downstairs? Do you expect me to stand here and see this place turned into a cheap barroom?

STEW
Now wait, don't get excited, Anne. There's no reason for that. Perhaps the boys have had a little too much to drink. That's all right. I'm sorry. I'll go right down and throw them out. That's no reason for you to take this attitude. After all, I certainly have a right to invite a few of my friends to my house, haven't I?

ANNE
(pointedly)
Your house?

STEW
(getting the implication;
after a pause)
O-o-oh, I get you--

(a knowing chuckle)
All right. All right. I don't blame you. I kinda forgot myself for a moment, there. That's what I call getting me told, isn't it, Anne?

Anne remains silent. That's exactly what she has done.

STEW
I suppose I've been boarding out this past year.

210. MEDIUM SHOT
He takes his coat off back of chair and slips into it.

STEW
(quietly; grimly)
All right, I'll tell you this--I don't _like_ your boarding house, lady--

As he gathers up loose manuscript, he continues ...

STEW
--and if it's all the same to you, I'm moving out.

ANNE
Stewart!

STEW
(hotly)
This is something I should have done a long time ago, only I didn't have sense enough to do it. No, I had to stick around here to try and make a success of something that I knew darn well was a failure from the very beginning. But no more. No more! So that's that.

ANNE
You can't walk out of here like this.

Throughout the scene, Stew is gathering his things together--and probably packing an overnight bag.

STEW
Oh I can't? Who's going to stop me? I'd like to see somebody stop me. If you think I'm going to stick around this joint just to look at this mausoleum, not on your life! You're going to make no stuffed shirt out of me. Now what do you think of that?

Mrs. Schuyler stalks majestically in.

MRS. SCHUYLER
What's going on here? Who is this woman?

STEW
(snappily)
Joan of Arc! What's it to you?

MRS. SCHUYLER
Heavens! The man's insane!

211. CLOSEUP - STEW

STEW
Sure I'm insane, but I've got some good news for you.
(points to himself)
This magnolia is leaving your sweet smelling vanilla joint. This bird in a cage is gonna button his own pants from now on. And that is what is known as telling the mother-in-law.

Gallagher's cry of joy is cut off by an icy look from Mrs. Schuyler.

GALLAGHER
Eurek--!

212. MEDIUM SHOT
Stew is stuffing things into a bag.

STEW
(heatedly to Anne)
You've done nothing but watch me - watch me! - ever since I've been here. Treated me like a thug, watched me like a hawk, mistrusted me. Every time I leave the house, that Jane--
(indicating Mrs. Schuyler)
--goes out and counts the silverware.

ANNE
That's ridiculous.

STEW
Fine! I don't blame her. I know I'm out of my own crowd. I should have had better sense in the beginning. But I'll stay in my own backyard from now on.

ANNE
You're acting like a child.

STEW
All right, I'm a child. Have it any way you want. But I'm going back to my own apartment, where I should have lived in the first place. But no, I got to listen to you and move here. All right. If you want to live with me, Anne, okay. But the sign outside will say "Mr. Stew Smith" and you'll have to be "Mrs. Stew Smith" or there's nothing doing. No more Anne Schuyler's husband--

He has his bag all packed by this time. He snaps it shut viciously, lifts it off the chair, picks up his hat, and notices Mrs. Schuyler staring open-mouthed at him.

STEW
(to Mrs. Schuyler, pointedly)
--and here's some more news for you. You can take your red room, your green room, your left wing and your right wing, and you know what you can do with them!

(to Gallagher)
Come on, Gallagher.

He brushes by Mrs. Schuyler and Anne, exiting.

ANNE
(exasperated)
Oh, Stewart!

EXT. SCHUYLER HOME - NIGHT

213. MEDIUM SHOT
Stew and Gallagher appear, coming through the iron gates.

214. MEDIUM MOVING SHOT
As Stew and Gallagher move off down the street, a ragged old panhandler comes wheedling up to them.

PANHANDLER
Pardon me, could you spare a dime for a cup of coffee?

Stew is struck by a sudden idea as he regards the bum intently.

STEW
Coffee? How would you like to be a Knight of the Garter?

PANHANDLER
(stupidly)
Huh! No--

Stew raises one foot, then the other, and quickly removes the solid gold garters which he presses into the bum's surprised hand.

STEW
(as he removes the garters)
Just a minute.
(to Gallagher)
Entertain the gentleman, Gallagher.
(to the panhandler)
There you are, my man - with those you can eat for a couple of months.

He walks away, leaving the bum staring dazedly at the luxurious pair of garters.

PANHANDLER
(an afterthought)
How about the socks?

215. MED. CLOSE SHOT
As Stew and Gallagher pass the Camera and go down the street, arm in arm. As they get past the Camera, Stew is seen to square his shoulders and throw out his chest. He shakes first one leg, and then the other, as if he were throwing off shackles.

216. CLOSER MOVING SHOT
Stew and Gallagher moving along. Gallagher has a peculiar expression as she glances at Stew. She has been deeply affected by the scene she has just witnessed. Stew's face is very thoughtful.

GALLAGHER
(comfortingly)
I wouldn't worry too much about it, Stew. She'll see it your way.

STEW

Huh?

(snapping out of it)

Oh, I'm not worrying about her - I'm worrying about that second act curtain, that's all.

Gallagher stares at him, realizing he is thinking more about the play than his split-up with his wife. Then she breaks into a grin.

GALLAGHER

Why, you're just a first-class chump! You just staged a scene that would play like a million dollars! How about that declaration of independence for the second act curtain?

Stew stops stock still and stares at her.

STEW

(almost reverently)

That's an idea, Gallagher - a great idea.

Gallagher happily links her arm in his and again they move down the street.

FADE OUT:

FADE IN

INSERT: CLOSE SHOT OF NAME PLATE OVER DOORBELL

"STEWART SMITH"

LAP DISSOLVE TO:

INSERT: SHEET IN TYPEWRITER
On it is being typed:

Act 3. Scene 1.

LAP DISSOLVE TO:

217. INT. STEW'S APARTMENT - DAY - MED. FULL SHOT
Inexpensive but comfortable. Stew is in his shirtsleeves. A battered old typewriter stands on the table with a sheet of blank paper in it. Stew is seated in a chair before it, and is picking out the letters, typing. He pauses, running up the roller to regard what he has written.

218. INT. STEW'S KITCHENETTE - MED. SHOT
Gallagher, in a little apron, is frying some ham and eggs. She looks up as she sees Stew from the doorway.

STEW

Hey, Gallagher!

GALLAGHER

Yeah?

STEW

How about my breakfast? How do you expect me to ring a curtain down on an empty stomach?

GALLAGHER

It'll be ready in a minute.

STEW
(accusingly)
Never mind that. If you can't get my breakfast ready - and can't get here on time in the morning - then you can go get yourself another job.

GALLAGHER
(in mock contrition)
Sorry, boss--

STEW
Don't be sorry. Just get the breakfast, that's all.

219 INT. STEW'S LIVING ROOM - MED. SHOT
There is a knock on the hall door.

Stew crosses and opens it.

220. CLOSER SHOT
As Stew opens the door. It reveals Dexter Grayson in the little hallway, immaculately clad, as usual. Stew regards him in frank surprise for a moment.

GRAYSON
Hello, Smith.

STEW
(puzzled)
Holy jumping swordfish!

GRAYSON
I suppose you know why I came ?

STEW
No, I have no idea - unless some of the silverware is missing.

GRAYSON
Now don't be absurd, Smith--
(as he brushes past, walking inside)
May I come in?

STEW
Surely, come right in.

GRAYSON
(as he sits down)
Thanks. May I sit down?

STEW
Surely, sit down. If I had known you were coming, I would have thrown you up a waffle.

GRAYSON
I don't eat waffles.

STEW
You don't.

221. MED. SHOT
Grayson sits stiffly on one of the Grand Rapids chairs. Stew remains standing, and waits silently for Grayson to speak. Grayson clears his throat.

GRAYSON
Anne asked me to come and see you about the divorce.

STEW
(with enlightened expression)
She did--?

GRAYSON
(uncomfortably)
She wants me to arrange the financial settlement.

STEW
Listen Grayson, I've got 106 bucks and 75 cents in the bank. Now Anne can have any part of that she wants, but she'd better hurry because I'm spending it awfully fast.

GRAYSON
(interrupting)
You don't seem to understand. Anne doesn't expect anything from you.

222. INT. STEW'S KITCHENETTE - MED. SHOT
Gallagher. Overcome by curiosity at the sound of voices, she leaves the frying eggs and goes quietly to the doorway and peeks out.

223. MED. SHOT
Grayson and Stew.

GRAYSON
We should like to know how much you would want to--

Stew stares off incredulously.

STEW
(interrupting)
Wait a minute. Do I get from you that she wants to pay me alimony?

GRAYSON
That's putting it crudely, but--

Stew starts advancing nervously toward him. Grayson, a bit alarmed, rises.

STEW
(closing in on him)
Remember what I told you about that twentieth crack? All right, you've just made it. Before you go unconscious I want you to get this through your nut.

GRAYSON
I beg your pardon.

STEW
Unconscious. You know, when you don't know anything. Your natural state. There are some people- you can't buy their self-respect for a bucket of shekels - well, I happen to be one of those guys.

224. CLOSE SHOT
Showing kitchen door open a crack. Gallagher's eyes are glistening as she watches and listens.

225. MED. CLOSE SHOT
Stew and Grayson.

GRAYSON
(weakly)
We just thought that--

STEW
(snaps)
Don't think. Let me do all the thinking. Now you go back to that Schuyler outfit and tell them that I didn't marry that dame for her dough and I don't want any of her dough now. I was too poor to buy her a wedding present when we got married, so I'm giving her a divorce for a wedding present. Now, stand up!

Grayson does so, completely intimidated by Stew's manner. Stew grabs him by the lapel.

GRAYSON
Yes.

STEW
And now for that twentieth crack--

Stew punches Grayson on chin and knocks him through the open door into the hall.

He slams door shut.

226. WIDER SHOT
Stew thrusts his hands into his pockets and walks thoughtfully back to the typewriter.

227. CLOSER SHOT
Stew standing staring down at the typewriter. He is still flushed with anger. Suddenly a thought strikes him, and his face breaks into a broad grin. He sits down quickly, and begins pounding away.

228. MED. SHOT
Gallagher enters from the kitchen, carrying a platter of ham and eggs and a coffee pot. She sets them on a small table and this is spread with a cloth. Then she crosses over to Stew.

GALLAGHER
(pretending ignorance)
Who was that?

STEW
(without looking up from his typing)
Grayson - Anne's lawyer.

GALLAGHER
What did he want?

STEW
Gallagher, that guy just dropped by to give us a great opening for the third act.

They sit at the little table.

229. CLOSER SHOT

GALLAGHER
What was the idea he gave you?

Stew dives into the ham and eggs.

STEW
It's a swell idea, Gallagher. How's this? The wife's family lawyer comes to see the kid, see - to talk over the divorce. Then this guy insults the poor but honest boy by offering him alimony - so the kid gets sore, socks the lawyer in the nose and throws him out. How's that for the beginning of the third act, huh?

GALLAGHER
Well, from now on the play will be easy. All you have to do is bring the wife back, have her say she's sorry, and then your play's over.

230. CLOSEUP - STEW
He looks over at Gallagher with a peculiar expression.

STEW
(vehemently - as he scoops out some melon)
What's the matter? Do you think I'm going to let that guy go back to his wife? Not on your life. He's got to go to the other girl.

231. CLOSEUP - GALLAGHER
She almost drops her coffee cup in a wild gleam of hope as she looks back at him. Gallagher tries hard to keep her voice steady.

GALLAGHER
(not sure of herself)
What other girl--?

232. MED. CLOSE SHOT OF THE TWO

STEW
The little O'Brien girl, of course - the one you suggested in the story.

GALLAGHER
(ecstatic, but still fighting)
But that's ridiculous! You can't make a sudden change like that.

STEW
Gallagher, what are you going to do - tell me how to write a play?

GALLAGHER
No.

STEW
There's nothing sudden about that--
(tensely)
He's always loved the girl, but he was such a sap he didn't have sense enough to tell her. Well, that's all right - we can fix that. He will

go to the little O'Brien girl, and - here, I'll
show you.

He gets to his feet, and comes around to her.

233. CLOSE TWO SHOT
Gallagher watches him a bit uncertainly.

STEW
(tenderly)
He goes to the little O'Brien gal and he says to
her - in some pretty words of some kind - something that you can write - he'll say--
(as if reading part - very emotional)
Darling, I'm sorry. I've been a fool all my
life. I've always loved you, only I didn't have
sense enough to see it. As quick as I can get a
divorce from my wife, I want you to marry me.
Then she'll look at him that way - yeah - then
they'll embrace, or something like that.
(they draw closer)
Then he'll kiss her, or something.

To demonstrate the point, Stew takes her in his arms and kisses her. They hold the kiss longer than is justified. Stew is swept away by his sudden emotion and clings to her desperately, while Gallagher's arms instinctively go around his neck.

Gallagher chokes back tears that persist in coming. She stifles a sob. Stew folds her in his arms

STEW
(tenderly)
What's the matter, Gallagher? What's the matter?

Gallagher buries her face in his shoulders.

FADE OUT.

THE END

Notes

1. Morkrum machines were an early printing-telegraph apparatus, first used in 1921, named for their trademark holder, Morkrum-Kleinschmidt Corp.

2. A "sob-sister," according to *The Pocket Dictionary of American Slang,* is "a woman news reporter who appeals to readers' sympathies with her accounts of pathetic happenings" (compiled by Harold Wentworth and Stuart Berg Flexner, Pocket Books, 1960).

3. This line is transcribed as "news mongrels" but it also sounds like "newsmongers." In the final draft it appears as "ruffians."

4. "Junior Leaguer" makes smart-aleck reference to the Junior League, a league of young women organized to participate in civic affairs, especially by volunteering their services. The league was founded in New York in 1901 and widespread in the United States by the 1930s.

5. Jeeves alludes to the highly efficient servant, one of the best-known characters of English writer and humorist P. G. Wodehouse, who was the title character of his 1925 novel *Jeeves.*

6. This joke pertains to the Smith Brothers, purveyors of popular cough drops in the United States, who were widely identified by their bearded likenesses on cough drop jars and boxes.

7. "Hey, ixnay - here's the ossbay" is Pig Latin for "Nix - here's the boss."

8. Riskin loved theater references. "Benedict" is not "Benedict Arnold," the notorious Revolutionary War traitor, but one spelling of "Benedick," the character in Shakespeare's *Much Ado About Nothing* who "begins the play by swearing never to get married and spends the rest of it in the process of breaking that vow" (from Joseph T. Shipley, *Dictionary of Word Origins,* Littlefield, Adams & Co, 1945).

9. Fagin is the adult leader of the gang of pickpockets, mostly young boys, in Charles Dickens's *Oliver Twist.*

10. "A Bird in a Gilded Cage," with music by Harry Von Tilzer and lyrics by Arthur J. Lamb, was one of the most popular turn-of-the-century ballads in America. Estimated sheet music sales were more than two million copies.

11. Two bits is one quarter, or twenty-five cents. "Six bits" is three quarters, apparently a lot of money for garters in those days.

12. The Four Hundred refers to the leading members of New York society. According to the *Merriam-Webster Pocket Dictionary of Proper Names* (compiled by Geoffrey Payton, Pocket Books, 1972), the expression came from a remark made in the 1980s by socialite Ward McAllister, who said that there were "only 400 people who really counted."

13. "Meadows" is possibly an oblique reference to a character in Bickerstaff's *Love in a Village,* who enters domestic service to escape an arranged marriage.

14. At least it *sounds* like "Laughing Waters." This is not in any draft of the script and appears to be an ad-lib. Bingy may be making an "Indian Chief" joke.

15. "Just a Gigolo" was a Viennese popular song recorded in the 1930s by various artists including Bing Crosby and Louis Armstrong. David Lee Roth revived it in a medley in 1985.

16. "Dempsey" was instantly recognized by 1930s movie audiences as Jack Dempsey, reigning American heavyweight from 1919 to 1926.

17. This probable ad-lib, somewhat garbled in the film, could be either "dips a beak" or "tips a drink," which mean the same thing. The phrase was added after the final draft.

18. "Cook's Tour" is well-traveled slang for any sightseeing excursion. It refers to Thomas Cook and Son, a venerable travel agency known for organizing foreign tours.

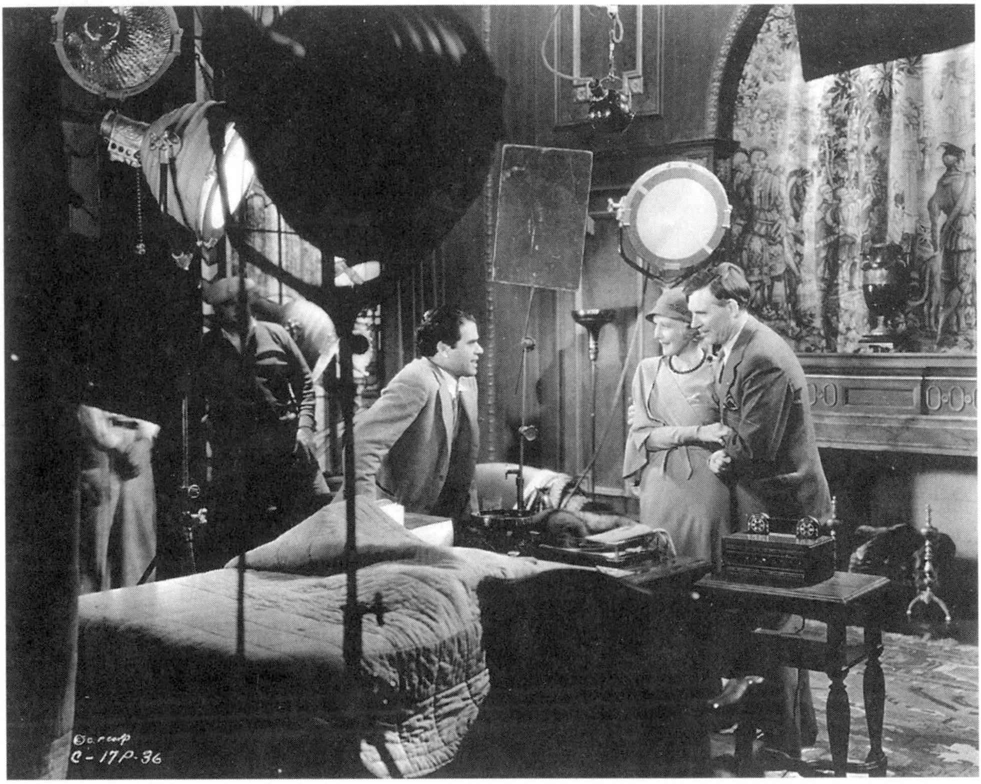

Frank Capra directing Kay Johnson and Walter Huston in a scene from *American Madness.*

American Madness

Columbia Pictures, 1932, 75 minutes

Produced by Harry Cohn

Directed by Frank Capra

Written by Robert Riskin

Photography by Joseph Walker

Edited by Maurice Wright

Cast: Walter Huston (*Dickson*), Pat O'Brien (*Matt*), Kay Johnson (*Mrs. Dickson*), Constance Cummings (*Helen*), Gavin Gordon (*Cluett*), Robert Ellis (*Dude Finlay*), Jeanne Sorel (*Cluett's Secretary*), Walter Walker (*Schultz*), Berton Churchill (*O'Brien*), Arthur Hoyt (*Ives*), Edward Martindel (*Ames*), Edwin Maxwell (*Clark*), Robert Emmett O'Connor (*Inspector*), Anderson Lawler (*Charlie*), Sterling Holloway (*Oscar*), Ralph Lewis, Pat O'Malley

FADE IN

1. EXT. BUILDING - DAY - LONG SHOT
Of a large, impressive-looking building on the corner of a busy, New York business street.

LAP DISSOLVE TO:

2. EXT. BUILDING - DAY - CLOSE SHOT
A dignified brass plate sign on the side of the building, reading: UNION NATIONAL BANK.

LAP DISSOLVE TO:

3. INT. FOYER OF BUILDING - MED. SHOT
Lower portion of high bronze doors, one side of which is partly opened. Sitting in front of the closed side is a uniformed officer, greeting, ad lib, the various employees as they enter.

LAP DISSOLVE TO:

4. INT. OF BANK - CLOSEUP
Of a cover being yanked off an adding machine.

CUT TO:

5. CLOSE SHOT AT SWITCHBOARD
A telephone operator, busily plugging in wires.

OPERATOR
(mechanically sweet voice)
Good morning ... Union National Bank ... Just a minute--

LAP DISSOLVE TO:

6. INT. ENTRANCE ROOM TO VAULTS - MED. SHOT
Of the inside of a massive vault door, made impressive by the shining, finely cut steel bolts and the many other intricate-looking instruments which adorn it.

CAMERA PANS UP to a clock overhead which registers 9:03.

A group of young men, paying tellers, are impatiently watching a teller struggle with the lock that will admit them to the vault.

TELLER
Come on, come on, Oscar, what are we waiting for?

2ND TELLER
What's the matter? Can't you find it?

3RD TELLER
Sneak up on it, boy!

4TH TELLER
Oscar, come on!

CHARLIE
Say, if it had lipstick on it, he'd find it!

They all laugh, as Oscar finds the combination.

OSCAR
Almonds to you![1] Almonds!

TELLERS
Now, now, Oscar - not almonds!

The CAMERA MOVES WITH THEM as they pass through the first portal.

CHARLIE
Nine o'clock and all is lousy!

1ST TELLER
Yes, I spend half of my life waiting for these time clocks to open. Say, where's Matt?

CHARLIE
Probably upstairs thinking up that daily joke.

2ND TELLER
That guy kills me with his wisecracks.

3RD TELLER
Say, when he comes in, let's put on a frozen face. Let's not smile.

They ad-lib agreement.

1ST TELLER
Shhh! Nix! Here he comes--

7. MED. SHOT
CAMERA PICKS UP Matt Brown, the chief teller, as he strides briskly in and begins turning the combination dial to the main vault. He is about twenty-six, a clean-looking, personable youngster. Several of the tellers are standing close to him, looking on.

MATT
How are you doing slaves?

TELLERS
Hello, Matt. How're you Matt?

Matt begins to work the combination of the main lock.

MATT
(with his back to them)
Say, did you boys ever hear the story of the pawnbroker with the glass eye?

1ST TELLER
No Matt, what is the story about the pawnbroker with the glass eye?

MATT
(as he continues to fiddle with the lock)
Well, I'll tell you. A fellow went into this shop to pawn his watch. The pawnbroker said, "I'll give you $50 for it, if you can tell me which is my glass eye." The fellow said, "All right, I'll do that. It's the right one." The pawnbroker said, "That's correct. But how did you know it was the right one?" The fellow

said, "Well, it's got more sympathy than the other one."

He turns, expecting their laugh, but is confronted by stone faces.

MATT

Sympathy! You know, the right one had more sym-pathy than the other one!

1ST TELLER

What's the matter? Can't you get this thing open?

Matt stares in disbelief, then gets the joke.

MATT

(contemptuously)

Six reasons why banks fail!

This cracks them all up, as a uniformed officer, who has been standing by, works a lever attached to the floor, which lowers a section of the floor, directly in front of the vault. This permits the vault door, which is sunk below the floor level, to swing open.

TELLERS

(ad-libbing)

I love your jokes, Matt! They're so entertaining! A very funny man!

8. MED. SHOT

Matt opens the inside door, made up of perpendicular steel bars. The tellers scurry into the cavernous-looking interior. Someone snaps on a light. CAMERA TRUCKS UP TO VAULT.

The back walls of the vault are lined with steel cabinets divided into many small compartments. On one side is a wall safe which is also opened by a combination and which contains the surplus cash carried by the bank. Matt is in charge of this. All around the room are numerous hand trucks - one for every teller. These trucks contain the cash in the charge of the individual tellers. While the tellers in the b.g. obtain their keys and open the drawers of their trucks, Matt examines the time clock which is attached to the inside of the vault door.

9. INT. VAULT - MED. CLOSE SHOT

At the door, as Matt enters and goes directly to the burglar alarm box to the left of the doorway. He leans over to throw off the burglar alarm switch.

CUT TO:

10. CLOSEUP - BURGLAR ALARM SWITCH

The handle of the switch points in the direction of a sign reading ON. Matt's hand comes into the scene and throws the switch up toward a sign reading OFF. This is done with no comment, it being a routine matter with Matt.

MATT

Come on, white collars. The day's started!

11. MED. SHOT

As the tellers file out with their trucks. Before they do, however, each one signs the cashbook. One or two exit silently.

12. CLOSE SHOT - MATT
As one of the tellers comes into scene. Matt examines the cashbook.

MATT
You're carrying too much money on you, Hank. You better turn some in tonight.

MATT
(as he goes)
Okay, Matt.

He exits out of scene.

MATT
How are you fixed?

TELLER
I'm okay, Matt.

MATT
(to another teller)
You've got enough?

2ND TELLER
I'll be all right.

Charlie, the last man, comes up.

CHARLIE
Say Matt, I'll have to have some money for those Manville payrolls.

MATT
How much?

CHARLIE
About twenty-four thousand.

MATT
(counting out money)
It was more than that last week.

CHARLIE
Yeah.

MATT
Here's twenty-five thousand.

He hands Charlie four stacks of bills. As Charlie is signing the cash book, Matt speaks:

MATT
Say, do me a favor, will you Charlie?

CHARLIE
Yeah.

MATT
Let me have ten bucks?

CHARLIE
(aghast)
Ten bucks? Say, if I had ten bucks, I'd quit.

MATT
Charlie!

CHARLIE
Yeah?

Charlie starts out. Matt follows him.

13. OUTSIDE OF VAULT - MED. CLOSE SHOT
As Charlie comes out, followed by Matt. CAMERA TRUCKS ALONG WITH THEM as they walk.

MATT
(as they walk)
I'll pay it back to you Saturday - on the level I will. Give a guy a break, will you? I've got to get it back in my account. If Helen ever finds out that I--

CHARLIE
(unsympathetically)
Baby, I can't give you anything but love ... [2]

LAP DISSOLVE TO:

14. INT. MAIN FLOOR OF BANK - BACKSTAGE
CAMERA TRUCKS with them as Charlie pushes his truck forward and Matt walks alongside of him. En route, CAMERA TAKES IN ATMOSPHERIC SHOTS of the general activity backstage of the bank

Male and female clerks stand around at various angles, checking away at adding machines. Several are assisted by someone who calls off figures to them as they record it on machines. We hear these figures read in a monotone as we pass them.

Matt is still trying to pry the ten dollars loose from Charlie.

MATT
Now listen Charlie. I'll give you an I.O.U. I'll give you a note, I'll pay your mortgage, it's a matter of life and death--

Ad-lib conversations from the other clerks distract his attention.

CHARLIE
Whose death?

MATT
It'll be yours if you don't kick in with that ten bucks.

CHARLIE
Say pal, did you ever hear of a Depression?

MATT
Aw, nerts!

Charlie arrives at his cage. CAMERA STOPS with them.

CHARLIE
Come over and see us sometime.

CAMERA CONTINUES TO FOLLOW Matt as he continues on to his cage, muttering half to himself.

MATT
I'm not asking you to pay off the Depression. I'm only asking you for ten bucks!

Another teller is busy in the cage next to him. Matt addresses him, referring to Charlie.

MATT
That mug reminds me of a guy with his second dollar.

TELLER
Yeah, what did he do with his first one?

MATT
Bought himself a pocketbook!

The teller laughs heartily.

15. MED. SHOT
THE CAMERA PICKS UP Helen as she crosses the main floor of the bank, reaches Matt's teller window and pushes it open.

MATT
Hello, Helen!

HELEN
(conspiratorially)
Matt, come here!

MATT
Why?

HELEN
Come here, honey!

He leans over, and she gives him a quick kiss.

MATT
Hey, look out, somebody's likely to see us!

HELEN
(already walking away)
Oh, is that so?

She quickly kisses him again, crosses back, and takes the grand stairs up to the outer office of the bank president as Matt watches with a grin.

16. INT. MAIN FLOOR OF BANK - FULL SHOT
Just then, a group of five or six important-looking men enter scene on the way to the conference room. One of the men looks towards Helen's desk.

17. MED. SHOT
On Helen and a secretary standing next to her.

SECRETARY
(to Helen)
Oh, oh. Look who's here.

18. MED. SHOT
The other clerks and tellers, noticing the newcomers as they file past.

TELLER
Hey, psst!

OSCAR
Oh, oh. Five ill winds.

TELLER
(standing next to Oscar)
And blowing no good for the old man, either.

19. CLOSER SHOT ON HELEN'S DESK
Shooting toward Helen.

HELEN
(acidly)
The four-and-a-half horsemen.[3]

GIRL
What are they doing here? There's no board meeting today.

HELEN
Search me.

By this time, the important group of men have reached Helen, and are passing her by, with perfunctory nods.

CLARK
(the most important of the important-looking men; to Helen)
Mr. Dickson in yet?

HELEN
Not yet, Mr. Clark.

CLARK
When he comes in, tell him we're waiting for him in the board room.

HELEN
Yes, sir.

CLARK
And tell him not to delay.

HELEN
Yes, sir.

The group of men file through the board room door, and out of sight.

GIRL
(to Helen)
Looks like trouble for your boss.

HELEN
Takes more than two tons of directors to make trouble for my boss.

GIRL
(as she turns to go)
Sez you!

20. INT. CONFERENCE ROOM - MED. SHOT
Taking in all of room. The directors are all here, and some sit around a long, narrow mahogany table. Clark, the sour-faced old

bird we saw previously talking to Helen, paces back and forth agitatedly.

CLARK
I've sent for the cashier, gentlemen. He has a list of the loans that Dickson made last month.

21. MED. CLOSE SHOT - CLARK
As he stops in his pacing a moment and addresses the directors further:

CLARK
And as I told you at breakfast, it is time we did something about it.

22. CLOSE SHOT - SCHULTZ
In thorough accord with Clark's violent attitude is Schultz, a German, whose instinctive conservatism rebels against Dickson's liberal banking methods.

SCHULTZ
Mr. Clark's right. Dickson will ruin this bank if we don't stop him.

AMES
(another conservative stalwart)
Looks to me as if we're in hot water already.

A very dignified but meek little old man, Jonathan Ives, tries horning in:

IVES
(feeble-voiced)
Gentlemen, I was just wondering--

23. MED. SHOT
As another of the directors, O'Brien, a large, bull-faced, thunderous-voiced contractor, rises to Dickson's defense. (O'Brien is always filing his nails, even while he talks.)

O'BRIEN
Personally, I think you're getting panic-stricken about nothing. Dickson's all right.

CLARK
(interrupting)
Oh, is he? We carry more unsecured paper than any other institution in the city. We're fools to tolerate it.

SCHULTZ
That's what I say. And the only way to end it is to get Dickson out.

24. CLOSE SHOT - O'BRIEN
He looks toward Schultz.

O'BRIEN
Don't make me laugh, Schultz!

25. MED. CLOSE SHOT - CLARK

CLARK
Dickson doesn't have to go. But he must agree to this merger with New York Trust--

O'BRIEN
What good will that do?

CLARK
What good will that do? Why, it will take control away from him. We'll put somebody else in charge, call in all doubtful loans, and be on safe ground again. That's what good it will do!

26. MED. CLOSE SHOT
Including Ives in scene with Clark and O'Brien. Ives is seated, O'Brien and Clark standing by table. Ives tries to speak again.

IVES
It has just occurred to me--

O'BRIEN
(interrupting)
You're wasting your time, I tell you. Dickson won't stand for it.

CLARK
He'll stand for it, if I have anything to say about it.

Just then they hear door open, and they all look towards door leading thru to main floor.

27. MED. CLOSE SHOT - CLUETT
As he shuts the door behind him. He is immaculately groomed, obviously cuts quite a dash with the women. He looks off toward the men as Clark's voice comes in:

CLARK'S VOICE
Ah - come in, Cluett.

CAMERA PANS WITH CLUETT as he comes forward and puts a paper on the table before Clark.

CLUETT
Here's the list.

CLARK
Yes, thank you.

CLUETT
Anything else?

CLARK
No. Nothing.

Cluett exits toward door again. Clark picks up the list and looks at it. Then he addresses the other men:

CLARK
Look at this. Just look at this. It's outrageous. Henry Moore - thirty-six thousand. Manny Goldberg - eighty-five hundred. Tony Consero - fifty-six thousand dollars. Joseph McDonald - eighteen thousand. Alvin Jones - sixty-six thousand dollars to a hotel that's on its last legs. I tell you, people get loans in this bank that couldn't borrow five cents anywhere else.

28. WIDER ANGLE
As the other men group around the loan list, which Clark has put back down on the table. They all scrutinize it carefully.

SCHULTZ
(to the men at large)
And on what? "Hunches," he calls it.

AMES
Some day he'll get a "hunch" about a man and give the bank away.

CLARK
He's almost done that already. Our chief teller, Matt Brown, is an example of that. He breaks into Dickson's house, holds him up, and the next day gets a job in the bank.

IVES
Well, as far as I'm concerned

SCHULTZ
A boy who should be in jail, handling a bank's cash!

CUT TO:

29. INT. MAIN FLOOR OF BANK - MED. CLOSE SHOT
Shooting toward Matt, inside the teller's cage, busily counting the money he is getting ready for Charlie.

Helen is outside the cage.

30. CLOSE SHOT
Shooting toward Helen.

HELEN
(skeptically)
What did you do with it?

MATT
With what?

HELEN
The ten dollars.

MATT
(quickly)
Oh, ten dollars--

HELEN
Yes.

MATT
(catches himself in time)
A friend of mine - yeah, really - his mother was terribly sick and she was dying, would you believe it?

31. CLOSE SHOT
Shooting toward Matt.

As she interrupts him:

HELEN
No.

MATT
Oh, you think I'm lying?

HELEN
Yes.

MATT
All right, I'm lying. Don't forget you called me a liar.

HELEN
Oh, Matt.

He reaches forward and takes her hands.

MATT
Oh honey, why don't we get married? Then you can handle it all.

Just then Oscar enters the scene, en route somewhere. He stops beside Matt, notices he and Helen are holding hands.

32. MED. CLOSE SHOT
As Helen and Matt separate guiltily.

OSCAR
Say, Matt! Matt! Did you hear the news?

MATT
No, what?

OSCAR
Pardon me. All the big shots are in a huddle, and it looks like Dickson's out on his ear.

Helen and Matt react to this piece of news. They look at one another. Apparently, it will have a definite effect on their lives.

MATT
(to Oscar)
Oh, you're kidding me, aren't you?

OSCAR
No, I'm not kidding. Everybody's talking about it. Ask her.

HELEN
I haven't heard about it.

OSCAR
Sure, everybody's talking about it.

33. CLOSE UP - MATT
As he speaks sadly.

MATT
If that's on the level, there goes my assistant cashier's job.

34. MED. CLOSE SHOT
Taking the three in.

OSCAR
Well, I just thought I'd drop by and cheer you up a bit.

As he turns to go out of scene, he looks at Matt.

OSCAR
I'll be seeing you, Matt - in the breadline.

CUT TO:

35. INT. CONFERENCE ROOM MED. - SHOT
The men are all gathered around the table now. Apparently, they have been discussing ways and means of ousting Dickson.

As we cut to this scene, Ives is pouring himself a glass of water.

IVES
That ham I had this morning was very salty--

36. CLOSER SHOT ON THE GROUP

CLARK
Gentlemen, let's get organized before Dickson gets here. Schultz, can I count on you?

37. CLOSE SHOT
On Schultz, who is seated next to Clark.

SCHULTZ
Absolutely.

CLARK
What about you, Ames?

38. CLOSE SHOT
On Ames, who is seated next to Schultz.

AMES
That's the way I feel about it.

CLARK
Ives, how about you?

39. CLOSE SHOT

IVES
Well, the way I look at it, it seems that--

CLARK
(interrupting)
All right. O'Brien?

40. CLOSE SHOT
At other end of table, where O'Brien is.

O'BRIEN
Well, you've got an awful fight on your hands. That's all I've got to say.

41. CLOSE SHOT
On Clark, determined.

CLARK
Gentlemen, I think it's time that we do fight.

CUT TO:

42. INT. MAIN FLOOR OF BANK - FULL SHOT
The outer offices of the bank are in this shot. A spacious stretch of desks occupied by clerks and junior officers, all busily at work.

A wizened old doorman is greeting clerks as they arrive.

CLERK
(passing by)
Hello, Gardiner.

GARDINER
Good morning. You're on time this morning. It's about time.

We see Dickson, looming in the doorway, for the first time.

43. CLOSE SHOT
As Dickson stops to speak to the doorman. Dickson is a man of about fifty, whose looks belie his years. There is a robustness and virility about him that is compelling. His very walk radiates power.

He now puts his hand on the old man's shoulder.

GARDINER
Good morning, Mr. Dickson.

DICKSON
John, how's your wife this morning?

GARDINER
(looking up, worship in his eyes)
Much better this morning, thank you.

DICKSON
Got a handkerchief?

Gardiner hurriedly produces a handkerchief, and starts to blow his nose.

GARDINER
Excuse me--

DICKSON
Wait a minute.
(he takes the handkerchief, and polishes the brass on Gardiner's uniform)
How do you feel this morning?

GARDINER
I'm feeling fine this morning.

DICKSON
That makes it unanimous. I feel all right too.

GARDINER
Thank you!

As Dickson exits from scene:

CUT TO:

44. TRUCKING SHOT WITH DICKSON
The smile on his face disappears as he sees something which annoys him.

DICKSON
(sternly)
Oh, Carter!

A young man looks up quickly. He is smoking a cigarette.

CARTER
Yes sir?

DICKSON
You know the rules about smoking ...

Carter quickly crushes out the cigarette. Even as he does so, Dickson reaches into his pocket and flips Carter a fresh one, which Carter pockets for later.

CARTER
Thank you, sir.

Now Dickson passes Matt's cage.

DICKSON
(catching Matt's attention)
Oh, Matt!

Matt looks up. Dickson tosses him a wink, and Matt winks back.

Dickson walks on towards his office. CAMERA TRUCKS AHEAD OF HIM. On the way he is greeted by his employees.

AD-LIB FROM EMPLOYEES
Good morning, Mr. Dickson. Etc., etc.

DICKSON
(pleasantly)
Morning. Good morning--

He is joined by Bill Saunders, a friend of his. Bill walks along with Dickson.

BILL
Hello, Tom.

DICKSON
(firmly, but pleasantly)
You here again? What do <u>you</u> want?

He does not stop. Continues his walk toward his office. Bill alongside of him.

BILL
(smiling)
What do you suppose anybody wants? Money, money, money!

DICKSON
Listen, I told you I wasn't interested in that deal, didn't I?

BILL
I want to know why.

Dickson notices a man, a janitor without a uniform, passing by.

DICKSON
(to the man)
Wait a minute. Where's your uniform?

JANITOR
I haven't any.

DICKSON
You haven't got a uniform?

JANITOR
No, sir.

DICKSON
My goodness, you ought to have a uniform. How much does one cost?

JANITOR
Why, I don't know.

DICKSON
You see Sampson. Tell him I sent you. You've got to have a uniform.

The man exits scene. Bill picks up the conversation where he left off.

BILL
Tom, I never had trouble getting credit from you before. When I was flat broke you gave me all the money I wanted. Now I come to you with a swell deal, and the greatest--

DICKSON
(interrupting)
I'll tell you why. I don't like the crowd you're mixed up with.
(softening)
Personally, you can have all the credit you want. But for that deal - not a cent.

BILL
But listen, Tom, I--

They have now reached the anteroom of Dickson's private chamber, where Helen sits at her desk.

45. INT. DICKSON'S OUTER OFFICE - MED. CLOSE SHOT
As Dickson comes up to Helen at her desk. A lady sits nearby. Dickson notices her.

DICKSON
Good morning, Mrs. Pembroke.

MRS. PEMBROKE
Good morning, Mr. Dickson.

DICKSON
Got my letter?

MRS. PEMBROKE
Yes, thank you.

DICKSON
Hello, Helen.

HELEN
Good morning.

DICKSON
Helen, you're becoming more beautiful every day. What are we going to do about it?

HELEN
I don't know.

DICKSON
Guess we'll just have to sacrifice the bank. When are you and Matt going to get married?

HELEN
(awkwardly)
Why - well, I--

DICKSON
Ummm. Stalling, eh?
(changing tone, professionally)
Anything new?

HELEN
Why, the directors are waiting for you in the board room.

DICKSON
Directors, eh? Long faces?

He gestures accordingly.

HELEN
(she trumps his gesture)
Longer.

DICKSON
(half-under his breath)
I haven't got any new stories for them this morning, either.

Mrs. Pembroke has been standing by, waiting to get a word in edgewise. CAMERA PANS SLIGHTLY with him to take in the lady:

MRS. PEMBROKE
Mr. Dickson?

DICKSON
Ah, Mrs. Pembroke. I spoke to Mr. Schaffer at the Guaranty. He's going to take care of that mortgage for you ...

During this speech the phone bell rings.

46. MEDIUM SHOT
As Helen picks up the phone and quietly answers it. Bill Saunders is standing nearby, still waiting to talk to Dickson again.

HELEN
(into phone)
Hello ...
(she turns to Dickson)
Mrs. Dickson on the phone.

Dickson comes over to the desk and as he picks up the receiver, he looks toward Mrs. Pembroke.

DICKSON
(to Mrs. Pembroke)
You'd better hurry over there. He's waiting for you.
(then into phone)
Hello, dear ...

47. CLOSE SHOT - DICKSON
As he continues, into phone:

DICKSON
Where are you? ... Sure, well, come on down right away. Huh? ... Yes, of course I remember. It's tonight.
(smiles)
See what a social hound I'm becoming! ... All right, goodbye, dear.

He hangs up. Mrs. Pembroke is waiting for him to finish. She has apparently been disappointed in the news he has for her.

MRS. PEMBROKE
But, Mr. Dickson, I thought you were going to take care of the mortgage. I only want ten thousand. The property is worth sixty.

DICKSON
(ill-at-ease)
Mr. Schaffer will take good care of you. He'll give you fifteen - maybe twenty ...

48. MED. CLOSE SHOT
He continues talking to the lady, trying to get rid of her.

DICKSON
Better hurry now. Goodbye. Good luck to you!

Mrs. Pembroke, bewildered, starts to leave.

MRS. PEMBROKE
(muttering)
Thank you.

CAMERA PANS WITH HIM as Mrs. Pembroke leaves.

DICKSON
(to Helen)
Oh, if Mrs. Dickson comes in, will you tell her to see Cluett if she needs any money?

Bill Saunders is still waiting. He corners Dickson.

BILL
What's the idea of turning her down? It sounds like a perfectly safe investment.

DICKSON
She's a widow. I don't like taking mortgages from widows.

BILL
(puzzled)
Why not?

49. CLOSE SHOT OF THE TWO
Shooting toward Dickson.

DICKSON
If she can't pay, I'll have to foreclose, won't I?

BILL
(dumbly)
Yes - sure--

DICKSON
(mimicking him)
Yeah - sure!

He turns to address a man below - the janitor without a uniform.

DICKSON
Oh, make that uniform blue.

JANITOR
Yes, sir.

Abruptly, he heads for the board room. Bill is still baffled by Dickson's queer reasoning. Suddenly, it dawns on him. He shakes his head admiringly.

CUT TO:

50. INT. CONFERENCE ROOM - MED. SHOT
Dickson enters.

DICKSON
(blithely; as he counts the board members present)
One - two - three - four - five. Seven more and you'd have a jury!

He grabs a walking cane and wields it like a golf putter.

DICKSON
Well, it's a nice morning, gentlemen. How about two foursomes of golf?

IVES
(eagerly)
Oh, I say, that would be ...

Ives's voice trails off as he realizes Clark is scowling at him.

DICKSON
(undeterred; still practicing his golf swing)
Say, you know, I found out something yesterday about hitting a golf ball. You've got to hit with the left hand, and from the inside out, it's the only way you can hit anything--

CLARK
(huffy)
I think, Mr. Dickson, we would like to have a little of your very valuable time here at the bank this morning, if you don't mind.

DICKSON
Oh, you would, eh? All right. If it's more important than golf, go ahead. What's on your mind?

CUT TO:

51. INT. LOBBY OF BANK - LONG SHOT
Shooting from one end of the lobby toward the front door. Depositors are scattered all over the place. Some at the windows. Some at the writing tables. Others sitting inside the railing, talking to junior executives. The scene is peaceful, though very active.

CAMERA STARTS TRUCKING FORWARD, passing en route, the different types of individuals who frequent the bank. People from all walks of life. CAMERA TRAVELS SLOWLY, picking up following little scenes.

TELLER
(at window)
The check is no good.

SADIE (A FEMALE CUSTOMER)
What?

CLERK
The check is no good. The man has no account here.

SADIE
Holy mackerel! I've been robbed.

CLERK
I'm sorry, madam.

SADIE
So am I. And don't call me madam!

CAMERA NEXT PICKS UP an elderly lady talking to a bank guard.

GUARD
Yes, ma'am, you can deposit your money here.

LADY
Is it safe?

GUARD
Absolutely.

LADY
It's his life insurance money, you know.

BANK GUARD
That's all right. You come with me, and I'll show you where to deposit your money.

CAMERA GOES PAST and now singles out three men who are coming forward. One glance and we know they are here for no kosher reason.

They are typical gangster types. One of them, the leader, is dressed in everything but the kitchen sink. Light fedora, stiff shirt and collar with stripes running perpendicularly. Flashy gray suit - spats - and walking stick. The other two are just tough hombres, but dressed to kill.

As they walk toward camera, they glance around the bank with a professional casualness, but obviously very much impressed. Their eyes rove around the place and finally land on some object where they stop.

CUT TO:

52. CLOSEUP - CHARLIE
As he quickly counts out several thousand dollars in bills.

CUT TO:

53. CLOSE SHOT - THREE RACKETEERS
Their eyes glisten. Their mouths water, as they watch Charlie off scene.

CUT TO:

54. MEDIUM SHOT
Inside the railing. Cluett emerges from his office and starts forward, business-like, when he suddenly stops in his tracks.

55. CLOSEUP - CLUETT
He stares off at the racketeers. A look of fright comes into his eyes. His impulse is to turn back.

56. CLOSE GROUP SHOT
The three gangsters. A quick flash. Their eyes light on Cluett off scene, and they glare menacingly at him.

LEADER
There he is! Good morning!

57. MED. CLOSE SHOT - CLUETT
He changes his mind about avoiding them. His face breaks into a feeble smile of affability as he walks toward them. CAMERA PANS WITH HIM as he approaches the three men, his hand outstretched in forced amiability.

CLUETT
(shaking)
Good morning! Who do you want to see?

The gangsters shake hands with him, their expressions remaining unchanged, which adds immeasurably to Cluett's discomfort.

LEADER
(flatly)
You.

1ST GANGSTER
(drawling)
Yeah. We wanna talk to you about a big deal.

There is a sinister significance in the manner in which he emphasizes "a big deal." Cluett is perceptibly ill-at-ease.

CLUETT
(uncertainly - sickly smile)
Oh, yes. Well, come right this way.

He opens the swinging gate in front of him, permitting the three racketeers to enter. They start for Cluett's office.

58. INT. ANTE ROOM DICKSON'S OFFICE - MED. CLOSE SHOT
Helen sits at her typewriter near a railing, overlooking the bank below. Another girl stands by her, both are staring off scene.

CUT TO:

59. INT. BANK LOBBY - MED. LONG SHOT
From Helen's angle.
Cluett and the three gangsters going into Cluett's office.

60. INT. ANTE ROOM OF DICKSON'S OFFICE - MED. CLOSE SHOT
Helen and other secretary.

HELEN
Hey Pat, come here! Look!

SECRETARY
(to Helen)
That's Dude Finlay, all right - I've seen his picture in the papers hundreds of times.

HELEN
I wonder what he's doing with Mr. Cluett.

SECRETARY
(still staring - thrilled - shuddering)
Gee, I'm scared. He's one of the toughest gangsters in town.

CUT TO:

61. INT. CONFERENCE ROOM - MED. LONG SHOT
Shooting down the length of the table. The men are all sitting around the large table. Dickson is on his feet.

DICKSON
(firmly)
Gentlemen, you're only wasting your time. There'll be no merger.

62. MED. CLOSE SHOT
As Dickson continues.

DICKSON
(the injustice kills him)
Why should I turn this bank over to anybody else? I've worked twenty-five years night and day to build it up, and now you're asking me to dump it into somebody's lap--
(with finality)
Nothing doing!

Schultz, who is seated near Dickson, looks up at him:

SCHULTZ
You can make a handsome profit on your stock.

DICKSON
I'm not interested in profits. I'm interested in the bank. In the depositors. They're my friends. They're looking to me for protection, and I'm not walking out on them.

Clark and O'Brien, also seated around close to Dickson.

CLARK
How are you protecting your depositors? By making a lot of idiotic loans!

O'BRIEN
(admonishing him)
Take it easy, Clark.

Ives, seated next to Schultz, becomes alarmed.

IVES
(still trying)
My dear friends ...

DICKSON
(unruffled, paying no attention to Ives)
It's all right. Let him go ahead. Let him speak his piece. I like it. Go on.

CLARK
All right. I'll speak my piece. Dickson, you've got to change your policy.

63. CLOSER SHOT
As Dickson retorts:

DICKSON
What's the matter with my policy? How many losses has this bank taken in the last twenty-five years?
(he looks around - silence)
I'll tell you. Not a single one!
(defiantly)
What's wrong with that kind of banking?

CLARK
(mumbles disdainfully)
Just pure luck!

64. CLOSE SHOT
Ames, seated beyond Ives, now speaks up:

AMES
Conditions have changed. These are precarious times. Banks today have got to be careful. And you've been more liberal than ever.

Dickson's voice comes in over scene:

DICKSON'S VOICE
Yes, and I'm going to continue to be liberal ...

65. CLOSEUP - DICKSON
As he continues:

DICKSON
The trouble with this country today is there's too much hoarded cash. Idle money is no good to industry. Where is all the money today? In the banks, vaults, socks, old tin cans, buried in the ground! I tell you, we've got to get the money in circulation before you'll get this country back to prosperity.

66. CLOSE SHOT - CLARK

CLARK
Who are we going to give it to? Men like Jones? Last week you made him an extra loan of fifty thousand dollars. Do you call that intelligent banking?

67. CLOSE SHOT - SCHULTZ AND DICKSON

SCHULTZ
He can't pay his bills. How do you expect him to pay us?

DICKSON
That's a fair question, Schultz. Now let's see how bad a risk Jones is. What's his history? He's been a successful business man for thirty-five years. Two years ago business started falling off. Today Jones needs money, and if he doesn't get it, he goes into bankruptcy and throws nine hundred men out of work. Answer - unemployment.

68. CLOSEUP - O'BRIEN
As he listens intently, Dickson's voice coming in:

DICKSON'S VOICE
It also means his creditors aren't paid. They're in trouble. They go to banks and are turned down ... more bankruptcies ...

69. CLOSEUP - DICKSON
As he continues:

DICKSON
It's a vicious circle, my friends, and the only place to cure it is right here at the source. Help Jones and you help the whole circle. Now, when Jones comes to me, I ask myself two questions. First - is he honest? Yes. Second - is he as good a business man as he was before? And the answer is - he's better.

70. CLOSEUP - CLARK
Showing his reaction, as part of Dickson's speech comes over scene:

DICKSON'S VOICE
He is not only older and wiser, but his present trouble has taught him precaution. In my estimation, gentlemen, Jones is no risk. Neither are the thousands of other Joneses throughout the country ...

71. CLOSEUP - SCHULTZ
To intercut with Dickson's speech.

72. CLOSEUP - AMES
To intercut with Dickson's speech.

73. CLOSEUP - IVES
To intercut with Dickson's speech.

74. MED. CLOSE SHOT
The group, as Dickson concludes his speech.

DICKSON
It's they who built this nation up to the richest in the world, and it's up to the banks to give them a break. Disraeli said security is the prosperity of the nation--[4]

AMES
(cutting him off)
Why, Disraeli didn't say anything of the kind.

DICKSON
Well, he should have said it. It's as true now as it was then. And let us get the right kind of security. Not stocks and bonds that zig-zag up and down, not collateral on paper, but character!

CLARK
(indignantly)
Character, hmmpf! That's your idea?

DICKSON
Not at all. That's Alexander Hamilton's idea[5] - the finest banking mind this country has ever known. Those are his exact words, gentlemen. Character! It's the only thing you can bank on, and it's the only thing that will pull this country out of the doldrums.

CUT TO:

75. INT. CLUETT'S PRIVATE OFFICE - MED. CLOSE SHOT
Cluett sits at his desk, his face drawn, panic-stricken. He is like an animal at bay. The leader of the trio, Dude Finlay, sits in a chair directly in front of Cluett. The other two men stand on either side of the desk.

DUDE
(menacingly)
You know what we do to welchers, Cluett, don't you?

CLUETT
(trembling)
I know, I know, Dude. Oh, I must have been crazy! I lost my head completely!

DUDE
That's <u>your</u> funeral. We've got fifty thousand dollars comin' to us.

CLUETT
(helplessly)
I haven't got it.

76. CLOSE SHOT - DUDE
Shooting past Cluett.

DUDE
(barking)
Then what did you want to gamble for? If you'd have beat _us_ out of fifty G's, you'd have been paid, wouldn't you? Well, we want our dough.

CLUETT
I'm sorry, Dude, but--I--

DUDE
That don't do us any good.

CLUETT
But after all, you can't take blood from a stone.

DUDE
(threateningly - quietly)
We can take blood from _anything_--
(pauses)
If it's comin' to us.

77. MED. CLOSE SHOT
Shooting toward Cluett. Dude on opposite side of desk, the other two men still standing by the desk.

A look of alarm spreads over Cluett's face. There is nothing hidden in this threat.

CLUETT
(wants time to think)
Perhaps if you'll wait a little while, I might be able--

ONE OF THE MEN
(snappily)
We waited long enough!

DUDE
(shrewdly - to the men)
Nix. Lay off.
(to Cluett)
Now - what's the use of getting excited, Cluett? It oughta be easy for you to lay your mitts on that kind of dough ...

78. CLOSE SHOT - CLUETT
Shooting past Dude, as Dude continues, slowly, deliberately:

DUDE
There's plenty of it in this bank - laying around loose.

Cluett looks up - horror-stricken.

CLUETT
(pop-eyed, choked voice)
Good heavens, man! You're not suggesting that I--

DUDE
Why not?

CLUETT
(perspiring freely)
Why, I couldn't do that ...!

DUDE
(flatly)
You don't have to do nothing.

Cluett looks up toward the men - then at Dude.

CLUETT
(slowly)
What do you mean?

DUDE
All you gotta do is fix a few things for <u>us</u>, and <u>we'll</u> do the rest, see?

There is a pause while Cluett stares at them, horrified, his confused mind trying to assimilate the ghastliness of their proposal. Suddenly he starts to rise.

79. MEDIUM SHOT
As Cluett gets to his feet and faces Dude across the desk.

CLUETT
No, no, I couldn't - I couldn't do anything like that. I--

Smack! The rest of his speech dies in his throat. The man to his right has slapped him across the face with his open palm. Taken unaware, Cluett's hand goes to his cheek. He stares at them, bewildered and frightened.

Cluett, feeling himself trapped and helpless, slowly sinks into his chair.

CUT TO:

80. INT. ANTEROOM DICKSON'S OFFICE - MED. SHOT
Helen sits at her typewriter. A very dignified, beautiful woman of thirty approaches her. She is Phyllis Dickson, Dickson's wife. She radiates refinement and culture.

MRS. DICKSON
(pleasantly)
Good morning, Helen.

81. CLOSER SHOT
At Helen's desk, as Helen looks up at Mrs. Dickson.

HELEN
How-do-you-do, Mrs. Dickson.

MRS. DICKSON
Is that busy husband of mine busy?

HELEN
(indicating conference room)
He's at a board meeting.

MRS. DICKSON
(not unexpected)
Board meeting. Oh, that means hours, I suppose.

HELEN
I'm afraid so.

MRS. DICKSON
Helen, did you ever try competing with a bank?

HELEN
No.

MRS. DICKSON
Well, take my word for it, and don't try it. It's useless! If it were some other woman, I could handle her, but after all, you can't scratch a bank's eyes out now, can you?

HELEN
Hardly.

82. CLOSE SHOT - MRS. DICKSON
Shooting past Helen.

MRS. DICKSON
Oh, well. I guess the only other thing for me to do is to go out and buy myself a few sticks of dynamite. When he comes out, you tell him I'll be back. He hasn't gotten rid of me!

HELEN
All right.

83. MEDIUM SHOT
Helen laughs as Mrs. Dickson leaves in the direction of Cluett's office.

CUT TO:

84. INT. CYRIL CLUETT'S OFFICE MED. CLOSE SHOT AT DOOR
The three racketeers are preparing to leave. Dude has his hand on the doorknob.

CLUETT
(nervously)
Dude - there's not any chance of my becoming involved in this, is there?

DUDE
You? No, you'll be all right, so long as you establish an alibi for tonight.

CLUETT
I know, but--

DUDE
Be sure you're with somebody responsible in case any questions are asked. Understand?

CLUETT
But Dude, listen - couldn't we make this some other time?

DUDE
(positively)
Listen, buddy, you're getting by pretty easy. Quit squawking!

Cluett looks at Dude, then at the others, and realizes he is helpless.

He opens the door and the men file out, silently. Cluett shuts the door and CAMERA PANS WITH HIM as he crosses back to his desk, shaking perceptibly. He reaches into a desk drawer and extracts a bottle of liquor.

As he takes a drink, Mrs. Dickson enters unannounced.

CUT TO:

85. MED. CLOSE SHOT
As Mrs. Dickson stands watching Cluett.

MRS. DICKSON
(playful reproach)
Oh, oh!

Cluett turns quickly. Upon seeing her, he makes an attempt to conceal the terror he feels.

CLUETT
(smiling feebly)
Oh, hello, Phyllis.

She advances toward him as he rises.

MRS. DICKSON
(shaking her head)
This won't do. Not during business hours ...

CLUETT
Why, I needed a--
(offering her drink)
Want one?

MRS. DICKSON
(screwing up her face)
Heavens, no! Do you mind putting up with me until the financial genius gets thru genius-ing?

CLUETT
No, no, of course not. Not at all. Oh, here.

As she takes out a cigarette, he offers her a light. Mrs. Dickson notices that he is rather nervous.

MRS. DICKSON
What is the matter with you? You're trembling!

86. CLOSE SHOT - CLUETT

CLUETT
(trying to be light)
Am I? Why, I - I don't know any reason why I should be, unless of course it's you ...

87. CLOSE TWO SHOT

MRS. DICKSON
Me?

CLUETT
Being alone with you has always done this to me. You know that.

MRS. DICKSON
For a celebrated bounder, that is an awful admission. Besides, I never knew that any female could do <u>this</u> to <u>you</u>.

CLUETT
Well, <u>you</u> can. You always could.

MRS. DICKSON
(smiling)
Liar! You're just suffering from lack of sleep.

He takes this as premature defeat, and heads back toward his desk.

MRS. DICKSON
(good-natured admonishment)
Here, here, here, now! Don't <u>you</u> go back to work on me, too. I'm getting tired of this. Besides, it's beginning to affect your looks--

CLUETT
(not understanding)
What is?

MRS. DICKSON
(finishing her little joke)
--running around. Not your work.
(Cluett laughs in relief)
You'd better start reforming, Cyril!

CLUETT
If I thought you were the slightest bit interested, I would.

MRS. DICKSON
Not bad, not bad at all. Do you know something? I've always been curious about your line.

CLUETT
Line?

MRS. DICKSON
Whatever it is that makes you such a riot with women.

He shrugs off the compliment.

MRS. DICKSON
(continuing)
Come on Cyril, try a little bit of it out on me. I haven't had any first-class blarney thrown at me since the day I was married.

CLUETT
(trying hard)
But you see, it isn't blarney where you're concerned.

MRS. DICKSON
(laughs)
Now let me see, what comes next?
(a mocking tone)
Oh yes, I know - what are you doing tonight, Phyllis?

88. CLOSEUP - CLUETT
He is suddenly reminded of his pact with Dude Finlay. Terror returns to his face.

CLUETT
Tonight?

He suddenly gets an idea. He was told to be with someone around midnight. Someone who would be an alibi for him. He stares off at Phyllis Dickson. Why not?

MRS. DICKSON
(continuing)
Doesn't that come next?

89. MED. CLOSE SHOT

CLUETT
Yes, yes, it does. What <u>are</u> you doing tonight, Phyllis?

MRS. DICKSON
See, we're getting along famously!

CUT TO:

90. INT. CONFERENCE ROOM - MEDIUM SHOT
Clark is in a state of agitation. The other directors seem worn by the ordeal. Dickson remains adamant.

DICKSON
Most of the creditors I know personally. I've seen them grow up in the community. I knew their fathers and mothers before them.

CLARK
I know, Dickson. That's all very well. But you're taking too many chances. In these times a bank should keep liquid in case of trouble. In case of emergency!

91. CLOSER SHOT AT THE TABLE
All the men in the scene.

DICKSON
I know what you mean by that. You want me to hang on to our cash. Well, I don't believe in it. The law demands that I carry a certain legal reserve, and I'm doing it. The rest of our money is out working ... working to help industry ... to help build up business ...

92. CLOSEUP - CLARK
As he almost shouts at Dickson.

CLARK
In the meantime, you're jeopardizing the safety of the bank. Well, we won't stand for it!

93. MED. CLOSE SHOT
Of the group, as Dickson turns to Clark.

DICKSON
You have to stand for it.

Meek little Ives once again tries to say something:

IVES
(exhausted)
But my dear friends ...

SCHULTZ
(interrupting)
You're forcing us to take action against you, Dickson.

Dickson looks at him:

DICKSON
Go ahead - take all the action you want!

He looks about at the others as he continues:

DICKSON
I'm running this bank my way. Get that clear!

CLARK
Gentlemen, you notice Mr. Dickson refuses to consider our wishes. He refuses an offer to merge with the New York Trust - the only thing that will put this bank on safe ground. He insists upon running a bank on so flimsy a thing as ... as faith!

DICKSON
Yes! You said it, Clark. That's the only thing that means anything to me.

94. CLOSEUP - CLARK
As Dickson's voice continues. Clark reacts appropriately.

DICKSON'S VOICE
Before I take a man into this bank, and before I extend credit to anyone, I satisfy myself on one thing - do I believe in him?

95. CLOSE PAN SHOT
On the other men - CAMERA PANNING from one to the other as Dickson's voice comes over the shot - finally CAMERA STOPS on Dickson.

DICKSON
So far, my judgement has been right one hundred per cent. One hundred per cent! When I start going wrong, you won't have to take any action. I'll turn the bank over to you. Then you can

merge all you want to. I won't be the fellow to
run it then. Good day, gentlemen!

He exits scene.

CAMERA TRUCKS AHEAD OF HIM as Dickson passes briskly through his outer office, stopping only to speak to Helen at her desk:

DICKSON
(cheerfully)
Helen, tell Matt I want to see him.

HELEN
Yes, sir.

CUT TO:

96. INT. CLUETT'S PRIVATE OFFICE - CLOSE SHOT - CLUETT AND PHYLLIS

CLUETT
(mid-stream)
--and after dinner, we could go--

MRS. DICKSON
(not at all angry)
Oh! Oh, no! I think I've done enough experimenting for one day. Congratulations, Cyril. You've convinced me that you're a philanderer of the very first order. I shall recommend you highly.

CLUETT
(simply)
Please, please don't laugh at me, Phyllis. I must see you tonight!

97. CLOSER SHOT OF THE TWO
Favoring Mrs. Dickson.

MRS. DICKSON
Tonight, Oh, never! Tonight I have reserved for a very special occasion. Believe it or not, it's our wedding anniversary. Tom doesn't probably even remember it. But then, they never do, do they?

CLUETT'S VOICE
No, they don't--

She shakes her head.

MRS. DICKSON
But I'm giving a party for him - a real, old-fashioned surprise party. Caps, bells, whistles, and everything. I'm really terribly excited about it. I've been planning it for months.

CLUETT
(after a pause)
Well--

MRS. DICKSON
(smiling)
Well, what?

CLUETT
(he won't give up)
Well, aren't you going to invite me?

MRS. DICKSON
(surprised)
You? No can do. It's all set. Just a few of Tom's closest friends.

CLUETT
Now Phyllis, if you don't invite me, I'm coming anyway.

MRS. DICKSON
Don't be silly, Cyril. These are respectable people. They'd probably bore you to death.

CLUETT
(desperate-sounding)
No, they won't. Not when you are there. Oh, please, be a sport. Please ask me.

MRS. DICKSON
(flattered, but a little suspicious)
Why are you so anxious?

CLUETT
(intense sincerity)
Don't you know?

MRS. DICKSON
No.

CLUETT
I want to be near you!

He steps closer to her.

MRS. DICKSON
What?

CLUETT
Don't you know I've been crazy about you for years?

MRS. DICKSON
(still flattered, lightly)
Now wait a minute, wait a minute ...

CLUETT
I've loved you ever since I can remember, long before you married Tom Dickson.

MRS. DICKSON
(still only half-believing)
Why, Cyril, you're insane--

CLUETT
No. No, I'm not. I deliberately avoided you. I was afraid of making a fool of myself. But I won't stand it any longer--

MRS. DICKSON
Cyril!

Before she realizes what has happened, he has swept her into his arms and crushes her to him. CAMERA PANS AWAY from them to the door to the outer office. The door opens and Matt steps in. He stops, suddenly, transfixed by what he sees off scene.

98. MEDIUM CLOSE SHOT
Phyllis Dickson in Cluett's arms (from Matt's angle). They suddenly become conscious of someone in the room and Phyllis struggles free, looking off scene toward Matt:

CUT TO:

99. CLOSE SHOT - MATT
From Cluett and Mrs. Dickson's angle.

He stares unbelievingly for a moment, and then collecting himself, turns and leaves the room, closing the door after him. CAMERA PANS BACK to Cluett and Mrs. Dickson. For a moment she is terribly upset.

CLUETT
Please forgive me, Phyllis. I lost my head for a minute. But I couldn't help it, Phyllis.

As she starts for the door, CAMERA PANS WITH HER. Cluett walks with her.

MRS. DICKSON
Please stop apologizing so much. You're making it far too important.

As they reach the door.

CUT TO:

100. INT. ANTE ROOM OF CLUETT'S OFFICE - MED. SHOT
Matt stands there, in a daze. Cluett's secretary is not there. He starts slowly forward, hardly knowing where he is going - CAMERA TRUCKING AHEAD OF HIM - there is a faraway look in his eyes. His hand clutches the list of payrolls but as far as he is concerned, it is entirely forgotten. Several people talk to him, but Matt walks on heedlessly. He can't get over the shock of what he just saw. He always had been under the impression that Dickson's home life was a happy one. He never dreamed that Phyllis Dickson represented anything but the height of circumspection. And now - Cyril Cluett, of all people!

Helen comes running into scene, all excited.

HELEN
(happily)
Matt, where have you been? Mr. Dickson wants to see you right away. Hurry up!

He turns around mechanically and continues to walk in the direction of Dickson's office - CAMERA TRUCKING AFTER HIM. Helen falls into step with him.

HELEN
Say, I just heard the merger isn't going thru. Isn't that grand?

MATT
(tonelessly)
Yeah, swell.

They reach Dickson's outer office. Matt crosses it and exits into the private office. Helen looks after him - her face falls in disappointment. Matt is acting very strangely. She thought he'd be elated. She stares unhappily at his forlorn figure as it disappears thru the door.

CUT TO:

101. INT. DICKSON'S PRIVATE OFFICE - MED. SHOT
Dickson sits at his desk when Matt enters. When he sees Matt, his face breaks into a broad, pleasant smile.

DICKSON
(grandly)
Well, Matt, get ready for the big moment. Starting tomorrow you become assistant cashier. How's that?

Matt crosses to the desk as Dickson is speaking.

102. CLOSE SHOT AT DESK
As Matt stops in front of Dickson. Matt cannot share Dickson's enthusiasm. The scene he just witnessed has taken the joy out of everything.

MATT
It's all right. Thanks.

DICKSON
And what's more, keep up the good work and who knows - some day you'll be the fellow sitting behind that desk ...
(the idea pleases him)
Not a bad thought, eh?

He suddenly notices Matt's lack of enthusiasm.

103. CLOSE SHOT OF THE TWO
Shooting toward Dickson.

He leans forward to look at Matt closely:

DICKSON
What's the matter? You don't seem very excited about it.

MATT
(feebly)
Sure, I think it's swell.

DICKSON
(scrutinizing him closely, very much hurt)
Say, come on. Show a little enthusiasm. What's the matter? Are you sick or something? Go on, fake it - even if it isn't real.

104. CLOSE SHOT - MATT
Shooting past Dickson.
Matt makes an attempt to snap out of it - and answers quickly.

MATT
Aw, I'm sorry, Mr. Dickson. It's just kind of sudden, that's all.
(working up a little enthusiasm)
Sure, I'm excited. I think it's great. Only, well, you've done so much for me already ... I'll never be able to thank you enough.

105. MEDIUM SHOT

DICKSON
Aw, go on, forget it. You came through, didn't you? That's all I wanted. A lot of them didn't think you would. You don't know how much satisfaction it's been to me. It's been swell. Well, when are you and Helen going to get married?

MATT
Well, I--

DICKSON
I suppose you want me to fix that up for you too, eh?

They are interrupted by the sudden appearance of Phyllis Dickson. Both men look up as she appears in the door.

106. CLOSE SHOT - MRS. DICKSON
As she stops in doorway. She glances fearfully, first at Matt and then at her husband, trying to sense whether Matt has said anything. She is quickly assured by Dickson's affable greeting.

107. MED. CLOSE SHOT
As Dickson comes toward her, arms extended:

DICKSON
Well, look who's here! Hello, dear.

MRS. DICKSON
Hello, darling.

He kisses her. Then throws his arms around her for an exaggerated "teddybear" hug. Over Dickson's shoulder, Phyllis looks gratefully at Matt.

108. CLOSE SHOT - MATT
He returns her glance. His eyes are unable to disguise his contempt.

109. MED. CLOSE SHOT
Dickson and Phyllis. He releases her.

DICKSON
If this isn't a red-letter day for Tom Dickson! First I trample on the Board of Directors, then I promote Matt here to assistant cashier, and now to complete the day I have a visit from my sweet and lovely and gorgeous wife. What a man, what a man!

MRS. DICKSON
(with a half-smile)
It's amazing that your sweet, lovely, gorgeous wife can ever get to see you.

DICKSON
Oooh! That has the earmarks!

He notices Matt, still standing there, uncomfortably.

DICKSON
(good-naturedly)
Are you still here? Go on - go to work! What do you think I pay you for?

Matt exits.

CUT TO:

110. INT. ANTE ROOM OF DICKSON'S PRIVATE OFFICE - MEDIUM SHOT
As Matt comes out and moves quickly forward as if anxious to get away from the embarrassing situation he found himself in. Helen, upon seeing him, jumps up.

HELEN
(excitedly)
What happened? What did he say? Did you get the job?

MATT
(dolefully)
Yeah.

111. CLOSE TWO SHOT
She is perplexed by his unenthusiastic attitude.

HELEN
What's the matter, Matt? Gee, I thought you'd be thrilled to death.

MATT
Come here.
(he takes her aside)
You know, a few minutes ago I was in Cluett's office and Mrs. Dickson was there.

HELEN
Well ...?

MATT
Well, he was making love to her.

Helen, although she had a vague suspicion, is shocked.

HELEN
(after a pause)
Oh Matt, you must be mistaken.

MATT
I tell you, I saw them!

Helen stares at him, horrified.

HELEN
In Cluett's office?

MATT
Yes, right in his office, the rat. I'd like to take a crack at that guy.

A telephone rings.

HELEN
(as she goes to answer the phone)
Wait a minute. Now don't go away ...

CUT TO:

112. INT. DICKSON'S PRIVATE OFFICE - MED. CLOSE SHOT
Dickson is seated with Mrs. Dickson on the arm of the chair.

DICKSON
(talking on the phone, as Mrs Dickson waits patiently)
Yes George ... yes, sure ... Oh, that's for tonight, eh? ... Yes, certainly, I'll be there ... Yes, we'll go down together and have dinner in Philadelphia ... Mrs. Dickson gets so upset ... That's right.... Yeah. ... Just as soon as the bank closes. ... Right. ... Goodbye. ...

He punches the intercom, speaks to Helen in the outer office.

HELEN'S VOICE
Yes?

DICKSON
Helen, I'm going to Philadelphia, just as soon as the bank closes. Make all the arrangements, will you?

HELEN'S VOICE
Yes, sir.

Mrs. Dickson looks visibly upset. Dickson can't help but notice.

DICKSON
What's the matter dear? What have I done now?

MRS. DICKSON
Nothing. Tom, I thought you were going out with me tonight.

DICKSON
Oh, I did have a date with you tonight, didn't I?

MRS. DICKSON
Yes.

DICKSON
I'm terribly sorry. I'd forgotten all about you. I'm so sorry, dear.

113. CLOSE SHOT OF THE TWO
Favoring Phyllis Dickson.

MRS. DICKSON
Now Tom, you simply cannot go to Philadelphia tonight. That's all there is to it.

DICKSON
But I have to go, dear. It's a very important banker's meeting.

MRS. DICKSON
(interrupting)
I don't care whether it's important or not. You said you were going out with me, and if you hadn't promised so faithfully, I wouldn't have gone and planned the whole thing.

DICKSON
Listen, it isn't so terribly important. We can go to the theatre any time.

MRS. DICKSON
The theatre?

114. MED. CLOSE SHOT

DICKSON
That's what it was you planned, wasn't it?

MRS. DICKSON
(after a slight hesitation)
Yes, of course.

DICKSON
You can take some of the girls. You can take Mildred — or Gwynn--

MRS. DICKSON
The girls! I don't suppose it ever occurred to you that I might go out and find myself an attractive young man ...

115. CLOSE SHOT OF THE TWO
Shooting toward Dickson, as he laughs boisterously.

DICKSON
Ho! Ho! Ho!

MRS. DICKSON
Ho, ho, ho, yourself! I wouldn't laugh if I were you. You may not suspect it, but I'm still attractive to some.

DICKSON
Listen, don't go around being attractive to anyone but me ...

MRS. DICKSON
Well ...

DICKSON
Don't you forget that I'm still the head man around here too. Now we'll get the tickets changed for tomorrow night. You and I are going out together. How's that?

MRS. DICKSON
Tomorrow night?

A buzzer sounds, and a visitor is announced on the intercom.

DICKSON
Yes?

VOICE
Mr. Gardner's here.

DICKSON
(answering the intercom)
Oh, yes. That's that lawyer. All right, let him have nine thousand.
(returning attention to his wife)
Yes sir, I'll step you around this town like you've never stepped before. We will have dinner at the St. Regis - then we'll go to a nice, snappy show - then a nightclub - we'll listen to soft music, and who knows? Ha! - I might break down and dance with you!

MRS. DICKSON
(still skeptical)
All right. I'll postpone the whole thing until tomorrow night.

DICKSON
(assuringly)
Happy now?

MRS. DICKSON
(mock-pouting)
No.

116. MEDIUM SHOT
He takes her in his arms and kisses her.

DICKSON
(tenderly)
Poor kid, you know, I <u>have</u> been neglecting you.

MRS. DICKSON
Oh, I don't care, darling. I love you, anyway.

A buzzer sounds again, and Dickson answers the intercom.

DICKSON
Yes?

HELEN'S VOICE
Mr. Sampson ...

DICKSON
All right. Send him in.

There is a knock on the door. Dickson moves away from his wife. He looks toward the door.

117. CLOSE SHOT AT DOOR
Sampson, an executive in the bank, enters. Sampson goes to Dickson with some papers in his hand. He lays the papers on the desk before Dickson.

DICKSON
Well, Sampson, what is it?

SAMPSON
Here's the data on the Clyde deal.

118. CLOSE SHOT AT DESK
Dickson is all absorbed.

DICKSON
Good. I'll take this along with me. Tell Clyde I'll see him tomorrow. I'm sick and tired of the delay.

SAMPSON
I'm afraid he's been stalling.

DICKSON
That's just exactly what he has been doing. This deal should have been closed weeks ago. Tell him to keep tomorrow open ...

SAMPSON
He says he can't get away in the daytime.

DICKSON
How about his nights? He's too busy running around. Tell him to keep tomorrow night open, come in and sign this thing, or I'll call this whole deal off.

SAMPSON
Yes, sir.

120. CLOSEUP - PHYLLIS DICKSON
She stands by a window, listening. There is despair in her look as she hears him making arrangements for tomorrow night. Dickson's voice comes over this shot:

DICKSON'S VOICE
I'm sick and tired of these people dilly-dallying. People who can't make up their minds ...

Mrs. Dickson's eyes close hopelessly, and she feels defeated. Again shut out from his scheme of things, she realizes he is incurable. On this picture of resignation:

FADE OUT:

FADE IN

INSERT: CLOCK OVER THE VAULT, reading 5:07

CAMERA PANS DOWN to open vault.

121. INT. VAULT - MED. SHOT
Inside, several of the tellers are putting their cash away. One of them is just entering with his truck.

MATT
Everybody in?

TELLER
I guess so.

MATT
Where's Charlie?

TELLER
(amused)
Charlie's upstairs as sore as a pup. He's out fourteen cents, and he can't find it.

AD-LIB VOICES
Good night. Good night, Matt.

CUT TO:

122. OUTSIDE OF VAULT - MED. CLOSE SHOT
Cyril Cluett is standing at the bottom of a spiral staircase from which he has just descended. He stops a second and watches Matt, off scene. Cluett has gloves on, his hat in his hand, preparatory to going home. Matt does not see Charlie.

CUT TO:

123. OUTSIDE OF THE VAULT - CLOSE SHOT
Matt and Helen standing near the vault door.

HELEN
What's keeping you?

MATT
Oh, Charlie again.

HELEN
Say Matt, you haven't done anything about what you saw today, have you?

MATT
(still upset)
Who? Cluett? No, not yet. But I'd like to take a crack at that stiff-necked, horse dollar.[6]

HELEN
Oh now, don't be silly.

MATT
(disgusted)
Can you imagine that guy? He was kissing her.

HELEN
Now you've got me worried, dear.
(she kisses him)
Promise me you won't butt in.

MATT
Okay, honey - but just the same I'd like to take a crack at that--

She puts her hand over her mouth:

HELEN
Shh ...!
(whispering)
I'll wait for you upstairs.

MATT
All right, dear.

She leaves. Matt remains standing, a far-away look in his eyes. It is obvious he is thinking about the thing seriously.

124. MEDIUM SHOT
The boys who were inside the vault now file out, having properly locked away their cash. At the same time, Charlie wheels in his truck.

MATT
(kidding him)
Where you been?

CHARLIE
(annoyed)
Where do you think I've been?
(pointing to truck)
I took the baby for a stroll in the park.

The men hurry out of sight, laughing. Charlie disappears into the vault. Matt enters the vault, his mind still preoccupied.

125. INTERIOR VAULT MED. SHOT
As Matt goes directly to the burglar alarm.

INSERT: BURGLAR ALARM
As Matt's hand comes into scene and throws the switch down toward sign reading ON.

BACK TO SCENE:
Matt starts to the vault door:

MATT
What's the matter, Charlie?

CHARLIE
I'm fourteen cents out, and it took me half an hour to find the mistake. And me with a date, too.

MATT
I remember once when your account checked.

CHARLIE
Yeah.

Matt goes to the time clock to check it up. He tinkers with it a moment.

CUT TO:

126. OUTSIDE OF VAULT - MED. CLOSE SHOT
Matt has just finished adjusting the time clock as Charlie comes out of the vault.

MATT
(pointing to time clock)
And listen, wise guy - I'm setting friend time clock for exactly nine o'clock, so no squawks out of you guys in the morning.

CHARLIE
(as he exits)
Say, don't annoy me. I got troubles of my own.

Matt smiles. He starts to shut the vault. He has it swinging half-way around when Cluett enters. When Matt sees Cluett, the smile dies on his lips.

CLUETT
Are the payrolls ready for tomorrow?

MATT
Yes, sir.

CLUETT
(peremptorily)
Let me see your cash book, will you?

MATT
Now?

CLUETT
Yes, now.

Matt looks at him a moment antagonistically. He has half a mind to talk to him right now, but he recalls Helen's admonitions and thinks better of it.

MATT
All right, sir.

He exits into vault. The moment he is gone, Cluett crosses quickly to the time clock.

INSERT: TIME CLOCK
As Cluett's gloved hand comes in and turns the indicator back to 12 o'clock.

127. INTERIOR VAULT - MED. CLOSE SHOT
Matt has opened a compartment and has brought out several sheets of paper. He goes thru them to find the one he wants.

INSERT: TIME CLOCK
Cluett's hand is seen throwing the switch up to indicator reading OFF.

BACK TO SCENE:
As Matt comes up to Cluett with a cash report. Cluett glances over it.

CLUETT
(returning sheet)
That's all right. But it seems to me you're carrying too much cash.

He exits. Matt glares belligerently at him.

CAMERA PANS with him as he returns the paper to compartment. He locks the compartment door, switches off the light in vault and CAMERA PANS WITH HIM as he starts out of the vault. As he swings the large vault door closed,

FADE OUT:

FADE IN

128. EXT. SIDEWALK IN FRONT OF APT. HOUSE - NIGHT - MED. SHOT
As a cab drives up to curb in the middle of a downpour, and stops.

129. INT. TAXICAB - CLOSE SHOT - CLUETT AND MRS. DICKSON
They are in evening clothes, apparently they had some drinks, as Phyllis is in a gay, frivolous mood.

CLUETT
(to driver)
Driver?

DRIVER'S VOICE
Yes.

CLUETT
Have you the correct time?

DRIVER'S VOICE
12:05.

CLUETT
12:05. Fine.

MRS. DICKSON
(looking out)
What's this?

CLUETT
My apartment.

MRS. DICKSON
(mock-melodramatic)
I knew I couldn't trust you. You told me you were taking me home.

CLUETT
Come on up for just a few minutes. We'll have just one drink, then we'll go.

MRS. DICKSON
(definitely)
No. I know the answer to that one.
(shaking her head)
I think you'd better take me home.

CLUETT
What's the matter? Afraid papa will spank?

130. CLOSER SHOT ON THE TWO

MRS. DICKSON
No. No, I'm afraid papa isn't that much interested. He's too busy rushing off to Philadelphia to make stuffy, old speeches at stuffy, old bankers' meetings. Too busy closing big, important deals--
(on second thought)
I think I will have a drink.

CLUETT
Good for you. Come on.

LAP DISSOLVE TO:

131. INT. CORRIDOR OUTSIDE CLUETT'S APT. - MED. CLOSE SHOT
Cluett and Mrs. Dickson emerge from the elevator and cross to his apartment, CAMERA FOLLOWING THEM. Cluett fumbles in his pocket for the key.

MRS. DICKSON
You know, there ought to be a Congressional Medal for men like you. America's comfort to misunderstood wives. I never thought I would find myself in that class.

CLUETT
Oh, you're not so badly off. There's something much worse than being a misunderstood wife.

MRS. DICKSON
What is that, Mr. Bones?[7]

CLUETT
A misunderstood bachelor.

Cluett smiles. He has the door open by now and stands aside to permit her to enter.

CUT TO:

132. INT. CLUETT'S APARTMENT - MED. CLOSE SHOT
At door. Phyllis Dickson has just stepped in, and Cluett follows. He closes the door and locks it.

CLUETT
(mock-melodramatic)
And now fair woman, I have you in my power.

MRS. DICKSON
(playing along)
I'm not afraid of you. You haven't got a moustache!

CLUETT
I'll grow a moustache by the time you get out of here.

CAMERA TRUCKS WITH THEM as he chases her into the next room. She alights on a piano bench, and runs her fingers up and down the scales. Suddenly Cluett stops. He stares off, a look of amazement in his face. Mrs. Dickson turns and follows his gaze and she, too, is startled.

CAMERA PANS QUICKLY over to the other side of the room. Matt sits on the edge of a chair waiting for them. He rises, looks off toward Cluett and Mrs. Dickson. As he starts forward, CAMERA PANS BACK to Cluett and Phyllis.

MRS. DICKSON
Why, Matt!

CLUETT
(when he recovers from his surprise)
What are _you_ doing here?

Matt enters the scene.

MATT
The butler said I could stay. I told him it was important.

CLUETT
Oh, yeah?

Cluett steps over to a bell cord and pulls it.

MATT
He's not here. He left at nine o'clock. He said you gave him the night off.

Cluett wheels around, infuriated.

CLUETT
What do you want?

133. CLOSE SHOT OF THE TWO
Favoring Matt.

MATT
(uncomfortably)
Well, I thought I'd like to have a little talk with you.

CLUETT
(sharply)
I'm listening.

MATT
(hesitatingly)
It's funny - now that I'm here, I don't know just how to go about it.
(a glance toward Mrs. Dickson)
You see, I kind of expected to find you here alone.

As Cluett starts away:

MATT
Do you mind stepping outside? We could talk--

134. MEDIUM SHOT
Cluett crosses to the door, where he stands, ready to open it. Mrs. Dickson stands by helplessly.

CLUETT
(a tone of dismissal)
Anything you have to say to me, you can say in the morning.

MATT
Oh no, Mr. Cluett, if it's all the same to you, I'd rather not wait. It's about you and Mrs. Dickson.

Cluett releases his hold on the doorknob. Mrs. Dickson looks at Matt uneasily - she is quickly sobering.

CLUETT
(aghast)
About me and ...

He crosses slowly toward Matt.

PHYLLIS
Why Matt, what are you talking about?

135. CLOSER SHOT OF THE THREE

MATT
(quickly)
I know I've got a lot of nerve butting in like this, but I just couldn't help it. I thought I could stop two people from doing something they'd be sorry for.

CLUETT
(livid)
I'm not interested in what you think.

MATT
You've no right to do this to her, Mr. Cluett. Why don't you think it over? It's only gonna get you into a lot of trouble.

CLUETT
I tell you, I'm not interested in your opinion.

MATT
(turns to Phyllis)
No? Then maybe _you'll_ understand, Mrs. Dickson. Oh, gee, he's crazy about you. Nobody knows it better than you. If he ever finds out, it'll kill him.

MRS. DICKSON
But Matt, you're mistaken about the whole thing. There isn't anything wrong. Mr. Cluett and I simply came here--

136. CLOSE SHOT - MATT & CLUETT
Shooting toward Matt.

CLUETT
(to Phyllis)
Phyllis, you don't have to explain anything.
(snappily, to Matt)
You'd do well to mind your own business.

MATT
(wheeling on him)
This is my business. Mr. Dickson's been like a father to me.
(his voice rising)
What has he ever done to you to deserve a deal like this?

CLUETT
(livid)
That will be just about enough! Now get out of here!

MATT
I guess I _have_ said enough.
(bitterly)
I'm just wasting my breath talking to you.

137. WIDER ANGLE
Taking in Mrs. Dickson, who stands slightly apart from the two men.

CLUETT
You're right for the first time. Now get out!

Matt ignores Cluett and looks toward Phyllis Dickson.

MATT
I'm appealing to you, Mrs. Dickson. Think what you're doing to him. You're passing up the whitest man on earth--
(flaring up)
--for a dirty, no-good.

Before he finishes the sentence, Cluett punches him. Matt, caught unawares, is thrown off balance and sent reeling. He drops between two chairs. Now, livid with rage, he pulls himself up, murder in his eyes. Cluett crosses quickly to a desk near the door, opens a drawer and extracts a revolver.

MRS. DICKSON
(frightened - cries out)
Cyril!

Matt, who was started toward Cluett, stops in his tracks upon seeing the gun.

138. CLOSE SHOT
Shooting toward Cluett.

CLUETT
(under his breath)
Now get out of here!

CAMERA PANS WITH MATT to the door.

MRS. DICKSON'S VOICE
Wait a minute, Matt!

Matt turns as she enters the scene.

MRS. DICKSON
I'll go with you.

CLUETT'S VOICE
But Phyllis!

Mrs. Dickson steps closer to Matt's side. Cluett comes up to them.

CLUETT
You needn't go on account of this idiot.

Matt has opened the door.

MATT
(quietly)
You better carry that around with you all the time - you're going to need it.

Matt follows Mrs. Dickson out, leaving Cluett glaring after them.

139. INT. OF BANK - NIGHT
A series of quick vignettes:

Cluett's watch, showing 12:07.

A wall clock, showing 12:07.

A night watchman, alerted by suspicious noise, creeping up to the vault.

The night watchman, shot by figures in the shadows.

A small number of men rush out of the vault, clutching money bags and toting guns.

The night watchman, getting off a shot, before he crumples to the floor.

FADE OUT:

FADE IN

140. INT. VAULT ROOM OF BANK - CLOSEUP ON DOOR
The vault door, partly opened. Over the shot we hear excited murmurs.

CAMERA STARTS TRUCKING BACK SLOWLY, until it takes in the full room. A fingerprint expert is working on the time clock for fingerprint impressions. The medical examiner bends over the body of the watchman, whose face is covered with a cloth. A detective in charge of the proceedings stands around, looking very officious.

DETECTIVE
What do you say, Doc?

DOCTOR
Oh, I'd say about eight or nine hours.

DETECTIVE
Well, you'd better call the coroner.

CAMERA CONTINUES TRUCKING BACK, until it passes a group of tellers and clerks in a huddle. They listen breathlessly as Oscar, the youngest of the tellers, relates his story. For the moment he is the center of attraction, and he revels in it.

OSCAR
(breathlessly)
I was the first one to see it. I was coming down the stairs, and there was the dead watchman at my feet. You coulda knocked me over with a pin.

AD-LIB FROM LISTENERS
(murmuring)
Gee ... Can you imagine ...

OSCAR
Do you see that clock? Right there. That's where the bullet hit. When I saw that, you coulda knocked me over with a pin.

CLERK
Was there much blood?

OSCAR
Blood!
(gesturing toward body)
Come on over fellas. I'll show you.

The clerks head toward the dead body, but are intercepted by the officious detective.

DETECTIVE
(officiously)
Get back there. I don't want anything touched until the Inspector gets here.

The clerks, awe-stricken, retreat.

CHARLIE
(running up)
Oscar, what's the matter?

OSCAR
I was the first one to see it. I was coming down the stairs, and there was the watchman lying dead at my feet.

CHARLIE
No kidding?

OSCAR
No kidding. When I saw it, you coulda knocked me over with a pin.

CHARLIE
Where's Matt?

OSCAR
Matt?

CHARLIE
Yeah. He'll have a tough time thinking up a wise-crack for this one ...

OSCAR
The detectives got Matt up there in Sampson's office.

CHARLIE
He has?

OSCAR
Yeah.

CLERK
Say, did Matt do it?

OSCAR
Don't look at me. I don't know.

TELLER
Say, he did look kinda funny yesterday, didn't you notice it?

OTHERS
Yeah, he did. I noticed it too.

OSCAR
You coulda knocked me over with a pin!

CUT TO:

141. INT. SAMPSON'S OFFICE - CLOSEUP - MATT'S FRIGHTENED FACE
He sits in a chair. The side of his face is swollen from Cyril Cluett's punch of the night before.

INSPECTOR'S VOICE
(like a tri-hammer)
Come on, come on. You might as well tell me the truth. What did you do with the money?

MATT
I didn't do it. I told you all I know, Inspector.

CAMERA TRUCKS BACK revealing the other occupants of the room. The Inspector leans over Matt, firing questions at him. Two detectives are also there, one at the door, the other near Matt. Helen stands in a corner, pale and fearful, looking on.

INSPECTOR
You turned off the burglar alarm, you set the time clock, came back at twelve and emptied the boxes, didn't you?

MATT
(rises in indignation)
I wasn't anywhere near this place--

INSPECTOR
(shoving him back down)
Sit down! When the watchman surprised you, you <u>shot</u> him - what'd you do with the gun?

MATT
(desperately)
I didn't do it! I haven't got a gun!

INSPECTOR
You used to carry a gun, didn't you?

142. MEDIUM SHOT
Sampson enters hesitantly.

SAMPSON
Pardon me, but I'd like to use my office for awhile!

INSPECTOR
(bellowing)
You use some other office!

Sampson exits scene hurriedly.

CUT TO:

143. INT. LOBBY OF BANK AT ENTRANCE - MED. CLOSE SHOT
The doorman, Gardiner, stands at the door, blocking a milling crowd, as Dickson, who apparently has already heard the news, enters.

PEOPLE
Come on, open up!

DICKSON
Good morning, everybody. What's the matter here? Open up the door. Come on, open this door.

GARDINER
Shall we let the people come in?

DICKSON
(snappily)
Of course, let them in! You're late now.

CAMERA TRUCKS WITH DICKSON as he proceeds toward interior of bank. Helen rushes into the scene and up to him. CAMERA STOPS.

HELEN
Oh, Mr. Dickson - they're going to arrest Matt. They think he did it!

DICKSON
Where is he now?

HELEN
In Mr. Sampson's office.

DICKSON
Now don't you worry about it.

He crosses in that direction, followed by Helen.

CUT TO:

143. INT. ANTE ROOM OF CLUETT'S OFFICE - MED. SHOT
Cluett comes out of his office, looks around cautiously and satisfied he is unobserved, walks toward front door of bank.

CAMERA PANS over to a corner of the ante room. Detective #3 is watching Cluett. As Cluett leaves, the detective follows.

144. INT. SAMPSON'S OFFICE - MED. SHOT
Matt is still seated, with the detectives grilling him.

INSPECTOR
Then you did it and you did it alone--

Dickson enters.

DICKSON
(to Matt)
What's the matter? What's going on here?
(to the Inspector)
This is ridiculous! You can't hold this boy on a vague suspicion.

145. CLOSER SHOT OF THE GROUP

INSPECTOR
I'm afraid I must, Mr. Dickson.

DICKSON
Why pick on _him_?

INSPECTOR
It's an inside job. That's a cinch. Whoever did it had a pretty good picture of the layout. Now Brown, here, is in charge of the vaults, isn't he?

DICKSON
Yes.

146. CLOSEUP - MATT
Over which comes Inspector's voice as he continues:

INSPECTOR'S VOICE
The burglar alarm was turned off. The time clock was set for 12 o'clock. What more do you want?

DICKSON'S VOICE
Somebody else could have done it, couldn't they?

INSPECTOR'S VOICE
He admits that he set the clock himself.

Matt looks up toward inspector.

MATT
I did. I set it for nine o'clock this morning.

147. MED. CLOSE SHOT - GROUP
As the Inspector turns to Matt:

INSPECTOR
Then who changed it?

MATT
(helplessly)
I don't know.

DICKSON
Wait a minute. Wait a minute.

The Inspector turns back to Dickson.

DICKSON
What time did this thing happen?

INSPECTOR
The clock opposite the vault was stopped by a bullet at 12:09.

DICKSON
All right. If the boy proves an alibi, he's all right, isn't he?

INSPECTOR
If he can do it, yes.

DICKSON
Why, certainly he can.
(to Matt)
Matt, now all you've got to do is tell them where you were last night, between twelve and twelve-thirty, and everything will be all right.

MATT
(averting Dickson's gaze)
I already told him I was home.

DICKSON
(to Inspector)
There you are.

INSPECTOR
That's what he says. I got a man from headquarters checking up on it now.

DICKSON
(confidently)
Good.
(to Matt, smiling)
You've got nothing to worry about. Soon as the report comes in, you'll be released.
(to Inspector)
And listen, don't talk so loud. Take it easy. Coast a little.

He exits scene.

148. INT. THE LOBBY OF THE BANK - FULL SHOT
Showing the normal activity of the bank in contrast to the turmoil going on inside. Just a few people scattered about.

CAMERA TRUCKS towards the other end of the lobby, establishing the calm and peace of the place along the way. CAMERA STOPS on a CLOSE SHOT at the bank telephone operator at the switchboard. Oscar, the young teller, is relating his story for the hundredth time.

OSCAR
Gee, what do you think? There was that watchman, that poor watchman, lying on the floor right in front of me. Oh, you coulda knocked me over with a pin!

OPERATOR
(wide-eyed)
You don't say! Dead?

OSCAR
Dead? He was lifeless! You know, I was the first one to see him. I was coming down the stairs, and there was the watchman lying on the floor, right in front of me. Dead! I tell you, you coulda knocked--

OPERATOR
(interrupting)
Yeah, I coulda knocked you over with a pin.

OSCAR
Yeah, you coulda--
(realizes he is getting the brush-off)
Oh - almonds to you! Almonds!

Oscar exits scene. The operator turns her attention to the switchboard, apparently Oscar has interrupted a conversation she has been having.

OPERATOR
Hello, Mame. This is Gert, again--
(pause)
Say, listen - I just heard something that'll make your head swim ... Listen to this ... Yeah, the bank was robbed last night. Yeah, over a hundred thousand dollars.

149. ANOTHER SWITCHBOARD OPERATOR - CLOSE SHOT

MAME
(into phone)
Who did it?

GERT
I don't know who did it, but the chief teller's in an awful jam.

MAME
Call me up later. I'm going to call up Lou now.

She pulls the plug, plugs in another wire.

MAME
Hello, Lou. Did you hear what happened over at the Union National Bank?
(a light flashes)
Wait a minute, Lou.
(plugs in wire)
Hello? Yes, sir. I'm trying to get them.
(pulls plug)
Yes, Lou, listen. They was robbed over two hundred thousand dollars. Can you beat that?

LAP DISSOLVE TO:

150. EXT. FRONT OF AN OFFICE BLDG. - MED. SHOT
Two men coming out of the building, engrossed in conversation.

MAN
Stole over a quarter of a million. Can you beat that?

The other man whistles in surprise.

2ND MAN
(whistling)
Whew! You can't laugh that off.

Several people in the crowd, overhearing them, turn and stare.

LAP DISSOLVE TO:

151. EXT. A STREET CORNER - MED. CLOSE SHOT
Of an old lady, pitiful expression, begging alms. Two gentlemen are beside her. One of them reaches in his pocket for a coin.

3RD MAN
I thought the Union National was pretty solid.

At the mention of the Union National, the old lady looks up, startled.

4TH MAN
I did too.

3RD MAN
Half a million is a lot of money. I wouldn't be surprised if they had to close their doors.

The first man drops a coin in the old lady's palm and they leave. The beggar woman, oblivious of the coin in her hand, stares unbelieving, at the departing men. Suddenly her face screws up in horror.

OLD LADY
Oh, good gracious!

She dashes out of scene.

LAP DISSOLVE TO:

152. EXT. A BOOTBLACK STAND - MEDIUM SHOT
A colored bootblack is brushing the coat of a customer.

MAN
Sammy, are you sure about that?

SAM
(emphatically)
Yes, suh! That messenga boy just tol' me that Mr. Dickson took it all hisself. And it was more than a million dollars.

MAN
More than a million dollars?

SAM
(breathlessly)
Cross my heart. And I sure hopes that man gets a long time in jail, too!

MAN
Never mind my shoes, Sam.

He hastily exits scene.

LAP DISSOLVE TO:

153. INT. A BARBER SHOP - MED. CLOSE SHOT
Taking in two chairs. The man on the right, being shaved, is in conversation with the barber.

CUSTOMER
Well, I always said the Union National was a phony bank.

The second customer sits straight up in his chair.

ANOTHER CUSTOMER
Union National?

BARBER WITH FRENCH ACCENT
You had money in that bank, too?

SECOND CUSTOMER
Yes. Something wrong?

BARBER WITH FRENCH ACCENT
(hysterical)
Mon dieu, mon dieu! Run, run!

Second customer dashes out of scene.

LAP DISSOLVE TO:

154. INT. A BAR - MED. CLOSE SHOT
Two men are in conversation. Another man is alone. One of the two men holding the conversation is the man of the bootblack episode.

MAN
(of bootblack episode)
I tell you, I got it from the best authority. Dickson got away with several million dollars.

155. CLOSE SHOT - 3RD MAN
He is just reaching for his glass, and starts to lift it to his lips when another man's voice comes into scene.

2ND MAN'S VOICE
Boy, that's the end of the Union National Bank. That's the trouble nowadays. You don't know who you can trust.

MAN
You said it.

The third man drops the glass and turns toward the two, panic-stricken.

156. MED. CLOSE SHOT OF THE THREE

3RD MAN
Say, is there something wrong with the Union National Bank?

2ND MAN
Something wrong? Brother, that ain't the half of it!

MAN
If you've got any money in there, you can just kiss it goodbye.

3RD MAN
(throatily)
Naw, you're kidding--

MAN
No, I'm not.

3RD MAN
Holy smoke!

He rushes out of the scene. The other two stare after him.

2ND MAN
(over-his-shoulder, to third man)
If you've got any friends, you'd better call them up too.

MAN
That's a good idea. I have friends of my own.

He dashes out of scene.

2ND MAN
(turning to bartender, who has been eavesdropping with interest)
Imagine that!

BARTENDER
What bank did you say that was?

2ND MAN
Union National Bank. They're broke. Haven't got a dime ...

LAP DISSOLVE TO:

157. PHONE MONTAGE
Quick cuts of excited phone conversations.

MAN
(into phone)
Listen, Jack, go down to the Union National and take your money out of there. Don't ask me how I know. I told you it's on the rocks. If you've got any friends, you'd better tell them too.

ANOTHER MAN
(into phone)
Better give all the men in your plant a couple of hours off to get their money out--

WOMAN
(into phone)
Tell Mrs. Hardy to tell everybody in the apartment house--

TOUGH GUY
(into phone)
All right. I'll get it or bust a few noses!

ANOTHER MAN
(into phone)
Holy smoke! I'll get right down there if I have to fly!

ANOTHER WOMAN
(into phone)
Run down there and get your money at once!

AD-LIB VOICES
(quick cuts - a rising tide - different languages)
Hello, dear ... Hurry! ... Union National is sunk! ... I told you to put it in the vault ... I don't know what's wrong with the bank ... I wouldn't trust anybody ... everybody's taking their money out ... Union National's broken ... Why take any chances? ... Hurry! Call the others! etc.

LAP DISSOLVE TO:

158. INT. LOBBY OF THE BANK - FULL SHOT
Showing in comparison to previous shot, the effect of the rumors. The lobby is buzzing with activity. Lines form in front of all the windows. Depositors crowd around the writing tables. There are not

enough pens to go around. Frantic hands reach over shoulders for withdrawal blanks. CAMERA MOVES FORWARD. Over the shot is heard the seething blend of many voices.

CAMERA STOPS ON a Teller and a Man.

TELLER
Closing your account?

MAN
Yes, sir. I'm closing my account. I wouldn't leave a nickel in this bank.

CAMERA STOPS ON a 2nd Man talking to a Woman.

2ND MAN
It's getting so a man's money ain't safe unless it's in his sock.

WOMAN
They're all a bunch of crooks.

2nd MAN
You said it.

CAMERA STOPS ON Jewish Man talking to a 4th Man standing next to him.

JEWISH MAN
Say, did I know the bank was going to go ca-flooey? What am I - a fortune teller or something?

CAMERA STOPS on a MED. CLOSE SHOT of Molly (the Zasu Pitts type). She is reaching over a man's shoulder to capture a withdrawal blank.

MOLLY
(fluttering)
Oh, my goodness! Oh, my goodness! Oh, my goodness!

MAN
What's the matter, lady?

MOLLY
Oh, mister, I gotta! I gotta!

MAN
Well, they only sign slips here.

MOLLY
Gimme your pen, please!

She grabs pen away from him. He turns to someone next to him.

MAN
Will you loan me that pen of yours? I'm in an awful hurry.

CAMERA MOVES ON to a CLOSE SHOT of a teller frantically beckoning Sampson.

TELLER
I need some more money! All of the depositors are withdrawing.

SAMPSON
I know, I know. I'll get you some.

He hurriedly exits scene.

CUT TO:

159. INT. SAMPSON'S OFFICE MED. SHOT
Inspector is still holding his ground. Matt sits dejectedly in the same place as before.

INSPECTOR
(to Dickson)
All I know is the bank's been robbed and a murder's been committed. The way I see it, Brown here looks guilty.

160. CLOSER SHOT ON GROUP

DICKSON
What are you talking about? He had no more to do with it than you did.

INSPECTOR
Maybe. But I'm taking no chances.
(emphatically)
Why, this kid's got a record.

DICKSON
So have you. So have I. So's everybody got a record. What difference does that make? You can't go around pinning crimes on people just because they--

He is interrupted by the sound of the door opening. He looks off toward door.

161. CLOSE SHOT AT DOOR
Sampson stands there, looking off toward the group.

SAMPSON
Mr. Dickson! Can I see you for a minute?

DICKSON'S VOICE
No, I'm busy. See me later.

SAMPSON
But this is important, Mr. Dickson. Looks like there's a run on the bank.

162. MED. CLOSE SHOT
Dickson and the others. Dickson looks off at Sampson, unbelievingly:

DICKSON
What? A run on the bank!

CAMERA PANS WITH HIM as he rushes over to the door to Sampson.

SAMPSON
The lobby's half filled now.

DICKSON
What are you talking about?

Dickson goes out the door, followed by Sampson.

163. OUTER OFFICES OF BANK - MED. CLOSE SHOT
As Sampson and Dickson come into the scene.

SAMPSON
(pointing in front of him)
Look!

Dickson looks in the direction in which Sampson points.

CUT TO:

164. INT. LOBBY OF BANK - LONG SHOT
From Dickson's angle.

This shot takes in the length of the bank. Clerks, bookkeepers, stenographers in the f.g., the lobby in the b.g. It seems a little more crowded than in previous shot.

CUT BACK TO:

164. OUTER OFFICES OF BANK - MED. CLOSE SHOT
Sampson and Dickson. Dickson's face clouds.

SAMPSON
They've been coming in steady all morning. I have called for some extra police.

DICKSON
(his eyes glued on the crowd)
All right. Send down to the vaults and have our reserve cash sent up here right away.

SAMPSON
We haven't much on hand, you know. If it gets any worse, I hope we don't have to close the doors.

165. CLOSE SHOT
Favoring Dickson.

He turns to Sampson.

DICKSON
(flaring up)
The bank's reputation wouldn't be worth a nickel after that. This is just a flurry, that's all. They've heard about the robbery and got panic-stricken. Listen, get ahold of our available securities and have them turned into cash. Wait a minute. Get my personal stuff and have that turned into cash too. Tell the boys anyone caught arguing with a depositor will be fired on the spot.

SAMPSON
Yes, sir.

166. MEDIUM SHOT
As Sampson leaves. Dickson starts out in the direction of Sampson's office. He is stopped by his name being called:

CLARK
Mr. Dickson!

Dickson turns. Clark and several directors appear.

CLARK
(grimly)
We want to talk to you.

DICKSON
What about?

CLARK
We'll discuss that in the board room.

He turns to follow, then is stopped by another voice.

DETECTIVE
Oh, Mr. Dickson! We got a check on Brown's alibi. Do you want to hear it?

DICKSON
(only a slight hesitation)
All right.
(to Clark)
I'll be with you in a minute, Clark.

CUT TO:

167. INT. SAMPSON'S OFFICE - MED. CLOSE SHOT
Dickson is by Matt's side. The Inspector is also in scene. Dickson puts a hand on Matt's shoulder.

DICKSON
Now don't worry, son. All you got to do is answer the questions they ask you, that's all.

CAMERA PANS TO THE DOOR as it opens and a detective enters, beckons to the inspector off scene.

168. MEDIUM SHOT
As the Inspector crosses to the new arrival, who whispers something in his ear. The others in the room watch them, interested. The Inspector whispers instructions to the detective, who leaves. The Inspector then crosses slowly to Matt.

169. MED. CLOSE SHOT
As the Inspector comes up to the group around Matt.

INSPECTOR
(carelessly)
So you were home last night?

MATT
(averting his gaze)
Yes.

INSPECTOR
What time did you get in?

MATT
(haltingly)
Well, about - uh - eleven o'clock.

INSPECTOR
Eleven o'clock, eh? Are you sure it was that?

MATT
Yes.

The Inspector turns away and CAMERA PANS WITH the Inspector as he crosses quickly to the door and beckons to the detective outside.

INSPECTOR
All right, Kelley.

Kelley returns to the room accompanied by a little old Irish woman. She looks around the room nervously. Inspector leads her toward Matt.

170. MED. SHOT OF GROUP
As everyone stares at her curiously.

INSPECTOR
(indicating Matt)
Do you know this young man, Mrs. Halligan?

MRS. HALLIGAN
Sure I do. He has the best room in me house. The one with the fancy wallpaper.

171. CLOSEUP - MATT
He feels himself cornered. The Inspector's voice comes over the shot.

INSPECTOR'S VOICE
Did you happen to be awake when he came in last night?

MRS. HALLIGAN
Yes, sir. I was having me hot mustard bath.

INSPECTOR
What time was it?

172. MED. CLOSEUP - GROUP
As Mrs. Halligan continues.

MRS. HALLIGAN
--for the rheumatism, you know.

INSPECTOR
What time was it, Mrs. Halligan?

MRS. HALLIGAN
It was late, I know. The Dooley sisters was already in. They work at a show, you know.

The Inspector is getting impatient.

INSPECTOR
What time was it?

MRS. HALLIGAN
Huh?

INSPECTOR
What time did Matt Brown get in?

MRS. HALLIGAN
Now, let me see - a half hour after the Dooley sisters - and the Dooley sisters never get home until after--

INSPECTOR
(snappily)
I don't care about the Dooley sisters - what time did <u>he</u> get in?

MRS. HALLIGAN
That's just what I'm trying to tell you, sir. It was a half hour after the Dooley sisters ...

INSPECTOR
Was it twelve o'clock?

173. MED. CLOSE SHOT
Dickson, Matt, and the rest of the group. Some show their amusement. Dickson and Matt, however, are serious. Mrs. Halligan's voice comes into scene.

MRS. HALLIGAN
No, it wasn't twelve 'cause the Dooley sisters ...

INSPECTOR'S VOICE
(interrupting her quickly)
Was it one o'clock?

174. CLOSE SHOT
Inspector and Mrs. Halligan.

MRS. HALLIGAN
Yes, I guess it was one, 'cause ...

INSPECTOR
(jumping her)
It couldn't have been earlier?

MRS. HALLIGAN
No. It wasn't earlier because ...

INSPECTOR
Yes, I know. Cause the Dooley sisters weren't in yet.

MRS. HALLIGAN
(firmly)
No - because me clock struck four, and when it strikes four, it's one.

INSPECTOR
(exasperated)
There you are!

175. MEDIUM SHOT
Matt speaks:

MATT
Aw, she doesn't know what she's talking about.

Mrs. Halligan looks at him, offended.

MRS. HALLIGAN
Who don't know?

She comes toward him threateningly.

MRS. HALLIGAN
Listen here, young man - nobody ever called me a liar yet and got away with it--

INSPECTOR
(coming after her, takes her arm)
That's all, Mrs. Halligan. Thanks.

Inspector leads her to the door. On the way Mrs. Halligan continues to mumble her protest against Matt's insult.

MRS. HALLIGAN
For two nickels I'd knock his block off. I never told a lie in me life.

She exits out of room.

176. MED. CLOSE SHOT
As Dickson steps closer to Matt.

DICKSON
(heartsick)
Is that true, Matt?

Inspector comes up to them now.

INSPECTOR
Of course it's true - and he knows it.

DICKSON
(tenderly)
Listen, Matt. If you don't tell the truth, I can't help you. Where were you last night?

MATT
(after a pause)
Aw, she was right. I didn't get in till after one o'clock.

Dickson is deeply disappointed.

MATT
(quickly - appealingly)
But I wasn't here, Mr. Dickson. Honest I wasn't ...

The Inspector barks at Matt:

INSPECTOR
Then where were you?

177. CLOSE SHOT
Favoring Dickson as he leans closer to Matt.

DICKSON
(to Inspector)
Wait a minute. Wait a minute.
(to Matt)
Matt, do you realize you're up against something? You're being charged with murder. It's serious, son. Now come on, I know you didn't do it.
(gestures toward Inspector)
But we've got to make them believe it. Come on, tell the truth, where were you last night?

MATT
(doggedly)
I can't tell you.

Matt maintains a determined silence.

DICKSON
(getting an idea)
Listen, if I get them out of the room, will you tell me?

Matt looks at him. Dickson is the only person he cannot tell his secret to.

MATT
No. I won't.

DICKSON
You're protecting somebody.

MATT
No, I'm not Mr. Dickson!

DICKSON
Yes, you are. You're protecting somebody. Now listen, it doesn't make any difference who it is. It can't be as important as this. Now come on, tell me. Where were you last night?
(a note of desperation)
Come on, don't be a fool. Matt, you trust me, don't you?

No reply from Matt. Dickson is heartsick. He turns, helplessly, away from Matt and walks out of Sampson's office.

CUT TO:

178. INT. THE LOBBY OF THE BANK - CLOSE SHOT
Of Gert, the telephone operator.

GERT
(all excited - into phone)
What a day, Mame! Everybody's coming in and drawing their money out.
(innocently)
Gee, Mame - I wonder what started it.

179. THE LOBBY OF THE BANK - LONG SHOT
Shouting from the offices. The lobby is now packed to the doors with frantic depositors. The low grumbling of before is now replaced by

vociferous condemnation of the bank and Dickson. Individual protestations are heard above the din of the crowd.

Dickson enters scene, and CAMERA TRUCKS AHEAD OF HIM as he quickly passes several tellers, giving them instructions to pay the depositors without delay. Sampson catches up with him.

SAMPSON
Look at them, Mr. Dickson. They're going crazy.

DICKSON
Did you get the case for the securities?

SAMPSON
Yes, sir.

DICKSON
Mine too?

SAMPSON
Yes, sir. But soon as our money runs out, they'll mob the place.

Dickson looks off toward the crowd.

DICKSON
The fools! If they only knew it, they're making things worse for themselves. Somebody starts a silly rumor, and they lose their heads.

SAMPSON
What'll we do?

DICKSON
I'll talk to them. Listen, go back and tell the boys to stall as much as possible. Tell 'em not to pay any attention to what I said. Tell 'em to verify every signature.

He leaves the scene as we

CUT TO:

180. LOBBY OF THE BANK - LONG SHOT
Taking in a greater portion of the lobby. Dickson comes into the scene in the b.g. and stands on the stairs, looking down at the crowd. He suddenly holds up his hand and shouts:

DICKSON
Take your time, folks. Don't get excited. Everybody stay in line. You'll all be taken care of. Don't worry about anything. Plenty of time for everything.

He has to raise his voice even louder.

DICKSON
Now listen, everybody! Listen to me!

Gradually their attention is attracted to him. All eyes are turned in his direction.

181. MED. CLOSE SHOT
Shooting toward Dickson, past the crowd.

Dickson standing on the stairs. The people looking up at him.

DICKSON
I want you to know that your money is safe. This bank is in excellent condition. If you've heard any reports to the contrary, it's based on malicious rumors.

AD-LIB FROM CROWD
Yeah? Maybe ...

MAN
It's a lotta hooey! We want our money!

DICKSON
All right. You'll get your money - every penny!

AD-LIB FROM CROWD
We want it now! We don't want no speeches!

182. CLOSE SHOT - DICKSON
As he addresses the crowd:

DICKSON
Listen to me now. It takes time. I've got seven paying tellers working just as fast as they can. If you'll all calm down, I'm making arrangements to keep the doors open until four o'clock this afternoon and you can be paid today.

183. MEDIUM SHOT OF THE CROWD
As they cheer their approval and return to their buddies.

184. MED. CLOSE SHOT
As Dickson starts back toward the offices, Sampson comes to meet him.

SAMPSON
We can't keep open till four o'clock. We haven't cash enough to last an hour.

DICKSON
Don't you think I know it?

They both start walking toward Dickson's office - CAMERA TRUCKING WITH THEM. As they pass the conference room, Schultz comes out and stops Dickson.

SCHULTZ
We're still waiting for you, Dickson.

Dickson looks up, studies Schultz a moment, as if trying to make up his mind whether to consult the Board of Directors or not.

CUT TO:

185. INT. DIRECTORS' ROOM - MED. SHOT
The door opens and Dickson enters, followed by Schultz. They all look up. Dickson goes up to them.

DICKSON
Well, gentlemen, we've got about one more hour to go. You know what that means?

186. MED. CLOSE SHOT
Dickson and the Directors.

DICKSON
(continuing)
We'll be forced to shut the doors. I've worked twenty-five years night and day to keep this bank alive. You've all made money out of it. Are you willing to help?

CLARK
(defiantly)
What do you mean, help?

DICKSON
I know that among you, you have at least a million dollars in various banks throughout the city. Get that money over here and I'll stop this run within five minutes.

CLARK
That sounds very simple, Dickson, but why should we jeopardize our personal fortunes?

DICKSON
I have everything I own in it. It's your bank as well as mine, isn't it?

187. CLOSE SHOT
Clark and Schultz.

CLARK
(this is just what he's been waiting for)
Oh, is it? Since when? Judging from the way you've ignored us, you wouldn't think so.

SCHULTZ
We tried to reason with you, but you wouldn't listen to us.

188. MED. CLOSE SHOT
Shooting toward Dickson.

CLARK
The depositors you were protecting were the first ones to pounce on you. You thought they were your friends. Why don't you go out there now and try and get some help from them?

DICKSON
Aw, they've gone crazy. You can't reason with a mob.

189. CLOSEUP - CLARK

CLARK
No. You can't reason with anyone else when you're in a jam. We pleaded with you to keep liquid, but you wouldn't listen to us. You preached to us about faith and a lot of other rubbish. Now you want our help. You want us to throw a lot of cash into a bank that you've

wrecked. All right. There's one way you can get it. Give us an option on your stock and resign as president.

190. CLOSEUP - DICKSON

DICKSON
(quietly - tense)
So, that's it, eh? You've waited a long time for this chance, haven't you?
(his voice rising)
Well, I'm not going to resign now - or ever.

191. WIDER ANGLE
Taking in the others at the table.

SCHULTZ
You have no choice.

DICKSON
I haven't? I'll shut the bank first.

CLARK
(terrified)
Say, you can't do that--

DICKSON
I can't? You just wait and see. If that run doesn't stop within the next hour, I'll shut the doors. You know what that means? The bank examiner will step in tomorrow. You'll be forced to liquidate. I'll insist upon it. The depositors will be paid one hundred cents on the dollar. What's left you gentlemen can have. But I'll guarantee there won't be enough to pay your next month's garage bill.

With which ultimatum, he crosses to the door and exits, CAMERA PANNING WITH HIM.

CUT TO:

192. INT. OUTSIDE CONFERENCE ROOM - MED. CLOSE SHOT
As Dickson barges out. He stops in front of the door, and looks off toward lobby.

193. INT. LOBBY OF BANK - FULL SHOT
Pandemonium has broken loose. Men and women are hysterical. The police battle with recalcitrant depositors in a desperate effort to maintain order. Strong men push weak ones out of the lines. Wild-eyed women jostle and scramble to get near the paying tellers. Sex and priority rights are totally disregarded. Above it all the din is deafening. Men and women are clamoring for their life's savings, ready to commit murder to retrieve their little stakes.

CUT TO:

194. OUTSIDE CONFERENCE ROOM - CLOSEUP - DICKSON
His face clouds. As he stands there watching the chaos, slowly the deep concern vanishes from his face and his jaw sets in grim determination. He starts toward the stairs.

CUT TO:

195. ENTRANCE OF BANK - MED. CLOSE SHOT
Cyril Cluett enters from outside, looking guiltily around. Then he starts forward and exits from scene. The moment he is gone, Detective #3, who followed him out, appears in the doorway and crosses in the direction taken by Cluett.

CUT TO:

196. OUTSIDE CONFERENCE ROOM - MEDIUM CLOSE SHOT
Dickson and Sampson.

SAMPSON
Mr. Dickson! Mr. Dickson!

DICKSON
Get all the big bills in the place. Take them out and get them changed. Get nothing but ones and fives. Distribute them among the tellers. Tell them to take their time. Stall as much as possible. Count and recount the money.

SAMPSON
Yes, sir.

DICKSON
I hate to do this, but I've got to have time to dig up some help. I think I know where I can get some real cash. Snap into it, Sampson. We will lick this thing yet.

He starts out of scene towards his office. CAMERA TRUCKS AFTER HIM, as he crosses past Helen, talking without breaking stride.

DICKSON
Come on in here, Helen. Bring your book. I want some numbers to try to get some action. Get Parker at the Union-Leeds - the Exchange ... Winslow and old man Harris at the Home Mortgage. Snap into it, Helen. Just as quick as you can.

HELEN
Yes, sir.

CUT TO:

197. INT. LOBBY OF BANK - FULL SHOT
Pandemonium, din and increasingly hysterical, pushing crowds.

CUT TO:

198. INT. CONFERENCE ROOM - MED. CLOSE SHOT
The directors apparently are having a battle of their own.

SCHULTZ
Look at that mob. They're going crazy.

AMES
You know, this run isn't doing the reputation of this bank any good.

IVES
My dear friends--

SCHULTZ
(interrupting)
How much longer is Dickson going to hold out?

O'BRIEN
You know Dickson as well as we do. He'll shut the doors before he gives up control.

CLARK
All right, let him! I'm sick and tired of hearing about him. If he wants to run the bank, let him do it. I don't want any part of it.

IVES
My dear friends--

CLARK
Oh, shut up!

CUT TO:

199. SOMEWHERE BACK OF TELLERS' CAGES - MEDIUM CLOSE SHOT
Sampson frantically advising tellers.

SAMPSON
Stall! Stall!

One teller faces an angry depositor.

TELLER
Er, is this your signature?

MAN
Certainly it's my signature. You've seen it often enough.

TELLER
I'm sorry, but I'll have to verify it.

CUT TO:

200. INT. DICKSON'S PRIVATE OFFICE - CLOSE SHOT - DICKSON
Seated at his desk, talking into the phone:

DICKSON
Hello, Parker. Listen. Listen, I've got to have a million dollars in cash, and I've got to have it quick.
(pause)
What?
(pause)
No, no, no. Tomorrow is no good. I need it now.
(pause)
Of course it's safe. Why, the bank's in excellent condition. You know that.

CUT TO:

201. INT. SAMPSON'S OFFICE - MED. SHOT
The Inspector is making preparations to take Matt down to headquarters.

INSPECTOR
You'd better tell Mr. Dickson we're taking Matt Brown downtown.

DETECTIVE
(to 2nd Detective)
Is the chief's car outside?

2ND DETECTIVE
Yes, sir.

INSPECTOR
Okay. Come on son. Let's go.

The detective takes Matt's arm and makes him get up from the chair.

Helen rushes into the room and into Matt's arms.

202. CLOSER SHOT
Helen clings to Matt.

HELEN
(sobbing)
Oh, Matt ...

MATT
(consoling her)
Don't cry, honey. Everything's gonna be all right.

The detective touches her shoulder, tenderly.

DETECTIVE
Sorry, sister.

Helen does not move. She clings to Matt, sobbing violently.

203. MED. CLOSE SHOT AT DOOR
As Detective #3 enters the room. CAMERA PANS WITH HIM as he crosses to the Inspector.

INSPECTOR
What did you find out, Mike?

MIKE
I've been trailing the cashier like you told me. You're right about that guy, chief. There's something screwy somewhere.

INSPECTOR
Never mind all that. What did you find out?

MIKE
He left here about an hour ago and went down to Dude Finlay's joint.

INSPECTOR
Dude Finlay?

MIKE
Yes, sir.

204. CLOSE SHOT - MATT & HELEN
Helen slowly lifts her head from Matt's shoulder. Her eyes widen as she hears the name of Dude Finlay. Mike's voice comes over this shot.

MIKE'S VOICE
He stayed about half an hour, and then he came right back here. He's in his office now.

INSPECTOR
(slowly dawning realization)
That's where I must have seen that guy--

Helen starts out of scene.

205. MEDIUM SHOT
As Helen leaves Matt's side and crosses to the Inspector and Mike.

HELEN
Did you say Dude Finlay?

INSPECTOR
Yes, why?

HELEN
He was in the bank yesterday.

206. CLOSER SHOT ON THE THREE

INSPECTOR
(suddenly alert)
He was here?

HELEN
He came to see Mr. Cluett.

INSPECTOR
Are you sure?

HELEN
Yes, sir.

207. CLOSE SHOT - MATT
As he listens intently to Helen and the Inspector

INSPECTOR'S VOICE
Who was with him?

HELEN'S VOICE
Two other men. They all went into Mr. Cluett's private office.

INSPECTOR'S VOICE
(pleased)
Now we're beginning to get somewhere.

208. MED. SHOT
Taking in all the people in the room. The Inspector turns to the detective and speaks quickly:

INSPECTOR
Kelly! You stay here with Brown.

(to Tim)
Tim, you and Mike come with me. We're going down to Cluett's office.

He crosses to the door, followed by Tim and Mike.

209. MED. CLOSE SHOT AT DOOR
As the Inspector turns back and calls:

INSPECTOR
Oh, Kelly - call me up in Cluett's office in about five minutes.

KELLY'S VOICE
What'll I say?

INSPECTOR
I don't care what you say. Sing "Mother Machree"[8] if you want to, but call me up.

Inspector, Tim and Mike go out.

CUT TO:

210. INT. LOBBY OF BANK - MEDIUM CLOSE SHOT
On the elderly lady depositor and bank guard, among the milling crowd.

GUARD
(above the din)
Quiet down, please! Take it easy, folks. Everything will be all right.

LADY
(to bank guard)
But you said it would be safe! It's his life insurance money. Oh, please, I'll go to the Old Ladies' Home if you don't do something, please!

GUARD
Please, lady. Please be quiet. Everything will be all right.
(leading the old lady - pushing a path through the crowd)
Open up here, folks. All right, folks, please!

CUT TO:

211. INT. DICKSON'S PRIVATE OFFICE - CLOSE SHOT DICKSON
Seated at his desk, talking into the phone:

DICKSON
Good heavens, man, you're taking no chances. No, I'm perfectly willing to sign everything over to you. What more do you want? I need action. I've got to have it within the next half hour.
(pause)
Yeah, sure - the board of directors turned me down, but you know why.
(pause)
Listen. Listen, read it. It wouldn't be a drop in the bucket to you.

(pause)
I see. Uh-huh. All right - ask me for a favor some time, will you?

He slams the phone down angrily.

CUT TO:

212. INT. CLUETT'S PRIVATE OFFICE - MED. CLOSE SHOT
Cluett sits at his desk. The Inspector stands in front of him.

INSPECTOR
(very suave)
I hope you don't mind me asking you a few questions, Mr. Cluett.

CLUETT
Of course, yes. Just what would you like to know, Inspector?

INSPECTOR
Where were you at twelve o'clock last night?

CLUETT
(much relieved)
That's very simple. I was home.

213. CLOSE SHOT - INSPECTOR AND CLUETT
Shooting toward Cluett

INSPECTOR
That _is_ simple, isn't it? I assume you can prove that if necessary.

CLUETT
(feeling very sure of himself)
Oh yes, of course. There was someone with me. A lady.

INSPECTOR
(smiling affably)
Looks like you're going to have no trouble at all. What was the lady's name, Mr. Cluett?

CLUETT
If you don't mind, Inspector, I'd rather not say - that is, unless it becomes absolutely essential. You see, she's married.

INSPECTOR
(a big understanding grimace)
Oh!

CLUETT
(smiling)
You understand?

INSPECTOR
(assuringly)
Why, of course.

The telephone rings at this point. Cluett turns to answer it.

CLUETT
Pardon me.

He picks up the receiver. The Inspector watches him closely.

214. WIDER ANGLE
As Cluett answers the phone.

CLUETT
Hello ... who? Yes, he's here.
(to Inspector)
It's for you, Inspector.

Cluett gets up out of his chair to permit Inspector to get to the phone.

INSPECTOR
Thanks.

CLUETT
(trying to be light)
Somebody must be in good humor. He was humming "Mother Machree."

INSPECTOR
(laughing)
It's one of the boys from headquarters. He always sings "Mother Machree" whenever he's got good news. Looks like this case'll be settled in no time.

215. CLOSEUP - CLUETT
His face clouds at this. He listens while Inspector's voice comes over scene:

INSPECTOR'S VOICE
Yeah, Kelly? Huh? Dude Finlay! Where do you got him?

Inspector pauses, waiting for a reply.

CUT TO:

216. INT. SAMPSON'S OFFICE - CLOSEUP DETECTIVE
Detective Kelly, speaking on the phone:

KELLY
(into phone)
I ain't got nobody here. I'm with Brown. Didn't you tell me to call you up in five minutes?

INSPECTOR'S VOICE
Sure.

CUT TO:

217. INT. CLUETT'S OFFICE - CLOSEUP - CLUETT
Cluett is terrified. The Inspector's voice continues:

INSPECTOR'S VOICE
Take him right down to headquarters.

Cluett starts to edge out of scene.

218. MED. SHOT
The Inspector is still holding receiver to his ear. Cluett has edged close to the door, his expression one of desperation.

The Inspector watches Cluett out of the corner of his eye as he continues.

INSPECTOR
(into phone)
Yeah. What? ... You don't mean Cyril Cluett, the cashier?
(long drawn-out)
Yeah-h-h-h-h.
(pause)
Well! Did Dude Finlay tell you that?

CUT TO:

219. INT. SAMPSON'S OFFICE - CLOSEUP - KELLY

KELLY
(into phone)
What? Dude Finlay? Sure, I got him here! You know, for a minute I didn't catch on ...

CUT TO:

220. INT. CLUETT'S OFFICE - MED. SHOT
On the Inspector.

INSPECTOR
(into the phone)
Yeah. We got him here right now. Yeah, yeah. Okay Kelly, good work. Looks like--

221. CLOSE SHOT - CLUETT
He feels himself trapped. He glances around the room quickly to determine his chances to escape. He keeps edging closer to the door with his back to it. His hands sneaks down and grabs hold of the doorknob.

Suddenly, Cluett snaps open the door and like a flash is out of the room.

222. MED. SHOT OF ROOM
As Cluett's figure disappears. The detectives are startled by the sudden move.

INSPECTOR
(hanging up receiver)
--get him!

The detectives dash out, Inspector following.

CUT TO:

223. SOMEWHERE IN THE CROWDED OUTER OFFICE - MED. CLOSE SHOT
Cluett hurries through.

224. EXT. TO MEN'S LOCKER ROOM - MED. CLOSE SHOT
At the door of the men's locker room. Cluett comes into scene and enters locker room.

CUT TO:

225. SOMEWHERE IN THE CROWDED OUTER OFFICE - MEDIUM SHOT
Inspector and detectives enter. Look around quickly.

DETECTIVE
(looking off, and spotting Cluett)
There he goes!

They rush out of scene, their hands on their guns, concealed.

CUT TO:

226. INT. MEN'S LOCKER ROOM - FULL SHOT
Metal lockers line the entire room. Cluett comes to door on other side of the room. Just as he gets there, he hears the detectives entering off scene. Quickly he changes his mind and springs into a space between a row of lockers and the wall, at the same time drawing his gun.

Inspector and detectives enter. The Inspector and one of the detectives advance into the room cautiously, holding their guns in front of them. Kelley, the other detective, shrewdly separates from them.

DETECTIVE
He must be here. There's only one door.

INSPECTOR
All right. Find him.

Cluett slips into a locker and closes the door behind him. They hear the noise off scene.

INSPECTOR
What was that noise?

DETECTIVE
Sounded like a locker.

INSPECTOR
A locker, eh? Well, search every one of them. He must be in one of 'em.

They search the lockers one by one, until the Inspector happens upon the one with Cluett inside. He leaps out, gun drawn.

227. CLOSE SHOT - CLUETT
From Inspector's angle.

CLUETT
Stand back Inspector, or I'll shoot. Drop that gun.

INSPECTOR
(calming tone)
All right, Jack, all right.

228. MED. CLOSE SHOT
The detective and Inspector. The detective drops his gun, but the Inspector keeps his levelled, toward Cluett, off scene:

INSPECTOR
Don't be a fool, Cluett. This is only going to make it worse for you.

CLUETT
Stand back, Inspector. Let me out of here, or
I'll shoot you!

He starts slowly forward.

The Inspector ignores the warning. He takes a few more steps forward.

229. CLOSEUP - CLUETT
From Inspector's angle.

CLUETT
I warn you, Inspector - I'll shoot!

He levels his gun.

230. CLOSEUP - KELLEY
He lifts his gun and aims for Cluett, off scene.

231. CLOSEUP - CLUETT
He is frightened, but desperate. He has his finger on the trigger, ready to fire.

CLUETT
(nervously)
If you take another step, I'll--

A shot is heard. The gun drops out of Cluett's hand. His arm goes limp. His face screws up in pain.

INSPECTOR
(rushing forward to grab him
- to the detectives)
Let me see it! Let me see it! It's only his finger. Get me a towel.
(to Cluett)
Now take it easy, buddy. Take it easy. All we want to do is talk to you.

CUT TO:

232. INT. A TELLER'S CAGE MED. - CLOSE SHOT
Shooting over the teller's shoulder.

People standing in line, an atmosphere of pandemonium and hysteria.

233. INT. DICKSON'S PRIVATE OFFICE - CLOSE SHOT - DICKSON
Still at phone. His coat is now off and flung across the desk. His face is worn. Perspiration rolls down his face. His appearance indicates he has been on the phone a long time.

DICKSON
(into phone - defeated)
You can't do a thing. You're up to your neck.
All right.

He listens. He is being turned down. He hangs up receiver. Over his face slowly comes a look of deep perturbation. He refers to a small notebook open on his desk. His finger runs down the list of names as he searches for another prospect.

CAMERA PANS ACROSS as Inspector and other detectives, with Cluett in custody, enter Dickson's office, all excited.

INSPECTOR
You were right, Mr. Dickson! Brown didn't have anything to do with it. Here's your man.

DICKSON
Why, you must be crazy. I've known this man for years.

INSPECTOR
He's just confessed. He's been mixed up with the toughest gangsters in town.

CAMERA PANS BACK to Dickson, as he stares, unbelievingly, at the shrunken figure of Cluett, who is trembling with fear.

234. CLOSER SHOT
Favoring Cluett and Dickson.

DICKSON
Confessed! Cluett, in heaven's name, what got into you?

CLUETT
(his voice shaking)
I don't know. It's all been like a crazy nightmare, Mr. Dickson.

DICKSON
What happened? You're not a thief. How'd you get mixed up with these kind of people?

CLUETT
Gambling - I owed them a lot of money. Last week I lost over fifty thousand dollars!

DICKSON
(shocked)
Fifty thousand dollars!

CLUETT
(hysterically)
But I didn't kill that man last night. Honest I didn't, Mr. Dickson!

235. CLOSEUP - CLUETT
As he continues:

CLUETT
(dully)
Yesterday they came to collect it. I begged them to wait. I wanted time to think, but they wouldn't listen to me.
(his voice rises)
They threatened to kill me if I didn't pay it! I was desperate! I didn't know what to do!

236. CLOSEUP - DICKSON
As he reacts to Cluett's confession. Cluett's voice continues over this shot.

CLUETT'S VOICE
(hoarsely - quickly)
Then they suggested that I help them rob the bank. All I had to do was turn off the alarm and

fix the time clock. It all sounded so easy. It seemed like a way out.

237. MED. CLOSE SHOT - GROUP
As Cluett continues:

CLUETT
(wildly)
I didn't know anybody was going to be killed!

The Inspector addresses Cluett:

INSPECTOR
What were you doing at Finlay's this morning?

CLUETT
They took my keys yesterday. I went there to get them back.

DICKSON
(desperately)
If you were in a jam, why didn't you come to me? I would have helped you out. You know that.

238. CLOSE SHOT
Favoring Cluett

CLUETT
I was crazy, I tell you, Mr. Dickson. I didn't know what I was doing. I wandered around in a daze. All I could think of was that they were going to kill me ...
(pleading desperately)
You'll stand by me, won't you, Mr. Dickson? You won't go back on me now, will you? I'll die if they send me to prison!

INSPECTOR
(practical)
Don't forget there's a dead watchman downstairs.

CLUETT
(wild-eyed)
I didn't kill him! I had nothing to do with that, I tell you! I was home in my apartment last night - I can prove it!

239. MED. CLOSE SHOT OF GROUP

INSPECTOR
(skeptically)
Claims he was there with a married woman. Doesn't want to mention her name.

CLUETT
(desperately - to Dickson)
He won't believe it, Mr. Dickson. But it's the truth - honest it is. I was in my apartment last night - ask your wife - she--

He stops dead. Suddenly he realizes what he is saying.

240. CLOSEUP - DICKSON
As he reacts electrically to the mention of his wife.

241. CLOSE SHOT - CLUETT
He slaps a hand over his mouth, as if to crush out anything further he might say. He stares wide-eyed and frightened at Dickson.

242. CLOSE TWO SHOT - DICKSON AND CLUETT
Dickson glares at Cluett, penetratingly. His brain slowly absorbs the revelation that Phyllis was in Cluett's apartment the night before.

DICKSON
(dully)
My wife? What's she got to do with you?

INSPECTOR
(out of the side of his mouth - to a detective standing next to him)
No wonder he didn't want to mention her name.

Dickson comes over to Cluett, grabs him by the arm.

DICKSON
What was my wife doing in your apartment last night?

CLUETT
(hysterically)
Nothing, nothing, Mr. Dickson. Don't pay attention to me. I don't know what I'm saying.

DICKSON
You just mentioned her name. What was she doing there? What was she doing in your apartment?

CLUETT
She just came up for a drink. Just for a few minutes.

Dickson grabs Cluett and shakes him.

DICKSON
(a shriek)
You're lying!

243. MED. CLOSE SHOT

INSPECTOR
Don't worry, Mr. Dickson. We'll find out whether he's telling the truth. I'll have a man from headquarters check up on it right away.

DICKSON
(hard)
You don't want to check up on anybody. I'll do all the checking up. Wait a minute.

CAMERA PANS WITH HIM as he crosses to his desk, and calls Helen on the intercom.

DICKSON
Helen!

HELEN'S VOICE
Yes?

DICKSON
Get Mrs. Dickson on the phone.

There is an awkward pause while Dickson waits. He is obviously agitated. Then the phone rings.

DICKSON
(answering it)
Listen, dear. I want to ask you something. I know it's a silly thing for me to ask you, but ... I want you to tell me the truth. Where were you last night?

CUT TO:

244. INT. DICKSON HOME - CLOSEUP - MRS. DICKSON

MRS. DICKSON
(into phone - disconcerted)
Last night? Er - why - uh, last night ...

CUT TO:

245. INT. DICKSON'S OFFICE - CLOSEUP - DICKSON

DICKSON
(very sombre)
Listen, dear. Now tell me the truth about this. Were you in Cluett's apartment?

CUT TO:

246. INT. DICKSON HOME - CLOSEUP - MRS. DICKSON

MRS. DICKSON
(into phone)
In Cluett's apartment? Well dear, you see, I ... I ...

CUT TO:

247. INT. DICKSON'S OFFICE - MED. CLOSE SHOT
Favoring Dickson, but showing Cluett and the others.

Dickson slowly puts the phone receiver down. His face is ashen. He is shaken to the core.

CLUETT
(miserably)
She wasn't to blame, Mr. Dickson. It wasn't her fault. Honest, it wasn't. I begged her to come up. She didn't--

DICKSON
(an explosion)
Get out, get out!

INSPECTOR
All right. Let's go.

The detectives get on either side of Cluett and silently they march him out of the room. Inspector and others follow, leaving Dickson alone. When they have gone out:

248. CLOSE SHOT - DICKSON
Left alone, he is a tragic figure. An incessant parade of disturbing thoughts tumble over each other in a hectic march across his chaotic mind. He grips his throbbing temples in an effort to crush out the torturous thought that Phyllis was involved in an intrigue with Cyril Cluett.

CUT TO:

249. INT. CONFERENCE ROOM - MED. SHOT
Most of the directors seem to be weakening. O'Brien is remaining staunch to Dickson. Clark alone, holds out.

O'BRIEN
Clark, you're insane to hold out any longer. Now let's get some money over here and stop this run.

AMES
If we close our doors, our stock won't be worth a nickel.

Meek little Ives once more tries to speak:

IVES
My dear friends, I--

O'BRIEN
(interrupting)
I'll lay you ten to one, Dickson won't give in.

250. CLOSER SHOT
Featuring Schultz and Clark, standing together.

SCHULTZ
Maybe they're right, Clark.

CLARK
(weakening)
All right, I'll go and have a talk with him.

As he starts to walk toward the door:

CUT TO:

251. INT. DICKSON'S PRIVATE OFFICE - FULL SHOT
Dickson sits at his desk, his head cupped in his hands. Clark enters thru door of outer office, quietly. He looks at Dickson a moment, then crosses to the desk.

CLARK
Oh, Dickson ...

252. CLOSE SHOT OF THE TWO
Shooting toward Dickson.

Dickson slowly looks up at Clark.

CLARK
(softly)
Dickson, I'd like to talk to you about the bank.

DICKSON
(heartsick)
The bank. All right. Do anything you want with it.

253. CLOSE SHOT - CLARK
His face lights up. This is a turn he never expected. He really came in to capitulate.

CLARK
(smoothly)
Now you're talking sense.
(alert)
We'll draw up the option on your stock - say, eighty dollars a share. How's that?

254. CLOSE SHOT - DICKSON
He is not even interested, speaks vaguely:

DICKSON
Eighty dollars? That's fine - anything you say.

He waves Clark away.

CLARK
Good, good. I'll draw it up at once.

255. MED. SHOT
As Clark starts out of Dickson's office, elated, Helen comes in.

HELEN
You want the rest of those numbers, Mr. Dickson?

DICKSON
(toneless)
Numbers? No, never mind.

She stares at him, surprised, backs out of the room.

CUT TO:

256. INT. OUTER ROOM OF DICKSON'S OFFICE - HELEN AND MATT
Immediately following:

MATT
What's he doing, honey? Is he getting any help?

HELEN
Something's happened. He isn't trying anymore.

MATT
They must have turned him down.

HELEN
Yes. He called some of the biggest people in town.

MATT
Sure, they'd turn him down. He ought to know that. I'm going in there and talk to him.

As he enters Dickson's office:

CUT TO:

257. INT. DICKSON'S OFFICE
CAMERA PANS ACROSS as Matt enters:

MATT
We haven't got much time left, Mr. Dickson. We've got to do something quick or it'll be too late.

DICKSON
(softly)
Why wouldn't you tell me where you were last night?

MATT
(ignoring the question)
You're not giving up, are you, Mr. Dickson?

DICKSON
Were you in Cluett's apartment?

MATT
(dismissively)
Oh, I can explain about that later. You're losing your bank - don't you realize what that means?

DICKSON
(gravely)
Was Mrs. Dickson there?

MATT
Listen, Mr. Dickson, don't let them lick you just because a couple of big shots turned you down. You've got more friends than anybody in this town. Little guys - guys who wouldn't be in business if it weren't for you. All you've got to do is--

DICKSON
(undeterred)
Wait a minute. Answer my question. Was Mrs. Dickson there?

MATT
(fumbling for words)
Well ... uh ... I ...

Dickson
She was, wasn't she? How long has this been going on? Do you know?

MATT
Aw, I don't know what you're talking about. All I know is that you're losing your bank and--

DICKSON
(firmly)
All right. That's all.
(poignantly)
Please, Matt.

Head bowed, Matt exits scene.

CUT TO:

258. INT. DICKSON'S OUTER OFFICE - MATT AND HELEN
Immediately following:

HELEN
Did you talk to him?

MATT
(downcast)
Yeah.
(he has a sudden inspiration)
I got an idea. Come on, let's get to a telephone.

They exit scene hurriedly.

CUT TO:

259. INT. DICKSON'S PRIVATE OFFICE - MED. CLOSEUP
All of his beliefs are shaken by this seeming betrayal. Dickson takes a framed photograph of Phyllis from his desk, gingerly sets it face down in the center drawer of his desk.

Also in the desk drawer is - he cannot help but notice - a gun.

CUT TO:

260. INT. CONFERENCE ROOM - CLOSE SHOT - CLARK
As he dictates to someone off screen:

CLARK
--a thirty-day option on ten thousand shares of stock of this company, now registered in the name of Thomas A. Dickson. Now make that in triplicate and get it to me just as fast as you can. Hurry!

CUT TO:

261. INT. SOMEWHERE IN THE BANK - CLOSE SHOT AT PAYROLL WINDOW
Shooting past cashier in f.g. towards line of laborers waiting to be paid.

Cashier stands in front of a tall counter upon which is a small metal box filled with currency. He is speaking into the phone by his side as scene opens.

He hangs up receiver and turns to the men on the other side of the window.

CASHIER
(speaking thru small window)
Sorry ladies and gentlemen, there's no more money. You'll have to go on to the next window.

He snaps the window shut, slams down cover of little metal box.

Angry ad-lib from line of laborers waiting to be paid.

CUSTOMER AD-LIBS
What do you mean there's no more money? etc.

Panicked shouting and pushing. In the center of the crowd, a woman faints.

CUT TO:

Another cashier, another window, another angry line of depositors.

CASHIER
That's all there is!

More pushing, shouting, angry ad-lib.

CUT TO:

262. INT. DICKSON'S OUTER OFFICE - MEDIUM CLOSE SHOT
Phyllis Dickson, serious-faced, comes up steps and thru ante room on the way to Dickson's private office.

She pounds on door of office. There is no reply from within. Standing next to her is a bank guard, uncertain about what to do. Throughout scene, there are b.g. sounds of melee in the bank.

MRS. DICKSON
(to bank guard)
Are you sure he's in there?

GUARD
Yes, ma'am. He must be in there. He hasn't come out.

She pounds on the door again.

MRS. DICKSON
(shouting)
Tom! Tom! Tom!
(to guard)
I've got to get in there. Can't you find me a key?

GUARD
(reaching into Helen's desk)
Yes, I think there's one right here in the drawer.

CUT TO:

263. INT. DICKSON'S PRIVATE OFFICE - FULL SHOT
As Mrs. Dickson rushes in.

Dickson is standing by a window.

264. CLOSE SHOT - MRS. DICKSON
She walks over to him - CAMERA PANNING WITH HER - and stands in back of him.

MRS. DICKSON
(softly - seriously)

Tom! Oh Tom, darling - I came to explain about last night ...

Dickson remains silent. Mrs. Dickson continues:

MRS. DICKSON
Cyril Cluett doesn't mean anything to me, Tom. I went out with him last night simply because ... well, I had begun to feel that I didn't have any part in your life. That I was an outsider. Tom, all we did was to go to the theatre, and then we went back to his apartment afterward for a drink. That's all it was. I didn't do anything wrong, Tom. I couldn't do anything wrong. I love you too much. You know that.

265. CLOSEUP - DICKSON
As he stares dully out the window.

Mrs. Dickson's voice coming over shot:

MRS. DICKSON
(breaking down - sobbing)
Oh, Tom! Tom!

CUT TO:

266. INT. SOMEWHERE IN BANK - MEDIUM CLOSE SHOT - MATT AND HELEN
Favoring Matt.

They are furiously working two phones, going down a list of people who owe Dickson and the bank a favor.

Although Matt has focus in the scene, Helen's voice is always in b.g., as she handles calls, making the same pitch.

MATT
(into phone - rat-a-tat)
Dickson's in a jam I tell you. The run's getting worse.

HELEN
(simultaneously)
Mr. Williams ...

MATT
(continuing)
The big guys have got the screws on him. You've got to come through for him, Mr. Conway. He came through for you a hundred times. If his friends don't help him, who is going to help him?

HELEN
(looking up from her own phone pitch)
Matt, look! There's Mr. Jones!

CUT TO:

267. INT. LOBBY OF BANK - MED. SHOT
As a man elbows his way thru the crowd to a receiving teller's window. He is accompanied by a bank guard, who sweeps the disbelieving crowd aside. He speaks loudly for everyone's benefit:

JONES
Any bank that Tom Dickson has anything to do with is all right. I'm putting my money in here. Why should you be afraid? Give him a chance. Tom Dickson is all right! He's perfectly square. I'm putting my money in this bank! I know what I'm doing!

He reaches a teller's window, which is closed. He pounds on it.

JONES
Open up! I want to put some money in here! I don't want to take any out!

A teller's face appears, somewhat astonished.

TELLER
(recovering composure)
Certainly, Mr. Jones! Certainly! Charlie!

CUT TO:

268. INT. SOMEWHERE IN BANK - MED. CLOSE SHOT - MATT AND HELEN

MATT
(into the phone - rat-a-tat)
They're starting to come in already. Yeah. Yeah. Well, listen. Don't waste any time. Get all the money you can lay your hands on, and bring it down here right away. Step on it.

He hangs up, dials another.

Helen has dialed another prospect also, and hands the phone to Matt.

MATT
(to Helen)
Who's this?
(into one phone)
Mr. Williams?
(into the other phone)
Mr. Gunther?
(to Helen)
I'll talk to both of them at once.
(holding both phones up to his mouth)
Listen, both you fellows. Dickson's in a jam. The run's getting worse. Those big guys got the screws on him. Yeah, both you fellows got to come thru for him. Listen, if his friends don't help him, who is going to help him? Now he came through for you a hundred times. Yeah, listen. They're starting to come in already. Yeah, listen. Both of you fellas - get all the money you can lay your hands on, and bring it down here right away. Both of you - step on it! All right.

CUT TO:

269. INT. LOBBY OF BANK - MED. SHOT
As several more people elbow their way thru the crowd on their way to teller's windows, speaking aloud.

MAN
(loudly)
Get out of my way. I got money I want to put into the bank.

CAMERA PANS WITH HIM and second man until they reach the receiving teller's window, where they fall into a line already containing ten or twelve people.

The second man shoves his way to the front, and addresses the teller:

2ND MAN
I want to make a deposit. Four thousand, six hundred dollars. He's the best man in the world. I believe in him.

CUT TO:

270. INT. DICKSON'S PRIVATE OFFICE - CLOSE TWO SHOT
Dickson and Phyllis Dickson. She is still explaining to him.

MRS. DICKSON
It doesn't matter what you think about me, there's something far more important. Those people down there. The bank, Tom. You can't give that up.

She is interrupted by sound of door opening. They look off.

271. CLOSE SHOT AT DOOR
As Sampson steps in. He looks off toward Dickson.

SAMPSON
Mr. Dickson! Come here a minute. Look at this. Something wonderful has happened. People are bringing deposits. You won't believe it until you see it. You have to come out.

272. CLOSE SHOT
Dickson and Mrs. Dickson. He shambles over towards the door.

273. INT. OUTSIDE OF DICKSON'S OFFICE - MED. CLOSE SHOT
As Sampson and Dickson come out from private office.

SAMPSON
(pointing off)
Look!

Dickson gazes in the direction he points.

CUT TO:

274. RECEIVING TELLER'S WINDOW - MEDIUM SHOT
From Dickson's angle.

The line has grown in size. Those trying to deposit their money are just as excited as those who want to draw it out.

MAN
(shouting)
Tom Dickson is a friend of mine! I'll put money in his bank any time!

ANOTHER MAN
(shouting)
Anybody who takes money out of this bank is crazy! I'm going to put a lot of money in! Here it is!

3RD MAN
I haven't got much, but here it is!

WOMAN
Tom Dickson can have all my money any time.

CUT TO:

275. INT. OUTSIDE OF DICKSON'S OFFICE - CLOSEUP
On Dickson, looking toward Receiving Teller's window. He stares at the miraculous spectacle, deeply moved. He can scarcely believe his own eyes. A smile grows on his face.

The sight of his friends coming to his rescue has an electrical effect on Dickson. It revives his fighting spirit. He sticks his jaw out determinedly. Without a word he turns and crosses to door of conference room.

CUT TO:

276. INT. CONFERENCE ROOM - FULL SHOT
Dickson flings the door open. Clark and the other directors are startled out of their business. Clark holds the necessary transfer papers in his hand.

DICKSON
Come out here you pawnbrokers - take a look at this!

CLARK
We've been waiting fifteen minutes--

DICKSON
(waving papers away)
You know what you can do with that! Come on, take a look at this! You'll see a demonstration of faith that's worth more than all the collateral in the world.

While he has been speaking, several of the directors have edged over to the door. They are perceptibly impressed.

277. MED. CLOSE SHOT - CLARK
He has remained unmoved, staring at Dickson, as if trying to determine what kind of ruse is this.

DICKSON'S VOICE
Come on boys! Come on Clark! It'll do your heart good.

CAMERA PANS WITH CLARK, as he crosses slowly to the door and looks out.

DICKSON
Look at that. They're shoving their hard-earned money across the counter with a ten to one chance against them.

278. CLOSER SHOT OF GROUP
As they edge out onto balcony overlooking scene.

DICKSON
If you fellas want to save this bank, get some real money over here right away.

O'BRIEN
(decisively)
That's enough for me, Dickson. I'm ashamed of myself. I'll have a hundred thousand dollars over here in five minutes.

O'Brien starts away and crosses to a phone.

Dickson turns to the others.

DICKSON
Now you're talking! Ames?

AMES
I'm sold.

He goes off.

DICKSON
All right. Schultz?

SCHULTZ
(only a moment's hesitation)
This _is_ your bank, Dickson, and I'm with you!

DICKSON
Ives?

279. CLOSE SHOT - IVES
At last he can say something.

IVES
(shaky voice)
My dear friends, that's what I've been trying to say all afternoon.

DICKSON
Go ahead and say it.
(turning to Clark)
Clark, you can do twice as much as any of them. How about you?

280. CLOSE SHOT - CLARK

CLARK
Oh, I don't agree with you, but if everybody's gone crazy, I'll go crazy too!

CUT TO:

281. INT. CONFERENCE ROOM - SERIES OF CLOSEUPS
As Clark and the other directors make their urgent phone calls

SCHULTZ
(into phone)
This is Ben Schultz talking. Send a hundred thousand cash over here to the Union National right away.

CLARK
(into phone)
Send all your available cash to Union National!

AMES
(into phone)
Currency - small denominations--

CLARK
(into phone)
--in tens and twenties--

IVES
(into phone)
Say, I want one hundred and fifty thousand dollars over here right away.
(listens)
I _am_ in my right mind. No, no, no. Not one hundred and fifty dollars. Say, listen you guys, one hundred and fifty _thousand_ dollars. Yes!

LAP DISSOLVE TO:

282. EXT. CITY STREET - LONG SHOT
A string of armored cars speed toward camera, accompanied by an escort of eight motorcycle cops. The procession heralds its approach by the piercing wail of sirens.

POLICEMAN
Open up!

LAP DISSOLVE TO:

283. INT. BANK - AT THE DOOR
A dozen policemen precede the entrance of a parade of uniformed guards, who carry in one hand sacks of money, their other hands clasped firmly on their guns. The crowd in the lobby stands aside, awe-stricken.

AD-LIB FROM COPS
Heads up--
Make way, there--
Hey, you, look out!

Murmurs of approval are heard from the crowd.

LAP DISSOLVE TO:

284. INT. BANK NEAR FRONT DOOR - MED. SHOT
As the crowd is leaving the bank. Everyone is smiling and happy. CAMERA SINGLES OUT VARIOUS INDIVIDUALS.

MAN
(to nearby man)
That's the trouble with people nowadays. They hear a crazy rumor, and right away they lose their heads. Not me! You didn't see me drawing my money out, did you?

LAP DISSOLVE TO:

285. INT. BANK - CLOSEUP - GERT
As she works the switchboard - the next day.

GERT
Good morning. Union National Bank. Just a minute ...

CUT TO:

286. INT. BANK VAULT - MEDIUM SHOT - GROUP OF TELLERS
As they gather for their morning ritual, waiting for Matt.

CHARLIE
Nine o'clock and all is lousy.

TELLER
Where's Matt?

CHARLIE
Ten to one he'll have a crack about the run yesterday.

TELLER
It's a cinch bet. I wouldn't take it.

2ND TELLER
If he pulls a gag about the run, we'll murder the guy. Murder him!

They hear Matt approaching, and gesture silence. Matt strides purposefully in. He works the mechanism on the vault. There is a long silence, during which nobody says anything, most surprisingly of all, not even Matt. Finally:

MATT
(after having opened the lock - turning to the group of expectant tellers)
Well, I suppose you guys had a good run for your money yesterday!

They tackle him to the ground.

CUT TO:

287. INT. BANK ENTRANCE MED. - CLOSE SHOT
As Dickson enters, and playfully pushes the hat down over Gardiner, the old bank guard's face. The bank guard adjusts his hat, annoyed, then sees it is the president of the bank.

GARDINER
(merrily)
Good morning, Mr. Dickson. My wife is <u>much</u> better this morning.

DICKSON
Well, that's too bad. Mine's all right too.

Guard puzzles over his non-sequitur for a moment, then smiles.

CAMERA TRUCKS AHEAD OF DICKSON, as he strides through the lobby, passing various individuals from opening scenes.

He spots the teller with a habit of smoking on the job.

DICKSON
Carter!

The teller, from Dickson's angle, holds up his empty hands. No cigarettes. Then, he opens his mouth and chews elaborately, showing that he has switched to gum.

Hellos and Good Mornings greet Dickson as he continues on his way. He passes the janitor in a new uniform, and stops him.

DICKSON
Well, well, well - got your uniform, eh?

JANITOR
Yes, sir.

DICKSON
Looks good. How much did it cost?

JANITOR
(proudly)
I don't know. Mr. Sampson bought it for me.

Dickson opens his jacket, affects an unenthusiastic perusal of his own well-worn suit of clothing.

DICKSON
(cheerfully)
Oh-oh. I guess I'll have to see Sampson myself.

CAMERA FOLLOWS HIM as he approaches Helen's desk outside his own private office. Helen looks up.

DICKSON
Good morning, Helen.

HELEN
Good morning.

DICKSON
Say, I know what's the matter with you. Matt!

Matt, hearing his name, dashes up to stand next to Dickson.

288. MED. CLOSE SHOT

DICKSON
I want you both to take the day off. Go downtown and get a license and get married right away!

MATT
(weakly)
But I haven't ...

DICKSON
I don't want to hear any more about it. If you don't get married, I'll fire both of you.

By now they are beaming. Dickson starts off, then has a second thought.

DICKSON
Helen, while you're downtown, you might stop in and make reservations for the bridal suite on the Berengaria[9] sailing next week.

MATT
Gee, thanks, Mr. Dickson--

HELEN
Oh!

DICKSON
(cutting him off)
Oh, no! It's not for you. You're only going to get married. Mrs. Dickson and I are going to go on the honeymoon.

With just the barest suggestion of a wink, he exits.

Matt looks at Helen:

MATT

Come, on slave.

They exit arm in arm.

FADE OUT.

<u>END</u>

Notes

1. "Almonds to you!" This remark, repeated later in the script, was not in the final draft. When Sterling Holloway was cast as Oscar, apparently his part was expanded, perhaps with some improvised dialogue on the set. One guess is that the line is an idiosyncratic variation on "Nuts!"

2. "I Can't Give You Anything But Love" was a Jimmy McHugh/Dorothy Fields song popularized on a hit record by Cliff "Ukelele Ike" Edwards.

3. The Four Horsemen of the Apocalypse are, of course, allegorical figures from the Bible, but Riskin, a sports enthusiast, is probably making reference to the Four Horsemen of football, "the name given by sportswriter Grantland Rice to the backfield of the University of Notre Dame's undefeated football team of 1924" (*The New Encyclopaedia Britannica,* Chicago, 1994).

4. British statesman Benjamin Disraeli, an uncommonly literate leader of the Tories in nineteenth-century England, served as prime minister twice and was renowned for his policies of democracy at home and imperialism abroad.

5. Alexander Hamilton was a leading Federalist, first Secretary of the United States Treasury (1789–1795) under President George Washington and founder of the Bank of the United States. He was mortally wounded in a famous duel with Aaron Burr.

6. This line is garbled on the screen. It is transcribed as "horse dollar." One guess is that it is a race-track term referring to an inferior racehorse.

7. Mr. Bones, according to the *Merriam-Webster Pocket Dictionary of Proper Names,* is "the end man in a minstrel show who plays on the bones "—clappers—"and like Mr. Tambo"—the tambourine man—"carries on humorous dialogue with Mr. Interlocutor"—the white-faced performer who asks questions of the end man (Geoffrey Payton, Pocket Books, 1972).

8. "Mother Machree" was a sentimental Irish song introduced by Chauncey Olcott, who wrote the music, in *Barry of Ballymore* on Broadway. It is also American slang for any alibi or sob story eliciting sympathy.

9. The *Berengaria* was German-built, a Cunard Line luxury passenger ship used in trans-Atlantic crossings from 1920 to 1938.

Peter Warne (Clark Gable) and Ellie Andrews (Claudette Colbert) in the famous hitchhiking scene from *It Happened One Night.*

It Happened One Night

Columbia Pictures, 1934, 105 minutes

Produced and directed by Frank Capra

Written by Robert Riskin, based on a story by Samuel Hopkins Adams

Photography by Joseph Walker

Edited by Gene Havlick

Musical direction by Louis Silvers

Art direction by Stephen Gooson

Costumes by Robert Kallock

Cast: Clark Gable (*Peter*), Claudette Colbert (*Ellie*), Walter Connolly (*Alexander Andrews*), Roscoe Karns (*Shapeley*), Jameson Thomas (*King Westley*), Alan Hale (*Danker*), Arthur Hoyt (*Zeke*), Blanche Frederici (*Zeke's Wife*), Charles C. Wilson (*Gordon*), Henry Wadsworth (*Drunk Boy*), Claire McDowell (*Mother*), Wallis Clark (*Lovington*), Hal Price (*Reporter*), Ward Bond, Eddy Chandler (*Bus Drivers*), Ky Robinson, Frank Holliday, James Burke, Joseph Crehan (*Detectives*), Milton Kibbee (*Drunk*), Matty Roubpert (*Newsboy*), Sherry Hall (*Reporter*), Mickey Daniels (*Vender*), George Breakston (*Boy*), Earl M. Pingree, Harry Hume (*Policemen*), Oliver Eckhardt (*Dykes*), Bess Flowers (*Secretary*), Fred Walton (*Butler*), Ethel Sykes (*Maid of Honor*), Edmund Burns (*Best Man*), Father Dodds (*Minister*), Eva Dennison (*Society Woman*), Eddie Kane (*Radio Announcer*), Harry Holman (*Manager Auto Camp*), Tom Ricketts (*Prissy Old Man*), Maidel Turner (*Manager's Wife*), Irving Bacon (*Station Attendant*), Frank Yaconelli (*Tony*), Harry C. Bradley (*Henderson*), Harry Todd (*Flag Man*), Bert Starkey, Rita Ross, Ernie Adams, Billy Engle, Allen Fox, Marvin Loback, Dave Wengren, Kit Guard (*Bus Passengers*).

PART ONE

The HARBOR at Miami Beach fades in, providing quick views of yachts, aquaplanes, and luxurious ship-craft lying at anchor in the calm, tranquil waters of tropical Florida. This dissolves to the NAME PLATE on the side of a yacht, reading "ELSPETH II," and this in turn to a YACHT CORRIDOR where a steward is standing in front of a cabin door, near a small collapsible table upon which there is a tray of steaming food. He lifts lids and examines the contents. A heavy-set sailor stands guard near the cabin door.[1]

STEWARD
Fine! Fine! She ought to like this.
(to the guard)
Open the door.

GUARD
(without moving)
Who's gonna take it in to her? You?

STEWARD
Oh, no.
(turning)
Mullison! Come on!

The view widens to include Mullison, a waiter. His eye is decorated with a "shiner."

MULLISON
Not me, sir. She threw a ketchup bottle at me this morning.

STEWARD
Well, orders are orders! Somebody's gotta take it in.
(he turns to someone else)
Fredericks!

The view moves to another waiter, who has a patch of bandage on his face.

FREDERICKS
Before I bring her another meal, I'll be put off the ship first.

STEWARD'S VOICE
Henri!

The view moves over to a Frenchman.

HENRI
(vehemently)
No, Monsieur. When I leave the Ritz you do not say I have to wait on crazy womans.

The view moves back to include the Steward and the others grouped around him.

ANOTHER WAITER (A COCKNEY)
My wife was an angel compared to this one, sir. And I walked out on her.

GUARD
(impatiently)
Come on! Make up your mind!

A petty officer approaches. He is blustering and officious, but the type that is feeble and ineffective. His name is Lacey.

LACEY
(talking quickly--staccato)
What's up? What's up?

There is a fairly close picture of the GROUP featuring Lacey and the Steward.

STEWARD
These pigs! They're afraid to take her food in.

LACEY
That's ridiculous! Afraid of a mere girl!
(he wheels on the steward)
Why didn't you do it yourself?

STEWARD
(more afraid than the others--stammering)
Why--I--well, I never thought about--

LACEY
(shoving him aside)
I never heard of such a thing! Afraid of a mere girl.
(moving to the tray)
I'll take it in myself.

They all stand around and watch him, much relieved. He picks up the tray and starts toward the door of the cabin.

LACEY
(as he walks--muttering)
Can't get a thing done unless you do it yourself.
(as he approaches the door)
Open the door.

We see him at the CABIN DOOR as the guard quickly and gingerly unlocks it.

LACEY
Afraid of a mere girl! Ridiculous.

Lacey stalks in bravely, the tray held majestically in front of him, while the steward and waiters form a circle around the door, waiting expectantly. There is a short pause, following which Lacey comes hurling out backwards and lands on his back, the tray of food scattering all over him. The steward quickly bangs the door shut and turns the key as the waiters stare silently.

The scene dissolves to the MAIN DECK of the yacht, first affording a close view of a pair of well-shod masculine feet, as they pace agitatedly back and forth. Then as the scene draws back, the possessor of the pacing feet is discovered to be Alexander Andrews, immaculately groomed in yachting clothes. In front of him stands a uniformed Captain, but Andrews, brows wrinkled, deep in thought, continues his pacing.

ANDREWS
(murmuring to himself)
On a hunger strike, huh?
(a grunt)
When'd she eat last?

CAPTAIN
She hasn't had a thing yesterday--or today.

ANDREWS
Been sending her meals in regularly?

CAPTAIN
Yessir. She refuses them all.

ANDREWS
(snappily)
Why didn't you jam it down her throat?

CAPTAIN
It's not quite that simple.
(he shakes his head)
I've dealt with prisoners in my time, but this one--

ANDREWS
Absurd!
(muttering)
All this fuss over a snip of a girl.
(suddenly)
I'm going down to see her myself.

He leaves with determination, followed by the Captain, and both are then seen walking in the direction of the cabin, Andrews grim.

CAPTAIN
This is dangerous business, Mr. Andrews. After all, kidnapping is no child's play.

But Andrews ignores him and merely stares grimly forward. They arrive in front of the cabin door, where Lacey is brushing himself off, and where a couple of waiters are picking up the last pieces of the broken dishes.

ANDREWS
What's this! What's happened here?

LACEY
(pathetically)
She refused another meal, sir.

ANDREWS
Get another tray ready. Bring it here at once.
(to the guard)
Open the door.

The Guard unlocks the door and Andrews enters. Then we get a view of the CABIN at the door, as Andrews enters and closes the door behind him. He looks around and his eyes light on his prisoner, following which the view swings over to ELLIE, a beautiful girl in her early twenties. At the moment, she holds a small vase over her head ready to heave it, and her eyes flash angrily. At sight of her new visitor, however, she lowers the vase and sets it on a small table.

ELLIE
What do <u>you</u> want?

Andrews doesn't stir from the door.

ANDREWS
What's this about not eating?

ELLIE
(sitting)
I don't want to eat!
(raising her voice)
And there's one more thing I don't want! Definitely! That's to see you.

She lights a cigarette. Andrews watches her a moment.

ANDREWS
Know what my next move is? No more cigarettes.

ELLIE
Why don't you put me in chains?

ANDREWS
I might.

ELLIE
(now seen at close range)
All right! Put me in chains! Do anything you want! But I'm not going to eat a thing until you let me off this boat!

She stares petulantly out at the blue sky, but Andrews comes over and sits beside her.

ANDREWS
(tenderly)
Come on, Ellie. Stop being silly. You know I'm going to have <u>my</u> way.

ELLIE
(moving away)
I won't stand for it! I won't stand for your running my life! Why do you insist on it!

ANDREWS
(still tender)
You ought to know why. Because--

ELLIE
(interrupting)
Yes. I know.
(she's heard it a million times)
Because I'm your daughter and you love me. Because you don't want me to make any mistakes. Because--

ANDREWS
(joining in)
Because marrying that fool King Westley is--

ELLIE
(snappily)
You're wasting your time. I'm already married to him.

ANDREWS
(sharply)
Not so far as *I'm* concerned, you're not.
(they are interrupted by a knock at the door)

ANDREWS
Yes?

The door opens and several waiters parade in with trays of steaming food.

ELLIE
(starting for them; threateningly)
How many times have I told you not to bring any food in here.

The waiters back up, frightened, but Andrews saves them.

ANDREWS
Wait a minute! Don't get excited! This isn't for you.
(to the waiters)
Put it right here.

Ellie glares at her father, and wanders over to the window seat, while the waiters occupy themselves setting the table. Andrews putters around the food, lifting the lids from which tempting aromas emanate. He shuts his eyes, murmuring "oohs" and "ahs."

A close-up of ELLIE shows her, too, drinking in the inviting aromas; and for a moment she weakens. A close view of ANDREWS shows him glancing toward Ellie to see her reaction; whereupon Ellie's face (again appearing in a close-up) freezes. Then Andrews and the waiters come into view.

FIRST WAITER
Anything else, Monsieur?

ANDREWS
No. Everything seems quite satisfactory. I may want some more of that delicious gravy. I'll ring.

WAITER
Very good, Monsieur.

The waiters bow their way out as Andrews pecks at the food.

ANDREWS
(making clucking noise)
Heavenly!

Now Ellie appears in the foreground, with Andrews at the table in the background.

ELLIE
(disdainfully)
Smart, aren't you! So subtle.

ANDREWS
(chewing on a mouthful of food)
If Gandhi had a chef like Paul, it would change the whole political situation in India.

ELLIE
You can't tempt me.
(shouting unnecessarily)
Do you hear? I won't eat!

ANDREWS
(quietly)
Please. I can't fight on an empty stomach. Remember what Napoleon said.

ELLIE
I hope you're not comparing yourself to Napoleon. He was a strategist. Your idea of strategy is to use a lead pipe.

Andrews eats silently while Ellie rants at him, walking around and puffing vigorously on her cigarette.

ELLIE
(muttering)
Most humiliating thing ever happened to me.
(shuddering)
A bunch of gorillas shoving me in a car! That crowd outside the justice of the peace--must have thought I was a criminal--or something.

A close view of ANDREWS intercuts with part of Ellie's speech. At the end of her speech he smacks his lips, enjoying the food with too great a relish. Then the two are seen together.

ELLIE
(after a pause--strongly)
Where are you taking me?

ANDREWS
(carelessly)
South America.

ELLIE
(aghast)
South America!

ANDREWS
We leave Miami in an hour. Soon's we get some supplies aboard.

ELLIE
(threateningly)
You'll have a corpse on your hands! That what you'll have. I won't eat a thing while I'm on this boat.

ANDREWS
(buttering bread)
In that event, we won't need so many supplies.

ELLIE
(exasperated)
What do you expect to accomplish by all this? I'm already married!

ANDREWS
I'll get it annulled.

ELLIE
You'll never do it! You <u>can't</u> do it!

ANDREWS
(now seen close as he speaks between snatches of food)
I'll do it if it takes every penny I've got. I'll do it if I have to bribe that musical comedy Justice of the Peace! I'll do it--if I have to prove that you were dragged in, staggering drunk. You probably were.
(he smacks his lips)
Mmm--mmm. This filet mignon is divine!

ELLIE
(seen with her father)
What've you got against King Westley?

ANDREWS
Nothing much. I just think he's a fake, that's all.

ELLIE
You only met him <u>once</u>.

ANDREWS
That was enough. Do you mind handing me the ketchup?

ELLIE
You talk as if he were a gigolo--or something.

ANDREWS
(rising--reaching for ketchup)
Never mind--I'll get it myself.
(he falls back in his chair)
Gigolo? Why, you took the word right out of my mouth. Thanks.

ELLIE
(seen closer now, with Andrews)
He's one of the best fliers in the country. Right now he's planning a trip to Japan.

ANDREWS
You're going to finance him, I suppose.

ELLIE
Why not? Look what he's doing for aviation. It takes courage to do what he does. And character! At least he's accomplished something worthwhile. I suppose you'd like to have me marry a business man. Well, I hate business men--particularly if <u>you're</u> a shining example.

He grins, not at all offended, knowing she doesn't mean it.

ELLIE
Your whole life is devoted to just one thing. To accumulate more money. At least there's romance in what he's doing.

ANDREWS
(unequivocally)
He's no good, Ellie, and you know it. You married him only because I told you not to.

ELLIE
(strongly)
You've been telling me what not to do since I was old enough to remember.
(screaming)
I'm sick of it!

And as Andrews ignores her, she starts moving around the table toward him.--Next she appears sitting on the edge of Andrews' chair, and she throws her arm around his shoulder.

ELLIE
(pleading sweetly)
Aw, listen, Dad. Let's not fight like this any more. I know you're worried about me--and want me to be happy. And I love you for it. But please try to understand. You're not being fair, darling. This isn't just a crazy impulse of mine. King and I talked about it a lot before we decided to get married. Look--why can't we give it a trial--let's say--for a year or so. If it's wrong, King and I will be the first to know it. We can get a divorce, can't we? Now, be a dear, and let me off the boat. Keeping me prisoner like this is so silly.

Andrews has been listening silently throughout the speech, giving no indication of his feelings in the matter.

ANDREWS
(unimpressed)
You'll be set free when the marriage is annulled.

A close-up of ELLIE, her eyes blazing angrily, shows her slowly edging away from her father, while he continues.

ANDREWS' VOICE
(carelessly)
So there's no use being a stubborn idiot.

ELLIE
(hissing)
I come from a long line of stubborn idiots!

ANDREWS
(again seen with her; calmly)
A time will come when you'll thank me for this.

ELLIE
(wildly)
I won't thank you! I'll never thank you!

ANDREWS
Please don't shout.

ELLIE
I'll shout to my heart's content! I'll scream if I want to.

ANDREWS
(reaching for it)
Ah! Coconut layer cake. Nice and gooey, too. Just the way I like it.

He is about to insert the first bite in his mouth when Ellie, her temper vanishing completely, overturns the small serving table, dumping its contents into her father's lap. The movement is so unexpected that Andrews, the fork still suspended near his mouth, stares at her stupefied. Then realizing what she has done, his eyes flash in anger. Dropping his fork, he rises and goes over to her, while she stands facing him defiantly. Without a word or warning, he slaps her a stinging blow across the cheek. For a moment she doesn't stir, her eyes widening in surprise, and staring at him unbelievingly. Then turning abruptly she bolts out of the door. Andrews remains motionless, his eyes shutting painfully; it is the first time he has struck her, and it hurts.

ANDREWS
(calling)
Ellie!
(and he starts for the door)

Next on the DECK, at the open cabin door, Andrews is seen, staring off at something and an amazed, frightened look comes into his eyes. Then, as viewed from his position at the cabin door, Ellie appears standing on the rail; and with a professional dive, she leaps into the water.

A full view of the DECK reveals the crew and the officers scurrying around, several of them shouting: "Somebody overboard!"

ANDREWS
It's my daughter! Go after her.

CAPTAIN
(shouting)
Lower the boats!

General excitement reigns; several of the crew dive into the water; others release the boat lines. Following this Ellie is seen swimming furiously against the giant waves. Next she appears as a small speck in the distance, while half a dozen of the crew are swimming in pursuit.

At the SIDE OF THE YACHT one of the boats has already been lowered, and two men jump in and grab the oars. The men seem to be gaining on Ellie. In the distance several small motor boats are anchored, and over the sides of the boats their owners are fishing. Ellie seems to be headed in their direction.

One of the motor boats appears closer. A middle-aged man sits on the stern, holding lazily to his line, his feet dangling in the water as the boat is tossed around by the turbulent waves. ELLIE is then again seen swimming. She looks back, and the next scene shows the men rowing toward her, and gaining on her. Thereupon we see Ellie ducking under the water.

The middle-aged fisherman is suddenly startled by Ellie's face which appears from under water, right between his legs. Ellie puts her finger up to her lips, warning him to shush, and he is too dumbfounded to say anything. As the pursuing boats come near, Ellie ducks under the water again and the boats scoot right by the fisherman. Then Ellie's head bobs up; she peers ahead of her, and seeing that her pursuers have passed her, she smiles victoriously.

ELLIE
(to the fisherman)
Thanks.
(and she starts swimming toward shore)

The scene dissolves to the DECK of the YACHT as Ellie's pursuers clamber aboard, Andrews waiting for them.

A MAN
Sorry, sir. She got away.

ANDREWS
(disappointed but proud)
Of course she got away--too smart for you.

CAPTAIN
What a hell cat. No controlling these modern girls.
(murmuring)
They're terrible!

ANDREWS
(resentfully)
Terrible! Nothing terrible about her. She's great! Marvelous youngster! Got a mind of her own. Knows just what she wants.
(smiling)
She's not going to get it though. She won't get very far. Has no money.

CAPTAIN
What about that diamond wrist watch she had on--she can raise some money on that?

ANDREWS
(his face falling)
Holy Smoke! I forgot all about that.
(to the officer by his side)
Send a wireless at once, "Lovington Detective Agency. Daughter escaped again. Watch all roads--all transports and railroad stations in Miami. Have your New York office keep tabs on King Westley. Intercept all messages. Want her back at all costs!"

OFFICER
Yessir.

The view draws in to afford a close-up of ANDREWS staring out at the sea, his face wreathed in a broad smile; then this fades out.

PART TWO

The RAILROAD STATION of an active terminal in Miami fades in. The view moves down to the entrance gate to the trains, passengers hurrying through it; then picks out two men, obviously detectives, who have their eyes peeled on everyone passing through. Then the view affords a glimpse of ELLIE, who stands watching the detectives. This scene wiping off, we see an AIR TRANSPORT, with several planes tuning up in the background. As passengers file through, several detectives stand around in a watchful pose. This scene wiping off,the front of a WESTERN UNION OFFICE comes into view. Several people walk in and out. At the side of the door, two detectives are on the lookout.

This scene also wipes off, revealing the WAITING ROOM of a BUS STATION. Over the ticket window there is a sign reading "BUY BUS TICKETS HERE," and a line forms in front of it. Here too there are two detectives.

FIRST DETECTIVE
We're wastin' our time. Can you picture Ellie Andrews ridin' on a bus?

SECOND DETECTIVE
I told the old man it was the bunk.

The view moves from them to ELLIE, who stands behind a post and is watching the two detectives apprehensively. As the two (viewed from her position) stand by the ticket window, one of them turns toward her. Thereupon, we see her slipping behind a post, concealing herself. Just then a little old lady approaches her.

OLD LADY
Here's your ticket, ma'am.

ELLIE
Oh, thank you. Thank you very much.
(she takes the ticket and change from the old lady, and hands her a bill)
Here.

OLD LADY
Oh, thank you. Thank you.

ELLIE
When does the bus leave?

OLD LADY
In about fifteen minutes.

ELLIE
Thank you.

She picks up a small overnight bag from the floor and hurries away. She crosses to the entrance ot the waiting room and disappears through the doors. The view then wings over to a telephone booth near the entrance. Clustered around the booth are half a dozen men of varied appearance. The inside of the booth is lighted, and a young man, Peter Warne, waves his hands wildly as he shouts into the phone, although it is impossible to hear what he is saying. A close inspection of the men surrounding the booth (the scene contracting to a close view) reveals them as being slightly and happily intoxicated. A short man approaches the door of the booth.

SHORTY
Hey, what's going on here? I'd like to use that phone.

FIRST MAN
(a reporter)
Shh! Quiet. This is history in the making.

SHORTY
What?

FIRST MAN
There's a man biting a dog in there.

SECOND MAN
(drunker than the rest)
Atta-boy, Petey, old boy! Atta-boy!--

PETER'S VOICE
I'm not going to stand for this any longer. In a pig's eye, you will!--

GROUP
Is that so? That's telling him, Petey old boy.

A close view of PETER WARNE in the telephone booth gives evidence of his having also imbibed freely.

PETER
(shouting into the phone)
Listen, monkey-face--when you fired me, you fired the best newshound your filthy scandal sheet ever had.

And the scene cuts to a New York NEWSPAPER OFFICE where the night editor, Gordon, his sleeves rolled up, sits at his desk shrieking into the phone.

GORDON
Say, listen, you wouldn't know a story if it reached up and kicked you in the pants.
(listening)
Yeah? Sure, sure, I got your copy. Why didn't you tell me you were going to write it in Greek? I'd start a new department.

PETER
(again seen close at the phone)
That was free verse, you gashouse palooka!

GORDON
(at the phone in the newspaper office)
Free verse, huh?
(shouting)
What the dickens was free about it? It cost this paper a gob of dough. Well, I'm here to tell you, it's not gonna cost us any more.

PETER
(in his phone booth)
That's okay by me! 'Cause as far as I'm concerned, I'm through with newspapers! See? I'm through with stupidity! I'll never write another newspaper story, for you or anybody else, if I have to starve.
(after a pause)
Yeah? What about my novel! When I get through with that--

GORDON
(in his office)
When you get through with that, I'll have a beard down to my ankles.
(at this point, Gordon's secretary enters)

SECRETARY
Mr. Gordon--

GORDON
(looking up)
Huh?

SECRETARY
Did you know he reversed the charges on that call?

GORDON
What!
(into the phone)
Say, listen you! When you get back to New York, take my advice and stay f-a-r away from this office--unless you don't care what happens to that funny map of yours.
(he bangs down the receiver viciously and glowers at the phone)

In the PHONE BOOTH Peter reacts to the phone being hung up on him. But he goes right on for the benefit of the boys.

PETER
(into the dead phone)
Oh, so you're changing your tune, eh? Well, it's about time. But it's going to do you no good, my tough friend. It's a little too late for apologies. I wouldn't go back to work for you if you begged me on your hands and knees! I hope this is a lesson to you!

He snaps up the receiver with a great pretense of outraged pride, following which the view expands to include his public.

MEN
Atta-boy, Peter. That's telling him, Peter.

The gang is full of admiration for the courageous way he talked to the boss as Peter staggers out of the booth.

PETER
Give me any of his lip, will he? Huh! I guess he knows now what I think of his job!
(expansively)
Is my chariot ready?

FIRST MAN
Your chariot awaiteth withouteth, oh mighty King.

MEN
Make way for the King. Long live the King. Make way.

With head held high, he struts majestically out of sight, followed by his admirers, following which the scene dissolves to the BUS STATION. His inebriated admirers stand around the entrance to a bus, while Peter stands on the steps, his suitcase in his hand.

PETER
(making a grand speech)
That's right, my friends. Cling to your jobs! Remain slaves the rest of your lives! Scum of the earth! Newspaper men! Not me! When I'm basking in the glorious arms of the Muse--what'll <u>you</u> be doing? Chasing news. You miserable worms. For what? A mere pittance! My heart goes out to you.
(with arms extended and in tremolo voice)
Good-bye.
(and with this he turns his back and enters the bus)

MEN
(in the same spirit)
Goodbye, Oh mighty King! Peace be with you, Courageous One!

ANNOUNCER'S VOICE
All aboard. Philadelphia, New York. All aboard.

GROUP
Look out. Get back. Farewell. Farewell.

PETER
Scram.

The scene cuts to the INTERIOR of the BUS as viewed from the front, the view moving forward, passing the conglomerate of unprepossessing human beings who occupy the seats. Every space is taken and the occupants seem hot and uncomfortable, which adds to their uninviting appearance. Mothers cling to crying babies. A Swedish farm hand and his young wife are already busy opening their basket of food prepared for the long journey. A surly-looking hoodlum traveling alone is slumped in his seat, his cap drawn carelessly over his eyes. The moving view passes these and other characters until it reaches one unoccupied seat in the car, unoccupied except for several bundles of newspapers.

Standing before the seat is Peter, his suitcase in his hand, speculating as to what disposition to make of the newspapers.

PETER
(calling)
Hey, driver! How about clearing this stuff away!

Several passengers (seen from his position in the back) crane their necks to scrutinize the intruder. Through a glass partition the driver can be seen receiving his last minute instructions from a superintendent, who stands on the running board, their voices indistinguishable. In answer to Peter's request, the driver glances back indifferently, and continues talking to the superintendent. A close view of PETER shows him arching his eyebrows, an amused acknowledgment of the disdainful attitude of the driver. He drops his suitcase and starts forward. Then we see him arriving at the glass partition, and Peter taps playfully on the pane with his fingernails, whereupon the driver turns and pulls the window down a few inches.

DRIVER
(annoyed)
Whadda you want!

PETER
(pleasantly)
If you'll be good enough to remove those newspapers I'll have a seat.

DRIVER
(irritably)
Okay! Okay! Keep your shirt on, young feller.
(with which remark the driver turns away from him)

PETER
(looking at the back of the driver's neck for a moment, then confidentially)
Just between you and me, I never intended taking it off.

He wheels around uncertainly and swaggers jauntily down the aisle toward the empty seat. En route he bestows genial smiles upon several of his disgruntled fellow passengers, and he stops in front of a robust lady who at the moment is breastfeeding her baby while a lighted cigarette dangles from her lips.

PETER
Personally, I was raised on a bottle.
(as the woman looks up at him, perplexed)
When I was a baby, I insisted on it. You know why?
(as the woman stares up stupidly)
I never liked the idea of getting cigarette ashes in my eyes.

He moves forward, leaving the woman unable to make head or tail of it; and assuming that he's crazy, she shrugs her shoulders and turns her attention to the baby.

Now PETER arrives at his seat, and whistling softly, raises the window. Unhurriedly, he picks the newspaper bundles up one by one and flings them out of the window. They hit the sidewalk below with a dull thud. Thereupon a close view of the DRIVER shows him reacting violently to Peter's unprecedented cheek, and starting down from his seat.

PETER has now cleared the seat of all the newspaper bundles and still whistling his favorite melody, he picks up his suitcase preparatory to placing it in the rack overhead. At this point, the driver enters the side door of the bus.

DRIVER
(pugnaciously)
Hey, wait a minute!

Peter, his arms holding the suitcase over his head, turns and glances at the driver, a quizzical look in his eyes.

DRIVER
(coming forward)
What do you think you're doing!

PETER
(turning)
Huh?

DRIVER
(bellowing)
The papers! The papers! Whadda you mean throwin' 'em out!

PETER
Oh--the papers--

He slowly lowers his arms and deposits the suitcase on the floor.

PETER
(now seen close, with the Driver)
That's a long story, my friend. You see, I don't like sitting on newspapers. I did once and all the headlines came off on my white pants.

DRIVER
Hey, whadda you tryin' to do--kid me?

PETER
Oh, I wouldn't kid you. On the level, it actually happened. Nobody bought a paper that day. They followed me all over town and read the news from the seat of my pants.

DRIVER
What're you gonna do about the papers? Somebody's gotta pick 'em up.

PETER
(turning to his suitcase)
It's okay with me. I'm not arguing.

DRIVER
(pugnaciously)
Fresh guy, huh! What you need is a good sock on the nose.

PETER
(turning back to him)
Look here, partner. You may not like my nose. But I do. It's a good nose. The only one I've got. I always keep it out in the open where anybody can take a sock at it. If you decide to do it, make sure you don't miss.

During his speech, Ellie enters from the rear and plunks herself into Peter's seat. Unseen by Peter, she places her small bag beside her.

DRIVER
(answering Peter; weakly)
Oh, yeah?

PETER
Now, that's a brilliant answer. Why didn't I think of it? Our conversation could have been over long ago.

DRIVER
Oh, yeah?

PETER
(exhausted)
You win!

Smiling, he turns to sit down. But the smile dies on his face when he finds his place occupied by Ellie, who stares out the window.

PETER
(now at close range, with Ellie)
Excuse me, lady--
(slowly)--
but that upon which you sit--is mine.

Ellie glances up at him--then down at her buttocks.

ELLIE
(eyes flashing)
I beg your pardon!

PETER
Now, listen. I'm in a very ugly mood. I put up a stiff battle for that seat. So if it's just the same to you--
(gesturing with thumb)
scram.

ELLIE
(ignoring him--calling)
Driver!

The driver, who has stopped to witness this new altercation, returns.

ELLIE
Are those seats reserved?

DRIVER
(pleased to discomfort Peter)
No. First come, first served.

ELLIE
(dismissing the whole thing)
Thank you.
(Peter, thwarted for a moment, just glares at her)

PETER
(also calling)
Driver!

DRIVER
Yeah?

PETER
These seats accommodate two passengers, don't they?

DRIVER
(hating to give in)
Maybe they do--and maybe they don't.

Peter lifts Ellie's overnight bag off the seat and drops it on the floor. Part of her coat covers the small space by her side. This he sweeps across her lap.

PETER
Move over, lady. This is a "maybe they do."

He plops into the seat, the other passengers around them heaving a sigh of relief. Ellie flashes him a devastating look and deliberately turns her back on him. But Peter suddenly looks down toward the floor, following which a close-up AT THEIR FEET reveals that Ellie's bag on the floor annoys Peter. With his foot he slowly moves it over to her, and Ellie's foot is seen pushing it back, whereupon Peter viciously kicks it over to her side again. Next we see Ellie glaring at him, picking up her bag, and standing on the seat depositing it on the rack overhead. But just then the bus starts forward with a lurch which unbalances her, and she falls backward right in Peter's lap. Their noses almost touch. Their eyes meet, and they glare at each other hostilely. Ellie quickly scrambles off and gets back in her seat, turning her back on him.

PETER
(amused)
Next time you drop in, bring your folks.

This dissolves to a COUNTRY ROAD, and the bus sways perilously as it speeds through the night, following which the view dissolves to the INTERIOR of the BUS, revealing Peter slumped in his seat, his hat drawn over his eyes. Ellie has her head thrown back, trying to sleep. But the swaying bus causes her head to roll from side to side uncomfortably, and finally she gives up.

ELLIE
(an order)
Tell that man not to drive so fast.
(at which Peter just cocks his head slightly)

PETER
Are you talking to me?

ELLIE
Yes. Tell that man to drive slowly.

Peter stares at her a moment, resenting her officious manner.

PETER
(pleasantly)
Okay.

And much to her surprise, he sighs deeply and relaxes to his former position, shutting his eyes. She glares at him crushingly.

The scene dissolves to another view of the BUS, disclosing the driver, and suddenly the bus comes to a stop.

DRIVER
(sticking his head in to face the passengers)
Rest station! Ten minutes!

The view draws back as some of the passengers rise. The men stretch their legs, and the women straighten out their skirts. A close view of Peter and Ellie then shows her rising. Peter accommodatingly shoves his feet aside for her to pass, and Ellie starts up the aisle. But she suddenly stops; looks back, first at her bag and then at Peter; decides to take her bag with her, and returns to take it. She reaches for it on the rack, Peter watching her, amused.

The scene dissolves to the outside of the REST STATION with several passengers walking briskly back and forth. The place is dimly lit by one or two lamp-posts, and Peter can be seen leaning against one of these posts, smoking a cigarette. The scene moving in, a close view of Peter shows him stealing a glance in the direction of Ellie. And a view, from his angle, reveals Ellie in the shadow of the bus, her bag at her feet. She slowly turns her head toward Peter and then quickly averts it.

PETER (seen close) speculates about her. He glances around the place, and the scene moves about, following his gaze. It takes in the other passengers, all obviously poor and uncultured. The moving view reaches Ellie. The contrast is perceptible. Thereupon, we see Peter reacting with comprehension: No doubt about it! She doesn't belong with these passengers. Then suddenly he sees something which startles him, and we see what it is: Directly in back of her, the young hoodlum passenger slyly lifts her overnight bag from the ground and starts running with it. Ellie is oblivious of his actions. PETER springs forward.

Ellie sees Peter coming toward her and is perceptibly startled. But Peter whizzes by her, and this amazes her even more. She shrugs her shoulders, perplexed, and resumes her smoking. In a few seconds Peter returns, puffing breathlessly.

PETER
He got away. I suddenly found myself in the middle of the brush and not a sign of the skunk.

ELLIE (seen close with PETER) doesn't know what he's talking about. She looks at him, puzzled.

ELLIE
I don't know what you're raving about, young man. And, furthermore, I'm not interested.

PETER
(taken aback)
Well--of all the--well--
(hard)
Maybe you'll be interested to know your bag's gone.

At this, Ellie wheels around and stares at the spot where her bag had been.

ELLIE
Oh, my heavens! It's gone!

PETER
(sarcastically)
Yeah. I knew you'd catch on eventually.

ELLIE
What happened?

PETER
That cadaverous-looking yegg[2] who sat in front of us, just up and took it. Boy, how that baby can run!

ELLIE
What am I going to do now?

PETER
Don't tell me your ticket was in it?

ELLIE
(opening her purse)
No, I've got that, all right. But my money. All I have here is four dollars. I've got to get to New York with it.

PETER
You can wire home for some money when we get to Jacksonville.

ELLIE
Why, no--I--
(catching herself)
Yes ... I guess I will.

PETER
(starting out)
I'll report it to the driver. About your bag, I mean.

ELLIE
(quickly)
No. I'd rather you didn't.

PETER
Don't be a fool. You lost your bag. The company'll make good. What's your name?

ELLIE
I don't want it reported!

PETER
Why, that's ridiculous! They're responsible for everything that--

ELLIE
(hotly)
See here, can you understand English! I don't want it reported!
(she starts away)
Please stay out of my affairs! I want to be left alone.
(with which she disappears from the scene)

A close-up of PETER shows him glaring after her.

PETER
(mumbling)
Why, you ungrateful brat!

The scene dissolves to the BUS, where all the passengers are scattering back to their seats; Peter is already seated, when Ellie arrives. A close view then shows her standing uncertainly for a moment, speculating whether to cross over his legs to get her place by the window. Peter feels her presence by his side and glances up. She tosses her head and plants herself in the seat in front of him, vacated by the young man who stole her bag. Peter takes the affront with a shrug and slides over gratefully to the coveted spot near the window.

The scene dissolves to a close view of Ellie and a recently arrived fat man next to her. She has her head thrown back in an effort to sleep, but the fat man, his hands clasped over his protruding stomach, snores disgustingly, and the rumble of the flying bus accompanies him. Suddenly the bus careens, the fat man falls against Ellie, and she awakens with a start and pushes him back. The fat man's snoring goes on uninterrupted, and Ellie relaxes again; but in a few seconds the procedure is repeated, and Ellie is beside herself. She looks around for somewhere to flee.

PETER, seated in back of her, in his customary slumped position, opens his eyes slightly. It is apparent he has been watching her for some time, for he grins at her discomfiture. Ellie's head turns in his direction and the grin leaves Peter's face. He shuts his eyes and pretends to be asleep. Ellie glances at Peter to make certain he is asleep. The fat man falls against her again and it is all she can stand. She starts to rise. Peter sees her coming and deliberately puts his hand on the seat next to him, still pretending to be asleep. Just as Ellie starts to sit, she notices his hand and is embarrassed. Gingerly she picks up his limp hand and places it on his knee. She then slides into the seat, sighing with relief, whereupon Peter opens his eyes and is amused. Slowly his head turns--and he scrutinizes her, soberly and appraisingly. Ellie slowly turns her head for a glimpse of Peter--and is startled to find him gazing at her. She turns forward, her jaw set forbiddingly.

The scene dissolves to the view of a ROAD. It is dawn, and in the distance, against the horizon, the bus, a mere speck, makes its lone way over the deserted country. This dissolves to a large SIGN, reading "JACKSONVILLE," and then into the BUS affording a close view of ELLIE and PETER. They are both asleep, her head resting comfortably on his shoulder, Peter's topcoat thrown over her. Then the view draws back. The bus is empty except for Ellie and Peter, the last few passengers are just leaving.

PETER's eyes slowly open. He looks down at the head on his shoulder and grins. With a sigh, he shuts his eyes again and resumes his slumber. Next, at the front of the bus, the DRIVER stands staring at Peter and Ellie in this intimate position and his mouth twists knowingly.

DRIVER
(murmuring)
Oh, yeah?

ELLIE stirs, squirms a little uncomfortably and with a sleepy grunt shifts her position. Just as she settles down, her eyes open. She stares out of the window with unseeing eyes, and then closes them dreamily, giving the impression that, still half conscious, she is trying to recall where she is. Apparently she does, for her eyes suddenly snap open and she lifts her head. Finally (in a scene including Peter), Ellie realizes that she has been sleeping on his shoulder, whereupon she straightens up, embarrassed.

ELLIE
Oh, I'm sorry--
(feebly smiling)
Silly, isn't it?

She looks around, and her finding herself alone with Peter adds to her embarrassment.

ELLIE
Everybody's gone.

She lifts her arms to adjust her hat and becomes conscious of his coat over her which slips. She stares at it thoughtfully for a moment--then at Peter.

ELLIE
(realizing that he put it there)
Oh, thank you.
(she hands him his coat; ill at ease)
We're in Jacksonville, aren't we?

PETER
Yes.

ELLIE
(nervously)
That was foolish of me. Why didn't you shove me away?

PETER
I hated to wake you up.
(she glances at him speculatively)
How about some breakfast?

ELLIE
No, thank you.
(she rises, anxious to get away)
Thank you so much.

Most uncomfortably, she edges away from him toward the front of the bus, Peter watching her leave, his interest definitely provoked.

The scene cuts to the STAND as Ellie emerges from the bus. At the foot of the steps is the driver.

ELLIE
How much time have I?

DRIVER
About a half hour.

ELLIE
I'm going over to the Windsor Hotel.

Peter appears in the door of the bus in the background, and a close view then shows him stopping to listen as he sees Ellie talking to the driver.

DRIVER'S VOICE
The Windsor! You'll never make it in time.

ELLIE'S VOICE
You'll have to wait for me.

DRIVER'S VOICE
(aghast)
Wait for you!

A smile flits across Peter's face; then a wider view shows Ellie leaving the driver.

ELLIE
(as she goes)
Yes. I may be a few minutes late

She disappears from sight, leaving the driver staring at her, dumbly; and Peter, standing in back of the driver, shakes his head in amazement.

The scene dissolves to the BUS STAND later that morning--at the same spot where the bus had previously been. It is no longer there, however. A huge crowd fills the space, and the view moving down through the crowd, singles Ellie out. She has just arrived and looks around helplessly. Finally she spots a uniformed terminal guard and approaches him.

ELLIE
(now next to the Guard)
Where's the bus to New York?

GUARD
Left twenty minutes ago.

ELLIE
Why, that's ridiculous! I was on that bus--I told them to wait!

GUARD
Sorry, Miss. It's gone.
(and he turns his back on her)

Ellie's face clouds. The crowds surge about her. She looks around thoughtfully. Suddenly her eyes open in surprise at something she sees, and the view then moves over to Peter, who sits on his suit-case, looking toward Ellie.

PETER
Good morning.

Peter is in the foreground, the guard is seen in the background. Ellie stares at Peter, perplexed.

PETER
Remember me? I'm the fellow you slept on last night.

ELLIE
Seems to me I've already thanked you for that.
(turning to guard)
What time is the next bus to New York?

GUARD
(turning)
Eight o'clock tonight.

ELLIE
Eight o'clock! Why, that's twelve hours!

GUARD
Sorry, Miss.

The Guard leaves the scene, and Ellie's disappointment is apparent.

PETER
(sarcastically)
What's the matter? Wouldn't the old meanies wait for you?
(Ellie glares at him, disdaining to reply--this angers him, and he continues hotly)
Say, how old are you anyway? Don't you know these busses work on a schedule? You need a guardian.

ELLIE
(starting away)
What are you excited about? <u>You</u> missed the bus, too.

Peter looks at her a moment before replying.

PETER
(quietly)
Yeah. I missed it, too.

There is a close view of the two. She turns to him. Her interest is provoked by his tone of voice. She glances up into his face.

ELLIE
Don't tell me you did it on *my* account!
(pause)
I hope you're not getting any idea that what happened last night is--
(she interrupts herself)
You needn't concern yourself about me, young man. I can take care of myself.

PETER
You're doing a pretty sloppy job of it.
(he reaches in his pocket)
Here's your ticket.

ELLIE
(surprised)
My ticket?

PETER
I found it on the seat.

ELLIE
(taking it)
Oh, thank you. Must have fallen out of my pocket.

While she is putting the ticket away in her purse, Peter speaks:

PETER
You'll never get away with it, Miss Andrews.
(this is a shock to Ellie)

ELLIE
(weakly)
What are you talking about?

PETER
Just a spoiled brat of a rich man. You and Westley'll make an ideal team.

ELLIE
(bluffing it through)
Will you please tell me what you're raving about!

PETER
You'll never get away with it, Miss Andrews. Your father'll stop you before you get half way to New York.

ELLIE
You must have me confused with--

PETER
(interrupting)
Quit kidding! It's all over the front pages, You know, I've always been curious about the kind of a girl that would marry King Westley.

He pulls a newspaper out of his pocket and hands it to her. Ellie glances at the headline hurriedly.

PETER
(while she reads)
Take my advice--grab the first bus back to Miami. That guy's a phony.

ELLIE
(looking up at him)
I didn't ask for your advice.
(she hands the paper back)

PETER
That's right. You didn't.

ELLIE
You're not going to notify my father, are you?

PETER
(looking at her squarely)
What for?

ELLIE
If you play your cards right, you might get some money out of it.
(a disdainful expression crosses his face)

PETER
I never thought of that.

ELLIE
(frantically)
Listen, if you'll promise not to do it, I'll pay you. I'll pay you as much as he will. You won't gain anything by giving me away as long as I'm willing to make it worth your while. I've got to get to New York without being stopped. It's terribly important to me. I'd pay now, only the only thing I had when I jumped off the yacht was my wrist watch and I had to pawn that to get these clothes. I'll give you my address and you can get in touch with me the minute you get to New York.

PETER
(furious)
Never mind. You know I had you pegged right from the start, you're the spoiled brat of a rich father. The only way you can get anything is to buy it. Now you're in a jam and all you can think of is your money. It never fails, does it? Ever hear of the word "Humility"? No, you wouldn't. I guess it never occurred to you to just say, "Please mister, I'm in trouble. Will you help me?" No; that'd bring you down off your high horse for a minute. Let me tell you something; maybe it'd take a load off your mind. You don't have to worry about me. I'm not interested in your money or your problems. You, King Westley, your father, you're all a lot of hooey to me.

He turns his back on her and leaves. A close-up of ELLIE shows her staring after him, her eyes blazing angrily.

In a TELEGRAPH OFFICE, Peter addresses a girl operator as he drops a telegram on the counter, which she reads.

PETER
(brusquely)
You send telegrams here?

OPERATOR
(recognizing him apparently, sarcastically)
I'm just fine thanks, and how are you?
(reading)
To "Joe Gordon, care of New York Mail, New York. Am I laughing. The biggest scoop of the year just dropped in my lap. I know where Ellen Andrews is--"
(looking up excitedly)
No, do you really?

PETER
(impatiently)
Go on. Go on send the telegram.

OPERATOR
"How would you like to have the story, you big tub of--of--"

PETER
Mush. Mush.

OPERATOR
"Tub of mush. Well try and get it. What I said about never writing another line for you still goes. Are you burning? Peter Warne." Well, that will be $2.60.

PETER
Send it collect.

OPERATOR
Collect?

Peter
(firmly)
Collect.

As the clerk takes the wire from him, scene fades out.

PART THREE

The BUS TERMINAL fades in. It is night now, and the rain comes down in torrents. People scurry around to get into the buses as the voice of an announcer is heard:

ANNOUNCER'S VOICE
Bus for blah-blah-blah-blah--Charleston--blah-blah-blah--and all points North to New York!

This dissolves to the interior of a BUS, which is practically filled. Peter is in his seat, reading a magazine, while Ellie enters hurriedly from the rear door and starts forward. As she approaches Peter, she hesitates a second, and deliberately passes him, plunking herself into a seat in the opposite aisle. Peter turns just as she gets seated. He glances at her indifferently.

A close view shows Ellie seated next to a man who sits reading a newspaper which covers his face. Her eyes are fixed forward, her lips set adamantly. A close-up of the MAN next to Ellie makes it plain that he is a typical drummer.[3] At the moment he is absorbed in a serial story, but suddenly he becomes aware of something at his feet, and without lowering the newspaper, his gaze slowly shifts downward. At this, the view moves down until it reaches Ellie's trim ankles. Her feet beat a regular tattoo on the floor; her extreme agitation is evident. The view moves back slowly, taking in Ellie's shapely leg as far as the knee. Then we see ELLIE and the DRUMMER as his gaze is still fixed on her leg. Slowly his face breaks into a lascivious grin, he lowers his paper, and turns for a scrutiny of her face. What he sees apparently delights him, for he drops his paper completely--and smiles broadly.

DRUMMER
Hi, sister--All alone? My name's Shapeley.
(Ellie favors him with a devastating look which is wasted on the drummer)
Might as well get acquainted. It's gonna be a long trip--gets tiresome later on. Specially for somebody like you. You look like you got class.
(he surveys her from head to foot)
Yessir! With a capital K.
(he chuckles at his own sally)
And I'm a guy that knows class when he sees it, believe you me.

A close-up of ELLIE, as Shapeley's voice continues, shows her glancing back at Peter, expecting him to come to her rescue.

SHAPELEY'S VOICE
Ask any of the boys. They'll tell you. Shapeley sure knows how to pick 'em. Yessir. Shapeley's the name, and that's the way I like 'em.

Ellie again looks toward Peter. But PETER seems to have found something of unusual interest in his magazine ... and we again see the harassed ELLIE and the irrepressible SHAPELEY, who continues.

SHAPELEY
You made no mistake sitting next to me.
(confidentially)
Just between us, the kinda muggs you meet on a hop like this ain't nothing to write home to the wife about. You gotta be awful careful who you hit up with, is what I always say, and you can't be too particular, neither. Once when I was comin' through North Carolina, I got to gabbin' with a good-lookin' mama. One of those young ones, you know, and plenty classy, too. Kinda struck my fancy. You know how it is. Well, sir, you could'a knocked me over with a Mack truck. I was just warming up when she's yanked offa the bus. Who do you think she was? Huh? Might as well give up. The girl bandit! The one the papers been writin' about.
(he pulls out a cigar, and continues--awed by the recollection)
Yessir, you coulda knocked me over with a Mack truck.
(he lights his cigar, takes a vigorous puff, and turns to her again)
What's the matter, sister? You ain't sayin' much.

ELLIE
(intending to freeze him)
Seems to me you're doing excellently without any assistance.
(this however only brings a guffaw from the drummer)

SHAPELEY
That's pretty good ... Well, shut my big nasty mouth!

A close-up shows ELLIE enduring more of this as Shapeley's voice continues:

SHAPELEY'S VOICE
... Looks like you're one up on me. Nothin' I like better than to meet a high-class mama that can snap 'em back at you. 'Cause the colder they are, the hotter they get, is what I always say.

Now Ellie and Shapeley are seen together, with Peter seen in the background.

SHAPELEY
Take this last town I was in. I run into a dame--not a bad looker, either--but boy, was she an iceberg! Every time I opened my kisser she pulls a ten strike on me. It sure looked like cold turkey for old man Shapeley. I sell office supplies, see? And this hotsy-totsy lays the damper on me quick. She don't need a thing--and if she did she wouldn't buy it from a fresh mugg like me. Well, says I to myself--Shapeley, you better go to work. You're up against a lulu. Well, I'm here to tell you, sister, I opened up a line of fast chatter that had that dame spinnin' like a Russian dancer. Before I got through she bought enough stuff to last the firm a year. And did she put on an act when I blew town!

Ellie has scarcely listened to him, and has divided her attention between glancing back at Peter and staring at Shapeley as if he were insane--none of which bothers Shapeley. He goes on with his merry chatter, blowing rings of smoke in the direction of the ceiling.

SHAPELEY
Yessir. When a cold mama gets hot--boy, how she sizzles! She kinda cramped my style, though. I didn't look at a dame for three towns.
(quickly)
Not that I couldn't. For me it's always a cinch I got a much better chance than the local talent.
(confidentially)
You see, they're kinda leery about the local talent. Too close to home. Know what I mean?

ELLIE has now reached the point where she could, without any compunction, strangle him.

SHAPELEY'S VOICE
(continuing over this glimpse of her desperation)
But take a bird like me--it's here today--and gone tomorrow. And what happens is nobody's business.

At this time she turns helplessly toward Peter, but we see PETER being deliberately oblivious of her presence, following which the three are seen, with Peter in the background.

SHAPELEY
But I don't go in for that kinda stuff--much. I like to pick my fillies. Take you, for instance. You're my type. No kiddin' sister. I could go for you in a big way. "Fun-on-the-side Shapeley" they call me, and the accent is on the fun, believe you me.
(this is all Ellie can stand)

ELLIE
(snappily)
Believe you me, you bore me to distraction.

(but Shapeley merely throws his head back and emits his characteristic guffaw)

SHAPELEY
(laughing)
Well, you're two up on me now.
(he holds up two fingers)

PETER
(approaching them)
Hey, you!

Shapeley's laugh dies down. He looks dumbly up at Peter, his two fingers still held in mid-air.

SHAPELEY
Huh?

PETER
(indicating his own seat)
There's a seat over there for you.

SHAPELEY
What's the idea?

PETER
I'd like to sit with my--uh--wife--if you don't mind.
(at which Shapeley's face falls)

SHAPELEY
(puzzled)
Wife?

PETER
Yeah. Come on--come on!

SHAPELEY
(rising)
Oh, excuse me.
(edging away)
I was just tryin'--you know--to make things pleasant.

And smiling sheepishly, he sidles over to Peter's seat, his two fingers still poised in air. Peter plants himself next to Ellie and totally ignoring her, opens his magazine, and resumes his reading. Then Ellie and Peter are seen close together. She looks up at him.

ELLIE
If you promise not to snap my head off, I'd like to thank you.

PETER
(without turning)
Forget it. I didn't do it for you. His voice got on my nerves.

She feels herself crushed, and ventures no further comment as Peter resumes his interest in his magazine.

A full view of the BUS follows, and there is silence for a while as the bus slows down and comes to a stop. Almost simultaneously a boy makes his appearance, selling magazines and candy.

BOY
Here you are, folks. Candy--popcorn--cigarettes--
magazines--

As Ellie and Peter are seen again, she turns and calls to the boy:

ELLIE
Here, boy!

PETER
(turning to her)
What'd you do? Wire one of your friends for
money?

ELLIE
(rummaging in her purse)
No. It'd be useless. Father'd get the wire before they would.

BOY
(as he enters)
Yes, ma'am?

ELLIE
A box of chocolates, please

PETER
(to the boy)
Never mind, son. She doesn't want it.
(he gestures with his thumb for the boy to leave)

BOY
(puzzled)
But the lady says--

ELLIE
Of course I do. What do you mean--

PETER
(to the boy)
Beat it!
(and the boy, frightened by his voice, leaves)

ELLIE
(resentfully)
You have your nerve!
(she starts to rise)
Here, boy--!

Peter snatches the purse out of her hand and takes the money out.
Ellie stares at him dumbfounded.

PETER
A dollar sixty! ... You had four dollars last
night! How do you expect to get to New York at
the rate you're going?

ELLIE
(vehemently)
That's none of your business.

PETER
(with finality)
You're on a budget from now on.

(he flings her purse back at her and pockets the money)

ELLIE
Now, just a minute--you can't--

PETER
Shut up!

He returns to his magazine, leaving her staring at him petulantly as the scene fades out.

PART FOUR

SOMEWHERE ON THE ROAD at night. This is apparently on the outskirts of a town. Two local policemen and our bus driver stand in the foreground near a police booth. The rain sweeps across their faces as they talk. The passengers in the bus, which stands in the background, stick their heads out, trying to hear what is going on.

FIRST POLICEMAN
You won't be able to pass till morning.

SECOND POLICEMAN
Not even then, if this keeps up.

Peter approaches the group and is then seen with the officers and the driver.

PETER
What's up?

FIRST POLICEMAN
Bridge washed out--around Dawson.

DRIVER
Looks like we can't go through till morning.

SECOND POLICEMAN
(his only contribution)
Not even then, if this keeps up.

FIRST POLICEMAN
Any of your passengers want a place to sleep--there's an auto camp up yonder a piece.

PETER
(interested)
Yeah? Where?

FIRST POLICEMAN
(pointing)
Up yonder. See the lights?

PETER
Yeah.

FIRST POLICEMAN
That's it. Dyke's Auto Camp.

PETER
Thanks.

He dashes toward the bus. Then he appears at the side door of the bus.

PETER
(calling)
Hey, Brat--!
(he is about to enter when he sees Ellie)

The view moves to the rear door of the bus. Ellie stands on the bottom step.

ELLIE
(haughtily)
Are you talking to me!

PETER
Yeah. Come on--we're stopping here for the night.

He disappears inside the bus through the side door. With an independent toss of her head, Ellie turns and also enters the bus, but through the rear door.

The scene dissolves to DYKE'S AUTO CAMP. Ellie stands alone on the porch of a small bungalow, sheltered from the rain. Over her head is a sign reading:

OFFICE--Dyke Auto Co.--P. D. Dyke, Prop.

She looks about her restlessly, giving the impression that she has been waiting for someone. Suddenly she is attracted by something and gazes in its direction. Then, as seen by Ellie in a long view, there appears, about twenty yards away, a small cabin, lighted on the inside; and from it Peter emerges accompanied by a man - presumably Mr. Dyke. We cannot hear what is being said; from their movements, however, it is apparent that an exchange of money is taking place. Dyke waves his hand in departure and starts toward Ellie. At the same time, Peter calls to her:

PETER
(shouting)
Hey! Come on! We're all set.
(saying which he enters the cabin)

Ellie hesitates a moment, then starts toward the cabin. Now she is hurrying across the open space. En route she passes Dyke.

DYKE
(as they pass)
Good evening. Hope you and your husband rest comfortably.

Ellie keeps on running, but suddenly she stops dead and looks back at Dyke, following which a close-up of ELLIE shows her eyes opening wide with astonishment. Her impulse is to call Dyke back, to make him repeat what he said--to make certain she heard him correctly. But Dyke is gone, and she turns and glances thoughtfully in the direction of the cabin. Then slowly the corners of her mouth screw up in an attitude of cynicism. So that's it, is it! He has given her no previous evidence of being "on the make"; yet now, with the first opportunity--. Her thoughts, however, are interrupted by Peter's voice:

PETER'S VOICE
Well, Brat--what do you say!

As she doesn't stir, there appears a close-up view of PETER standing in the doorway of the cabin, looking toward Ellie.

PETER
(impatiently)
Come on! Come on! What are you going to do? Stand there all night?
(he disappears inside)

For a long moment, ELLIE is lost in speculation as to how to proceed. Then, tossing her head defiantly, with her lips set grimly, she starts toward the cabin until she reaches it, stops in the doorway and peers in. As she does this, there is a view of the inside of the CABIN, as seen by her at the door. Except for two cots on either side of the room, a few sticks of cane furniture, a small table upon which stands an oil burner for cooking, the place is barren. At the moment Peter is attaching a clothes line across the center of the room. His suitcase is already open. And now Ellie steps inside, surveying the place contemptuously. But Peter, with his back to her, is oblivious of her presence; and as he works, he hums his favorite melody. Ellie finally breaks the silence.

ELLIE
(sarcastically)
Darn clever, these Armenians.

PETER
(seen close as he turns)
Yeah. Yeah, it's a gift.
(but he finishes his hammering and turns to his suitcase)

ELLIE
(seen with Peter)
I just had the unpleasant sensation of hearing you referred to as my husband.

PETER
(carelessly)
Oh, I forgot to tell you. I registered as Mr. and Mrs.
(the matter-of-fact way in which he says this causes her eyebrows to lift)

ELLIE
Oh, you did? What am I expected to do--leap for joy?

PETER
I kind of half expected you to thank me.

ELLIE
Your ego is colossal.

PETER
(blithely)
Yeah. Yeah, not bad. How's your's?

There is silence for a moment, and Peter proceeds with the unpacking of his suitcase. As she watches him, Ellie's mood changes from one of anger to that of sarcasm.

ELLIE
(appearing in a close-up, her face disdainful)
Compared to you, my friend, Shapeley's an amateur.
(sharply)
Whatever gave you an idea you can get away with this! You're positively the most conceited--

PETER'S VOICE
(interrupting)
Hey, wait a minute!
(appearing beside her)
Let's get something straightened out right now. If you've any peculiar ideas that I'm interested in you, forget it. You're just a headline to me.

ELLIE
(frightened)
A headline? You're not a newspaper man, are you?

PETER
Chalk up one for your side. Now listen, you want to get to King Westley, don't you? All right, I'm here to help you. What I want is your story, exclusive. A day-to-day account. All about your mad flight to happiness. I need that story. Just between you and me I've got to have it.

ELLIE
Now isn't that just too cute? There's a brain behind that face of yours, isn't there? You've got everything nicely figured out, for yourself, including this.

PETER
This? Oh, that's a matter of simple mathematics. These cabins cost two bucks a night and I'm very sorry to inform you, wifey dear, but the family purse won't stand for our having separate establishments.
(he goes back to the business of laying out his things)

ELLIE
(starting to leave)
Well, thank you. Thank you very much, but--you've been very kind.
(but the rain outside causes her to hesitate)

PETER
Oh, yeah? It's all right with me. Go on out in the storm, but I'm going to follow you, see? Yeah. And if you get tough I'll just have to turn you over to your old man right now. Savvy? Now that's my whole plot in a nutshell. A simple story for simple people. Now if you behave yourself, I'll see that you get to King Westley; if not, I'll just have to spill the beans to papa. Now which of these beds do you prefer? This one? All right.

While he speaks he has taken the extra blanket from the cot and hung it over the clothes line. This manages to divide the room in half.

A close view at the door shows Ellie watching him with interest.

ELLIE
(sarcastically)
That, I suppose, makes everything--uh--quite all right.

PETER
(the previous scene returning)
Oh, this?--I like privacy when I retire. I'm very delicate in that respect. Prying eyes annoy me.
(he has the blanket spread out now)
Behold the walls of Jericho![4] Maybe not as thick as the ones that Joshua blew down with his trumpet, but a lot safer. You see, I have no trumpet.
(taking out pajamas)
Now just to show you my heart's in the right place, I'll give you my best pair of pajamas.

He flings them over to her, and she catches them and throws them on her cot. Throughout the scene she hasn't budged from the door, but Peter now prepares to undress.

PETER
Do you mind joining the Israelites?

ELLIE
You're not really serious about this, are you?

PETER
(seen at close range, going about the job of undressing very diffidently)
All right, don't join the Israelites. Perhaps you're interested in how a man undresses.
(and he hangs his coat over the chair)
Funny thing about that. Quite a study in psychology. No two men do it alike.
(now his shirt is coming off)

A close view of ELLIE shows her standing stubbornly.

PETER'S VOICE
I once knew a chap who kept his hat on until he was completely undressed.
(chuckling)
Made a comical picture ...

As the scene includes both of them, Peter spreads his shirt over his coat.

PETER
Years later his secret came out. He wore a toupee.

He lights a cigarette diffidently while she remains brazenly watching him, her eyes flashing defiantly.

PETER
I have an idiosyncrasy all my own. You'll notice my coat came first--then the tie--then the shirt--now, according to Hoyle,[5] the pants should come next. But that's where I'm different.

(he bends over)
I go for the shoes first. After that I--

ELLIE
(unable to stand it any longer)
Smart aleck!

And thoroughly exasperated, she goes behind the blanket, and plops on the cot. She sits on the edge, debating what to do, feeling herself trapped. Her impulse is to leave, if only to show this smart aleck he's not dealing with a child, and she rises impetuously and moves to the window.

A close view at the WINDOW shows her looking out. The downpour has not abated one bit, and the heavy raindrops clatter against the window pane in a sort of challenge to Ellie, whose jaw drops. She turns slowly back to the room, and as she does so her eyes light on the cot. It looks most inviting; after all, she hasn't had any rest for two nights. She falls on the cot again, her shoulders sagging wearily. Following this, the view reveals both sides of the blanket. Peter is already in his pajamas.

PETER
Still with me, Brat?
(there is no answer from Ellie)
Don't be a sucker. A night's rest'll do you a lot of good. Besides, you've got nothing to worry about. The Walls of Jericho will protect you from the big bad wolf.

A close view shows ELLIE glancing over at the blanket. Despite her self, the suggestion of a smile flits across her face.

ELLIE
You haven't got a trumpet by any chance, have you?

PETER gets the idea and smiles broadly.

PETER
Not even a mouth organ.

Pulling the covers back, he prepares to get into bed, humming as he does so.

PETER
(humming to himself)
Who's afraid of the big bad wolf--
The big bad wolf, the big bad wolf.
(louder)
She's afraid of the big bad wolf,
Tra-la-la-la-la--
(he springs into bed)

Ellie smiles, and wearily she pulls her hat off her head. She sits this way a moment, thoughtfully; then, determined, she looks up.

ELLIE
Do you mind putting out the light?

PETER
Not at all.

(he leans over and snaps it off)

The room is thrown into darkness except for a stream of light coming in the window from the night-light outside the camp. Visible are Peter's face and arms as he stares ceilingward, while on Ellie's side all we can see of her is her silhouette, except for such times as she gets in direct line with the window. There are glimpses of her as she moves around in the process of undressing, and we see, or rather sense, her dress dropping to the floor. She now stands in her chemise; this being white silk, it stands out more prominently against the darkness. She picks up the pajamas and backs into a corner, following which a close-up of her head and shoulders shows her glancing apprehensively toward Peter's side of the room; and holding the pajamas in front of her with one hand, with the other she slips the strap off her shoulders. She flings her "slip" over the blanket.

PETER, on his side of the room, looks toward the blanket, and reacts to the "slip" coming into sight. Then other undergarments join the "slip" on the blanket.

PETER
(hoarsely)
Do you mind taking those things off the Walls of Jericho?
(a pause)
It's tough enough as it is.

ELLIE'S VOICE
Oh, excuse me.
(and we see the underthings flipped off the blanket.)

Ellie's side of the room appears, showing her crawling quickly into bed, pulling the covers over her and glancing apprehensively in Peter's direction--following which a close view shows PETER being very conscious of her proximity. The situation is delicate and dangerous; the room is atingle with sex. He turns his gaze toward the blanket. The view moves to the BLANKET, remaining on it a moment. It is a frail barrier. The view then moves back to Peter, whose eyes are still on the blanket, his face expressionless. A close view of ELLIE, next shows that she, too, has her eyes glued on the blanket, a little fearfully. She turns her head and gazes at the ceiling for a moment. Then suddenly her eyes widen--and she sits up abruptly.

ELLIE
(seriously)
Oh, by the way--what's your name?

PETER
(seen close; turning his head toward her)
What's that?

ELLIE
(both sides of the blanket coming into view)
Who are you?

PETER
Who, me? Why, I'm the whippoorwill that cries in the night. I'm the soft morning breeze that caresses your lovely face.

ELLIE
(interrupting)
You've got a name, haven't you?

PETER
Yeah. I got a name. Peter Warne.

ELLIE
Peter Warne? I don't like it.

PETER
Don't let it bother you. You're giving it back to me in the morning.

ELLIE
(flopping back on her pillow as she mumbles)
Pleased to meet you, Mr. Warne ...

PETER
The pleasure is all mine.

There is silence between them for a few seconds.

PETER
I've been thinking about you.

ELLIE'S VOICE
Yes?

PETER
You've had a pretty tough break at that. Twice a Missus and still unkissed.

Ellie doesn't like the implication, and glares in his direction as Peter's voice continues:

PETER'S VOICE
(meaningly)
I'll bet you're in an awful hurry to get back to New York, aren't you?

ELLIE
(hard)
Goodnight, Mr. Warne.
(she turns over)

PETER
Goodnight.

He also turns his head toward the wall, and the scene fades out.

PART FIVE

A long view of the SKY, in the early morning, fades in. In the dim distance there is a speck, which, as it comes nearer, turns out to be an airplane. The drone of its motors becomes louder and louder. Then the view cuts to the CONTROL COCKPIT of the PLANE revealing TWO PILOTS.

FIRST PILOT
(shouting to other)
The old man's screwy!

SECOND PILOT
(who can't hear him)
What's 'at?

FIRST PILOT
(louder)
I said, the old man's screwy!

SECOND PILOT
(nodding his head in agreement)
Yeah!

FIRST PILOT
(cupping his mouth)
The dame's too smart for him.

SECOND PILOT
(nodding again, then leaning over)
How'd you like to be married to a wild cat like that?

The First Pilot grimaces in disgust, grabs his nose between his fingers, and goes through the motion of ducking under water. And as they both laugh, the scene cuts to the CABIN of the plane, a privately built plane which has all the equipment of a passenger ship. Andrews and one of his secretaries, a conservative-appearing man of middle age, lean over a table. This being a closed cabin, the roar of the motors scarcely interferes with the dialogue.

SECRETARY
Here's another wire, sir. This one's from Charleston.
(as there is a close view of the two)
"Checking every northbound train. Also assigned twenty operatives to watch main highways. No success yet. Will continue to do everything possible." Signed: Lovington Detective Agency, Charleston.

ANDREWS
Any others?

SECRETARY
Yessir.
(holding up stack of wires)
There's a report here from every State along the East coast. Want to hear them?

ANDREWS
(impatiently)
What do they say?

SECRETARY
They're practically all the same, sir.
(he shrugs his shoulders to indicate there is no news)

ANDREWS
(muttering)
Amateurs!

SECRETARY
They're the finest detective agency in the country, sir.

Andrews doesn't answer him. He puffs furiously on his cigar, glances out of the window, and turns irritably to a phone by his side. He snaps up the receiver and presses a button, following which the scene cuts to the CONTROL COCKPIT, where a light flashes on the instrument board, and the pilot picks up the receiver.

PILOT
Yes, sir?

ANDREWS
(seen in the cabin)
I thought I made it clear I was in a hurry to get to New York?
(bellowing)
What are we crawling for!

In the control cockpit, the pilot reacts to the complaint and glances at his speed indicator. We then see the SPEED INDICATOR registering 180 miles an hour. The pilot looks aghast.

PILOT
(yelling into phone)
We've got her wide open, sir.

ANDREWS
(irascibly)
Well, step on it! Step on it!

He bangs up the receiver and stares moodily out of the window. It is plain that he is worried. The view then includes his secretary, Henderson.

HENDERSON
I hope she's all right, sir.

ANDREWS
(sharply)
Of course she's all right. What do you think can happen!

HENDERSON
(intimidated)
Nothing, sir!

ANDREWS
Then shut up about it!

Thereupon the view cuts to a close-up of an airplane motor in rapid motion, and this dissolves to the AUTO CAMP CABIN next morning, a close view showing ELLIE peacefully sleeping. But the drone of the plane overhead disturbs her, and she moves restlessly.

ELLIE
(murmuring in her sleep)
Darn planes--

She squirms around uncomfortably, and finding it impossible to resume her slumber, opens her eyes. The sun pouring in through the window causes her to squint. She sits up and stares outside, puzzled. Then remembering where she is she looks toward the other side of the cabin, listening for some sign of life. But there is none and she relaxes. She falls back on the pillow, pulling the covers over her.

Now PETER enters from the outside with an armful of foodstuffs, which he dumps on the table. He looks toward Ellie.

PETER
Hey--you not up yet? Come on--come on!

ELLIE'S VOICE
What time is it?

PETER
Eight o'clock.

He goes to the blanket which hangs between the two cots and throws something over it to Ellie.

PETER
Here--

ELLIE
(catching the package)
What is it?
(opening the package)
Why, it's a toothbrush! Thanks.
(noticing her dress hanging freshly pressed)
You--you had it pressed.

PETER
(getting things ready for breakfast)
Come on! Hurry up! Breakfast'll be ready in no time.

ELLIE
Why, you sweet thing, you. Where'd you get it pressed?
(at this the view moves with him and he goes to the blanket)

PETER
Listen, Brat--I'm going to count to ten. If you're not out of bed by then I'm going to yank you out myself.

A close view of ELLIE shows her being stubborn, but alarmed.

PETER'S VOICE
(counting quickly)
One--two--three--four--five

ELLIE
(panic-stricken)
Why, you bully. I believe you would.

PETER'S VOICE
--six--seven--eight--nine--

ELLIE
(screaming)
I'm out! I'm out!

And she jumps out of bed, throwing the cover around herself, following which Peter is seen going back to the table.

PETER
You'll find the showers--and things--right back of the second cottage.
(at this Ellie sticks her head over the blanket)

ELLIE
(aghast)
Outside!

PETER
Certainly, outside. All the best homes have 'em outside.

ELLIE
I can't go out like this.

PETER
Like what?

ELLIE
Like this. I have no robe.

PETER
Here--take mine.

He flings his robe over to her, and she disappears behind the blanket.

PETER
But make it snappy.

Now Ellie has got into his robe, and appears on his side. The robe is too large for her and she makes a comical figure. As she enters, she tries to maintain her customary dignity.

ELLIE
(dignifiedly)
Where'd you say the showers--and things--were?
(Peter turns; when he sees her he laughs)

PETER
(appraisingly)
Hey--you're little, aren't you?

ELLIE
Where is the shower?

PETER
Your hair's cute like that. You should never comb it.

ELLIE
(leaving haughtily)
I'll find it myself.

She slams the door viciously, but Peter rushes over to the window to watch her; and as viewed by him, Ellie appears next walking to the showers outside the cabin. She holds her head high and struggles valiantly to maintain as much dignity as she can muster under the circumstances. Then in the cabin, at the window, Peter watching Ellie, chuckles at her, shaking his head in amusement. He starts toward the table, and the scene cuts to a moving view outside the cabins, with Ellie walking past several cottages on her way to the showers. Several people stop to stare at her until she reaches her destination. There are two wooden shacks adjoining, each having a sign on them; one reads, "Showers--Men"--the other, "Showers--Women." In front of the women's shower there are several unappetizing-looking fat women waiting, and with them is a small girl. Ellie crosses over to the women's shower and disappears inside, the waiting women staring at her, puzzled. A moment elapses and Ellie backs out, being pushed by a woman, part of whose naked body is visible, and whose voice is heard in protest:

WOMAN
Can't a body have some privacy around here?

The women who are waiting chuckle at Ellie's embarrassment as she stands aside. They certainly are making a monkey out of her decorum. The little girl keeps eyeing Ellie, fascinated.

LITTLE GIRL
(pointing)
Don't she look funny, Mama?

Ellie, wheeling on the little girl, crushes her with a devastating look, so that the little girl cringes against her mother's skirt. Ellie goes to the end of the line to await her turn, following which close-ups show the LITTLE GIRL slowly turning her head to look at Ellie, and ELLIE noticing the little girl staring at her, whereupon Ellie sticks her tongue out at her. And, in a scene which includes both, the little girl retaliates by sticking her tongue out also.

This dissolves to a view of ELLIE coming out of the showers. At the same time Shapeley comes out of the men's shower, and upon seeing Ellie, his face lights up.

SHAPELEY
Hello, sister.

Ellie ignores him, and walks toward her cabin. But Shapeley falls into step with her.

SHAPELEY
Sorry about last night. Didn't know you were married to that guy. Shoulda told me about it right off.
(he chuckles)
There I was, gettin' myself all primed for a killin', and you turn out to be an old married woman.

The scene cuts to the door of PETER'S CABIN as Peter comes out, stands in the doorway, and is surprised to see Ellie and Shapeley, who are then seen (from his angle) talking. Thereupon PETER is seen again as his lip curls up a little jealously; he returns to the cabin, following which we again see Ellie and Shapeley walking. He notices the robe she is wearing, and he looks down toward her feet, the view moving down to show Ellie's legs and feet. The pajama legs are seen protruding below the robe, the cuffs of which she has turned up. Then the view moving back up to Ellie and Shapeley, he lifts her robe playfully.

SHAPELEY
Hey, what's this? Wearing Papa's things? Now that's cute. That's what I call real lovey-dovey. Yessir.

ELLIE
(stopping--her eyes blazing)
If you don't get out of here, I'll slap that fresh mouth of yours.

SHAPELEY
(startled)
Sorry--I didn't mean to--

ELLIE
(sharply)
Get out!

SHAPELEY
Okay. I was just trying to make conversation.

Ellie leaves him abruptly, and the scene cuts to the CABIN, where Peter is now busy setting the small table. Ellie enters after a moment, while Peter has his back to the door.

PETER
(without turning)
High time you got back.

ELLIE
I met some very interesting women at the showers. We got to chatting about this and that. You know how time flies.

She disappears behind the blanket, following which we see Peter's side of the cabin, while Ellie's voice continues from behind the blanket.

ELLIE'S VOICE
We must come back to this place often. You meet the nicest people!

Her head bobs up over the blanket now and again as she dresses.

ELLIE
I saw the little Pussinfoos girl. She's turned out quite a charming creature.

Peter ignores her chatter, except for an annoyed glance once in a while.

ELLIE
Very outspoken, too. Said I looked funny. Wasn't that cute?

PETER
Hurry up and get dressed.

ELLIE
(sticking her head over blanket)
Why, Peter! Don't you want to hear about our lovely friends?

PETER

If you didn't waste so much time on that wise-cracking drummer--we'd have been through with breakfast by this time.

A close view shows ELLIE in the process of buttoning her dress. She looks up, having recognized a tinge of jealousy in his voice, which intrigues her. She starts to the other side of the blanket. Then we see her joining Peter in his part of the cabin.

ELLIE

Well, I hope you're not going to dictate whom I can talk to.

PETER

I know a couple of truck drivers I'd like to have you meet sometime.
(setting a plate for her)
Come on, sit down.

ELLIE

Thank you.
(sitting down to the table; referring to the food)
My, my! Scrambled eggs.

PETER

Egg. One egg--doughnuts--black coffee. That's your ration till lunch. Any complaints?

ELLIE

(cheerily)
Nope. No complaints.

PETER

I'd have gotten you some cream but it meant buying a whole pint.

ELLIE

("sweetly")
Why, you don't have to apologize, Mr. Warne. You'll never know how much I appreciate all this.

PETER

(gruffly)
What makes you so disgustingly cheerful this morning?

ELLIE

Must be the Spring.

PETER

I thought maybe--uh--"believe you me" told you a couple of snappy stories.

ELLIE

He apologized for last night.
(carelessly)
Said he didn't know we were married.

PETER
(passing her a doughnut)
Just shows you how wrong a guy can be. Doughnut?

ELLIE
Thanks.
(embarrassed)
You think this whole business is silly, don't you? I mean running away and everything.

PETER
(easily)
No. No. It's too good a story.

ELLIE
Yes, you do. You think I'm a fool and a spoiled brat. Perhaps I am, although I don't see how I can be. People who are spoiled are accustomed to having their own way. I never have. On the contrary, I've always been told what to do and how to do it and where and with whom. Would you believe it? This is the first time I've ever been alone with a man!

PETER
Yeah?

ELLIE
It's a wonder I'm not panic stricken.

PETER
Um. You're doing all right.

ELLIE
Thanks. Nurses, governesses, chaperones, even body-guards. Oh, it's been a lot of fun.

PETER
One consolation; you can never be lonesome.

ELLIE
It has its moments. It got to be a sort of game to try to outwit father's detectives. I--I did it once; actually went shopping without a body-guard. It was swell. I felt absolutely immoral. But it didn't last long. They caught up with me in a department store. I was so mad I ran out the back way and jumped into the first car I saw. Guess who was in it?

PETER
Santa Claus?

ELLIE
King--King Westley was in it.

PETER
Oh. Is that how you met him?

ELLIE
Um-hm. We rode around all afternoon. Father was frantic. By 6 o'clock he was having all the rivers dragged.
(she has been "dunking" her doughnut throughout this, Peter watching her)

PETER
Say, where did you learn to dunk, in finishing school?

ELLIE
(indignantly)
Aw, now, don't you start telling me I shouldn't dunk.

PETER
Of course you shouldn't. You don't know how to do it. Dunking's an art. Don't let it soak so long. A dip and plop, into your mouth. If you let it soak so long, it'll get soft and fall off. It's all a matter of timing. I ought to write a book about it.

ELLIE
Thanks, professor.

PETER
Just goes to show you. Twenty millions and you don't know how to dunk.

ELLIE
I'd change places with a plumber's daughter any day.

But before he can answer, they are interrupted by voices directly outside their window, and the view moves with Peter as he goes to the door, which he opens slightly. Thereupon Dyke is seen in conversation with two men outside the CABIN.

DYKE
(protesting loudly)
You can't go around bothering my tenants. I tell you, there's no girl by that name here. Besides, how do I know you're detectives?

FIRST DETECTIVE
Show him your credentials, Mac. I'll look around.

At this, Peter closes the door and turns to Ellie.

PETER
Detectives!

ELLIE
(petrified)
That's Father at work. What'll I do?
(appealingly, to him)
Peter, what'll I do?

PETER
Don't look at me. I didn't marry King Westley.

Ellie runs around the room picking up her stuff and murmuring, "Oh, my goodness!" She reaches the window.

ELLIE
(now seen close, at the window)
Maybe I could jump out of the window.
(tremulously)
Do you think they'd see me?

PETER'S VOICE
(suddenly)
Come here, you little fool!

She starts toward him. We then see him plunking her in a chair:

PETER
Sit down!

He rumples her hair and sticks a few hairpins in her mouth. He now stands aside and deliberately talks loud enough to be heard outside.

PETER
(practically shouting)
Yeah. I got a letter from Aunt Betty. She says if we don't stop over at Wilkes-Barre she'll never forgive us.

ELLIE
(a close-up showing her staring at him in bewilderment)
What are you talking about?

At this, Peter rushes over to her and clamps his hand over her mouth.

PETER
(with his hand over her mouth)
The baby is due next month--and they want us to come.

Ellie looks up at him, and realizes what he's doing, she nods to him that it's all right, whereupon he removes his hand from her mouth. And now one of the detectives approaches the FRONT DOOR of the cabin. When he hears Peter's voice, he stops to listen.

PETER'S VOICE
She says she saw your sister Ethel the other day, and she's looking swell.

The detective knocks on the door. At this we again see inside of the cabin as Peter whispers to Ellie to say "Come in."

ELLIE
(calling)
Come in!

The moment she does, Peter rushes behind the hanging blanket. He has his head stuck over it, waiting for the detective to enter, and the moment the door opens Peter ducks. The detective takes a step inside the room.

PETER'S VOICE
(from behind blanket)
I hope Aunt Betty has a boy, don't you? She's always wanted a boy. I think we'll stop over in Wilkes-Barre this trip, darling. Give the family a treat.

A close view shows Ellie and the detective. They have been staring at each other.

ELLIE
(very sweet, calling to Peter)
There's a man here to see you, Sweetheart.

PETER'S VOICE
Who--me?
(appearing from behind the blankets; pleasantly)
Want to see me?

DETECTIVE
(who hasn't taken his eyes off Ellie)
What's your name?

ELLIE
(innocently)
Are you addressing me?

DETECTIVE
Yeah. What's your name?

PETER
(stepping in front of him)
Hey, wait a minute! You're talking to my wife! You can't walk in here and--what do you want, anyway?

DETECTIVE
We're looking for somebody.

PETER
Well, look your head off--but don't come bustin' in here. This isn't a public park.

While Peter has been speaking, the second detective and Dyke have entered. They walk over to Peter, the First Detective, and Ellie.

PETER
I got a good mind to sock you right in the nose.

FIRST DETECTIVE
Take it easy, son. Take it easy.

SECOND DETECTIVE
(crowding forward)
What's up?

The Second Detective's eyes fall on Ellie and he stops to stare at her suspiciously. He takes a photograph out of his pocket which he inspects.

DYKE
(explains)
These men are detectives, Mr. Warne.

PETER
(shouting)
I wouldn't care if they were the whole police department. They can't come in here and start shooting questions at my wife!

ELLIE
(appearing very domestic)
Don't get excited, Peter. They just asked a civil question.

PETER
(turning on her; very sarcastic)
There you go again! How many times did I tell you to stop butting in when I have an argument?

ELLIE
(sharply; entering into the spirit of the pretense)
Well, you don't have to lose your temper!

PETER
(mimicking her)
You don't have to lose your temper!
(in his own voice)
That's what you told me the last time too. Every time I step in to protect you. At the Elk's dance[7] when that big Swede made a pass at you--

ELLIE
He didn't make a pass at me! I told you a million times!

The two detectives and Dyke are seen watching the other two, who are now out of sight.

PETER'S VOICE
(screaming)
Oh, no! I saw him! He kept pawing you all over the dance floor!

ELLIE'S VOICE
He didn't! You were drunk!

PETER
(now seen with Ellie)
Oh, so now I was drunk!

ELLIE
Well, you were!

PETER
I'm sorry I didn't take another sock at him.

ELLIE
Yeah, and gotten yourself arrested!

PETER
Aw, nuts! You're just like your old man! Once a plumber always a plumber! There isn't an ounce of brains in your whole family!

ELLIE
(starting to cry)
Peter Warne, you've gone far enough. I won't stand being insulted like this another minute.

Ellie goes over to her cot, and starts picking up her hat and things, whereupon Dyke, very much affected, turns to the detectives.

DYKE
Now look what you've done!

FIRST DETECTIVE
(apologetically)
Sorry, Mr. Warne. But you see, we're supposed to check up on everybody.

SECOND DETECTIVE
We're looking for a girl by the name of Ellen Andrews. You know--the daughter of the big Wall Street mug.

A close-up of ELLIE appears as their voices are heard.

FIRST DETECTIVE'S VOICE
Your wife sure looks like her. Don't she, Mac?

SECOND DETECTIVE'S VOICE
She sure does.

PETER
(the entire group coming into view)
Well, I hope you find her.
(to Ellie)
Quit bawling! Quit bawling!

The detectives start out, accompanied by Dyke, who is still concerned about the disturbing of his tenants. As they disappear out the door, we hear Dyke's voice:

DYKE'S VOICE
I told you they were a perfectly nice married couple.

Their voices die. Peter stands in the middle of the room watching them go. From her side, where she has been stalling, Ellie peers out of the window until the detectives vanish. She starts toward Peter.Then they appear together, both staring out until the detectives are well out of sight. Finally, Peter closes the door and turns to her.

PETER
(seriously)
It'll be a dirty trick on Aunt Betty if it turns out to be a girl after all.

This brings laughter from them both. But Peter suddenly sobers, and he looks at her thoughtfully.

PETER
Say, you were pretty good. Jumping in like that. Got a brain, haven't you?

ELLIE
You weren't so bad yourself.

PETER
We could start a two-person stock company. If things get tough--we can play some small town auditoriums. We'll call this one "The Great Deception."[8]

ELLIE
Next week "East Lynne."

PETER
After that "The Three Musketeers."
(he strikes a pose)
I'd make a great D'Artagnan.

ELLIE
How about Cinderella--or a real hot love story?

PETER
No mushy stuff. I'm running this troupe.

ELLIE
(fighting)
Oh, you are! Who made you the manager?

PETER
I did! It was my idea, wasn't it?

ELLIE
You always want to run everything.

PETER
If you don't like it, you can resign from the company.

ELLIE
I refuse to resign!

PETER
Then I'll fire you. I'll do all the parts myself.

They are interrupted by the door being flung open. Dyke sticks his head in the door.

DYKE
Your bus leaves in five minutes.

PETER
Holy jumping--! We haven't started to pack yet!

And they both scurry around, throwing things carelessly into Peter's suitcase, as the scene fades out.

PART SIX

GORDON'S OFFICE fades in, and Gordon is at his desk as his secretary enters.

SECRETARY
Here's another wire from Peter Warne.

GORDON
Throw it in the basket.
(as the secretary starts to do so)
What's it say?
(reading)
"Have I got a story! It's getting hotter and hotter. Hope you're the same."

Gordon snatches the wire out of her hand and tears it viciously into bits.

GORDON
Collect?

SECRETARY
Yes.

GORDON
Don't accept any more.

The scene dissolves to ANDREWS' NEW YORK OFFICE--a richly appointed place, awe-inspiring in its dignified furnishings, which shriek of wealth. Andrews paces back and forth in back of his desk. Sitting before him is a man of fifty, with very rugged features. He is Lovington, head of the detective agency bearing his name. When the scene opens, Andrews is holding forth:

ANDREWS
Three days! Three whole days! And what have you accomplished!--
(in a close view at the desk)
All you've shown me is a stack of feeble reports from those comical detectives of yours. I want action, Lovington!

LOVINGTON
We can't do the impossible, Mr. Andrews.

ANDREWS
What I'm asking isn't impossible. My daughter is somewhere between here and Miami. I want her found!

LOVINGTON
I've put extra men on, all along the way.

ANDREWS
It's not enough!
(suddenly)
Are you certain she's not with King Westley?

LOVINGTON
No. He's been trailed twenty-four hours a day since this thing started. He can't even get a phone call we don't know about.

ANDREWS
(who has been pressing several buttons on his desk)
I'm worried, Lovington. After all, something might have happened to her.
(he is interrupted by the entrance of several employees)

ONE OF THEM
Yessir?

ANDREWS
(seeing them)
Oh, Clark--want you to arrange for a radio broadcast--right away--coast to coast hook-up! Offer a reward of ten thousand dollars for any information leading to her whereabouts.

CLARK
(leaving)
Yessir.

ANDREWS
Brown--

BROWN
Yessir?

ANDREWS
Send the story out to the newspapers.
(he rips a picture of Ellie on the desk out of its frame)
Some of the out of town papers may not have a picture of her. Here--wire this to them I want it to break right away.

As he hands the picture to Brown, the view moves in to a close-up of the PICTURE which dissolves to a close-up of the same picture in a newspaper, and as the view draws slowly back we see the headline over it, which reads

"DAUGHTER OF BANKER DISAPPEARS
TEN THOUSAND DOLLARS REWARD"

The view then draws back to reveal SHAPELEY reading the newspaper. He stares long and absorbedly at the picture. Then slowly he turns his head toward the rear of the bus, and the view following his gaze passes a group of men singing "The Man On the Flying Trapeze." They are huddled together, and accompanied by a man who plays a guitar. Then the view continues moving until it reaches Peter and Ellie who join in the song, and a close-up of ELLIE shows her eyes sparkling as she sings gaily.

SHAPELEY looks back at Ellie, and apparently comes to the conclusion that his suspicions are correct, for he quickly folds the newspaper, casting a surreptitious glance around to make certain he is not being watched. A diabolical smirk spreads over his face.

A full view of the interior of the bus shows most of the occupants joining in the fun, singing. They seem unmindful of the discomfiture caused by the rocking of the bus, which throws them against each other. Then the view draws in to a front seat in which sit a woman and a small boy of ten. The woman's face is haggard and she sways uncertainly, her eyes half closed. Her small son's frightened face peers up at her.

BOY
(in a trembling voice)
What'sa matter, Ma? Don't you feel all right?

The woman struggles valiantly to recover her composure. She presses her son's small hand in a feeble effort at assurance.

A close view of Ellie and Peter shows ELLIE singing more boisterously than the rest, doing the comical song with exaggerated gestures. But suddenly her face clouds, at something she sees.

ELLIE
(touching Peter's arm)
Peter!
(as he turns)
There's something the matter with that woman.
She looks ill.

Peter follows her gaze, whereupon we see the WOMAN. Her head rolls weakly, a pained expression on her face.

ELLIE
(again seen with Peter; sympathetically)
I better go over and see her.

PETER
Don't be silly. Nothing you can do. Must be
tough on an old woman--a trip like this.

ELLIE
(worried)
Yes.

We see the other passengers around Ellie and Peter enjoying themselves. One of them pokes her.

MAN
Hey, Galli-Curci,[9] come on--get onto it!
(poking Peter)
You, too, McCormack.

Ellie and Peter snap into it; they are just in time for the long wail which precedes the chorus:

ELLIE AND PETER
(singing)
"O-o-o-oh--He flies through the air with the
greatest of ease--
This daring young man on the flying trapeze--"

At this the scene cuts to the ROAD. The bus is caught in a muddy road, full of ruts, and at the moment wavers dangerously at an angle. The left front wheel is stuck in a deep hole, and the engine roars and clatters as the driver feeds the gas. Finally the bus moves forward, extricating the wheel; but just as it does, the right front wheel falls into another mud hole on the other side, and this time the bus seems hopelessly stuck, a close-up of the RIGHT WHEEL showing it revolving desperately, but in vain. The mud splashes in all directions, and the wheel seems to sink deeper and deeper. Thereupon this view cuts to the inside of the BUS. The bus is tilted over at an extreme angle, which has thrown Ellie into a corner on the floor, where she now crouches in an undignified position. She looks like a turtle, her head being invisible.

ELLIE
(sticking her head out)
Thank the man for me, Peter. This is the first comfortable position I've had all night.

Peter, amused, is assisting her to her feet. The guitarist has continued his playing uninterrupted, and as Peter lifts Ellie, he sings:

PETER
(singing)
"She flies through the air with the greatest of ease.
This darin' young maid on the flying trapeze--
(grunting)
Her movements are graceful--all men does she please--"

A close view of the WOMAN and the LITTLE BOY now shows the latter terrifiedly watching his mother, whose head sags wearily. Finally she topples forward in a swoon.

BOY
(with a moan)
Ma! Ma! What'sa matter with you?
(tears stream down his cheeks)
Somebody help me! Somethin's happened to her!

The music stops abruptly. Everyone looks up, startled. Ellie starts forward, followed by Peter. Passengers closely group around the woman and chatter. "She's fainted. Look how pale she is."

Peter and Ellie step up.

PETER.
Get some water, somebody.
(to the boy)
Let me get in here, son.

Ellie goes out of sight to get water. The boy cries audibly, terror-stricken, but gets out of Peter's way, and Peter lifts the woman up and stretches her across the seat. Ellie comes back with water which she silently hands to Peter, who administers to the woman and when she slowly opens her eyes, makes her drink the water. The woman looks around, bewildered.

PETER
(consolingly)
That's better. You're all right now. Just took a little nose-dive, that's all.

He assists her in sitting up. The boy's wailing is heard, and he now rushes over and throws his arms around his mother.

BOY
(crying)
Ma--oh, gee, Ma--!

His mother clings to him, but still feeling faint, her head sways. Peter looks up at Ellie and gives her a sign to sit down beside the woman. ELLIE sits down beside her. Peter takes the boy by the shoulders.

PETER
Come on, son. Better give your mother a chance to snap out of it.
(as the boy emits a heart-breaking sob)
It's all right, son. She'll be okay in a couple of minutes.

He leads the boy away, while Ellie places her arm around the woman.

ELLIE
You'd better rest. It's been a hard trip, hasn't it?

The scene cuts to a close view of SHAPELEY who has his eye peeled on Peter, watching him, and we next see Peter and the boy, who is still sobbing quietly. They are now standing away from the other passengers.

BOY
We ain't ate nothin' since yestidday.

PETER
What happened to your money?

BOY
Ma spent it all for the tickets. She didn't know it was gonna be so much.
(with a new outburst)
We shouldn'a come, I guess, but Ma said there's a job waitin' for her in New York--and if we didn't go, she might lose it.

PETER
Going without food is bad business, son. Why didn't you ask somebody?

BOY
I was gonna do it, but Ma wouldn't let me. She was ashamed, I guess.

Peter reaches into his pocket for a bill, just as Ellie approaches them.

ELLIE
She'll be all right, soon's she gets something to eat.

Peter has extracted a single bill and dips in his pocket for a smaller one. Before he can find anything, however, Ellie takes the one he has in his hand and gives it to the boy.

ELLIE
Here, boy--first town we come to, buy some food.

(Peter glances at the empty hand and then at Ellie)

BOY
I shouldn't oughta take this. Ma'll be angry.

ELLIE
(confidentially)
Just don't tell her anything about it. You don't want her to get sick again, do you?

BOY
(a sob in his voice)
No-o. But I shouldn't oughta take the money.
(to Peter)
You might need it.

PETER
Me? Forget it, son.
(rumples his hair--smiling)
I got millions.

BOY
(also smiling)
Thanks.

ELLIE
(her arm around the boy)
Come on. Let's go back to your mother.

She leaves with the boy, Peter watching her a moment, impressed by her display of humanness, before turning and leaving the scene, following which a close-up shot of SHAPELEY watching Peter, then also rising and starting out.

On the ROAD, the driver is now standing in front of the mud-hole, staring at the sunken wheel dolefully, as several people stray into the scene.

DRIVER
That storm sure made a mess outa these roads.

PETER
(appearing, and seeing the trouble)
Holy Smokes! You'll never get out yourself! Better phone for some help.

DRIVER
Phone for help?
(unhappily)
We're right in the middle of nowhere. There isn't a town within ten miles of here.

Shapeley is just entering the outskirts of the group. He stops, looks in the direction of Peter speculatively. He has the newspaper stuck in his pocket, which he caresses tenderly. The scene expanding, Peter is then seen leaving the group.

SHAPELEY
(as Peter approaches)
What's up?

PETER
Looks like we're going to be stuck for a long time.
(he starts away)

SHAPELEY
(calling to him)
Say, Buddy—

Peter turns, and looks at him quizzically, and the two are then seen close together.

SHAPELEY
Like to have a look at my paper?

He has taken it out and has it opened as he hands it to Peter. The headlines concerning Ellie and her picture shriek out at Peter. This startles him for a moment, but he manages to recover his poise.

SHAPELEY
Travelin' like this, you kinda lose track of what's goin' on in the world.

PETER
(guardedly)
Thanks.
(he glances from the newspaper to Shapeley, wondering how much he suspects)

SHAPELEY
If you wanna get anywhere nowadays, you gotta keep in touch with all the news, is what I always say.

PETER
(eyeing him expectantly)
That's right.

SHAPELEY
(pointing to paper)
Take that story there, for instance. Be kinda sweet if we could collect that ten thousand smackers.

PETER
(non-committally)
Yeah--wouldn't it?

SHAPELEY
It's a lotta dough. If I was to run across that dame, you know what I'd do?

PETER
What?

SHAPELEY
I'd go fifty-fifty with you.

PETER
Why?

SHAPELEY
Cause I'm a guy that don't believe in hoggin' it, see? A bird that figures that way winds up behind the eight ball,[10] is what I always say.

PETER
What's on your mind?

SHAPELEY
(hard)
Five G's--or I crab the works.

PETER
You're a pretty shrewd baby.
(looking around)
We better get away from this gang. Talk this thing over privately.

And the view moves with them as Peter leads the way toward a clump of bushes off the side of the road, Shapeley following. They are concealed from the rest of the passengers.

PETER
Lucky thing, my running into you. Just the man I need.

SHAPELEY
(smiling broadly)
You're not making any mistake, believe you me.

PETER
I can use a smart guy like you.

SHAPELEY
(expansively)
Say listen, when you're talkin' to old man Shapeley, you're talking to--

PETER
(suddenly)
Do you pack a gat?[11]

A close view of the TWO shows the smile dying on Shapeley's face. He looks up quickly.

SHAPELEY
Huh?

PETER
A gat! A gat!
(feeling him)
Got any fireworks on you?

SHAPELEY
(weakly)
Why--no--

PETER
(carelessly)
That's all right. I got a couple of machine guns in my suitcase. I'll let you have one of them.

(Shapeley is beginning to realize he is in for something he hadn't bargained for, and stares speechlessly at Peter, who continues blandly)
Expect a little trouble up North. May have to shoot it out with cops.

The perspiration starts appearing on Shapeley's brow (as we see him in a close-up). Peter's voice continues:

PETER'S VOICE
(with emphasis)
If you come through all right, your five G's are in the bag. Maybe more. I'll talk to the "Killer"--see that he takes care of you.

SHAPELEY
(finally finding his voice)
The Killer?

PETER
(seen with Shapeley; watching the latter to gauge the effect of his words)
Yeah--the "big boy"--the Boss of the outfit.

SHAPELEY
(shakily)
You're not kidnapping her, are you?

PETER
(tough)
What else, stupid! You don't think we're after that penny-ante reward, do you?
(contemptuously)
Ten thousand bucks? Chicken feed! We're holding her for a million smackers.

SHAPELEY
(stammering)
Say, look! I didn't know it was anything like this, see--and--

PETER
What's the matter with you! Gettin' yellow?

SHAPELEY
(raising his voice, pleadingly)
But I'm a married man. I got a couple of kids. I can't get mixed up with--

PETER
(gripping his arm)
Sh-sh-sh--! Soft pedal, you mug!--before I--
What're you trying to do? Tell the whole world about it!
(low and menacingly)
Now listen, you're in this thing--and you're <u>staying</u> in! Get me? You know too much.

SHAPELEY
(frightened out of his wits)
I won't say anything. Honest, I won't.

PETER
Yeah?--How do I know?
(he reaches into his coat threateningly)
I gotta good mind to plug you.
(arguing with himself)
I shouldn't take any chances on you.

SHAPELEY
(breaking down)
You can trust me, Mister. I'll keep my mouth shut.

PETER.
Yeah?
(he glares at Shapeley a moment silently, as if making up his mind)
What's your name?

SHAPELEY
Oscar Shapeley.

PETER
Where do you live?

SHAPELEY
Orange, New Jersey.

PETER
Got a couple of kids, huh?

SHAPELEY
Yeah. Just babies.

PETER
You love them, don't you?

SHAPELEY
(sensing the threat; horrified)
Oh, gee, Mister--you wouldn't--you ain't thinkin' about--

PETER
(threateningly)
You'll keep your trap shut, all right.

SHAPELEY
(quickly)
Sure--sure--I'll keep my trap shut. you can depend on me, Mister.

PETER
If you don't--Ever hear of Bugs Dooley?

SHAPELEY
No.

PETER
Nice guy. Just like you. But he made a big mistake, one day. Got kind of talkative. Know what happened? His kid was found in the bottom of the

river. A rock tied around its neck. Poor Bugs! He couldn't take it. Blew his brains out.

(Shapeley can't stand much more of this. He is ready to keel over)

SHAPELEY

Gee! That musta been terrible.

(righteously)

I guess he had it coming to him though. But don't you worry about me. I don't talk. I never talk. Take my word for it. Gee, I wouldn't want anything to happen to my kids.

PETER

Okay. Just remember that. Now beat it.

SHAPELEY

(grabbing Peter's hand and shaking it gratefully)

Oh, thanks, thanks, Mister. I always knew you guys were kind-hearted.

PETER

(putting his hand away)

Come on, scram! And stay away from that bus.

SHAPELEY

Sure. Anything you say.

As he says this, he backs away from Peter, following which a close-up of PETER shows a twinkle in his eye and then, as seen by Peter, Shapeley appears walking hurriedly away. When he thinks the distance is safe he starts running. He slips and falls in the mud, picks himself up, and continues his race for life.

The scene dissolves to the ROAD, at night, with Ellie and Peter walking along. It is apparent they have been trudging like this for a long time.

ELLIE

Poor old Shapeley. You shouldn't have frightened him like that.

PETER

At the rate he started, he's probably passed two state lines by this time. The exercise is good for him.

ELLIE

Yes, I noticed he was getting a little fat lately.

(she grabs her side)

Ouch!

PETER

What's the matter?

ELLIE

(grimacing)

I was never built for these moonlight strolls.

(protesting)

Why did <u>we</u> have to leave the bus?

PETER
I don't trust that chatterbox.

The scene dissolves to the banks of a narrow STREAM at night. Peter is bending over, removing his shoes, and we see the two closer as they talk.

PETER
First town we hit in the morning, you better wire your father.

ELLIE
Not as long as I'm alive.

PETER
Okay with me, if you can stand the starvation diet.

ELLIE
What do you mean--starvation?

PETER
It takes money to buy food.

ELLIE
Why, haven't you--?

PETER
(interrupting)
Not a sou. I had some before the fainting scene.

ELLIE
You didn't give that boy all your money?

PETER
I didn't give him anything. You were the big-hearted gal. How about wiring your father now?

ELLIE
Never! I'll get to New York if I have to starve all the way.

PETER
(rising -uttering a deep sigh)
Must be some strange power Westley has over you women.
(he now has his shoes off and ties them to each other)
How do you expect to get there?

ELLIE
To New York?

PETER
Yeah.

ELLIE
I'm following you.

PETER
Aren't you afraid of me?

ELLIE
(confidently)
No.

PETER
(looking at her)
Okay. Hang on to these.

As he bends down in front of Ellie, he gets a firm grip around her legs and throws her over his shoulder like a sack. She squeals, terrified, but Peter ignores this; and with his right hand, which is free, he lifts the suitcase and starts walking across the stream. Ellie's first fright is gone and she now rather enjoys the sensation of being carried by Peter. She lets herself go completely limp, still clinging to his shoes, which she carries by the string. As they walk, the dangling shoes keep hitting Peter's backside.

PETER
I wish you'd stop being playful.

ELLIE
(thereupon holding the shoes out at a safe distance)
Sorry.
(Peter takes several more laborious steps before either of them speaks)

ELLIE
It's the first time I've ridden "piggy-back" in years.

PETER
This isn't "piggy-back."

ELLIE
Of course it is.

PETER
You're crazy.

ELLIE
(after a silence for several seconds)
I remember distinctly Father taking me for a "piggy-back" ride--

PETER
And he carried you like this, I suppose.

ELLIE
Yes.

PETER
(with finality)
Your father didn't know beans about "piggy-back" riding.

ELLIE
(another silence before she speaks again)
My uncle--Mother's brother--had four children ... and I've seen <u>them</u> ride "piggy-back."

PETER
I don't think there's a "piggy-back" rider in your whole family. I never knew a rich man yet who was a good "piggy-back" rider.

ELLIE
That's silly.

PETER
To be a "piggy-backer" it takes complete relaxation--a warm heart--and a loving nature.

ELLIE
And rich people have none of those qualifications, I suppose.

PETER
Not a one.

ELLIE
You're prejudiced.

PETER
Show me a good "piggy-back" rider and I'll show you somebody that's human. Take Abraham Lincoln, for instance--a natural "piggy-backer."
(contemptuously)
Where do you get off with your stuffed-shirt family?
(turning)
Why, your father knew so much about "piggy-back" riding that he--

In his excitement he wheels around to speak to her, forgetting that as he turns she goes with him. Not finding her at his right, he swings around to his left. Naturally he takes Ellie with him--and realizing his mistake he mutters:

PETER
Aw, nuts!

He proceeds on his way, walking faster than before. They continue this way silently for some time. Finally Ellie breaks the silence.

ELLIE
(persistently)
My father was a <u>great</u> "piggy-backer."

Peter raises his eyes heavenward in thorough disgust, then calmly hands his suitcase to her.

PETER
Hold this a minute.

Ellie takes the suitcase from him, and his hand now free, he delivers a resounding smack on her backside, so that Ellie lets out a yelp.

PETER
(taking the suitcase)
Thank you.

The scene dissolves to the edge of a cow PASTURE, at night, and Ellie and Peter are revealed climbing under a barbed wire fence, following which the scene dissolves to a HAYSTACK, in front. Peter sets his bag down and surveys the layout, Ellie watching him.

PETER
(to himself)
This looks like the best spot.

ELLIE
We're not going to sleep out here, are we?

PETER
I don't know about you, but I'm going to give a fairly good imitation of it.

And he busies himself laying out a bed for her, pulling hay from the stack and spreading it out on the ground. Ellie wanders aimlessly and then moves to a rock, where she sits and watches Peter.

ELLIE
(after a pause; coyly)
Peter--

PETER
(as a close view shows him still arranging her bed; grumbling)
What?

ELLIE'S VOICE
I'm hungry.

PETER
(without looking up)
Just your imagination.

ELLIE
(seen at the rock, while Peter is out of sight)
No, it isn't. I'm hungry and--and scared.

PETER'S VOICE
You can't be hungry and scared at the same time.

ELLIE
(insisting)
Well, I am.

PETER
(as both he and Ellie are seen in their respective places)
If you're scared it scares the hunger out of you.

ELLIE
(argumentatively)
Not if you're more hungry than scared.

PETER
(impatiently)
All right. You win. Let's forget it.

ELLIE
(after a pause)
I can't forget it. I'm still hungry.

PETER
(tearing his hair; screaming)
Holy Smokes! Why did I ever get mixed up with you!

This brings silence, and he goes on building a bed for her. Then a close-up of Ellie shows her watching him. Her eyes soften. A very definite interest in him is slowly but surely blossoming, and the fact that he is making her bed adds to the intimacy of the scene. A close view of PETER shows him concentrating on his task, but he pauses a moment and turns to glance at her. It is a devouring look, which he quickly dispels by working more feverishly on her bed.

PETER
(muttering while he works)
If I had any sense, I'd have been in New York by this time.
(he emphasizes his feelings by yanking viciously at the hay as both of them are now seen)
Taking a married woman back to her husband. Humh! What a prize sucker I turned out to be.
(He has her bed ready; without glancing at her)
Come on--your bed's all ready.

She watches him a moment, then rising slowly, starts toward Peter. Then she stands over her bed, surveying it speculatively.

ELLIE
I'll get my clothes all wrinkled.

PETER
(sharply)
Well, take them off.

ELLIE
(shocked)
What!

PETER
(shouting)
All right! Don't take them off. Do whatever you please. But shut up about it.

She flashes him a petulant, offended glance but it is lost on Peter, who has his back to her, and meticulously, she slips to her knees and proceeds to stretch out on the hay. The hay bed is bumpy and hard and she has quite a difficult time getting comfortable; her efforts to do so are accompanied by painful sighs. A close view shows PETER stopping to watch her, and his look is sympathetic and solicitous. Then while Ellie groans and sighs and pounds the hay with her palm, Peter steps out of sight. Ellie is unaware of his departure, so busily occupied is she with her makeshift bedding. She squirms around unhappily and finally stretches out, deciding to make the best of it. She lies on her back, her hands clasped under her head, looking up at the stars.

ELLIE
(seen close, as she is lying back on hay bed)
You're becoming terribly disagreeable lately. Snap my head off every time I open my mouth.

(she waits for a reply, but receives none)
If being with me is so distasteful to you, you can leave.
(independently)
You can leave any time you see fit. Nobody's keeping you her.
(martyr-like)
I can get along.

She waits a second and then turns to see what effect this has on him. The fact that Peter is gone doesn't quite register at first. She looks around calmly, then is puzzled, and finally she becomes panicky. She sits up with a start.

ELLIE
(murmuring, frightened)
Peter--
(there is a pause while she listens, but nothing stirs, and there is more apprehension in her voice)
Peter!

Real terror comes into her face, and she is ready to cry. She gets to her feet.

ELLIE
(with a terrified outcry)
Peter!!

At this he comes running into the scene; under his arm he has a watermelon.

PETER
What's the matter?

ELLIE
(relieved)
Oh, Peter--
(she throws her arms around his neck and sobs freely)

PETER
(hoarsely)
What's got into you?

ELLIE
(clinging to him)
Oh, Peter! I was so scared.

With his free hand he removes her arm from around his neck and starts away.

PETER
(setting the watermelon down)
I wasn't gone more than a minute. Just went out to find you something to eat.

ELLIE
(a sob still in her voice)
I know--but--

PETER
(kicking the melon over to her)
Here. Eat your head off.

ELLIE
I don't want it now.

PETER
(vehemently)
Thought you were hungry!

ELLIE
I was--but--

PETER
But what!

ELLIE
I was so scared--that it scared--

PETER
(exasperatedly)
Holy Jumping Catfish! You can drive a guy crazy.

He kicks the melon viciously out of sight, and without any particular preparation or fuss, he flops down on his bed, following which Ellie goes to her bed and lies down, too. Then a close view of ELLIE appears, and at the moment she looks far removed from the spoiled, pampered, self-reliant brat of Alexander Andrews. Instead, she is a helpless baby, clinging to Peter's protective wing. She'd be ever so grateful right now for a little civility on his part, for a little tenderness and understanding, and she glances over at him, hopefully. PETER, however, stares up at the stars, dreamily; and we then see ELLIE turning away from him, disappointed. Still, the minute Ellie turns her head, Peter looks at her out of the corner of his eye, and it's a long and steady gaze. Then suddenly he gets an idea and rises. He finds his topcoat and goes to her.

PETER
Might get chilly later on.
(he spreads it over her)
Better use this.

As he bends down to tuck her in, their faces are seen in close proximity. Ellie, tremulous and fearful, has her eyes peeled on him. The situation is imminent with danger; anything is likely to happen at this moment; and she is frightened and expectant--she knows how weak she would be, if he suddenly crushed her in his arms. Peter avoids her gaze. He, too, is a bit shaky. The temptation is there and his resistance is waning. He tucks her in and quickly turns away. Ellie's eyes, however, never leave him. Immediate danger has vanished, and it leaves her a little regretful.

A close view of PETER, as he walks over to a rock and sits down, shows him nervously taking out a cigarette and lighting it.

PETER
You've had a lot of men crazy about you, haven't you?

ELLIE doesn't respond. She has the scrutinizing, speculative look of a girl who feels herself falling in love with someone who is practically a stranger to her, as a result of which she is frightened. Then a wider view includes both of them and we see that Peter, too, fights valiantly against a mounting interest in this girl, who epitomizes everything he dislikes. He creates the impression in the following scene that in his analysis of her he is trying to dissuade himself from something he is bound to regret. His attack on her, consequently, is overly vicious.

PETER

I guess you've pretty much had your own way with them. That's your trouble mostly. You've <u>always</u> had your own way. That's why you're such a mess now.

He pauses a second, waiting for a protest, but Ellie offers none; she is too much absorbed in her own confusing emotions. A close view then shows PETER taking a long puff on his cigarette and exhaling the smoke, watching it vanish before he speaks.

PETER

(suddenly)

You know what generally happens to people like you? You get your values all mixed up. You attach all the importance to the wrong things. Right now, for instance, there's only one thought in your mind--to get back to King Westley.

He waits for a reaction, but a close view shows ELLIE absorbed, and she remains silent. Peter's voice continues.

PETER'S VOICE

Comical part of it is, it isn't what you want at all. In a couple of weeks you'll be looking for the nearest exit ...

(now seen with her)

People like you spend all your life on a merry-go-round. I guess that's what makes you so dizzy.

(he rises and paces a few moments)

You're always chasing after something. At least you think you are. Truth is, you're just running away.

(emphatically)

From yourself, mostly. 'Cause you're miserable. You hate yourself. The world's full of people like you. Don't know what they want.

ELLIE

Do you know?

PETER

Sure.

ELLIE

What?

PETER

(flatly)

Nothing.

(after a pause)

Nothing you'd give two cents for.

ELLIE
(seen close)
Try me.

PETER'S VOICE
I just want to be let alone, that's all. Life's swell if you don't try too hard. Most people want to get a strangle-hold on it. They're not living. They're just feverish.
(now appearing with her)
If they didn't get themselves all balled up with a lot of manufactured values, they'd find what they want. Peace and calm. When you get right down to it, what's all the shootin' for, will you tell me? After all, you can only eat three meals a day, only sleep in one bed--
(looking up)
Right now, that hay feels pretty good to you, doesn't it? Sure it does. 'Cause you were tired--and it's the only thing around.

ELLIE
You sound like a hobo.

PETER
I am. I only work when I have to. Two years ago I got a notion and went to China. There was a war going on. Swell! After a while it got stale. I went down to Tahiti. Just lay on the beach for six months. What could be sweeter?

ELLIE
Doesn't sound very exciting.

PETER, seen close, looks at her for a long time before speaking:

PETER
I guess not. I'd have given odds it wouldn't mean anything to you.
(he goes over and flops down on his own side of hay)
There were moments when I had hopes. When I--aw, I'm wasting time. You're destined to be a dope the rest of your life.
(contemptuously)
I pity you. Goodnight.

He turns over with a finality that precludes any further discussion, following which a close-up of ELLIE reveals that her eyes are wide open, staring thoughtfully up at the sky. The scene fades out slowly.

PART SEVEN

A ROAD fades in. It is day now, and Peter and Ellie are trundling along. Ellie limps, and wears an unhappy expression on her face.

ELLIE
What are you thinking about?

PETER
By a strange coincidence, I was thinking of you.

ELLIE
(pleased)
Really?

PETER
Yeah. I was just wondering what makes dames like you so dizzy.

ELLIE
What'd you say we're supposed to be doing?

PETER
Hitch-hiking.

ELLIE
Well, you've given me a very good example of the hiking--
(strongly)
where does the hitching come in?

PETER
(amused at her)
A little early yet. No cars out yet.

She spies a rock and heads for it. Then we see her seated on the rock.

ELLIE
If it's just the same to you, we'll sit right here till they come.
(Peter comes over, sets his bag down, and prepares to wait)
Got a toothpick?

PETER
No. But I've got a penknife.
(he extracts one from his pocket which he snaps open)

ELLIE
Hay--in my teeth.

She points to her front teeth, and Peter flicks the hay out of her teeth.

PETER
There it is. Better swallow it. We're not going to have any breakfast.

ELLIE
Needn't rub it in.
(Peter takes a carrot out of his coat pocket and starts nibbling on it; Ellie looks up at this)
What're <u>you</u> eating?

PETER
Carrots.

ELLIE
Raw?

PETER
Uh-huh. Want one?

ELLIE
(emphatically)
No!!
(as Peter smacks his lips with satisfaction)
It's a wonder you couldn't get me something _I_ can eat.

PETER
You don't think I'm going around panhandling for you.
(he takes a bite)
Best thing in the world for you--carrots. Had a tough time getting them. If that farmer ever caught me--goodnight!

ELLIE
I hate the horrid stuff.

While she speaks a car roars by at terrific speed. Peter and Ellie both jump up.

PETER
I wish you wouldn't talk too much. We let a car get away.
(Ellie goes back to her rock, despondently)

ELLIE
What if nobody stops for us?

PETER
Oh, they'll stop, all right. It's a matter of knowing how to hail them.

ELLIE
You're an expert, I suppose.

PETER
Expert! Going to write a book on it. Called the "Hitch-Hikers Hail."

ELLIE
There's no end to your accomplishments.

PETER
You think it's simple, huh?

ELLIE
(exaggeratedly)
Oh, no!

PETER
Well, it _is_ simple. It's all in the thumb, see? A lot of people do it--
(waving)
like this.
(he shakes his head sadly)
But they're all wrong. Never get anywhere.

ELLIE
Tch! Tch! I'm sorry for the poor things.

PETER
But the thumb always works. Different ways to do it, though. Depends on how you feel. For instance, number one is a short, jerky movement--
(he demonstrates)
That shows independence. You don't care if they stop or not. 'Cause you got some money in your pocket, see?

ELLIE
Clever.

PETER
Number two is a wider movement--a smile goes with that one--like this.
(he demonstrates)
That means you got a couple of brand new stories about the farmer's daughter.[12]

ELLIE
You figured that all out yourself, huh?

PETER
Oh, that's nothing. Now take number three, for instance. That's a pip. It's the pathetic one. When you're broke--and hungry--and everything looks black. It's a long movement like this--
(demonstrating)
--with a follow through.

ELLIE
Amazing.

PETER
Hm? Yeah, but it's no good if you haven't got a long face with it.

In the distance a car is heard approaching, and Ellie looks up quickly.

ELLIE
(excitedly)
Here comes a car!

PETER
(alert)
Now watch me. I'm going to use Number One. Keep your eye on that thumb, baby, and see what happens.

Peter steps forward into the road and does his thumb movement. The car approaches, but speeds right by, spreading a cloud of dust in Peter's face, leaving him staring at the departing car, nonplussed. Thereupon ELLIE (seen close) glances up at him, a satirical expression on her face.

ELLIE
(sarcastically)
I'm still watching your thumb.

Peter is still looking after the car.

PETER
Something must have gone wrong. I guess I'll try number two.

ELLIE
When you get up to a hundred, wake me up.

Another car is heard coming, and Peter steps forward, prepared to hail it. Then this dissolves to a long view of the ROAD as a stream of cars of every description speeds forward ("toward the camera") and vanishes. The view moving in to the side of the road, Peter is seen still in the same spot. He waves his arms, jerks his thumb, indulges in all sorts of gyrations, while Ellie remains slumped on her rock, completely worn out.

Now Ellie watches Peter out of the corner of her eye, her face expressionless. Peter continues his arm waving--but slows down like a mechanical toy which has run out. He finally gets down to just thumbing his nose at the passing vehicles; and then thoroughly wearied, he flops down on a rock near Ellie.

PETER
I guess maybe I won't write that book after all.

ELLIE
Yes. But look at all the fun you had.
(as he glares at her)
Mind if I try?

PETER
(contemptuously)
You! Don't make me laugh.

ELLIE
You're such a smart aleck! Nobody can do anything but you. I'll show you how to stop a car--and I won't use my thumb.

The scene widens as she rises and steps forward.

PETER
What're you going to do?

ELLIE
Mind your own business.

She lifts her skirt to above her knees and pretends to be fixing her garter. Her very attractive leg is in full display. Almost instantly, we hear the screaming and grinding of quickly applied brakes, and Peter looks up astonished.

The scene wiping off, we then get a closer view of Ellie and Peter sitting in the back of an open Ford. It is a broken-down, rickety affair of the 1920 vintage. Ellie grins victoriously up at Peter, who stares ahead of him, glumly.

ELLIE
You might give me a little credit.

PETER
What for?

ELLIE
I proved once and for all that the limb is mightier than the thumb.

PETER
Why didn't you take all your clothes off? You could have stopped forty cars.

ELLIE
We don't need forty cars.

Peter glares at her, and Ellie's eyes twinkle mischievously, following which we get a wider view which includes the driver of the car, Danker. He is a man of about thirty, a heavy set, loose chinned person; at the moment he is singing an aria from some opera. He suddenly stops, turning to Ellie and Peter in the back seat.

DANKER
So you've just been married, huh? Well, that's pretty good. If I was young, that's just the way I'd spend my honeymoon--hitch-hiking. Y-e-s s-i-r!

And for no reason except that he cued himself into it, he bursts forth into song gustily.

DANKER
(singing)
"Hiking down the highway of love on a honeymoon.
Hitch-hiking down--
Down-down-down the highway
Down--."

Ellie and Peter in the back of the car react to the noise Danker makes.

PETER
Hey, hey, aren't you afraid you'll burn out a tonsil?

DANKER
Tonsil? Me? No! Me burn a tonsil?
(singing)
"My tonsils won't burn--
As life's corners I ...

PETER
(giving up)
All right, let it go.

DANKER
(completing his last line)
... turn."

The scene dissolves to the front of a LUNCH WAGON on a deserted road, and Danker's car drives into the scene and stops. Then we see Danker turning to Ellie and Peter.

DANKER
How about a bite to eat?

ELLIE
(quickly)
Why, I think that would be--

PETER
(stopping her)
No, thanks. We're not hungry.

DANKER
(sentimentally)
Oh, I see, young people in love are never hungry.

PETER
No.

DANKER
(singing as he leaves them)
"Young people in love
Are very seldom hungry.
People in love
Are very seldom hungry ... "

When he is out of sight, Peter glares at Ellie.

PETER
What were you going to do? Gold dig him for a meal?[13]

ELLIE
(defiantly)
Why not? I'm hungry.

PETER
Eat a carrot.

ELLIE
Never!
(she starts out of car)
I'm going in and ask him--

PETER
(grabbing her arm)
If you do, I'll break your neck.

She looks up at his glowering face, realizes he means it, and wilts under his dominant gaze.

PETER
Let's get out and stretch our legs.

Peter gets out, followed by Ellie, and they walk away from the car. Both are silent. At the DOOR of the LUNCH WAGON, then, Danker comes out and looks around furtively. Ellie and Peter, as seen by him, appear, walking away, following which the view moves over to the Ford and drops down to a close-up of Peter's suitcase. Now Danker looks about quickly and starts toward his car. He springs into the car, steps on the starter, and is off.

ELLIE and PETER hear the motor. They wheel around, and their eyes widen in surprise.

PETER

Hey!

He flings his coat at Ellie and dashes after the Ford. He is then seen running after it when the car turns around a bend in the road. Peter continues the pursuit. This scene wiping off, the FORD now makes its appearance around the bend, and as it approaches, Peter is seen at the wheel. He looks like he's just been through a fight. And as Peter rides in, Ellie comes running toward him.

ELLIE

(a note of great relief in her voice)

Oh, Peter! What happened? Are you all right?

PETER

Come on--get in.

ELLIE

(noticing a gash in his cheek)

Oh, you've been hurt! There's a cut on--

PETER

(impatiently)

Come on! come on!

(at this she runs around to get in the other side)

ELLIE

(as she runs)

What happened?

PETER

(as we see them closer)

Just a road thief. Picks people up and runs off with their stuff. What a racket!

(by this time she is in the car)

ELLIE

What'd you give him for the car?

PETER

A black eye.

(thereupon the car moves out of sight)

A close view shows Peter and Ellie driving along in the Ford. Peter looks ahead, uncommunicatively. Ellie glances up at him, and it is plain that something's on her mind.

ELLIE

(a little self-consciously)

Look--uh--how are the--uh--carrots holding out? Any left?

Peter glances at her. He knows what a concession this is on her part, and he smiles sympathetically.

PETER

(tenderly)

You don't have to eat the carrots.

(as she looks her surprise)

Just passed a pond with some ducks in it.

ELLIE

(with a cry of joy)

Darling!

She reaches up and kisses his cheek, and Peter beams happily.

PETER
(looking worried)
Haven't much gas left in this thing. Got to start promoting some.
(throwing her his coat)
Better take the things out of the pocket of that coat. Ought to be good for ten gallons.

The scene fades out.

PART EIGHT

ANDREWS' STUDY fades in, affording a close view of King Westley. He answers every description we have had of him. He is a stiff, handsome, stuffed-shirt gigolo. He sits in a chair, leaning on a cane, his gloves loosely in his hand. The view then moves back to reveal Andrews, who, from the opening of the scene, is speaking as he paces around the room.

ANDREWS
I haven't changed my mind, Westley, I want you to understand that! I don't like you! I never have! I never will! That's clear enough, isn't it?

KING
You've made that quite evident--with all your threats of annulment.
(confident)
Well, it hasn't bothered me for a minute. Ellie and I got married because we love each other. And she's proving it; as far as I'm concerned there's going to be no annulment.

ANDREWS
(hard)
You've got a good thing and you're hanging on to it, huh?
(Andrews smiles in a very superior manner)
All right, you win. I'll just have to get used to you. I admit I'm licked. But only because I'm worried. I've had detectives all over the country searching for her. I've seen thousands of photographs. Fortune tellers, nuts, every crank in the country has written me.
(quietly)
Haven't slept one night this week. If I don't find her, I'll go crazy.

WESTLEY
I might have been able to help if it weren't for you. I've been watched so closely, I--

ANDREWS
(impatiently)
Yes. I know. Well, you can help now. I issued a statement yesterday that I've withdrawn my objections. Begging her to come home. I haven't heard from her. Apparently she doesn't trust me.

WESTLEY
Why should she? After all--

ANDREWS
(interrupting)
All right. That's why I sent for you.
(pointing to next room)
There's a room full of reporters out there. I want you to make a statement--that you've had a talk with me--that we've reached an understanding--that if Ellen comes home, I won't interfere with your marriage. Will you do that?

WESTLEY
If you really mean it, I will.

ANDREWS
(strongly)
Of course I mean it! I don't care whom she's married to--
(softly)
--as long as I can get her back.
(he starts out)

As Andrews opens the door, a number of reporters enter.

ANDREWS
Come in, boys. This is my--uh--this is King Westley.
(Westley rises)
He has a statement to make.

REPORTERS
Hello, Westley ... How do you do.
(they group around him)

The scene dissolves to the side of a lonely ROAD at night. First there is a close-up of a newspaper headline, which reads.

ANDREWS WITHDRAWS OBJECTION
Magnate and Aviator Reconciled
"Everything all right. Come home, darling," says Westley.

Then the view draws back revealing that the newspaper is in the hands of Ellie, who sits in the car alone, gazing at the headlines. Then Peter's voice is heard.

PETER'S VOICE
All right, Brat.

At the sound of his voice, she is startled, and she quickly folds the paper and throws it out of sight. She starts to get out of the car.

ELLIE
(as she scrambles out of the car just as Peter comes up to her)
Any luck?

PETER
Yeah. He finally agreed to let us have a room.

ELLIE
What about money?

PETER
Talked him out of it. He thinks we're going to stay a week. I'll have to think of something before morning.

ELLIE
That's swell!

PETER
I'm glad you think so. If you ask me, it's foolish. I told you there's no sense in our staying here tonight. We could make New York in less than three hours.

ELLIE
I couldn't arrive in New York at three in the morning. Everybody's in bed.

PETER
(after a pause)
Okay.
(with a wave of his hand)
Cottage Number Three.

As they start toward it, the scene cuts to the OWNER'S CABIN. The owner of the auto camp and his wife are standing at window, looking out. She is a hatchet-faced shrew. He is meek and docile.

WIFE
There you go--trustin' people again. How many times did I tell you--

OWNER
He looked like an upright young feller to me, Ma.

WIFE
Yeah. They're all upright till they walk out on you.

OWNER
Said he was gonna stay a week.

WIFE
Mebbe.

OWNER
Worst comes to the worst, we got his car for security.

WIFE
(unconvinced)
I don't trust him.

The scene cuts to the inside of a CABIN not unlike the previous auto camp cabin in which Peter and Ellie spent a night. Peter's opened suitcase is on a chair, over which he leans. Ellie walks around, puffing at a cigarette.

PETER
(without looking up)
Well, here we are on the last lap.

Ellie crosses to the window and stares out moodily. Peter removes several things from his suitcase and lays them on the bed. There is a strained silence between them, as both are lost in their own thoughts. A close view of PETER as he putters abstractedly with the contents of his bag creates the impression that he empties it tonight rather ruefully. It somehow spells finis to their adventure.

PETER
(strangely)
Tomorrow morning, you'll be in the arms of your husband.

ELLIE (seen close) turns away from the window and looks at Peter. She stares this way for a long moment before speaking.

ELLIE
(in a still, small voice)
Yes. You'll have a great story, won't you?

PETER
(dryly)
Yeah, swell.

Peter takes the rope out of his bag. It is the one used for the "Walls of Jericho" previously. He lays it aside and then, remembering, retrieves it. For a moment he holds it in his hand, speculatively; then turning, proceeds to tack it up. The noise of the tacking attracts Ellie's attention, and Ellie (again seen close) turns and looks toward Peter.

ELLIE
Is that the Walls of Jericho going up?

PETER'S VOICE
Yep! The Walls of Jericho.
(at which she turns back to the window)

PETER (also seen close) stretches the rope across the room and tacks the other side.

PETER
(then reaching for blanket)
We certainly outsmarted your father.
(he throws the blanket over the rope)
I guess you ought to be happy.

There is no response from her, a close view revealing that she quite obviously isn't happy. They are now separated by the blanket, and Peter gets her pajamas from his suitcase and throws them over the blanket.

ELLIE
Thank you.
(there is silence while Peter starts undressing)

ELLIE
(suddenly)
Am I going to see you in New York?

PETER
(laconically)
Nope.

ELLIE
Why not?

PETER glances up at the "Walls of Jericho" and after a speculative pause, speaks quietly.

PETER
I don't make it a policy to run around with married women.

A close-up of ELLIE, disclosing only her neck and shoulders, shows her slipping out of her clothes. She pauses--then looks up.

ELLIE
No harm in your coming to see us.

PETER'S VOICE
Not interested.
(at this Ellie's face falls, this is a definite rebuff)

ELLIE
(weakly)
Won't I ever see you again?

PETER (seen close) is now getting into his pajamas.

PETER
What do you want to see _me_ for? _I've_ served my purpose. I brought you back to King Westley, didn't I?
(his mouth screws up bitterly)
That's what you wanted, wasn't it?

ELLIE is already in bed, staring up at the ceiling.

ELLIE
Peter, have you ever been in love?

PETER crawls into bed.

PETER
I probably did the world a great favor at that. Got two pinheads out of circulation.
(he reaches over and lights a cigarette)
Cupid thinks he's doing something when he brings two lovers together. What good's that? _I'm_ bringing two pains-in-the-neck together. I think I'll start an institution--hang out a shingle.

The view now widens to include both sides of the blanket. Ellie doesn't hear a word of Peter's attack. She is too intent on her own thoughts.

ELLIE
Haven't you ever _wanted_ to fall in love?

PETER
Me?

ELLIE
Yes. Haven't you thought about it at all? Seems to me you could make some girl wonderfully happy.

PETER
(disdainfully)
Maybe.
(after a pause)
Sure--sure, I've thought about it. Who hasn't? If I ever met the right sort of a girl, I'd--
(interrupting himself)
Yeah, but where you going to find her--somebody that's real--somebody that's alive? They don't come that way any more.

ELLIE'S disappointment is apparent.

PETER
(seen close)
I've even been sucker enough to make plans.
(a long puff on his cigarette)
I saw an island in the Pacific once. Never been able to forget it. That's where I'd like to take her. But she'd have to be the sort of a girl that'd jump in the surf with me on moonlight nights--and love it as much as I did.
(he loses himself in his romantic contemplations)
You know, those nights when you and the moon and the water all become one--when something comes over you--and you feel that you're part of something big and marvelous.
(sighing)
Those are the only places to live. Where the stars are so close over your head that you feel you could reach right up and stir them around.

A close-up of ELLIE at this point shows that she is affected by his stirring description of a heaven--from which she is excluded, as she listens to him continuing.

PETER'S VOICE
Certainly I've been thinking about it. Boy, if I could ever find a girl who's hungry for those things--

PETER (again seen close) has disposed of his cigarette and now stares dreamily heavenward.

PETER
I'm going to swim in the surf with her--I'm going to reach up and grab stars for her--I'm going to laugh with her--and cry with her. I'm going to kiss her wet lips--and--

Suddenly stopping, he turns his head slowly, sensing Ellie's nearness; and the view, drawing back to include Ellie, shows her standing at his bedside, looking down at him yearningly.

Then we see them close together: Peter's face is immobile. Ellie drops to her knees.

ELLIE
(fervently)
Take me with you, Peter. Take me to your island. I want to do all those things you talked about.

Peter stares at her lovely face. His heart cries out with an impulse to crush her in his arms.

PETER
(after a long pause; hoarsely)
Better go back to your bed.

ELLIE
(simply)
I love you.

PETER
(arguing with himself)
You're forgetting you're married.

ELLIE
(tensely)
I don't care. I love you. Nothing else matters. We can run away. Everything'll take care of itself.
(begging)
Please, Peter. You can't go out of my life now. I couldn't live without you.
(in a choked voice)
Oh, Peter--

Sobbing, she lays her head on his breast and throws her arms around him. All is quiet for a moment as Ellie's head rests on his breast, while Peter struggles with an overwhelming urge to pour out his heart to her.

PETER
(scarcely audible)
Better go back to your bed.

There is a lengthy pause, neither of them stirs. Then Ellie slowly raises her tear-stained face and gets to her feet.

ELLIE
(whispering)
I'm sorry.

She turns and disappears behind the blanket. Peter remains motionless. Then a close view shows ELLIE, as she gets into bed, sobbing quietly. She hides her face in the pillow to suppress her sobs. It is the first time in her life that she has been so deeply hurt. A close view next shows PETER reaching over for a cigarette, which he lights. All his movements are thoughtful, meditative. He leans back and stares at the ceiling, until we see only the cigarette in his mouth as it emits slowly rising puffs of smoke. This dissolving, the cigarette is seen to be burnt three quarters down, a long, frail ash hanging perilously on. PETER is then seen as he removes the cigarette from his mouth and crushes it in a tray. He leans back on the pillow and for a moment he is quiet. Then glancing over in Ellie's direction, he calls to her:

PETER
(softly calling)
Hey, Brat--!
(a pause)
Did you mean that? Would you really go?
(he waits for a response, but none comes. He tries again)
Hey, Brat--

He listens--all is quiet. He slips his covers off and crosses to the blanket, and peers over it. She is asleep. Her tear-stained face rests on the pillow, her arm extends over her head. It is a childlike posture.

PETER is watching her tenderly. He speculates whether to awaken her and decides against it. He starts away. Peter tiptoes around the room for a few moments, deep in thought. Then as an idea which he has been turning over in his mind begins to take form, he hastily begins dressing.

The scene dissolving, Peter is seen completely clothed and starting for the door when he thinks of something. He turns back, grabs his suitcase, stops to throw a kiss to Ellie, and goes out into the night. Thereupon the scene wipes off, disclosing a GAS STATION along the road at night. Here Peter is talking to a station attendant.

PETER
All I'm asking is enough gas to get me to New York. The bag's worth twenty-five dollars.

MAN
(hesitatingly)
Yeah, but I got a bag. My wife gave me one for Christmas.

PETER
("high-pressuring" him)
Listen, man--I'll tell you what I'll do. When I come back in the morning, I'll buy it back from you and give you ten dollars profit? What do you say?

MAN
(looking at Peter's hat)
I ain't got a hat--

PETER
What?

MAN
I ain't got a hat.

PETER
(promptly putting it on his head)
Well, you got one now.--Come on, fill 'er up.

While he is still talking the scene dissolves to a view of Peter driving furiously, a broad, happy grin on his face, following which several scenes wipe off in succession (denoting the passage of time)--scenes of Peter driving at high speed, causing several cows to amble out of the way; of the CAR driving into the Holland Tunnel, and of the BACK ROOM of a SPEAKEASY where Peter stands in front of a small desk upon which there is a typewriter. Near him is a swarthy Italian.

PETER
Fine! That's fine, Tony. Now get me a drink and make sure nobody disturbs me for half an hour.

ITALIAN
(going out)
Sure. Sure, Pete.

As Peter plants himself in front of the machine, the scene dissolves to a close-up of the typewriter carriage upon which are typed the words:

"--and that's the full and exclusive story of Ellen Andrews' adventures on the road. As soon as her marriage to King Westley is annulled, she and Peter Warne, famous newspaperman--and undoubtedly the most promising young novelist of the present era--will be married."

The view drawing back, Peter re-reads the last sentence, smiles contentedly, and as he yanks out the sheet, the scene wipes off disclosing the outside of GORDON'S OFFICE, the sign on the door reading: "Office--Mr. Gordon." Gordon's secretary is at her desk as Peter breezes in.

PETER
(rumpling her hair)
Hello, Agnes.

AGNES
Better not go in. He'll shoot you on sight.

PETER
(entering)
I haven't been shot at for days.

In GORDON'S OFFICE, Gordon is at his desk. He looks up when Peter enters.

GORDON
(rising to his full height menacingly)
Get out of here!

PETER
(advancing)
Wait a minute, Gordon--I--

GORDON
(quietly)
Get out!

Peter reaches his side, and grabs him by the arms.

PETER
Joe, listen--

GORDON
Don't "Joe" me.

PETER
Okay, Joe. Listen--you know I've always liked you. Anytime I could do you a great turn--anytime I ran into a story that looked good--I always came running to you, didn't I? Well, I got one now. Those wires I sent you were on the level. It's the biggest scoop of the year. I'm giving it to you, Joe.

GORDON
You mean about the Andrews' kid?

PETER
That's it.
(tapping his pocket)
I got it all written up. Ready to go. All I want is a thousand dollars.

Upon hearing this GORDON is ready to jump out of his skin.

GORDON
A thousand dollars!
(furiously)
Get out of this office before I throw you out bodily.

PETER
Don't get sore, Joe. This is something you got to do for me. I need a thousand dollars--and I need it quick. I'm in a jam.

GORDON
(softening)
What's the thousand bucks for?

PETER
To tear down the Walls of Jericho.

GORDON
What!

PETER
Never mind ... Listen--suppose I should tell you that Ellen Andrews is going to have her marriage annulled.

GORDON
Huh?

PETER
That she's going to marry somebody else.

GORDON
You're drunk.

PETER
Would an exclusive story like that be worth a thousand bucks to you?

GORDON
If it's on the level.

PETER
Well, I got it, Joe.

GORDON
Who's she gonna marry?

PETER
(taking out the story from his pocket)
It's all right here. Give me the thousand and it's yours.

GORDON
(skeptically)
I wouldn't trust you as far as I could throw that desk.

PETER
Wait a minute, Joe. Use your bean. I couldn't afford to hand you a phoney yarn, like that. I'd be crazy. There isn't a newspaper in the country'd give me a job after that! I could go to jail!

GORDON
I'd put you there myself.

PETER
Sure. I wouldn't blame you, either.

GORDON
Who's the guy she's gonna marry?

PETER
I am, Joe.

GORDON
(his eyes widening)
You!

PETER
Yeah.

GORDON
Now I _know_ you're drunk.
(he grabs his hat)
I'm going home. Don't annoy me any more.

PETER
(running after Gordon as the latter starts out)
For heaven's sake, Joe--stop being an editor for just a minute.
(he grabs his arm)
We've been friends for a long time, haven't we? You ought to know when I'm serious. This is on the level.

Gordon is affected by the sincere note in Peter's voice.

PETER
I met her on a bus coming from Miami. Been with her every minute.
(hoarsely)
I'm in love with her, Joe.

GORDON
Well, I'll be--

PETER
Listen, Pal--you've got to get this money for me. Now. Minutes count. She's waiting for me in an auto camp outside of Philadelphia. I've got to get right back. You see, she doesn't know I'm gone.
(self-consciously)
A guy can't propose to a girl without a cent in the world, can he?

While Peter has been speaking Gordon stares into space thoughtfully.

GORDON
What a story!
(picturing it)
On her way to join her husband, Ellen Andrews falls in love with--
(alert--grabbing paper out of Peter's hand)
Lemme see that a minute.

He moves to his desk excitedly, and Peter, a gleam of hope in his eyes, joins him, following which the scene cuts to the SHACK of the camp owner and wife in the early morning. The owner is suddenly startled out of his sleep by the voice of his wife calling, "Zeke! Zeke!" He looks up, just as she rushes into the room.

WIFE
I told you! I told you, you couldn't trust him! He's gone!

OWNER
Who?

WIFE
That feller last night, that's who! He was gonna stay a week, huh? Well, he's skipped. Took the car with him, too. We wouldn't have known a thing about it until morning if I hadn't took that magnesia.
(pulling at him)
Come on, get up, don't lay there. Let's do something about it.

Thereupon the scene cuts to the AUTO CAMP CABIN affording a close view of ELLIE tossing restlessly in her sleep. Suddenly there is a loud banging on the door, and Ellie, startled, awakens. The pounding continuing, Ellie looks around, frightened. The door suddenly bursts open, and the owner and wife enter. They both glance over at Peter's side.

WIFE
See that. They're gone!

OWNER
(timidly)
Looks like it, don't it?
(suddenly he sees Ellie)
Here's the woman, ma.

WIFE
(full of fight--glaring at Ellie)
Oh!!

ELLIE

(in a close view at Ellie's Bed as the owner and his wife come up to her; timidly--sitting up)

What's the matter?

WIFE

Where's your husband, young lady--

ELLIE

Husband?

WIFE

Yes--if he _is_ your husband.

ELLIE

Isn't he here?

WIFE

No, he ain't! And the car's gone, too.

ELLIE

(bewildered)

Why, he'll be back.

WIFE

Yeah? What makes you think so! He took his suit-case and everything.

(Ellie is perceptibly startled by this piece of news)

Kinda surprised, huh? It's just like I told you, Zeke. They ain't married a'tall ...

There is a close view of ELLIE as the wife's voice continues uninterruptedly:

WIFE'S VOICE

... could tell she was a hussy just from the looks of her.

Ellie is lost in thought, trying to adjust herself to the idea of Peter's leaving her like this. She scarcely hears what is being said.

OWNER'S VOICE

Hey! You! Got any money?

ELLIE

(snapping out of her trance)

Why--no.

WIFE

(the three now seen together)

Then--you'll have to _git_!

OWNER

Yeah, you'll have to _git_.

ELLIE

Why, you can't put me out in the middle of the--

WIFE
Serves you right. Oughta be careful who you take up with on the road. You can't go plyin' your trade in my camp.

ELLIE
But can't you wait until morning--

WIFE
Ain't gonna wait a minute.

OWNER
Not a minute!

WIFE
Better start gettin' into your clothes.

OWNER
Yeah.

WIFE
(glaring at him)
Zeke.
(he looks up startled)
Git!

OWNER
(disappointed)
Yes, Ma.

As Zeke leaves, the Wife plunks herself in a chair, grimly determined to wait until Ellie gets dressed and out.

ELLIE
Can I use your telephone? I want to talk to New York.

WIFE
You ain't gonna stick <u>me</u> for no phone calls. You can go down to the Sheriff's office.

The scene thereupon cuts to the EXTERIOR of the AUTO CABIN as Ellie emerges, the Wife standing in the doorway. In the foreground several people are scattered around the courtyard. One woman washes stockings under a pump. A man is changing the tire on his car. Ellie comes down the steps and crosses the courtyard.

WIFE
(shouting to her)
And listen, next time better keep away from here. I run a <u>respectable</u> place.

Ellie does not turn, but walks straight forward, trying to maintain her poise. The people in the courtyard turn to stare at her, and one of them snickers.

The scene dissolves to GORDON'S OFFICE as Peter is pocketing the money. Gordon is fondling the story.

PETER
Thanks, Pal. You saved my life.

GORDON
(waving the story)
Okay, Pete.
(he drops the story on the desk and escorts Peter out, his arm around his shoulder)
For my dough,
(smiling)
you're still the best newspaperman in the business.

They reach the door, which Peter opens. Then they appear at the DOORWAY. Through the open door the secretary stares dumbfounded at their friendliness.

GORDON
S'long, kid. And good luck.

Outside GORDON'S OFFICE, Peter kisses the secretary as he passes through.

PETER
'Bye, Agnes. You're beautiful. All women are beautiful!
(he goes out)

Gordon is immediately electrified into action.

GORDON
Oh, boy! What a yarn! What a yarn!
(suddenly)
Get me Hank on the phone. Gotta hold up the morning edition.

While he speaks he dashes back to his desk. We then see him in his office.

SECRETARY'S VOICE
There's Hank.

GORDON
(grabbing phone)
Hank! Listen. Hold the morning edition. Break down the front page. Gonna have a completely new layout--Send a couple of re-write men in here. Don't do a thing--I got a story that'll make your hair curl.

During his speech, his other phone has been ringing persistently. He has ignored it until now. He picks up receiver:

GORDON
(into the second phone)
Yeah. Yeah. Don't annoy me. I'm busy.
(he bangs up receiver, and turns back to the first phone)
Listen, Hank! Dig out all the Andrews pictures. Get Healy out of bed. I want a cartoon right away.
(the second phone rings impatiently, but Gordon ignores it)
With King Westley in it. He's waiting at the church. Big tears streaming down his face. His bride hasn't shown up. Old Man Andrews is there,

too. Laughing his head off. Everything exaggerated. You know--Now snap into it!
(he bangs up the receiver, and grabs the second phone, speaking into it impatiently)
Yeah. Yeah. What is it?

A close view of GORDON, as he listens, shows his eyes widening with amazement.

GORDON
What!--Ellen Andrews! You're crazy!

This cuts to a TELEPHONE BOOTH where a reporter is seen speaking excitedly.

REPORTER
Yeah. She just phoned her father from an auto camp to come and get her. He's getting a police escort. Westley's going along, too. She's been traveling by bus. The moment she read that her father and Westley made up, she phoned in.

Back in GORDON'S OFFICE Gordon is seen still at the phone.

GORDON
You sure that's right! Say, you haven't been drinking, have you! Okay--grab a car--and stay with them.
(he hangs up the receiver and grabs the first phone)
Put Hank on.
(shouting)
Agnes!
(as the secretary hurries in)
Get me a doctor. I'm about to have a nervous breakdown.
(she stares at him dumbly as he speaks into the phone)
Hank--forget everything I just told you. I was just having a nightmare!
(he hangs up--and turns to Agnes)
Call up the police department! Tell 'em to find Peter Warne. Send out a general alarm. I want the dirty crook pinched.

He picks up Peter's story and flings it viciously into the wastebasket.

AGNES
(starting out)
Yessir.
(two re-write men come in, passing Agnes)

MEN
You want us?

GORDON
(wheeling around)
Yeah. Shove everything off the front page. Ellen Andrews just phoned her father--she's coming home. The moment she heard the old man withdrew his objections, she gave herself up. Spread it all over the place. Here's your lead: "Love Triumphant!" Step on it!

MEN
(leaving)
Yessir.

Gordon goes to his desk, mumbling to himself. His eye lights on the waste basket containing Peter's story, and he is about to kick it when he stops. He stares at it thoughtfully, reaches down, lifts it out--runs through it hastily--and then stares into space, deep in thought.

The scene dissolves to an open ROAD, in the morning, as Peter flies over it in his Ford. He beams happily. He passes a gasoline truck and waves cheerily to the driver. This dissolves to a close-up of an AUTO SIREN accompanied by a prolonged wail, then to a ROAD, that morning, as four motorcycles, two abreast, speed forward, followed by a luxurious limousine, which in turn is trailed by a car filled with reporters. Next, in the LIMOUSINE, Andrews is seen in the back seat. He is accompanied by King Westley--Henderson--Lovington, and a police inspector.

HENDERSON
I knew she was safe.

LOVINGTON
(sighing)
Certainly gave us a run for our money.
(but Andrews is too overwhelmed with joy to listen to any of this)

ANDREWS
(anxiously)
Can't you get them to go any faster?
(at this the Inspector leans over to talk to chauffeur)

This dissolves to a deserted ROAD, Peter at the wheel of his car. His high spirits find expression in his efforts to sing.

PETER
(singing)
"I found a million dollar baby--"

He is interrupted by the song of a meadowlark, whistling its strange melody. Peter listens to it a second time, then answers its call by imitating it. The meadowlark whistles again, and Peter is highly amused.

PETER
(waving his hand--to the meadowlark)
Okay, Pal. Be seein' you.

Just then the sound of sirens is heard in the distance. Peter glances back, and as the sirens come nearer, he pulls over to the side of the road. There follows a full view of the ROAD, with Peter in the foreground at the side as the police cavalcade whizzes by accompanied by the shrieking sirens. Thereupon PETER (seen close) gets an idea.

PETER
(to his Ford)
Come on, Dobbin, old boy. We got a police escort.

He applies the gas and shoots out of sight, following which a full view of the road shows Peter's car trying to catch up with the parade. It outdistances him, however, and we see PETER in the Ford pressing his body forward to help the car make time. His foot pushes the accelerator down to the floor. But the police cars are now out of sight, and Peter gives up.

PETER
(seen close; to the car--with exaggerated dramatics)
Dobbin, me lad. You failed muh. I'm afraid you're gittin' old.

Thereupon the scene dissolves to a small town ROAD, where at the door of a Sheriff's office a policeman is standing on guard. The reporters hang around in front of him. Several yokels look on. The limousine and motor cycles are at the curb. And now, in a closer view, at the DOOR the policeman on guard steps aside as the door opens and Ellie, her father, and King Westley emerge. King has his arm around her. The moment they appear in the doorway, cameras click and several reporters surround them.

REPORTERS
Will you make a statement Miss Andrews? Was it an exciting experience? How did you travel?

ANDREWS
(brushing them aside)
Later, boys, later. See her at home.

They cross the sidewalk--to the waiting limousine, as cameras click.

The scene dissolves to a ROAD, with Peter still driving. He is, however, as before, in excellent form, and is singing lustily. Suddenly, however, his eyes widen and he pulls on his brake; the car screeches and moans--and comes to a stop.

PETER
Take it easy, Dobbin. Remember your blood pressure.

We find Peter directly in front of a slow moving freight train. Several hoboes stick their heads out of a car, and Peter waves to them. The hoboes look puzzled for a minute and then wave back. The view then swings over to an opening between the cars affording a flash of the police parade on the other side, apparently on its way back.

PETER amuses himself by talking to an old flagman.

PETER
Better get that toy train out of here. I'm in a hurry.

The Flagman grins at him in reply. By this time the last car is in sight, and Peter gets all set to move. He stops, however, to wave to a couple of brakemen on the rear platform.

In the meantime, the motorcycles have started forward, and the sirens begin their low, moaning wail. Peter, attracted, turns, and over Peter's shoulder we see the parade starting. As the limousine passes, we get a glimpse of the inside. Ellie lies back on King Westley's shoulder. He has his arm around her as they pass out of sight. Thereupon a close view of PETER shows him reacting to what he saw. He turns his head quickly to stare at the disappearing car, a look of astonishment and bewilderment in his eyes. Slowly he turns his head forward, staring ahead of him blankly; he can't quite make it out. Then gradually the significance of it all strikes him--and his mouth curls up bitterly.

The scene wiping off, a series of NEWSPAPER HEADLINES come into view:

"ELLEN ANDREWS RETURNS HOME."
"MARRIAGE HALTED BY FATHER TO BE RESUMED"
"ELLEN ANDREWS AND AVIATOR TO HAVE CHURCH WEDDING"
"LOVE TRIUMPHS AGAIN"
"PARENTAL OBJECTION REMOVED IN FAVOR OF LOVERS"
"CANNOT THWART LOVE SAYS FATHER OF ELLEN ANDREWS"
"GLAD TO BE HOME SAYS ELLEN"

This dissolves to the anteroom of a NEWSPAPER OFFICE. The place is alive with activity, and copies of newspapers are lying around, bearing headlines relating to the Andrews story. Peter, a bewildered, stunned expression on his face, enters and crosses funereally toward Gordon's office. Several people standing around look up.

PEOPLE
Hi, Pete--Didya see this? Ellen Andrews is back. Gonna marry that Westley guy after all--What a dame! What a dame!

Peter pays no attention to any of this. He reaches Gordon's door, which is open. He walks directly past Agnes and enters the office. She looks up at him, puzzled. Then in GORDON'S OFFICE, Peter walks to Gordon's desk and lays the roll of bills on it. Agnes enters, watching him anxiously.

AGNES
Gordon's out back some place.
(seeing the money, she looks up, surprised)

PETER
See that he gets that, will you, Agnes? Tell him I was just kidding.
(he goes out)

As Agnes stares after him, puzzled, Gordon dashes in from a back door.

GORDON
You can't get a thing done around her unless--

AGNES
Peter Warne was just in.

GORDON
Huh? What?

AGNES
Left this money. Said to tell you he was just kidding.

GORDON
(looking at the money)
Where is he?

The scene cuts to the OUTER OFFICE and CORRIDOR, as seen over Gordon's shoulder through the open door. Peter is seen walking out. Gordon hurries after him.

GORDON'S VOICE
Hey, Pete!

At the sound of Gordon's voice, Peter turns, and Gordon comes over to him.

PETER
Hello, Joe. Sorry. Just a little gag of mine. Thought I'd have some fun with you.

GORDON
(understanding)
Yeah. Sure. Had me going for a while.

PETER
Wouldn't have made a bad story, would it?

GORDON
Great! But that's the way things go. You think you got a swell yarn--then something comes along--messes up the finish--and there you are.

PETER
(smiling wryly)
Yeah, where am I?

GORDON
(slipping a bill in his coat pocket)
When you sober up--come in and see me.

PETER
(a whisper)
Thanks, Joe.

He leaves, Gordon watching him sympathetically, and the scene fades out.

PART NINE

The LAWN of the ANDREWS ESTATE fades in. It is morning and at the moment the place is a beehive of activity. Dozens of butlers and maids hustle around setting tables. Floral decorations are being hung by men on ladders. In the background on a platform, a twenty-piece orchestra is getting ready, accompanied by the scraping of chairs, adjusting of music stands, unpacking of instruments.

The scene cuts to ANDREWS' STUDY: King Westley is seated, and Andrews walks around him. They are both dressed in striped trousers, frock coat, etc.

ANDREWS
Well, here we are; it's all set. You're finally going to be married properly.
(he waves toward the window)
With all the fanfare and everything.

(shaking his head)
I still don't know how it happened--but you're going to be my son-in-law whether I like it or not. I guess you're pleased.

KING
Why, naturally, I--

ANDREWS
(drily)
Naturally.
(with vehemence)
You're going to become a partner in a big institution. It's one of the largest in the world.

KING
You talk as if--

ANDREWS
Someday perhaps, you might even take charge.

A close view of ANDREWS shows him looking around his study despairingly.

ANDREWS
(murmuring)
The thought of it makes me shudder.

KING'S VOICE
(confidently)
You might be surprised.

ANDREWS
I hope so. However, that'll take care of itself.
(taking a new tack)
There's another responsibility you're taking on. One that I'm _really_ concerned about.

KING'S VOICE
What's that?

ANDREWS
My daughter.

KING
(the two now seen again; lightly)
Ellie? Oh, she's no responsibility.

ANDREWS
No? Say, listen--I've devoted a whole lifetime trying to tame that wildcat. Toughest job I ever tackled. Ever hear of J. P. Clarkson? Biggest man in the country, isn't he? Well, I tamed _him_. Got him eating out of the palm of my hand. I've browbeaten financiers, statesmen, foreign ministers--some of the most powerful people in the world--but I've never been able to do a thing with her. She's been too much for me. I'm glad you think it's easy.

(he bends over him)
Now listen--if you'll do what I tell you, perhaps I might develop a little respect for you. You never can tell.

KING
What would you like to have me do?

ANDREWS
Sock her!

A close view of KING shows him looking up, surprised, as Andrews' voice continues.

ANDREWS' VOICE
Sock her at least once a day. Do it on general principles. Make her know you're the boss and never let her forget it. Think you can do that?

KING
It's quite an assignment--

ANDREWS
Try. Do me a favor. Try. It's your only chance. And hers, too. Do that for me--and maybe we'll be friends--
(muttering)
Maybe.
(he holds out his hand)
Do we understand each other?

KING
(taking his hand--rising)
Yes, sir.

ANDREWS
(dismissing him)
Fine. I'll see you at the reception.

He withdraws his hand, which he looks at disgustedly--the result of a jellyfish handshake.

KING
Oh, by the way, Mr Andrews, I thought of a great stunt for the reception.
(as Andrews looks at him quizzically)
I'm going to land on the lawn in an autogyro.[14]
What do you think of that!

A close view of ANDREWS shows him staring off at King in complete disgust.

ANDREWS
You thought that up all by yourself, huh?

KING
(unabashed)
Why, it'll make all the front pages. A spectacular thing like that--

ANDREWS
(hard)
Personally, I think it's stupid!
(humoring a child)
But go ahead. Have a good time. As long as Ellie doesn't object.

KING
Oh, no. She'll be crazy about it. Well, see you later. I'm going out on the lawn and arrange for landing space.
(holding out his hand)
Goodbye.
(but Andrews turns his back on him)

ANDREWS
We've done that already.

KING
(smiling)
Yes, of course.

He turns and leaves; Andrews watching him go, shaking his head sadly.

ANDREWS
Autogyro! I hope he breaks his leg.

Andrews starts out, and the scene cuts to the HALLWAY as Andrews enters from the study. A maid coming down the stairs, he calls to her:

ANDREWS
Oh--Mary--

MARY
Yes, sir?

ANDREWS
How is she?

MARY
(hesitantly)
Why--uh--she's all right, sir.

ANDREWS
What's the matter? Anything wrong?

MARY
Oh, no, sir. No different than--

ANDREWS
Yes. I know. Still in the dumps, huh?

MARY
Yessir. If you'll excuse me, sir--she sent me for a drink.
(she leaves)

Andrews stands a moment thoughtfully and then starts up the stairs, following which the scene dissolves to the UPSTAIRS CORRIDOR in front of Ellie's door. Andrews enters and knocks several times. Receiving no response, he gingerly opens the door.

Next Andrews enters ELLIE'S BEDROOM and looks around. The view swings around the room, following his gaze. It focuses on Ellie, who reclines on a sofa, in her bridal outfit, her head resting on the back. She stares moodily, unhappily up at the ceiling. The view then expanding to include both father and daughter, Andrews is seen staring at her a moment sympathetically. He senses something is wrong.

ANDREWS
(after a pause)
Ellie--

ELLIE
(jumping up with a start)
Oh, hello, Dad.

ANDREWS
(a close view as he goes over to her)
I knocked several times.

ELLIE
Sorry. Must have been day-dreaming.
(to hide her confusion, she reaches for a cigarette)

ANDREWS
(with forced lightness)
Well, everything's set. Creating quite a furor, too. Great stunt King's going to pull.

ELLIE
(in a faraway voice)
Stunt?

ANDREWS
Landing on the lawn in an autogyro.

ELLIE
Oh, yes. I heard.

ANDREWS
(noting her listlessness)
Yes. Personally, I think it's silly, too.

As he continues talking, the view moves with Ellie, who wanders over to a window overlooking the lawn and stares out, lost in thought.

ANDREWS' VOICE
(he goes over the Ellie)
You look lovely. Are you pleased with the gown?
(as Ellie does not seem to hear him, he becomes worried)
Ellie!

ELLIE
(turning and looking at him blankly)
Huh?
(it just penetrates)
Oh--the gown--
(distantly)
Yes, it's beautiful.

ANDREWS
(tenderly)
What's the matter, Ellie? What's wrong?

ELLIE
Nothing.
(she walks over to table and crushes her cigarette)

ANDREWS
You've been acting so strangely since you returned. I'm--I'm worried. I haven't bothered to ask you any questions--I--
(waving his hand toward the lawn)
Isn't all this what you wanted?
(receiving no answer from Ellie)
You haven't changed your mind about King, have you?

ELLIE
(too quickly)
Oh, no.

ANDREWS
If you have, it isn't too late. You know how I feel about him. But I want to make you happy. You gave me such a scare--I--when I couldn't find you.
(smiling feebly--meaning his heart)
You know, the old pump isn't what it used to be.

ELLIE
(her hand on his arm)
Sorry, Dad. I wouldn't hurt you for the world. You know that.

She moves away from him and sits on the sofa, and Andrews watches her a moment and crosses over to her. He sits beside her, placing an arm affectionately around her shoulder.

ANDREWS
(tenderly)
Ellie--what is it? Aren't you happy, child?

At this point she finally breaks, and impulsively buries her face on his breast.

ANDREWS
(after a pause, hoarsely)
I thought so. I knew there was something on your mind.
(there are audible sobs from Ellie)
There--there!

They remain thus quietly for some time. Finally Andrews breaks the silence.

ANDREWS
What is it, darling?
(receiving no answer)
You haven't fallen in love with somebody else, have you?

As this brings an audible sob from Ellie, Andrews lifts up her chin.

ANDREWS
(looking into her eyes)
Have you?
(Ellie turns her head away, a little ashamed of her tears)

Ellie now rises and walks miserably away from him, dabbing her eyes. Andrews, watching her, realizes he has hit upon the truth. He walks over to her.

ANDREWS
I haven't seen you cry since you were a baby. This must be serious.
(Ellie is silent)
Where'd you meet him?

ELLIE
On the road.

ANDREWS
(trying to cheer her)
Now, don't tell me you fell in love with a bus driver!

ELLIE
(smiling)
No.

ANDREWS
Who is he?

ELLIE
I don't know very much about him.
(in a whisper)
Except that I love him.

ANDREWS
(the great executive)
Well, if it's as serious as all that--we'll move heaven and earth to--

ELLIE
(quickly)
It'll do no good.
(wryly)
He despises me.

ANDREWS
Oh, come now--

ELLIE
He despises everything I stand for. He thinks I'm spoiled and pampered, and selfish, and thoroughly insincere.

ANDREWS
Ridiculous!

ELLIE
He doesn't think so much of you either.

ANDREWS
(his eyes widening)
Well!

ELLIE
He blames you for everything that's wrong about me. Thinks you raised me stupidly.

ANDREWS
(smiling)
Fine man to fall in love with.

ELLIE
(whispering)
He's marvelous!

ANDREWS
Well, what are we going to do about it? Where is he?

ELLIE
(sadly)
I don't know.

ANDREWS
I'd like to have a talk with him.

ELLIE
It's no use, Dad. I practically threw myself at him.
(she shrugs futilely)

ANDREWS
Well, under the circumstances, don't you think we ought to call this thing off?

ELLIE
No, I'll go through with it.

ANDREWS
But that's silly, child. Seeing how you feel, why--

ELLIE
It doesn't matter.
(tired)
I don't want to stir up any more trouble. I've been doing it all my life. I've been such a burden to you--made your life so miserable--and mine, too. I'm tired, Dad. Tired of running around in circles. He's right, that's what I've been doing ever since I can remember.

A close-up of ANDREWS shows him watching Ellie, as her voice continues.

ELLIE'S VOICE
I've got to settle down. It really doesn't matter how--or where--or with whom.

ANDREWS
(seriously--impressed)
You've changed, Ellie.

ELLIE
(seen with Andrews; sighing)
Yes, I guess I have.
(sincerely)
I don't want to hurt anybody any more. I want to get away from all this front page publicity. It suddenly strikes me as being cheap and loathsome. I can't walk out on King now. It'll make us all look so ridiculous.
(she shrugs resignedly)
Besides, what difference does it make?
(inaudibly)
I'll never see Peter again.

ANDREWS
Is that his name?

ELLIE
Yes. Peter Warne.

She starts to walk away when she is attracted by her father's surprise at the mention of the name.

ANDREWS
Peter Warne!
(his hand has instinctively gone to his inside pocket)

ELLIE
(noticing this)
Why? Do you know him?
(but Andrews withdraws his hand. Apparently he has changed his mind)

ANDREWS
(evasively)
Oh, no--no.

ELLIE
(suddenly anxious)
You haven't heard from him, have you, Dad?

ANDREWS
(obviously guilty)
Why, no ... Don't be silly.

ELLIE
Oh, please, Dad--

She has reached into his pocket and has extracted a letter, which she hurriedly opens and reads, following which we see a LETTER in Peter's handwriting. It is addressed to: "Alexander Andrews, 11 Wall Street." It reads:

"Dear Sir:
I should like to have a talk with you about a financial matter in connection with your daughter.
Peter Warne."

Ellie is then seen reading and re-reading the note. Her face clouds and then slowly changes to an expression of complete disillusionment.

ELLIE
(her voice strident)
Looks like that was his only interest in me. The reward.

ANDREWS
(taking the note from her)
I'm sorry you read it.

ELLIE
Are you going to see him?

ANDREWS
I suppose so.

ELLIE
(hard)
Certainly! Pay him off. He's entitled to it. He did an excellent job. Kept me thoroughly entertained. It's worth every penny he gets.

She paces agitatedly, Andrews watching her silently. He knows what an awful blow to her pride this must be. Mary now enters with a cocktail tray which she sets on the table.

ELLIE
Thanks, Mary. That's just what I need.
(she pours herself a cocktail)

MARY
Mr. King Westley is on his way up.

ELLIE
Fine--Fine! Have him come in.

ANDREWS
(mumbling)
I'll be going.
(he goes out behind Mary)

Ellie swallows her drink and starts pouring herself another, as King enters.

ELLIE
(upon seeing him)
Well, if it isn't the groom himself! You're just in time, King.

A close view of the TWO shows King taking her in his arms.

KING
How are you, Ellie?
(he gives her a kiss, which she accepts perfunctorily--but he insists upon being ardent)
Are you happy?

ELLIE
(releasing herself)
Happy? Why shouldn't I be happy? I'm getting the handsomest man in captivity.
(handing him a drink)
Here you are, King. Let's drink.
(she holds her glass out)
Let's drink to <u>us</u>.

(she drains the glass; pouring another, as she continues)
We finally made it, didn't we?

KING
You bet we did.

ELLIE
It's up to you now. I want our life to be full of excitement, King. We'll never let up, will we? Never a dull moment. We'll get on a merry-go-round and never get off. Promise you'll never let me get off? It's the only way to live, isn't it? No time to think. We don't want to stop to think, do we? Just want to keep going.

KING
Whatever you say, darling.

ELLIE
I heard about your stunt. That's swell, King. Just think of it--the groom lands on the lawn with a plane. It's a perfect beginning for the life we're going to lead. It sets just the right tempo.
(handing him a drink)
Come on, King. You're lagging.
(they both drink)

In ANDREWS' STUDY, Andrews walks around the room, perceptibly affected by his visit with Ellie. He keeps turning Peter's letter over in his hand, apparently debating in his mind what to do with it. He finally gets an idea--and determinedly crosses to the phone. Then the scene cuts to a HOTEL ROOM. First there is a close-up of a NEWSPAPER--a tabloid bearing a heading which reads: "LOVE TRIUMPHANT."

"Interrupted Romance of Ellen Andrews and King Westley Resumed, as Father Yields. Wedding Reception to be Held on Andrews' Lawn."

Below this is a page of pictures, and the view turns to each photograph. The first picture is of Ellie and King on a beach. The title over the picture reads: "Where they met." The second picture shows them in the cockpit of a plane, the heading reading: "Where they romanced." The next picture is of a small frame house with a shingle on it reading: "Justice of the Peace." Over the photograph is a caption: "Where they were married." The next picture is of the Andrews yacht, and the title reads: "Where she was taken." Finally, the view moves down to the bottom of the page to a picture of Ellie and King, with her father between them, in front of Sheriff's office. Caption reads: "Where love triumphed." Over these pictures the phone bell has been ringing.

And now PETER is seen staring, expressionless, at the newspaper. Suddenly he becomes conscious of the phone ringing; he looks up--then goes to it.

PETER
(into the phone)
Hello ... Yes? ... Who? ... Oh ... Why can't I see you at your office?

The scene cuts to ANDREWS' STUDY, affording a close view of ANDREWS at the phone.

ANDREWS
I leave for Washington tonight. May be gone several weeks. Thought perhaps you'd like to get this thing settled.

This cuts to the HOTEL ROOM where PETER is at the phone.

PETER
Yeah, but I don't like the idea of walking in on your jamboree ... Just between you and me--those things give me a stiff pain.

ANDREWS
(seen in his office)
You needn't see anybody. You can come directly to my study. I'd appreciate it very much if--

PETER
(at his phone)
No--no. What the deuce do I want to--

His eyes fall on something, and there follows a close view of a tabloid newspaper, featuring the heading: "Love Triumphant" and containing the pictures of Ellie and King. The view then moves down to feature headline reading "Groom to Land on Bride's Lawn."

"King Westley plans to drop in an autogyro on the lawn of Andrews estate ... "

Peter's mouth screws up disdainfully.

PETER
(into the phone)
Yeah, wait a minute. Maybe I will come over. I'd like to get a load of that three-ring circus you're pulling. I want to see what love looks like when it's triumphant. I haven't had a good laugh in a week.
(he is still at the phone as the scene dissolves)

Then the LAWN of the ANDREWS ESTATE dissolves in. It is now filled with guests, who wander around, chattering gaily. The orchestra plays. A captain of waiters in the foreground instructs his men.

CAPTAIN
I want everything to be just so. When the ceremony starts, you stand on the side--<u>still</u>. No moving around--no talking, <u>comprenez</u>?

The view cuts to a ROADWAY leading to the estate, and Peter is seen driving up in his Ford and squeezing in between two Rolls-Royces. The uniformed chauffeurs glare at him. But Peter springs nonchalantly out of his car.

PETER
(blithely, as he passes them)
Keep your eye on my car when you're backing up, you guys.

And as he goes, the chauffeurs look at each other, surprised. The scene dissolves to ANDREWS' STUDY, where a butler stands in front of Andrews who is seated at his desk.

ANDREWS
Show him in.

The Butler leaving, a close view shows ANDREWS reaching over and snapping on a dictograph concealed somewhere on his desk. The office coming into view again, we see Andrews rising and awaiting Peter's entrance. After a moment Peter comes in, removes his soft felt hat, and tucks it under his arm.

ANDREWS
Mr. Warne?

PETER
Yeah.

ANDREWS
Come in. Sit down.

Peter advances into the room, looking around curiously. His air is frigid, contemptuous as Andrews studies him, and he makes no move to sit. Andrews waves to a chair and sits down himself. Peter flops into the nearest chair.

ANDREWS
(seen close with Peter; after a pause)
I was surprised to get your note. My daughter hadn't told me anything about you. About your helping her.

PETER
That's typical of your daughter. Takes those things for granted.
(too restless to sit, he jumps up)
Why does she think I lugged her all the way from Miami--
(vehemently)
for the love of it?

ANDREWS
Please understand me. When I say she didn't tell me anything about it, I mean not until a little while ago. She thinks you're entitled to anything you can get.

PETER
(bitterly)
Oh, she does, huh? Isn't that sweet of her! <u>You don't</u>, I suppose.

ANDREWS
(shrugging)
I don't know. I'd have to see on what you base your claim. I presume you feel you're justified in--

PETER
(seen close now)
If I didn't I wouldn't be here!
(he reaches into his pocket)
I've got it all itemized.

(and he throws the paper on Andrews' desk)

ANDREWS picks up the paper and glances at it. After a moment, he looks at Peter, studying him interestedly; then he returns to the paper, and reads its contents:

"Cash outlay	8.60
Topcoat	15.00
Suitcase	7.50
Hat	4.00
3 shirts	4.50
Total	39.60"

Andrews looks up from the paper. This is a twist he hadn't anticipated, and he doesn't quite know how to handle it.

PETER
(now seen closer with Andrews)
I sold some drawers and socks, too; I'm throwing those in.

ANDREWS
And this is what you want--thirty nine dollars and sixty cents?

PETER
Why not? I'm not charging you for the time I wasted.

ANDREWS
Yes, I know--but--

PETER
What's the matter? Isn't it cheap enough? A trip like that would cost you a thousand dollars! Maybe more!

ANDREWS
Let me get this straight. You want this thirty-nine sixty in addition to the ten thousand dollars?

PETER
What ten thousand?

ANDREWS
The reward.

PETER
(sharply)
Who said anything about a reward!

ANDREWS
(smiling)
I'm afraid I'm a little confused. You see, I assumed you were coming here for--

PETER
(impatiently)
All I want is thirty-nine sixty. If you'll give me a check I'll get out of this place. It gives me the jitters.

ANDREWS
You're a peculiar chap.

PETER
(irritably)
We'll go into that some other time.

ANDREWS
The average man would go after the reward. All you seem to--

PETER
Listen, did anybody ever make a sucker out of you? This is a matter of principle. Something you probably wouldn't understand.
(he burns at the thought)
When somebody takes me for a buggy ride I don't like the idea of having to pay for the privilege.

ANDREWS
You were taken for a buggy ride?

PETER
Yeah--with all the trimmings. Now, how about the check. Do I get it?

A close-up indicates that ANDREWS has been studying Peter throughout the scene. He is now completely won over.

ANDREWS
(smiling)
Certainly.
(he opens a checkbook and writes it out)

While Andrews writes, Peter wanders around the room in an attitude of bitter contempt. Andrews rises and goes to him.

ANDREWS
Here you are.
(as Peter takes the check)
Do you mind if I ask you something frankly?
(Peter just looks at him without responding)
Do you love my daughter?

PETER
(evasively, while folding the check)
A guy that'd fall in love with your daughter should have his head examined.

ANDREWS
That's an evasion.

PETER
(putting the check into a wallet)
She grabbed herself a perfect running mate. King Westley! The pill of the century!
(pocketing wallet)
What <u>she</u> needs is a guy that'd take a sock at her every day--whether it's coming to her or not.

A close view of the TWO shows Andrews smiling: Here is a man!

PETER
If you had half the brains you're supposed to have, you'd have done it yourself--long ago.

ANDREWS
Do you love her?

PETER
(going for his hat as he replies)
A normal human being couldn't live under the same roof with her, without going nuts.
(going to the door)
She's my idea of nothing!

ANDREWS
I asked you a question. Do you love her?

PETER
(snapping it out)
Yes!
(as Andrews smiles)
But don't hold that against me. I'm a little screwy myself.

He snaps the door open and goes out, following which ANDREWS is seen watching the door, his eyes twinkling, and the scene cuts to the DOWNSTAIRS HALLWAY as Peter comes through, moving on to the front door. But just as he reaches it, Ellie enters, accompanied by half a dozen men and holding a cocktail in her hand. They see each other almost simultaneously, and both stop, glaring.

PETER
(looking her over contemptuously)
Perfect! Now you look natural.

At this Ellie leaves her group and comes toward Peter, and a close view shows them together, glaring at each other.

ELLIE
(icily)
I hope you got your money.

PETER
You bet I did.

ELLIE
Congratulations.

PETER
Same to you.

ELLIE
Why don't you stay and watch the fun? You'll enjoy it immensely.

PETER
I would. But I've got a weak stomach.

He wheels around and goes through the door, Ellie looking after him, her eyes blazing. The drone of a plane motor outside is heard, and several people rush down the stairs, all excited.

GUESTS
Here comes King! He's just coming down! Hurry up, everybody! Come on, Ellie!

Immediately there is a general excitement, as guests hurry through the hallway on the way to the lawn. But Ellen does not move--she remains staring blankly at the door through which Peter went until Andrews enters from his study.

ANDREWS
I just had a long talk with him.

ELLEN
(her voice breaking)
I'm not interested.

ANDREWS
Now, wait a minute, Ellie--

ELLIE
(sharply)
I don't want to hear anything about him!

She walks away from him, and Andrews, frustrated, looks at her helplessly. Thereupon the scene dissolves to a full view of the LAWN. The orchestra is playing Mendelssohn's Wedding March. The lawn is crowded with guests. In the background we see the autogyro idling. A closer view shows a small platform, serving as an altar. Over it there is an arbor of roses. Back of the altar stands a minister, ready. A reverse view reveals a long, narrow, carpeted pathway leading to the house. Both sides are lined with guests, who are murmuring excitedly. At the moment, King Westley and his best man are marching solemnly toward the altar. Back of the altar we see a high platform upon which are several newsreel men who are grinding their cameras.

The guests, of whom close glimpses are caught, are now peering over each other's shoulders. King and his best man have reached the altar, and the music of the wedding march comes to a stop. The orchestra leader is looking around, apparently waiting for a signal. At the DOOR of the HOUSE a very "prissy" middle-aged man waves his handkerchief and nods his head to the orchestra leader. The orchestra leader acknowledges the signal by nodding his head--turns to his men--waves his baton, and the orchestra starts playing, "Here Comes the Bride."--The guests whisper to each other excitedly. A great deal of stirring takes place.

The door of the house slowly opens--and a parade of small flower girls emerges. They march, taking each step carefully, while they strew flowers along the path. They are well out of the way when Ellie, on the arm of her father, appears in the doorway. A view of the guests shows that they cannot contain themselves. Murmurs of "Here she comes," and "Doesn't she look beautiful?" are heard. The newsreel men on their platform behind the altar bestir themselves. This is what they've been waiting for!

ELLIE and her FATHER (seen close) now make their way to the altar. Ellie's face is solemn, and her jaws set.

ANDREWS
(whispering out of the side of his mouth)
You're a sucker to go through with this.

Ellie glances at him out of the corner of her eye--and quickly turns forward again.

ANDREWS
That guy Warne is O.K. He didn't want the reward.

Ellie keeps her eyes glued in front of her, remaining expressionless.

ANDREWS
All he asked for was thirty-nine dollars and sixty cents ... that's what he spent on you. It was a matter of principle with him--says you took him for a ride.

This registers on Ellie and she raises her eyes--but her reaction is only slightly perceptible.

A close view of a GROUP OF GUESTS shows two girls looking enviously in the direction of the bride.

A YOUNG GIRL
(whispering)
I wish I were in her shoes.

SECOND GIRL
Yes. She certainly is lucky.

ELLIE and her FATHER are seen again, and ANDREWS is still whispering to her.

ANDREWS
He loves you, Ellie. Told me so.

This brings a definite reaction, which she quickly covers up.

ANDREWS
You don't want to be married to a mug like Westley.

At this there is a close view of Westley--there is a satisfied smirk on his face.

ANDREWS
I can buy him off for a pot of gold, and you can make an old man happy, and you wouldn't do so bad for yourself. If you change your mind, your car's waiting at the back gate.

Ellie gives no indication of her intentions. Her face remains immobile. And now Ellie and her father have reached the altar. The "prissy" man is placing them in position. The big moment has arrived. The guests are all atwitter. But a close view of ELLIE shows that she realizes that her fate is closing in on her. She looks around for a means of escape.

MINISTER
(starting the ceremony)
Dearly beloved, we are gathered together here in the sight of God and in the face of this company to join together this man and this woman in holy matrimony. If any man can show just cause why they may not lawfully be joined together, let him speak now or else hereafter forever hold his

peace. King, wilt thou have this woman to be thy wedded wife? So long as ye both shall live?

KING

I will.

MINISTER

Ellen, wilt thou have this man to be thy wedded husband so long as ye both shall live?

Then, seen at the ALTAR, Ellie makes her decision. She reaches down, takes a firm hold on her train and, pushing several people aside, runs out of the scene. Those at the altar look up, surprised, and the most startled of all is KING himself.

KING

(calling after her)

Ellie!

He starts to go after her--but finds Andrews in his way while the outcries of the guests rise in chorus.

GUESTS

What's happened? Where's she going?

On the platform, the newsreel men, a look of astonishment on their faces, decide to follow Ellie.

A MAN

Get her, Mac! She's ducking!

And, as viewed by the newsreel men, Ellie is seen in the distance dashing through the gates. The guests stare dumbfounded. Following this, Andrews and King are seen together in the crowd.

KING

(helplessly)

What happened?

ANDREWS

(blandly)

I haven't the slightest idea.

But his mouth twitches as he tries to keep from smiling. As King runs out of sight Andrews gets out a cigar and lights it--a happy smile on his face which he now doesn't try to conceal.

Outside the FRONT GATE Ellie is seen in a fast roadster, as she starts away with a plunge. Her eyes sparkle. A crowd of people dash up, headed by King. They stop dead when they see the car disappear. On the LAWN the commotion runs high, and the guests chatter their amazement. A close view of ANDREWS shows him smiling with satisfaction.

The scene dissolves to ANDREWS' OFFICE, where Andrews is regaling himself with a whiskey and soda. He is in a pleasantly inebriated mood when his SECRETARY enters.

ANDREWS
(as he picks up the phone that has started ringing)
Don't want to talk to--don't want to talk to anybody. Don't want to see anybody.

SECRETARY
But it's King Westley on the phone.

ANDREWS
Ooooooh.
(into the phone)
Hello my would-be ex-son-in-law. I've sent you a check for a hundred thousand. Yes. That's the smartest thing you ever did, Westley, not to contest that annulment. That's satisfactory, isn't it? Yeah. Well, it ought to be. Oh I'm not complaining. It was dirt cheap.
(as he hangs up)
Don't fall out of any windows.

SECRETARY
(placing a telegram on the desk)
There's another wire from Peter, sir. They're in Glen Falls, Michigan.

ANDREWS
(reading it)
"What's holding up the annulment, you slow poke? The Walls of Jericho are toppling."
(to the Secretary)
Send him a telegram right away. Just say. "Let 'em topple."

This dissolves to the exterior of an AUTO CAMP very much like the other camps at which Peter and Ellie stayed. The owner's wife is talking to her husband.

WIFE
Funny couple, ain't they?

MAN
Yeah.

WIFE
If you ask me, I don't believe they're married.

MAN
They're married all right. I just seen the license.

WIFE
They made me get 'em a rope and a blanket, on a night like this.

MAN
Yeah?

WIFE
What do you reckon that's for?

MAN
Blamed if I know. I just brung 'em a trumpet.

WIFE
(puzzled)
A trumpet?

MAN
Yeah. You know, one of those toy things. They sent me to the store to get it.

WIFE
But what in the world do they want a trumpet for?

MAN
I dunno.

The scene moves to the cabin occupied presumably by Peter and Ellie. The windows are lighted. There is a blast from a trumpet, and as the lights go out a blanket is seen dropping to the floor, and the scene fades out.

Notes

1. The opening scene was greatly trimmed back in the film from the version indicated by the script. Riskin made a point of using his lengthier opening sequence in the 1943 publication of the script in *Twenty Best Film Plays,* while appending the "revised opening sequence" as a footnote. The "revised opening sequence" reads as follows:

ANDREWS
Hunger strike, eh? How long has this been going on?

CAPTAIN
She hasn't had anything yesterday or today.

ANDREWS
Send her meals up to her regularly?

CAPTAIN
Yes, sir.

ANDREWS
Well, why don't you jam it down her throat?

CAPTAIN
Well, it's not as simple as all that, Mr. Andrews.

ANDREWS
Ah! I'll talk to her myself. Have some food brought up to her.

CAPTAIN
Yes, sir.

ELLIE
I'm not going to eat a thing until you let me off this boat.

ANDREWS
Aw, come now, Ellie. You know I'll have my way.

ELLIE
Not this time, you won't. I'm already married to him.

ANDREWS
But you're never going to live under the same roof with him. I'll see to that.

ELLIE
Can't you get it through you head that King Westley and I are married? Definitely, legally, actually married. It's over, it's finished. There's not a thing you can do about it. I'm over twenty-one and so is he.

ANDREWS
Would it interest you to know that while you've been on board, I've been making arrangements to have your marriage annulled?

ELLIE
Annulled? I'll have something to say about that and so will King.

ANDREWS
Yes, I expect him to. Ah, the victuals. Come in. Come in.

ELLIE
I thought I told you not to bring any food in here.

ANDREWS
Now wait a minute. This isn't for you. Put it right down here.

ELLIE
Smart, aren't you? So subtle.

ANDREWS
Strategy, my dear.

ELLIE
I suppose it was strategy sending those gorillas down to drag me away from that Justice of the Peace. Your idea of strategy is to use a lead pipe.

ANDREWS
I've won a lot of arguments with a lead pipe.

ELLIE
Outside of the fact that you don't like him, you haven't got a thing against King.

ANDREWS
He's a fake, Ellie.

ELLIE
He's one of the best flyers in the country.

ANDREWS
He's no good and you know it. You married him only because I told you not to.

ELLIE
You've been telling me what not to do ever since I can remember.

ANDREWS
That's because you've always been a stubborn idiot.

ELLIE
I come from a long line of stubborn idiots.

ANDREWS
Well, don't shout. You may work up an appetite.

ELLIE
I'll shout if I want to. I'll scream if I want to.

ANDREWS
All right, scream.

ELLIE
If you don't let me off this boat, I'll break every piece of furniture in this room.

ANDREWS
Here, here, hero. Have a nice piece of juicy steak. You don't have to eat it; just smell it. It's a poem.

2. "Yegg" is somewhat outdated vernacular that originally meant any thief but came to mean, especially in the 1930s, a hobo-thief traveling by the freights.

3. A "drummer" is a traveling salesman. Shapeley the drummer is one of Riskin's most idiomatic characters. Most of his slang is familiar or easily decipherable. A "Mack truck" (as in "You coulda knocked me over with a Mack truck," country cousin to a similar line in *Platinum Blonde*, "You coulda knocked me over with a pin") is a trademark heavy-duty truck. An "iceberg" is an unemotional person; a "kisser" is one's mouth; a "ten-strike" is a complete knockdown of all ten pins in the game of bowling. "Cold turkey" is sudden deprivation. A "hotsy-totsy," the noun form of the exclamatory "hotsie-totsie," indicates a thoroughly satisfactory dame; a "lulu" is a remarkable type; a "filly," in this context, is a young girl.

4. Joshua, the successor to Moses, was one of the Israelites who arrived at the border of Canaan after their flight from Egypt. One of twelve sent to spy out the land, Joshua reported that it was "fruitful but inhabited" by "giants, sons of Anak." This so frightened the Israelites that they decided to return to Egypt, despite Joshua's pleading. The Lord punished the Israelites by decreeing they should wander forty years in the wilderness, and among the adults only Joshua and Caleb (one of his fellow spies) were allowed to enter the Promised Land. "Joshua led the people in its conquest, in the course of which the walls of Jericho fell flat at the sound of his trumpets in one battle and the sun stood still in another" (from *Benét's Reader's Encyclopedia*, Third Edition, Harper & Row, 1987).

5. "According to Hoyle" is synonymous with "according to the rules of the game." Britisher Edmond Hoyle (1672–1769) wrote a famous, authoritative book on all card games and other indoor sports.

6. At a finishing school young, well-to-do ladies are trained in cultural subjects, public activities, and social etiquette.

7. The Elks refers to a longtime American fraternal organization with Masonic-type rituals. The Benevolent and Protective Order of Elks was founded in 1868. In *Meet John Doe,* when Bert and Old Sourpuss suddenly feel neighborly, Old Sourpuss shakes Bert's hand like an "old lodge brother."

8. "East Lynne" refers to an 1861 novel by Mrs. Henry Wood, later dramatized as a tear-jerker by traveling troupes and thus familiar to Victorian era music-hall and small-town audiences.

9. These were the names of contemporary personages. Amelita Galli-Curci was an Italian-American coloratura soprano, "not excelled by any coloratura of her day," from 1909 to her 1930 retirement, according to *The Concise Columbia Encylopedia* (Avon Books, 1988). John McCormack was the reigning Irish-American tenor during the same period, popular with Chicago and Boston audiences, especially, and known for his operas, concerts, and recordings (*The Concise Columbia Encyclopedia).*

10. More slang from Shapeley the drummer: "G's," "smackers," "dough," and "bucks" are all dollars in various amounts. "Behind the eight ball" indicates a losing position, as in a game of eight-ball pool.

11. "Gat," was well known to audiences of Warner Brothers gangster films in the 1930s as a colloquialism for any firearm, but usually a revolver or pistol.

12. The "farmer's daughter" was notorious as the object of prurient jokes by traveling salesmen and other wayfarers of the road.

13. "Gold dig" is not often seen as a verb. A "gold digger" is a girl or woman who befriends a man and becomes his lover or wife solely for the purpose of exploiting him for his money. Warner Brothers popularized the term in the musical film *Golddiggers of 1933.*

14. An "autogyro" or "autogiro" is a trademarked aircraft that utilizes a rotating wing, or rotor, similar to a helicopter but with "a conventional engine propeller combination in addition to the rotor to pull the vehicle through the air like a fixed-wing aircraft" (from *Encyclopedia of Science and Technology,* McGraw-Hill, 1992).

Frank Capra (far right) on the set of *Mr. Deeds Goes to Town* with Gary Cooper and Jean Arthur.

Mr. Deeds Goes to Town

Columbia Pictures, 1936, 115 minutes

Produced and directed by Frank Capra

Written by Robert Riskin, based on a story by Clarence Budington Kelland

Photography by Joseph Walker

Edited by Gene Havlick

Musical direction by Howard Jackson

Art Direction by Stephen Gooson

Costumes by Samuel Lange

Special effects by E. Roy Davison

Cast: Gary Cooper (*Longfellow Deeds*), Jean Arthur (*Babe Bennett*), George Bancroft (*MacWade*), Lionel Stander (*Cornelius Cobb*), Douglas Dumbrille (*John Cedar*), Raymond Walburn (*Walter*), Margaret Matzenauer (*Madame Pomponi*), H. B. Warner (*Judge Walker*), Warren Hymer (*Bodyguard*), Muriel Evans (*Theresa*), Ruth Donnelly (*Mabel Dawson*), Spencer Charters (*Mal*), Emma Dunn (*Mrs. Meredith*), Wryley Birch (*Psychiatrist*), Arthur Hoyt (*Budington*), Stanley Andrews (*James Cedar*), Pierre Watkin (*Arthur Cedar*), John Wray (*Farmer*), Christian Rub (*Swenson*), Jameson Thomas (*Mr. Semple*), Mayo Methot (*Mrs. Semple*), Margaret Seddon (*Jane Faulkner*), Margaret McWade (*Amy Faulkner*), Russell Hicks (*Dr. Malcolm*), Gustav von Seyffertitz (*Dr. Frazier*), Edward Le Saint (*Dr. Fosdick*), Charles [Levison] Lane (*Hallor*), Irving Bacon (*Frank*), George Cooper (*Bob*), Gene Morgan (*Waiter*), Walter Catlett (*Morrow*), Edward Gargan (*2nd Bodyguard*), Paul Hurst (*1st Deputy*),

Paul Porcasi (*Italian*), Franklin Pangborn (*Tailor*), George F. ["Gabby"] Hayes (*Farmers' Spokesman*), Mary Lou Dix (*Shop Girl*), George Meeker (*Brookfield*), Barnett Parker (*Butler*), Patricia Monroe, Lillian Ross (*Hat Check Girls*), Peggy Page (*Cigarette Girl*), Janet Eastman (*Shop Girl*), Bud Flannigan [Dennis O'Keefe] (*Reporter*), Dale Van Sickel (*Lawyer*), Harry C. Bradley (*Anderson*), Edwin Maxwell (*Douglas*), Billy Bevan (*Cabby*), Ann Doran (*Girl on Bus*), Cecil Cunningham, Bess Flowers, Beatrice Curtis, Beatrice Blinn, Pauline Wagner, Frank Hammond, Charles Sullivan, Flo Wix, Hal Budlong, Ethel Palmer, Juanita Crosland, Vacey O'Davoren.

FADE IN

EXTERIOR - MONTAGE
1. Quick shots of a car speeding around curves in a mountainous region. The car jumps a bridge, hurtles into space, crashes in a fireball. Followed by newsboys hawking special editions, people on streetcorners buying and reading newspapers with a succession of banner headlines:
"MARTIN W. SEMPLE, FINANCIER, DIES IN ITALY,"
"CIVIC LEADER KILLED IN AUTO ACCIDENT,"
"DISCLOSURE OF BANKER'S WILL AWAITED" and finally
"SEMPLE HEIR AS YET UNKNOWN"

DISSOLVE TO:

INTERIOR - EDITOR'S OFFICE, DAILY MAIL
2. CLOSE SHOT
of Mac, the editor, at his desk, barking into the telephone.

MAC
Say listen, Corny, who do you think you're talking to? If the Semple attorneys don't know who the heir is, who does?
(listens)
Aw, come on Corny, I've done you a lot of favors. What do you say - who's getting the Semple dough?

CUT TO:

INTERIOR - CEDAR'S PRIVATE OFFICE
3. CLOSE SHOT
Of Cornelius Cobb - a hardened ex-newspaperman, customarily impatient, grouchy and nervous - victim of the New York tempo. His friends call him "Corny."

COBB
(on the phone)
You're asking the wrong guy, Mac. I'm only a press agent.

THE CAMERA PULLS BACK GRADUALLY TO REVEAL a plush law office, leather chairs and shelves of books. Arthur Cedar, attorney, briskly enters scene and seats himself at his desk. Cedar is in the neighborhood of fifty - grey-templed - dignified - sharp. Cobb is using the phone on his desk. Cedar glances at him.

CEDAR
Newspaperman?

COBB
(covering mouthpiece - confidentially)
Wants to know who the heir is.

CEDAR
(firmly)
Hang up.

COBB
(returning to the phone)
Sorry, Mac, I can't. Yeah, Mac. Sure, but I ain't the attorney--

CEDAR
(more firmly)
Hang up.

THE CAMERA PULLS BACK FURTHER TO REVEAL another attorney at one end of the desk, reviewing a pile of papers.

COBB
(continuing)
Mr. Cedar is, and I haven't seen him in two days.
(hangs up the phone)
Listen, Cedar, we've got to do something about the newspapers.

CEDAR
(barely glancing up)
I'm not interested in the newspapers.

COBB
But it's a great story. Somewhere in this country a guy is walking into twenty million bucks.

CEDAR
Yes, I know. My first concern is to locate the lucky man. When I do, it's your job to keep the newspapers away from him.

COBB
(resignedly)
It's okay with me as long as my weekly stipend keeps coming in.

THE CAMERA PULLS BACK TO A FULL SHOT as two men rush in with a flurry of excitement. One of them is Anderson, an obsequious employee of Cedar's. With him is another lawyer, one of the Cedar brothers.

ANDERSON
We located him, Mr. Cedar! We found out where he is.

CEDAR
Good!

FIRST BROTHER
Yes, John, we got him.

ANDERSON
Here's the report: Longfellow Deeds, single, 28, lives in Mandrake Falls, Vermont.

CEDAR
(glancing at the report)
Thank heaven.

FIRST BROTHER
Better wire him right away, John.

CEDAR
I'll do no such thing. I'm going there myself. You're going with me too, Anderson - and you too, Cobb.

He pushes a button on the intercom.

VOICE
Yes?

CEDAR
Make three reservations on the first train out to Mandrake Falls, Vermont.

VOICE
(skeptically)
Where?

CEDAR
Mandrake Falls.
(begins to spell as scene fades)
M-A-N--

CUT TO:

EXT. A STATION

4. MEDIUM SHOT
It is a pleasantly rural scene - with just a handful of local characters scattered about. At one end of the platform - some mail - newspapers - and a few pieces of freight are being loaded. Cedar, Cobb and Anderson stand in front of a welcome sign. The three obviously are out of their element here - obviously "City folks."

Over their shoulders. We hear Cobb's voice as he reads:

COBB'S VOICE
Welcome to Mandrake Falls -
Where the scenery enthralls -
Where no hardship e'er befalls -
Welcome to Mandrake Falls.

5. MEDIUM SHOT
Cobb and Cedar exchange glances.

COBB
That's pretty.

CEDAR
Are you sure this is the town he lives in?

ANDERSON
Yes sir, Mr. Cedar. This is the town all right.

CEDAR
Well, I dropped everything at the office - I hope it's not a wild goose chase.

ANDERSON
No, sir. We checked it thoroughly. He lives here all right.

COBB
Ah! I spy a native. Let's ask him.

CAMERA MOVES WITH THEM as they cross to a small, one-story old brick building, covered with ivy. This is the ticket and freight office combined. In front of it is a very old man, a stoop-shouldered rail agent with a face of a million wrinkles - puttering around some packages.

CEDAR
(as they approach)
Good morning.

AGENT
(glances up)
Morning, neighbors. Morning.

He picks up a package and disappears into the building. Cedar and Cobb look at each other.

COBB
That's an excellent start. At least we've broken the ice.

The old man returns to his pile of packages.

CEDAR
I say, my friend, do you know a fellow by the name of Longfellow Deeds?

AGENT
Deeds?

CEDAR
Yes.

AGENT
Yes, sir. Yes, indeedy. Everyone knows Deeds.

CEDAR
Yes, I--

He again disappears.

COBB
Must be a game he's playing.

The old man shows up again.

CEDAR
We'd like to get in touch with him. It's very important.

AGENT
Who's that?

CEDAR
Deeds! Who do you think I'm talking about?

AGENT
Oh, yes - Deeds. Fine fellow. Very democratic. You won't have no trouble at all. Talk to anybody.

Whereupon the old man carries another package inside. Cobb is properly exasperated now.

CEDAR
I guess we'd better try somebody else.

COBB
No, we won't! The next time that jumping jack comes out, I'll straddle him while you ask him your questions.

The old man emerges from the building and looks up at them as if he's never seen them before.

AGENT
Morning, neighbors.

6. TWO SHOT - COBB AND AGENT (FEATURING COBB)
Cobb grabs the old man as he turns to head back into the building.

COBB
Remember us? We're the fellows who were here a minute ago.

AGENT
Oh, yes. Yes, indeedy. I never forget a face.

He turns again but Cobb holds him by the arm and sets him down on a small packing case.

COBB
Listen, Pop, we've come all the way from New York to look up a fellow by the name of Deeds. It's important - <u>very</u> important!

AGENT
(releasing his arm)
You don't have to get rough, neighbor. All you got to do is ask.

COBB
Then please pretend, for just one fleeting moment, that I'm asking. Where does he reside?

AGENT
Who?

Cobb turns away in disgust. Anderson steps forward.

7. CLOSE SHOT - THE THREE

ANDERSON
Longfellow Deeds - where does he live?

AGENT
Oh, that's what you want! Well, why didn't you say so in the first place instead of beating around the bush? Those other fellows don't know what they're talking about.
(as he exits scene)
Come on, I'll take you there in my car. If they'd only explained to me what they wanted, there would be no trouble.

He leaves Cobb and Cedar staring after him killingly.

DISSOLVE TO:

INT. LONGFELLOW'S LIVING ROOM

8. MEDIUM SHOT
A little old lady, Mrs. Meredith, answers a knock at the door. Cedar, Cobb and Anderson stand there, with the old man at their heels. Mrs. Meredith is a sweet, soft-voiced, timid and fluttery little creature.

MRS. MEREDITH
Oh, will you come in please, gentlemen?

CEDAR
Is Mr. Deeds in?

MRS. MEREDITH
No - he's over to the park arranging for the bazaar, so's to raise money for the fire engine.
(to old man)
Mal, you shoulda knowed he was in the park.

AGENT
Knew it all the time. But these men said they wanted to see the house.
(mumbling as he exits)
Can't read their minds if they don't say what they want.

9. GROUP SHOT
Cobb glares after him exasperatedly. Mrs. Meredith turns to Cobb and Cedar.

MRS. MEREDITH
Come in, please. Come in. Can I get you a cup of tea?

CEDAR
No, thanks.

MRS. MEREDITH
Sit down. Sure I couldn't get you a glass of lemonade or something?

CEDAR
That's very kind of you. Are you related to him?

MRS. MEREDITH
No, I'm his housekeeper.

CEDAR
Well, we'd like to find out something about him. What does he do for a living?

MRS. MEREDITH
He and Jim Mason own the Tallow Works. But that's not where he makes his money. He makes most of it from his poetry.

10. CLOSE SHOT - THE THREE
Featuring Cobb.

COBB
(skeptically)
He writes poetry?

MRS. MEREDITH
Oh, my goodness, yes. Longfellow's famous. He writes all those things on postcards. You know, for Christmas - and Easter - and birthdays. Sit down, please.

She reaches over to a desk and picks one up.

MRS. MEREDITH
Here's one - he got $25 for this one.

11. CLOSEUP - MRS. MEREDITH
As she reads - with feeling:

MRS. MEREDITH
"When you've nowhere to turn - and you're filled
with doubt -
Don't stand in midstream, hesitating,
For you know that your mother's heart cries out -
'I'm waiting, my boy, I'm waiting.'"
(she looks up)
Isn't that beautiful?

12. CLOSEUP - COBB
His eyes open unbelievingly.

MRS. MEREDITH'S VOICE
Isn't it a lovely sentiment?

COBB
(flatly)
Yeah.

A dog enters, racing toward the door, scratching at it and whining.

MRS. MEREDITH
(as she heads toward the door)
Here he is now.

She opens the door and goes out, with the dog racing ahead.

COBB
(to Cedar - sotto voce)
I suggest you break it to him gently. He's liable to keel over from the shock.

Mrs. Meredith re-appears. We hear her voice as she comes through the doorway.

MRS. MEREDITH
They've been waiting a long while.

Longfellow Deeds trails behind her.

LONGFELLOW
Who are they?

MRS. MEREDITH
I don't know.

CEDAR
(standing - formally)
Mr. Longfellow Deeds?

LONGFELLOW
Yes.

CEDAR
How do you do.

LONGFELLOW
(shaking hands)
How do you do.

CEDAR
(extending card)
I'm John Cedar - of the New York firm of Cedar, Cedar, Cedar and Budington.

13. CLOSE SHOT - GROUP
Featuring Cobb. He watches Longfellow who is glancing at the card.

LONGFELLOW
(reads to himself)
Cedar, Cedar, Cedar and Budington.
(looks up; smiles)
Budington must feel like an awful stranger, hmm?

Cobb's eyes pop at the nifty.[1]

CEDAR
Mr. Cornelius Cobb and Mr. Anderson.

They exchange greetings. Longfellow gestures to chairs.

LONGFELLOW
You gentlemen make yourselves comfortable.

COBB AND ANDERSON
Thanks.

14. MEDIUM SHOT
Longfellow crosses to his tuba near a chair. He takes a mouthpiece out of his pocket.

LONGFELLOW
New mouthpiece. Been waiting two weeks for this. Kids keep swiping them all the time. They use 'em for bean shooters.
(he blows a note)
What can I do for you gentlemen?

MRS. MEREDITH
You gentlemen going to stay for lunch?

CEDAR
(right to the point; ignoring her)
I'd like to ask you a few questions.

LONGFELLOW
All right.

Longfellow looks at them strangely and sits down beside his tuba.

CEDAR
Mr. Deeds, are you the son of Dr. Joseph and Mary Deeds?

LONGFELLOW
Yes.

CEDAR
Are your parents living?

LONGFELLOW
Why, no.

CEDAR
Mr. Deeds, does the name of Martin W. Semple mean anything to you?

LONGFELLOW
Not much. He's an uncle of mine, I think. I never saw him, but my mother's name was Semple, you know.

CEDAR
Well, he passed on. He was killed in a motor accident in Italy.

LONGFELLOW
He was? Gee, that's too bad. If there's anything I can do to--

While he speaks, he has been adjusting the tuba between his legs and now sucks on the mouthpiece, preparatory to playing.

CEDAR
I have good news for you, sir. Mr. Semple left a large fortune when he died. He left it all to you, Mr. Deeds. Deducting the taxes, it amounts to something in the neighborhood of $20,000,000.

15. CLOSEUP - LONGFELLOW
His lips are over the mouthpiece of the tuba. His only reaction to the startling news is to lift his eyes in Cedar's direction.

16. GROUP SHOT

MRS. MEREDITH
How about lunch? Are the gentlemen going to stay - or not?

LONGFELLOW
Of course they're going to stay.
(to the gentlemen)
She's got some fresh orange layer cake. You know, with the thick stuff on the top?
(to Mrs. Meredith)
Sure, they don't want to go to the hotel.

Mrs. Meredith leaves. Cobb and Cedar have watched this by-play, open-mouthed, and are now even more astounded to see Longfellow blow into his tuba.

17. CLOSER SHOT - THE THREE

CEDAR
(over the noise of the tuba)
Perhaps you didn't hear what I said, Mr. Deeds! The whole Semple fortune goes to you! $20,000,000!

LONGFELLOW
Oh, yes, I heard you all right. $20,000,000. That's quite a lot, isn't it?

COBB
Oh, it'll do in a pinch.

LONGFELLOW
(impressed)
Yes, indeed. I wonder why he left me all that money? I don't need it.

He resumes his 'Oom-pahs.'

18. CLOSE SHOT - CEDAR AND COBB
Staring, unbelievingly.

DISSOLVE TO:

INT. AN ALCOVE
19. FULL SHOT
The three men sit around a table, having lunch. By Longfellow's side is, as expected, the tuba.

CEDAR
Mr. Cobb here is an ex-newspaperman associated with your uncle for many years - as a sort of buffer.

LONGFELLOW
Buffer?

COBB
Yeah. A glorified doormat.

CEDAR
Yes. You see, rich people need someone to keep the crowds away. The world's full of pests. Then there's the newspapers to handle. One must know when to seek publicity - and when to avoid it.

During Cedar's speech, Longfellow seems to have been lost in his own thoughts.

20. CLOSE SHOT - LONGFELLOW AND COBB
Favoring Longfellow.

LONGFELLOW
Cedar, Cedar, Cedar and Budington. Funny, I can't think of a rhyme for Budington.

COBB
Why should you?

LONGFELLOW
Well, whenever I run across a funny name, I always like to poke around for a rhyme. Don't you?

COBB
Nah.

LONGFELLOW
I've got one for Cobb--

21. CLOSE SHOT - THE GROUP

LONGFELLOW
"There once was a man named Cobb,
Who kept Semple away from the mob.
Came the turn of the tide
And Semple - he died -
And now poor Cobb's out of a job!"

COBB
Sounds like a two weeks' notice to me.

LONGFELLOW
Huh?

COBB
I've gotten the 'backaroo' in many ways - but never in rhyme.

LONGFELLOW
Oh, I don't mean that. I'm sure I'm going to need your help.

COBB
Oh, that's different if it's just poetry.

22. WIDER ANGLE
As Mrs. Meredith enters with coffee which she pours.

CEDAR
Are you a married man, Mr. Deeds?

LONGFELLOW
Who - me? No.

MRS. MEREDITH
No, he's too fussy for that. That's what's the matter with him. There are lots of nice girls right here in Mandrake Falls who're dying to be married--

LONGFELLOW
Don't pay any attention to her.

MRS. MEREDITH
He's got a lot of foolish notions - about saving a lady in distress.

LONGFELLOW
Now you keep out of this!

CEDAR
(diplomatically)
Saving a lady in distress, eh? Well, I suppose we all have dreams like that when we are young.
(rising)
Incidentally, we'd better get started. You'll have to pack.

LONGFELLOW
What for?

CEDAR
You're going to New York with us.

LONGFELLOW
When?

COBB
This afternoon - at four o'clock.

LONGFELLOW
I don't think we've got any suitcases.

MRS. MEREDITH
Well, we could borrow a couple from Mrs. Simpson. You know, she went to Niagara Falls last year.

LONGFELLOW
I'm kind of nervous. I've never been away from Mandrake Falls in my life. Kind of like to see Grant's Tomb, though.

CEDAR
(all business)
I can understand that.
(rises to go)
We'll take a walk around town, meet you at the train at four o'clock.
(shakes his hand)
Congratulations, Mr. Deeds. You're one of the richest men in the country. We'll see you later.
(to Mrs. Meredith)
Goodbye and thank you.

COBB
See you later, kid.

ANDERSON'S VOICE
(as he too exits)
Good day, sir.

They exit.

23. TWO SHOT - LONGFELLOW AND MRS. MEREDITH

LONGFELLOW
Hear what he said? You know how much twenty million is?

MRS. MEREDITH
I don't care how much it is. You sit right there and eat your lunch. You haven't touched a thing.

Longfellow nibbles at some food, staring into space thoughtfully.

DISSOLVE TO:

EXT. STATION

24. LONG SHOT

The whole town is out. The band is playing "He's a Jolly Good Fellow" - the crowd sings. It's a festive occasion. A large, awkwardly painted sign looms over everyone's head. It reads:

FAREWELL
LONGFELLOW DEEDS
THE PRIDE OF MANDRAKE FALLS

25. MEDIUM SHOT - CEDAR AND ANDERSON

They peer anxiously around, looking for someone, when Cobb dashes in.

COBB
(breathlessly)
I can't find him.

CEDAR
You can't?

COBB
I looked everywhere. I even went to his house. It's locked up.

ANDERSON
He probably had a change of heart.

CEDAR
He wasn't very anxious to come in the first place.

COBB
(looking on)
Here comes the train.

Cedar glances off.

26. LONG SHOT (STOCK)

Of train approaching.

27. CLOSE SHOT - CEDAR AND COBB

The band has already begun and is now in the midst of "For He's A Jolly Good Fellow."

At this moment, as he looks off, a startled expression comes into Cobb's eyes. He grabs Cedar by the arm - who glances in the direction he points.

COBB
Look!

CEDAR
What?

COBB
That tuba player!

28. MEDIUM SHOT - THE BAND
With Longfellow, in his customary position, blowing on his tuba.

CONTINUATION SCENE 27
Cedar and Cobb stare, wide-eyed, as the song is finished.

COBB
Well, now I've seen everything.

DISSOLVE TO:

EXT. STATION
29. LONG SHOT
In the b.g. is the train with Longfellow standing on the observation platform, clutching his tuba. On either side of him is Cedar and Cobb. In the f.g. the crowd yells its farewell. Several of them stuff baskets of fruit into his hands. The band plays "Auld Lang Syne."

30. CLOSE SHOT
Over Longfellow and Cobb's shoulders. As the train begins pulling out. Longfellow smiles wanly and waves.

LONGFELLOW
Goodbye, Mrs. Meredith! Goodbye, Jim! Bye, Buddy! Goodbye, everybody!
(a pause)
Gosh, I've got a lot of friends.

Cobb looks up into Longfellow's face - affected by the scene.

DISSOLVE TO:

INT. TRAIN DRAWING ROOM
31. FULL SHOT
Longfellow is slumped in his seat, his legs sprawled out, his eyes ceilingward - in deep thought. Cobb sits across from him. Cedar enters, hangs up his coat, hat and cane.

COBB
(opening a snifter - generously)
Have a drink?

LONGFELLOW
(distractedly)
No, thanks.

Cobb and Cedar exchange a look.

CEDAR
Will you have a cigar?

LONGFELLOW
No, thank you.

Cedar sits down.

CEDAR
(breaking the silence)
I wouldn't worry if I were you. Of course, a large fortune like this entails a great responsibility - but you'll have a good deal of help. So don't worry. Leave everything to me.

LONGFELLOW
Oh, I wasn't worried about that.

CEDAR
No?

LONGFELLOW
I was wondering where they're going to get another tuba player for the band.

Cobb has just finished taking a drink and can't help but nearly spit it out.

FADE OUT:

FADE IN

32. LONG SHOT (STOCK)
The 20th Century crossing the Harlem River.

DISSOLVE TO:

33. ANOTHER STOCK SHOT
Of the 20th Century going under the street level on Park Avenue.

DISSOLVE TO:

34. CLOSE SHOT OF OFFICE DOOR
Upon which we read: "CEDAR, CEDAR & BUDINGTON - ENTRANCE." CAMERA PULLS BACK to take in Cedar, who opens the door and walks through.

INT. GENERAL OFFICE
35. CLOSE TRUCKING SHOT
With Cedar as he strides across the room - in business-like fashion. He comes to a door marked "PRIVATE OFFICES." He pushes this door opens and disappears.

MAN'S VOICE
(as Cedar passes by)
Hello, John. Where have you been?

CEDAR
(as he walks briskly)
I've been fishing.

In the background is typical office hub-bub.

CEDAR
(to a secretary as he passes)
Good morning, Celia.

SECRETARY
Good morning, Mr. Cedar.

A chorus of "Good Morning, Mr. Cedar!" issues from the clerks. A secretary looks up.

INT. PRIVATE OFFICES
36. CLOSE TRUCKING SHOT
With Cedar - as he passes through the room - arriving at a door marked "JOHN CEDAR, PRIVATE." He goes through the door.

INT. CEDAR'S PRIVATE OFFICES - ANTEROOM

37. FULL SHOT

Cedar breezes in and speaks to a secretary.

CEDAR

Good morning. Where are they?

SECRETARY

Waiting for you in the other office.

He strides across the room to still another door marked "PRIVATE" and he disappears.

DISSOLVE TO:

INT. CEDAR'S PRIVATE OFFICE

38. FULL SHOT

A group of associates sit around in large leather chairs, as Cedar barges in.

CEDAR

(beaming)

Good morning. Hello, boys.

The men come to life. Some rise - others lean forward. Two of them are brothers of Cedar - tall and athletic. The third is a small, frightened-looking man. He is Budington.

MEN

(ad lib)

Hello, John.
What happened?
Well, what's he like?

CEDAR

We've got nothing to worry about. He's as naive as a child.

BUDINGTON

John--

CEDAR

Close that door.

(into dictograph)

Will you get Mrs. Cedar on the phone, please?

FIRST BROTHER

Come on, John. What happened?

CEDAR

(to associates)

The smartest thing I ever did was to make that trip.

BUDINGTON

(anxiously)

John, did you get the - uh--

39. MED. SHOT - GROUP
Favoring Cedar.

CEDAR
(interrupting)
No, Budington, I didn't get the Power of Attorney. But don't worry, I will.
(beaming to his brothers)
I asked him last night what he was going to do with the money, and what do you suppose he said?

THE TWO BROTHERS
(gathering around him)
What?
I can't imagine.

CEDAR
He said he guessed he'd give it away.

THE TWO BROTHERS
(laughing)
Give it away!?
The boy must be a nit-wit!

Budington hasn't enjoyed the joke - his mind still on their problem.

ONE OF THE BROTHERS
Well, John, you had the right hunch!

BUDINGTON
John, if you don't mind my saying so - we can't afford to

CEDAR
(irascibly)
I know, Budington. We can't afford to have the books investigated right now. You must have said that a thousand times already.

BUDINGTON
But what if they fall into somebody else's hands, why - uh--

CEDAR
Well, it hasn't happened yet - has it?

BUDINGTON
(wailing)
But a half million dollars! My goodness, where are we going to get--

CEDAR
(exploding)
Will you stop worrying! It was I who got old man Semple to turn everything over to us, wasn't it? And who got the Power of Attorney from him! All right, and I'll get it again!
(pause - change of tone)
I'll take it easy. Those books'll never leave this office.

DISSOLVE TO:

INT. AN APARTMENT

40. MEDIUM SHOT

George Semple, a ne'er-do-well, prominent for the pouches under his eyes and a perpetual nose-twitch, is sprawled out in a chair reading a newspaper. A nagging wife walks around him.

WIFE

A yokel! Nothing but a yokel! Your uncle must have been mad to leave all that money to him! You're as closely related to him as he is, and what did you get?

She storms around the room. George merely twitches his nose but says nothing.

WIFE

(slaps the paper George is reading)

I say, what did you get?

GEORGE

Stop yelling. Can I help it if my uncle didn't like me?

WIFE

I told you to be nice to him. Ten years we've been waiting for that old man to kick off. And then we were going to be on Easy Street. Yeah - on Easy Street!

GEORGE

Oh, shut up! It's too late now, and you're a nuisance!

WIFE

That's just what I'm going to be - a nuisance. I'm going to be a nuisance until I get hold of some of that money!

DISSOLVE TO:

INT. EDITOR'S OFFICE, DAILY MAIL

41. FULL SHOT

The editor stands in front of his desk. Four or five reporters in front of him - several photographers. In the b.g., leaning against the wall near the door, apparently indifferent, is Babe Bennett. The editor, Mac, is haranguing them.

MAC

(as he blows his nose)

He's news! Every time he blows his nose, it's news. A corn-fed bohunk like that falling into the Semple fortune is hot copy ... But it's got to be personal. It's got to have an angle. What does he think about? How does it feel to be a millionaire! Is he going to get married! What does he think of New York! Is he smart? Is he dumb? ... A million angles!

42. CLOSE SHOT - BABE

She has a string in her hand which she keeps flicking, trying to get a knot into it - in the manner of cowboys with a rope. Mac's voice continues over scene:

43. MEDIUM SHOT
Of them all, as Mac continues:

MAC
He's been here three days, and what have you numbskulls brought in! Any halfwit novice could have done better!

REPORTER'S VOICE
Yeah, we tried too--

MAC
Am I talking too loud? Or annoying anybody?

REPORTER
You know Corny Cobb. He's keeping him under lock and key.

MAC
Cobb, Cobb! Never mind about Cobb. Use what little brains you've got! Find out something yourselves, you imbecilic stupes! Now get out of here before I really tell you what I think of you. Come on, get out!

They scramble to their feet. One of the reporters mumbles something as he passes Mac on the way to the door.

REPORTER
(Mumbles.)

MAC
(alert)
What was that?

REPORTER
(thinking fast - covering up)
Huh? I said you had dirty plaster.

44. MED. CLOSE SHOT AT DOOR
As Babe is still flicking her string, trying to get a knot. The reporters file past her on their way out. Just as the last one is approaching, she succeeds in doing the trick.

45. MEDIUM SHOT
As Mac turns to Babe.

MAC
You too! Thought I could depend on you, but you're getting as bad as the rest of them.

He grabs up a handful of papers and starts out.

BABE
(flicking the string)
Look, I can do it!

MAC
What's gotten into you, Babe? I remember the time when you'd blast this town wide open before you'd let Cobb get away with a thing like this.

46. CLOSE TWO SHOT

BABE
Oh, he's not getting away with anything.

MAC
(excited)
Listen, Babe - get me some stuff on this guy, and you can have--

BABE
Can I have a month's vacation?

MAC
With pay!

BABE
With pay!

MAC
Uh-huh.

BABE
(casually, as she starts away)
Leave four columns open on the front page tomorrow.

47. MEDIUM SHOT
As Babe crosses to door.

MAC
Now you're talking, Babe. I'll keep the whole front page open. What are you going to do?

BABE
(at door)
Have lunch.

She exits. Mac's face lights up happily.

DISSOLVE TO:

EXT. RESIDENCE

48. LONG SHOT
Of a large, imposing-looking residence.

INT. LONGFELLOW'S BEDROOM

49. MEDIUM SHOT
Longfellow stands awkwardly between two tailors - who chalk and pin a suit on him. After a few seconds of silence:

LONGFELLOW
It's the first time I ever had a suit made on purpose.

The tailors smile accommodatingly as CAMERA PULLS BACK and we discover that both Cedar and Cobb are present. Cobb is slumped in a chair, and Cedar is carefully putting some papers away in a portfolio.

CEDAR
It's merely a suggestion. I don't wish to press the point, Mr. Deeds, but if you'll give me your Power of Attorney we'll take care of everything. It'll save you a lot of petty annoyances. Every shark in town will be trying to sell you something.

LONGFELLOW
Oh, yes, there've been a lot of them around here already. Strangest kind of people. Salesmen - politicians - moochers - all want something. I haven't had a minute to myself. Haven't seen Grant's Tomb yet.

CEDAR
Well, you see, your uncle didn't bother with that sort of thing. He left everything to us. He traveled most of the time, and enjoyed himself. You should do the same thing, Mr. Deeds.

LONGFELLOW
Besides wanting to be my lawyer, you also want to handle my investments too?

CEDAR
Yes. That is to say--

LONGFELLOW
Well, outside of your regular fee, how much extra will it cost?

CEDAR
(too quickly)
Oh - nothing. No extra charge.

LONGFELLOW
That involves a lot of extra work, doesn't it?

CEDAR
(generously)
Yes, but that's an added service a firm like Cedar, Cedar, Cedar and Budington usually donates.

LONGFELLOW
Budington. Funny, I can't think of a rhyme for Budington yet.

50. WIDER ANGLE
As a butler stands in the doorway.

BUTLER
The gentlemen from the opera are still waiting in the board room, sir. They're getting a trifle impatient, sir.

LONGFELLOW
They are? I forgot all about them.
(to Cobb)
What do you think they want?

CEDAR
Well, your uncle was Chairman of the Board of Directors. They probably expect you to carry on.

COBB
(rising)
I'll tell those mugs to keep their shirts on, that you'll be right down.

LONGFELLOW
Thanks
(suddenly)
Oh, did you send that telegram to Jim Mason?

COBB
Jim Mason? Oh, yeah. Yeah. No, I didn't send it. I've got it written out, though. Here it is.
(reaches into his pocket and reads)
"Arthur's been with the Tallow Works too long. STOP. Don't think we should fire him. Longfellow."

LONGFELLOW
Fine. Send it right away. I don't want him to fire Arthur.

COBB
Oh, sure. Sure. We don't want to fire Arthur.

LONGFELLOW
He was the last baby my father delivered, Arthur was.

CEDAR
I think you ought to give this matter some thought, Mr. Deeds.

LONGFELLOW
Huh?

CEDAR
I mean, about the Power of Attorney.

LONGFELLOW
Oh, yes. Yes, I will.

Cobb has stalled long enough to hear Longfellow's decision before he goes out of the room.

LONGFELLOW
I'll give it a lot of thought. There was a fellow named Winslow here a little while ago, wanted to handle my affairs for nothing too. It puzzles me why these people all want to work for nothing. It isn't natural. So I guess I'd better think about it some more.

51. MEDIUM SHOT
Longfellow, Cedar and the two tailors.

TAILOR
That's that.

LONGFELLOW
You go to an awful lot of work to keep a fellow warm, don't you?

TAILOR
Yes, sir.

A butler enters again.

BUTLER
A Mr. Hallor to see you sir.

CEDAR
(quickly)
Did you say Hallor?

BUTLER
Yes, sir.

CEDAR
Well, don't let him in.

LONGFELLOW
Why not? Who is he?

CEDAR
A lawyer representing some woman with a claim against the estate.
(to butler)
Tell him to see me at my office.

LONGFELLOW
Well, if he has a claim, we'd better see him.
(to butler)
Send him in.

The butler disappears.

CEDAR
He's capable of causing you a lot of trouble, Mr. Deeds.

LONGFELLOW
How can he make any trouble for me? I haven't done anything.

The butler reappears, followed by Hallor. The minute he appears, Cedar speaks up belligerently.

CEDAR
I thought I told you to take up this matter with me, Hallor.

52. MED. CLOSE GROUP SHOT

HALLOR
I'm a little tired of being pushed around by you, Mr. Cedar - I don't care how important you are.
(to Longfellow)
Mr. Deeds, I represent Mrs. Semple.

LONGFELLOW
(eyebrows raised)
Mrs. Semple?

HALLOR
Yes. Your uncle's common-law wife. She has a legal claim on the estate.

CEDAR
We'll let the courts decide what her legal position is.

HALLOR
You wouldn't dare go into court with a case like this - and you know it!

He turns to Longfellow, who has listened to them studyingly.

HALLOR
I leave it to you, Mr. Deeds. Can you conceive of any court not being in sympathy with any woman who gave up the best years of her life for an old man like your uncle?

LONGFELLOW
What kind of wife did you say she was?

HALLOR
Common-law wife. On top of that, there's a child.

LONGFELLOW
A child? My uncle's?

HALLOR
Yes, sir.

LONGFELLOW
That's awful. The poor woman should be taken care of immediately.

HALLOR
(pleased)
I'm glad to see you're willing to be reasonable, Mr. Deeds.

LONGFELLOW
If she was his wife, she should have all the money. That's only fair. I don't want a penny of it.

He yanks his trousers off and hands them to the tailor.

CEDAR
Don't make any rash promises--

As the tailors exit, Cobb returns.

COBB
You'd better get right down there. That opera mob is about to break into the Mad Song from "Lucia."[2]

LONGFELLOW
(to Hallor)
Oh, I don't want to keep them waiting any longer. They're important people.
(to Cobb)
I wish you'd go along with me, Cobb. They're all strangers to me.

HALLOR
Well, what about it, Mr. Deeds?

LONGFELLOW
(getting into robe - to Hallor)
You'll excuse me, won't you? I'll be right back.

He exits with Cobb.

INT. CORRIDOR
53. MED. TRUCKING SHOT
As Longfellow and Cobb come out and start down corridor.

LONGFELLOW
Gee, I'm busy. Did the opera people always come here for their meetings?

COBB
Uh-huh.

LONGFELLOW
That's funny. Why is that?

COBB
(wisely)
Why do mice go where there's cheese?[3]

INT. BOARD ROOM
54. FULL SHOT
A group of eight distinguished-looking men sit around a long table, awaiting Longfellow's arrival. At the head of the table is a Mr. Douglas.

DOUGLAS
From what I'm led to believe, the young man's quite childish. I don't think we'll have any difficulty in getting him to put up the entire amount. After all, it's only a matter of $180,000.

CHORUS OF VOICES
A drop in the bucket for him.
An excellent idea!
Why not? ...

DOUGLAS
(slyly)
You know, gentlemen, we're really very fortunate the young man is so sympathetic toward music.
(winking)
He plays the tuba in the town band.

MAN
(who has been watching at door)
Here he comes.

DOUGLAS
Good.

There is a shuffle of preparation.

DISSOLVE TO:

INT. DIRECTOR'S ROOM
55. SAME SCENE
With Longfellow and Cobb present. Longfellow looks around, completely awed.

DOUGLAS
Now, gentlemen, the first order of business will be the election of a new Chairman of the Board.

A MAN
(rising)
As a sentimental gesture toward the best friend opera ever had, the late Mr. Semple, I think it only fitting that his nephew, Mr. Longfellow Deeds, should be made our next Chairman. I therefore nominate him.

A VOICE
Second.

DOUGLAS
All those in favor ...

EVERYBODY
Aye.

DOUGLAS
Carried.
(rises)
My congratulations, Mr. Deeds.

56. CLOSER SHOT
Featuring Longfellow.

LONGFELLOW
(self-consciously)
I'm Chairman?

DOUGLAS
(humoring a child)
Oh yes, of course - you've just been elected.

LONGFELLOW
(to Cobb)
I'm Chairman.

COBB
(dryly)
Happy voyage.

DOUGLAS
Right here, Mr. Deeds.

57. WIDER ANGLE
As Longfellow is led to the president's chair. Douglas sits next to him.

DOUGLAS
Now, the next order of business is the reading of the Secretary's minutes ...

A VOICE
Move we dispense with it.

ANOTHER VOICE
Second.

DOUGLAS
All in favor?

CHORUS OF VOICES
Aye!

Longfellow looks his surprise.

DOUGLAS
I think they can be dispensed with. We're ready now for the reading of the Treasurer's report.

A VOICE
Move we dispense with it.

ANOTHER VOICE
Second.

DOUGLAS
All in favor?

CHORUS OF VOICES
Aye!

DOUGLAS
Quite right! Now, gentlemen, the next business will be--

58. MED. CLOSE SHOT
Featuring Longfellow, as he interrupts:

LONGFELLOW
Wait a minute. What does the Chairman do?

DOUGLAS
Why, the Chairman presides at the meetings.

LONGFELLOW
That's what I thought. If you don't mind, I'm rather interested in the Treasurer's report. I'd like to hear it.

There is an uncomfortable shuffle. For a few minutes, no one speaks. From the rear, a tall man rises.

59. CLOSE SHOT
Featuring treasurer.

TREASURER
The treasurer reports a deficit of $180,000 for the current year.

60. CLOSE SHOT - LONGFELLOW
He is stunned.

LONGFELLOW
A deficit! You mean we've lost that much?

61. WIDER ANGLE
To include all at table.

DOUGLAS
You see, Mr. Deeds, the opera is not conducted for profit.

LONGFELLOW
It isn't? What is it conducted for?

DOUGLAS
Why, it's an artistic institution--

LONGFELLOW
We own an opera house, don't we?

A VOICE
We do.

LONGFELLOW
And we give shows?

DOUGLAS
We provide opera.

LONGFELLOW
But you charge. I mean, you sell tickets?

VOICE
Of course.

LONGFELLOW
And it doesn't pay?

DOUGLAS
That's impossible. The opera has never paid.

LONGFELLOW
(conclusively)
Well, then, we must give the wrong kind of shows.

Cobb smiles. The directors are stumped.

62. MED. CLOSE SHOT
Featuring Douglas and Longfellow.

DOUGLAS
The wrong kind! There isn't any wrong or right kind. Opera is opera!

LONGFELLOW
I guess it is. But I personally wouldn't care to be head of a business that kept losing money. That wouldn't be common sense. Incidentally, where is the $180,000 coming from?

DOUGLAS
Well, we were rather expecting it to come from you.

LONGFELLOW
Me?!

DOUGLAS
Naturally.

LONGFELLOW
Excuse me, gentlemen, there's nothing natural about <u>that</u>.

He is suddenly startled. His ears prick up.

63. SHOT OF DIRECTORS
They all stare at Longfellow. Over scene comes the low wailing cry of a siren, which increases in volume as it gets closer to the building.

64. MEDIUM SHOT
Longfellow jumps up.

LONGFELLOW
Hey, a fire engine!

He rushes to the window and peers out. The others stare unbelievably. The shriek of the siren finally dies down. Longfellow turns back.

LONGFELLOW
(admiringly)
Gee, that was a pip![4]
(as he goes back to his seat)
We expect we're going to have one like that in Mandrake Falls pretty soon — with a siren, too.

There is a pause while he gets seated.

LONGFELLOW
Now, where were we?

65. MED. CLOSE SHOT AT TABLE

DOUGLAS
You see, Mr. Deeds, the opera is not conducted like any ordinary business.

LONGFELLOW
Why not?

DOUGLAS
Because it just isn't a business, that's all!

LONGFELLOW
Well, maybe it isn't to you, but it certainly is a business to me, if I have to make up a loss of $180,000. If it's losing that much money, there must be something wrong. Maybe you charge too much. Maybe you're selling bad merchandise. Maybe lots of things. I don't know. You see, I expect to do a lot of good with that money. And I can't afford to put it into anything that I don't look into. That's my decision for the time being, gentlemen. Goodbye, and thank you for making me Chairman.

66. MED. SHOT - DIFFERENT ANGLE
He exits, followed by Cobb, whose eyes shriek his admiration. The directors watch them leave, flabbergasted. Cobb's head reappears in doorway.

COBB
Gentlemen, you'll find the smelling salts in the medicine chest.

He disappears. The Board of Directors stare in dumb stupefaction at the door.

WIPE OFF TO:

INT. LONGFELLOW'S BEDROOM
67. MED. SHOT
As Longfellow enters. Hallor and Cedar rise.

LONGFELLOW
Sorry to keep you waiting so long. Those opera people are funny. They wanted me to put up $180,000.

HALLOR
What about it, Mr. Deeds?

LONGFELLOW
Why, I turned them down, naturally.

HALLOR
No, I mean - about my client.

LONGFELLOW
Oh - we'll have to do something about the common wife.

Longfellow's valet, Walter, enters and holds up a full dress suit.

WALTER
Tails tonight, sir?

LONGFELLOW
What - tails?
(turns and sees it)
Why, that's a monkey suit![5] Do you want people to laugh at me? I never wore one of those things in my life.

WALTER
Yes, sir.

The tailors are leaving.

TAILOR
(shaking hands with Longfellow)
Goodbye, and thank you sir.

LONGFELLOW
Goodbye.
(turning to the others)
Wants me to wear a monkey suit.

Cedar and Hallor smile accommodatingly. Walter hands him a pair of trousers.

68. CLOSER SHOT OF GROUP
As Longfellow starts getting into the trousers.

HALLOR
Of course, we don't want to appear greedy, Mr. Deeds.

LONGFELLOW
Huh?

HALLOR
I say we don't want to appear greedy.

LONGFELLOW
Oh. That.

Walter has gotten down on his knees and holds the ends of the pants.

LONGFELLOW
What do you think you're doing?

WALTER
Why, I'm assisting you, sir.

LONGFELLOW
Get up from there. I don't want anybody holding the ends of <u>my</u> pants. Get up from there!

WALTER
(rising)
Yes, sir.

LONGFELLOW
(to others)
Imagine that - holding the ends of my pants!

Hallor smiles feebly - his impatience growing.

HALLOR
Mrs. Semple is entitled by law to one-third of the estate.

LONGFELLOW
(to Walter)
And don't ever get down on your knees again, understand?

WALTER
No, sir.

LONGFELLOW
(to Hallor)
Excuse me. What did you say?

HALLOR
Mrs. Semple is entitled to one-third of the estate.

LONGFELLOW
One-third? That's about $7,000,000 isn't it?

HALLOR
(quietly)
Well, we didn't expect that much. I'm sure I can get her to settle quietly for one million.

CEDAR
If there's any talk of settlement, Hallor, take it up with me at the office.

HALLOR
I'll do no such thing--

LONGFELLOW
That's right. Don't you go to his office. There's only one place you're going, and that's out the door.

Hallor looks up, surprised.

HALLOR
You're making a mistake, Mr. Deeds.

LONGFELLOW
Oh no, I'm not. I don't like your face. Besides, there's something fishy about a person who would settle for a million dollars when they can get seven million. I'm surprised that Mr. Cedar, who's supposed to be a smart man, couldn't see through that.

HALLOR
Now wait a minute, buddy--

69. MED. SHOT
Longfellow crosses to bell cord and pulls it.

LONGFELLOW
There's one nice thing about being rich - you ring a bell and things happen. When the servant comes in, Mr. Hallor, I'm going to ask him to show you to the door. Many people don't know where it is.

HALLOR
No use in getting tough. That'll get you nowhere, Mr. Deeds.
(strongly)
You know, we've got letters.

As a butler enters, Longfellow turns to him.

LONGFELLOW
Will you show Mr. Hallor to the front door?

BUTLER
Yes, sir.

70. CLOSE SHOT AT DOOR
As Hallor gets to it. Longfellow grabs him by the shirt front and half lifts him off the floor.

LONGFELLOW
And listen, there isn't any wife - there aren't any letters - and I think you're a crook. So you better watch your step.

He shoves Hallor violently and he stumbles out of scene. Cobb enters to Longfellow, his hand extended.

COBB
I can't hold out on you any longer. Lamb bites wolf.
(shakes his head)
Beautiful.

LONGFELLOW
Only common sense.

71. MED SHOT
Cedar has been most uncomfortable through the scene, but now suavely assumes an admiring attitude.

CEDAR
(a forced smile)
I can't hold out any longer either, Mr. Deeds.
(holds out his hand)
Being an attorney for you will be a very simple affair.

LONGFELLOW
You're not my attorney yet, Mr. Cedar. Not till I find out what's on your mind. Suppose you get the books straightened out quick so I can have a look at them.

CEDAR
Yes, of course, if you wish. But you must be prepared. This sort of thing will be daily routine.
(picks up his hat)
If it becomes annoying, you let me know. Goodbye, Mr. Deeds. Goodbye, sir.

Longfellow shakes his hand. Cedar exits. Longfellow stares after him disgustedly, wiping his hands with his handkerchief.

LONGFELLOW
Even his hands are oily.

Walter has entered and holds up a coat for Longfellow.

COBB
Well, how about tonight? What would you like in the way of entertainment?

LONGFELLOW
Entertainment?

72. CLOSE TWO SHOT

COBB
Your uncle had a weakness for dark ones, tall and stately. How would you like yours? Dark or fair, tall or short, fat or thin, tough or tender?

LONGFELLOW
What're you talking about?

COBB
Women! Ever heard of 'em?

LONGFELLOW
Oh.

COBB
Name your poison and I'll supply it.

LONGFELLOW
Some other time, Cobb. Some other time.

COBB
Okay, you're the boss.
(as he goes)
When your blood begins to boil, yell out. I'll be seeing you!

73. MED. SHOT
As Cobb exits. Longfellow turns to Walter, the valet.

LONGFELLOW
He talks about women as if they were cattle.

WALTER
Every man to his taste, sir.

LONGFELLOW
Tell me, Walter, are all those stories I hear about my uncle true?

WALTER
Well, sir, he sometimes had as many as twenty in the house at the same time.

LONGFELLOW
Twenty! What did he do with them?

WALTER
That was something I was never able to find out, sir.

WIPE OFF TO:

EXT. CORRIDOR
74. MED. SHOT
Longfellow, exiting his bedroom, wearing a coat and hat. He comes to the top of a grand staircase, looks around slyly and sees that no one is watching. He slides down the bannister and touches the statue at the bottom for good luck.

He starts for the door. When he gets there he finds his way barred by two husky-looking mugs. He looks up surprised.

FIRST BODYGUARD
Hey, you going out?

LONGFELLOW
Why yes. Isn't that all right?

2ND BODYGUARD
No. Don't ever want to go out without telling us.

LONGFELLOW
Who are you?

BODYGUARDS
We're your bodyguards.

LONGFELLOW
Oh, yeah.

2ND BODYGUARD
Yeah, Mr. Cobb said stick to your tail no matter what.

LONGFELLOW
That's very nice of Mr. Cobb but I don't want anybody sticking to my tail no matter what.

FIRST BODYGUARD
Sorry, mister. Orders is orders.

LONGFELLOW
Is that so?

2ND BODYGUARD
Yes, sir. We gotta get you up in the morning - and we gotta put you to bed at night.

FIRST BODYGUARD
Only it's all right. No matter what we see - we don't see nuttin', see?

LONGFELLOW
(smiling)
That's going to be fun.

2ND BODYGUARD
Some people like it.

Longfellow glances around the room thoughtfully, then continues:

LONGFELLOW
Uh, will you do something for me before we go out?

FIRST BODYGUARD
Sure!

The first bodyguard eagerly takes out a pistol. The second bodyguard slaps it away.

2ND BODYGUARD
(to first bodyguard)
Put that away, slug!
(to Longfellow)
At your service!

LONGFELLOW
I got a trunk in that room. Will you get it out for me?

2ND BODYGUARD
Certainly.

FIRST BODYGUARD
With pleasure.

The two bodyguards accommodatingly enter a closet. The moment they are gone, Longfellow closes the door calmly and turns the key.

BODYGUARDS
(ad-lib)
Hey, hey! We're your bodyguards. You can't do this!

Longfellow whistles as he exits.

DISSOLVE TO:

<u>EXT. FRONT OF HOUSE</u>

75. MED. CLOSE SHOT
Longfellow comes out, glances over the horizon. The air is filled with a slight drizzle and he sighs happily.

CUT TO:

<u>INT. TAXI CAB</u>

76. CLOSE SHOT
Babe and two photographers, Bob and Frank, are huddled conspiratorially in the back seat of a taxi cab.

BABE
(pointing)
There he is. Yep, that's him.

BOB
That's who?

BABE
Get the cameras ready and follow me.

FRANK
What are you going to do?

BABE
Never mind. Follow me and grab whatever you can get.

BOB
I suppose it's going to be the same old thing.

FRANK
I tell you that dame's nuts.

BOB
Right.

CUT TO:

EXT. FRONT OF HOUSE

77. MED. CLOSE SHOT
Longfellow is exiting front gate.

78. MED. SHOT
From his angle. Out of the shadows a girl comes into view and staggers forward. She reaches a tree and clutches it weakly Then her strength failing, she crumples to the ground.

79. MED. CLOSE SHOT
Longfellow's eyes widen in apprehension as he starts forward - CAMERA FOLLOWING HIM. He reaches the girl and bending down, lifts her head. We see it is Babe Bennett. Her eyes are closed, apparently in a dead faint.

80. CLOSE SHOT - LONGFELLOW AND BABE - LOW ANGLE
Longfellow studies her face for a moment, then starts to lift her. As he does so, her eyes open and she looks up at him, feigning bewilderment.

LONGFELLOW
You fainted.

BABE
(feebly)
Oh, did I? I'm sorry ...

She struggles to get to her feet.

81. WIDER ANGLE
Longfellow tries to assist her.

LONGFELLOW
Can I help you?

BABE
No, thank you. I'll be all right.

LONGFELLOW
Look, this is my house. I'd like to--

BABE
Oh, no, really - I'll be all right.

LONGFELLOW
What happened?

BABE
Well, I guess I walked too much. I've been looking for a job all day. I found one, too. I start tomorrow.

(backing away)
You've been awfully kind. Thank you very much.

As she leaves him, Longfellow watches her, full of sympathy. She takes a few steps and, again feigning weakness, falls against the iron fence, clutching it. Longfellow rushes to her assistance.

82. CLOSE TWO SHOT

LONGFELLOW
(looking around)
Hey, taxi!

CUT TO:

INT. TAXI CAB
83. CLOSE SHOT

BOB
(to driver)
Hey, stupe! Follow that cab they just got into, will you? Hurry up! Step on it!

FRANK
Come on, come on!

BOB
Hurry up!

DISSOLVE TO:

INSERT: AN ELECTRIC SIGN:
"TULLIO'S -- EAT WITH THE LITERATI"

DISSOLVE TO:

INT. TULLIO'S
84. MED. CLOSE SHOT
A corner table, surrounded by ferns, at which Longfellow and Babe sit. She's still eating.

LONGFELLOW
Feel better now?

BABE
Mmm, it tastes so good. Mr. Deeds, I don't know how I can ever thank you.

LONGFELLOW
Tell me more about yourself.

BABE
Well, I guess I've told you almost everything there is to tell. My folks live in a small town near Hartford. I'm down here alone trying to make a living.
(hanging her head)
Oh, I'm really just a nobody.

Longfellow spots a strolling violinist. He furtively beckons the fellow over. The musician leans into them with romantic strains.

BABE
(as the musician finishes and strolls away)
Oh, that was so lovely. Thank you.

LONGFELLOW
You were a lady in distress, weren't you?

BABE
(looks up)
What?

LONGFELLOW
Oh - uh - nothing.

85. WIDER ANGLE
As a waiter enters the scene and begins removing dishes.

LONGFELLOW
Waiter! Has anybody come in yet?

WAITER
Huh? Oh, no. Nobody important.

LONGFELLOW
Be sure and point 'em out to me, won't you?

WAITER
Uh-huh.

LONGFELLOW
I'm a writer myself, you know

The waiter throws Longfellow a sidelong glance of complete boredom.

WAITER
Uh-huh.

LONGFELLOW
I write poetry.

WAITER
Uh huh.

He exits.

86. CLOSE TWO SHOT - BABE AND LONGFELLOW

BABE
You've been having quite an exciting time here, haven't you? All those meetings and business deals and society people - haven't you been having fun?

LONGFELLOW
No. That is, I didn't--
(pause - while he looks at her)
Until I met you. I like talking to you, though--
(moodily)
Imagine my finding you right on my doorstep.

87. WIDER ANGLE
The waiter enters again.

WAITER
Brookfield just came in.

LONGFELLOW
Oh, the poet? Where?

WAITER
Over at that big round table. The one that looks like a poodle.

Longfellow stares off scene - his eyes full of worship.

LONGFELLOW
(to Babe)
Look - there's Brookfield, the poet.

BABE
(looks also)
Really?

88. MED. SHOT
From their angle, to show people at a table, engaged in conversation.

89. MED. CLOSE SHOT
At Longfellow's table. He stares off at them, awed. Babe watches his face.

90. MED. SHOT - AUTHOR'S TABLE
A group of five men, drinking - as the waiter enters.

WAITER
(confidentially - indicating Longfellow)
Pardon. Longfellow Deeds, who just inherited the Semple fortune, wants to meet you.

BROOKFIELD
Oh, yes. I read about him. He writes poetry on postcards.

HENABERRY
Let's invite him over. Might get a couple of laughs. Getting rather dull around here.

MORROW
It's always dull here.

BROOKFIELD
(rising)
I'll get him.

HENABERRY
Good.

DISSOLVE TO:

91. MED. SHOT - ROUND TABLE
At which they are all seated now. Babe sits next to Longfellow, who is the center of attraction. Brookfield is just finishing introductions.

BROOKFIELD
Henaberry, Mr. Morrow, Bill - this is Mr. Deeds and his fiancée from Mandrake Falls.

THE GROUP
(ad-lib)
How do!
Hello!
Nice to meet you!

LONGFELLOW
Nice of you to ask us to come and sit with you. Back home we never get a chance to meet famous people.

BILL
(calling waiter)
Waiter! A little service here.

THE GROUP
(ad-lib)
Yes!
Mr. Deeds is a distinguished poet.
A drink for Mr. Deeds!

HENABERRY
He's a poet. Have a drink.

LONGFELLOW
No - I don't want it, thank you.

HENABERRY
Why, you must drink! All poets drink!

92. MED. CLOSE SHOT - THE GROUP

BILL
Tell us, Mr. Deeds. How do you go about writing your poems? We craftsmen are very interested in one another's methods.

HENABERRY
Yes. Do you have to wait for an inspiration, or do you just dash it off?

LONGFELLOW
(self-consciously)
Well, I don't know. I--

HENABERRY
Mr. Morrow, over there, for instance, just dashes them off.

MORROW
Yes. That's what my publishers have been complaining about.

They all laugh superficially.

93. CLOSE SHOT GROUP - BABE AND LONGFELLOW
Babe glances up at Longfellow, to see if he's aware that he is being laughed at. But he apparently isn't.

LONGFELLOW
(laughing feebly)
Your readers don't complain, Mr. Morrow.

MORROW'S VOICE
Oh, thanks. Thanks.

BROOKFIELD
How about you, Mr. Deeds?

LONGFELLOW
Well, I write mine on order. The people I work for just tell me what they want and then I go to work and write it.

BROOKFIELD
Amazing! Why, that's true genius!

HENABERRY
Yes. Have you any peculiar characteristics when you are creating?

LONGFELLOW
Well, I play the tuba.

They all laugh.

MORROW
I've been playing the harmonica for forty years - didn't do me a bit of good.

94. CLOSE SHOT - GROUP

BROOKFIELD
You wouldn't have one in your pocket, would you, Mr. Deeds?

LONGFELLOW
(smiling)
What? A tuba?

They all laugh.

BROOKFIELD
No, a postcard - with one of your poems on it.

Longfellow is beginning to sense he is being kidded.

LONGFELLOW
(his face sober)
No.

HENABERRY
You mean to tell me you don't carry a pocketful around with you?

BROOKFIELD
Too bad! I was hoping you'd autograph one for me.

HENABERRY
I was too.

BILL
Quite right.

95. MED. GROUP SHOT
As they keep on. Longfellow has his eyes levelled on each speaker in turn, obviously cognizant of their ill concealed jibes.

HENABERRY
Wait a minute, boys. Perhaps Mr. Deeds would recite one for us.

THE OTHER'S VOICES
(ad-lib)
Yes!

BROOKFIELD
That's a very good idea. Nothing like a poet reciting his own stuff.

ONE OF THE OTHERS
How about a Mother's Day poem, Mr. Deeds?

HENABERRY
Exactly! Give us one that wrings the great American heart.

THE GROUP
(ad-lib)
Yes.

Babe has been watching Longfellow, interested. Now, when their voices die down - and they wait expectantly - he speaks quietly.

LONGFELLOW
(deeply hurt)
I guess I get the idea. I guess I know why I was invited here. To make fun of me.

96. MED. SHOT - GROUP

SEVERAL VOICES
(ad-lib)
Oh, come now.
I wouldn't say that.

HENABERRY
Look, he's temperamental.

LONGFELLOW
(levelling off at him)
Yeah, what if I am? What about it?

Henaberry's face sobers.

LONGFELLOW
(simply)
It's easy to make fun of somebody if you don't care how much you hurt 'em.
(to Brookfield)
I think your poems are swell, Mr. Brookfield, but I'm disappointed in you. I know I must look funny to you, but maybe if you went to Mandrake Falls you'd look just as funny to us. Only nobody would laugh at you and make you feel ridiculous -'cause that wouldn't be good manners.

97. CLOSE SHOT - LONGFELLOW
As he rises, continuing:

LONGFELLOW
I guess maybe it is comical to write poems for postcards, but a lot of people think they're good. Anyway, it's the best I can do. So if you'll excuse me, we'll be leaving. I guess I found out that all famous people - aren't big people ...

98. MED. SHOT
The group watches him silently as he leaves the table accompanied by Babe. For a moment they are nonplussed - then they break into raucous laughter - all but Morrow.

99. CLOSE TRUCKING SHOT
With Longfellow and Babe as they take several steps. Then he abruptly stops.

LONGFELLOW
(turning to them)
There's just one thing more. If it weren't for Miss Dawson being here with me, I'd probably bump your heads together.

BABE
(quickly)
Oh, I don't mind.

Longfellow stares at her for a moment.

LONGFELLOW
Then I guess maybe I will.

He starts back toward the table.

100. MED. SHOT AT TABLE
Protectively, Brookfield and Henaberry rise from their chairs. But they are too late, for Longfellow clips Brookfield on the chin first with his left fist - and with his right catches Henaberry on the jaw. The punches are almost simultaneous. The surprise attack catches the men off-guard and they fall backward. A waiter rushes forward to escort Longfellow and Babe out.

WAITER
(calling out)
Manager!

Morrow, who never budged from his chair, and who has watched Longfellow with great admiration, now rises to catch up to him.

MORROW
(an outcry)
Eureka!

INT. FOYER OF TULLIO'S

101. MED. SHOT
As Morrow catches up to Longfellow and Babe, who are on their way out. The waiter is shooing people away.

WAITER
Step aside, step aside!

Morrow barges forward. Longfellow and Babe turn.

MORROW
(obviously groggy with drink)
Say fellow, you neglected me - and I feel very put out.
(points to his chin)
Look, sock it right there, will you? Lay one right on the button,[6] but sock it hard.

102. CLOSE SHOT - THE THREE

LONGFELLOW
That's all right. I got it off my chest.

MORROW
The difference between them and me is I know when I've been a skunk. You take me to the near est news-stand and I'll eat a pack of your post-cards raw. Raw!

Longfellow and Babe smile. As Morrow continues to speak, he sways drunkenly and would fall over backwards a couple of times in midsentence if the alert Longfellow didn't have a clutch on his collar.

MORROW
Oh, what a magnificent deflation of smugness. Pal, you've added ten years to my life! A poet with a straight left and a right hook - delicious! Delicious! You're my guest from now on - forever and a day - even unto eternity!

LONGFELLOW
Thanks, but Miss Dawson and I are going out to see the sights.

MORROW
Fine, fine. Swell, You just showed me a sight lovely to behold, and I'd like to reciprocate. Listen, you hop aboard my magic carpet--
(Longfellow catches him before he falls backward in his enthusiasm)
--thanks - and I'll show you sights that you've never seen before.

LONGFELLOW
I'd kind of like to see Grant's Tomb - and the Statue of Liberty.

103. CLOSE SHOT - GROUP
Favoring Morrow.

MORROW
Well, you'll not only see those, but before the evening's half through, you'll be leaning against the Leaning Tower of Pisa - you'll mount Mt. Everest. I'll show you the Pyramids and all the little Pyramiddes, leaping from sphinx to sphinx. Pal, how would you like to go on a real, old-fashioned binge?

LONGFELLOW
(puzzled)
Binge?

MORROW
Yes. I mean the real McCoy. Listen, you play saloon with me, and I'll introduce you to every wit, every nit-wit, and every half-wit in New York. We'll go on a twister that'll make Omar the soused philosopher of Persia[7] look like an anemic on a goat's milk diet.

Longfellow saves him - once again - from crashing over.

104. CLOSE SHOT - GROUP
Featuring Longfellow.

LONGFELLOW
(vaguely)
That ought to be fun.

MORROW
Fun? Say, listen, I'll take you on a bender that will live in your memory as a thing of beauty and joy forever.
(to someone off)
Boy! Boy! My headpiece!

He exits from the scene. CAMERA FOLLOWING HIM.

MORROW
(to the world in general)
Oh, Tempora! Oh, Moeraes! Oh, Bacchus![8]

He bumps into a woman, who glares at him.

WOMAN
Oh, you're drunk.

MORROW
(unmindful)
Oh, you're right.

105. CLOSEUP - BABE AND LONGFELLOW

LONGFELLOW
(to Babe)
I guess if we go with him, we'll see things, huh?

She looks up at his face, amazed at his innocence.

BABE
Yes, I guess we will.

FADE OUT:

INT. MAC'S OFFICE

106. MED. SHOT
Mac is reading the story, eyes sparkling. Babe is sprawled in a chair, doing tricks with a coin.

MAC
(reads)
"'I play the tuba to help me think.' This is one of the many startling statements made by Longfellow Deeds - New York's now Cinderella Man - who went out last night to prove that his uncle, the late M.W. Semple - from whom he inherited $20,000,000 - was a rank amateur in the art of 'standing the town on its cauliflower ear' ..."[9]

He looks up.

MAC
Cinderella Man! That's sensational, Babe! Sensational!

BABE
It took some high-powered acting, believe me.

MAC
Did it?

BABE
I was the world's sweetest ingenue.

MAC
Is he really that big a sap?

107. CLOSE SHOT - THE TWO
Favoring Babe.

BABE
He's the original. There are no carbon copies of that one.

MAC
Cinderella Man! Babe, you stuck a tag on that hick that'll stick to him the rest of his life. Can you imagine Cobb's face when he reads this?

BABE
If we could sell tickets, we'd make a fortune.

She covers the coin with palm of other hand, and the coin disappears. But Mac is too excited to pay any attention.

MAC
How'd you get the picture?

BABE
Had the boys follow us.

MAC
Marvelous!
(reads again)
"At two o'clock this morning, Mr. Deeds tied up traffic while he fed a bagful of doughnuts to a horse. When asked why he was doing it, he replied: 'I just wanted to see how many doughnuts this horse would eat before he'd ask for a cup of coffee.'"
(laughs)
Beautiful! What happened after that?

BABE
I don't know. I had to duck to get the story out. He was so far along he never even missed me.

MAC
When're you going to see him again?

BABE
Tonight, maybe.
(looks at her watch)
I'll phone him at noon.
(explaining)
Oh, my lunch hour. I'm a stenographer, you know. Mary Dawson.

108. MED. SHOT - THE TWO
Favoring Mac.

MAC
(laughing)
You're a genius, Babe - a genius!

BABE
I even moved into Mabel Dawson's apartment - in case old snoopy Cobb might start looking around.

MAC
(all excited)
Good! Good! Stay there. Don't show your face down here. I'll tell everybody you're on your vacation. They'll never know where the stories are coming from. Stick close to him, Babe - you can get an exclusive story out of him every day for a month. We'll have the other papers crazy.
(starts for her)
Babe, I could kiss you!

109. WIDER ANGLE

BABE
(sidestepping)
Oh, no. No. Our deal was for a month's vacation - with pay.

MAC
Sure.

BABE
With pay!

She is out the door.

MAC
(yelling after her)
You'll get it, Babe. You'll get it.

DISSOLVE TO:

INT. LONGFELLOW'S BEDROOM

110. CLOSE SHOT
Walter leans over the bed violently, shaking Longfellow, who is lost in drunken sleep.

WALTER
Mr. Deeds - Mr. Deeds, sir - you really must get up. It's late!

LONGFELLOW
(without budging - without opening his eyes)
You're Walter, aren't you?

WALTER
Yes, sir.

LONGFELLOW
I just wanted to make sure.

111. CLOSE SHOT - WALTER
He smiles.

WALTER
If you'll permit me to say so, sir, you were out on quite a bender last night, sir.

112. CLOSE SHOT - LONGFELLOW
Longfellow opens one eye - and then the other, blinking. As consciousness returns to him, he glances around the room as if to get his bearings.

LONGFELLOW
Bender? You're wrong, Walter. We started out to a binge but we never got to it.

113. MED. CLOSE SHOT - THE TWO
Walter offers him a drink on a tray.

WALTER
(humoring him)
Yes, sir.

LONGFELLOW
What's that?

WALTER
A Prairie Oyster, sir.[10]

LONGFELLOW
(slow to comprehend anything)
Prairie? Oysters?

WALTER
Yes, sir. It makes the head feel smaller.

Longfellow takes it and downs it in one swig.

LONGFELLOW
(his face finally reacting)
Oh. Oh!
(remembering)
Has Miss Dawson called yet?

WALTER
Miss Dawson, sir? No, sir. No Miss Dawson has called, sir.

LONGFELLOW
She was a lady in distress. She wouldn't let me help her. Got a lot of pride. I like that.

WALTER
Oh, I do too, sir.

LONGFELLOW
I'd better call her up and apologize. I don't remember taking her home last night.

WALTER
I'd venture to say, sir, you don't remember much of anything that happened last night, sir.

114. CLOSE SHOT - THE TWO
Favoring Longfellow.

LONGFELLOW
What do you mean? I remember everything! Hand me my pants - I wrote her phone number on a piece of paper.

WALTER
You <u>have</u> no pants, sir.

Longfellow looks up slowly. Walter goes on:

WALTER
You came home last night - <u>without</u> them.

LONGFELLOW
(after a double take)
I did what!

WALTER
As a matter of fact, you came home without any clothes. You were in your - uh - shorts. Yes, sir.

LONGFELLOW
Oh, don't be silly, Walter. I couldn't walk around in the streets without any clothes. I'd be arrested.

WALTER
That's what the two policemen said, sir.

LONGFELLOW
What two policemen?

WALTER
The ones who brought you home, sir. They said you and another gentleman kept walking up and down the streets, shouting: "Back to nature! Clothes are a blight on civilization! Back to nature!"

Longfellow watches his face, fascinated. Slowly it is all coming back to him.

LONGFELLOW
Listen, Walter, if a man named Morrow calls up, tell him I'm not in. He may be a great author, but I think he's crazy. The man's crazy, Walter.

115. REVERSE ANGLE
Favoring Walter.

WALTER
Yes, sir. By the way, did you-

Longfellow slowly swings out of bed into a sitting position. Walter kneels to put on Longfellow's slippers. Longfellow balks, points, silently reminding Walter that he has broken his promise not to kneel down in front of him.

LONGFELLOW
(pointing)
Please!

WALTER
But how'll I put on the slipper, sir?

Longfellow's expression begs no disagreement. Walter stands, fumbling with the shoes from a stooped posture.

WALTER
(continuing)
Yes, sir. I beg pardon, sir, but did you ever find what you were looking for, sir?

LONGFELLOW
Looking for?

WALTER
You kept searching me last night, sir. Going through my pockets. You said you were looking for a rhyme for Budington.

LONGFELLOW
(flatly)
Better bring me some coffee, Walter.

WALTER
Very good, sir.
(remembering)
Oh, I beg pardon. A telegram came for you, sir.
(he hands the telegram to Longfellow)
I'll get you some <u>black</u> coffee, sir.

116. MEDIUM SHOT
Following Walter's exit. Longfellow quickly opens the telegram. His face clouds. At this moment, Cobb comes bursting into the room - a newspaper in his hand.

COBB
(wildly)
Did you see all this stuff in the papers?

LONGFELLOW
(holding out telegram)
Arthur wants to quit!

COBB
Arthur! Who's Arthur?

LONGFELLOW
He's the shipping clerk at the Tallow Works. Wants a $2 raise - or he'll quit.

COBB
(he goes crazy)
What do I care about Arthur! Did you see this stuff in the paper? How'd it get in there? What'd you do last night? Who were you talking to?

He flings the paper on the bed. Longfellow glances at it, and his face clouds.

COBB
(while Longfellow reads)
And what'd you do to those bodyguards? They quit this morning. Said you locked them up.

LONGFELLOW
Oh, they insisted on following me.

117. TWO SHOT

COBB
(wildly)
What do you think bodyguards are for?

LONGFELLOW
(glances up)
What do they mean by this - "Cinderella Man!"

COBB
Are those stories true?

118. CLOSE SHOT - LONGFELLOW AND COBB
Longfellow has his eyes glued on the paper.

LONGFELLOW
I don't remember. "Cinderella Man!" What do they mean by that?

COBB
They'd call you <u>anything</u> if you gave them half a chance. They've got you down as a sap.

LONGFELLOW
(calmly)
I think I'll go down and punch this editor on the nose.

COBB
(quickly)
No, you don't! Get this clear: Socking people is no solution for anything.

119. TWO SHOT

LONGFELLOW
Sometimes it's the <u>only</u> solution.

COBB
Not editors. Take my word for it. Not editors!

LONGFELLOW
If they're going to poke fun at me, I'm going to--

COBB
(bends over, earnestly)
Listen. Listen, Longfellow. You've got brains, kid. You'll get along swell if you'll only curb your homicidal instincts - and keep your trap shut. Don't talk to anybody! These newshounds are out gunning for you.

LONGFELLOW
(referring to paper)
But what about this "Cinderella Man"?

COBB
That's my job. I'll take care of that. I'll keep that stuff out of the papers - if you'll help me. But I can't do anything if you go around talking to people. Will you promise me to be careful from now on?

LONGFELLOW
Yes, I guess I'll have to.

COBB
(mopping his brow)
Thank you.
(as he goes)
If you feel the building rock, it'll be me blasting into this editor.

120. MED. SHOT
He exits. During the scene Walter has entered with a tray, which he has adjusted on Longfellow's knee.

LONGFELLOW
Cobb's right. I mustn't talk to anybody.

BUTLER
(entering)
Miss Dawson on the phone, sir.

LONGFELLOW
(alertly)
Who? Miss Dawson?

BUTLER
Yes, sir.

LONGFELLOW
Fine. I'll talk to her. Give me the phone, quick. She's the only one I'm going to talk to from now on.

As the butler scurries around for the phone,

DISSOLVE TO:

EXT. TOP OF FIFTH AVENUE BUS - NIGHT - (PROCESS)

121. CLOSE SHOT - BABE AND LONGFELLOW
Longfellow looks around, absorbed. Babe watches him.

LONGFELLOW
It's awfully nice of you to show me around like this.

BABE
I enjoy it.

LONGFELLOW
The Aquarium was swell. If I lived in New York, I'd go there every day. I'll bet you do.

BABE
Well, I'd like to - but I have a job to think of.

EXT. STREET

122. MED. CLOSE SHOT - A TAXI
Directly behind the bus. A man's head is stuck out of taxi window. We recognize it as one of the photographers, Bob.

BOB
(to driver)
Hey, flap-ears![11] You better keep following that bus!

DRIVER'S VOICE
Keep your shirt on!

INT. THE TAXI - PROCESS

123. CLOSE SHOT - BOB AND FRANK
Two photographers, with their equipment. They keep their eyes glued on the bus in front. They return to their seats.

BOB
It don't look as though we're gonna get any pictures tonight.

FRANK
Babe ought to get him drunk again.

EXT. TOP OF BUS

124. CLOSE SHOT - BABE AND LONGFELLOW

BABE

Got any news--

(catches herself)

I mean, has anything exciting been happening lately?

LONGFELLOW

Sure. I met you.

BABE

(laughs)

Oh. What's happening about the opera?

LONGFELLOW

Oh, that - well, we had another meeting. I told them I'd go on being Chairman if--

(explaining)

I'm Chairman, you know.

BABE

Yes, I know.

LONGFELLOW

I told 'em I'd play along with them if they lowered their prices - and cut down expenses - and broadcast.

BABE

What did they say?

LONGFELLOW

Gosh, you look pretty tonight.

BABE

What did they say?

LONGFELLOW

Huh? Oh. They said I was crazy. Said I wanted to run it like a grocery store.

BABE

What are they going to do?

LONGFELLOW

(leans over close to her)

Do you always wear your hair like that?

125. WIDER SHOT

At this point, two girls pass by, chattering. One girl has a paper open.

FIRST GIRL

Isn't it a scream - "Cinderella Man!" The dope!

2ND GIRL

I'd like to get my hooks into that guy.

FIRST GIRL
Don't worry. Somebody's probably taking him for plenty.

They are gone. Longfellow glares after them. Babe is afraid to look up.

LONGFELLOW
(quietly)
If they were men, I'd knock their heads together.

Babe is silent. Longfellow watches her for a moment.

126. CLOSE SHOT - THE TWO
Favoring Longfellow.

LONGFELLOW
Have you seen the papers?

BABE
Uh-huh.

LONGFELLOW
That's what I like about you. You think about a man's feelings. I'd like to go down to that newspaper and punch the fellow in the nose that's writing that stuff--

127. MED. CLOSE SHOT - THE TWO
She looks up, startled.

LONGFELLOW
--"Cinderella Man!" I guess pretty soon everybody will be calling me "Cinderella Man."

Babe has had an uncomfortable time of it - and quickly changes the subject.

BABE
Would you like to walk the rest of the way? It's so nice out.

LONGFELLOW
Yes.

BABE
Yeah, let's.

She jumps up from her seat, and Longfellow follows.

<u>INT. THE TAXI</u>
128. MED. CLOSE SHOT
Favoring the taxi driver.

DRIVER
Hey, wise guys. He's getting off.

This sets off a mad scramble.

BOB AND FRANK
(ad-lib)
Hey, come on!

Pull over to the curb!

DISSOLVE TO:

EXT. RIVERSIDE DRIVE - GRANT'S TOMB
129. MED. CLOSE SHOT - LONGFELLOW AND BABE
He stands across the street from Grant's Tomb, looking solemn. His eyes moist. She is unaware of his emotion.

BABE
Come on, don't you want to see it?

INT. THE TAXI
130. MED. SHOT - BOB AND FRANK

FRANK
Feast your eyes. Grant's Tomb!

BOB
Is that it?
(to driver)
Hey, beetle-puss! The Tomb!

131. MED. CLOSE SHOT - LONGFELLOW AND BABE
As they approach the monument.

BABE
There you are. Grant's Tomb. I hope you're not disappointed.

LONGFELLOW
(throatily)
It's wonderful.

BABE
To most people, it's an awful letdown.

LONGFELLOW
(in awe)
Huh?

BABE
I say, to most people it's a washout.

LONGFELLOW
That depends on what they see.

BABE
(looks up at him)
Now, what do _you_ see?

132. CLOSEUP - LONGFELLOW

LONGFELLOW
Me? Oh, I see a small Ohio farm boy becoming a great soldier. I see thousands of marching men. I see General Lee with a broken heart, surrendering, and I can see the beginning of a new nation, like Abraham Lincoln said. And I can see that Ohio boy being inaugurated as President--
(dreamily)
Things like that can only happen in a country like America.

133. CLOSEUP - BABE
To intercut with above speech. During his recital, she watches his face, fascinated. Her impulse is to laugh, but she finds that she can't.

LONGFELLOW
(overcome - he almost chokes on his final words)
Excuse me!

FADE OUT:

INT. PRIVATE OFFICES
134. MED. CLOSE SHOT
A switchboard operator fielding calls.

SWITCHBOARD OPERATOR
Sorry, Mr. Hopper. Mr. Cedar won't answer his phone. Sorry.

OFFICE CLERK
(passing by)
Say, what's going on in the boss's office?

SWITCHBOARD OPERATOR
Search me. The three 'Cs' and little 'B' have been in there for over an hour.

INT. CEDAR'S PRIVATE OFFICE
135. FULL SHOT
Cedar paces the floor. His brothers look worried. Budington is enthroned at Cedar's desk.

BUDINGTON
I don't want to be critical, John, but here it is--

CEDAR
(pouncing on him)
Yes, I know. A week's gone by and we haven't got the Power of Attorney yet!

BUDINGTON
Yes, but you said--

CEDAR
(walking way from him)
I don't care what I said. I can't strangle him, can I!

FIRST BROTHER
It's ridiculous for us to have to worry about a boy like that.
(crosses to desk)
Look at these articles about him! "Cinderella Man!" Why, he's carrying on like an idiot.

BUDINGTON
Exactly what I was saying to my wife when this--

FIRST BROTHER
Who cares what you were saying to your wife?

There is a moment's awkward silence. The silence is broken by the buzzing of the dictograph. Cedar crosses to it and snaps the button.

136. CLOSE SHOT AT DESK
As secretary's voice comes over dictograph:

CEDAR
Yes?

SECRETARY'S VOICE
Mr. and Mrs. Semple are still waiting.

CEDAR
(irritated)
I can't help it. Let them wait!

He snaps the dictograph off.

137. MED. SHOT GROUP

FIRST BROTHER
Those people have been in to see me every day this week.

2ND BROTHER
Who are _they_?

CEDAR
(dismissing it)
Relatives of old man Semple.

FIRST BROTHER
They keep insisting they should have some nuisance value.

CEDAR
Nuisance value?

FIRST BROTHER
They say if it hadn't been for Deeds, _they'd_ have gotten all the money.

CEDAR
(suddenly)
Nuisance value.
(thinks a minutes - crosses to door)
Maybe they have! Maybe they have! Maybe they have!
(opens door)
Mr. and Mrs. Semple, please. How do you do?

The others all stand around - as the Semples enter.

MRS. SEMPLE
We've been trying to--

138. MED. CLOSE SHOT - CEDAR AND THE SEMPLES

CEDAR
(smoothly cutting her off)
I'm so sorry to have kept you waiting. How are you, sir? I don't know what my secretary could

have been thinking to keep you waiting this long.
(to one of his brothers)
Will you bring the chairs? Quickly. Will you have a cigar, Mr. Semple?

MR. SEMPLE
Thanks.

Semple takes the cigar - rather flabbergasted at all the sudden attention showered upon him.

DISSOLVE TO:

EXT. ROOF OF TALL BUILDING - NIGHT

139. MED. SHOT - LONGFELLOW AND BABE
From over their shoulders, looking down on the lights and teeming activity of Times Square.

BABE
There's Times Square.

LONGFELLOW
You can almost spit on it, can't you?

BABE
Why don't you try?

He does try. The wind blows it back on him. She laughs, takes out a handkerchief and wipes it off his coat.

BABE
(as she wipes)
Oh! It's breezy up here.

He doesn't say anything right away.

BABE
You're worried about those articles they're writing about you, aren't you?

LONGFELLOW
I'm not worrying any more. I suppose they'll go on writing them till they get tired. You don't believe all that stuff, do you?

A guilty look spreads over Babe's face.

BABE
Oh, they just do it to sell the newspapers, you know.

LONGFELLOW
Yeah, I guess so. What puzzles me is why people seem to get so much pleasure out of hurting each other. Why don't they try liking each other once in a while?

An awkward pause.

BABE
Shall we go?

DISSOLVE TO:

EXT. CENTRAL PARK - NIGHT
140. MED. TRUCKING SHOT
As Babe and Longfellow walk.

BABE
(spotting a park bench)
Here's a nice place.

LONGFELLOW
Yeah. Anyway, there aren't any photographers around.

EXT. PARK - BEHIND SOME BUSHES
141. MEDIUM SHOT
Bob and Frank, sneaking around in the bushes.

142. CLOSE SHOT - LONGFELLOW AND BABE

BABE
You know, you said something to me when you first met me that I've thought about a great deal.

LONGFELLOW
What's that?

BABE
You said I was a lady in distress.

LONGFELLOW
Oh, that--

BABE
What did you mean by that?

LONGFELLOW
Nothing--

There is a pause.

LONGFELLOW
Have you got a - are you - uh - engaged or anything?

143. CLOSEUP - BABE
The corners of her mouth go up in sympathetic amusement.

BABE
No. Are you?

LONGFELLOW'S VOICE
No.

BABE
You don't go out with girls very much, do you?

LONGFELLOW'S VOICE
I haven't.

BABE
Why not?

144. CLOSE SHOT - THE TWO
Favoring Longfellow.

LONGFELLOW
Oh, I don't know.

BABE
You must have met a lot of swell society girls since you've been here. Don't you like them?

LONGFELLOW
I haven't met anybody here that I like, particularly. They all seem to have the St. Vitus Dance.[12]
(awkwardly)
Except you, of course.
(a pause)
People here are funny. They work so hard at living - they forget how to live.
(thoughtfully; leans back)
Last night, after I left you, I was walking along and looking at the tall buildings and I got to thinking about what Thoreau said. They created a lot of grand palaces here - but they forgot to create the noblemen to put in them.

145. REVERSE ANGLE
Favoring Babe. She stares at him curiously.

LONGFELLOW
I'd rather have Mandrake Falls.

BABE
_I'm_ from a small town too, you know.

LONGFELLOW
(interested)
Really?

BABE
Probably as small as Mandrake Falls.

LONGFELLOW
(finding a kindred soul)
Gosh! What do you know about that!

Babe leans her head back in a reminiscent mood. We get a feeling that, for the moment, she has forgotten she is Babe Bennett, out on a story.

BABE
Ah, it's a beautiful little town, too. A row of poplar trees right along Main Street. Always smelled as if it just had a bath.

146. MED. CLOSE SHOT - THE TWO
Longfellow watches her face intently.

BABE
I've often thought about going back.

LONGFELLOW
You have?

BABE
Oh, yes. I used to have a lot of fun there when I was a little girl. I used to love to go fishing with my father. That's funny. He was a lot like you, my father was. Talked like you, too. Sometimes he'd let me hold the line while he smoked - and we'd just sit there for hours. And after awhile, for no reason, I'd go over and kiss him and sit in his lap. He never said very much but once I remember him saying: "No matter what happens, honey, don't complain."

LONGFELLOW
He sounds like a person worth while knowing.

There is a pause while Longfellow watches her, and she is lost in thought.

BABE
(continuing)
He played in the town band, too.

LONGFELLOW
He did? I play the tuba--

BABE
Yeah, I know.

LONGFELLOW
What did he play?

BABE
The drums. He taught me to play some.

LONGFELLOW
He did?

BABE
Yes. I can do "Swanee River." Would you like to hear me?

LONGFELLOW
(enthusiastically)
Sure!

147. MEDIUM SHOT
She picks up a couple of branches. With the two sticks she drums on the bench seat - and sings "Swanee River."

When she is finished, though clearly delighted, he shows her a long face of mock-disappointment.

BABE
Oh, I suppose _you_ could do better.

LONGFELLOW
Sure. I can sing "Humoresque."

BABE
"Humoresque"? I'll bet you don't even know how it goes.

LONGFELLOW
Sure. Look! You sing it over again, and I'll do "Humoresque" with you.

BABE
It had better be good.

She starts again, and he sings "Humoresque" in counterpoint to her drumming.

CUT TO:

EXT. PARK - BEHIND SOME BUSHES

148. CLOSE SHOT - BOB AND FRANK
They wait with their camera. When they hear the singing, they look up, and then at each other in surprise.

BOB
I wonder if they'd want to make it a quartet.

FRANK
Shhh!

149. MEDIUM SHOT
Longfellow and Babe. They are having a grand time with their singing. A policeman saunters into the scene and stands watching them for a few seconds, without their being conscious of his presence. He smiles, shakes his head and passes on out of scene. Over the shot we hear the low moan of a siren in the distance.

150. CLOSE SHOT - THE TWO
They reach the climax of their song - and laugh joyously. At this moment, the shrieking of the siren is nearer and louder. Longfellow looks up quickly. Excited, he jumps up and runs toward street. Babe looks up, surprised.

LONGFELLOW
(as he runs off)
Fire engine! Fire engine! I want to see how they do it. Wait for me, will you?

151. CLOSE SHOT - BOB AND FRANK BEHIND BUSHES
Frank grabs the camera.

FRANK
Looks like the evening is not going to be wasted!

152. MEDIUM SHOT
They dash by the policeman, who looks up, startled.

153. LONG SHOT
As the fire engine slows down - and people are beginning to gather. We see Longfellow running toward the truck and hopping aboard.

154. MED. SHOT AT FIRE TRUCK
As Longfellow jumps on.

FRANK
Hello - what do <u>you</u> want?

LONGFELLOW
(short salute)
Captain Deeds - fire volunteer - Mandrake Falls.

FIREMAN
(amused)
Hi, Cap! Boys, meet the Captain!

155. LONG SHOT - REVERSE ANGLE
Bob and Frank running with their cameras toward Longfellow.

DISSOLVE TO.

INT. LIVING ROOM OF MABEL DAWSON'S STUDIO
156. CLOSEUP
Of typewriter carriage. It contains a paper upon which the following is typed:

"CINDERELLA MAN FIRE-EATING DEMON"
"Longfellow Deeds, 'The Cinderella Man,' last night threw a 'defy' into the teeth of the New York Fire Department, that when it comes to extinguishing conflagrations - they had better look to their laurels--"

CAMERA PULLS BACK and we find Babe, staring at the sheet of paper in front of her. Her eyes have a distant look.

157. FULL SHOT
Several feet away from her Mabel Dawson stands in front of an easel, working silently on a painting. She dabs at it and turning, pauses a moment to watch Babe, who at the moment rests her forehead on the typewriter carriage.

MABEL
(softly)
What's the matter, hon?

BABE
(quickly)
Nothing.

Babe is too much absorbed to hear this. Getting no response, Mabel turns and studies her for a few seconds.

MABEL
What's up, Babe? Something's eating you.

BABE
No. It's nothing.

MABEL
My unfailing instinct tells me something's gone wrong with the stew.

BABE
(murmuring)
Don't be ridiculous.

She again resumes her typing. Mabel crosses to her and looks over her shoulder.

MABEL
You haven't gotten very far, have you? That's where you were an hour ago. Come on, let's knock off and go down to Joe's. The gang's waiting for us.

BABE
(jumping up)
I can't write it, Mabel! I don't know what's the matter with me.

Babe lights a cigarette. Mabel studies her.

MABEL
(quietly)
Uh-huh. I think I can tell you.

The phone bell rings. Mabel picks it up.

158. CLOSE SHOT AT PHONE

MABEL
(into phone)
Hello ...
(listens)
Yes, she's here. Who wants her?
(listens)
Who?
(listens)
Oh, yes. Yes, just a moment.
(her hand over the mouthpiece)
It's him - whatcha-ma-call-him - the "Cinderella Man." The "Cinderella Man"!

Babe grabs the phone.

BABE
Hello.

INT. LONGFELLOW'S BEDROOM
159. CLOSE SHOT - LONGFELLOW
Who lies dressed in bed, phone in hand.

LONGFELLOW
(into phone)
Couldn't sleep. Kinda wanted to talk to you. Do you mind?

INT. MABEL'S LIVING ROOM
160. CLOSE SHOT - BABE AT PHONE

BABE
(sincerely)
No - not at all. I couldn't sleep either.

INT. LONGFELLOW'S BEDROOM
161. CLOSE SHOT - LONGFELLOW
At phone.

LONGFELLOW
I wanted to thank you again for going out with me.
(listens)
Huh? Well, I don't know what I'd do without you. You've made up for all the fakes that I've met.

CONTINUATION SCENE 160

BABE
Well, that's very nice. Thank you.

CONTINUATION SCENE 161

LONGFELLOW
You know what I've been doing since I got home? Been working on a poem.
(listens)
It's about you.
(listens)
Sometimes it's kinda hard for me to say things - so I write 'em.

CONTINUATION SCENE 160

BABE
(touched)
I'd like to read it some time.

She listens for a moment, apparently moved by his sweetness.

CONTINUATION SCENE 161

LONGFELLOW
Maybe I'll have it finished next time I see you.
(listens)
Will I see you soon?
(listens)
Gosh, that's swell, Mary.
(listens)
Good night.

He hangs up, and lies back - enthralled.

CONTINUATION SCENE 160

BABE
Good night.

INT. APT. LIVING ROOM
162. MED. CLOSE SHOT - AT PHONE

BABE
Mabel, that guy's either the dumbest, the stupidest, the most imbecilic idiot in the world - or he's the grandest thing alive. I can't make him out.

163. MED. CLOSE SHOT - THE TWO

MABEL
(knowingly)
Uh-huh.

BABE
I'm crucifying him.

MABEL
People have been crucified before.

BABE
Why? Why do we have to do it?

MABEL
You started out to be a successful newspaper woman, didn't you?

BABE
Yeah, then what?

MABEL
(shrugging)
Search me. Ask the Gypsies.

BABE
Here's a guy that's wholesome and fresh. To us he looks like a freak. You know what he told me tonight? He said when he gets married he wants to carry his bride over the threshold in his arms.

MABEL
The guy's balmy.

BABE
Is he? Yeah, I thought so, too. I tried to laugh, but I couldn't. It stuck in my throat.

MABEL
Aw, cut it out, will you? You'll get me thinking about Charlie again.

BABE
He's got goodness, Mabel. Do you know what that is?

MABEL
Huh?

BABE
No - of course you don't. We've forgotten. We're too busy being smart-alecks.
(sits at her typewriter)
Too busy in a crazy competition for nothing.

FADE OUT:

FADE IN

SERIES OF INSERTS:

"Cinderella Man Fire-Eating Demon--
Punches Photographer."

DISSOLVE TO:

"Cinderella Man to Reform Opera--

Must be put on paying basis - or else - says post-card poet."

DISSOLVE TO:

"Madame Pomponi, Famous Opera Singer, To Launch Deeds on Social Career"

DISSOLVE TO:

INT. LONGFELLOW'S BEDROOM

164. MEDIUM SHOT
Longfellow is in bed in his pajamas, playing the tuba. Walter enters.

WALTER
I beg pardon, sir. I beg pardon, sir.

Longfellow stops, looking daggers at him.

WALTER
Madame Pomponi is on the telephone, sir.

LONGFELLOW
Who?

WALTER
Madame Pomponi. She says everything is all set for the reception.

LONGFELLOW
What do you mean by coming in here when I'm playing?

WALTER
But she's on the telephone--

LONGFELLOW
Get out.
(pointing)
The evil finger's on you. Get out!

Walter hurries out. Longfellow jumps up and chases him down the grand staircase. Longfellow stops at the top of the stairs, struck by an idea.

INT. GRAND STAIRCASE

165. WIDE ANGLE
Showing Walter at the bottom of the stairs and Longfellow at the top.

LONGFELLOW
Stop!

Walter halts. Longfellow gives a shout from the top of the stairs. There is a discernible echo.

LONGFELLOW
Hey, did you hear that?

WALTER
What, sir?

Longfellow gives another shout. There is another echo. He tries it again - louder. Another echo. It is all very satisfactory.

WALTER
(pleased)
Why, that's an echo, sir!

LONGFELLOW
You try it.

WALTER
(timidly)
Me, sir?

LONGFELLOW
(an order)
Yeah.

Walter gives a bird-like hoot. There is an echo.

LONGFELLOW
(firmly)
Louder.

Walter gives a louder hoot. And louder. Each time, an echo.

A butler in a bathrobe emerges to see what all the hullabaloo is about. Longfellow spots him.

LONGFELLOW
(to butler)
You try it.

BUTLER
Me, sir?

But the butler clearly relishes the opportunity. He gives a little high-pitched squeak.

LONGFELLOW
Louder!

The butler tries it again - much better. Another man-servant has emerged. Longfellow points to him.

LONGFELLOW
You try it!

The man-servant tries it - very raspy, another tone altogether.

LONGFELLOW
(waving like a conductor)
All together!

A symphony of hoots, shrieks, barks and echoes.

LONGFELLOW
Again!

The household staff do it again.

LONGFELLOW
(surveying the scene - then, dramatically)
Let that be a lesson to you.

With that, Longfellow spins on his heel and returns to his bedroom.

There is a pause. The butler takes command of the other two.

BUTLER
(gesturing imperiously)
Go back to your room, both of you!

Walter and the man-servant hasten to exit.

The butler waits until nobody is looking, then gives one, final hoot. He murmurs to himself with satisfaction as he exits.

DISSOLVE TO:

EXT. LONGFELLOW'S HOME - NIGHT
166. LONG SHOT
Limousines arriving - from which guests emerge - in full evening dress.

INT. DRAWING ROOM - NIGHT
167. MED. SHOT AT DOOR
Madame Pomponi greets a group of guests. Ad-lib chatter is heard. From inside music emanates.

AD-LIB CHATTER
Oh, hello darling
So good of you to come.
Sweet of you to ask me.
Where is he?
I'm just dying to see the "Cinderella Man."

CAMERA MOVES SWIFTLY among groups of people picking out vignettes of conversation. Longfellow is the hot topic.

A husband and a wife whispering:

A HUSBAND
Shh! - he may hear you.

A WIFE
Even if he heard you, he wouldn't understand.

A man and a woman gossiping:

A MAN
I hear he still believes in Santa Claus.

A WOMAN
Will he be Santa Claus? That's what I want to know.

Another man holding forth to two elegantly-dressed women:

ANOTHER MAN
Have you all got your slippers ready for the "Cinderella Man"?

WOMEN
(ad-lib)
Yes, I have.

Everybody laughs.

FIRST WOMAN
With $20,000,000, he doesn't have to have looks!

2ND WOMAN
He won't have it long with that Pomponi woman hanging around him.

Two women in evening dress twittering like birds:

FIRST WOMAN
(to other woman)
My dear, I hear he can't think unless he plays his tuba!

DISSOLVE TO:

INT. MABEL'S BEDROOM

168. FULL SHOT
Babe is listlessly packing her few things in a small handbag. She slowly and meticulously folds a silken undergarment, wrapping it in tissue. Her eyes have a distant look. Mabel watches her, concerned. There is a long pause before either of them speaks.

MABEL
(breaking the silence)
You're a fool, Babe.

BABE
I just couldn't stand seeing him again.

MABEL
Running away is no solution.

169. MED. CLOSE SHOT - THE TWO
Babe is unresponsive.

MABEL
(after a pause)
What'll I tell him if he calls up?

BABE
Tell him I had to leave suddenly. I got a job in China - some place.

MABEL
You're acting like a school girl.

BABE
(suddenly - tensely)
What else can I do? Keeping this up is no good. He's bound to find out sometime.
(softly)
At least I can save him that.

They are suddenly startled by the boisterous entrance of Bob and Frank, whose voices are heard as they barge in.

170. MEDIUM SHOT
Babe, not wishing to explain to them, hides her bag - and follows Mabel to greet them in the living room.

<u>INT. LIVING ROOM</u>
171. MED. FULL SHOT
The boys cross to a table and drop their cameras.

BOB AND FRANK
Say, where is everybody? Come on, Babe - the artillery's ready.

Mabel enters. Babe stands in doorway.

MABEL
(by way of greeting)
It's those two sore spots again.

BOB
You shoulda been down to the office today, Babe.

FRANK
Yeah. Mac threw Cobb out again.

BOB
Boy, was he burning.

FRANK
(reaching for a bottle)
Just one little drink and then we're ready to shoot.

MABEL
(grabbing it away)
Just a minute. No, you don't.

BABE
We're not going out tonight.

BOB
Thought you had a date with him.

172. CLOSE SHOT - BABE

BABE
It's off. He's having a party at his house.

173. MED. CLOSE SHOT
Frank, Bob and Mabel.

FRANK
Say, what's the matter with her <u>now</u>!

MABEL
You wouldn't know if I drew you a diagram. Now, run along and peddle your little tin-types.

BOB
What is this? Throwing us out of here's getting to be a regular habit.

There is a knock on the door. They all look up.

174. CLOSE SHOT AT DOOR
As Mabel opens the door slightly. We see Longfellow. Mabel's eyes open in surprise.

LONGFELLOW
Is Mary Dawson here? I'm Longfellow Deeds.

175. CLOSE SHOT - BOB AND FRANK
They stand - stupefied.

176. CLOSE SHOT - MABEL
She waves her hand back of her, for them to hide.

MABEL
(loud - for the boys)
Oh! Oh, yes, of course. Longfellow Deeds. Come in. Step in, please.

177. CLOSE SHOT - BOB AND FRANK
They duck behind the sofa, CAMERA PANNING WITH THEM.

178. FULL SHOT
Longfellow enters. Mabel closes the door behind him, watching him speculatively. Longfellow turns to Mabel.

LONGFELLOW
You're Mabel - her sister - aren't you?

MABEL
(flustered)
Huh? Oh, yes - yes, of course. Her sister. Yes, I've been her sister for a long time.

LONGFELLOW
Is she home?

MABEL
Yeah. What?

LONGFELLOW
Is Mary home?

They look at each other stupidly - smiling feebly.

179. CLOSE SHOT ON TABLE
Featuring the camera. A hand comes in from behind the sofa and yanks the camera out of sight.

180. MEDIUM SHOT
Mabel and Longfellow still standing, looking at each other.

MABEL
Oh, Mary? Yes, of course. Well, I don't know whether she's home or not. I'll see.

As she turns, Babe appears in doorway.

MABEL
Why there she is! Of course she's home.
(feebly)
Stupid of me ...

BABE
Hello.

LONGFELLOW
Hello, Mary. I waited in the park for you over an hour. I thought maybe you'd forgotten.

181. MED. CLOSE SHOT - LONGFELLOW AND BABE
Mabel in b.g.

BABE
I didn't think you could come with the party and everything.

LONGFELLOW
Oh, I wouldn't let them stop me from seeing you. So I threw them out!

BABE
You threw them out!

182. CLOSER SHOT

MABEL
You mean--
(gesturing with hands)
--by the neck or something?

LONGFELLOW
Sure. They got on my nerves, so I threw 'em out.

Mabel raises her eyebrows.

LONGFELLOW
I guess that'll be in the papers tomorrow. It will give 'em something else to laugh at.

183. CLOSEUP - BABE
Her face clouds - miserably.

LONGFELLOW'S VOICE
(lightly)
I don't mind though. I had a lot of fun doing it.

BABE
(quickly)
Would you like to go for a walk?

184. MED. CLOSE SHOT

LONGFELLOW
Yes, if it isn't too late.

BABE
(going to bedroom)
I'll get my hat.

She disappears, leaving Mabel and Longfellow again staring at each other, self-consciously. Mabel smiles, ill-at-ease.

LONGFELLOW
Nice day out - er, nice night - wasn't it? - isn't it?

MABEL
(tremulously)
Yes, lovely. We've had a lot of nice weather lately.

LONGFELLOW
(after a pause)
It would be a nice night to go for a walk, don't you think?

MABEL
Oh yes, I think it'd be a swell night to go for a walk. A nice long one.

185. CLOSE SHOT - BEHIND SOFA
Bob and Frank, holding their breaths.

186. MEDIUM SHOT
Babe comes out of bedroom.

BABE
Ready?

LONGFELLOW
Gosh, she looks better every time I see her.

BABE
(vaguely)
Thank you.

She crosses to the door.

LONGFELLOW
(to Mabel)
Goodnight. Don't worry. I won't keep her out late.

MABEL
Thank you so much. Good night.

They exit. Mabel sighs relievedly. The boys jump from their crouching positions.

FRANK
(wobbling forward)
Ow! My foot's asleep!

BOB
(grabbing camera)
Come on - let's go!

Frank grabs <u>his</u> camera and both bolt toward the door. Mabel gets there one step ahead of them, and blocks their path.

MABEL
No, you don't. Just a minute. No more photographs.

DISSOLVE TO:

EXT. FRONT OF BABE'S HOME
187. CLOSE TRUCKING SHOT
As they walk slowly down the front steps.

LONGFELLOW
The reason why I wanted to take a walk, Mary, is 'cause I wanted to talk to you.

BABE
Let's just walk, okay?

LONGFELLOW
All right.

188. CLOSE TRUCKING SHOT
As they walk along a foggy street, on their faces.

LONGFELLOW
Mary, I'm going home.

BABE
Are you? When?

LONGFELLOW
In a day or so, I think.

BABE
I don't blame you.

189. CLOSE TWO SHOT
Continuing on them, as they slowly walk around the block.

LONGFELLOW
A man ought to know where he fits in. I just don't fit in around here. I once had an idea I could do something with the money, but they kept me so busy here, I haven't had time to figure it out. I guess I'll wait till I get back home.

There is a long pause. Both lost in their own thoughts.

LONGFELLOW
Do you mind if I talk to you, Mary? You don't have to pay any attention to me.

BABE
No, I don't mind.

LONGFELLOW
All my life, I've wanted somebody to talk to. Back in Mandrake Falls, I always used to talk to a girl.

BABE
A girl?

LONGFELLOW
Oh, an imaginary one. I used to hike a lot through the woods and I'd always take this girl

with me so I could talk to her. I'd show her my pet trees and things. Sounds kind of silly but we had a lot of fun doing it.
(smiling)
She was beautiful.
(then moodily)
I haven't married 'cause I've been kinda waiting. You know, my mother and father were a great couple. I thought I might have the same kind of luck. I've always hoped that some day that imaginary girl would turn out to be real.

They have arrived back at the front steps of Babe's home.

LONGFELLOW
Well, here we are again.

BABE
Yes, here we are again.
(after a pause)
Good night.

LONGFELLOW
(then, quickly - his voice faltering)
Mary - I - excuse me--

190. CLOSE TWO SHOT
Favoring Babe. She cuts him off, her voice shaking.

BABE
Goodbye, darling. Don't let anybody hurt you again - ever. They can't anyway. You're much too real. You go back to Mandrake Falls. That's where you belong - goodbye!

191. WIDER ANGLE
She runs up the steps.

LONGFELLOW
Mary--

She stops and turns. He walks up close to her.

192. CLOSER SHOT - THE TWO

LONGFELLOW
You know the poem I told you about? It's finished.

His hand goes to his breast pocket - and then slowly is withdrawn - without bringing out the poem.

LONGFELLOW
Would you like to read it? It's to you.

BABE
(scarcely audible)
Yes, of course.

He now takes the poem out. The paper is folded. He hands it to her and she slowly unfolds it. Just as she is about to read Longfellow lays a hand on her arm.

LONGFELLOW
(a little frightened)
You don't have to say anything, Mary. You can tell me tomorrow what you think.

She looks into his eyes, but does not respond. Then she holds the paper up and begins reading. Longfellow watches her anxiously.

193. CLOSEUP - BABE
Reading softly:

BABE
"I tramped the earth with hopeless beat -
Searching in vain for a glimpse of you.
Then heaven thrust you at my very feet,
A lovely angel - too lovely to woo."

The last words come with difficulty. Babe's eyes are slowly welling up.

194. CLOSE SHOT - THE TWO
Babe continues reading:

BABE
"My dream has been answered, but my life's just as bleak,
I'm handcuffed and speechless in your presence divine -
For my heart longs to cry out, if it only would speak,
'I love you, my angel be mine, be mine.' "

Her voice is choked when she finishes. She does not look up until she refolds the paper. He stands close to her, waiting expectantly. Finally, she glances up. Her cheeks are moist, and her face clouded. Impulsively, she throws her arms around his neck, kissing him.

BABE
Oh, darling!

Longfellow's arms encircle her and for a few moments they remain in an emotional embrace.

LONGFELLOW
(huskily)
You don't have to say anything now. I'll wait till tomorrow - till I hear from you.

195. CLOSEUP - BABE
Her eyes are beset with fears. She loves him - but knows how hopeless it all is. She slowly starts freeing herself from his embrace.

196. MED. CLOSE SHOT - THE TWO
As Babe, weeping softly, frees herself from his embrace.

Longfellow gives a yelp of joy and leaps down the steps. He trips over a garbage pail and bumps into passersby, making a racket as he zigzags down the street and out of scene.

A VOICE
(shouting)
Hey, what's the big idea?

FADE OUT:

FADE IN

INT. NEWSPAPER OFFICE - DAY
197. CLOSE SHOT - MAC
Behind his desk.

MAC
Stop it, Babe! Stop it! What do you mean, you're quitting! You might as well tell me I'm quitting.

As he speaks, CAMERA DRAWS BACK to reveal Babe near a window, peering out moodily. Mac crosses over to her side.

MAC
What's bothering you, huh?

BABE
(after a pause)
Last night he proposed to me.

MAC
Proposed to you! You mean he asked you to marry him?

BABE
Yes.

MAC
(alert)
Why, Babe - that's terrific!
(sees it in print)
"Cinderella Man Woos Mystery Girl! Who is the Mysterious Girl That--"

BABE
Print one line of that, and I'll blow your place up!

198. MED. CLOSE SHOT - THE TWO

MAC
Sorry, Babe. Sorry. It would have made a swell story. I just got carried away. That's too bad. So he proposed to you, huh?
(intrigued)
What a twist! You set out to nail him - and he--

BABE
(bitterly)
Yeah. Funny twist, isn't it?

MAC
(suddenly)
Say, you haven't gone and fallen for that mug, have you?

Babe's silence is eloquent.

MAC
Well, I'll be--

He places an arm tenderly around her shoulder.

MAC
That's tough, Babe.

Babe smiles wryly.

MAC
(interested)
What're you going to do?

BABE
(walking away)
I'm going to tell him the truth.

MAC
Tell him you're Babe Bennett? Tell him you've been making a stooge out of him?

BABE
I'm having lunch with him today. He expects an answer. It's going to be pretty.

MAC
You're crazy! You can't do that!

199. MED. CLOSE SHOT - THE TWO
Over their shoulders, from behind, as Mac comforts her.

BABE
He'll probably kick me right down the stairs. I only hope he does.

MAC
I'll put you on another job. You need never see him again, eh?

BABE
That's the rub.

MAC
Oh, as bad as that, huh?

BABE
(far-away)
Telling him is the long shot - I'm going to take it.

He watches her sympathetically. Babe sighs resignedly.

BABE
(looking around)
Well, it was fun while it lasted, Mac. I'll clean out my desk.

She leaves him. Mac is deeply moved by her problem.

DISSOLVE TO:

INT. GRAND STAIRCASE

200. WIDE SHOT

As Longfellow, in a buoyant mood, emerges from his room and slides down the bannister of the grand staircase.

INT. INTIMATE DINING ROOM

201. MEDIUM SHOT

Table is set for two. Two butlers putter around. Longfellow enters full of expectant enthusiasm. He is in his shirt sleeves. He hovers over them, checking their preparations.

LONGFELLOW

How's it going? Okay?

BUTLER

Yes, quite all right. Thank you, sir.

LONGFELLOW

(picking up a salt shaker and examining it)

Gold, eh?

BUTLER

(as he continues his puttering)

Yes, sir.

LONGFELLOW

Fourteen carat?

BUTLER

Yes, sir.

LONGFELLOW

Is that the best you've got?

BUTLER

Oh, yes sir.

LONGFELLOW

(seizing on another detail)

Those flowers are too high. Won't be able to see her.

(lifts a bowl of flowers off)

Get a smaller bowl, will you?

BUTLER

(repeating his command as he hands the bowl to the other butler)

A smaller bowl of flowers.

2ND BUTLER

(exiting with flowers)

Yes, sir. A smaller bowl of flowers.

LONGFELLOW

(to butler)

Did you get that stuff I was telling you about?

BUTLER

Stuff, sir?

LONGFELLOW
That goo. That stuff that tastes like soap.

BUTLER
Oh, yes, sir. Here it is, sir. The pate de fois gras, sir.

LONGFELLOW
Yeah, that's fine. Have a lot of it because she likes it.

BUTLER
Yes, sir.

The other butler returns with a small bowl of flowers which he places in the center of the table

LONGFELLOW
Now you got the idea. Fine.

He sits in one of the chairs and leans forward in an imaginary conversation with Babe - his lips move but we hear nothing.

LONGFELLOW
(motions to butler)
Sit over there, will you?

BUTLER
Me sir?

LONGFELLOW
Yes.

The butler sits.

LONGFELLOW
Yes. You're too tall. Slink lower, will you?

The butler does it.

LONGFELLOW
More. Now forward.

They are practically nose to nose over the flowers.

BUTLER
(seriously)
How is this, sir?

LONGFELLOW
(rising)
Perfect! Perfect!

BUTLER
I wish you luck, sir.

LONGFELLOW
Thank you. Now don't touch a thing. Leave everything as it is.

He hurries toward his bedroom.

DISSOLVE TO:

INT. BEDROOM
202. FULL SHOT
Longfellow enters.

LONGFELLOW
(yelling)
Walter! Walter! Walter, where are you?

Walter enters, panic-stricken.

WALTER
Yes, sir. What is it, sir? Anything happened3

203. MED. CLOSE SHOT

LONGFELLOW
Anything happened? I've got to get dressed! I can't meet her like this!

WALTER
But she isn't due for an hour, sir.

LONGFELLOW
An hour? What's an hour! You know how time flies, Walter. My tie? Get it.

WALTER
Yes, sir. Very good, sir. Here it is right here, sir. There, sir.

While putting it on, he sings "Humoresque" loudly and gaily.

204. MEDIUM SHOT
At this moment, Cobb bursts in - his face grim:

COBB
Just as I suspected, wise guy! I don't mind you making a sap out of yourself - but you made one out of me, too.

LONGFELLOW
(to Walter - merrily)
Will you tell the gentleman I'm not in?

COBB
Mary Dawson, huh? Mary Dawson, my eye. That dame took you for a sleigh ride that New York will laugh about for years. She's the slickest, two-timing, double-crossing--

At the mention of the name, Longfellow turns for the first time.

205. CLOSEUP - LONGFELLOW
His face goes livid, as Cobb's voice continues:

LONGFELLOW
(between clenched teeth)
What are you talking about?

206. MEDIUM SHOT
Longfellow has started out toward him. In two long strides, Longfellow has grabbed Cobb by the shirt-front, ready to strangle him.

COBB
All right. Go ahead. Sock away, and then try to laugh this off.

With his free hand, he reaches into his coat pocket. He unrolls a newspaper. Longfellow shifts his glance over to the photograph in the newspaper Cobb holds up, and slowly his grip on Cobb relaxes. He takes the newspaper.

207. CLOSEUP - LONGFELLOW
As he looks at the picture.

INSERT: PICTURE OF BABE BENNETT
Under which is the following:

"Louise (Babe) Bennett - wins Pulitzer Prize for reportorial job on Macklyn love triangle."

BACK TO SCENE
Longfellow stares long and unbelievingly at the picture.

208. MED. CLOSE SHOT - COBB AND LONGFELLOW

COBB
(adjusting his clothes)
She's the star reporter on The Mail. Every time you opened your kisser, you gave her another story. She's the dame who slapped that monicker on you - "Cinderella Man." You've been making love to a double dose of cyanide!

LONGFELLOW
(an outcry)
Shut up!

Longfellow, stunned, crosses to the bed - CAMERA PANNING WITH HIM. He slumps down and continues staring at picture.

209. MEDIUM SHOT
Cobb crosses to phone and picks up receiver.

CUT TO:

INT. NEWSPAPER OUTER OFFICE
210. MED. CLOSE SHOT
Babe is at her desk. She has just finished rummaging through her desk. Many articles are on top. Mac is by her side. Babe flicks the pages of a small loose-leaf book, and hands it to Mac.

BABE
This is for you, Mac. The names of all the headwaiters in town. You can always buy a bit of choice scandal from them at reasonable prices.

MAC
Aw, listen Babe, I can't let you quit now. You're not going through with this thing, are you?

Babe shakes her head with finality, as the phone bell rings.

MAC
(picking up receiver)
I've seen 'em get in a rut like you before - but they always come back.
(into phone)
Hello ... Yes. Just a minute.

He holds the receiver out to her.

MAC
It's for you. In a couple weeks you'll get the itch so bad, you'll be working for nothing.

BABE
(into phone)
Hello ...

INT. LONGFELLOW'S BEDROOM
211. MEDIUM SHOT
Cobb is at the phone.

COBB
Babe Bennett? Just a minute.

He listens and hands phone to Longfellow.

LONGFELLOW
(into phone)
Hello, Mary?

INT. NEWSPAPER OUTER OFFICE
212. CLOSE SHOT - BABE

BABE
(at phone)
Oh, hello darling.

Her face goes dead as she realizes she is speaking to Longfellow.

INT. LONGFELLOW'S BEDROOM
213. CLOSE SHOT - LONGFELLOW

LONGFELLOW
(at phone; strained)
Is it you who's been writing those articles about me?

INT. NEWSPAPER OUTER OFFICE
214. CLOSE SHOT - BABE
At phone.

BABE
Why - uh - I was just leaving - I'll be up there in a minute--
(listens)
Look - uh, yes, I did - but I was just coming up to explain--

The words die in her throat. She looks dully at the receiver.

INT. LONGFELLOW'S BEDROOM

215. CLOSEUP - LONGFELLOW

BABE'S VOICE
(coming over phone)
Oh listen, darling, wait a minute! Please! Lis-
ten--

He hangs up. His face is a dead mask, every illusion shattered. Slowly, a wry smile appears on his face and, rising, he wanders around the room in deep abstraction. Cobb and Walter watch him sympathetically.

Longfellow is silent a long time.

216. MEDIUM SHOT
As a butler enters.

BUTLER
I beg pardon, sir. Shall I serve the wine with
the squab, sir?

Longfellow doesn't hear him.

BUTLER
(tries again)
I beg pardon, sir.

217. CLOSEUP - COBB
His face softens.

COBB
If I knew you were going to take it so hard, I
woulda kept my mouth shut. Sorry.

218. MEDIUM SHOT
As finally Longfellow speaks, without turning.

LONGFELLOW
(quietly)
Pack my things, Walter. I'm going home.

WALTER
Yes, sir.

He immediately busies himself.

DISSOLVE TO:

INT. CORRIDOR

219. WIDE SHOT
Longfellow emerges from his bedroom, walking briskly toward the staircase, immediately followed by Cobb and Walter. Walter is loaded down with suitcases. Longfellow is wearing coat and hat.

COBB
(trying to keep up with Longfellow)
You shouldn't be running away like this. What's
going to happen to the Estate?

LONGFELLOW
They can have the Estate.

As they approach the staircase, a commotion is heard from stairs. Cobb hurries ahead to see what is going on.

INT. GRAND FOYER

220. MEDIUM SHOT
Two butlers are struggling with a wild-eyed man of middle age. They shout in unison.

BUTLERS (simultaneously)	FARMER
You can't come up here! He's not home, I tell you! We'll send for the police!	Let me go! I wanna see him! I wanna see that guy! Let me go!

They continue to struggle as Cobb reaches them.

COBB
What's going on here?

The man yanks himself free.

FARMER
There he is! I just wanted to get a look at him.

He sees Longfellow over Cobb's shoulder.

FARMER
There you are! I just wanted to see what kind of a man you were!

He struggles to thrust Cobb aside.

221. FULL SHOT
Favoring Longfellow, who has reached the bottom of the staircase and watches the man warily.

FARMER
(wildly)
I just wanted to see what a man looks like that can spend thousands of dollars on a party - while people around him are hungry! The "Cinderella Man," huh? Did you ever stop to think how many families could have been fed on the money you pay out to get on the front pages?

Cobb forcibly restrains the man.

COBB
Come on! Take him out of here!

FARMER
Let me go!

LONGFELLOW
(an order)
Let him alone.

FARMER
Let me alone!
(threateningly)
If you know what's good for you - you'll let me get this off my chest!

(to Longfellow)
How did you feel feeding doughnuts to a horse? Get a kick out of it, huh? Got a big laugh?
(sarcastically)
Did you ever think of feeding doughnuts to human beings! No!

Longfellow stares at him.

WALTER
(quietly)
Shall I call the police, sir?

LONGFELLOW
No!
(to man)
What do _you_ want!!

FARMER
Yeah - that's all that's worrying you. What do I want? A chance to feed a wife and kids! I'm a farmer. A job! That's what I want!

LONGFELLOW
A farmer, eh! You're a moocher, that's what you are! I wouldn't believe you or anybody else on a stack of bibles! You're a moocher like all the rest of them around here, so get out of here!

FARMER
Sure - everybody's a moocher to you. A mongrel dog eating out of a garbage pail is a moocher to you!

COBB
(starting to push him towards the door)
This won't do you any good--

The man shoves him away, suddenly whips out a gun and levels it at him.

FARMER
Stay where you are, young feller. Get over there.

Cobb backs away and the man points the gun at Longfellow, who remains staring at him, immobilely.

FARMER
(tensely)
You're about to get some more publicity, Mr. Deeds! You're about to get on the front page again! See how you're going to like it this time!
(voice rises)
See what good your money's going to do when you're six feet under ground. You never thought of that, did you? No! All you ever thought of was pinching pennies - you money-grabbing hick! You never gave a thought to all of those starving people--

(his voice wavers)
--standing in the bread lines--
(huskily)
--not knowing where their next meal was coming from! Not able to feed their wife and kids.
(voice breaks)
Not able to--

He can't go on. A sob escapes. He reaches up and brushes away a tear with a rough hand. It seems to bring him to his senses. He glances down and seeing the gun in his hand - stares at it in surprise. He realizes what he was about to do.

FARMER
(scarcely audible)
Oh!

222. MED. SHOT - THE GROUP
The man slumps into a chair and the gun drops to the floor. Cobb bends quickly and picks it up. Longfellow never moves.

FARMER
(dead voice - staring into space)
I'm glad I didn't hurt nobody. Excuse me.

He turns his head slowly and peers at them with non-seeing eyes, then suddenly he hides his face in his hands and sobs.

FARMER
(muffled)
Crazy. You get all kinds of crazy ideas.

Longfellow watches him pityingly.

FARMER
Sorry. I didn't know what I was doing.

The rest of it seems to come out of him effortfully - his voice breaking.

FARMER
Losing your farm after twenty years' work - seeing your kids go hungry - a game little wife saying "Everything's going to be all right."
(stridently)
Standing there in the bread lines. It killed me to take a handout.
(pathetically)
I ain't used to it.
(resigned)
Go ahead and do what you want with me, mister.
(scarcely audible)
I guess I'm at the end of my rope.

He sobs openly. While he was speaking, Longfellow was peering into the man's face intently. As the man finishes

DISSOLVE TO:

EXT. INTIMATE DINING ROOM
223. CLOSE SHOT
At the table that was all set for Babe. The man sits, eating. He seriously bends over his food. Longfellow sits opposite him - his eyes glued on the man, absorbed in profound thought.

MAN
(tentatively)
Can I take some of this home with me?

Longfellow nods.

DISSOLVE TO:

INSERT: NEWSPAPER HEADLINES

"LONGFELLOW DEEDS TO GIVE FORTUNE AWAY
Huge farming district to be divided into ten acre farms - fully equipped - at a cost of eighteen million dollars."

WIPE OFF TO:

INSERT: SECOND NEWSPAPER HEADLINE

"DEEDS' PLAN STARTLES FINANCIAL WORLD"

WIPE OFF TO:

INSERT: THIRD NEWSPAPER HEADLINE

"STAFF OF WORKERS INVESTIGATE APPLICANTS"

WIPE OFF TO:

INSERT: FOURTH NEWSPAPER HEADLINE

"THOUSANDS OF UNEMPLOYED STORM DEEDS HOME FOR FARM DONATIONS"

WIPE OFF TO:

EXT. LONGFELLOW DEEDS' HOME

224. LONG SHOT
A mob of shouting men and women clamor at the gates, being jostled around by the police.

INT. LONGFELLOW'S DRAWING ROOM

225. FULL SHOT
It has been transformed into an office. Longfellow sits at one end of the room. Clerks are at several desks. On one side and leading out into the hall, is a long line of men waiting to be interviewed.

VOICE
Go on. Step lively.

226. MED. SHOT
At Longfellow's desk. He has a two days' growth of beard and looks worn. Next to him is a clerk. In front of him is an applicant.

LONGFELLOW
(as the camera moves in on him)
Are you married?

APPLICANT
Yes, sir.

LONGFELLOW
Any children?

APPLICANT
No, no children.

LONGFELLOW
All right, Mr. Dodsworth. I think you'll qualify.
(he hands him a form)
Take this to that desk over there for further instructions.

APPLICANT
(gratefully - exiting)
Thank you very much.

LONGFELLOW
Next, please.

A man steps forward and stands in front of his desk.

227. MED. CLOSE SHOT AT DESK
Longfellow, clerk and applicant.

LONGFELLOW
(to clerk)
How many does that make?

CLERK
You've okayed 819.

LONGFELLOW
(wearily)
Is that all?

CLERK
That's all.

LONGFELLOW
It's going awfully slow. We need 1100 more.
(phone rings)
Hello ... oh, yes. Yes. The water development seems okay - but I don't like the road layout yet. Come up tonight about ten and bring the maps. Right.

He hangs up.

228. WIDER ANGLE
As the farmer in previous sequence approaches.

FARMER
Here's the order for the plows. We got a good price on them.

LONGFELLOW
That's fine. Thanks. I'll look 'em over later.

FARMER
Oh, Mr. Deeds--

Longfellow looks up. Farmer goes on:

FARMER
--my wife wanted me to tell you she--
(hesitates)
--she prays for you every night.

LONGFELLOW
(embarrassed)
Well, thanks, I - uh--
(to applicant in front of him)
How do you do? What is your name?

RANKIN
George Rankin, sir.

While Longfellow writes--

229. CLOSE SHOT AT A DESK
Cobb is on the phone.

COBB
(into phone)
No! No! We're not buying any bulls. What's that? Listen, fellow, bull's what I've been selling all my life!

He slams down the receiver.

INT. CEDAR'S OFFICE
230. MEDIUM SHOT
Cedar behind his desk. In front of him is Henry Semple and his nagging wife. Cedar shoves a paper in front of Semple.

CEDAR
We have very little time. He's ordered me to turn everything over to him immediately. We have to work fast before he disposes of every penny.

WIFE
See! I told you something could be done. I knew it all the time. Sign it, dear.

SEMPLE
(hesitating)
We may get into trouble.

WIFE
Oh, don't be so squeamish.

CEDAR
There are millions involved. After all, you have your legal rights. You're his only living relatives.

231. CLOSE SHOT AT DESK
As Semple picks up the paper.

SEMPLE
What's it say?

WIFE
That's your agreement with Mr. Cedar, if we win.

CEDAR
You see, my end is going to be rather expensive. I have a lot of important people to take care of. I have the legal machinery all set and ready to go. I've been working on nothing else for the last week. You say the word, and we'll stop this yokel dead in his tracks.

WIFE
Sign it!

SEMPLE
Oh, all right.

With the perturbed expression still on his face, Semple reaches over to sign the document. Simultaneously, Cedar flicks a button on his dictagraph.

CEDAR
(into dictagraph)
Charlie, we're off! Papers all set?

VOICE
All set.

CEDAR
Okay, then. Go to it.
(afterthought)
And, Charlie--

VOICE
Yeah?

CEDAR
Find out who wrote those newspaper articles and subpoena them right away.

VOICE
Okay.

DISSOLVE TO:

INT. LONGFELLOW'S DRAWING ROOM
232. MEDIUM SHOT
A large, raw-boned Swede stands before Longfellow.

LONGFELLOW
What is your name?

SVENSON
Christian Svenson.

LONGFELLOW
Farmer?

SVENSON
Yes, ma'am.

LONGFELLOW
Where is your farm?

SVENSON
South Dakota north.

LONGFELLOW
South Dakota - north?

SVENSON
South Dakota - but on the top.

LONGFELLOW
Oh. Oh!

233. WIDER ANGLE
Cobb enters, very businesslike.

COBB
What about your knocking off for lunch?

LONGFELLOW
Not hungry. I want to get through this work in a hurry, and then I want to go home. What price did you get on those trucks?

COBB
Come on, come on. What are you trying to do, kid? Keel over? You haven't been out of this house in two weeks.

LONGFELLOW
(tired)
Well, maybe I will have a sandwich.
(to Swede)
Do you mind waiting a few minutes?

SVENSON
(undoing paper package)
Oh, sure, sure. If you like to have a sandwich, I can give you one, please.

He brings out two huge sandwiches, and hands one to Longfellow.

LONGFELLOW
(smiling)
Thanks. Thank you. Never mind, Cobb.

He takes it, and he and the Swede silently eat. Longfellow looks up.

LONGFELLOW
Good.

The Swede smiles. Longfellow nibbles his sandwich, then glances around the room. His gaze rests on:

234. LONG SHOT
Of the long line of applicants waiting for an audience.

235. MEDIUM SHOT

LONGFELLOW
(calls to Cobb)
Cobb! Get lunch for the rest of them.

COBB
(entering)
What? There must be 2000 of them out there.

LONGFELLOW
Well, that doesn't make 'em any less hungry.

COBB
Okay, Santa Claus. 2000 lunches.

He exits. Longfellow glances over at the line, smiling.

236. FULL SHOT
In front of the line there is a slight scuffle, as a man is being pushed forward by some others. He mumbles a protest, tries to get back into position, but the men push him forward again.

GROUP
(ad-lib)
Go on, say something. Say something!

237. CLOSEUP - LONGFELLOW
He looks up inquiringly.

238. MED. CLOSE SHOT - MEN IN LINE
The man finally is resigned, and stands shifting, ill-at-ease, his head hanging bashfully.

MAN
Mr. Deeds, the boys here wanted me to say a little something. They just wanted me to say that--
(clears his throat)
Well, they wanted me to say that--
(quickly gets it out)
We think you're swell - and that's no baloney.

MAN'S VOICE
Say something more!

239. CLOSE SHOT - LONGFELLOW
He smiles self-consciously.

240. MED. CLOSE SHOT OF MEN
The spokesman apparently has not finished yet. Directly behind the line, three officious-looking men have made their appearance and wait for him to conclude.

MAN
Give me a chance, fellas. We're all down and out - but when a fellow like you comes along, kinda gives us a little hope - and they just wanted me to say--

It's as far as he gets - as the three strangers break their way through the line and approach Longfellow's desk.

ONE OF THE SHERIFFS
(ad-lib)
Break it up.

241. MED. SHOT AT DESK

FIRST DEPUTY SHERIFF
(pointing to Longfellow)
That's him.

2ND DEPUTY SHERIFF
Are you Longfellow Deeds?

LONGFELLOW
(looks up)
Yes?

FIRST DEPUTY SHERIFF
Sheriff's office.
(shows paper)
We've got a warrant to take you into custody.

LONGFELLOW
(without moving)
A what?

FIRST DEPUTY SHERIFF
A warrant for your arrest. You'll have to come along with us.

Cobb enters.

COBB
What's up? What do _you_ mugs want?

FIRST DEPUTY SHERIFF
I don't know nothing, buddy. All I know is the Sheriff gives me an insanity warrant to execute.

COBB
Insanity! Who's says he's insane?

They all turn to Charlie, who comes forward.

CHARLIE
The complainant is a relative of the late Martin Semple. The charges are that Mr. Deeds is insane and incapable of handling the Estate.

COBB
Oh, somebody got panic-stricken about his giving his dough away, eh?
(to sheriff)
Where do you think you're going to take him?

FIRST DEPUTY SHERIFF
To the County Hospital.

CHARLIE
Of course, that's only temporary. A hearing will follow immediately.

242. CLOSEUP - LONGFELLOW
As he speaks quietly.

LONGFELLOW
That's fine. Just because I want to give this money to people who need it, they think I'm crazy.
(cynically)
That's marvelous. That makes everything complete.

243. WIDER ANGLE
To include group.

FIRST DEPUTY SHERIFF
Let's get going!

COBB
Wait a minute! Not so fast. We're going to get a lawyer. I'll call Cedar.

LONGFELLOW
(thoroughly disillusioned)
No, don't bother.

CHARLIE
As a matter of fact, I'm from Mr. Cedar's office. He represents the complainant.

COBB
Oh.

Longfellow glances up at him and smiles bitterly.

FIRST DEPUTY SHERIFF
Well, let's go. We're wasting a lot of time.

He goes to one side of Longfellow, and his partner to the other. They take Longfellow by the arms. He glances down casually and, suddenly, violently pushes the deputies away from him. They are thrown backward; their eyes widen in surprise.

LONGFELLOW
(calmly rising)
All right, I'll go. But get your hands off me!

244. MEDIUM SHOT
Longfellow starts to walk forward, accompanied by Cobb - and the two deputies and Charlie fall in behind them.

THE SHERIFFS
(ad-lib)
Make way! Make way!

245. CLOSE SHOTS OF CLERKS
To be intercut with above scene. They stare, petrified, and mumble to each other.

246. MEDIUM SHOT
Of the farmers and other applicants. The line has fallen out and they stand in a bunch, staring pathetically and hopelessly at the departing group.

247. CLOSEUP OF THE FARMER
Who stands in f.g. of bunch. What is taking place has slowly penetrated his befuddled brain. The disappointment he feared is here. His body imperceptibly sags, his eyes dim - all hope having gone out of them.

FADE OUT:

FADE IN

INSERT: SIGN reading: "COUNTY HOSPITAL"

DISSOLVE THRU TO:

INT. CORRIDOR OF HOSPITAL
248. MEDIUM SHOT
A guard sits at a desk near a door, talking on the telephone.

GUARD
(on phone)
Yes, most everybody in town has been here to see him. Yes, sir. I won't. Goodbye--

Babe rounds the corner quickly, heading for the door. The guard hurriedly hangs up and stands to block her.

GUARD
Sorry, lady--
(recognizes her)
Oh, it's you again.

BABE
Oh, please! I've got to see him.

GUARD
Now listen, sister, for the fourteenth and last time he don't want to see nobody.

BABE
(pleading)
Will you just give him my name?

GUARD
(confidentially)
Listen, toots, just between us, there ain't a thing in the world the matter with that guy till I mention your name, then he goes haywire!

Babe winces under the blow.

INT. HOSPITAL ROOM
249. MEDIUM SHOT
Longfellow is seated by the far wall, peering moodily out the window. Cobb paces about. Suddenly, he wheels on Longfellow.

COBB
What are you going to do - just sit back and let them railroad you? It's as pretty a frameup as ever hit this rotten town! If you'd just let me get you a lawyer!

Longfellow pays no attention to him.

250. MED. CLOSE SHOT
As Cobb continues.

COBB
(raises his voice)
You can't walk into that courtroom without being ready to protect yourself in the clinches. Cedar's too smart. With the array of talent he's got lined up against you - you're cooked!

Longfellow is still unresponsive. Cobb thinks a moment, watching him studiously; then pleading tenderly:

COBB
Listen, pal - I know just how you feel. A blonde in Syracuse put me through the same paces. I came out with a sour puss - but full of fight. Come on, you don't want to lay down now.

Longfellow is still unresponsive.

COBB
Do you realize what's happening? They're trying to prove that you're nuts! If they win the case, they'll shove you in the bughouse. The moment they accuse you of it, they have you half licked. You've got to fight!

Longfellow disregards him and Cobb sighs, resignedly.

INT. CORRIDOR OUTSIDE DOOR

251. MED. CLOSE SHOT
The guard is reading his paper. Babe is still waiting, pacing.

GUARD
Go on, sit down, won't you?

252. MED. CLOSE SHOT AT DOOR
As Cobb comes out. The guard gets up to check the door is locked.

GUARD
So long, Mr. Cobb.

Cobb, in a troubled frame of mind, doesn't respond and starts down corridor - CAMERA TRUCKS WITH HIM. Babe catches up with him.

BABE
Corny!

Cobb doesn't stop. Babe grabs his arm:

BABE
Corny!

Cobb stops.

253. CLOSE TWO SHOT
Cobb glares at Babe belligerently.

BABE
I've got to see him! I've got to talk to him!

COBB
Haven't you done enough damage already?

BABE
(ignoring his attack)
Somebody's got to help him! He hasn't got a chance against Cedar. Look, I've been all over town talking to everybody. I've got Mac all lined up - and the paper's behind him. And I can get him Livingston, too. With a lawyer like Livingston, he's got a fighting chance.

COBB
(coldly)
You're wasting your time. He doesn't want any lawyers. He's sunk so low, he doesn't want help from anybody.
(bitterly)
You can take a bow for that.
(huskily)
As swell a guy as ever hit this town, and you crucified him! For a couple of stinking headlines! You've done your bit - now stay out of his way!

He exits abruptly, leaving Babe staring despairingly at his disappearing back, his brutal diatribe ringing harshly in her ears.

FADE OUT:

FADE IN

INSERT: NEWSPAPER HEADLINES

"DEEDS SANITY HEARING TODAY!
Simple Heir Charged With Incompetency! 'Should Be Confined To An Institution,' Declares Cedar.

"Longfellow Deeds Refuses Counsel; Remains Incommunicado."

"Farmers Aroused At Efforts to Balk Their Benefactor."

"Police Surround Courthouse In Anticipation Of Outbreak."

DISSOLVE TO:

<u>EXT. COURTHOUSE</u>
254. LONG SHOT
Of an unruly mob being jostled by the police.

<u>INT. CORRIDOR OF COURTHOUSE</u>
255. LONG SHOT
The corridor is jammed with curious public endeavoring to gain entrance. Perspiring police fight to keep them back.

<u>INT. COURTROOM</u>
256. FULL SHOT
It is practically full. The few empty seats are being quickly filled. People stumble over each other to find a seat. The judge is not yet at his bench. There is a general chatter of excitement and anticipation.

257. MED. SHOT - FRONT OF COURTROOM
Among the spectators Babe sits beside Mac. She stares, expressionless. Mac glances at her sympathetically.

258. MED. SHOT
Featuring the farmer who broke into Longfellow's house. Near him is the Swede we saw - and others.

259. SHOT INSIDE RAILING
Cedar and his assistants arrange their papers. Two dignified gentlemen, psychiatrists, await action, arms folded. Near them is Henry Semple, the complainant, his nose twitching nervously. By his side is his wife, sparkling expectantly.

260. SHOT AT LONG TABLE
At which sit a dozen newspaper reporters.

261. MED. CLOSE SHOT
From a side door Longfellow enters, accompanied by his guard. Immediately the place is astir. As he advances to a chair in front of a table--

262. MED. FULL SHOT - COURTROOM
Necks crane for a glimpse. Whispered conversations take place.

263. CLOSE SHOT - HENRY SEMPLE
He looks guilty, nose twitching more violently than ever.

SEMPLE
(to Cedar)
Here he is!

264. CLOSE SHOT - BABE AND MAC
Babe sits up, her eyes riveted on Longfellow. Impulsively she starts to rise, but Mac puts a restraining hand on her.

265. MED. CLOSE SHOT
Longfellow turns neither to left nor right. He is slumped low in his chair, staring solemnly into space. Cobb breaks into scene and sits down beside him.

COBB
(full of excitement)
Cedar just sent for me. Wants to make a settlement. Here's your chance to get out of the whole mess. What do you say?

He gets no response from Longfellow.

There is a stir in the courtroom.

266. MED. LONG SHOT
The bailiff calls out as the Judge proceeds to his bench.

BAILIFF
Quiet, please! The Supreme Court of the State of New York, County of New York, is now in session, the Honorable John May, Judge, presiding. Be seated.

267. MED. CLOSE SHOT
To include Judge and Longfellow.

JUDGE
The court wishes to warn those present that it will tolerate no disturbances.
(to Longfellow)
Regarding the sanity hearing of Longfellow Deeds, are you represented by counsel, Mr. Deeds?

Almost imperceptibly, Longfellow shakes his head no. The Judge looks troubled. There is a stir in the courtroom.

JUDGE
I understand that you have no counsel, Mr. Deeds. In fact, that you have no intention of defending any of these charges. Now, if you wish to change your mind, the hearing can be postponed.

Getting no response from Longfellow, the Judge shrugs his shoulders.

JUDGE
Proceed.

DISSOLVE TO:

INT. COURTROOM
268. MEDIUM SHOT
Cedar is on his feet.

CEDAR
(addressing the court)
--and in the interests of my client, the only other living relative of the late Martin W. Semple, we cannot permit a fortune so huge to be dissipated by a person whose incompetency and abnormality we shall prove beyond any reasonable doubt.

269. PANNING SHOT OF SPECTATORS

CEDAR'S VOICE
I have before me a series of articles written by a newspaper woman who was an eye-witness to his conduct ever since he came to New York.

CAMERA STOPS on Babe and Mac. Cedar's voice goes on:

CEDAR
She tells how, in the midst of a normal conversation, he would suddenly begin playing his tuba. She tells of his attacks upon several of our eminent writers - for no apparent reason. In fact, there are many instances not recorded in these articles in which Mr. Deeds satisfied an unnatural desire to smash people up without provocation.

270. MED. SHOT - FRONT OF COURTROOM

CEDAR
I, myself, unable to keep pace with his mental quirks, and constantly fearful of assault, turned down an opportunity to represent him as his attorney. This newspaper woman, whom we have subpoenaed to testify, tells how he tied up traffic for an hour feeding doughnuts to a poor horse. And by his own statement, waiting for that horse to ask for a cup of coffee.

There is laughter in the courtroom - which quickly subsides when the Judge pounds his gavel.

CEDAR
We have photographs to substantiate this little episode, and other photographs showing Mr. Deeds jumping upon a fire engine. This scarcely sounds like the action of a man in whom the disposition of twenty million dollars may safely be entrusted. This writer of these articles - a woman whose intelligence and integrity in the newspaper world is unquestioned - held him in such contempt that she quite aptly named him "The Cinderella Man."

271. CLOSEUP - LONGFELLOW

CEDAR'S VOICE
We have witnesses here from Mandrake Falls, his own home town, who will tell of his conduct throughout his lifetime, proving that his derangement is neither recent nor a temporary one.

Longfellow's interest is only slightly aroused. He lifts his eyes in a casual glance around him.

272. MED. CLOSE SHOT
Featuring Cedar.

CEDAR
We have others who will tell of his unusual behavior when he invited the great leaders of the musical world to his home, and then proceeded to forcibly eject them. Only recently when he was in the County Hospital for observation, he not only refused to be examined by these gentlemen, the state psychiatrists, but he actually made a violent attack upon them.

273. CLOSE SHOT - THE JUDGE
As Cedar continues talking, CAMERA PULLS BACK to WIDER SHOT.

CEDAR
In these times, with the country incapacitated by economic ailments, and endangered with an undercurrent of social unrest, the promulgation of such a weird, fantastic and impractical plan as contemplated by the defendant, is capable of fomenting a disturbance from which the country may not soon recover. It is our duty to stop it! Our government is fully aware of its difficulties and can pull itself out of its economic rut without the assistance of Mr. Deeds, or any other crackpot.

274. MED. PANNING SHOT
Of farmers, the Swede and others.

CEDAR'S VOICE
His attempted action must therefore be attributed to a diseased mind afflicted with hallucinations of grandeur, and obsessed with an insane desire to become a public benefactor.

275. CLOSE SHOT AT FRONT OF COURTROOM
Featuring Cedar.

CEDAR
(suddenly)
Your Honor, at this time, we would like to call our first witness: Miss Louise - Babe - Bennett.

276. FULL SHOT
There is a mild stir, and all wait expectantly for Babe to appear.

CLERK
Miss Bennett, please.

Babe, eyes on Longfellow, slowly walks to the stand.

277. CLOSEUP - LONGFELLOW
He has his face averted and doesn't look at her.

278. MEDIUM SHOT
Babe continues to rivet her eyes on Longfellow, as she is sworn in.

CLERK
Raise your right hand, please.

She does so.

CLERK
Do you solemnly swear the testimony you may give before this court to be the truth, the whole truth and nothing but the truth, so help you God?

BABE
I do.

CLERK
State your right name, please.

BABE
Louise Bennett.

CLERK
Take the stand.

279. MED. CLOSE SHOT AT WITNESS STAND
As Cedar steps up to question Babe. Judge in f.g.

CEDAR
Miss Bennett, are you employed by the Morning Mail?

There is no answer. Babe continues to stare off at Longfellow, hoping he will look up. Cedar speaks to her again:

CEDAR
I must ask you to direct your attention to me.

But Babe's attention remains focused on Longfellow.

BABE
(appealing to Judge)
Your Honor, this is ridiculous!

JUDGE
Please answer the questions.

BABE
(wildly)
The whole hearing's ridiculous! That man's no more insane than you are.

The suddenness of her outbreak is startling. The Judge pounds his gavel.

280. WIDER ANGLE - FRONT OF COURTROOM
The Judge pounding his gavel.

JUDGE
Miss Bennett please!

CEDAR
This is outrageous!

BABE
(rising to stand)
It's obviously a frameup! They're trying to railroad this man for the money they can get out of him!

CEDAR
Your Honor!

The Judge pounds his gavel throughout her speech.

JUDGE
(highly)
Young lady, another outburst like that and I shall hold you in contempt! We're not interested in your opinion of the merits of this case. You're here to testify. Sit down and answer the questions. Proceed.

Cedar beams victoriously.

CEDAR
Thank you, Your Honor. Are you employed by the Morning Mail?

BABE
(sharply)
No!

Cedar's eyes widen in surprise. There is a light stir.

CEDAR
(threateningly)
You are under oath, Miss Bennett. I ask you again - are you employed by the Morning Mail?

BABE
(irritably)
No! I resigned last week!

281. CLOSE SHOT - LONGFELLOW
As Cedar proceeds without interruption.

CEDAR'S VOICE
Well, prior to that time - were you employed by the Morning Mail?

BABE'S VOICE
(laconically)
Yes.

282. CLOSE SHOT AT WITNESS STAND - BABE AND CEDAR

CEDAR
Were you given an assignment to follow the activities of Longfellow Deeds?

BABE
Yes.

CEDAR
Did you subsequently write a series of articles about him?

BABE
Yes!

CEDAR
(holding them up)
Are these the articles?

BABE
Yes!

CEDAR
Were you present when all these things took place?

BABE
Yes!

CEDAR
Are they true!

BABE
NO!!

CEDAR
But they _did_ take place?

BABE
They're colored! Just to make him look silly!

CEDAR
And you saw them happen?

BABE
Yes, but I--

CEDAR
(preemptorily)
That's all, Miss Bennett.

BABE
(half shrieking)
It isn't all! I'd like to explain--

CEDAR
(brusquely)
That's all, Miss Bennett. That's all.

283. MEDIUM SHOT
A bailiff takes Babe by the arm.

BAILIFF
Come on, miss - come on!

CEDAR
(simultaneously, to Judge)
Your Honor, I'd like to submit these articles as evidence.

Babe struggles away from the bailiff.

BABE
(frantically)
Let go of me!
(steps up to Judge; wildly)
What kind of hearing is this? What are you trying to do - persecute the man? He's not defending himself. Somebody's got to do it!

Throughout her tirade, the Judge has been angrily pounding his gavel.

JUDGE
Miss Bennett, please!

284. CLOSER SHOT
Featuring Babe and Judge.

BABE
I've got a right to be heard! I've attended dozens of cases like this. They're usually conducted without any formality at all. Anybody can be heard! My opinion is as good as these quack psychiatrists. I know him better than they do.

JUDGE
Miss Bennett, if you have quite finished, I should like to inform you that one more utterance from you and I shall place you under arrest.
(leans back)
I'm willing to hear anything anyone has to say - but I insist on it being done in an orderly fashion. When you have learned to show some respect for this court, you may return.
(dismissing her)
Until then, you'd better go back to your seat and calm down.

BAILIFF
This way, miss.

285. WIDER ANGLE
As Babe is led away, there is another courtroom stir.

BAILIFF'S VOICE
Order in the court!

When Babe is out of sight, the Judge turns to Longfellow.

JUDGE
Mr. Deeds, have you anything to say in defense of these articles?

286. CLOSE SHOT - LONGFELLOW AND COBB
Longfellow shakes his head. Cobb glances to him helplessly.

287. CLOSE SHOT - JUDGE
He shrugs.

JUDGE
Mr. Deeds?
(again no reply)
Mark these Exhibit A for the plaintiff.

CLERK
Yes, Your Honor.

JUDGE
Proceed.

288. CLOSE SHOT - BABE
As she sits down beside Mac - who places an affectionate arm around her shoulders.

DISSOLVE TO:

289. MED. SHOT - FRONT OF COURTROOM
Two old ladies are being led to the witness stand. Their eyelids flutter excitedly as they go.

290. CLOSE SHOT - LONGFELLOW
He looks up, sees the old ladies and smiles at them friendily.

291. MED. CLOSE SHOT AT JUDGE'S BENCH
Against the drone of the clerk, who swears witnesses in:

CEDAR
The Falkner sisters are rather timid, Your Honor, and wish to be together. If the court pleases, I will only have one of them testify.

JUDGE
(impatiently)
Yes! Yes! Let's get on with it.

Cedar turns to them.

292. MED. CLOSE SHOT AT WITNESS STAND
As Cedar addresses one of the old ladies.

CEDAR
What is your name, please?

JANE
Jane Falkner. This is my sister, Amy.

AMY
(agreeing)
Yes - Amy.

CEDAR
I'll direct my questions to you, Miss Jane. You can answer for both. Do you know the defendant, Mr. Longfellow Deeds?

The two old ladies look at each other, then in the direction in which Cedar points.

JANE
Oh yes, yes - of course we know him.

CEDAR
(a little nervously)
How long have you known him?

Jane turns to her sister, and they whisper to each other.

JANE
(turns to Cedar)
Since he was born.

AMY
Yes. Elsie Taggart was the midwife.

JANE
He was a seven-months baby.

CEDAR
Thank you, that's fine. Do you see him very often?

The two old ladies have their whispered conference again.

JANE
Most every day.

AMY
Sometimes twice.

JUDGE
(irascibly)
Must we have the echo?

CEDAR
Suppose you just answer, Miss Jane. Now, will you tell the Court what everybody at home thinks of Longfellow Deeds?

The two old ladies consult each other once more.

JANE
They think he's pixilated.

AMY
Oh yes, pixilated.

JUDGE
(leaning forward)
He's what?

CEDAR
(concerned)
What was that you said he was?

JANE
Pixilated.

AMY
Uh-huh.

CEDAR
(patiently)
Now, that's a rather strange word to use, Miss Jane. Can you tell the court exactly what it means?

While the two ladies go into a huddle:

293. CLOSE SHOT - PSYCHIATRISTS
As one of them speaks up.

PSYCHIATRIST
Perhaps I can explain, Your Honor. The word pixilated is an early American expression - derived from the word 'pixies,' meaning elves. They would say, 'The pixies had got him,' as we nowadays would say a man is 'balmy.'

294. MEDIUM SHOT
The Judge nods his understanding. The Falkner sisters nod in pleasant agreement. Cedar sighs victoriously.

CEDAR
Is that correct?

JANE
Uh-huh.

AMY
Uh-huh.

JUDGE
Now tell me, why does everyone think he's - uh - pixilated? Does he do peculiar things?

295. MED. SHOT TOWARD WITNESS STAND

JANE
(after conferring with Amy)
He walks in the rain, without his hat, and talks to himself.

AMY
Sometimes he whistles.

JANE
And sings.

CEDAR
Anything else?

JANE
Recently he gave Chuck Dillon a thumping.

AMY
Blacked his eye.

CEDAR
And why?

JANE
For no reason, I guess. He always does it. We always run into the house when we see him coming.

AMY
Never can tell what he's going to do.

JANE
He sure is pixilated.

AMY
Oh, yes - he's pixilated all right.

CEDAR
Thank you, ladies. That's all.

Cedar beams. The old ladies leave to resume their seats.

DISSOLVE TO:

296. CLOSE SHOT IN WITNESS STAND
A policeman in uniform.

POLICEMAN
They kept hollering: "Back to Nature! Back to Nature!" I thought they looked harmless enough so I took them home. I never thought he was cracked.

WIPE OFF TO:

297. CLOSE SHOT IN WITNESS STAND
The waiter at "Tullio's."

WAITER
I'm a waiter. He kept pressing me to point out the celebrities, and so help me Hannah I'm coming out of the kitchen a coupla minutes later and there he is moppin' up the floors with them. I never figured he was a guy looking for trouble.

WIPE OFF TO:

298. CLOSE SHOT IN WITNESS STAND
Mme. Pomponi.

MME. POMPONI
(expostulating)
He threw us out bodily! But bodily!

WIPE OFF TO:

299. MED. CLOSE SHOT IN WITNESS STAND
Of one of the bodyguards on witness stand.

BODYGUARD
We was hired as his bodyguard, see? Well, the first crack out of the box, he throws us in a room and locks the door, see? Now, if a thing like that gets around in our profession, we'd get the bird - see? So I says to my partner, "Let's quit this guy, he's nuts!"

WIPE OFF TO:

300. CLOSE SHOT IN WITNESS STAND
A Cockney cabman.

CABMAN
I'm very fond of Clara, sir. She's a nice 'orse. And when this bloke 'ere started feedin' 'er doughnuts, I yelled down to him, "Mind what you're doin' down there! Mind what you're doing'!" Of course I wouldn't mind, sir, but Clara won't eat nothin' but doughnuts, now.

WIPE OFF TO:

301. WIDE SHOT[13]
Of one of the photographers (Bob) and enlarged photographs of Longfellow's antics.

BAILIFF'S VOICE
Come to order.

CEDAR
Your Honor, I wish to call your attention to these exhibits. Mr. Davis, do you recognize these reproductions?

BOB
Sure, they're good enlargements. Where'd you have them made?

CEDAR
Did you make the originals of them?

BOB
Sure. I took the originals. Taking pictures is my business. I photograph a lot of nuts.

WIPE OFF TO:

As Cedar speaks.

CEDAR
And now, Your Honor, if the court pleases, I shall call upon Dr. Emil Von Holler, if he will be good enough to give us his opinion. Dr. Von Holler, as you know, is the eminent Austrian psychiatrist - probably the greatest authority on the subject in the world. At present he is in this country on a lecture tour, and has graciously volunteered his services. Dr. Von Holler?

While he is still speaking,

VOICE OF BAILIFF
Dr. Von Holler!

DISSOLVE TO:

302. WIDER ANGLE
As the clerk finishes swearing Dr. Von Holler in.

CLERK
Do you solemnly swear the testimony you are about to give in the cause now pending before this court shall be the truth, the whole truth and nothing but the truth, so help you God? State your right name, please.

VON HOLLER
(a slight Austrian accent)
Emil Von Holler.

CLERK
Take the stand.

303. MED. CLOSE SHOT AT WITNESS STAND
On Von Holler and Cedar.

CEDAR
Now Dr. Von Holler, will you kindly tell the court what your opinion is on this case?

VON HOLLER
This is purely a case of manic depression. In cases of this kind, patients sometimes go on for years before being detected.

He turns to one of the psychiatrists, sitting with the Judge.

VON HOLLER
You remember, Dr. Fosdick, in my last book there are some very fine examples.

DR. FOSDICK
(nodding)
Uh-huh.

VON HOLLER
Especially, the one of the young nobleman, you remember?

DR. FOSDICK
Oh, yes. Yes, of course Dr. Von Holler. Very interesting.

VON HOLLER
It reminds me very much of this one. Nicht wahr?

DR. FOSDICK
Ja.

VON HOLLER
It takes so long to detect them--
(to Judge)
--because their mood changes so often and so quickly. Now, Your Honor, may I show you? May I use the chart?

JUDGE
By all means.

He moves to a blackboard. There are chalk marks on it. A straight line runs diagonally across the center. Other lines run zig-zag over and below this center line.

VON HOLLER
(indicating chart)
Below here, they are extremely depressed, melancholy, impossible to live with, and often become violent.
(running a line up)
From this mood the manic depressive might gradually change until they reach this state.
(he reaches the center line)
Here is lucidity. Here they are perfectly normal. As normal as you or I--
(smiling)
--assuming, of course, that we are normal.
(he starts up with chalk)
Then, the mood changes again until--
(chalk reaches top)
--they reach this state, a state of highest exaltation. Here everything is fine. Here the world is beautiful. Here they are so elated - how do you express it?
(quickly, as it comes to him)
--they would give you the shirt off their backs!

CEDAR
Dr. Von Holler, how would you say that applied to Mr. Deeds's case?

VON HOLLER
The symptoms are obvious.
(points to top line)
When he was here, on top of the wave, he felt nothing but kindliness and warmth toward his fellow-men. He wanted them around him. So he decided he would give a big reception. But in the meantime, his mood has changed.
(chalk goes down)
He is now at the bottom of the wave - depressed - melancholy. So, when his guests arrive, he throws them out. They are now his imaginary enemies.

304. CLOSE SHOT - LONGFELLOW
As Von Holler's voice continues:

VON HOLLER'S VOICE
Other instances of high elation are when he plays his tuba, when he writes his poetry, when he chases fire engines in his desire to help humanity. This is contrasted with his present mood, which is so low that even the instinct for self-preservation is lacking.

305. MED. SHOT FRONT OF COURTROOM
Von Holler still continues:

VON HOLLER
Oh, the man is verrukt. Your Honor, this is decidedly a case of a manic depressive.

CEDAR
Thank you, Dr. Von Holler.

Dr. Von Holler returns to his seat.

CEDAR
Your Honor, we rest.

306. FULL SHOT - COURTROOM
There is a shifting of bodies, and a renewed interest, as they wait for the next move. The Judge and his own two experts go into an inaudible huddle.

307. CLOSE SHOT - COBB AND LONGFELLOW
Longfellow is slumped in his seat, head down.

COBB
Come on, what're you going to do? Let them get away with it? They got you cooked.

Longfellow does not budge.

There is an expectant stir in the courtroom among the spectators and rows of reporters.

308. MED. CLOSE SHOT - THE JUDGE AND HIS EXHIBITS
Judge comes out of his huddle and glances at Longfellow.

JUDGE
(leaning forward)
Mr. Deeds, before the court arrives at a decision, isn't there anything you wish to say?

309. CLOSE SHOT - LONGFELLOW AND COBB
Longfellow shakes his head slightly.

COBB
(whispering)
Come on - don't be a sap!

CONTINUATION SCENE 308
The Judge watches him a few moments, hesitatingly, and then turns to his experts.

310. MED. SHOT - NEWSPAPER REPORTERS

A REPORTER
He's sunk.

311. CLOSE SHOT - CEDAR AND HIS CLIENTS, ASSISTANTS ETC.
They smirk confidently.

312. CLOSE SHOT - BABE AND MAC
She stares, panic-stricken.

313. MED. SHOT
Of the Swede, the farmer, and others. Their faces show their resentment.

314. MED. SHOT FRONT OF COURTROOM

JUDGE
(to the two experts)
You both concur?

EXPERTS
(ad-lib)
Oh, positively.

The Judge emerges from his consultation with his experts and addresses Longfellow.

JUDGE
Mr. Deeds, in view of the extensive testimony and your continued silence and upon recommendation of the doctors, the Court considers it advisable for your own safety that you be committed to an institution as prescribed by law. You need medical attention, Mr. Deeds.
(shrugs)
Perhaps in a little while--

Suddenly the air is rent with the shrill voice of Babe.

BABE
No! No! No! Wait a minute!

All are startled and look up. Babe runs right to the Judge.

BABE
You can't do it! You've got to make him talk.

CEDAR'S VOICE
Your Honor, I object!

She turns directly to Longfellow - leaning over close to him.

315. CLOSE SHOT - BABE AND LONGFELLOW

BABE
(pleading softly)
Oh, darling, please. I know everything I've done. I know how horrible I've been. No matter what happens, if you never see me again, do this for me.

JUDGE'S VOICE
Miss Bennett, please!

BABE
(frantically)
You said I could speak! You said I could have my say if I were rational. I'm rational. Please, let me take the witness chair.

316. WIDER ANGLE

BABE
He must be made to defend himself before you arrive at a decision.

JUDGE
Very well. Take the stand.

Babe goes up to the witness stand and sits down.

BABE
Oh, thank you!

CEDAR
(shouting)
Your Honor, what she is saying has no bearing on the case. I object.

JUDGE
Let her speak.

BABE
I know why he won't defend himself! That has a bearing on the case, hasn't it? He's been hurt! He's been hurt by everybody's he met since he came here, principally by me. He's been the victim of every conniving crook in town. The newspapers pounced on him - made him a target for their feeble humor.

317. CLOSE SHOT - BABE

BABE
I was smarter than the rest of them! I got closer to him so I could laugh louder. Why shouldn't he keep quiet? Every time he said anything it was twisted around to sound imbecilic.

318. CLOSEUP - BABE
As she continues.

BABE
He can thank me for it! I handed the gang a grand laugh. This is a fitting climax to my sense of humor.

319. WIDER ANGLE
As Cedar protests.

CEDAR
But Your Honor - this is preposterous!

The Judge waves him down with a dismissing gesture of his hand.

BABE
Certainly I wrote those articles. I was going to get a raise - and a month's vacation! But I stopped writing them when I found out what he was all about! When I realized how real he was.

320. CLOSE SHOT - LONGFELLOW
As Babe's voice continues:

BABE'S VOICE
He could never fit in with our distorted viewpoint because he's honest and sincere - and good. If that man is crazy, Your Honor, the rest of us belong in straight-jackets.

321. MED. SHOT
Cedar jumps up.

CEDAR
Your Honor, this is absurd. The woman's obviously in love with him.

BABE
What's that got to do with it?

CEDAR
(shouting)
Well, you are in love with him, aren't you?

BABE
(shouting back)
What's that got to do with it?

CEDAR
(louder)
You are, aren't you?

BABE
(just as loud)
Yes!!!

322. CLOSEUP - LONGFELLOW
To be intercut during her speech. At first he merely glances up at her speculatively. Finally, he begins to show some interest.

323. MED. SHOT FRONT OF COURTROOM
Cedar turns to the Judge.

CEDAR
Your Honor, her testimony is of no value. Why shouldn't she defend him? It's a tribute to American womanhood - the instinct to protect the weak. I'm not saying that nobody likes the boy. I cherish a fond affection for him myself. But that doesn't mean to say--

In the middle of his speech, Mac - the editor - appears at his elbow.

MAC
When the windbag here gets through, Your Honor, I'd like to verify what Miss Bennett said. I'm her editor. When she quit her job, she told me what a swell fellow this man was. And anything Babe Bennett says is okay with me.

JUDGE
If you have anything to say, you will take the stand.

MAC
I've already said it, Your Honor. I just thought I'd like to get my two cents in.

As he starts to go, CAMERA PANNING WITH HIM, he passes Longfellow. He nudges him.

MAC
Don't be a sucker, pal. Stand up and speak your piece.

He disappears to his seat.

COBB
Your Honor, I've got a couple of cents I'd like to put in--

JUDGE
Sit down!

COBB
I've been with this man ever since he came to New York--

324. MED. SHOT
Shooting toward the Judge. He pounds his gavel, interrupting Cobb.

JUDGE
Sit down! There will be no further interruptions.

Almost simultaneously with the Judge's speech, the farmer, somewhere in the audience, rises to his feet.

FARMER
How about us, Mr. Deeds!

325. MED. SHOT
Shooting toward audience. As the farmer finishes, a dozen others are on their feet.

CROWD
(ad-lib)
Yes! What about us, Mr. Deeds!
You're not going to leave us out in the cold!
They're trying to frame you, Mr. Deeds!

The turmoil is general, with bailiffs running to quiet them. The Judge pounding his gavel, incensed.

BAILIFF'S VOICE
Order! Order!

JUDGE
(when quiet reigns)
In the interest of Mr. Deeds, I have tolerated a great deal of informality. But if there is one more outburst, I shall have the courtroom cleared.

LONGFELLOW
Your Honor--

JUDGE
(surprised)
Yes?

LONGFELLOW
I'd like to get in my two cents' worth.

JUDGE
Take the stand!

There is a general stir of excitement - and whispering.

326. CLOSE SHOT - BABE
Her eyes sparkle happily.

327. CLOSE SHOT - CEDAR AND CLIENTS
The clients look up at Cedar, concerned. Cedar comforts them with a confident grimace.

328. MED. SHOT
To include Longfellow, Judge, and others around them. Longfellow hesitates.

JUDGE
Proceed.

LONGFELLOW
Well, I don't know where to begin. There's been so many things said about me that I--

329. CLOSE SHOT AT WITNESS STAND
Longfellow continues:

LONGFELLOW
About my playing the tuba. Seems like a lot of fuss has been made about that. If a man's crazy just 'cause he plays the tuba, then somebody better look into it, 'cause there are a lot of tuba players running around loose. Of course, I don't see any harm in it. I play mine whenever I want to concentrate. That may sound funny to some people - but everybody does something silly when they're thinking. For instance, the Judge here is an O-filler ...

330. WIDER ANGLE
Front of courtroom.

JUDGE
A what?

LONGFELLOW
An O-filler. You fill in all the spaces in the O's, with your pencil.
(points to desk)
I was watching you.

The Judge looks down at a paper in front of him.

INSERT: OF A PRINTED DOCUMENT
Of some sort. All the O's and P's and R's have the white spaces pencilled in.

331. CLOSEUP - JUDGE
As he looks up from the document. He is a trifle self-conscious. Laughter comes from the courtroom.

LONGFELLOW'S VOICE
That may make you look a little crazy, Your Honor, just sitting around filling in O's - but I don't see anything wrong 'cause that helps _you_ to think. Other people are doodlers.

JUDGE
Doodlers?

332. MED. SHOT - FRONT OF COURTROOM

LONGFELLOW
That's a name we made up back home for people who make foolish designs on paper when they're thinking. It's called doodling. Almost everybody's a doodler. Did you ever see a scratch pad in a telephone booth? People draw the most idiotic pictures when they're thinking. Dr. Von Holler, here, could probably think up a long name for it, because he doodles all the time.

Dr. Von Holler, who is in the middle of some doodling, flinches. A roar of laughter comes from the spectators. Longfellow reaches over to where Dr. Von Holler sits and picks up a piece of paper.

LONGFELLOW
(to Dr. Von Holler)
Thank you.
(returning to the stand)
This is a piece of paper he was scribbling on.
(scrutinizes it)
I can't figure it out. One minute it looks like a chimpanzee - and the next minute it looks like a picture of Mr. Cedar.
(hands it to him)
You look at it, Judge.

The Judge, with a serious mien, takes the paper.

INSERT: OF PAPER
It is a doodle face.

BACK TO SCENE:
Dr. Von Holler is somewhat uncomfortable.

LONGFELLOW
Exhibit A - for the defense.
(after a pause)
Looks kind of stupid, doesn't it, Your Honor? But I guess that's all right if Dr. Von Holler has to doodle to help him think. That's his business. Everybody does something different. Some people are--
(demonstrates)
ear-pullers - some are nail-biters--
(pointing)
That Mr. Semple over there is a nose-twitcher.

333. CLOSE SHOT - SEMPLE AND HIS WIFE
He looks up, startled, his nose twitching more violently than ever. The courtroom rocks with laughter.

His wife, in her nervousness, pulls at her fingers.

LONGFELLOW'S VOICE
And the lady next to him is a knuckle-cracker.

Mrs. Semple quickly drops her hands in her lap, as the courtroom again fills with laughter.

334. CLOSE SHOT - COBB
He swings a key-ring around his forefinger. Suddenly he realizes Longfellow might get to him, and he hastily palms the keys and shoves them in his pocket.

335. MED. CLOSE SHOT - NEWSPAPER REPORTERS
One is leaning forward, listening intently - biting the end of his pencil. The one next to him nudges him and silently points to the pencil in his mouth. The reporter gets the idea and, smiling sheepishly, yanks it out of his mouth.

336. MED. CLOSE SHOT - FRONT OF COURTROOM

LONGFELLOW
So you see, everybody does silly things to help them think.
(in conclusion)
Well, I play the tuba.

337. CLOSE SHOT - MAC
As he bursts forth.

MAC
Nice work, toots!

The crowd echoes him with shouts and laughter.

338. CLOSE SHOT - JUDGE
He glares off scene at Mac, reprimandingly.

339. CLOSE SHOT - BABE
She is amused at the embarrassment Longfellow has caused them all.

340. CLOSE SHOT - CEDAR AND HIS CLIENTS
They squirm uncomfortably.

341. MED. CLOSE SHOT AT WITNESS STAND
Longfellow in chair - Judge at bench, b.g.

JUDGE
Mr. Deeds, do you recall forcibly ejecting people from your home?

LONGFELLOW
Oh, yes. Yes. About my throwing those people out of my house. Mrs. Pomponi told the truth. I did throw them out because I didn't want the party in the first place. I didn't invite anybody. Mrs. Pomponi did all that. They just came to see what kind of a freak the "Cinderella Man" was. I don't know how people like that are supposed to act, Your Honor, but if that Pomponi woman is an example, I'll stick to simple folks. She just came in, talked my ear off, and took charge of everything. If I were a friend of hers, I'd have her examined.

342. MED. SHOT OF COURTROOM
Featuring Longfellow. Cedar, who cannot stand it any longer, jumps to his feet.

CEDAR
Your Honor, this is becoming farcical. I demand that Mr. Deeds dispense with side remarks and confine himself to facts! Let him explain his wanderings around the streets in underclothes, his feeding doughnuts to horses!

JUDGE'S VOICE
Proceed.

LONGFELLOW
Mr. Cedar's right. Those things do look kind of bad, don't they? But to tell the truth, Your Honor, I don't remember them. I guess they happened, all right, because I don't think a policeman would lie about a thing like that, but I was drunk. It was the first time I was ever drunk in my life. It's probably happened to you, some time. I mean, when you were younger, of course.

The Judge clears his throat in embarrassment. Several women giggle. The Judge sternly pounds his gavel.

343. CLOSE SHOT - LONGFELLOW

LONGFELLOW
It's likely to happen to anybody. Just the other morning I read in the paper about Mr. Cedar's own son - about how he got drunk and insisted on driving a taxi-cab, while the driver sat inside. Isn't that so, Mr. Cedar? Isn't that so, Mr. Cedar?

344. MED. SHOT OF COURTROOM
All eyes have turned to Cedar.

345. CLOSE SHOT - CEDAR
His eyes are beginning to blaze angrily.

CEDAR
Your Honor, I object.

JUDGE
Proceed.

346. MEDIUM SHOT

LONGFELLOW
Now about the Falkner sisters. That's kind of funny. I mean about Mr. Cedar going all the way to Mandrake Falls to bring them here. Do you mind if I talk to them?

JUDGE
Not at all.

Longfellow turns. Everybody stretches to get a better look at them.

LONGFELLOW
Jane, who owns the house you live in?

347. CLOSE SHOT - THE SISTERS
The girls consult with each other.

JANE
Why, you own it, Longfellow.

AMY
Yes, you own it.

LONGFELLOW'S VOICE
Do you pay any rent?

JANE
(after conferring with Amy)
No, we don't pay any rent.

AMY
Good heavens, no! We never pay rent.

348. WIDER ANGLE
As Longfellow continues questioning:

LONGFELLOW
Are you happy there?

JANE
Oh, yes.

AMY
Yes, indeed.

LONGFELLOW
Now, Jane, a little while ago you said I was pixilated. Do you still think so?

JANE
(after the usual conference)
Why, you've always been pixilated, Longfellow.

AMY
Always.

LONGFELLOW
(smiling)
That's fine. I guess maybe I am.
(seriously)
Now tell me something, Jane. Who else in Mandrake Falls is pixilated?

Jane turns to her sister and this time they go into a prolonged huddle. It is apparently a difficult thing to figure out. Finally they come out of it.

JANE
Why, <u>everybody</u> in Mandrake Falls in pixilated - except us.

AMY
Uh-huh.

349. MED. SHOT OF SPECTATORS
There is an outburst of laughter which the Judge quickly quells with his gavel.

350. MED. SHOT - DIFFERENT ANGLE

LONGFELLOW
Now, just one more question. Do you see the Judge here? He's a nice man, isn't he?

JANE & AMY
Uh-huh.

LONGFELLOW
Do you think he's pixilated?

JANE
(quickly)
Oh, yes.

AMY
Yes, indeedy.

There is more laughter. More pounding of the judiciary gavel.

351. CLOSE SHOT - CEDAR
He feels his case slowly crumbling.

352. CLOSE SHOT - BABE
She can scarcely conceal her elation.

353. MED. SHOT - FRONT OF COURTROOM

JUDGE
Mr. Deeds, you haven't yet touched upon a most important thing. This rather fantastic idea of yours to want to give away your entire fortune. It is, to say the least, most uncommon.

LONGFELLOW
Oh yes, I was getting to that, Your Honor.

CAMERA MOVES TO CLOSER SHOT, featuring Longfellow and Judge, as former continues:

LONGFELLOW
Suppose you were living in a small town and getting along fine, and suddenly somebody dropped $20,000,000 in your lap. Supposing you discovered that all that money was messing up your life, was bringing a lot of vultures around your neck, and making you lose faith in everybody. You'd be a little worried, wouldn't you? You'd feel that you had a hot potato in your hand, and you'd want to drop it. I guess Dr. Von Holler would say you were riding on--
(points to chart)
--those bottom waves, 'cause you wanted to drop something that was burning your fingers.

354. MEDIUM SHOT
Cedar springs to his feet.

CEDAR
(shouting)
If this man is permitted to carry out his plan, repercussions will be felt that will rock the foundations of our entire governmental system!

The Judge has pounded him into silence.

JUDGE
Please, Mr. Cedar!
(to Longfellow)
Proceed.

355. MED. CLOSE SHOT AT WITNESS STAND

LONGFELLOW
Personally, I don't know what Mr. Cedar's raving about. From what I can see, no matter what system of government we have, there will always be leaders and always be followers.

356. MED. CLOSE SHOT
Farmers in audience, as Longfellow's voice continues:

LONGFELLOW'S VOICE
It's like the road out in front of my house. It's on a steep hill. Every day I watch the cars climbing up. Some go lickety-split up that hill on high--

357. FULL SHOT

LONGFELLOW
--some have to shift into second - and some sputter and shake and slip back to the bottom again. Same cars - same gasoline - yet some make it and some don't. And I say the fellows who can make the hill on high should stop once in a while and help those who can't.

358. MEDIUM SHOT

LONGFELLOW
(making his point)
That's all I'm trying to do with this money. Help the fellows who can't make the hill on high.

359. CLOSE SHOT - LONGFELLOW

LONGFELLOW
(hotly)
What does Mr. Cedar expect me to do with it? Give it to him - and a lot of other people who don't need it?
(rising; sarcastically)
If you don't mind, Your Honor, I'll ride on those top waves for a minute.
(calls out)
Hey, all you fellows out there! All those who applied for a farm, stand up!

360. REVERSE ANGLE
Showing most of the audience struggling to their feet.

361. MED. CLOSE SHOT - WITNESS CHAIR

LONGFELLOW
See all those fellows? They're the ones I'm trying to help. They need it!
(pointing)
Mr. Cedar and that Mr. Semple don't need anything. They've got plenty! It's like I'm out in a big boat and I see one fellow in a rowboat who's tired of rowing and wants a free ride - and another fellow who's drowning. Who would you expect me to rescue? Mr. Cedar, who just got tired of rowing and wants a free ride? Or those men out there who are drowning? Any ten-year-old child will give you the answer to that.
(to farmers etc. in courtroom)
All right, fellows. Thank you. Sit down.

362. MEDIUM SHOT - FRONT OF COURTROOM

LONGFELLOW
Now, my plan is very simple. I was going to give each family ten acres - a horse, a cow and some seed. And if they work the farm for three years, it's theirs. Now, if that's crazy, maybe I ought to be sent to an institution. But I don't think it is. And what's more, Mr. Cedar doesn't either.
(vehemently)
Just before the hearing started, he offered to call the whole thing off if I made a settlement with him. So you see, he wouldn't think I was crazy if he got paid off.

363. CLOSE SHOT - CEDAR
He jumps to his feet, highly incensed.

CEDAR
It's a lie!

JUDGE
Mr. Cedar!

CEDAR
Mr. Deeds is drawing on his warped imagination!

364. CLOSE SHOT - LONGFELLOW
As he listens to Cedar, watching him antagonistically.

CEDAR'S VOICE
I've never heard anything so colossally stupid in my life!

Longfellow's eyes narrow resentfully.

365. WIDER ANGLE
To include Longfellow, Cedar and Judge.

CEDAR
It's an insult to our intelligence to sit here and listen to his childish ravings.

Throughout his speech the Judge has been pounding his gavel. Longfellow has his eyes levelled off on Cedar.

JUDGE
(when quiet reigns)
You will please permit Mr. Deeds to finish.

CEDAR
But Your Honor--

JUDGE
Mr. Cedar!

Cedar, grumblingly, remains standing. Judge asks Longfellow:

JUDGE
Anything else, Mr. Deeds?

LONGFELLOW
(eyes still on Cedar)
No.
(changes his mind; turns to Judge)
Yes. There's just one more thing I'd like to get off my chest before I finish.

JUDGE
Proceed.

LONGFELLOW
Thank you, Your Honor.

He rises to his feet, takes one step forward, and clouts Cedar flush on the jaw. As Cedar falls into the arms of an associate, pandemonium breaks loose.

BAILIFF'S VOICE
Order! Order! Order in the court!

366. FULL SHOT OF COURTROOM
The Judge pounds his gavel. There are cries of approval from the spectators. In the midst of the commotion--

DISSOLVE TO:

<u>INT. COURTROOM</u>

367. MED. PANNING SHOT
Showing spectators, waiting breathlessly for a decision. All eyes are on the Judge.

368. CLOSE SHOT AT BENCH
The Judge holds a whispered conversation with his experts.

369. CLOSE SHOT - BABE
She is apprehensive.

370. CLOSE SHOT - LONGFELLOW
He glances furtively at Babe, off scene.

371. MED. SHOT OF FARMERS
Leaning forward. Their entire future hangs in the balance.

372. MED. CLOSE SHOT AT BENCH
The Judge comes out of the huddle; his face is very stern.

BAILIFF'S VOICE
Remain seated and come to order. The Court is again in session.

JUDGE
Before the Court announces its decision, I want to warn all who are here that the police have orders to arrest anyone creating a disturbance.

373. QUICK FLASHES
Of Babe - Cobb - Longfellow - Mac - the farmers.

374. INSERT: CLOSE SHOT - JUDGE
The Judge's preface augurs ill.

375. CLOSEUP - CEDAR
His mouth curls up in a contented grimace.

376. FULL SHOT - COURTROOM
All eyes are upon the Judge, who clears his throat.

JUDGE
(serious mien)
Mr. Deeds, there has been a great deal of damaging testimony against you. Your behavior, to say the least, has been most strange.

An audible gasp is heard from audience. Judge goes on:

JUDGE
But in the opinion of the Court, you are not only sane, but you are the sanest man that ever walked into this courtroom. Case dismissed!

The shout that greets this is tumultuous. The Judge smiles warmly, and clasps Longfellow's hand. Immediately, Longfellow is surrounded by a crowd of people who come running down the aisles.

377. CLOSE SHOT - CEDAR AND GROUP
They sit, stunned, disappointed. Mrs. Semple turns to her husband and slaps him.

MRS. SEMPLE
You nose-twitcher!

Budington rises to confront Cedar.

BUDINGTON
Oh, I knew it! I knew it! You, you--

Cedar disgustedly pushes him in the face, aside.

378. CLOSE SHOT - BABE
She smiles ecstatically, too excited to move. Suddenly she rises.

379. MEDIUM SHOT
As Babe tries to get to Longfellow, but finds herself on the fringe of a jubilant crowd in the center of which is Longfellow. She tries to break through, but finds it impossible. Desperately, she jumps on a chair and tries frantically to get a glimpse of him. At that moment, several farmers have lifted Longfellow on their shoulders.

380. FULL SHOT - COURTROOM
As jubilantly, Longfellow is carried out on the shoulders of the excited crowd.

381. MEDIUM CLOSE SHOT
As Babe frantically tries to reach Longfellow, but is jostled aside. The parade envelops her.

382. LONG SHOT FROM REAR
The shouting mob is heading for the door at end of courtroom. Everyone crowds forward.

383. CLOSE SHOT IN REAR
Babe is left helplessly out.

DISSOLVE TO:

384. FULL SHOT OF COURTROOM
Empty - except for the Falkner sisters, still whispering to each other, and Babe, sitting helpless and forlorn.

385. CLOSE SHOT - BABE
Her eyes are filled. Dismally she starts forward. We hear a rising commotion from the outside, at this moment.

386. WIDER ANGLE
Longfellow running toward camera with the mob, shouting, back of him. He reaches courtroom, slams the doors shut behind him. Babe, attracted by the noise, looks up. He runs toward her, and swoops her up in his arms.

387. CLOSE SHOT - JANE & AMY

JANE
He's still pixilated.

AMY
He sure is.

388. CLOSE SHOT - BABE AND LONGFELLOW
She kisses him over and over again. He looks around and over his shoulder at the mob, a little dazed. Finally, he notices her effort, and gives her one passionately back.

All that is heard is the cheering of the crowd outside and the Columbia music.

FADE OUT.

THE END

Notes

1. A "nifty" is an especially clever joke.

2. "The Mad Song" is a famous aria from Gaetano Donizetti's opera *Lucia di Lammermoor* (1835).

3. This punch line was an eleventh-hour addition, an improvement on the version in the final draft: "Why did Mohammed go to the mountain?"

4. A "pip," an excellent or remarkable thing, is short for the less commonly used "pippin." A pippin is a seedling apple of good quality, hence the saying, "It's a pippin!"

5. A "monkey suit," usually describing fancy or formal dress, was a disparaging allusion to the outfit worn by an organ grinder's monkey.

6. "Right on the button" means "on the point of the chin."

7. "Omar, the soused philosopher of Persia" can only refer to Omar Khayyam, the eleventh-century astronomer, mathematician, and poet best known for his "Rubaiyat."

8. "Oh, Tempora!" may refer to time, or the temples of the skull. The Moeraes are the Greek goddesses of fate. Bacchus is another name for Dionysus, Greek god of fertility.

9. "Standing the town on its cauliflower ear" means, in effect, turning the town on its head, or upside down. "Cauliflower ear" usually refers to an ear swollen from repeated blows in boxing. Riskin liked the term, which occurs also in *Platinum Blonde*.

10. Prairie oysters is a post-hangover drink comprised of a raw egg yolk mixed into Worcestershire sauce, hot sauce, salt, and pepper.

11. "Flap-ears" is a Riskinism meaning "big-ears."

12. "St. Vitus dance" is an expression derived from a god of the Baltic Slavs who was adored with hysterical dances. His name, Svanto-Vid, was altered to Sanctus Vitus or Saint Vitus with the encroachment of Christianity. The third-century Christian martyr, St. Vitus, was invoked against Sydenham's chorea, a nervous disorder also known as St. Vitus's dance, which is marked by chaotic muscle movements, especially of the limbs and extremities.

13. Present-day versions of *Mr. Deeds* contain variant dialogue trims of the long courtroom finale, which probably reflects some minor tinkering after initial release of the film in 1936. Missing in most theatrical prints and video versions are Bob's testimony and the display of the enlarged photographs (shot 301) and Deeds's rebuttal to Madame Pomponi (shot 341). The Madame Pomponi subplot, important in "Opera Hat," figured in initial Riskin drafts, but kept shrinking in subsequent drafts of the script until finally it became a mere sidelight in the film.

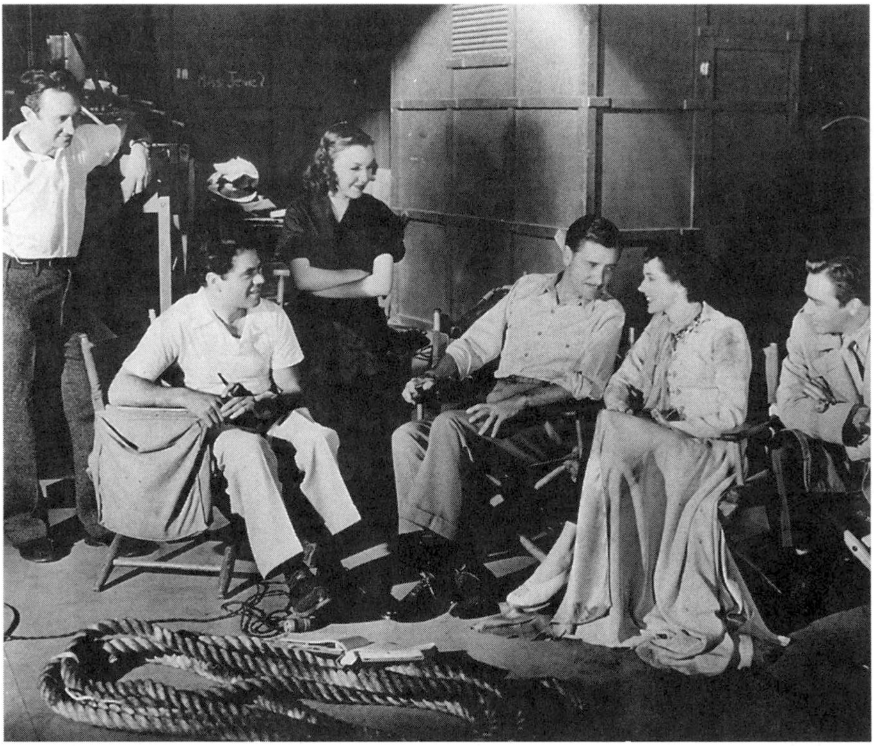

From left to right, during a break in filming *Lost Horizon,* are an unidentified person, Frank Capra, Margo, Ronald Colman, Jane Wyatt, and John Howard.

Lost Horizon

Columbia Pictures, 1937, 133 minutes

Produced and directed by Frank Capra

Written by Robert Riskin, based on the novel by James Hilton

Photography by Joseph Walker

Music by Dimitri Tiomkin

Edited by Gene Havlick and Gene Milford

Musical direction by Max Steiner

Art direction by Stephen Gooson

Set design by Babs Johnstone

Costumes by Ernest Dryden

Special effects by E. Roy Davidson and Ganahl Carson

Cast: Ronald Colman (*Robert Conway*), Jane Wyatt (*Sondra*), Edward Everett Horton (*Alexander P. Lovett*), John Howard (*George Conway*), Thomas Mitchell (*Henry Barnard*), Margo (*Maria*), Isabel Jewell (*Gloria Stone*), H. B. Warner (*Chang*), Sam Jaffe (*High Lama*), Hugh Buckler (*Lord Gainsford*), John Miltern (*Carstairs*), Lawrence Grant (*1st Man*), John Burton (*Wynant*), John T. Murray (*Meeker*), Max Rabinowitz (*Seiveking*), Willie Fung (*Bandit Leader*), Wryley Birch (*Missionary*), John Tettener (*Montaigne*), Boyd Irwin (*Assistant Foreign Secretary*), Leonard Mudie (*Senior Foreign Secretary*), David Clyde (*Steward*), Neil Fitzgerald (*Radio Operator*), Val Durand (*Talu*), Ruth Robinson (*Missionary*), Margaret McWade (*Missionary*), Noble Johnson (*Leader of Porters*),

Dennis D'Auburn (*Aviator*), Milton Owen (*Fenner*), Victor Wong (*Bandit Leader*), Carl Stockdale (*Missionary*), Darby Clarke (*Radio Operator*), George Chan (*Chinese Priest*), Eric Wilton (*Englishman*), Chief Big Tree (*Porter*), Richard Loo (*Shanghai Airport Official*), Beatrice Curtis, Mary Lou Dix, Beatrice Blinn, Arthur Rankin (*Passengers*), The Hall Johnson Choir.

LOST HORIZON

FADE IN[1]

Over the titles we see SUPERIMPOSED the snow-capped mountains leading to Shangri-La.

CLOSE-UP of an impressive-looking book. The covers open and the pages turn. The first page reads:

> In these days of wars and rumors of wars - haven't you ever dreamed of a place where there was peace and security, where living was not a struggle but a lasting delight?

The second page reads:

> Of course you have. So has every man since Time began. Always the same dream. Sometimes he calls it Utopia - sometimes the Fountain of Youth - sometimes merely "that little chicken farm."

The third page reads:

> One man had such a dream and saw it come true. He was Robert Conway - England's "Man of the East" - soldier, diplomat, public hero -

The fourth page reads:

> Our story starts in the war-torn Chinese city of Baskul, where Robert Conway has been sent to evacuate ninety white people before they are butchered in a local revolution.

The fifth and final page reads:

> Baskul - the night of March 10, 1935.

DISSOLVE TO:

EXT. BASKUL FLYING FIELD - NIGHT

1. LONG SHOT
The field is aflare with floodlights - on one side is an office building - on the other are hangars. The whole field is filled with Chinese refugees running around wildly. An Army transport is in front of the office building, motors going.

2. REVERSE SHOT
Showing in the distance, probably several miles away, the effect of a burning city, which is Baskul. Over the shot we hear the steady boom-boom of gunfire. In the f.g., we see the silhouetted figures of Chinese running away from Baskul and toward the Camera, their personal packs on their backs.

3. MED. CLOSE SHOT
Toward office building. Conway comes out of the building, followed by a small group of white people with frightened faces. They have to fight their way through a horde of milling Chinese.

4. MEDIUM SHOT
As Conway and group finally reach the plane where Conway forces the white people in. In this he is aided by his brother, George, a young and vigorous Englishman. The pilot sticks his head out of the cockpit.

PILOT
Conway, we can't take more than seven!

Conway pulls a passenger out and gives the pilot a signal to start.

CONWAY
(to passenger)
All right. I'm sorry. There will be another plane in a minute. All right - go on.

5. LONG SHOT
Motors roar, and the plane starts to move, scattering those of the Chinese who were unfortunately too close to the ship. Conway and George rush back into the office building.

INT. LARGE OFFICE ROOM

6. FULL SHOT
There are about thirty white refugees, men, women and several children. They all lift their panicky faces to Conway and George as they enter. A barrage of questions are flung at them.

AD-LIB
Are there any more planes? Do you think the bandits will come here? Please take my wife next, Mr. Conway!

CONWAY
Wait, wait! Everybody, wait! There are plenty of planes coming. Now everybody have patience. Everything will be all right.

He crosses to a back room.

GEORGE
You have nothing to worry about. Leave everything to my brother.

INT. RADIO ROOM

7. MEDIUM SHOT
As Conway enters to speak to operator.

RADIO OPERATOR
Yes, sir - with seven passengers aboard.

RADIO SPEAKER
Seven passengers? Good.

CONWAY
Get me Shanghai.

OPERATOR
I'm talking to them now, sir.

CONWAY
Hello? Hello?

RADIO SPEAKER
Hello. Hello.

CONWAY
(into mike)
Conway speaking. Is Colonel Marsh there?

COLONEL'S VOICE
Right here, Conway. Go ahead.

8. CLOSE SHOT
As Conway continues into mike.

CONWAY
Colonel, I need more planes. I've still about twenty people to get out. Where are those planes you promised us?

COLONEL'S VOICE
We sent everything we could find, Conway.

CONWAY
They better get here soon or I can't be responsible--

9. WIDER ANGLE
As George rushes in.

GEORGE
Bob! I think I hear motors!

CONWAY
(listening - then into mike)
Colonel, wait a minute, they may be here now!
(to George)
Say George, get down on that field and guide those planes in when they get here.

GEORGE
Yes.

He starts for the door.

CONWAY
And be sure that none of the natives get in.

GEORGE
(exiting)
Yes.

CONWAY
Hello? Colonel?

COLONEL'S VOICE
Hello, Conway. Yes?

CONWAY
Thanks - and take care of that liver of yours.

COLONEL'S VOICE
Oh, ho - my word!

INT. OFFICE ROOM
10. FULL SHOT
As Conway enters.

CONWAY
All right, get ready everybody. The planes are here.

The people crowd around him pleading for priority.

CONWAY
One at a time. Children first. Where are they? Come on now, and stand over here.

A woman pushes some children forward.

CONWAY
Where's the mother?

PRIEST
(standing nearby)
They're orphans, Mr. Conway.

CONWAY
I see. All right.
(directing people aside - pulling out an old lady)
Well, you come - right over here - and you, and you--
(looking off scene)
--come on--

OLD MAN
What about us, Mr. Conway?

CONWAY
Gentlemen, please wait your turn.

11. CLOSE SHOT
A girl slouched in a corner. We meet Gloria Stone, a surly, wan-looking prostitute.

GLORIA
You'd better take some of those squealing men with you first. They might faint on you. I'll wait.

12. CLOSE SHOT - CONWAY
Something of a smile crosses his face.

CONWAY
Just as you say!

Just then, a terrific explosion is heard in the distance.

13. FULL SHOT
All the lights go out. Everybody starts screaming.

CONWAY
(sharply)
Whoa! Don't lose your heads now - I'll see what it is.

He dashes out.

EXT. OFFICE BUILDING
14. CLOSE SHOT AT DOOR
Conway rushing out, meets George coming back.

GEORGE
The power house - they've blown it up! The planes can't land without lights.

CONWAY
(thinking fast)
Come on! We'll burn the hangar. That will make light for them!

He grabs a lantern and dashes off.

15. MEDIUM SHOT
As they run through the screaming mob toward the hangar.

INTERIOR HANGAR
16. FULL SHOT
It is filled with Chinese refugees clinging to their household goods. Conway and George enter. Conway speaks to them in Chinese, ordering them out. Some hesitate, and they have to push the terror-stricken waiting coolies out. When they have all left, Conway opens the spigots of several gasoline tanks, waits for the fuel to spill on the ground, then tosses a lantern on the fuel, igniting a blaze. At the same moment, he and George dash for the door.

EXTERIOR FIELD
17. LONG SHOT
Conway and George rush out of hangar. When they are at a fairly safe distance, the building bursts into flames.

DISSOLVE TO:

18. LONG SHOT
Against a background of the burning hangar, a plane is just leaving the ground, as another one is landing.

19 MEDIUM SHOT
Of Conway, signalling.

CONWAY
All right, go ahead!
(to George)
We go on to the next plane. Bring out any people that are left.

GEORGE
Right, Bob.

20. REVERSE ANGLE - LONG SHOT
Shooting toward the burning city of Baskul in the distance. We see the bandits coming, flashing bayonets, in pursuit of screaming refugees.

21. MED. SHOT FRONT OF OFFICE BUILDING
Conway emerges, followed by Gloria, and an American, Barnard. CAMERA FOLLOWS THEM to the ship just as the pilot, Fenner, is climbing down from cockpit.

CONWAY
Hello, Fenner.

FENNER
(broad grin)
Hello, Conway. Having a little trouble?

CONWAY
You never mind me. Get this gadget off the ground.

George is pushing off Chinese.

GEORGE
Bob, these are all that are left.

CONWAY
(to George)
Come on! Quick! This way.

22. MED. SHOT AT PLANE
When Conway and others approach, George helps Gloria Stone up, while Conway faces the mob, punching at those who try to wedge their way forward. Finally one of them manages to get his foot on the step, and Conway pushes him violently.

23. CLOSE SHOT - MAN
Who staggers back and falls, sprawling. As he hits the ground, he yells:

MAN
You can't leave me here, you blighter.[2] I'm a British subject!

We meet Alexander P. Lovett.

24. MEDIUM SHOT
Conway looks his surprise and lifts him off the ground.

25. CLOSE SHOT - A CHINAMAN
Glaring off toward Conway, picks up a board and starts toward Conway.

26. MED. CLOSE SHOT ENTRANCE TO SHIP
George emerges in time to see the Chinese lift the board and about to clout Conway on the head. George moves quickly, puts out his left hand, wards off the blow and with his right he punches the Chinese, who reels out of the scene.

GEORGE
Look out, Bob!

27. MEDIUM SHOT
A shadowy figure materializes in the cockpit, and clubs Fenner from behind. He shoves Fenner aside and takes his place.

28. MEDIUM SHOT
Conway pushes George up and starts to mount himself. He looks off - and what he sees startles him.

CONWAY
(yells off)
All right, Fenner! Go ahead!

29. LONG SHOT
Of what Conway sees. Several trucks loaded with bandits - in makeshift uniforms - come tearing up the road - come to a stop. Some fire toward plane - others are setting up machine guns. Droves of refugees scramble to cover.

INT. PLANE
30. FULL SHOT
Already present are Barnard, an American; Gloria Stone, the prostitute; and Lovett, whom we saw dressed as a Chinese. Conway slams the door shut - looks off - then cries:

CONWAY
Get down on the floor, everybody. Go ahead, Fenner!

They all fall on their faces.

GEORGE
Fenner, let's go!

31. MED. CLOSE SHOT
Of the new pilot setting the controls and lifting the plane into flight.

EXT. FIELD
32. LONG SHOT
As the plane swings around - taxies crazily - and leaves the ground, accompanied by gunfire of the bandits.

INT. PLANE
33. FULL SHOT
The occupants are still on the floor. Conway rises and glances out of a window, warily.

CONWAY
(mumbling)
Well, I guess we're out of range.
(to others)
Everybody all right?

There are murmurs of "Yes" "I'm all right" - as they raise themselves.

GEORGE
Whew! That was close.

34. MEDIUM SHOT
Conway starts for the back seat and suddenly sees Lovett.

CONWAY
Where did _you_ come from?

LOVETT
I'm Alexander P. Lovett, sir.

CONWAY
Why aren't you registered through our office?

GEORGE
(chiming in)
It would serve you right if you were left behind.

LOVETT
(high-pitched voice)
How could I know that a war was going to break out right over my head!
(a grave injustice)
Right over my head. Oh, my word! I tell you, those Chinese were pouncing on me from every direction. I had to get into these ridiculous clothes in order to escape.

CONWAY
Where were you hiding?

LOVETT
Hiding? Oh, no. Hunting - I was in the interior - hunting fossils. This morning I looked up suddenly--

CONWAY
I know - and a war broke out right over your head.

GEORGE
The next time you're in wild country like this, keep in touch with the British Consul.

CONWAY
Aha - very good, Freshie.[3] Very good. You'd better put his name on the list and make out a report later.

He proceeds to the back seat. Barnard, the American, who is in front of Lovett, leans over toward him.

35. MED. CLOSE SHOT - THE TWO
Barnard and Lovett.

BARNARD
I beg your pardon, brother. What did you say you were hunting?

LOVETT
Fossils.

BARNARD
Fossils, huh?

LOVETT
I'm a paleontologist.

BARNARD
(blankly)
A what?

LOVETT
A paleontologist.

BARNARD
Oh, I see.

Lovett produces a small box clutched under his arm.

LOVETT
I have here a discovery that will startle the world. It's the vertebrae from the lumbar of a Megatherium,[4] found in Asia.

BARNARD
Well, what do you know about that!

LOVETT
Found in Asia!

BARNARD
Uh-huh.

LOVETT
When I get home I shall probably be knighted for it.

BARNARD
Knighted! You don't say. Do you mind if I take a look at it?

LOVETT
(proudly)
Not at all.

He lifts the lid and Barnard peeks inside.

INSERT: OF BOX
Wrapped carefully in absorbent cotton is something that resembles a dry chicken bone.

BACK TO SCENE:
Barnard reaches for the box, but Lovett pulls it away from him.

BARNARD
Sorry.

LOVETT
This is the only thing I was able to save when those heathens surrounded me.

BARNARD
(he is allowed to take it out and examine it - unimpressed)
Uh-huh.

LOVETT
You see, from this vertebrae I shall be able to reconstruct the entire skeleton.

BARNARD
Wait a minute, you expect to be knighted for finding that soupbone?

LOVETT
It was the vertebrae of a Megatherium - found in Asia.

BARNARD
Yeah, I remember. You said that before.

LOVETT
Sir Henry Derwent was knighted, and he never got beyond the mesozoic era.

Barnard stares at Lovett unbelievingly.

BARNARD
Ah, poor fellow.

Lovett glares at him resentfully, and snaps the lid shut on his box.

LOVETT
Yes, it just shows--
(taking offense)
I don't know why I'm talking to you. I don't know you. Who are you?

BARNARD
(turns away)
Okay, brother.

LOVETT
Don't call me brother.

BARNARD
Okay, sister.
(chuckles to himself)
No offense. No offense!

36. CLOSE SHOT - GLORIA AND BARNARD
Gloria sits slumped in her seat, looking glumly out. Barnard glances at her curiously. Finally he makes a friendly overture.

BARNARD
Cigarette?

Gloria turns her head, surveys Barnard coldly, and without responding, turns back.

BARNARD
I say, will you have a cigarette?

GLORIA
No.

BARNARD
(unabashed)
Say, you're an American, aren't you?

GLORIA
(irascibly)
Say, listen - will you go and annoy the rest of your playmates? Let me alone!

He shrugs his shoulders and slides back into his seat.

37. FULL SHOT
All is silent for a moment. Conway is writing on a small pad - which he rests on an uplifted knee. George is rummaging through a closet - rear of the cabin.

38. MED. SHOT - GEORGE AND CONWAY
Conway still writes, undisturbed. George reaches into the closet and emerges with a bottle of whiskey. His face lights up.

GEORGE
(holds up bottle)
Hello! Look what _I_ found!

He crosses to Conway.

GEORGE
Just what I needed too.

CONWAY
(looks up - smiling)
You?

GEORGE
Just this once, Bob. I feel like celebrating. Just think of it, Bob - a cruiser sent to Shanghai just to take you back to England. You know what it means.
(hands him cup)
Here you are. Don't bother about those cables now. I want you to drink with me.
(holds his cup up)
Gentlemen, I give you Robert Conway - England's new Foreign Secretary.

Conway watches him, amused. George gulps down his drink.

CONWAY
(after a slight hesitation - downing his drink)
Hurray!

GEORGE
How I'm going to bask in reflected glory!
(dreamily)
People are going to point to me and say, "There goes George Conway - brother of the Foreign Secretary."

CONWAY
Don't talk nonsense. Give me the bottle.

Conway takes the bottle from him and pours himself a second drink.

GEORGE
That's why they're sending for you, Bob. With all these foreign entanglements, it was bound to happen. They need you.

Conway, with a poured drink in hand, laughs.

GEORGE
All right, you can laugh if you want to. But who else can they get? Who else is there in all of England half the fighter, half the diplomat, who

has half your knowledge of the foreign situation? They can't stop you now, Bob.

Conway moodily pours himself a third. He downs the drink as we

DISSOLVE TO:

INT. PLANE

39. CLOSE SHOT OF CONWAY

We find Conway, asleep in his seat, his head on his hands. George approaches and tenderly spreads a jacket over his shoulders. Conway stirs, opens an eye.

CONWAY

(drunkenly)

Hello, Freshie. Did you make that report out yet?

GEORGE

Yes, Bob.

CONWAY

Did you say we saved ninety white people?

GEORGE

Yes.

CONWAY

Hurray for us. Did you say that we left ten thousand natives down there to be annihilated? No, you wouldn't say that. They don't count.

GEORGE

You'd better try to get some sleep, Bob.

CONWAY

Just you wait until I'm Foreign Secretary. Can't you just see me, Freshie, with all those other shrewd, little Foreign Secretaries?

(confidentially - screws up face)

You see, the trick is to see who can out-talk the other. Everybody wants something for nothing, and if you can't get it with smooth talk, you send an army in. I'm going to fool them, Freshie. I'm not going to have an army. I'm going to disband mine. I'm going to sink my battleships - I'm going to destroy every piece of warcraft. Then when the enemy approaches we'll say, "Come in, gentlemen - what can we do for you?" So then the poor enemy soldiers will stop and think. And what will they think, Freshie? They'll think to themselves - "Something's wrong here. We've been duped. This is not according to form. These people seem to be quite friendly, and why should we shoot them?" Then they'll lay down their arms. You see how simple the whole thing is? Centuries of tradition kicked right in the pants--

(pause - drily)

--and I'll be slapped straight into the nearest insane asylum.

He starts to pour himself another drink.

GEORGE
You'd better not drink any more, Bob. You're not talking sense.

Conway downs the drink, and then chuckles cynically.

CONWAY
Don't worry, George. Nothing's going to happen. I'll fall right into line. I'll be the good little boy that everybody wants me to be. I'll be the best little Foreign Secretary we ever had, just because I haven't the nerve to be anything else.

GEORGE
Do try to sleep, Bob.

CONWAY
Huh? Oh, sure, Freshie. Good thing, sleep.

He grunts and squirms. George tucks him in.

CONWAY
Did you ever notice the sunrise in China, George? Ah, you should. It's beautiful.

He gets settled. George relaxes and, leaning back, shuts his eyes.

40. LONG SHOT OF CABIN
It is quiet. All are asleep. CAMERA MOVES FORWARD SLOWLY until it reaches the glass panel leading to the cockpit. The pilot's face turns. Instead of Fenner we see a strange, Mongolian face - with sharp, piercing eyes. A half-smile plays across his mouth.

EXT. SHOT OF PLANE
41. LONG SHOT OF PLANE
Flying at high speed against a moonlit sky. We stay on the shot until it vanishes, a mere speck, over the horizon.

DISSOLVE TO:

EXT. SHOT DAWN
42. LONG SHOT
The morning sun peeks over a mountain top. From the same direction, as if arriving with the sun, the ship looms up, and comes roaring toward us.

INT. PLANE
43. FULL SHOT
All are asleep except Lovett, who fidgets on his seat. Then Barnard stirs - opens his eyes - and stretches. As he does so, he sees that Lovett is awake.

BARNARD
Good morning, Lovey.

LOVETT
I beg your pardon.

BARNARD
I say, good morning, Lovey.

LOVETT
Good morning--
(catches himself)
Look here, young man.

BARNARD
Eh?

LOVETT
I didn't care for 'sister' last night, and I don't like 'Lovey' this morning. My name is Lovett - Alexander, P.

BARNARD
I see.

LOVETT
I see.

BARNARD
Well, it's a good morning, anyway.

LOVETT
I'm never conversational before I coffee.

Barnard glances out of the window, looks around outside thoughtfully.

BARNARD
Wait a minute. Is it a good morning? Say, we're supposed to be travelling east, aren't we?

LOVETT
Why, of course. Yes.

BARNARD
Well, it looks to me as if we're travelling west.

LOVETT
That's ridiculous.

BARNARD
Is it?

LOVETT
It certainly is.

BARNARD
Look here--

LOVETT
Any child knows how to tell direction. Any child. I don't care where the child is - in the air, on the earth, or in the sea. If you face the rising sun, your right hand is the north, and your left hand is the south--

BARNARD
I always get it twisted because I'm left-handed.

LOVETT
Oh, really?

BARNARD
Yes.

LOVETT
Well, you just reverse it. Your left hand is--
(tries to explain - gets confused and irritated)
What difference does it make what 'hand' you are? The north is the north!

BARNARD
Uh-huh. All I know is - the sun rises in the east, and we're going away from it.

LOVETT
Now you're irritating and absurd!

44. CLOSE SHOT - LOVETT
As he sulks by himself, looks around - locates the sun in back of him - smiles - satisfied he's right, throws a condescending glance over at Barnard - then suddenly his face clouds - the whole thing dawns on him.

LOVETT
(jumps up shrieking)
Oh, my word - of course - yes. Boy! Boy, we're travelling in the wrong direction! Wake up! We're going in the wrong direction!

45. FULL SHOT
Conway is still asleep.

GEORGE
(concerned for Conway)
Couldn't you arrange to make a little less noise?

LOVETT
I tell you, we're going west, and Shanghai is east of here!

GEORGE
Be quiet! Fenner's the best pilot in China. He knows what he's doing.

LOVETT
(not quite reassured)
It's Fenner.

BARNARD
He might have lost his way.

LOVETT
Of course. That's what I told them last night. You can't expect a man to sail around in the dark.[5]

During this George has been looking around - he rises.

GEORGE
All right, all right. Calm yourself. I'll talk to Fenner.

He crosses to panel leading to cockpit, CAMERA FOLLOWING HIM. When he gets there he knocks on the window.

GEORGE
Fenner! I - I say--

George knocks again. From the cockpit side - the small shade suddenly snaps up - and George finds himself staring into the face of the mysterious pilot. He takes an instinctive step backward. The pilot turns his head. CAMERA ANGLE WIDENS as George keeps backing up until he gets to Conway. George turns to Conway and shakes his shoulder.

GEORGE
Bob! Bob!

Conway stirs in his sleep, slowly opens his eyes, yawns and stretches. Throughout it, George speaks.

GEORGE
Wake up! Something's happened! It isn't Fenner in the cockpit!

Conway looks at him, glances off toward the others, and back at George.

CONWAY
(dismissing him with a gesture)
Oh, stop it!

GEORGE
The bloke up there looks a Chinese, or a Mongolian, or something.

BARNARD
We're nowhere near Shanghai. We're going in the opposite direction.

This interests Conway and he looks out of the window.

CONWAY
We're over the desert. That's funny.

Then rising, he crosses to cockpit. The others watch him expectantly.

46. GROUP SHOT - AROUND COCKPIT
Conway pounds on the panel. The face of the pilot appears in sight. Conway tries to ask him something in Chinese. The pilot glares at them for a second, then a gun is shoved out at them. Instinctively they back away.

CONWAY
Charming chap.

BARNARD
(not being funny)
Nice puss to meet in a dark alley.

The ship lurches - and they are thrown off balance. The panel has been snapped shut.

CONWAY
Well, that's that, I guess.

BARNARD
Wonder what's happened to Fenner.

LOVETT
Yes. And who is _he_? How'd _he_ get there?

BARNARD
Do you suppose we stopped someplace during the night and changed pilots?

CONWAY
No. That's not possible! If we had landed, we all would have been awakened.

LOVETT
Of course. We never left the air. I know - I didn't sleep the whole night long.

CONWAY
(with finality)
That fellow got on at Baskul.

LOVETT
What's he doing? Where's he taking us? He may be a maniac for all we know.

George, who has disappeared during the above, now returns, with a monkey wrench in his hand. Conway stops him.

CONWAY
George, what are you going to do?

GEORGE
I'm going to drag him out and force him to tell us what his game is.

LOVETT
Good.

CONWAY
What if he refuses?

LOVETT
We'll smash his face in. That's what we'll do.

CONWAY
Brilliant!
(a sweeping gesture)
Can anyone here fly a plane?

There is a general chorus of "no--not I," etc.

CONWAY
(takes wrench from George's hand)
Well, George, that's no good.

Conway throws the monkey wrench into a corner.

CONWAY
I guess we're in for it.

LOVETT
In for what?

CONWAY
I don't know. He must have had some purpose in taking the plane away from Fenner.
(starts for his seat)
When he lands, we'll find out.

LOVETT
You mean to tell me you're not going to do anything until we land?

CONWAY
What do you suggest?

LOVETT
Why, you - you-- Look here - he may dash us to pieces!

CONWAY
It might afford you a great deal of relief.
(sitting)
Now gentlemen, I'm going back to sleep. Oh, and I was having such a peaceful dream.
(curling up)
As soon as he lands, let me know.

He shuts his eyes and leans back. The others watch him for a second - and wander back to their seats.

47. CLOSE SHOT - GLORIA AND BARNARD
Gloria is apparently indifferent to their predicament. As Barnard watches her, a little bitter smile plays around her mouth.

48. CLOSE SHOT - GEORGE
He stares out of the window and is suddenly startled.

EXT. SHOT OF PLANE
49. LONG SHOT
Of the plane with its nose turned downward in a sharp descent.

INT. CABIN OF PLANE
50. MEDIUM SHOT
George is on his feet.

GEORGE
(excited)
We're heading down! We're going to land!

Everyone looks out. George rushes to Conway and nudges him.

GEORGE
(breathlessly)
Bob, we're landing!
(pointing out)
Bob, we're coming to a village!

Conway sits up and looks out.

EXT. SHOT OF PLANE
51. MEDIUM SHOT
Plane starting toward ground. All we can see are mountain tops.

INT. PLANE
52. MEDIUM SHOT
They all stare out of the windows. Conway peers intently.

DISSOLVE TO:

EXT. SHOT FROM AIRPLANE
53. LONG SHOT
From angle in cabin of plane. Through the window, directly below we see a large open space at the foot of the hills. The plane is headed for it.

54. LONG SHOT
We see a swarm of strange-looking natives, scantily attired, but bearing bayonets, running toward the plane.

INT. PLANE
55. MEDIUM CLOSE SHOT
Of George and Conway, as the ship hits the ground, bouncing and swaying perilously.

EXT. MOUNTAINOUS COUNTRY
56. MEDIUM SHOT
As the plane taxies across the uninhabited space.

INTERIOR PLANE
57. MED. CLOSE SHOT AT DOOR
Conway and George ready to get out. As Conway turns to open the door, he looks off and is startled by something he sees. George follows his gaze, and a bewildered expression comes into his eyes, too.

EXTERIOR OF PLANE
58. LONG SHOT
Shooting through door. The strange-looking natives have surrounded the plane and are closing in.

INTERIOR PLANE
59. MEDIUM SHOT
Conway and George both instinctively wheel around toward the opposite side. But from that direction too, a horde of natives dash toward them. Conway hesitates a second, and like a flash springs for the door. But he stops again, as he opens the door.

EXTERIOR OF PLANE
60. MEDIUM SHOT
To include door of plane. Conway finds himself staring into the threatening mouths of half a dozen rifles, and quickly shuts the door.

GEORGE
What are these people?

CONWAY
I don't know. I can't get the dialect.

EXTERIOR OF PLANE
61. MEDIUM SHOT THROUGH WINDOW
We see the pilot and several natives in single file as they come toward the plane, buckets in hand. In b.g., one of them lowers a bucket into a well in the ground.

GEORGE
Look - they're loading up with gasoline.

EXTERIOR OF PLANE
62. SEVERAL SHOTS
The gas is being loaded. Natives on horseback dash back and forth shouting and signalling. Camels can be glimpsed among the horses. There is tremendous disorder and commotion.

63. LONG SHOT
The ship leaves the ground. The natives stand around, curiously watching.

INTERIOR PLANE
64. MEDIUM SHOT
Conway is pacing. The occupants sit by their open windows.

CONWAY
Imagine having all that fuel there, waiting for us!
(he sits down)
George, something tells me our journey is just beginning.

LOVETT
Where are we going? Huh?

BARNARD
(pointing)
If you ask me, we're heading straight for those mountains.

EXTERIOR SHOT
65. LONG SHOT
We see the plane against the sky. In the b.g., there is nothing but snow-covered mountains.

DISSOLVE TO:

INSERT: A sign reading "Shanghai Municipal Airport."

INT. AIRPORT
66. MEDIUM CLOSE SHOT
A Chinese officer is on the phone.

CHINESE OFFICER
A Douglas plane[6] from Baskul with Conway and four others aboard are missing. Unreported between here and Baskul.

QUICK SHOTS of:
A switchboard operator besieged by calls.
A telegraph secretary furiously typing.
Newspapers being run off a press.

INT. FOREIGN OFFICE
67. CLOSE SHOT
Of a high official of the British Foreign Office.

HIGH OFFICIAL
(holding forth to his secretary)
Make it very emphatic that His Majesty's Government will hold the Chinese government and all Chinese governors of Chinese provinces responsible for the complete safety of Robert Conway.

THE CAMERA PULLS BACK to reveal other foreign department officials and functionaries arriving in the midst of his speech.

HIGH OFFICIAL
Good morning, gentlemen

FUNCTIONARIES
(ad-libbing)
Good morning, etc.

OFFICIAL
No news yet, sir?

HIGH OFFICIAL
It's fantastic. The plane couldn't disappear into thin air.
(turning to secretary of the group)
And cable Lord Gainsford at Shanghai. Leave no stone unturned to find Conway.
(turning back to foreign officials)
And Robertson?

ROBERTSON
Yes, sir?

HIGH OFFICIAL
Better get a postponement of the Far East conference. We can't afford to meet those nations without Conway.

INT. PLANE
68. MED. SHOT
The occupants are hunched up in the corner of their seats. What little clothes they have, and what few blankets, are bundled around them. All the windows are shut.

INSERT: ALTOMETER
Registering a height of 10,000 feet.

69. FULL SHOT
There is silence for a moment before Barnard speaks.

BARNARD
It can't be kidnapping. They wouldn't be taking us so far on such a dangerous trip. No sense to it.

No one responds to his speculation and he lapses into silence.

70. MED. SHOT
To include George, Conway and Lovett.

GEORGE
What do you make of it, Bob? You must have some idea?

Conway shrugs.

CONWAY
Huh? I give it up. But this not knowing where you're going is exciting anyway.

LOVETT
Well, Mr. Conway, for a man who is supposed to be a leader, your do-nothing attitude is very disappointing.

GEORGE
What do you want him to do?

LOVETT
I don't know. I'm a paleontologist, not a Foreign Secretary.

Lovett slips back into his corner and pulls his coat over his face.

INSERT: OF ALTOMETER
Registering above 10,000 feet. We STAY on it as it climbs and climbs to 15,000 feet.

EXT. MOUNTAINOUS COUNTRY
71. Showing the plane high over mountain peaks.

DISSOLVE TO:

EXT. SHOT OF PLANE - NIGHT
72. LONG SHOT
Against a moonlit sky, we see a lone speck - the plane as it flies high above the mountains. It appears to be traveling through endless space.

INT. PLANE
73. MED. SHOT
The atmosphere is pervaded with a feeling of utter futility. The occupants are still slumped in the corners of their seats.

74. CLOSE SHOT - GLORIA AND BARNARD
Gloria has a fit of coughing. She grabs her throat - as she gasps for breath. Barnard, himself feeble and exhausted, glances over at her sympathetically.

75. WIDER SHOT
Including Lovett, George, and Conway. Lovett sits with his chin helplessly on his chest, his mouth ludicrously open, his eyes popping. George, his teeth clenched, struggles against a desire to sob. Conway looks at him feelingly.

76. CLOSE SHOT - GEORGE AND CONWAY
Conway's eyes never leave George, who finally unable to control himself, emits a sob - and rather ashamed, slaps his hand over his mouth and turns away.

CONWAY
Oh George, come on.

GEORGE
(suddenly - tensely)
It's not knowing that's so awful, Bob. Not knowing where you're going, or why, or what's waiting when you get there.

George, with an effort, stifles another outbreak.

CONWAY
We got above that storm.

INSERT: OF ALTOMETER
At 20,000 feet - and while we stay on it - keeps mounting.

INTERIOR CABIN
77. FULL SHOT
Deathly silence. Gloria has her hands to her ears, rocking in pain. Suddenly her voice rents the air.

GLORIA
Oh! Oh! I can't stand it any longer!

She jumps up and moves about frantically.

GLORIA
(screaming)
Take us down! I can't stand this pain any longer! Let me out of here I say! I can't stand it any longer!

She runs to one of the ship's doors and pounds on it with her fist, then tries to shove it open. A blast of frigid air throws her back. George and Conway manage to pry her off and pull her away. Sobbing pitifully, she lets Conway steer her back to her seat, where she bundles up in torturous pain. For a moment nothing is heard but her stifled moans.

BARNARD
Take it easy, sister.

Unexpectedly the cockpit panel opens, and the pilot tosses something out in Gloria's direction.

CONWAY
(grabbing for it)
It's oxygen!
(he rigs it up for her)
Now take it with your teeth. That's right - bite.

GLORIA
(struggling)
Let me alone.

CONWAY
Now, now. Come on now. That's right. Now, bite.

She resumes her sobbing quietly.

DISSOLVE TO:

<u>EXT. PLANE</u>
78. LONG SHOT
Of the plane at twilight, fading into deepest night.

<u>INT. PLANE</u>
79. FULL SHOT
Of the cabin at night, everyone frozen in despair. All of a sudden there is a loud, sputtering noise from the outside. They all react - listen for a moment - until the noise dies completely. Now nothing is heard - not even the motor.

AD-LIB
(breaking the silence)
What's that! What's happening?

CONWAY
(immediately on his feet)
He must have run out of fuel.

BARNARD
Look! Look down there!

<u>EXT. PLANE</u>
80. LONG SHOT
The plane gradually tilting downward.

<u>INT. PLANE</u>
81. FULL SHOT
The ship sways several seconds and finally rights itself.

<u>EXT. PLANE</u>
82. LONG SHOT
Of what they see from plane. Vast snow-covered mountain peaks, with no sign of a stretch big enough to land.

83. LONG SHOT
The plane sways perilously in the cross wind.

<u>INTERIOR PLANE</u>
84. MEDIUM SHOT
They are all silent - waiting prayerfully. Conway turns to the others - his voice electric with authority.

CONWAY
George - everybody - better get back towards the tail! He may nose her over. Into the corner, quick! George - cushions, blankets!

They obey his command.

<u>EXTERIOR SHOT OF PLANE</u>
85. LONG SHOT
We see the plane nearing the ground, sailing over some smaller hills.

<u>INTERIOR PLANE</u>
86. MED. CLOSE SHOT
With Conway in front of them, the others are crouching in the corner. There are ad-libs of fearful assurances while they hand around cushions and blankets.

EXTERIOR SHOT OF PLANE

87. LONG SHOT
Just as the ship hits the ground for the first time.

INTERIOR PLANE

88. MED. CLOSE SHOT
The occupants brace themselves for the jolt. The ship hits and bounces several times and finally stops. Its nose seems to bury itself in the ground. The people are lifted high into the air where they remain, suspended for a few seconds, terror-stricken. Then, accompanied by grinding, crackling sounds, the ship flops back and falls on its side. For a moment there is stark silence - while the people do not stir. A look of relief spreads over their faces.

CONWAY
Everybody all right?

The passengers offer dazed replies: "Okay - yeah - I think so." Meanwhile, Conway has opened the door. A swirling mass of snow greets them, so that they have to force their way out.

EXTERIOR OF PLANE

89. MEDIUM SHOT
George and Conway fight their way down from the plane in the blinding snow. George quickly runs around to the other side. Conway crosses to the cockpit, and clambers aboard.

90. CLOSE SHOT IN THE COCKPIT
Lit only by the dashboard light. Conway sticks his head in from the outside. His eyes which have been flashing with determination suddenly sober. CAMERA PANS OVER to pilot, who is slumped over, his chin resting on his chest.

91. MEDIUM CLOSE SHOT
George pops into view on the opposite side, just as Conway has found the pilot's gun beside him on the seat.

GEORGE
What is it? Has he fainted?

CONWAY
It looks like it.
(sniffing)
Smell those fumes?

Conway hops up beside the pilot. George follows suit.

CONWAY
(handing gun to George)
Here George, take the gun. Hold the lights. I'm going to search him before he comes to.
(while searching)
We might find something interesting.
(finds something)
Hello - what's this? A map!
(hands it to George)

He resumes his search enthusiastically. Suddenly he stops. The utter limpness of the pilot's body gives him pause. He lifts up his chin, stares into his face - pulls up his eyelid and then places a hand over his heart. He turns slowly toward George, who has been watching his brother intently.

CONWAY
He's dead.

GEORGE
Dead?

George stares unbelievingly.

CONWAY
It must have happened the moment he hit the ground.
(a pause)
Let's take a look at this map.

Conway holds the map under the dashboard light. He studies it painstakingly, and his tense expression changes to one of deep concern. George's eyes are glued on him.

GEORGE
What is it?

CONWAY
See that spot?

GEORGE
Yes.

CONWAY
That's where we were this morning. He had it marked. Right on the border of Tibet. Here's where civilization ends. We must be a thousand miles beyond it - just a blank on the map.

GEORGE
(afraid to ask)
What's it mean?

CONWAY
It means we're in unexplored country - country nobody ever reached.

George stares at him, wide-eyed, the gravity of their situation slowly penetrating his terrorized mind. Conway's thoughts are interrupted by a knock on the panel, and he looks up.

92. MED. CLOSE SHOT THROUGH GLASS PANEL
We see the faces of Barnard and the others. We hear their voices inquiring - "Hey, Conway, what's happening?" - "What's up?" - "Where are we?" - "What'd you find out?"

93. CLOSE SHOT - CONWAY AND GEORGE
Conway turns to George.

CONWAY
George, our chances of getting out of this are pretty slim. But it's up to us.
(a nod toward cabin)
We can't have three hysterical people on our hands.

He enters the cabin through the cockpit.

INT. CABIN OF PLANE
94. MEDIUM SHOT
As Conway enters, he is met by a volley of questions.

AD-LIB
What do you say? What'd you find out?

CONWAY
(interrupting - cheerily)
Everything's all right. The pilot won't trouble us any more. He's - he's dead.

This is met by a series of exclamations.

AD-LIB
Dead? How did it happen?

CONWAY
Probably a heart attack.

BARNARD
What are we going to do?

CONWAY
Well, there's nothing we can do until the morning.

95. CLOSE SHOT
Taking in George as he enters from cockpit. His terror-stricken eyes look dully before him. He stops in the doorway.

CONWAY
The storm will probably die down by then. My suggestion is that we better all try and get a good night's rest.

96. MEDIUM SHOT
Over the shoulders of Gloria, Barnard and Lovett as they face Conway, who sits down.

GEORGE
(fiercely)
Why don't you tell them the truth?

97. FULL SHOT
They all wheel around and face George.

GEORGE
Why don't you tell them we're a million miles from civilization, without a chance of getting out of here alive? It's slow starvation - that's what it is. It's a slow, horrible death!

When the significance of this outburst finally sinks into the chaotic minds of his listeners, they turn to Conway hopefully, certain he will refute it. But Conway looks beyond them at George. From his noncommittal silence, they realize that George's statement is the truth. They slip into their seats. The place is heavy with a fatalistic silence. George slowly crosses to his seat near Conway, avoiding his accusing eyes. Suddenly the air is rent with harsh, bitter laughter from Gloria. They all look up.

GLORIA
Well, that's perfect! Just perfect! What a kick I'm going to get out of this!

She emits another outburst of semi-hysterical laughter.

98. CLOSE SHOT - GROUP
Favoring Gloria. The bitterness of a lifetime in her voice.

GLORIA
(grimly satisfied)
A year ago a doctor gave me six months to live. That was a year ago! I'm already six months to the good. I'm on velvet.[7] I haven't got a thing to lose--
(semi-hysterical)
But you! - you, the noble animals of the human race, what a kick I'm going to get out of watching you squirm for a change.
(her voice cracks completely)
What a kick!

She flops into her seat and buries her head in her hands. For quite a while all we hear are her stifled sobs.

99. CLOSE SHOT - CONWAY AND GEORGE
George throws sidelong glances at his brother, feeling his guilt.

100. FULL SHOT
Shooting from front of plane, taking in entire cabin. The only sound that comes in on the tragic quiet is the low moaning of the wind outside. A feeling of doom has descended upon the five people.

FADE OUT:

FADE IN

101. LONG SHOT
Shooting toward the mountains which seem to imprison the valley below. The snowstorm, treacherous in its fury, seems to threaten the valley with complete obliteration.

102. MEDIUM SHOT
Of the plane, tilted over on its side. It is fully covered with snow. CAMERA PANS UP TO LOVETT AND BARNARD, shivering in their blankets as they pace worriedly.

INTERIOR OF PLANE
103. MEDIUM SHOT
George and Conway are missing. Lovett turns from the window.

LOVETT
They've been gone for three hours.

The others appear disinterested in this observation.

LOVETT
Left us here to rot. That's what they've done. Heroes of the newspapers!

BARNARD
All right, all right. Keep quiet.

Lovett sees something through the window.

EXTERIOR OF PLANE
104. MEDIUM SHOT - THROUGH WINDOW OF PLANE
George and Conway are seen walking briskly toward the plane, their few clothes a scant protection against the biting wind.

INTERIOR PLANE
105. FULL SHOT

LOVETT
Here they come!

The others quickly glance up, just as Conway and George clamber aboard. Conway has a serious mien, but George is full of vigor and enthusiasm.

GEORGE
Hello, everybody.

He holds out his hat which he has been carrying, bottom side up.

GEORGE
Well, we found some food.

Barnard and Lovett rush to him.

GEORGE
No chance of our starving now.

When they see the contents of his hat, their faces fall.

LOVETT
What is it?

GEORGE
Mountain grass. It's good, too. Here, have some. I've read of people lasting thirty days on this stuff.

They grab handfuls. He goes on:

GEORGE
Listen, my brother and I have worked out a plan. If we use our heads, we should be able to keep alive for weeks, until he gets back.

LOVETT & BARNARD
Gets back? Where's he going?

GEORGE
He doesn't know. But he's starting out right away in the direction of India. Sooner or later he's bound to run into somebody - a tribe or something.

BARNARD
Yeah?

106. CLOSE SHOT - CONWAY
Throughout the previous scene he has been busily occupied making preparations. Out of the baggage hold he has brought some blankets and rope and has been wrapping his feet in them. As George speaks, he looks up and smiles.

GEORGE
Now here's the idea. We found a cave over by that small hill. After we bury the pilot, we're moving in. We can have a fire there. I shouldn't be surprised to see Bob back within a week.

Conway's smile dies on his face. We get a feeling he is attempting a futile journey, and is fully aware of it. He resumes the roping of his feet - his movements mechanical.

107. MED. CLOSE SHOT - GROUP
Barnard and Lovett all attention as George speaks. Gloria, off to one side, has her eyes peeled on Conway intently.

108. CLOSE SHOT - GLORIA AND CONWAY

GLORIA
You haven't got a Chinaman's chance[8] of getting out of this country alive, and you know it.

Conway stares at her blankly.

BARNARD
Cave, eh? Where?

GEORGE
(pointing)
Over by that hill.

Barnard peers out the plane window.

BARNARD
Hey - look!

GEORGE
Look, Bob!

109. FULL SHOT
They all look up and glance out.

EXTERIOR OF PLANE
110. LONG SHOT THROUGH WINDOW
From their angle. In the distance, just appearing over the top of a hill, we see a caravan of natives approaching. They are not close enough to distinguish who or what they are, but that they are human beings is apparent.

INTERIOR PLANE
111. MEDIUM SHOT
Conway takes in the unbelievable sight. We hear the exultant exclamations of the others. Barnard and Lovett start out of the plane.

LOVETT
(looking around)
Where are they? Do you see them?

BARNARD
Yes!

LOVETT
Do you think they're cannibals?

EXTERIOR OF PLANE

112. MEDIUM SHOT
Where George, Lovett and Barnard wait, a trifle awe-stricken. Conway joins them. Gloria has stayed inside.

113. MED. LONG SHOT
The approach of the caravan from the viewpoint of the group. It comprises some twenty Tibetans, attired in sheepskins, fur, hats and boots. Somewhere in the middle of the single file is Chang, an elderly Chinese. Chang steps forward as their leader.

114. MED. SHOT (MOVING)
As Conway leaves his group and meets the oncoming party. He approaches Chang and bowing courteously, greets him in Chinese. Chang turns his head slowly and speaks in perfect Oxfordian English.

CHANG
I am from a nearby Lamasery.
(holding out his hand)
My name is Chang.

115. MEDIUM SHOT
George, Barnard and Lovett.

GEORGE
Why, he's speaking English.

LOVETT
English!

CONWAY
(shaking hands)
And mine's Conway.

CHANG
How do you do?

CONWAY
You've no idea, sir, how unexpected and very welcome you are. My friends and I - and the lady in the plane - left Baskul night before last for Shanghai, but we suddenly found ourselves travelling in the opposite direction--

LOVETT
At the mercy of a mad pilot.

CONWAY
We'd be eternally grateful if you--

CHANG
(interrupting)
Where is your mad pilot?

CONWAY
He must have had a heart attack, or perhaps the fumes. When the plane landed he was dead.

GEORGE
We were just going to bury him when you came along.

CHANG
(preoccupied)
Pardon me--

Chang turns to some of his men and issues an order in a foreign tongue, obviously instructions to take care of the pilot.

CONWAY
(when Chang is through)
So, if you will be good enough to direct us to your Lamasery--

116. MED. CLOSE SHOT - GROUP
Favoring Chang.

CHANG
I shall consider it an honor to accompany you and your friends.

He issues a command to his men and turns to Conway.

CHANG
You will need suitable clothes for the journey. It is not particularly far, but quite difficult.

CONWAY
Thank you.

Several men have hopped into the scene while he has been speaking. They come forward with boots - sheepskins - fur caps, etc. As they start to get into these new clothes:

DISSOLVE TO:

117. LONG SHOT
As the caravan starts its journey back up the hill. All five people are now attired in their newly acquired outfit.

118. SERIES OF SHOTS
Showing the party on various stages of what looks like a humanly impossible journey. We see them first climbing - then across long vastnesses of flat land. Each succeeding time we see them, their feet drag more wearily. Their breathing becomes more difficult. These pictures finally

DISSOLVE TO:

EXT. NARROW TABLELAND

119. MED. LONG SHOT
Halfway up a mountainside. The procession is just starting around a hairpin curve. They are forced to travel on a narrow ledge overlooking a deep ravine.

120. CLOSE SHOT - LOVETT, BARNARD AND GLORIA
As they cling against the rocky sides and glance apprehensively down into the abyss below.

121. CLOSE SHOT - GLORIA
Close by to Barnard. Gloria's face is wan and haggard. Every upward move seems to require a Herculean effort. She stops and has a fit of coughing.

DISSOLVE TO:

EXT. MOUNTAIN TRAIL
122. LONG SHOT
Of the snake-like moving party. They have reached quite a height although the peak of the mountain they are ascending towers high above them. The cutting wind moans treacherously as it caroms off the mountainside. A heavy mist envelops them.

123. SERIES OF SHOTS
As the snake-like line approaches a narrow, treacherous footbridge and makes a slow, difficult crossing in heavy weather.

EXT. MOUNTAIN TOP
124. MED. SHOT
Of the group. They round a curve and come upon a narrow crevice which opens up into a passageway. One by one they step through, assisted by the natives. On the other side, they sigh relievedly. Oddly, the wind has stopped, the chill has lessened. They look up to inspect their surroundings and a startled look comes into their eyes.

124. MED. CLOSE SHOT
Of Conway as he glances casually around. What he sees leaves him transfixed. He stares unbelievingly before him for a long time.

EXT. SHOT OF SHANGRI-LA
125. LONG SHOT
From angle at mountain top.

A sight that is both magnificent and incredible. The eye-filling horizon before them throws out a softness and a warmth that is breathless. On the left is a group of colored pavilions that seem as if suspended on the mountainside. Down below, in the hazy distance, is a valley which gives one the impression of a huge tapestry, superb in its blending of soft colors. In every direction, wherever one might gaze, there is a feast of strange and heavenly beauty.

126. MED. CLOSE SHOT
As Chang approaches Conway.

CHANG
Welcome to Shangri-La.

EXT. MOUNTAIN TOP
127. MED. SHOT - GROUP
Conway's group and Chang. Chang smiles as he watches their astonished faces. Conway turns from the rare magnificence of Shangri-La, unhampered by the wind and storm they had just encountered, and looks backward, in the direction from which they came to assure himself he is the victim of a nightmare. Chang, watching him, answers him before he can express his astonishment.

CHANG
(a wave of his hand)
You see, we are sheltered by mountains on every side. A strange phenomena for which we are very grateful.

DISSOLVE TO:

EXT. A GARDEN
128. SERIES OF SHOTS
As the group approaches the beautiful and peaceful Shangri-La.

129. MED. SHOT
At the foot of a wide marble stairway as the caravan stops.

LOVETT
It's magic!

130. CLOSER SHOT
On the group, as they look around and feast their eyes on the grandeur of the place.

131. CLOSE SHOT - CONWAY
Glancing around at his picturesque surroundings.

132. PANNING SHOT
Following Conway's gaze. In an upper window of a tower, their faces glued to the pane, are two robed Lamas who stare down curiously. CAMERA PANS OVER to a very narrow terrace covered almost completely by a floral arbor. In it stands a statuesque woman of rare beauty. She looks down at Conway intently.

133. CLOSE SHOT - CONWAY
As he returns her gaze, impressed by her beauty.

GEORGE'S VOICE
Come along, Bob. Coming, Bob?

134. CLOSE SHOT - CONWAY
His eyes still on the girl above. He starts up the steps, staring at her, then stumbles.

135. CLOSE SHOT - THE GIRL
Laughing at his embarrassment.

136. CLOSE SHOT - CONWAY
He smiles up at her.

DISSOLVE TO:

INT. A DINING ROOM
137. FULL SHOT
It suggests nothing we might expect to see in this forsaken place. The motif is neither Oriental nor religious - but rather a delicately appointed room, subdued in tones. At the moment, no one is present except servants who silently set the table.

INT. A CORRIDOR
138. MED. TRUCKING SHOT
Of Lovett peering worriedly toward dining room door. He sees two servants who flank the entrance and steps back hesitantly. Barnard emerges from a room across the hall, and Lovett beckons to him. Both are attired in flowing robes not unlike the one worn by Chang.

LOVETT
Mr. Barnard, I do not like this place. I definitely do not like this place.

BARNARD
Will you stop squawking!

LOVETT
Look at me. Look at what they gave me to wear.

BARNARD
You never looked better in your life. As soon as our clothes are cleaned, they're going to give them back to us, Lovey.

They have reached the doorway of the dining room and halt. Two servants bow and scrape and lead them in.

BARNARD
Something tells me this means food. Come on!

LOVETT
I just feel as though I'm being made ready for the executioner.

INT. DINING ROOM
139. MEDIUM SHOT
As the servants show Lovett and Barnard to their places.

BARNARD
(taking in the food)
Yeah? If this be execution, lead me to it.

LOVETT
That's what they do with cattle just before the slaughter. Fatten them.

BARNARD
Uh-huh. You're a scream, Lovey.

LOVETT
Please don't call me Lovey.

At this moment Conway and George enter.

CONWAY
That was refreshing! Oh, ho - the food looks good!

He takes something off the table and nibbles at it.

BARNARD
Some layout they got here. Did you get a load of the rooms? You couldn't do better at the Ritz.

LOVETT
All the conveniences for the condemned, if you ask me.

Conway looks at him and smiles.

BARNARD
Don't mind Lovey. He's got the misery.

LOVETT
Mr. Conway, I don't like this place. I don't like it. It's too mysterious.

CONWAY
It's better than freezing to death down below, isn't it?

BARNARD
I'll say.

INT. GLORIA'S ROOM[9]
140. FULL SHOT
It is in semi-darkness. The moon sends a stream of light through the windows. Outside we see the outline of towering mountains. Spread across the bed - her clothes unchanged - is the body of Gloria - her face sunk deep in the pillows.

141. MED. CLOSE SHOT
Gloria emits wracking coughs. After a few moments - she sits up. Her cheeks are wet - her hair disheveled - her eyes bloodshot. We get an impression of someone who has suffered for hours. Finally, her coughing begins again - and unable to stand it, she rises and paces the floor - then she crosses to the window and looks down, CAMERA PANNING WITH HER - and into her eyes has come a grim, determined expression.

142. LONG SHOT
From Gloria's point of view.

She is staring at the chasm below her.

CONTINUATION SCENE 141
Gloria continues to peer below - and her coughing resumes.

INT. CORRIDOR
143. MEDIUM SHOT
As Chang comes down the corridor - hears the coughing and stops.

INT. GLORIA'S ROOM
144. FULL SHOT
Chang enters and watches Gloria for a moment before speaking.

CHANG
Is there something I can do for you?

Gloria wheels around and glares at him.

GLORIA
What do you want?

CHANG
I've offered you some warm broth. I thought perhaps—

GLORIA
You get out of here! If any of you men think you can come busting in here—

She cannot finish as she is attacked by a fit of coughing.

CHANG
Please calm yourself. You'll soon be well if you do.

GLORIA
(through fits of coughing)
I don't need any advice from you! Get me a doctor!

CHANG
I'm sorry, but we have no doctors here.

GLORIA
(looks up quickly)
No doctors?
(bitterly)
That's fine. That's just fine.

CHANG
Please let <u>me</u> help you.

GLORIA
Sure, you can help me! You can help me jump over that cliff! I've been looking and looking at the bottom of that mountain, but I haven't got the nerve to jump!

CHANG
(quietly)
You shouldn't be looking at the <u>bottom</u> of the mountain. Why don't you try looking up at the top sometimes?

GLORIA
(her voice cracking)
Don't preach that cheap, second-hand stuff to me!
(a sob escapes)
Go on, beat it. Beat it!

She flings herself across the bed, coughing uncontrollably. Chang watches her sympathetically for a few seconds.

CHANG
(before turning away)
Peace be with you, my child.

<u>INT. DINING ROOM</u>
145. FULL SHOT
They all look up as Chang enters. He is escorted to his place at the head of the table by two servants who stand on either side of his chair.

CHANG
(jovially)
Good evening. Good evening, my friends. Oh no, no, no, please sit down. I hope you found everything satisfactory.

BARNARD & CONWAY
Swell. Excellent.

CHANG
(sees that no one has started)
You shouldn't have waited for me.

BARNARD
Where's the girl? Miss Stone.

CHANG
She's remaining in her room. She isn't feeling very well.
(to others)
Now please go on without me. I eat very little.

146. MEDIUM SHOT
Shooting down the long table toward Chang. He sits up straight - studying them - as the others bend over their food.

DISSOLVE TO:

INT. DINING ROOM
147. MEDIUM SHOT
The meal is over. Conway sips from a wine glass.

BARNARD
Well, there's certainly nothing wrong with that meal!

CHANG
Thank you.

CONWAY
And the wine - excellent.

CHANG
I'm glad you like it. It's made right here in the valley.

LOVETT
Now that dinner is over, if you'll excuse us, we're very anxious to discuss ways and means of getting back home.

GEORGE
The first thing we want to do is to cable the Foreign Office. All of England is waiting to hear about my brother. There's a cruiser at Shanghai ready to take him back.

CHANG
Really? Well, as regards cabling, I'm afraid I can't help. Unfortunately, we have no wire-less here. As a matter of fact, we have no means of communication with the outside world.

George stares at him suspiciously - and then turns to Conway for his reaction - but Conway is apparently disinterested in the whole conversation.

BARNARD
Not even a radio?

CHANG
It's always been a source of deep regret, but the mountains surrounding us have made reception almost impossible.

GEORGE
In that event, we better make arrangements to get some porters immediately. Some means to get us back to civilization.

CHANG
Are you so certain you are away from it?

GEORGE
As far away as I ever want to be.

CHANG
Oh, dear.

LOVETT
Of course, the porters will be very well paid - that is, within reason.

CHANG
I'm afraid that wouldn't help. You see, we have no porters here.

LOVETT
No porters here!!

CHANG
No.

BARNARD
What about those men we met this morning?

CHANG
Yes. Those are our own people. They never venture beyond the point where you were met this morning. It is much too hazardous.

148. CLOSE SHOT - CONWAY
To intercut with above speech.

He has remained quiet throughout the scene, apparently interested only in a paper in front of him, upon which he has been writing.

INSERT: What has been occupying Conway's interest. It is a picture of Chang which he has been listlessly drawing.

BARNARD
How do you account for all this? Who brought it in?

149. FULL SHOT
They all turn to Chang expectantly.

CHANG
Oh, yes. There is a tribe of porters some five hundred miles from here. That is our only contact with the outside world. Every now and again, depending upon favorable weather of course, they make the journey.

GEORGE
How can we get in touch with them?

CHANG
In that respect, you are exceedingly fortunate. We are expecting a shipment from them almost any time now--

LOVETT
What exactly do you mean by "almost any time now"?

CHANG
Well, we've been expecting this particular shipment for the past two years.

BARNARD
Two years!?

CHANG
Yes.

Barnard and Lovett look shocked. George starts to say something, but the words choke in his throat.

CHANG
But I can assure you, gentlemen, if there is a prolonged delay, Shangri-La will endeavor to make your stay as pleasant as possible.
(rising)
And now if you will excuse me, it is getting late. I do hope you all sleep well. Good night.

The servants move his chair back. Before he goes, however, he turns to Conway.

CHANG
Good night, Mr. Conway.

Conway, a little surprised at the distinction in his behalf, nods.

CONWAY
Good night, sir.

Chang exits. There is a hushed silence following Chang's departure.

LOVETT
That's what I mean - mysterious. Mr. Conway, I don't like that man. He's too vague.

GEORGE
(concerned)
We didn't get much information out of him, did we Bob?

CONWAY
It seems to me we should be grateful. We were in a bad mess this morning.
(a wave of his hand)
After all, this is quite pleasant. Why not make ourselves comfortable until the porters do arrive?

While he was speaking, the muted strains of a violin float into the room. Conway rises.

150. MEDIUM SHOT
As Conway crosses to a balcony door.

BARNARD
That's what I say. What do you say to a rubber of bridge? I saw some cards in the other room.

CONWAY
Not for me, thanks. No, I'm too weary.

He disappears onto the balcony. George watches him go.

BARNARD
(slightly effeminate)
How about you Lovey? Come on. Let's you and I play a game of honeymoon bridge.

LOVETT
(distractedly)
I'm thinking.

BARNARD
Thinking? What about some double solitaire?

LOVETT
As a matter of fact, I'm very good at double solitaire.

BARNARD
No kidding?

LOVETT
Yes.

BARNARD
Then I'm your man.
(starts away)
Come on, Toots.

Lovett detests the pet names, but follows. George thinks a moment - and crosses to balcony.

EXT. BALCONY
151. MEDIUM SHOT
Conway is listening moodily to the soulful music. George wanders in beside him.

CONWAY
Hello, George.
(looking out)
Cigarette?

GEORGE
Thanks.
(lights the cigarette - after a pause)
I suppose all this comes under the heading of adventure.

CONWAY
We've had plenty of it the last few days.

GEORGE
It's far from over, from what I can see. This place gives me the creeps, hidden away like this - no contact with civilization. Bob, you don't seem concerned at all.

CONWAY
Oh, I'm feeling far too peaceful to be concerned about anything.
(moodily)
I think I'm going to like it here.

GEORGE
You talk as though you intend on staying.

CONWAY
(turns to him)
Something happened to me, when we arrived here, George, that - well - did you ever go to a totally strange place, and feel certain that you've been there before?

GEORGE
What are you talking about?

CONWAY
(back to earth)
I don't know.

GEORGE
You're a strange bird. No wonder Gainsford calls you the man who always wanted to see what was on the other side of the hill.

152. TWO SHOT - CONWAY AND GEORGE
Conway's point of view, studying George.

CONWAY
Don't you ever want to see what's on the other side of the hill?

GEORGE
What could there be except just another hill? In any event, I'm not curious. At the moment, it seems to me we should be concerned about getting home. I'd give anything to be in London right now.

CONWAY
Of course you would. If ever we get out of this place, the thing for you to do is to take that job with Helen's father.

GEORGE
What do you mean <u>if</u> we should get out?

CONWAY
(evasively)
Did I say "if"?

GEORGE
(interrupting)
That's what you said.

CONWAY
Well - I mean--

GEORGE
What's on your mind, Bob? You talk as though we're going to have trouble getting out of here.

153. CLOSE TWO SHOT - FAVORING CONWAY

CONWAY
George, I've been putting things together. Do you notice the resemblance between those natives and the pilot? And why did those clothes materialize so conveniently when they met us at the plane? Chang himself just said that they never venture beyond that point. What brought them there? Unless it was to meet us?

GEORGE
(catching on)
Chang's first question was about the pilot.

CONWAY
Uh-huh.

GEORGE
There must be some connection between the plane and this place. They must have deliberately brought us here. Why, Bob? What reason could they have for doing a thing like that?

CONWAY
That's what's on the other side of the hill.

FADE OUT:

FADE IN

EXT. OF VALLEY - DAY
154. LONG SHOT FROM A TOWER ROOM
Shooting over shoulders of two men in f.g.

We see a beautiful picture of the valley below. There is a tranquility here that is beatific. CAMERA PULLS BACK. The two men are revealed as Conway and Chang. They stand on a terrace of one of the tower rooms.

CHANG
It's three thousand feet, practically straight down to the floor of the valley. The Valley of the Blue Moon, as we call it. There are over two thousand people in the Valley besides those here in Shangri-La.

CONWAY
Who and what is Shangri-La? You?

CHANG
Goodness, no!

CHANG
So there are others?

CHANG
Oh, yes.

CONWAY
Who, for instance?

CHANG
In time you will meet them all.

155. CLOSE SHOT - THE TWO - FAVORING CONWAY
He watches Chang's face searchingly, then smiles.

CONWAY
For a man who talks a great deal, it's amazing how unenlightening you can be.

CHANG
(laughs)
There are some things, my dear Conway, I deeply regret I may not discuss.

CONWAY
You know, that's the fourth time you've said that today. You should have a record made of it.

CHANG
(evasively)
Shall we go inside? I should so like to show you some of our rare treasures.

INT. A TOWER

156. FOLLOW SHOT WITH GEORGE
On a spiral staircase. Looking surreptitiously around, he backs his way up. CAMERA FOLLOWS HIM as he reaches the top of the landing. Here he stops and glances around the corner down a corridor.

INT. CORRIDOR

157. MEDIUM SHOT
CAMERA FOLLOWS GEORGE as he peers into several rooms searchingly. He finally arrives at one and enters.

INT. A ROOM

158. FULL SHOT
George enters and looks around. It is dimly lit and apparently unoccupied. He crosses to a desk and picks up several objects, scrutinizing them closely.

159. CLOSE SHOT OF THE GIRL, MARIA - IN ALCOVE
She sits, a tapestry board on her lap, watching George with keen interest.

160. CLOSE SHOT - GEORGE
He opens a book and glances at its contents.

161. MED. SHOT TO INCLUDE BOTH
Maria surveys his back appraisingly.

MARIA
Good afternoon.

George wheels around, startled, and stares at her intently.

GEORGE
(starts backing out)
Excuse me—

MARIA
(appealingly)
Please don't go.

George hesitates at door.

MARIA
Tea will be served any moment.

162. CLOSE SHOT - GEORGE
He watches her with grave speculation for a long moment, then slowly moves toward her.

MARIA
(a winning smile)
Won't you come in?

George still maintains a serious mien, as their eyes meet.

MARIA
My name is Maria. Won't you sit down?

INT. LIBRARY
163. FULL SHOT
It is a huge room. The walls are lined with impressive tomes. Chang is showing Conway around.

164. MEDIUM SHOT
Conway has just finished browsing through one of the books.

CONWAY
By the way, what religion do you follow here?

CHANG
We follow many.

A look of surprise spreads over Conway's face.

CHANG
(thoughtfully)
To put it simply, I should say that our general belief was in moderation. We preach the virtue of avoiding excesses of every kind, even including--
(he smiles)
--the excess of virtue itself.

165. CLOSER SHOT - THE TWO

CONWAY
That's intelligent.

CHANG
We find, in the Valley, it makes for better happiness among the natives. We rule with moderate strictness and in return we are satisfied with moderate obedience. As a result, our people are moderately honest and moderately chaste and somewhat more than moderately happy.

CONWAY
How about law and order? You have no soldiers or police?

CHANG
Oh, good heavens, no!

CONWAY
How do you deal with incorrigibles? Criminals?

CHANG
Why, we have no crime here. What makes a criminal? Lack, usually. Avariciousness, envy, the desire to possess something owned by another. There can be no crime where there is a sufficiency of everything.

CONWAY
You have no disputes over women?

CHANG
Only very rarely. You see, it would not be considered good manners to take a woman that another man wanted.

CONWAY
Suppose somebody wanted her so badly that he didn't give a hang if it was good manners or not?

CHANG
(smiling)
Well, in that event, it would be good manners on the part of the other man to let him have her.

166. CLOSE SHOT - THE TWO - FAVORING CONWAY

CONWAY
That's very convenient. I think I'd like that.

CHANG
You'd be surprised, my dear Conway, how a little courtesy all around helps to smooth out the most complicated problems.

167. MED. CLOSE SHOT - THE TWO
Chang smiles. Conway scarcely hears the last speech, for his attention has been caught by the playing of a piano. He stops to listen. Chang has walked out of scene.

168. MEDIUM SHOT
Conway locates the direction whence the music comes, goes to a doorway where he stops.

169. CLOSE SHOT - CHANG
He realizes Conway did not follow him and turns. When he sees Conway, his face clouds - and he starts toward him.

170. CLOSE SHOT AT DOOR
Conway watches someone through door with grave interest. Chang enters scene and follows his gaze.

<u>INT. MUSIC ROOM</u>

171. FULL SHOT
From doorway. It is a spacious, high-ceilinged room, oddly shaped, and except for a piano, a harp and several chairs, is otherwise sparsely furnished. At the extreme end, the room is set off by an alcove of stained glass extending from the ceiling to the floor, where it finishes with a deep window seat. At the piano we see an old man - and by his side is the girl Conway saw last night. They finish playing and both laugh heartily.

172. CLOSE SHOT AT DOORWAY
Conway finds her laughter infectious - and smiles.

173. CLOSE SHOT - GIRL AND MAN AT PIANO
In the midst of her laughter, the girl sees Conway, off scene, and her face sobers - self-consciously.

174. CLOSE SHOT AT DOORWAY
Chang quickly takes Conway by the arm.

CHANG
At some time in the future you will have the pleasure of meeting her.

Conway turns for one last glimpse of the girl, and then turns to Chang, looking up at his face, puzzled and amused.

CONWAY
Some man had better get ready to be very courteous to me.

175. CLOSEUP - THE GIRL
She continues to stare off toward the door, her eyes alight with a keen interest.

DISSOLVE TO:

<u>INT. CORRIDOR</u>

176. FOLLOW SHOT WITH CONWAY AND CHANG

CONWAY
But Mr. Chang, all these things - books, instruments, sculpture - do you mean to say they were all brought in over those mountains by porters?

CHANG
They were.

CONWAY
Well, it must have taken—

CHANG
Centuries.

CONWAY
Centuries! Where did you get the money to pay for all those treasures?

CHANG
Of course we have no money as you know it. We do not buy or sell or seek personal fortunes because, well, because there is no uncertain future here for which to accumulate it.

INT. A ROOM

177. CLOSE SHOT - THE TWO

They have arrived in a small room, where they pause. Chang reaches into a bowl of large nuts, cracks one, and hands the nut to Conway. Then he does the same for himself. During the following scene, both are eating nuts from the bowl.

CONWAY

That would suit me perfectly. I'm always broke. How did you pay for them?

CHANG

Our Valley is very rich in a metal called gold, which fortunately for us is valued very highly in the outside world. So we merely ...

CONWAY

--buy and sell?

CHANG

Buy and - sell? No, no, pardon me, exchange.

CONWAY

(chuckling)

I see. Gold for ideas. You know Mr. Chang, there's something so simple and naive about all of this that I suspect there has been a shrewd, guiding intelligence somewhere. Whose idea was it? How did it all start?

CHANG

That, my dear Conway, is the story of a remarkable man.

CONWAY

Who?

CHANG

A Belgian priest by the name of Father Perrault, the first European to find this place, and a very great man indeed. He is responsible for everything you see here. He built Shangri-La, taught our natives, and began our collection of art. In fact, Shangri-La is Father Perrault.

CONWAY

When was all this?

CHANG

Oh, let me see - way back in 1713, I think it was, that Father Perrault stumbled into the Valley, half frozen to death. It was typical of the man that, one leg being frozen, and of course there being no doctors here, he amputated the leg himself.

CONWAY

(shocked)

He amputated his own leg?

CHANG
Yes. Oddly enough, later, when he had learned to understand their language, the natives told him he could have saved his leg. It would have healed without amputation.

CONWAY
Well, they didn't actually mean that.

CHANG
Yes, yes. They were very sincere about it too. You see, a perfect body in perfect health is the rule here. They've never known anything different. So what was true for them they thought would naturally be true for anyone else living here

CONWAY
Well, is it?

CHANG
Rather astonishingly so, yes. And particularly so in the case of Father Perrault himself. Do you know when he and the natives were finished building Shangri-La, he was 108 years old and still very active, in spite of only having one leg?

CONWAY
108 and still active?

CHANG
You're startled?

CONWAY
Oh, no. Just a little bowled over, that's all.

CHANG
Forgive me. I should have told you it is quite common here to live to a very ripe old age. Climate, diet, mountain water, you might say. But we like to believe it is the absence of struggle in the way we live. In your countries, on the other hand, how often do you hear the expression, "He worried himself to death?" or, "This thing or that killed him?"

CONWAY
Very often.

CHANG
And very true. Your lives are therefore, as a rule, shorter, not so much by natural death as by indirect suicide.

CONWAY
(after a pause)
That's all very fine if it works out. A little amazing, of course.

CHANG
Why, Mr. Conway, you surprise me!

CONWAY
I surprise you? Now that's news.

CHANG
I mean, your amazement. I could have understood it in any of your companions, but you - who have dreamed and written so much about better worlds. Or is it that you fail to recognize one of your own dreams when you see it?

CONWAY
Mr. Chang, if you don't mind, I think I'll go on being amazed - in moderation, of course.

CHANG
(chuckles)
Then everything is quite all right, isn't it?

They exit scene together.

EXT. GARDEN[10]
178. MED. CLOSE SHOT
On a garden bench Gloria slumps languidly. Suddenly we hear Barnard's voice, yelling. Gloria quickly turns her back. Barnard runs into scene.

BARNARD
Honey, it's terrific! Terrific! I just saw something that will make your hair stand on end. You see those hills over there? Gold! Gold! Popping right out of them! Tons of it!
(conspiratorially)
Now look, you keep this under your hat, because if those other monkeys hear about it, they'll declare themselves in. But if I can mine that stuff, I'll throw a bombshell into Wall Street. Now look, I've got a plan - and if I--

Gloria begins coughing heavily. Barnard notices how pale and haggard she looks.

BARNARD
Aw say, honey, you aren't feeling well, are you? Look, don't pay too much attention to what those doctors tell you. I've seen an awful lot of people fool them, and I've got a hunch that this place is going to be good for you. Honest, I have.
(waits for her reaction - receives none)
Come on now. Come on. You be a good kid, and snap out of it, and I'll cut you in on the gold deal. Look, I'm going up and make a deal with Chang - right now.

He enthusiastically exits scene.

INT. LOVETT'S ROOM
179. CLOSE SHOT
Lovett enters warily, sits down at his desk and begins to write in his journal.

INSERT OF WHAT HE WRITES:

THE DIARY OF ALEXANDER P. LOVETT
2nd Day at Shangri-La
"This place is too mysterious!"

He looks up, sees himself in a mirror and gives a start. Then, chuckling to himself reassuringly, he looks around warily and continues to write.

DISSOLVE TO:

EXT. SOMEWHERE IN SHANGRI-LA

180. FULL SHOT
It is a bright, cheery morning. Conway is drinking in the beauty of his surroundings. He comes into the area where the horses are stabled. Two men are busily grooming the horses.

CONWAY
(cheerily)
Good morning!

MEN
Good morning, Mr. Conway!

CONWAY
Oh, you speak English, do you?

MEN
Yes, sir.

ONE OF THE MEN
Would you like to take a ride, Mr. Conway?

CONWAY
No, thanks. Not just now.

Suddenly, Conway is startled by the sound of hoof-beats and, looking up, is in time to see 'the girl' of the previous sequence (Sondra) fly by him on a horse - screaming delightedly. As she passes him, she waves.

CONWAY
(instantly changing his mind)
Well, I think I will take that ride!

181. MED. SHOT - CONWAY
As he rides off in pursuit of her.

182. SEVERAL SHOTS OF THE CHASE
Showing Sondra successfully eluding him - as he closes in on her.

183. MED. LONG SHOT - BOTTOM OF A HILL
Sondra whizzes by. As we stay on the shot - Conway rides through in exciting pursuit.

184. ANOTHER ANGLE
Showing Sondra disappearing behind a mountain waterfall. Conway dashes up, but she is lost from sight. He wheels around several times - and unable to find her, looks puzzled. Finally, giving up, he starts slowly back. After a few moments he is startled by her laughter, and glances around.

185. LONG SHOT
From his view - shooting upward. High up - near the summit of the hill - we see Sondra - waving and laughing. Then she swings her horse around and disappears.

186. CLOSEUP - CONWAY
As he smiles - amused and interested.

DISSOLVE TO:

187. LONG SHOT - SONDRA
As she swims in a mountain stream, apparently in the buff. From a distance, we see her climb onto a rock to dry off.

188. CLOSEUP - SONDRA
As she shakes her shimmering hair.

189. MEDIUM SHOT - CONWAY
He has caught up to her tethered horse and is skulking around trying to find out where she is.

190. CLOSE SHOT - A SQUIRREL
A squirrel, near to Sondra, chatters excitedly.

191. CLOSE SHOT - SONDRA
She can apparently understand the squirrel's warning. She hurries to dive back into the water and swim to the other side. She comes up, spots Conway and watches him from hiding, behind some bushes.

192. MEDIUM SHOT - CONWAY
Conway has discovered her clothing and is constructing a kind of scarecrow on a bush out of them. As a crowning touch, he adds a flower to the effigy, his eyes twinkling at his little joke. With one final glance over his shoulder, he turns to leave.

193. CLOSE SHOT - SONDRA
She stifles her laughter as he vanishes from view.

DISSOLVE TO:

INT. DINING ROOM - NIGHT

194. FULL SHOT
Lovett and Barnard are at the table waiting for the others. Several servants are in the b.g. George paces nervously in front of the door.

195. MED. SHOT AT TABLE
Lovett and Barnard. Barnard nibbles at something.

BARNARD

Bah! Fossils! Why? What for? Running around digging up a lot of old bones! You didn't dig yourself out of one of those holes by any chance, did you?

Lovett is about to reply, when he realizes he is being made fun of, and gives a tentative chuckle.

INT. CORRIDOR

196. MEDIUM SHOT
Conway is coming down the corridor. George comes out of door to dining room and starts forward. Conway walks along in a cheerful mood, singing as he goes, a Cockney song.

GEORGE
(forces a smile)
You seem gay. Did you find out anything?

197. CLOSE TRUCKING SHOT WITH THEM
As they walk back toward dining room door.

CONWAY
Well - I heard that if you want a man's wife, she's yours, if he's got any manners.

GEORGE
Nothing about the porters yet?

CONWAY
Porters?

GEORGE
Good heavens, Bob, we've been here two weeks and we haven't found out a thing.

CONWAY
Well, we haven't been murdered in our beds yet, George, have we?

GEORGE
I'm afraid the porters are just a myth.
(tensely)
I guess we never will know why we're here, or how long we're going to be held prisoners.

CONWAY
Shhh!

They have reached the door and start into dining room.

INT. DINING ROOM
198. MEDIUM SHOT
As Conway and George enter, Barnard calls to them:

BARNARD
Hey, hurry up, you slow-pokes - I'm starved!

CONWAY
(imitating Chang as he takes his chair)
Please! Please! Do not wait for me! I eat so very little.

Barnard laughs heartily. George, surily silent, enters and drops in his seat. At the same moment, Gloria comes into the room.

GLORIA
Good evening.

The men greet her, all rising.

BARNARD
Well, I'm certainly glad to see that it's all finally organized.
(to servant)
Okay, handsome. Dish it out, and make it snappy.

As he sits, he looks over at Gloria and something in her face arrests him.

BARNARD
Hey, what's happened to you?

GLORIA
(self-consciously)
Nothing. Why?

BARNARD
Why, you look beautiful.

CONWAY
That's unkind. Doesn't Miss Stone always look beautiful?

199. MED. CLOSE SHOT AT TABLE
Featuring Gloria, Barnard and Conway.

BARNARD
(suddenly)
I got it! It's your make-up. You've got none on.

Gloria busies herself with her soup, self-consciously.

BARNARD
And say, honey, you look a million per cent better. Wholesome, kind of - and clean. You take a tip from me, and don't you ever put that stuff on your face again. Why, it's like hiding behind a mask.

LOVETT
Ha, ha - who are you to be talking about a mask? What do you mean? You've been wearing a mask ever since we met you.

BARNARD
Have I?

LOVETT
It's very strange, you know. You've never told us anything about yourself. Who are you, anyway? Why don't you take your mask off for once!

CONWAY
(lightly)
Yes. Unbosom yourself, Mr. Hyde.[11]

BARNARD
(his face has become serious)
All right, I will! I'll let my hair down! Why not? It can't make any real difference now.
(after a pause)
Hey Lovey, were you ever chased by the police?

Lovett is halted in his tracks - soup spoon halfway up to his mouth.

LOVETT
Certainly not.

200. CLOSE SHOT - BARNARD

BARNARD
Believe me, it's no fun. When you fellas picked me up at Baskul, they'd been on my tail for a year.

LOVETT
(skeptical)
The police?

BARNARD
Uh-huh.
(after another pause)
Did you ever hear of Chalmers Bryant?

CAMERA PULLS BACK to include the others. They look shocked.

CONWAY
(the first one to make the connection)
Chalmers Bryant!

BARNARD
Bryant's Utilities - that's me.

George is the only one unconcerned. He is deeply absorbed in thought - his food has remained untouched. Lovett suddenly explodes.

LOVETT
I knew it. I knew I had a reason for hating you! Sir, you're a thief.

GLORIA
He never stole anything from _you_, did he?

LOVETT
I have 500 shares of Bryant Utilities that I bought with money that I saved for 20 years teaching school, and now I couldn't sell it for postage stamps.

201. MED. SHOT - GROUP
Featuring Barnard.

BARNARD
That's too bad. I got a half million shares. My whole foundation! And now look at me!

LOVETT
A colossal nerve you have sitting there and talking about it so calmly - you, the swindler of thousands of people--

BARNARD
You know, that's what makes the whole thing so funny. A guy like me starts out in life as a plumber - an ordinary, everyday, slew-footed[12] plumber - and by the use of a little brains, mind you, he builds up a gigantic institution, employs thousands of people, becomes a great civic leader. And then the crash comes - and overnight he's the biggest crook the country ever had.

LOVETT
You are a thief, sir, and a swindler, and I, for one, will be only too glad to turn you over to the police when we get back.

George can't stand it any longer.

GEORGE
(suddenly - hoarsely)
What do you mean - "when we get back"?

The sharpness of his voice startles the others.

GEORGE
What makes you think we're ever going to get back? You may not know it, but you're all prisoners here. We were deliberately kidnapped and brought here - and nobody knows why--

He rises to his feet.

GEORGE
Well, I'm not content to be a prisoner. I'm going to find out when we're going to get out of this place.
(whips out a revolver; grimly)
I'll make that Chinese talk if it's the last thing I do!

He starts out.

202. MEDIUM SHOT
Before anybody can realize what his intentions are, he has bolted out of the room.

CONWAY
(calling)
George!

Starts after him.

<u>INT. CORRIDOR</u>
203. MEDIUM SHOT
As George strides determinedly out into the hall, yelling.

GEORGE
Chang! Chang!

Suddenly he sees a native servant and his eyes pop insanely. CAMERA PANS WITH HIM as he strides across to the servant and grabs him by the shirt-front.

GEORGE
(shaking servant violently)
Where is he? Where's Chang? Where is he? Where's Chang, or I'll blow your brains out!

Conway has caught up with him and wrestles him away from the servant, who stumbles off in fright.

CONWAY
George, what do you think you're doing?

GEORGE
Let me go, Bob!

George pushes Conway away from him and starts down the corridor.

CONWAY
George, come back!

GEORGE
Chang! Chang! Chang!

George spies another servant.

GEORGE
Come here, you! Come here!

The servant, frightened by his voice, turns suddenly and starts running. George levels his revolver and sends a stream of bullets after the fleeing servant, who miraculously manages to skate around a corner, unharmed. Conway runs into scene, reaching George, and with a quick flip of his left hand he smacks him over his revolver arm - and with his right, he punches him flush on the jaw.

CONWAY
George, you idiot!

George reels for a moment and slumps to the floor.

204. CLOSE SHOT
As the others trail in.

BARNARD
Had to sock him, eh?

Conway pockets the gun and, bending over George, a pained expres sion on his face, starts to lift him.

DISSOLVE TO:

INT. CONWAY'S ROOM
205. MED. CLOSE SHOT
Conway brings George in, followed by the others. He drapes him across his bed. Conway stands by his side, looking down at him, deeply concerned. After a moment, Conway shakes him and George awakens with a start.

GEORGE
Let me up! Let me up!

CONWAY
All right. Sorry, George.

George groans and turns away.

206. MED. SHOT TOWARD DOOR
On Barnard, Lovett and Gloria. Barnard wanders over to Conway, who appears lost in thought.

BARNARD
Say Conway, is it true about us being kidnapped?

Conway shrugs.

BARNARD
(louder)
I say, is it true about us being kidnapped?

Conway suddenly is aroused from his reverie by someone he sees off scene. He looks up alertly.

CONWAY
Mr. Chang!

Chang enters scene, beaming charmingly.

CONWAY
Do you mind stepping in here for a moment?

207. FULL SHOT
As Chang enters. He bows courteously to the others, who stand in front of George's bed. Conway shuts the door and turns the key. He crosses to a door leading to another room - and locks this one, also. Chang watches him curiously. The others, including George, who is now alert, are puzzled and somewhat impressed. Then Conway comes to Chang.

CONWAY
Won't you sit down?

Chang sits, his placidity unchanged. Conway pulls up a chair in front of him.

CONWAY
(very quietly)
Mr. Chang, you have been very kind to us - and we appreciate it. But for some reason we are being held prisoners here, and we want to know why.

208. CLOSE SHOT - BARNARD, LOVETT AND GLORIA
As Conway's voice continues, talking to Chang:

CONWAY
Personally, I don't mind at all. I'm enjoying every minute of it.
(dead serious)
But my brother is not of the same opinion, nor are the others.
(after a pause)
It's time we were told what it's all about.

209. MED. SHOT - GROUP
Conway still continuing:

CONWAY
We want to know why we were kidnapped, why we are being kept here, but most important of all - do we get the porters, and when?
(much too suavely)
Until we get this information, my dear Mr. Chang, I am very much afraid we cannot permit you to leave this room.

There is a pause while the eyes of all are centered on Chang's face.

CHANG
(after a pause)
You know, it's very, very strange, but when you saw me in the corridor, I was actually on my way to you. I bring the most amazing news.
(impressively)
The High Lama wishes to see you, Mr. Conway.

LOVETT
The High Lama! Who in blazes is he?!

BARNARD
Yeah. I though you ran this joint.

CONWAY
Mr. Chang - High Lamas or Low Lamas, do we get the porters?

CHANG
The High Lama is the only one from whom any information can come.

GEORGE
Don't believe him, Bob. He's just trying to get out.

LOVETT
Yes.

BARNARD
Sounds like a stall to me.

CONWAY
One moment. You say the High Lama is the only one who can give us any information?

CHANG
The only one.

CONWAY
And he can arrange for the porters to take us back?

CHANG
The High Lama arranges everything, Mr. Conway.

CONWAY
Well, then he's the man I want to see.
(to Chang)
Will you come along?

Conway unlocks the door. When he has opened it, he turns.

CONWAY
Better wait here until I get back. We'll soon know where we stand.

INT. CORRIDOR IN HIGH LAMA'S QUARTERS

210. MED. TRUCKING SHOT
With Conway and Chang. Chang walks in a high state of expectancy. Conway is grim. They climb a narrow spiral staircase.

211. MED. CLOSE SHOT
They proceed up the stairs until they arrive at a large, impressively ornate double door which seems to open automatically the moment they approach. Chang remains without. The moment Conway steps over the threshold, the doors swing closed.

INT. HIGH LAMA'S CHAMBER[13]

212. MED. SHOT
As the doors swing shut. Conway turns and realizes Chang is no longer with him.

213. CLOSE SHOT AT DOOR
Conway stands still, glancing around the room, which is lit so dimly that nothing definite is distinguishable.

214. FULL SHOT
To show what Conway sees. For the moment, practically nothing. As his eyes become adjusted to the darkness, he begins to sense the architecture and furnishings of the room. But as yet no sign of life. SLOW PAN SHOT reveals it to be a dark-curtained and low-ceilinged room, furnished rather simply. Very sombre, indistinct tapestries drape the back walls. While the CAMERA FOLLOWS CONWAY'S GAZE, MOVING SLOWLY AROUND, a voice is heard.

HIGH LAMA'S VOICE
(soft and friendly)
Good evening, Mr. Conway.

CAMERA QUICKLY SWINGS OVER to the nethermost corner of the room where, scarcely visible, sits an old man of indeterminate age. In the gloom only the outlines of his pale and wrinkled face can be seen. It yields an effect of a fading antique portrait.

215. CLOSE SHOT - CONWAY
He stares, motionless, at the eerie vision.

216. MED. SHOT OF ROOM

HIGH LAMA
Please come in.

Conway comes forward warily until he stands within a few feet of the old man, his eyes riveted upon him.

HIGH LAMA
Sit here, near me. I am an old man and can do no one any harm.

CONWAY
Are you the High Lama?

HIGH LAMA
Yes.

217. CLOSE SHOT - THE TWO
As Conway, expressionless, sits down opposite the High Lama.

HIGH LAMA
I trust you have been comfortable at Shangri-La, since your arrival.

CONWAY
Personally, I've enjoyed your community very much. But my friends do not care for this mystery. They are determined to leave as soon as--

While he has been speaking, his eyes have been gradually taking in the details of the old man. The CAMERA QUICKLY FOLLOWS HIS GAZE - to crutches leaning against the man's throne - then, looking down, to his legs, one of which appears to have been amputated.

218. CLOSEUP - CONWAY

CONWAY
(awe and amazement)
It's astonishing - and incredible, but--

219. CLOSE SHOT - THE TWO

HIGH LAMA
What is it, my son?

CONWAY
You're the man Chang told me about! You're the first - who - two hundred years ago -
(reverently)
--you're still alive, Father Perrault!

HIGH LAMA
Sit down, my son.
(pause)
You may not know it, but I've been an admirer of yours for a great many years.

Conway evinces surprise.

HIGH LAMA
Oh, not of Conway the empire-builder and public hero. I wanted to meet the Conway who in one of his books, said, "There are moments in every man's life when he glimpses the eternal."

The quotation captures Conway's interest - and his eyes widen.

HIGH LAMA
That Conway seemed to belong here. In fact, it was suggested that someone be sent to bring him here.

CONWAY
That I be brought here? Who had that brilliant idea?

HIGH LAMA
Sondra Bizet.

CONWAY
(secretly pleased)
Oh, the girl at the piano?

HIGH LAMA
Yes. She has read your books and has a profound admiration for you, as have we all.

CONWAY
Of course I have suspected that our being here is no accident. Furthermore, I have a feeling that we're never supposed to leave. But that, for the moment, doesn't concern me greatly. I'll meet that when it comes. What particularly interests me at present is, why was I brought here? What possible use can I be to an already thriving community?

HIGH LAMA
We need men like you here, to be sure that our community will continue to thrive. In return for which, Shangri-La has much to give you. You are still, by the world's standards, a youngish man. Yet in the normal course of existence, you can expect twenty or thirty years of gradually diminishing activity. Here, however, in Shangri-La, by our standards your life has just begun, and may go on and on.

CONWAY
But to be candid, Father, a prolonged future doesn't excite me. It would have to have a point. I've sometimes doubted whether life itself has any. And if that is so, then long life must be even more pointless. No, I'd need a much more definite reason for going on and on.

HIGH LAMA
We have reason. It is the entire meaning and purpose of Shangri-La. It came to me in a vision, long, long, ago. I saw all the nations strengthening, not in wisdom, but in the vulgar passions and the will to destroy. I saw their machine power multiply until a single weaponed man might match a whole army. I foresaw a time when man, exulting in the technique of murder, would rage so hotly over the world that every book, every treasure, would be doomed to destruction. This vision was so vivid and so moving that I determined to gather together all the things of beauty and culture that I could and preserve them here against the doom toward which the world is rushing.
(pause)
Look at the world today! Is there anything more pitiful? What madness there is, what blindness, what unintelligent leadership! A scurrying mass of bewildered humanity crashing headlong against each other, propelled by an orgy of greed and brutality. The time must come, my friend, when this orgy will spend itself, when brutality and the lust for power must perish by its own sword. Against that time is why I avoided death and am here, and why you were brought here. For when that day comes, the world must begin to look for a new life. And it is our hope that they may find it here. For here we shall be with their books

and their music and a way of life based on one
simple rule: Be Kind.
(pause)
When that day comes, it is our hope that the
brotherly love of Shangri-La will spread
throughout the world.
(pause)
Yes, my son, when the strong have devoured each
other, the Christian ethic may at last be fulfilled, and the meek shall inherit the earth.

A long silence ensues during which Conway, so engrossed is he in all he has just heard, scarcely notices the Lama, who has risen slowly and now stands before him. The Lama reaches down and gently touches him on the shoulder.

CONWAY
(scarcely audible)
I understand you, Father.

Conway kisses the High Lama's hand.

HIGH LAMA
You must come again, my son. Good night.

Conway slowly rises to his feet and turns to leave scene.

INT. UPPER CHAMBER

220. MED. CLOSE SHOT AT DOOR TO LAMA'S CHAMBERS
Conway comes through. He walks as if in a trance. CAMERA PULLS BACK as he continues on his way - bearing an expression of deep absorption.

DISSOLVE TO:

INT. LOWER CORRIDOR

221. MED. SHOT
As Conway walks toward an open door at the end of corridor leading to the garden. Lovett emerges from one of the rooms and sees him. He beckons to those inside and almost immediately they come out and start toward Conway.

222. MED. CLOSE SHOT NEAR GARDEN DOOR
Conway, just about to exit, when the others catch up to him.

AD-LIB
We thought you were never coming back!
What'd you find out?
When do we leave?

Conway stares at them blankly.

GEORGE
What about the porters?

CONWAY
(vaguely)
Porters?

GEORGE
Didn't you find out anything about the porters?

CONWAY
Why - I'm sorry - but I--

He starts away from them, but they crowd around him.

AD-LIB
What were you doing all this time? You've been gone for hours.

GEORGE
For heaven's sake, Bob, what's the matter with you? You went out there for the purpose of--

CONWAY
George. George - do you mind? I'm sorry, but I can't talk about it tonight.

He leaves them.

EXT. GARDEN - NIGHT

223. MED. CLOSE SHOT
Shooting toward garden through open doorway. Conway walks away from the crowd in f.g., all staring at him, nonplussed. We see Conway walk through the garden in b.g. and disappear.

224. CLOSEUP - GEORGE IN DOORWAY
He stares at his brother, off, fearfully.

EXT. SOMEWHERE IN THE VALLEY

225. FULL SHOT
Of a pleasant and peaceful place. Conway is walking along moodily, drinking in the pastoral beauty.

226. MED. TRUCKING SHOT WITH CONWAY
As he walks along. He comes to a spot where a man and a woman are tilling the soil, and stops to watch them. The man looks up and, seeing Conway, makes a friendly bow and doffs his hat. Conway also bows. The woman curtsies prettily and smiles. Conway doffs his hat in acknowledgement.

He is in a cheerful frame of mind and continues his walk - CAMERA CONTINUING WITH HIM. He greets several other people. Upon seeing him, they also bow and doff their hats. Conway does likewise.

EXT. SOMEWHERE IN THE VALLEY - DAY

227. FULL SHOT
Conway is walking along a street in the valley. It is a quaint thoroughfare, unlike anything we have ever seen before. The small, one-story huts along its very narrow sidewalk are of singularly varied architecture - giving the impression of being "homemade." As a result of this, no two are alike. Only one characteristic about them is similar - their cleanliness. Something about the atmosphere is fresh and wholesome and peaceful. In front of several of the huts native women sit - some weaving on a tapestry board, some nursing babies, some asleep, and some just sitting. The keynote is contentment.

228. MED. TRUCKING SHOT
With Conway, walking along. As he passes, the women smile at him in the most friendly fashion. From inside these homes, soft and soothing music emanates. At the end of the street, Conway finally arrives at a garden spot. The suddenness of this is startling, too - because of its beauty. Sighing contentedly, Conway throws himself at the foot of an overhanging tree, and leans against the trunk.

229. CLOSE SHOT - CONWAY
He throws his head back, shuts his eyes - in a restful and contemplative mood. He remains this way quietly for a few seconds, when he is attracted by the singing of a chorus of children's voices. He glances around.

230. LONG SHOT
From Conway's angle. In the shadow of a row of overhanging trees which form an arch, a group of fifteen or twenty children sing a hymn, or nursery song - in English. Sondra (the violin girl of previous scenes) stands in front of them, a baton in hand, conducting them.

231. CLOSE SHOT - CONWAY
He smiles at the sight - and springing to his feet starts in their direction.

232. MED. SHOT
Of Sondra and the children, as Conway saunters into the scene behind her. He finds himself a comfortable place under a tree and sits down. The children, still singing, have seen his approach and crane their necks curiously.

233. CLOSE SHOT - SONDRA
She waves her baton and sings with the children. Then she notices they are being distracted and casually turns her head. She is some what startled at seeing Conway, but quickly recovers her composure, and smiles wanly.

234. CLOSE SHOT - CONWAY
He smiles also.

CONWAY
Do you mind?

235. WIDER ANGLE
To include Sondra, Conway and some of the children. They finish the song, and Conway applauds. Sondra curtsies prettily. She turns to the children.

SONDRA
This is Mr. Conway, children.

236. MED. SHOT
In unison the twenty children curtsey.

CHILDREN
(all together - sing-song)
Good morning, Mr. Conway.

CONWAY
How do you do?

CHILDREN
Very well, thank you.

Conway scrambles to his feet and does an exaggerated bow. Sondra laughs delightedly.

SONDRA
All right, children. We will now sing—

She lifts her baton and the thin, piping voices fill the air.

237. CLOSEUP - CONWAY
He lights a cigarette and, leaning against a tree, studies Sondra's face - impressed by her beauty.

238. CLOSEUP - SONDRA
She slyly glances backward, and a self-conscious smile covers her face.

239. MED. SHOT
As a child from the ranks breaks and comes to Sondra, who leans down to listen to the child - who whispers in her ear. Sondra, murmuring, "Of course, dear" and still waving her baton is, for the moment, uncertain what to do. Then turning to Conway, holds out the baton to him.

SONDRA
Do you mind?

Conway snaps out of his reverie and jumps forward.

CONWAY
Not at all.

He takes the baton from her.

SONDRA
Thank you.

And, taking the child by the hand, she exits.

240. CLOSE SHOT - CONWAY
Conducting the chorus in all seriousness - albeit a trifle awkwardly. He turns his head to watch Sondra, and when he looks forward again, finds himself off-beat. To cover his embarrassment, he smiles foolishly.

241. MED. SHOT
They come to the end of the song, but Conway, whose eyes are searching for Sondra, is oblivious of this and continues to conduct mechanically. The children break into laughter.

242. MED. CLOSE TRUCKING SHOT
With Sondra as she returns with the child clinging to her. As she turns a bend, she looks up, surprised.

243. CLOSE SHOT - SONDRA
As she laughs heartily.

244. CLOSE SHOT - CONWAY

CONWAY
All right, children. Now teacher is going to be very busy this afternoon, so school's dismissed!

The children break into squeals and race off. THE CAMERA FOLLOWS THEM as they cross a footbridge, gleefully doff their clothes and with yelps and cries leap into a stream.

245. MED. SHOT - CONWAY AND SONDRA
Favoring Conway.

CONWAY
Oh, please. I hope you're not going to run away this time.

SONDRA
(extending her hand)
My name's Sondra.

CONWAY
I hope you'll forgive me for--

He hears curious, fluttering music coming from somewhere.

CONWAY
(looking around)
You know, each time I see you, I hear that music. What is it?

SONDRA
Oh, you mean my pigeons.

THE CAMERA SHOWS PIGEONS swirling overhead.

Sondra pulls a miniature flute from one of her pocket.

SONDRA
(showing him)
It's these little flutes that I attached to their tails. See? Come along with me, and I'll show you how I put them on.

They exit scene.

INT. PIGEON HOUSE

246. MED. CLOSE SHOT
Of a large coop where pigeons are bred and raised. The pigeons flutter around, landing on Sondra and Conway, as she shows him her collection with pride. She grabs one pigeon and ties one of the miniature flutes to its legs.

SONDRA
You see, this is how we tie them on. And by varying the size of the flutes, I can get any notes I wish. The wind does the rest. Here's a little fellow who lost his!

She grabs another pigeon, ties a flute to its legs.

CONWAY
(wonderingly)
Was this your idea?

SONDRA
Yes. Hold this pigeon.

CONWAY
You suggested my being brought here, didn't you? What gave you the idea I'd fit in?

SONDRA
That was easy. I read your books.

CONWAY
Oh, you've read my books. You do more things! What have my books got to do with it?

SONDRA
I saw a man whose life was empty.

CONWAY
A man whose life was empty!

SONDRA
Oh, I know. It was full of this and full of that. But you were accomplishing nothing. You were going nowhere, and you knew it.

Conway scrutinizes her face intently.

SONDRA
As a matter of fact, all I saw was a little boy whistling in the dark.

CONWAY
A little boy whistling in the dark!? Do you realize that there is a British cruiser waiting at Shanghai, smoke pouring out of its funnels, tugging at its moorings, waiting to take Mr. Conway back to London? Do you know that at this minute there are headlines shrieking all over the world the news that Conway is missing? Does that look like a man whose life is empty?

SONDRA
(after a pause)
Yes.

CONWAY
(good-naturedly)
You're absolutely right. And I had to come all the way to a pigeon house in Shangri-La to find the only other person in the world who knew it. May I congratulate you?

She laughs merrily and shakes his hand.

SONDRA
I really only brought you here to show you my pigeons!

CONWAY
Don't worry about the pigeons. From now on, you can put flutes on my tail and bells on my feet!

She turns to leave, and he follows, exiting scene.

DISSOLVE TO:

<u>EXT. SOMEWHERE ON TOP OF A HILL</u>

247. MEDIUM TRUCKING SHOT
Sondra and Conway, walking. This spot is on top of a hill overlooking the splendor of the valley below.

248. CLOSER TRUCKING SHOT
They walk along silently for a few seconds, while Conway studies her face speculatively.

CONWAY
There are so many questions I'd like to ask you, I hardly know where to begin.

SONDRA
I'll help you. To begin with, you'd like to know what I'm doing here. Whether I was born here.

CONWAY
Thank you.

SONDRA
Well, I was <u>almost</u> born here. It took place in that wild country beyond the pass. My father and mother were in a party of explorers who got lost and wandered around for a year. When Chang found us, only Father and I were alive. But he was too weak to climb the pass. He died on the way. I was brought up here by Father Perrault himself.

CONWAY
Father Perrault! I envy you. I talked to him last night.

SONDRA
Yes, I know.

CONWAY
Father Perrault. Of course I can't quite get used to this age thing.

He steals a sideways glance at her. She is greatly amused.

SONDRA
(satisfying his obvious curiosity)
I'm thirty.

CONWAY
Oh, you're going to make life very simple.

249. MED. SHOT
As they arrive at a scenic overlook. It is getting toward dusk.

CONWAY
(wonderingly)
It's inconceivable.

SONDRA
What is?

CONWAY
All of it. Father Perrault and his magnificent history. This place, hidden away from the rest of the world, with its glorious concepts, and now you come along and confuse me entirely.

SONDRA
I'm sorry. I thought I was to be the light. But why do I confuse you? Am I so strange?

CONWAY
On the contrary, you're not strange. And that in itself is confusing. I have the same idea about Shangri-La. The sense that I've been here before, that I belong here.

SONDRA
I'm so glad.

CONWAY
I can't quite explain it, but everything is somehow familiar. The very air that I breathe. The Lamasery, with its feet rooted in the good earth of this fertile valley, while its head explores the eternal. All the beautiful things I see, these cherry blossoms, you - all somehow familiar.
(chuckles to himself)
I've been kidnapped and brought here against my will. A crime, a great crime, yet I accept it amiably, with the same warm amiability one tolerates only from a very dear and close friend. Why? Can you tell me why?

SONDRA
Perhaps because you've always been a part of Shangri-La without knowing it.

CONWAY
I wonder.

SONDRA
I'm sure of it. Just as I'm sure there's a wish for Shangri-La in everyone's heart. I have never seen the outside world. But I understand there are millions and millions of people who are supposed to be mean and greedy. Yet I just know that secretly they are all hoping to find a garden spot where there is peace and security, where there's beauty and comfort, where they wouldn't have to be mean and greedy. Oh, I just wish the whole world might come to this valley.

CONWAY
Then it wouldn't be a garden spot for long.

She laughs as they exit scene.

EXT. SOMEWHERE IN SHANGRI-LA[14]
250. TRUCKING SHOT
Barnard is bringing a reluctant Lovett along on an excursion into the Valley. They pass friendly natives and farmers at work.

LOVETT
I don't know why I associate with you, Mr. Barnard - or Mr. Chalmers Bryant - or Mr. Embezzler - or whatever your name may be.

BARNARD
Just call me Barney.

LOVETT
Barney? Why should I? Never! We have nothing in common. Hmmpf, Barney! What effrontery!

BARNARD
Okay, Lovey.

LOVETT
And this trip to the valley. I can't imagine why I'd allow you to drag me down here. Why, we don't know anything about these people. We're not even armed!

BARNARD
They're very nice people - except that they've got horns.

LOVETT
(alarmed at first)
Horns?

Barnard points to sheepherders with their long horns.

BARNARD
(chuckles)
Yeah. You know.

LOVETT
Horns? What kind of horns?

Lovett sees his point, starts to chuckle, but still looks wary.

BARNARD
Here, here! Come on. They won't hurt you.

DISSOLVE TO:

EXT. A WATERFALL
251. MEDIUM SHOT
Barnard has encountered some beautiful native girls, and they have surrounded him with their hospitality - plying him with wine and food. Lovett is off scene.

BARNARD
Okay, honey, all I want is a glass of wine! Thanks very much.

NATIVE GIRL
Please sit down.

BARNARD
This is fine. This is swell. No, just a drink. I've been walking and I'm a little thirsty, you see? That's all right. I don't just happen to be very hungry. Say look, all I asked for was a glass of water. Look here, I've got to have some help with this.
(looking around anxiously)
Now, Lovey! Where is Lovey?

252. CLOSE SHOT
Of Lovett, lagging behind and missing out on all the fun.

LOVETT
Mr. Barnard?

253. MEDIUM SHOT
Favoring Barnard as Lovett comes into view.

BARNARD
Hey Lovey, come here! Lovey, I asked for a glass of wine and look what I got. Come on, sit down.

LOVETT
So that's where you are. I might of known it. No wonder you couldn't hear me.

BARNARD
You were asked to have a glass of wine. Sit down!

LOVETT
And be poisoned out here in the open?

BARNARD
Certainly not!

NATIVE GIRL
(to Lovett)
For me, won't you please have a glass of wine?

LOVETT
I never drink wine in the daytime.

BARNARD
(as he is poured a glass anyway)
There you are!

LOVETT
(raising the glass to his lips)
This doesn't obligate me in any way.

NATIVE GIRL
No.

DISSOLVE TO:

EXT. A CLEARING

254. FULL SHOT
A merry Lovett has had too much to drink. Now he is entertaining a group of native children, who are huddled at his feet. Other natives watch the entertainment. Bernard, watching from one side, is losing patience.

LOVETT
--then the bears came right into the bedroom and the little baby bear said, "Oh, somebody's been sleeping in my bed." And then the mama bear said, "Oh dear, somebody's been sleeping in my bed!" And then the big papa bear, he roared, "And somebody's been sleeping in my bed!" Well, you have to admit the poor little bears were in a quandary!

BARNARD
I'm going to sleep in my bed. Come on, Lovey!

LOVETT
(continuing)
They were in a quandary, and--

BARNARD
Come on, Lovey.

LOVETT
Why? Why 'come on' all the time? What's the matter? Are you going to be a fuss budget all your life? Here, drink it up! Aren't you having any fun? Where was I?

BARNARD
In a quandary.

They all laugh.

LOVETT
I'm telling this story! I'm telling it.
(continuing)
Yes, the poor little bears didn't know what to do, you see, because somebody had been sleeping in their bed.

A CHILD IN THE AUDIENCE
Who slept in their beds?

NATIVE GIRL
(the one who poured him a drink of wine--alluringly)
Who was it, Lovey?

LOVETT
(smitten)
Oh, you call me Lovey, eh?
(to Barnard)
Look at those eyes? There's the devil in those eyes!

DISSOLVE TO:

INT. LOVETT'S BEDROOM
255. CLOSE SHOT
Following Lovett as he enters, unusually chipper, singing "Here we go gathering nuts in May ... " He is in such a good mood that he improvises the lyrics, putting Shangri-La in with his la-la-las. After glancing out the window, Lovett sits down and pulls out his journal. He writes:

INSERT:

APRIL 4TH
24TH DAY AT SHANGRI-LA. FEEL SO GOOD I COULD SOW A WILD OAT--

He pauses, looks up, opens the compact box at his side and looks at himself confidently and admiringly in the mirror. Returning to his journal, he adds:

INSERT:

--OR TWO.

EXT. GARDEN - DAY
256. MED. SHOT (MOVING)
With George as he disconsolately walks. He is startled by the sound of Maria's voice calling him. CAMERA PANS with him as he crosses to a sheltered spot where Maria sits on a garden bench.

GEORGE
Hello, Maria.

He fumbles for a cigarette.

257. MED. CLOSE SHOT

MARIA
(a little hurt)
You promised to come for tea yesterday. I waited for so long.

GEORGE
I'm sorry.
(chagrined to discover he has no cigarettes left)
I haven't even got any cigarettes left!

MARIA
I'll make some for you!
(pleading)
You will come today?

GEORGE
(after a pause)
Perhaps.

MARIA
(tenderly)
Please say you will. The days are so very long and lonely without you.
(a whisper)
Please ...

GEORGE
All right, I'll be there.

MARIA
(happily)
Thank you.

GEORGE
(suddenly)
You'll tell me some of the things I want to know, won't you? You'll tell me who runs this place. And why we were kidnapped. And what they're going to do with us!

258. CLOSEUP - MARIA
From the moment he starts to speak, her face clouds. George's voice continues without interruption.

GEORGE'S VOICE
Chang's been lying about those porters, hasn't he?

She runs off, frightened.

INT. ELSEWHERE IN THE GARDEN
259. MED. CLOSE SHOT
Following Conway and Sondra as they stroll peacefully hand in hand amongst the sculpted shrubbery and rows of flowers. There is a sudden pealing of bells. The two of them look off and pause, their gaze momentarily captured by picturesque snowcapped peaks in the distance.

CONWAY
(moved)
Beautiful! I'm waiting for the bump.

SONDRA
Bump?

CONWAY
When the plane lands at Shangri-La and wakes us all up.

She gives him a pinch.

CONWAY
Ouch!

SONDRA
(chuckling)
You see, it's not a dream.

CONWAY
You know, sometimes I think that it's the other that's the dream. The outside world. Have you never wanted to go there?

SONDRA
Goodness, no. From what you tell me about it, it certainly doesn't sound very attractive.

CONWAY
It's not so bad, really. Some phases are a little sordid, of course. That's only to be expected.

SONDRA
Why?

CONWAY
Oh, the usual reasons. A world full of people struggling for existence.

SONDRA
Struggling, why?

CONWAY
Well, everybody naturally wants to make a place for himself, accumulate a nest egg, and so on.

SONDRA
Why?

CONWAY
You know, if you keep on asking that, we're not going to get anywhere. And don't ask me why.

SONDRA
I was just going to.

CONWAY
It's the most annoying word in the English language. Did you ever hear a child torture his parent with it?

(mimicking)
Mother's little darling musn't stick her fingers in the salad bowl. Why? Because it isn't lady-like to do that. Why? Because that's what forks are made for, darling.

SONDRA
(joining in)
Why, mother?

CONWAY
Because mother read it in a book somewhere, and if mother's little darling doesn't take her fingers out of the salad bowl this instant, mother's going to wring her little neck.

Sondra laughs heartily.

SONDRA
(teasingly)
Would you like to wring my little neck?

CONWAY
I'd love it!

SONDRA
Why?

Conway makes a grab for her and she spurts away. He chases her across part of the garden, and past the fountain catches up with her. He reaches to place his hands around her neck.

SONDRA
(laughing)
I'm sorry. I'm very sorry.

He hesitates, studying her intently.

260. CLOSE-UP
They kiss.

SONDRA
(when they break)
I've thought about it for years.
(softly)
I knew you'd come. And I knew if you did - you'd never leave.
(a whisper)
Am I forgiven for sending for you?

CONWAY
Forgiven.
(a pause)
You know, when we were on that plane, I was fascinated by the way its shadow followed it. That silly shadow racing along over mountains and valleys, covering ten times the distance of the plane. It was always there to greet us with outstretched arms when we landed. And I've been thinking that somehow you're that plane, and I'm that silly shadow. That all my life I've been rushing up and down hills, leaping rivers, crashing over obstacles, never dreaming that one day that beautiful thing in flight would land on this earth and into my arms.

They kiss again.

DISSOLVE TO:

INT. LIVING ROOM
261. MEDIUM SHOT
Chang is being visited by Lovett, who has lost his petrified manner.

LOVETT
Amazing, Mr. Chang. This place is amazing! And that marble quarry in the valley is simply magnificent. Oh, I've looked around. I've seen everything. Your woodworkers and your clothweavers - they all seem so very, very happy.

CHANG
Yes.

LOVETT
You may not know it, Mr. Chang, but right here you have Utopia.[15]

CHANG
You've very kind Mr. Lovett.

262. CLOSE SHOT - THE TWO

LOVETT
I don't mean it in that sense. I only give credit where credit is due.
(pauses - sincerely)
Er, Mr. Chang, I'm very anxious to have you realize that I never for a moment believed that ridiculous kidnapping story.

CHANG
Oh, I'm so glad.

LOVETT
Simply preposterous. Do you know what I did last night? Last night, Mr. Chang, I held a sort of a self-inventory. I said to myself last night, Mr. Chang, I said, "Lovey"--
(catches himself - looks around)
Mr. Lovett! "Mr. Lovett," I said, "you are an ungrateful fool ... "

CHANG
Why, no.

LOVETT
"Ungrateful fool ...!" Those were my very words to myself last night. "Here are these people in Shangri-La doing everything in their power to make our stay comfortable and happy and I haven't done one single thing to show my appreciation."

CHANG
Now, what would you like to do?

LOVETT
Well, Mr. Chang, I thought, with your permission of course, and while I'm waiting for these porters, I would like to organize classes for those children in the valley and teach them something practical and something useful. Geology.

CHANG
Splendid!

LOVETT
Isn't it? Isn't it! You know I was a professor for twenty years? - and a very good one.

CHANG
I'm sure you were. When would you like to start?

LOVETT
Oh, immediately.

CHANG
(offering his handshake)
Then it's done.

LOVETT
Oh, thank you. Thank you!

CHANG
Thank you.

<u>EXTERIOR GARDEN</u>
263. MEDIUM SHOT
Conway sits on a bench - Barnard leans over him, showing him a map - a-twitter with an idea.

BARNARD
You see? You get the idea? From this reservoir here I can pipe in the whole works. Oh, I'm going to get a great kick out of this. Of course it's just to keep my hand in, but with the equipment we have here, I can put a plumbing system in for the whole village down there. Can rig it up in no time.
(aghast)
Do you realize those poor people are still going to the well for water?

264. CLOSER SHOT - THE TWO

CONWAY
(a twinkle in his eye)
It's unbelievable.

BARNARD
Think of it! In times like these.

CONWAY
Say, what about that gold deal?

BARNARD
Huh?

CONWAY
Gold. You were going to--

BARNARD
(interrupting)
Oh - that! That can wait. Nobody's going to run off with it.
(full of business)
Say, I've got to get busy. I want to show this whole layout to Chang.
(exiting)
So long. Don't you take any wooden nickels.

CONWAY
All right.

He disappears. We hear him whistling, something joyous. Probably "The Old Gray Mare Ain't What She Usta Be"--

265. CLOSEUP - CONWAY
As he watches Barnard go, pleased at the metamorphosis that's taking place in him. Suddenly he sees George and jumps up.

CONWAY
George.

266. MED. LONG SHOT
From Conway's angle. George has just made his appearance.

CONWAY
George!

George keeps on going and Conway runs toward him.

267. MED. CLOSE SHOT
As Conway catches up to George--and takes him by the arm.

CONWAY
(sincerely)
George - you're behaving like a child. You haven't opened your mouth in two weeks.

GEORGE
(coldly)
I don't see that there's anything to say.

And releasing his arm, he leaves Conway abruptly.

268. CLOSEUP - CONWAY
As a look of deep pain comes into his face. He stands for several seconds - looking helplessly - and despairingly in George's direction.

FADE OUT:

FADE IN

INT. LIVING ROOM
269. MEDIUM SHOT
Chang and Conway playing chess. Conway leans over the board, a faraway expression on his face. Chang leans over - moves a 'man' into position.

CHANG
I'm afraid that does it.

Conway looks up - aroused from his reverie. He glances over the board.

CONWAY
Yes. I'm afraid it does.

CHANG
Shall we have another?

CONWAY
(rises)
No thanks. Not tonight if you don't mind.

He crosses to a window and glances out. Chang looks up and sees Maria in doorway.

CHANG
Come in, my dear.

270. CLOSE SHOT - MARIA
In doorway. She seems slightly embarrassed.

MARIA
Sorry. I didn't mean to interrupt.
(self-consciously)
I thought Mr. Conway's brother was here.
Excuse me.

She leaves.

271. CLOSE SHOT - CONWAY AND CHANG

CHANG
Charming, isn't she?

CONWAY
Yes, charming.

CHANG
Your brother seems quite fascinated by her.

CONWAY
Why not? She's an attractive young woman.

CHANG
Young? She arrived here in 1888. She was 20 at the time. She was on her way to join her be-trothed - when her carriers lost their way in the mountains. The whole party would have per-ished but for meeting some of our people.

CONWAY
(hands in the air)
Amazing! She still doesn't look over 20. When is she likely to grow old in appearance?

CHANG
Not for years. Shangri-La will keep her youthful indefinitely.

CONWAY
Suppose she should leave it?

CHANG
Leave Shangri-La! That's not likely. You couldn't drive her out.

CONWAY
No, I mean about her appearance. If she should leave the valley - what would happen?

CHANG
Oh, she'd quickly revert in her appearance to her actual age.

CONWAY
(shaking his head)
It's weird.
(a pause)
Chang, how old are you?

CHANG
Age is a limit we impose upon ourselves. You know, each time you Westerners celebrate your birthday, you build another fence around your minds.

They are interrupted by the entrance of George.

GEORGE
(stridently)
Oh, there you are! You're just the man I'm looking for.

272. WIDER ANGLE
As George comes up to them. He is livid with rage. He crosses directly to in front of Chang.

GEORGE
A fine trick! Smart, aren't you? What a pack of lies you told us about those porters! Of course the minute they arrive, we can make arrangements to leave. If they take us. But you knew very well you'd tell them not to!

273. THREE SHOT - FAVORING GEORGE

CHANG
Now, my dear boy. You shouldn't--

GEORGE
(snapping at him)
You've been lying to us ever since we got here! Apparently it's worked with some people. Perhaps it's because they lack the courage to do anything about it. But not me, Chang. You're up against the wrong man. I'll get out of here, if I have to blow this fantastic place into the valley! I'll get out--porters or no porters!

And with this threat, he storms out of the room.

CHANG
You must prevail upon him not to attempt the journey. He could never get through that country alive.

CONWAY
(tensely)
I can't let him go alone. It's suicide!

He exits abruptly. Chang watches him depart, deeply upset.

INT. HIGH LAMA'S CHAMBER
274. MEDIUM SHOT
Conway sits in the same place before the Lama.

LAMA
Yes, of course, your brother is a problem. It was to be expected.

CONWAY
I knew you'd understand. That's why I came to you for help.

LAMA
You must not look to me for help. Your brother is no longer my problem. He is now your problem, Conway.

CONWAY
Mine?

LAMA
Because, my son, I am placing in your hands the future and destiny of Shangri-La.
(pause)
For I am going to die.

There is a pause during which Conway cannot conceal his amazement at this simple statement.

LAMA
I knew my work was done when I first set eyes upon you.

275. CLOSEUP - CONWAY AND LAMA
Conway is too awed and impressed to utter a sound. The High Lama finally resumes.

LAMA
I have waited for you, my son, for a long time. I have sat in this room and seen the faces of newcomers. I have looked into their eyes and heard their voices - always in hope that I might find you. My friend, it is not an arduous task that I bequeath, for our order knows only silken bonds. To be gentle and patient, to care for the riches of the mind, to preside in wisdom, while the storm rages without.

CONWAY
Do you think this will come in my time?

276. MED. CLOSE SHOT - THE TWO

HIGH LAMA
You, my son, will live through the storm. You will preserve the fragrance of our history, and add to it a touch of your own mind. Beyond that, my vision weakens.
(pause - magisterially)
But I see in the great distance a new world starting in the ruins - stirring clumsily - but in hopefulness, seeking its vast and legendary treasures. And they will all be here, my son, hidden behind the mountains in the Valley of the Blue Moon, preserved as if by a miracle.

The voice of the Lama, toward the last, seems to fade out. Conway, thoroughly engrossed, half-consciously waits for it to continue. Following a protracted silence, he slowly turns toward the Lama. A breeze blows through the room, ruffling curtains on the window.

277. CLOSE SHOT - THE HIGH LAMA
From whose face the glow has faded. There is nothing left but a dark-shadowed mask.

278. CLOSEUP - CONWAY
He stares, uncertainly, for a long while, with a slow realization that the High Lama is dead. Quite unaware that he is being moved emotionally, tears well up in his eyes. While still sitting this way, unable to stir, he becomes conscious of activity around him.

279. MEDIUM SHOT
As two servants, unbeckoned, arrive - only to peer, solemn-faced, at the Lama. Then, in intervals of seconds, groups of Lamas, hitherto unseen, enter softly and silently, and gather around the High Lama. We hear indistinguishable murmurs that might or might not be prayers. Conway is only vaguely aware of their presence - and after a few moments, scarcely conscious of what is actuating his movements, he drifts away from the murmuring Lamas, and walks in the direction of the door.

DISSOLVE TO:

INT. BARNARD'S ROOM

280. MEDIUM SHOT
Barnard and Gloria are on their knees on the floor. Before them they have spread a large map or chart. Barnard is enthusiastically outlining his plans.

BARNARD
Look, honey. We run the pipes through here, and we connect with the main water line here.

GLORIA
Pipes? Where are you going to get pipes?

BARNARD
Oh, that's a cinch. I'll show them how to cast pipes out of clay.

This is as far as they get for George at this moment barges in.

GEORGE
There you are! Barnard, you'd better get your things together. We're leaving.

BARNARD
Leaving?

GEORGE
Yes. I've just been talking with the porters. They're going to take us. We've got clothing, food, everything. Come on!

BARNARD
When are you going to start?

GEORGE
Right this very minute! The porters are waiting for us on the plateau. And that Chinaman thought he could stop me. Come along.

BARNARD
I think I'll stick around. I'll leave with the porters on their next trip.

GEORGE
You mean you don't want to go?

BARNARD
Well - I'm--

GEORGE
I see. You're afraid of going to jail, eh?

BARNARD
Well, no. You see, I got this plumbing business--

GEORGE
All right! If you insist on being an idiot, I'm not going to waste time coaxing you.
(to Gloria)
How about you?

BARNARD
Oh, no - you don't want to go yet, honey.
(before she can answer)
She'll stick around too.
(to Gloria)
Is that right?

GLORIA
(beaming)
If you want me to!

BARNARD
Sure - sure. Don't you worry. I'll take care of you.

GEORGE
All right, suit yourself. But just remember you had your chance.

As he starts out, Lovett enters.

GEORGE
How about you? Do you want to go?

LOVETT
Go? Where?

GEORGE
Home. Away from here. I've got porters to take us back.

281. CLOSE TWO SHOT - GEORGE AND LOVETT

LOVETT
Oh, my dear boy, I'm sorry. That's impossible. Why, I have my classes all started.

GEORGE
(irritablY)
I don't care what you've got started. Do you want to go?

LOVETT
Well - no - I think I'd better wait. Yes, yes. I will. I'll wait.

GEORGE
(grumbling as he goes)
You'll wait till you rot!

LOVETT
(glowering after him)
Yes.
(does a double-take)
Barney!

BARNARD
Lovey!

Lovett immediately dismisses George from his mind and his face brightening, he starts toward Barnard and Gloria.

282. MED. CLOSE SHOT
As Lovett joins the two on the floor.

LOVETT
Hello, Gloria.

GLORIA
Hello.

LOVETT
Barney, I've just finished translating one of the most interesting old tablets you can imagine. It told me all about the origin of the Masonic symbols and--

BARNARD
That's swell, Lovey. I want to show you something. Look!

He proudly displays his map.

LOVETT
Oh my, isn't that pretty! What is it?

BARNARD
Plumbing. Everything modern. I'm going to run pipes all through the village--

As all three heads go into a huddle.

INT. CONWAY'S ROOM

283. CLOSE SHOT
Conway stands in front of a window - his arms extended across - peering out moodily. He is watching a solemn and slow-moving procession of torchlight-bearers - the funeral rites of the High Lama - accompanied by cermonial music and drum-beating.

284. LONG SHOT
Shooting over his shoulder.

Getting his view of the magisterial procession.

285. CLOSE SHOT
Conway, as he thoughtfully surveys the surroundings of which he has just become master.

286. CLOSE SHOT - AT DOOR
George appears in the doorway. He looks around and espies Conway. For a moment he stands uncertainly, and finally enters.

GEORGE
(softly)
Bob--

287. MEDIUM SHOT
As Conway turns - and seeing him, evinces no emotion whatsoever.

CONWAY
(a murmur)
Hello, George.

George looks at him peculiarly. Conway's behavior is odd in view of their strained relationship.

GEORGE
Well, you can stop worrying about everything now, Bob. I've made arrangements to leave. If you'll let me close that window, I can talk to you. That noise is driving me crazy.

He closes the window.

GEORGE
I said we're getting out of here. Back to civilization. I made a deal with the porters. They brought in a load of books or something, and they're leaving tomorrow at dawn. They're waiting for us five miles outside the valley. Come on, get your things together. Where's your top coat?

288. CLOSE SHOT - THE TWO

CONWAY
You can't leave, George.

GEORGE
Why not? What's going to stop me?

CONWAY
(pleading)
You mustn't. You've got to stay here now.

GEORGE
(sharply)
Stay here?!
(more softly)
What's the matter with you, Bob? You've been acting strangely ever since we came here.
(no response from Conway)
I've never seen you like this. Why can't we leave? What's stopping us?

Conway combats an impulse to tell him the whole story.

CONWAY
(impulsively)
Something grand and beautiful, George. Something I've been searching for all my life. The answer to the confusion and bewilderment of a lifetime. I've found it, George, and I can't leave it. You mustn't either.

GEORGE
I don't know what you're talking about. You're carrying around a secret that seems to be eating you up. If you'll only tell me about it.

CONWAY
I will, George. I want to tell you. I'll burst with it if I don't. It's weird and fantastical and sometimes unbelievable, but so beautiful!
(pause)
Well, as you know, we were kidnapped and brought here ...

While he is speaking, we slowly

DISSOLVE TO:

289. SAME SCENE:
As Conway is concluding his story.

CONWAY
... And that's the whole story, George. He died as peacefully as the passing of a cloud's shadow. His last words to me were, "I place in your hands, my son, the future and destiny of Shangri-La." Now you know why I can't leave.

George listens to him intently, his face a mask of apprehension. He stares at his brother for some time and finally rises and walks around for a few moments.

GEORGE
(running his hand through his hair)
Well, I - I really don't know what to say. Except that you must be completely mad.

CONWAY
So you think I'm mad?

GEORGE
What else can I think after a tale like that? Good heavens, Bob, things like that don't happen today. We're living in the twentieth century.

CONWAY
So you think it's all nonsense, huh?

290. MED. SHOT - THE TWO

GEORGE
I think you've been hypnotized by a lot of loose-brained fanatics. Why, I wouldn't believe it if I heard it in an English monastery. Why should I swallow it here in Tibet? How do you know the things they told you are true? Did they show you any proof?

CONWAY
I don't need any proof.

GEORGE
(contemptuously)
I knew there was a reason I hated this place. I'd give half my life to fly over it with a load of bombs just for what they've done to you. How do you know the things they told you are true? Did they show you any proof? All this talk about the Lamas being hundreds of years old. How do you know? Did you see their birth certificates?
(some more pacing)
I can't believe it, Bob. A bunch of decrepit old men sit around and dream about reforming the world. And you, Bob Conway - two-feet-on-the-ground Conway - want to join them. It's horrible.

CONWAY
Is that all my story meant to you?

GEORGE
What else could it mean to me? It's obviously a lot of bunk.

CONWAY
Then you'd better go, George. This is no place for you.

GEORGE
It's no place for you, Bob. Think of what's waiting for you. Do you want to stay here until you're half dead? Until your mind starts corroding like the rest of them?

CONWAY
Please, George. I don't want to talk about it anymore.

GEORGE
You've got to talk about it. What about me? You said they stole that plane to bring you here. I didn't want to come. You owe me some responsibility.

CONWAY
I'm tired of owing you things. You're free to go. Go ahead.

GEORGE
(suddenly)
It's that girl - that girl has twisted and turned--

CONWAY
Enough! Never mind the girl!
(a tense moment of silence)
Well, why don't you go?

Conway has sunk into a chair. George kneels before him, pleading.

GEORGE
Look here, Bob, Ever since I can remember, you've looked after me. Now I think you're the one that needs looking after. I'm your brother, Bob. If there's something wrong with you, let me help you.

CONWAY
(a murmur)
Oh, George ...

GEORGE
Besides, I - I don't feel like making that trip alone, Bob.

CONWAY
George, you couldn't possibly stay here, could you?

GEORGE
I'd go mad!

CONWAY
(after a moment's hesitation)
George, I may be wrong, I may be a maniac. But I believe in this, and I'm not going to lose it.
(warmly)
You know how much I want to help you, but this is bigger, stronger if you like than brotherly love. I'm sorry, George. I'm staying.

GEORGE
(after a long pause)
Well, I can't think of anything more to say. Goodbye, Bob.

They shake hands warmly. George turns to leave.

CONWAY
(just as George reaches the door)
George, are you sure of the porters? About their taking care of you, I mean?

GEORGE
(turning back)
Oh yes. It's all set. Maria made the arrangements.

CONWAY
(glances up - surprised)
Maria?

GEORGE
Yes, the little Russian girl.

CONWAY
What's she got to do with it?

GEORGE
She's going with me.

Conway looks his extreme amazement.

CONWAY
(suddenly - wild)
George, you're crazy!

As he says this he jumps to his feet. George is startled by his tone and manner.

CONWAY
(wheeling)
You can't take her away from here!

GEORGE
(confidently)
Why not?

CONWAY
(strongly)
Because you can't. Do you know what will happen to her if she leaves Shangri-La? She's a fragile thing that can only live where fragile things are loved. Take her out of this valley and she'll fade away like an echo.

GEORGE
(slowly)
What do you mean - "fade away like an echo"?

CONWAY
She came here in 1888!

291. CLOSE SHOT - THE TWO
Favoring George. He laughs hollowly. He runs his hand through his hair. He stares unbelievingly at Conway.

GEORGE
This would be funny - if it wasn't so pathetic.
Why, she isn't a day over twenty!

CONWAY
You're wrong, George.

GEORGE
I'm not wrong. She told me so. Besides, she wouldn't have to tell me. I'd know anyway.
(significantly)
I found out a lot of things last night.
(quickly)
I'm not ashamed of it either. It's probably one of the few decent things that's ever happened in this hellish place.

292. MED. CLOSE SHOT - THE TWO
Conway stares at him.

GEORGE
(cynically)
So everyone is serenely happy in Shangri-La? Nobody would ever think of leaving?
(vehemently)
It's all just so much rot! She's pleaded with me ever since I came here to take her away from this awful place. She's cried in my arms for hours, for fear I'd leave her behind. And what's more, she's made two trips to the plateau to bribe the porters - for me!

CONWAY
(doesn't want to believe it)
I don't believe it! I don't believe a word of it!

GEORGE
All right. I'll prove it to you! You believe everything they've told you - without proof! I'll prove my story!

As he speaks he has crossed to door leading to adjoining room. Conway's eyes are glued on him.

GEORGE
Come in a minute.

After a few seconds Maria appears in the doorway and stands there timidly.

GEORGE
Come in.

She steps forward.

293. MED. SHOT - THE THREE

GEORGE
(shrewdly)
I've got some bad news for you, Maria. My brother and I have decided we can't take you along.

Maria's face collapses.

MARIA
(small, frightened voice)
You can't take me?

She rushes to George and throws her arms around him.

MARIA
But you promised me! You promised to take me with you!

Over her shoulder George looks victoriously at Conway, who cannot believe his ears. Suddenly Maria wheels on Conway.

MARIA
It's all your fault! It was all arranged until he spoke to you! Why can't you leave us alone?

CONWAY
Do you mean to tell me you want to leave Shangri-La?

MARIA
I'll die if I have to stay here another minute! I've waited a long time for this chance to go, and you're not going to stop me now. If I have to, I'll go alone. It was I who bribed the porters. If it weren't for me, you'd never get out!

CONWAY
I thought the porters had instructions from the High Lama not to take anyone.

MARIA
The High Lama? Who pays any attention to him? The porters laugh at the High Lama. All they want to know is how much gold he will give them. Well, I gave them more gold. I've been stealing it for a year. I'd do anything to get out of this place. To get away from that High Lama - the one who calls himself Father Perrault! Why, he's been insane for years!

CONWAY
Father Perrault is dead.

MARIA
He's dead? That's fine. You won't see me shedding any tears over him!
(pleading)
Oh George, you must take me with you!

CONWAY
(quietly)
Aren't you afraid to leave? You don't want to look like an old woman, do you?

MARIA
Old woman? Chang told you that, didn't he?

CONWAY
Yes.

MARIA
I thought so! He tells everyone I'm old. He wants them to stay away from me. He can't stand it when anyone comes near. He's punished me for every minute I've spent with George. If it weren't for him, I would have been out of here long ago, but he always stops me. Six months ago, I tried to escape and he locked me in a dark room. I nearly went crazy.
(pause)
Look at me, Mr. Conway, do I look like an old woman? Is this the skin of an old woman? Look into my eyes and see if these are the eyes of an old woman?

GEORGE
She was kidnapped and brought here two years ago just as we were, Bob.

CONWAY
(thrown)
I don't believe it! I can't believe it. She's lying.
(wildly)
You're lying. You're lying! Every word you've been saying is a lie! Come on, say it!

He has backed her into a corner and is nearly throttling her.

CONWAY
You're lying, aren't you?

MARIA
No, Mr. Conway, I'm not lying. What reason could I have for lying? The chances are that we'll never come out of that horrible trip alive, but I'd rather die out there in a snowstorm and be buried alive, than to stay here one more minute now.

Thoroughly disillusioned, Conway emits a few cynical chuckles - shakes his head - stares blankly for a moment.

CONWAY
(dead voice)
You say the porters are waiting for us?

GEORGE
Yes.

CONWAY
The clothes?

GEORGE
(alertly)
Yes, everything!

CONWAY
What about the others?

GEORGE

I've already asked them. They're afraid to make the trip. We'll have to send an expedition back after them.

CONWAY
(business-like)
Come on! We're wasting time!

Conway dashes around and collects his things.

MARIA
Are you taking me?

CONWAY
Yes, of course. Certainly. Come on!

They start out the door and we ...

DISSOLVE TO:

EXT. IN THE GARDEN

294. MED. CLOSE TRUCKING SHOT
Conway, George and Maria on their way out of the main building. The funeral procession continues around them. The two men walk together, Maria behind. George is cheerful and buoyant.

GEORGE
It won't be long now before we're in London. Can't you just see everyone when we pop out of the blue!

Conway's jaw is set grimly.

295. MED. SHOT
As Conway, George and Maria continue.

GEORGE
We'll have them breathless when they hear our story.

While he speaks, Conway turns his head around, looking for a glimpse of Sondra.

296. MEDIUM SHOT - CHANG
As he hurries out of the building and looks out at them from a roof terrace.

297. CLOSE SHOT - MOVING WITH CONWAY
As he continues to look back in Sondra's direction, although he keeps in step with George.

GEORGE'S VOICE
You had me worried for a while. I thought you were gone completely.

Conway turns his head away.

298. THREE SHOT (MOVING)
Conway, George and Maria. George glances up at Conway.

GEORGE
(sincerely - grinning)
Lucky thing for me you snapped out of it, too. You saved my life. I never could have made it alone.

CONWAY
What was that?

GEORGE
I was saying--

CONWAY
Can't you shut up? Must you go on babbling like an idiot?

George looks up, startled.

299. LONG SHOT
Sondra has come running out to stand anxiously beside Chang.

300. MED. CLOSE SHOT
Sondra and Chang.

SONDRA
What's happened? Where's Bob?

CHANG
He's going, my child.

SONDRA
Going?

CHANG
But he will return.

SONDRA
Oh no! No! Bob!

Shouting, she rushes off and the CAMERA FOLLOWS HER as she races down a long flight of stairs, calling out Conway's name.

301. TRUCKING CLOSEUP - SONDRA
As she runs, calling out Conway's name and weeping.

302. A SERIES OF SHOTS
Showing Conway, George and Maria - accompanied by a dozen or more porters - as they approach the mountain opening where they first entered Shangri-La.

303. CLOSEUP - CONWAY
He hesitates at the opening, looks back one more time. His eyes show confusion and defeat. George, ahead, calls out to him to hurry.

304. TRUCKING MEDIUM SHOT - SONDRA
As she stumbles up the trail to the opening, minutes behind. The wind howls on the other side. She cries and weeps, calling out Conway's name, but he can no longer be seen.

DISSOLVE TO:

305. A SERIES OF SHOTS
Which should be a group of portraits - showing the group's seemingly impossible journey back to civilization. These pictures should be accompanied by music in the appropriate mood.

306. NIGHT SHOT
Accompanied by the porters, they trudge laboriously through snow-ridden plains.

DISSOLVE TO:

307. DAY
The whole caravan are seen in the distance, clambering up a mountain-side - hoisted by ropes.

DISSOLVE TO:

308. NIGHT
In the middle of a vast plain. They attempt to put up tents, which proves futile, as a raging snowstorm rips the canvas from its moorings.

DISSOLVE TO:

309. DAY
The large group are seen lowering themselves in single file down a ledge alongside a ravine. The wind howls.

DISSOLVE TO:

310. DAY
A mountain pass somewhere with a hailstorm swiping viciously across their faces. They edge their way pre-cautiously across a narrow ledge. Suddenly the girl loses her bearings - slips - screams - and is caught by Conway just in time to save her from falling down the side of the jagged mountain.

DISSOLVE TO:

311. MED. SHOT - NIGHT
Maria has one arm around George and the other around Conway - limping. She has her head down. They trudge silently. The porters are off in the distance, leaving them behind.

MARIA
(collapsing)
I can't stand it. I can't go on anymore! I've got to rest.

She stumbles and they help her up. George looks off toward the porters helplessly.

MARIA
(hysterical)
How long is this going to go on? I can't stand it, I say.

312. MED. SHOT
Of the porters, laughing at their distress.

313. MED. SHOT - THE THREE

GEORGE
Bob, can't you get them to wait for us? They're leaving us farther behind every day.

CONWAY
There's nothing that would suit them better than to lose us, but we must go on.
(to Maria - gently)
Come on.

MARIA
No, I can't! I can't! You've got to let me rest! You've got to let me rest!

CONWAY
(calling out to the porters)
Hey!

314. MED. SHOT
Of the porters, still laughing. The lead porter whips out a gun and fires at them for sport.

315. MED. SHOT - THE THREE
They are in no danger. The porters are too far off.

GEORGE
(contemptuously)
Target practice again! One of these days they're going to hit us.

CONWAY
(wryly)
As long as they keep on aiming at us, we're safe.
(to Maria)
Come now, child.

They start to move again.

316. MED. SHOT
Of the porters. They are still laughing, and now others have drawn out their guns. Firing off wildly, they trigger an ominous thunder overhead.

317. MED. SHOT - THE THREE
Looking up, they see an avalanche beginning.

318. A SERIES OF SHOTS
Of the avalanche, picking up strength and fury as it crashes downhill, sweeping over the porters and crushing them to death.

319. CLOSE SHOT - THE THREE
An immense silence comes over them. Conway and George can only stare, dazed and frightened. The only sound is Maria, sobbing.

DISSOLVE TO:

320. MEDIUM SHOT - DAY
A scene in which Conway carries the girl on his back. George walks behind. The wind continues to howl.

321. CLOSEUP - GEORGE
Staring at the girl's face as it hangs over Conway's back. Suddenly, his eyes widen.

322. CLOSEUP - MARIA
A distorted view of her. Youth and beauty seem to be vanishing.

323. CLOSEUP - GEORGE
His eyes are glued on her.

GEORGE
(a frightened whisper)
Bob! Bob! Look at her face, Bob! Her face! Look at her face!

DISSOLVE TO:

324. MEDIUM SHOT - NIGHT
On the backs of the two men, who bend over Maria. CAMERA DRAWS BACK as they straighten up. Both stare down aghast at the girl, whom we do not see.

325. ANOTHER ANGLE
To include the girl.

326. MED. SHOT OF THE THREE
The only illumination comes from the moon. We cannot get a clear view of her face. But what we see seems to us to be small, withered and aged. She is dead. The men stare at her intently.

327. CLOSE SHOT - THE TWO MEN
Who watch her, immobile. George looks despairing. Slowly his head turns toward the cliff behind him - and his eyes become alert with an idea. His face lights up with great determination. He lets out a piteous howl, and breaks away, racing out of scene.

Conway turns sharply and is horrified.

CONWAY
George! George!

328. A SERIES OF SHOTS
George stumbling toward the cliff, Conway chasing him. George, falling head over heels, rocking on the edge - then plummeting over, falling down, down into the darkness.

329. WIDER SHOT
Conway, at the end of the cliff, peering starkly downward.

DISSOLVE TO:

330. A SERIES OF SHOTS
As Conway soldiers on, alone, through howling wind and snow.

DISSOLVE TO:

331. MED. SHOT - NIGHT
On Conway, struggling against a cyclonic wind. He tops a rise, stumbles, falls over, and rolls down the mountainside, until finally he comes to a stop, mounded by snow. Slowly, he begins to rise and start again.

DISSOLVE TO:

332. DAWN
As the sun comes up, Conway emerges from the whiteness, feeling his way forward with a walking stick. He walks with the pain and effort of a blind man, and just as he manages to cross a bridge spanning a great chasm, the bridge collapses. He stumbles on.

DISSOLVE TO:

333. DAY
Conway, looking haggard and more dead than alive, stumbles out onto more dry and level terrain. He collapses to the ground.

EXT. NATIVE VILLAGE DAY
334. MEDIUM SHOT
A group of Chinese in front of huts. They look up, see something off and commence shouting excitedly in their native tongue.

335. MEDIUM LONG SHOT
Conway's body from their angle.

DISSOLVE TO:

336. A SERIES OF SHOTS
Newspaper headlines:

"Conway Found Alive in Chinese Mission"

Similar headlines follow. Newsboys hawk bulletin editions to milling crowds. Top-level government dignitaries confer.

FADE OUT:

FADE IN

INT. FOREIGN OFFICE
337. FULL SHOT - OUTER SECTION
CAMERA MOVES FORWARD passing a series of desks and clerks until it reaches a clerk who is opening several cablegrams. Finally he comes to one which causes his eyes to pop. Muttering something under his breath which sounds like "Good heavens!" - and without taking his eyes off the cablegram, he rises and starts away.

338. MED. TRUCKING SHOT - CLERK
As he strides across to the end of the outer office - to a glass-panelled door upon which we read "ASSISTANT TO THE FOREIGN SECRETARY" - through which he disappears.

INT. OFFICE OF ASSISTANT
339. FULL SHOT
As the clerk enters, full of excitement.

CLERK
Cable from Gainsford.

ASSISTANT SECRETARY
Oh, read it!

CLERK
(reading)
"Leaving today for London with Conway aboard S.S. Manchuria. Conway can tell nothing of his experiences. Is suffering from complete loss of memory. Signed, Gainsford."

ONE OF THE OTHERS IN THE ROOM
Loss of memory?

ASSISTANT SECRETARY
All right, give it to the press.

CLERK
All of it?

ASSISTANT SECRETARY
Yes. Might as well - all of it.

CLERK
Yes, sir.

ASSISTANT SECRETARY
I'll dispatch a convoy to meet him.

340. A SERIES OF SHOTS
More newspaper headlines reporting that Conway has amnesia and other details of his homeward journey.

FADE OUT:

FADE IN

INT. OFFICE OF ASSISTANT
341. FULL SHOT
Another clerk enters with haste, bearing another cablegram.

CLERK
Conway's gone again! Run out! Listen to this! From Gainsford.

ASSISTANT SECRETARY
Let me have it.
(takes it and reads aloud)
"Aboard the S.S. Manchuria. Last night Conway seemed to recover his memory. Kept talking about Shangri-La, telling a fantastic story about a place in Tibet. Insisted upon returning there at once. Locked him in room but he escaped us and jumped ship during night at Singapore. Am leaving ship myself to overtake him, as fearful of his condition. Wrote down details of Conway's story about Shangri-La which I am forwarding. Lord Gainsford."

342. A SERIES OF SHOTS
More newspaper headlines indicating Gainsford has abandoned his pursuit of Conway and returned to London.

FADE OUT:

FADE IN

INT. A GRILL ROOM OF A FASHIONABLE CLUB

343. FULL SHOT
A scattering of men are present - some at the bar - others at tables.

344. MED. SHOT IN A BOOTH
Several men are seated.

CARSTAIRS
(looking off)
Here's Gainsford now.

They all look off.

345. LONG SHOT
From their view. We see Gainsford standing in the doorway, looking around. He spies them and starts forward.

346. MEDIUM SHOT
As Gainsford arrives at the booth. The men rise with extended hands.

AD-LIB
Well, it's good to see you back, Lord Gainsford! Thought you were never coming.

MEEKER
Will you have a drink? Sit down.

347. MED. CLOSE SHOT AT TABLE
As Gainsford shakes hands with them, and sits down.

GAINSFORD
Yes. Scotch and soda. I'm parched.

ROBERTSON
Here you are, ready and waiting.

He pushes on in front of him.

CARSTAIRS
We're most eager to know what you've discovered.

AD-LIB
Any news of Conway?
Where is he?
Did you bring him back?

All this is said as Gainsford drains his glass.

GAINSFORD
(setting glass down)
Gentlemen, you see before you a very weary old man, who has just ended a chase that lasted nearly ten months.

MEEKER
Do you mean to tell me you never caught up with him?

GAINSFORD
Since that night that he jumped off the ship until two weeks ago, I've been missing him by inches.

WYNANT
You don't mean it!

AD-LIB
Think of it!

ROBERTSON
He was as determined as that to get back?

GAINSFORD
Determined! Gentlemen, in the whole course of my life, I have never encountered anything so grim. During these last ten months, that man has done the most astounding things. He learned how to fly, stole an army plane and got caught, put into jail, escaped ... all in an amazingly short space of time. But this was only the beginning of his adventures.
(leaning forward)
He begged, cajoled, fought, always pushing forward to the Tibetan frontier. Everywhere I went, I heard the most amazing stories of the man's adventures. Positively astounding. Until eventually, I trailed him to the most extreme outpost in Tibet.

348. CLOSE GROUP SHOT
Favoring the other men, as Gainsford continues.

GAINSFORD
Of course he had already gone. But his memory - ah - his memory will live with those natives for the rest of their lives. The Man Who Was Not Human, they called him. They'll never forget the devil-eyed stranger who six times tried to go over a mountain pass where no other human being dared to travel, and six times was forced back by the severest storms. They'll never forget the madman who stole their food and clothing - whom they locked up in their barracks - but who fought six of their guards to escape.

349. MED. CLOSE GROUP SHOT
Gainsford still continues.

GAINSFORD
Why, their soldiers are still talking about their pursuit to overtake him, and shuddering at the memory. He led them the wildest chase through their own country, and finally he disappeared over that very mountain pass that they themselves dared not travel.
(takes a drink)
And that, gentlemen, was the last that any known human being saw of Robert Conway.

WYNANT
Think of it!

CARSTAIRS
By jove, that's what I call fortitude!

ROBERTSON
Tell me something, Gainsford. What do you think of his talk about Shangri-La? Do you believe it?

GAINSFORD
(thinks a moment)
Yes - yes, I believe it.
(sincerely)
I believe it, because I _want_ to believe it.

They all watch his face, impressed by his tone.

350. CLOSE SHOT - GAINSFORD
As he lifts his glass.

GAINSFORD
Gentlemen, I give you a toast. Here is my hope that Robert Conway will find his Shangri-La!

351. CLOSE GROUP SHOT
They all raise their glasses.

GAINSFORD
(softly)
Here is my hope that we _all_ find our Shangri-La.

They are all impressed by the sincerity in his voice - and as their glasses come together - CAMERA MOVES UP TO A CLOSEUP OF THEM and as the music starts - the picture

DISSOLVES TO:

EXT. SOMEWHERE IN TIBET - NIGHT
352. CLOSEUP
MOVING IN FRONT OF CONWAY - as he walks forward with a steady step - his head held high - his eyes sparkling - snow pelting his face.

353. LONG SHOT
Over his silhouetted back.

As he walks away from the CAMERA, and we STAY WITH HIM a long time as he approaches a hill.

DISSOLVE TO:

354. ANOTHER LONG SHOT
He has now ascended to the middle of the steep hill - his gait unchanged. THE CAMERA PANS UP to the summit of the incline - and we see that beyond it the horizon is filled with a strange warm light. Conway's figure - in silhouette - disappears over the hill - bells ring - and as the music begins to swell[16]

FADE OUT.

THE END

Notes

1. Up until the final draft of March 23, 1936, the film script began with a scene in which a cable is received by the Foreign Secretary, bringing the news that Conway has been found alive aboard the S.S. Manchuria. Then there ensued a long sequence aboard the steamer with Gainsford and his friends (who reappear in the last sequence in the film) and an amnesiac Conway. There is a shipboard concert after which Conway sits down at the piano and plays a musical piece which he says was composed by Chopin, although there is no record of such a piece. Against all logic he insists it was taught to him by one of Chopin's pupils. He becomes agitated and begins to murmur the name "Shangri-La," as memory comes flooding back. As he starts to tell Gainsford about the night at Baskul when it all began, the story unfolds in flashback. This frame-flashback appears to have been filmed, fell victim to severe cuts after the early audience previews, and is not represented in the "restored" *Lost Horizon.*

2. A "blighter" is a mild British expletive for someone held in low esteem.

3. The only explanation for the meaning of "Freshie" occurs in the frame-flashback of the script, the prelude that was cut from the final film, when Conway reminds Gainsford that his brother George is affectionately nicknamed "The Freshman." You will notice that this term of endearment, offered a couple of times in the establishing scenes, disappears thereafter from the script.

4. In other words, Lovett possesses a bone from the region between the lowest rib and pelvis of a large extinct ground sloth of the family Megatheriidae.

5. This sounds like "You can't expect a man to steer around in the dark" but is represented in the continuity transcript as "sail around in the dark."

6. A "Douglas plane" was an aircraft made by Douglas Aircraft of Santa Monica, California. The twin-engined plane shown in *Lost Horizon* is probably a DC-4, the four-engined version of the DC-3, which was otherwise referred to, especially by Britishers, as "the Dakota."

7. "Living on velvet" was common vernacular. "Velvet" means a net profit or money in excess of what is expected; it signifies, in this context, living on unexpected or borrowed time.

8. The phrase "Chinaman's chance," meaning extremely poor odds, seems an inappropriate choice of words here. It derives from the California gold rush of 1849, when Chinese worked inferior or abandoned prospector sites in hopes of mining gold; continued use of the phrase reflects anti-Chinese prejudice in modern society.

Riskin the humanist was sometimes insensitive to racial differences. In the *Lost Horizon* script, the Chinese in crowd scenes are sometimes referred to as "coolies," which distinctly denigrates them as unskilled laborers. In *Meet John Doe,* Willoughby makes an ill-considered remark, in the scene where he informs Ann Mitchell that he has dreamed about her getting married. She passes his dream off "lightly," according to the script, saying the groom was probably "a tall, handsome Ubangi," that is, a Central African native. "No, not that bad," Willoughby replies.

9. This scene between Gloria and Chang was the first of several major expository scenes cut by Capra from the final film and later reconstructed for the "restored" *Lost Horizon.* Although deleted from theatrical prints in 1937, Chang's reference to Gloria in the next sequence ("She's remaining in her room. She isn't feeling well.") nonetheless preserved the continuity without obvious gaps.

10. This scene between Barnard and Gloria, deemed expendable by Capra, was missing in the final film and reconstructed for the "restored" *Lost Horizon.* The character of Gloria probably suffered the most loss of screen time when the cuts were made.

11. This is a glancing reference to the evil Mr. Hyde, the opposite side of the good Dr. Jekyll, from Robert Louis Stevenson's 1886 classic novel, *The Strange Case of Dr. Jekyll and Mr. Hyde.*

12. A "slew-foot" is awkward or clumsy—a stumblebum.

13. This long scene between Conway and the High Lama was condensed and abbreviated in the final film, then restored to its original length in the 1977 re-release of *Lost Horizon.*

14. This scene between Lovett and Barnard, from their excursion into the Valley extending into the recitation of the Three Bears, was dropped from the final film and reconstructed for the "restored" *Lost Horizon.*

15. The original Utopia, it is worth remembering, was a Pacific island called "Nowhere," imagined by Sir Thomas More to be an idyllic place, governed according to the ideals of English humanism. It provided a stark contrast with the socially diseased state of sixteenth-century Britain.

16. The last line of dialogue from the transcript prepared for New York State censors indicates that the final shot in the first released version of the *Lost Horizon* was of Sondra, waiting for Conway, on the mountain top:

SONDRA
It's he. It's Mr. Conway! Go! Tell Chang!
Bob! Bob!

This was cut after opening engagements and is missing from today's video versions, including the "restored" version of *Lost Horizon.*

Curtain call: on the set of *Meet John Doe* are an unidentified person, James Gleason, Barbara Stanwyck, Robert Riskin, Frank Capra, Gary Cooper, Walter Brennan, and Spring Byington.

Meet John Doe

Warner Brothers, 1941, 125 minutes

Produced and directed by Frank Capra

Written by Robert Riskin, based on a story
by Richard Connell and Robert Presnell

Photography by George Barnes

Music by Dimitri Tiomkin

Edited by Daniel Mandell

Musical direction by by Leo F. Forbstein

Art direction by Stephen Gooson

Gowns by Natalie Visart

Special effects by Jack Cosgrove

Cast: Gary Cooper (*Long John Willoughby*), Barbara Stanwyck (*Ann Mitchell*), Edward Arnold (*D. B. Norton*), Walter Brennan (*The Colonel*), Spring Byington (*Mrs. Mitchell*), James Gleason (*Henry Connell*), Gene Lockhart (*Mayor Lovett*), Rod La Rocque (*Ted Sheldon*), Irving Bacon (*Beany*), Regis Toomey (*Bert Hanson*), Ann Doran (*Mrs. Hanson*), J. Farrell MacDonald (*Sourpuss Smithers*), Warren Hymer (*Angelface*), Harry Holman (*Mayor Hawkins*), Andrew Tombes (*Spencer*), Pierre Watkin (*Mannett*), Stanley Andrews (*Bennett*), Charles C. Wilson (*Charlie Dawson*), Vaughn Glaser (*Governor*), Sterling Holloway (*Dan*), Mike Frankovich, Knox Manning, Selmer Jackson, John B. Hughes (*Radio Announcers*), Pop Dwyer (*Aldrich Bowker*), Mrs. Brewster

(*Mrs. Gardner Crane*), Pat Flaherty (*Mike*), Carlotta Jelm, Tina Thayer (*Ann's Sisters*), Bennie Bartlett (*Red, Office Boy*), Sarah Edwards (*Mrs. Hawkins*), Edward Earle (*Radio M.C.*), James McNamara (*Sheriff*), Emma Tansey (*Mrs. Delaney*), Frank Austin (*Grubbel*), Edward Keane (*Relief Administrator*), Lafe McKee (*Mr. Delaney*), Edward McWade (*Joe, Newsman*), Guy Usher (*Bixler*), Walter Soderling (*Barrington*), Edmund Cobb (*Policeman*), Billy Curtis (*Midget*), Johnny Fern (*Lady Midget*), John Hamilton (*Jim, Governor's Associate*), William Forrest (*Governor's Associate*), Charles K. French (*Fired Reporter*), Edward Hearn (*Mayor's Secretary*), Bess Flowers (*Newspaper Secretary*), Hank Mann (*Ed, A Photographer*), James Millican (*Photographer*), The Hall Johnson Choir.

MEET JOHN DOE

Ext. Bulletin Office - Sidewalk.

Close-up: Of a time-worn plaque against the side of a building. It reads:

THE BULLETIN
"A free press for a free people."

While we read this, a pair of hands come in holding pneumatic chisel which immediately attacks the sign. As the lettering is being obliterated,

Dissolve to: Close-up: A new plaque on which the lettering has been changed to:

THE NEW BULLETIN
"A streamlined newspaper for a streamlined era."

Cut to: Int. Bulletin outer office. Full shot: Of a mid-western newspaper office.

Med. shot: At a door at which a sign-painter works. He is painting HENRY CONNELL's name on the door. It opens and a flip office boy emerges. The painter has to wait until the door closes in order to resume his work.

Full shot: Of the outer office. The activity of the office seems to suddenly cease, as all eyes are centered on the office boy.

Med. shot--panning: With the office boy--who has a small sheet of paper in his hand. He walks jauntily to a desk, refers to his paper, points his finger to a woman, emits a short whistle through his teeth, runs a finger across his throat and jerks his thumb toward managing editor's office. The woman stares starkly at him while her immediate neighbors look on with sympathy. The office boy now goes through the same procedure with several other people. All watch him, terror written in their eyes.

Med. shot: Toward CONNELL's office door where painter works. It opens and three people emerge. Two men and a girl. The girl is young and pretty. All three look dourful. The painter again has to wait for the door to shut before resuming his work. The two men exit. The girl suddenly stops.

Close shot: Of the girl. Her name is ANN MITCHELL. She stands, thinking, and then suddenly, impulsively, wheels around. Camera pans with her as she returns to CONNELL's office door, flings it open and disappears. The painter remains poised with his brush, waiting for the door to swing back. There is a slight flash of resentment in his eyes.

Int. CONNELL's office. Full shot: CONNELL is behind his desk on which is a tray of sandwiches and a glass of milk, half gone. Near him sits POP DWYER, another veteran newspaperman. ANN crosses to CONNELL's desk.

CONNELL
(on phone)
Yeh, D. B. Oh, just cleaning out the deadwood. Okay.

ANN
(supplicatingly)
Look, Mr. Connell ... I just can't afford to be without work right now, not even for a day. I've got a mother and two kid sisters to ...

Secretary enters. (Her name is Mattie.)

SECRETARY
More good luck telegrams.

ANN
Well, you know how it is, I, I've just got to keep working. See?

CONNELL
Sorry, sister. I was sent down here to clean house. I told yuh I can't use your column any more. It's lavender and old lace![1]
(flicks dictograph button)

MATTIE
(over dictograph)
Yeah?

CONNELL
Send those other people in.

MATTIE
(over dictograph)
Okay.

ANN
I'll tell you what I'll do. I get thirty dollars a week. I'll take twenty-five, twenty if necessary. I'll do anything you say.

CONNELL
It isn't the money. We're after circulation. What we need is fireworks. People who can hit with sledge hammers--start arguments.

ANN
Oh, I can do that. I know this town inside out. Oh, give me a chance, please.

She can get no further, for several people enter. They are cowed and frightened. ANN hesitates a moment, then, there being nothing for her to do, she starts to exit. She is stopped by CONNELL's voice.

CONNELL
All right, come in, come in! Come in!
(to Ann)
Cashier's got your check.
(back to others)
Who are these people? Gibbs, Frowley, Cunningham, Jiles--
(to Ann at door)
Hey, you, sister!

Ann turns.

CONNELL
Don't forget to get out your last column before you pick up your check!

ANN's eyes flash angrily as she exits.

Int. Outer Office. Med. shot: ANN storms out. The painter again has to wait for the door to swing back to him.

Int. ANN's office. Full shot: ANN enters her office and paces around, furious. A man in alpaca sleeve-bands enters. His name is JOE.

JOE
You're a couple o' sticks[2] shy in your column, Ann.

ANN
(ignores him, muttering ...)
A big, rich slob like D. B. Norton buys a paper--and forty heads are chopped off!

JOE
Did you get it, too?

ANN
Yeah. You, too? Oh, Joe ... oh, I'm sorry darling ... why don't we tear the building down!

JOE
Before you do, Ann, perhaps you'd better finish this column.

ANN
Yeah. Lavender and old lace!

Suddenly she stops pacing. Her eyes widen as a fiendish idea strikes her.

ANN
Wait, Joe--wait!

She flops down in front of her typewriter.

ANN
(muttering)
Wants fireworks, huh? Okay!

She begins to pound furiously, her jaw set.

Close-up: Of ANN. Eyes flashing as she types.

Close-up: Of JOE, watching her. The wild look in her eye and the unnatural speed of her typing causes him to stare dumbly at her.

Med. shot: ANN bangs away madly. Finally she finishes. She whips the sheet out of the typewriter, hands it to JOE.

ANN
Here.

As JOE takes it, ANN begins to empty the drawers of her desk.

Close-up: Of JOE reading what ANN has written.

JOE
(reading)
"Below is a letter which reached my desk this morning. It's a commentary on what we laughingly call the civilized world. 'Dear Miss Mitchell: Four years ago I was fired out of my job. Since then I haven't been able to get another one. At first I was sore at the state administration because it's on account of the slimy politics here we have all this unemployment. But in looking around, it seems the whole world's going to pot, so in protest I'm going to commit suicide by jumping off the City Hall roof!' Signed, A disgusted American citizen, John Doe.'"

JOE pauses to absorb this.

JOE
(continues reading)
"Editor's note ... If you ask this column, the wrong people are jumping off roofs."

JOE glances up toward ANN, in mild protest.

JOE
Hey, Ann, this is the old fakeroo, isn't it?

Full shot: ANN has just about accumulated all her things. JOE stares at her, knowing it's a fake.

ANN
Never mind that, Joe. Go ahead.

JOE shrugs, shakes his head, and exits. ANN stuffs her things under her arm and also goes.

Int. Outer office: Med. shot: Voices ad lib--"Awfully sorry you're not going." "Good-bye." (Laughing)

ANN comes out. Suddenly, she stops, gets another idea, picks up a book from a desk, and reaches back to heave it.

Med. shot: At CONNELL's office door. The sign-painter has just finished CONNELL's name, and as he leans back, pleased, wiping his brushes, the book flies in. The painter lifts his head slowly, his wrath too great to find utterance.

Dissolve to: Int. GOVERNOR JACKSON's office: Close-up: Of two of GOVERNOR'S ASSOCIATES.

MAN
(reading newspaper)
"... and it's because of the slimy politics that we have all this unemployment here."
(agitated)
There it is! That's D. B. Norton's opening attack on the Governor!

2ND MAN
Why Jim, it's just a letter sent in to a column.

JIM
No, no. I can smell it. That's Norton!

While he speaks, the GOVERNOR has entered.

GOVERNOR
Good morning, gentlemen. You're rather early.

MEN
'Morning. 'Morning, Governor.

GOVERNOR
You're here rather early.

JIM
(pushes paper over to him)
Did you happen to see this in the New Bulletin, Governor?

He emphasizes the word "new" cynically.

GOVERNOR
Yes. I had it served with my breakfast this morning.

2ND MAN
Jim thinks it's D. B. Norton at work.

JIM
Of course it is!

GOVERNOR
Oh, come, Jim. That little item? D. B. Norton does things in a much bigger way ...

JIM
This is his opening attack on you, Governor! Take my word for it! What did he buy a paper for? Why did he hire a high-pressure editor like Connell for? He's in the oil business! I tell you, Governor, he's after your scalp!

GOVERNOR
All right, Jim. Don't burst a blood vessel, I'll attend to it.
(flips button on dictograph)
Get me Spencer of the Daily Chronicle, please.

Dissolve to: Int. SPENCER's office: Med. shot: SPENCER is on the telephone.

SPENCER
Yes. Yes. I saw it, Governor ... and if you ask me that's a phoney letter. Why, that gag has got whiskers on it. Huh? Okay, I'll get the Mayor and maybe the Chamber of Commerce to go after them.
(into dictagraph)
Get Mayor Lovett on the phone!

Int. MAYOR's office: Med. shot: Of MAYOR's secretary.

SECRETARY
(picking up phone)
Hello? Sorry, the Mayor's busy on the other phone.

Camera pans over to the MAYOR who is fatuous and excitable.

MAYOR
(into telephone)
Yes, I know, Mrs. Brewster. It's a terrible reflection on our city. I've had a dozen calls already.

SECRETARY enters scene.

SECRETARY
Spencer of the Chronicle.

MAYOR
Hold him.
(into phone)
Yes, Mrs. Brewster, I'm listening.

The SECRETARY lays down the receiver.

Dissolve to: Int. corner of a bedroom: Close shot: Of MRS. BREWSTER--stout and loud. She is propped up in bed--a breakfast tray on her lap--the newspaper by her side.

MRS. BREWSTER
I insist that this John Doe man be found and given a job at once. If something isn't done. I'll call out the whole Auxiliary[3]--yes, and the Junior Auxiliary, too. We'll hold a meeting and see--

Cut to: Int. MAYOR's office: Med. shot: Of MAYOR. He lays the receiver down and we continue to hear MRS. BREWSTER's voice. MAYOR picks up SPENCER's phone.

MAYOR
Yes, Spencer. Who? The Governor? Well, what about me? it's my building he's jumping off of! And I'm up for re-election, too!

SECRETARY
Shh!

MAYOR
(to Secretary)
What are you doing? Get Connell at the Bulletin!
(to Spencer)
Why, he's liable to go right past my window,
(suddenly--to Sec'y--excitably)
What was that?!

SECRETARY
What?

MAYOR
Out the window! Something just flew by!

SECRETARY
I didn't see anything.

MAYOR
(semi-hysterical)
Well, don't stand there, you idiot. Go and look. Open the window. Oh, why did he have to pick on my building?

The SECRETARY, telephone in hand, peers out window.

MAYOR
Is there a crowd in the street?

SECRETARY
No, sir.

MAYOR
Then he may be caught on a ledge! Look again!

SECRETARY
I think it must have been a sea-gull.

MAYOR
A sea-gull? What's a sea-gull doing around the city hall? That's a bad omen, isn't it?
(picks up Mrs. Brewster's phone)

SECRETARY
Oh, n-no, sir. The sea-gull is a lovely bird.

MAYOR
(into telephone)
I-it's all right, Mrs. Brewster. It was just a sea-gull.
(catches himself)
Er, nothing's happened yet! No, I'm watching. Don't worry. Ju-just leave it all to me!

The SECRETARY holds out another phone. The MAYOR drops MRS. BREWSTER's phone again, and her voice is still heard.

MAYOR
(into Spencer's phone)
Spencer, I'll call you back.

Secretary has gotten CONNELL on the phone--hands phone to MAYOR.

MAYOR
Hello! Connell! This is--
(to Secretary)
What are you doing?
(back to phone)
This is the Mayor.

Int. CONNELL's office: Full shot: CONNELL is on the phone. POP DWYER is draped in a chair nearby.

CONNELL
Yes, Mayor Lovett! How many times are you gonna call me? I've got everybody and his brother and sister out looking for him. Did you see the box I'm running?

He picks up the front page of the Bulletin; we see a four column box on the front page.

CONNELL
(reading)
"An appeal to John Doe. 'Think it over, John. Life can be beautiful,' says Mayor. 'If you need a job, apply to the editor of this paper ...'" " and so forth and so forth ... Okay, Mayor. I'll let you know as soon as I have something! What? ... Well, pull down the blinds!
(he hangs up)

The door opens and a man enters. His name is BEANY. Walks fast, talks fast and accomplishes nothing. Outside, we see the painter trying once more to get his sign painted. He reaches in--and pulls the door to.

BEANY
I went up to Miss Mitchell's house, boss. Boy, she's in a bad way.

CONNELL
Where is she?

BEANY
Hey, do you know something? She supports a mother and two kids. What do you know about that?

CONNELL
(controlling his patience)
Did you find her?

BEANY
No. Her mother's awful worried about her. When she left the house she said she was going on a roaring drunk. Er, the girl, I mean!

CONNELL
(barking)
Go out and find her!

BEANY
Sure. Hey, but the biggest thing I didn't tell you ...

CONNELL picks up telephone.

CONNELL
Hello! ... Yeh?

BEANY
Her old man was Doc Mitchell. You know, the doc that saved my mother's life and wouldn't take any money for it? You remember that? Okay, boss, I'll go and look for her.

BEANY exits, knocking over an ash-stand.

CONNELL
(into phone)
Holy smokes, Commissioner. You've <u>had</u> twenty-four hours! Okay, Hawkshaw, grab a pencil. Here it is again. She's about five foot five, brown eyes, light chestnut hair and as fine a pair of legs as ...

The door opens, ANN stands there--CONNELL sees her.

CONNELL
(into phone--staring at Ann)
... ever walked into this office.

Med. shot: At door. The sign painter is slowly beginning to lose patience. He again reaches in--pulls the door shut--glaring at ANN.

Close-up: Of ANN.

ANN
(innocently)
Did you want to see me?

Wider shot: CONNELL, without moving, stares at her.

CONNELL
(quietly--sizzling)
No. I've had the whole army and navy searching for you because that's a game we play here every day.

ANN
I remember, distinctly, being fired.

CONNELL
That's right. But you have a piece of property that still belongs to this newspaper. And I'd like to have it!

ANN
What's that?

CONNELL
The letter.

ANN
What letter?

CONNELL
The letter from John Doe.

ANN
Oh!

CONNELL
The whole town's in an uproar. We've got to find him. The letter's our only clue.

ANN
(simply)
There <u>is</u> no letter.

CONNELL
We'll get a handwriting expert to--
(suddenly realizes what she has said)
What!

ANN
There is no letter.

He stares at her for a moment, flabbergasted--exchanges a look with POP--crosses to the back door--shuts it--then comes back to face her.

Close shot: ANN and CONNELL.

CONNELL
Say that again.

ANN
There is no letter. I made it up.

CONNELL looks at her a long moment and then up at POP.

CONNELL
(repeating dully)
You made it up.

ANN
Uh-huh. You said you wanted fireworks.

Wider shot: As he recovers from the shock, and then wheels on ANN again.

CONNELL
Don't you know there are nine jobs waiting for this guy? Twenty-two families want to board him free? Five women want to marry him, and the Mayor's practically ready to adopt him? And you ...

As CONNELL glares at her the door springs open and BEANY enters.

BEANY
I just called the morgue, boss. They say there's a girl there--

CONNELL
Shut up!

Close-up: Of BEANY. He is startled by this--and then stares pop-eyed as he sees ANN.

BEANY
Ann! Say, why didn't yuh--

CONNELL
Beany!

Med. shot: At the door. The painter is beginning to grind his teeth. He pulls the door shut, viciously.

Wider shot: To include all.

POP
Only one thing to do, Hank. Drop the whole business quickly.

CONNELL
How?

POP
Run a story. Say John Doe was in here, and is sorry he wrote the letter and--

CONNELL
(jumps in quickly)
That's right. You got it! Sure! He came in here and I made him change his mind. "Bulletin editor saves John Doe's life." Why, it's perfect. I'll have Ned write it up.
(into dictograph)
Oh, Ned!

NED'S VOICE
Yeah?

CONNELL
I got a story I want yuh to--

ANN
Wait a minute!

She rushes over--snaps the dictograph off.

Med. shot: Of ANN, leaning on CONNELL's desk.

ANN
Listen, you great big wonderful genius of a newspaperman! You came down here to shoot some life into this dying paper, didn't you?

CONNELL blinks under the attack. POP and BEANY move into the scene.

ANN
Well, the whole town's curious about John Doe and, boom, just like that you're going to bury him. There's enough circulation in that man to start a shortage in the ink market!

CONNELL
(thoroughly bewildered)
In <u>what</u> man!

ANN
John Doe.

CONNELL
What John Doe?

ANN
Our John Doe! The one I made up! Look, genius-- Now, look. Suppose there <u>was</u> a John Doe--and he walked into this office. What would you do? Find him a job and forget about the whole business, I suppose! Not me! I'd have made a deal with him!

CONNELL
A deal?

ANN
Sure! When you get hold of a stunt that sells papers you don't drop it like a hot potato. Why, this is good for at least a couple of months. You know what I'd do? Between now and let's say, Christmas, when he's gonna jump, I'd run a daily yarn starting with his boyhood, his schooling, his first job! A wide-eyed youngster facing a chaotic world. The problem of the average man, of all the John Does in the world.

Two shot: ANN and CONNELL. Despite himself, he's interested in her recital.

ANN
Now, then comes the drama. He meets discouragement. He finds the world has feet of clay. His ideals crumble. So what does he do? He decides to commit suicide in protest against the state of civilization. He thinks of the river! But no, no, he has a better idea. The City Hall. Why? Because he wants to attract attention. He wants to get a few things off his chest, and that's the only way he can get himself heard.

CONNELL
So?

Full shot: Of the whole group. BEANY grins in admiration. CONNELL has leaned back in his chair, his eyes glued on ANN.

ANN
So! So he writes me a letter and I dig him up. He pours out his soul to me, and from now on we quote: "I protest, by John Doe." He protests against all the evils in the world; the greed, the lust, the hate, the fear, all of man's inhumanity to man.

Arguments will start. Should he commit suicide or should he not! People will write in pleading with him. But no! No, sir! John Doe will remain adamant! On Christmas Eve, hot or cold, he goes! See?

She finishes, takes a deep breath--awed, and at the same time proud of her accomplishment.

Close shot: Of CONNELL. He just stares at ANN.

CONNELL
(after a pause--quietly)
Very pretty. Very pretty, indeed, Miss Mitchell. But would you mind telling me who goes on Christmas Eve?

ANN
John Doe.

CONNELL
(loses control--screams)
What John Doe?

ANN
(screams right back)
The one we hire for the job, you lunkhead!

There is silence for a moment.

CONNELL
(breaking silence--speaks with a controlled patience)
Wait a minute. Wait a minute. Lemme get this through this lame brain of mine. Are you suggesting we go out and hire someone to say he's gonna commit suicide on Christmas Eve? Is that it?

ANN
(nodding)
Well, you're catching on.

CONNELL
Who, for instance?

ANN
Anybody! Er, er--Beany'll do!

Close-up: BEANY. He is petrified.

BEANY
Why sure--Who? Me? Jump off a--Oh, no! Any time but Christmas. I'm superstitious.

Full shot: BEANY backs away from them--and when he gets to the door makes a dash for it.

Int. Outer office: Med. shot: At door. As BEANY comes dashing out, he almost upsets the painter from the stool. When the door is shut, the name of "Connell" which he has been printing is all smudged over. The painter stares at it, helplessly for a second, and then--unable to stand it any more, rises, throws his brush violently to the floor--after completely smearing the sign himself.

Full shot:

CONNELL
(sighing)
Miss Mitchell, do me a favor, will you? Go on out and get married and have a lot o' babies--but stay out o' newspaper business!

POP
Better get that story in, Hank, it's getting late.

ANN
(to CONNELL)
You're supposed to be a smart guy! If it was raining hundred dollar bills, you'd be out looking for a dime you lost some place.

CONNELL
Holy smokes! Wasting my time listening to this mad woman.

He crosses to his desk just as NED enters from the back door.

NED
Look, Chief! Look what the Chronicle is running on John Doe. They say it's a fake!

CONNELL turns sharply.

Close-up: Of ANN. She was just about giving up, when she hears this--and her eyes brighten alertly.

Med. shot: At CONNELL's desk. CONNELL--reading the paper--becomes incensed.

CONNELL
Why, the no-good--low-down--
(reading)
"John Doe story amateur journalism. It's palpably phoney. It's a wonder anyone is taking it seriously." What do yuh think of those guys!

ANN has walked into scene while CONNELL is reading.

ANN
That's fine! That's fine! Now fall right into their laps. Go ahead. Say John Doe walked in and called the whole thing off. You know what that's going to sound like on top of this!

CONNELL
(doesn't like Ned hearing all this)
That's all, Ned. Thank you.

NED
All right.

NED, puzzled, exits. CONNELL comes away from his desk and walks around.

CONNELL
(fighting spirit)
"Amateur journalism", huh? Why, the bunch of sophomores! I can teach them more about--

But he is interrupted by the front door being flung open. On the threshold stands BEANY.

BEANY
Hey, boss. Get a load of this.

CONNELL
(joins him in the doorway)
What?

BEANY
Look!

Med. shot: Over their shoulders. In the outer office are a large group of derelict-looking men. Some standing--some sitting--some leaning. It looks like the lobby of a flophouse had been transplanted.

Close shot: Beany and Connell.

CONNELL
What do they want?

BEANY
They all say they wrote the John Doe letter.

Med. shot: POP and ANN have walked over and also peer out.

CONNELL
(amused, turns)
Oh, they all wrote the letter?

ANN pushes CONNELL aside--talks to BEANY.

ANN
Tell them all to wait.

She shuts the door and turns to CONNELL.

ANN
Look, Mr. Connell--one of those men is your John Doe. They're desperate and will do anything for a cup of coffee. Pick one out and you can make the Chronicle eat their words.

Close-up: Of CONNELL. A broad smile slowly spreads over his face.

CONNELL
I'm beginning to like this.

Med. shot: POP looks worried.

POP
If you ask me, Hank, you're playing around with dynamite.

CONNELL
No, no, no, the gal's right. We can't let the Chronicle get the laugh on us! We've got to produce a John Doe now.
(muttering)
Amateur journalism, huh!
(starts for door)
I'll show those guys.

ANN
Sure--and there's no reason for them to find out the truth, either.
(significantly)
Because, naturally, *I* won't say anything.

CONNELL turns sharply, stares at her a moment puzzled, then grins.

CONNELL
(grinning)
Okay, sister, you get your job back.

ANN
Plus a bonus.

CONNELL
What bonus?

Close-up: Of ANN. She takes the plunge. She is a little frightened at her own nerve, but she is going to brazen it out.

ANN
(tries to drop it casually)
Oh, the bonus of a thousand dollars the Chronicle was going to pay me for this little document. You'll find it says, er: "I, Ann Mitchell, hereby certify that the John Doe letter was created by me--"

Med. shot: As she speaks, she gets the "little document" out of her bag, hands it to CONNELL who glares at her, takes the paper and starts to read. Ann leans over his shoulder. POP peers over his other shoulder.

CONNELL
I can read. I can read!

ANN
Sorry.

She backs away. CONNELL continues reading her confession.

CONNELL
So you think this is worth a thousand dollars, do you?

ANN
(very carelessly)
Oh, the Chronicle would consider it dirt cheap.

CONNELL
Packs everything, including a gun.
(flings paper on desk)
Okay, sister, you've got yourself a deal. Now let's take a look at the candidates. The one we pick has gotta be the typical average man. Typical American that can keep his mouth shut.

POP
Show me an American who can keep his mouth shut and--I'll eat him.

CONNELL
(opens door)
Okay, Beany, bring 'em in one at a time.
(he steps back and rubs his hands in anticipation)

Wipe to: Montage: Half a dozen different types of hoboes appear--and in each instance ANN shakes her head, negatively.

Wipe to: Close shot: Of a TALL CHAP, head hanging shyly.

Two shot: Of ANN and CONNELL. They are impressed.

Full shot: ANN and CONNELL exchange hopeful glances and begin slowly walking around the new candidate.

Close-up: Of TALL CHAP. He feels awkward under this scrutiny.

Wider shot: CONNELL stops in his examination of the man.

CONNELL
Did you write that letter to Miss Mitchell?

TALL CHAP
(after a pause)
No, I didn't.

ANN, CONNELL and POP evince their surprise.

CONNELL
What are you doing up here then?

TALL CHAP
Well, the paper said there were some jobs around loose. Thought there might be one left over.

They study him for a second, then ANN walks over close to him.

Two shot: ANN and TALL CHAP.

ANN
Had any schooling?

TALL CHAP
Yeah, a little.

ANN
What do you do when you work?

TALL CHAP
(slight pause)
I used to pitch.

ANN
Baseball?

TALL CHAP
Uh-huh. Till my wing[4] went bad.

ANN
Where'd you play?

TALL CHAP
Bush leagues mostly.[5]

Med. shot: To include the rest of them. They have their eyes glued on his face. ANN is very much interested.

CONNELL
How about family? Got any family?

TALL CHAP
(after a pause)
No.

CONNELL
Oh, just traveling through, huh?

TALL CHAP
Yeah. Me and a friend of mine. He's outside.

CONNELL nods to the others to join him in a huddle. He crosses to a corner. They follow.

Close three shot: They speak in subdued voices.

CONNELL
Looks all right--

ANN
He's perfect! A baseball player. What could be more American!

CONNELL
I wish he had a family, though.

POP
Be less complicated <u>without</u> a family.

ANN
Look at that face. It's wonderful. They'll believe <u>him</u>. Come on.

Close-up: Of TALL CHAP. He is a strange, bewildered figure. He knows he is being appraised, but doesn't know why. He fingers his hat nervously and looks around the room. Suddenly he is attracted by something.

Close-up: Of tray of sandwiches on CONNELL's desk.

Close-up: Of TALL CHAP. He swallows hard. His eyes stare at the sandwiches hungrily.

Med. shot: Over his shoulder. Shooting toward the huddling group. It breaks up. They walk toward him.

Med. shot: Another angle.

CONNELL
What's your name?

TALL CHAP
Willoughby. John Willoughby, Long John Willoughby they called me in baseball.

ANN
Er, would you, er, would you like to make some money?

JOHN
Yeah, maybe.

NOTE: Henceforth in this script he shall be referred to as JOHN DOE.

ANN
Would you be willing to say you wrote that letter--and stick by it?

JOHN
Oh, I get the idea. Yeah, maybe.

There is an appraising pause, and CONNELL again signals them to join him in a huddle. They exit to their corner.

Close-up: Of JOHN. His eyes immediately go to the sandwiches.

Close-up: Of tray, with sandwiches and milk, on desk.

Close-up: Of JOHN. His eyes riveted on tray. He glances, speculatively, over toward them and then back to the tray.

Med. shot: Of the huddled group.

ANN
That's our man. He's made to order.

CONNELL
I don't know. He don't seem like a guy that'd fall into line.

ANN
(it's significant to her)
When you're desperate for money, you do a lot of things, Mr. Connell. He's our man, I tell you.

Suddenly, they are startled by a loud thud: they all look around sharply.

ANN
He's fainted! Get some water quickly!

As all three rush to him.

CONNELL
Hurry up, Pop.

ANN
Oh.

CONNELL
(to John)
Right here. Sit down.

JOHN
Huh?

ANN
Are you all right?

JOHN
Yeah, I'm all right.

Dissolve to: Int. ANN's office. Close-up: Of JOHN--sitting at ANN's desk, just completing a meal--and still eating voraciously.

Camera draws back and we find another bindle-stiff sitting beside JOHN, packing food away in silence. He is the friend JOHN referred to. He is much older and goes by the name of COLONEL.

Camera continues to pull back revealing ANN who sits nearby, watching them sympathetically.

Close shot: JOHN and the COLONEL. They continue eating. JOHN glances up and catches ANN's eye. He smiles self-consciously.

Close-up: Of ANN. She, too, smiles warmly.

Med. shot: They continue to eat silently.

ANN
How many is that, six? Pretty hungry, weren't you?

COLONEL
Say, all this John Doe business is batty, if yuh ask me.

ANN
Well, nobody asked yuh.

COLONEL
Trying to improve the world by jumping off buildings. You couldn't improve the world if the building jumped on you!

JOHN
(to Ann)
Don't mind the Colonel. He hates people.

ANN
He likes you well enough to stick around.

JOHN
Oh, that's 'cause we both play doohickies.[6] I met him in a box car a couple o' years ago. I was foolin' around with my harmonica and he comes over and joins in. I haven't been able to shake him since.

Full shot: Suddenly, he starts to play the overture from "William Tell." The COLONEL whips out an ocarina and joins him. ANN stares, amused. The door opens and CONNELL and BEANY barge in, followed by half a dozen photographers.

CONNELL
All right, boys, here he is.

ANN
(jumping up)
No, no, no! You can't take pictures of him like that--eating a sandwich--and with a beard!

She waves the photographers out, and shuts the door.

CONNELL
But, he's gonna jump off a building!

ANN
Yes, but not because he's out of a job. That's not news! This man's going to jump as a matter of principle.

CONNELL
Well, maybe you're right.

ANN
We'll clean him up and put him in a hotel room--under bodyguards. We'll make a mystery out of him.
(suddenly)
Did you speak to Mr. Norton?

CONNELL

(nods)

Thinks it's terrific. Says for us to go the limit. Wants us to build a bonfire under every big shot in the state.

ANN

Oh, swell! Is that the contract?

(seeing paper in CONNELL's hand)

CONNELL

Yes.

(sees the COLONEL)

What's he doing here?

ANN

Friend of his. They play duets together.

CONNELL

Duets? But can we trust him?

ANN

Oh!

JOHN

I trust him.

CONNELL

Oh, you trust him, eh? Well, that's fine. I suppose he trusts you, too?

ANN

Oh, stop worrying. He's all right.

COLONEL

(insulted)

That's--

CONNELL

Well, okay. But we don't want more than a couple o' hundred people in on this thing. Now the first thing I want is an exact copy of the John Doe letter in your own handwriting.

ANN

I got it all ready. Here.

CONNELL

Well, that's fine. Now I want you to sign this agreement. It gives us an exclusive story under your name day by day from now until Christmas. On December twenty-sixth, you get one railroad ticket out of town, and the Bulletin agrees to pay to have your arm fixed. That's what you want, isn't it?

JOHN

Yeah, but it's got to be by Bone-Setter Brown.

CONNELL

Okay, Bone-Setter Brown goes. Here, sign it. Meanwhile, here's fifty dollars for spending money. That's fine. Beany!

BEANY
Yeah, Boss?

CONNELL
Take charge of him. Get him a suite at the Imperial and hire some bodyguards.

ANN
Yeah, and some new clothes, Beany.

BEANY
Do you think we better have him de-loused?

CONNELL
Yeh, yeh, yeh.

BEANY
Both of 'em?

CONNELL
Yes, both of 'em! But don't let him out of your sight.

ANN
Hey, Beany, gray suit, huh?

BEANY
Yeah.

CONNELL
Okay, fellows.

ANN
Take it easy, John Doe.

JOHN and the COLONEL follow BEANY out.

CONNELL
(turns to Ann)
And you! Start pounding that typewriter. Oh, boy! This is terrific! No responsibilities on our part. Just statements from John Doe and we can blast our heads off.

ANN
(interrupting)
Before you pop too many buttons, don't forget to make out that check for a thousand.

CONNELL
(grimaces)
Awwwww!

Dissolve to: Int. Living-room of suite.

Full shot: The door opens and BEANY enters. He is followed by JOHN and the COLONEL. JOHN glances around, impressed. The COLONEL looks glum.

Med. shot: At door. As JOHN exits scene into the room, tailed by the unhappy COLONEL. BEANY beckons someone out in the corridor.

BEANY
Okay, fellas.

Three bruisers stand in the doorway.

BEANY
Now, lemme see. You sit outside the door. Nobody comes in, see. You two fellas sit in here.

As they reach for chairs,

Cut to: Med. shot: JOHN is pleased as his gaze wanders around the room.

JOHN
Hey, pretty nifty, huh?

COLONEL
You ain't gonna get me to stay here.

JOHN
Sure, you are.

COLONEL
No, sir. That spot under the bridge where we slept last night's good enough for me.

While he speaks, JOHN has managed to get a glimpse of himself in a mirror--admiring his new suit.

BELL HOP
Hey, what'll I do with this baggage?

BEANY
Aw, stick 'em in the bedroom.

COLONEL
Gimme mine. I ain't staying! You know we were headed for the Columbia River country before all this John Doe business came up. You remember that, don't yuh?

JOHN
Sure. I remember ... Say, did your ears pop coming up in the elevator? Mine did.

COLONEL
Aw, Long John ... I tell you--it's no good. You're gonna get used to a lotta stuff that's gonna wreck you. Why, that fifty bucks in your pocket's beginning to show up on you already. And don't pull that on me neither!
(as John brings out harmonica)

JOHN
Stop worrying, Colonel. I'm gonna get my arm fixed out of this.

Wider shot: As BEANY enters scene with box of cigars.

BEANY
Here's some cigars the boss sent up. Have one.

JOHN's eyes light up.

JOHN
Hey, cigars!

He grabs one and stuffs it in his mouth.

BEANY
(to Colonel)
Help yourself.

COLONEL
Naw.

JOHN flops into a luxurious chair--and immediately ANGELFACE holds a light up for his cigar. JOHN looks up, pleased.

JOHN
Say, I'll bet yuh even the Major Leaguers don't rate an outfit like this.

ANGELFACE
(hands him a newspaper)
Here. Make yourself comfortable.
(turns to the Colonel)
Paper?

COLONEL
(sharply)
I don't read no papers and I don't listen to radios either. I know the world's been shaved by a drunken barber and I don't have to read it.

ANGELFACE backs away, puzzled.

COLONEL
(crosses to John)
I've seen guys like you go under before. Guys that never had a worry. Then they got ahold of some dough and went goofy. The first thing that happens to a guy--

BEANY
Hey, did yuh get a load of the bedroom?

JOHN
No.

BEANY beckons to him to follow, which JOHN does with great interest.

Int. bedroom: Full shot: As BEANY and JOHN puff luxuriously on their cigars and examine the room.

COLONEL
(in doorway)
The first thing that happens to a guy like that--he starts wantin' to go into restaurants and sit at a table and eat salads--and cup cakes--and tea--
(disgusted)
Boy, what that kinda food does to your system!

JOHN pushes on the bed and is impressed with its softness.

COLONEL
The next thing the dope wants is a room. Yessir, a room with steam heat! And curtains and rugs

and 'fore you know it, he's all softened up and he can't sleep 'less he has a bed.

Close-up: Of BEANY. He stares, bewildered, at the COLONEL.

Wider shot: JOHN turns and crosses to window.

JOHN
(as he goes)
Hey, stop worrying, Colonel. Fifty bucks ain't going to ruin me.

COLONEL
I seen plenty of fellers start out with fifty bucks and wind up with a bank account!

BEANY
(can't stand it any more)
Hey, whatsa matter with a bank account, anyway?

COLONEL
(ignoring him)
And let me tell you, Long John. When you become a guy with a bank account, they got you. Yessir, they got you!

BEANY
Who's got him?

COLONEL
The heelots!

BEANY
Who?

JOHN
(at the window)
Hey. There's the City Hall tower I'm supposed to jump off of. It's even higher than this.

BEANY
Who's got him?

COLONEL
The heelots!

Close-up: JOHN opens window and leans out.

Close-up: Of BEANY. His eyes pop; he's petrified.

Med. shot: JOHN stretches far out of the window, and quickly bounces back.

JOHN
Wow!

At the same time BEANY springs to his side and yanks him back.

BEANY
Hey, wait a minute! You ain't supposed to do that till Christmas Eve! Wanta get me in a jam?

JOHN
(twinkle in his eye)
If it's gonna get you in a jam, I'll do you a favor. I won't jump.

He exits to the living room.

Int. living room: Full shot: As JOHN enters, flicking ashes from his cigar, grandly, the COLONEL leaves the doorway, still pursuing his point.

COLONEL
And when they get you, you got no more chance than a road-rabbit.

BEANY
(dogging the COLONEL)
Hey. Who'd you say was gonna get him?

JOHN
Say, is this one of those places where you ring if you want something?

BEANY
Yeah. Just use the phone.

The thought of this delights JOHN.

JOHN
Boy! I've always wanted to do this!

He goes to the phone.

BEANY
Hey, Doc, look. Look, Doc. Gimme that again, will yuh? Who's gonna get him?

COLONEL
The heelots!

BEANY
Who are they?

Two shot: The COLONEL finally levels off on BEANY.

COLONEL
Listen, sucker, yuh ever been broke?

BEANY
Sure. Mostly often.

COLONEL
All right. You're walking along--not a nickel in your jeans--free as the wind--nobody bothers you--hundreds of people pass yuh by in every line of business--shoes, hats, automobiles, radio, furniture, everything. They're all nice, lovable people, and they let you alone. Is that right?

Close-up: Of BEANY--nodding his head, bewildered.

COLONEL'S VOICE
Then you get hold of some dough, and what happens?

BEANY instinctively shakes his head.

Two shot: The COLONEL takes on a sneering expression.

COLONEL
All those nice, sweet, lovable people become heelots. A lotta heels.
(mysterioso)
They begin creeping up on you--trying to sell you something. They've got long claws and they get a strangle-hold on you--and you squirm--and duck and holler--and you try to push 'em away--but you haven't got a chance--they've got you! First thing you know, you own things. A car, for instance.

BEANY has been following him, eyes blinking, mouth open.

COLONEL
Now your whole life is messed up with *more* stuff--license fees--and number plates--and gas and oil--and taxes and insurance--

Close shot: Of the LUGS at the door. One of them listens with a half-smile on his face. The other, more goofy, looks bewildered. He has been listening--and now, slowly rises, ears cocked, frightened by the harrowing tale. Camera retreats before him--as he slowly walks nearer to BEANY and the COLONEL. Meantime, we continue to hear the COLONEL'S voice.

COLONEL'S VOICE
... and identification cards--and letters--and bills--and flat tires--and dents--and traffic tickets and motorcycle cops and court rooms--and lawyers--and fines--

Wider shot: The LUG steps up directly behind BEANY--and the two horrified faces are close together--both staring at the COLONEL.

COLONEL
And a million and one other things. And what happens? You're not the free and happy guy you used to be. You gotta have money to pay for all those things--so you go after what the other feller's got--
(with finality)
And there you are--you're a heelot yourself!

Close shot: Of the two heads of BEANY and the LUG. They continue to stare, wide-eyed, at the COLONEL.

Wider shot: As JOHN approaches the COLONEL.

JOHN
(smiling)
You win, Colonel. Here's the fifty. Go on out and get rid of it.

COLONEL
(as he goes)
You bet I will! As fast as I can! Gonna get some canned goods--a fishing rod, and the rest I'm gonna give away.

ANGELFACE
(aghast)
Give away?

JOHN
(calling)
Hey. Get me a pitcher's glove! Got to get some practice.

ANGELFACE
Say, he's giving it away! I'm gonna get me some of that!

BEANY
Hey, come back here, yuh heelot!

JOHN
(on the phone)
Will you send up five hamburgers with all the trimmings, five chocolate ice cream sodas, and five pieces of apple pie? No, apple, with cheese. Yeah. Thank you.

JOHN hangs up.

The COLONEL has just reached the door when it flies open and Ann comes in with photographer EDDIE--she sees JOHN all dressed up.

ANN
Hello there. Well, well! If it isn't the man about town!

EDDIE
All set, Ann?

ANN
(coming out of it)
Huh? Oh, yes. Let's go.
(she backs away)
Now, let's see. We want some action in these pictures.

JOHN
Action?

ANN
Um-hum.

JOHN winds up in pitching pose--his left leg lifted up high.

EDDIE
That's good.

ANN
No, no, no. This man's going to jump off a roof.

EDDIE
Oh.

ANN
Here. Wait a minute. Let me comb your hair. Sit down. There. That's better.

Close shot: She combs his hair--straightens his tie--etc. He inhales the fragrance of her hair and likes it--winks to the others. She poses JOHN's face and looks it over.

ANN
You know, he's got a nice face, hasn't he?

ANGELFACE
Yeh--he's pretty.

JOHN gives him a look and starts to get up slowly.

ANN
Here. Sit down!
(to ANGELFACE)
Quiet, egghead!
(back to JOHN)
All right, now, a serious expression.

JOHN
(laughing)
Can't. I'm feeling too good.

ANN
Oh, come on, now. This is serious. You're a man disgusted with all of civilization.

JOHN
With all of it?

ANN
Yes, you're sore at the world. Come on, now.

JOHN
Oh, crabby guy, huh?

He tries scowling.

ANN
Yeah. No, no!
(laughing)
No! No, look. You don't have to smell the world!
(the men laugh)

JOHN
Well, all those guys in the bleachers think--

ANN
Never mind those guys. All right, stand up. Now let's see what you look like when you protest.

JOHN
Against what?

ANN
Against anything. Just protest.

JOHN
(laughing)
You got me.

ANN
Oh, look. I'm the umpire, and you just cut the heart of the plate with your fast one and I call it a ball. What would you do?

JOHN
(advances toward her)
Oh, yuh did, huh?

ANN
Yes!

JOHN
Why can't you call right, you bone-headed, pig-eared, lop-eared, pot-bellied--

ANN
Grab it, Eddie, grab it!

Eddie takes the picture.

A Montage: Of Newspaper inserts featuring John Doe's picture.

"I protest against collapse of decency in the world."
"I protest against corruption in local politics."
"I protest against civic heads being in league with crime."
"I protest against state relief being used as political football."
"I protest against County Hospitals shutting out the needy."
"I protest against all the brutality and slaughter in the world."

Close-up: Superimposed over all of the above is a circulation chart--showing the circulation of the Bulletin in a constant rise.

Dissolve to: Int. GOVERNOR's study: Med. shot: The GOVERNOR paces furiously. In front of him are several associates.

GOVERNOR
I don't care whose picture they're publishing. I still say that this John Doe person is a myth. And you can quote me on that. And I'm going to insist on his being produced for questioning. You know as well as I do that this whole thing is being engineered by a vicious man with a vicious purpose--Mr. D. B. Norton.

As he finishes saying this, Dissolve to: Ext. D. B.'s estate:

Close-up: Of D. B. NORTON. Camera pulls back and we find him on horseback.

Reverse long shot: We discover that he is watching the maneuvers of a motorcycle corps who are in uniform. They are being drilled by TED SHELDON.

Med. shot: As a groom rides toward D. B.

GROOM
Mr. Connell and Miss Mitchell are at the house, sir.

D. B.
Oh, they are? All right, come on.

Dissolve to: Int. D. B.'s study: Med. shot--panning: As ANN, D. B. and CONNELL enter and cross to D. B.'s desk.

ANN
(as they walk)
Personally, I think it's just plain stupidity to drop it now.

They reach D. B.'s desk and stop.

ANN
You should see his fan mail! Thousands! Why, it's going over like a house afire!

Close-up: Of D. B. He studies her a moment before he turns to CONNELL.

D. B.
What are you afraid of, Connell? It's doubled our circulation.

Wider shot: To include all three.

CONNELL
Yeah, but it's got everybody sore. Ads are being pulled--the Governor's starting a libel suit--what's more, they all know John Doe's a phoney--and they insist on seeing him.

ANN
Well, what about it? Let them see him! We'll go them one better. They can also hear him.
(to D. B.)
You own a radio station, Mr. Norton. Why not put him on the air?

Close-up: Of D. B. He admires her fight.

CONNELL'S VOICE
Watch out for this dame, D. B. She'll drive you batty!

ANN
Ohh!

Wider shot: To include all three.

CONNELL

Look. We can't let 'em get to this bush-league pitcher and start pumping him. Good night! No telling what that screwball might do. I walked in yesterday--here he is, standing on a table with a fishing pole flycasting. Take my advice and get him out of town before this thing explodes in our faces!

ANN

If you do, Mr. Norton, you're just as much of a dumb cluck as he is! Excuse me.

CONNELL

(to Ann--hotly)

No, you've got yourself a meal ticket and you hate to let go.

ANN

Sure, it's a meal ticket for me. I admit it, but it's also a windfall for somebody like Mr. Norton who's trying to crash national politics.

(she turns to D. B.)

That's what you bought the newspaper for, isn't it? You wanta reach a lotta people, don't you? Well, put John Doe on the air and you can reach a hundred and fifty million of 'em. He can say anything he wants and they'll listen to him.

Close-up: Of D. B. Fascinated by ANN.

Wider shot: CONNELL stares at her derisively. D. B. is completely absorbed.

ANN

All right, let's not forget the Governor, the Mayor and all small fry like that. This can arouse national interest! If he made a hit around here--he can do it everywhere else in the country! And you'll be pulling the strings, Mr. Norton!

Close-up: Of D. B. His eyes have begun to light up with extensive plans.

Wider shot: D. B. continues to study ANN with deep interest. Then he turns to CONNELL.

D. B.

Go down to the office and arrange for some radio time.

CONNELL

(protesting)

Why, D. B., you're not going to fall for--

D. B.

(interrupting sharply)

I want it as soon as possible.

CONNELL
(shrugging)
Okay. I just came in to get warm, myself. Come on, let's go.

He starts out. ANN picks up her bag, prepared to follow CONNELL.

D. B.
Er, don't you go. I want to talk to you.

CONNELL goes. ANN waits, somewhat nervously.

D. B.
(when CONNELL is gone)
Sit down.

Med. two shot: ANN and D. B. D. B. studies her for a moment.

D. B.
... Er, this John Doe idea is yours, huh?

ANN
Yes, sir.

D. B.
How much money do you get?

ANN
Thirty dollars.

D. B.
(probingly)
Thirty dollars? Well, er, what are you after? I mean, what do you want? A journalistic career?

ANN
Money.

D. B.
(laughs)
Money? Well, I'm glad to hear somebody admit it. Do you suppose you could write a radio speech that would put that fellow over?

ANN
Oh, I'm sure I can.

D. B.
Do it, and I'll give you a hundred dollars a week.

ANN
A hundred dollars!

D. B.
That's only the beginning. You play your cards right and you'll never have to worry about money again. Oh, I knew it.

ANN'S eyes brighten with excitement. They are interrupted by the arrival of TED SHELDON, in uniform.

D. B.

(to TED)

Hello. Whenever there's a pretty woman around, er--

(laughing)

This is my nephew, Ted Sheldon, Miss Mitchell.

ANN

How do you do.

TED

How do you do!

D. B.

All right, Casanova. I'll give you a break. See that Miss Mitchell gets a car to take her home.

TED

Always reading my mind, aren't you?

ANN

(laughing)

Thank you very much for everything.

D. B.

And, Miss Mitchell--I think from now on you'd better work directly with me.

ANN

Yes, sir.

They exit. D. B. walks to the door, a pleased expression on his face.

Close-up: Of D. B. His face wreathed in a victorious smile.

Fade-out.

Fade-in: Int. ANN's living room: Close shot: Of ANN. She sits at a typewriter reading something she has written. Suddenly, impulsively, she yanks the sheet out of the machine and flings it to the floor. As she rises, camera pulls back. We find the floor littered with previously unsuccessful attempts to get the speech written. For a moment, ANN paces agitatedly, until she is interrupted by a commotion.

Med. Shot: At door. ANN's two sisters, IRENE and ELLEN, aged nine and eleven--and dressed in their sleeping pajamas, dash in, squealing mischievously. Camera pans with them as they rush to ANN and leap on her.

ANN

Oh! Hey! Oh, hey! I thought you were asleep!

ELLEN

We just wanted to say good night, Sis.

They embrace and kiss her.

ANN

Oh, oh! Oh, you little brats! You're just stalling. I said good night!

Med. shot: At door. ANN'S MOTHER appears in the doorway. She is a prim little woman--her clothes have a touch of the Victorian about them--her hair is done up in old-fashioned style, her throat is modestly covered in lace.

MOTHER
(above the din)
Come, come, come, children. It's past your bedtime.

ELLEN
Oh, all right.

MOTHER
Go on!

ELLEN
Come on, Pooch! Come on, come on.

MOTHER
Now, keep Pooch off the bed.

The CHILDREN exit, squealing. ANN'S MOTHER goes to ANN's desk and searches for something.

ANN
Stick a fork through me! I'm done. I'll never get this speech right.

MOTHER
Oh, yes you will, Ann dear ... you're very clever.

ANN
Yeah, I know. What are you looking for?

MOTHER
Your purse. I need ten dollars.

ANN
What for? I gave you fifty just the other day.

MOTHER
Yes, I know, dear, but Mrs. Burke had her baby yesterday. Nine pounds! And there wasn't a thing in the house--and then this morning the Community Chest[7] lady came around and--

ANN
And the fifty's all gone, huh? Who's the ten for?

MOTHER
The Websters.

ANN
The Websters!

MOTHER
You remember those lovely people your father used to take care of? I thought I'd buy them some groceries. Oh, Ann, dear, it's a shame, those poor--

ANN
You're marvelous, Ma. You're just like Father used to be. Do you realize a couple of weeks ago we didn't have enough to eat ourselves?

MOTHER
Well, yes, I know, dear, but these people are in such need and we have plenty now.

ANN
If you're thinking of that thousand dollars, forget it. It's practically gone. We owed everybody in town. Now, you've just gotta stop giving all your money away.

Her MOTHER looks up, surprised at her tone.

MRS. MITCHELL
Oh, Ann, dear!

Close-up: ANN realizes she has spoken sharply to her MOTHER and immediately regrets it. Her face softens.

Med. shot: As ANN crosses to her MOTHER--and places an arm around her shoulder, tenderly.

ANN
Oh, I'm sorry, Ma. Oh, don't pay any attention to me. I guess I'm just upset about all this. Gee whiz, here I am with a great opportunity to get somewhere, to give us security for once in our lives, and I'm stuck. If I could put this over, your Mrs. Burke can have six babies!

MOTHER
Do you mean the speech you're writing?

ANN
Yeah, I don't know. I simply can't get it to jell! I created somebody who's gonna give up his life for a principle, hundreds of thousands of people are gonna listen to him over the radio and, unless he says something that's, well, that's sensational, it's just no good!

MOTHER
Well, honey, of course I don't know what kind of a speech you're trying to write, but judging from the samples I've read, I don't think anybody'll listen.

ANN
What?

MOTHER
Darling, there are so many complaining political speeches. People are tired of hearing nothing but doom and despair on the radio. If you're going to have him say anything, why don't you let him say something simple and real, something with hope in it? If your father were alive, he'd know what to say.

ANN
Oh, yes, Father certainly would.

MOTHER
Wait a minute ...

ANN
Huh?

MRS. MITCHELL crosses to a desk, finds a key and unlocks a compartment. ANN watches her, curiously.

Close shot: MRS. MITCHELL extracts a diary from the compartment, which she handles very tenderly.

Camera pans with her as she goes back to ANN.

MOTHER
That's your father's diary, Ann.

ANN
Father's ... I never knew he had a diary.

MOTHER
There's enough in it for a hundred speeches, things people ought to hear nowadays. You be careful of it, won't you dear? It's always helped keep your father alive for me.

ANN
(holds MOTHER's hand to her cheek)
You bet I will, Ma.

Her mother abruptly leaves.

Close-up: ANN turns her attention to the diary. As she opens it, her eyes sparkle expectantly. She becomes interested in the first thing she sees.

Dissolve to: Int. corridor of hotel.

Med. shot: At door of JOHN's suite. A crowd of people are around the door trying to crash it. The LUG on guard stands before the door.

LUG
Wait a minute. John Doe don't wanta sign no autographs.

INQUIRER
Well, what does he do all day?

LUG
What does he do all day? He's writin' out his memories!

Cut to: Int. living room.

Med. shot: BEANY is on the telephone. He is apparently weary from answering them all day.

BEANY
Sorry, lady. you can't see Mr. Doe. He wants to be alone. No, no, he just sits around all day and commutes with himself.

Camera swings around to JOHN. He stands in the middle of the floor, his pitcher's glove on, playing an imaginary game of ball. He winds up and throws an imaginary ball.

Close-up: Of the COLONEL. He wears a catcher's mitt--and smacks it as if he just caught the ball.

BEANY
(umpiring)
Ba-ll!

COLONEL
I don't know how you're gonna stand it around here till after Christmas.

Full shot: At the door are the two LUGS, watching the imaginary ball game. The COLONEL takes a couple of steps over home plate, and throws the "ball" back to JOHN who picks it up out of the air.

COLONEL
(as he steps back behind the plate)
I betcha yuh ain't heard a train whistle in two weeks.

He crouches on his knees--and gives JOHN a signal.

BEANY
St-rike!

COLONEL
I know why you're hangin' around--you're stuck on a girl--that's all a guy needs is to get hooked up with a woman.

Close shot: Of JOHN. He shakes his head, and waits for another sign. When he gets it, he nods. He steps onto the mound--winds up and lets another one go. This is apparently a hit, for his eyes shoot skyward, and he quickly turns--watching the progress of the ball as it is flung to first base. From his frown we know the man is safe.

Close shot: Of the two LUGS, ANGELFACE and MIKE. ANGELFACE is seriously absorbed in the game. MIKE leans against the wall, eyes narrowed, a plan going on in his head.

ANGELFACE
(seriously)
What was that? A single?

Close-up: Of JOHN.

JOHN
(explaining)
The first baseman dropped the ball.

Close-up: Of ANGELFACE.

ANGELFACE
(shouting at "firstbaseman")
Butterfingers!
(back to John)
That's tough luck, Pal.

Med. shot: JOHN disregards him completely. He is too much absorbed with the man on first. He now has the stance of a pitch without the windup.

COLONEL
When a guy has a woman on his hands--the first thing he knows his life is balled up with a lot more things--furniture and--

Close shot: Of JOHN. He catches the "ball"--gets into position--nods to his catcher--raises his hands in the air, takes a peek toward first base--and suddenly wheels around facing camera, and whips the "ball" toward first base. Almost immediately his face lights up.

Close-up: Of ANGELFACE.

ANGELFACE
Did you get him?

Close-up: Of JOHN. He winks.

BEANY
(umpiring)
You're out!

Full shot: JOHN flips the glove off his hand so that it dangles from his wrist--and massages the ball with his two palms.

ANGELFACE
That's swell! What's this--the end of the eighth?

JOHN
Ninth!

He steps into the "pitcher's box".

Wider shot: Just as they take their positions, the LUG, from outside, partly opens the door.

LUG
Hey, Beany! There's a coupla lugs from the Chronicle snooping around out here!

BEANY immediately comes from background.

BEANY
Come on, Angelface! Gangway!

As they reach the door, the LUG speaks to ANGELFACE.

LUG
What's the score, Angelface?

ANGELFACE
Three to two--our favor.

LUG
Gee, that's great!

Close-up: Of JOHN. He has heard this and grins mischievously. He starts winding up for another pitch.

Close-up: Of MIKE. He looks around mischievously, then turns to JOHN.

MIKE
You've got swell form. Must have been a pretty good pitcher.

Wider shot: JOHN is just receiving the ball.

JOHN
Pretty good? Say, I was just about ready for the major leagues when I chipped a bone in my elbow. I got it pitchin' a nineteen-inning game!

MIKE
Nineteen!

JOHN
Yep. There was a major league scout there watching me, too. And he came down after the game with a contract. Do you know what? I couldn't lift my arm to sign it. But I'll be okay again as soon as I get it fixed up.

MIKE
(picks up newspaper--sighing)
That's too bad.

JOHN
What do you mean, too bad?

MIKE
(pretending distraction)
Huh? Oh, that you'll never be able to play again.

JOHN
Well, what are you talking about? I just told you I was gonna get a--

MIKE
(interrupting carelessly)
Well, you know how they are in baseball--if a guy's mixed up in a racket--

JOHN
(walking over)
Racket? What do you mean?

MIKE
Well, I was just thinking about this John Doe business. Why, as soon as it comes out it's all a fake, you'll be washed up in baseball, won't you?

JOHN
Y-yeah. Gee, doggone it, I never thought about that. Gosh!

MIKE
And another thing, what about all the kids in the country, the kids that idolize ball players? What are they gonna think about you?
(shakes his head)

Close shot: Of the COLONEL. He has dropped his glove--flopped into a chair--and has taken out his ocarina.

JOHN'S VOICE
Hey, did you hear that, Colonel?

The COLONEL nods, disinterestedly, and begins to play.

Wider shot: JOHN ponders his dilemma for a second.

JOHN
I gotta figure some way out of this thing!

COLONEL
The elevators are still runnin'.

MIKE
(carelessly)
I know <u>one</u> way you can do it.

JOHN
How?

MIKE
Well, when you get up on the radio, all you have to do is say the whole thing's a frame-up. Make you a hero sure as you're born!

John thinks this over, but something troubles him.

JOHN
Yeah, but how am I gonna get my arm fixed?

MIKE
Well, that's a cinch. I know somebody that'll give you five thousand dollars just to get up on the radio and tell the truth.

COLONEL
(eyes popping)
Five thousand dollars?

MIKE
Yeah. Five thousand dollars. And he gets it right away. You don't have to wait till Christmas.

COLONEL
Look out, Long John! They're closing in on you!

JOHN
(ignores COLONEL)
Say, who's putting up this dough?

MIKE
Feller runs the Chronicle.
(takes it out of his pocket)
Here's the speech you make--and it's all written out for you.

JOHN takes it.

Close-up: Of the COLONEL.

COLONEL
(eyes heaven-ward)
Five thousand dollars! Holy mackerel! I can see the heelots comin'. The whole army of them!

MIKE
It's on the level.

Close-up: Of JOHN.

Dissolve to: Int. broadcasting station:

Close shot: TELEPHONE OPERATORS.

1ST GIRL
No, I'm sorry. Tickets for the broadcast are all gone. Phone the Bulletin.

2ND GIRL
Sorry. No more tickets left.

Med. shot: Crowd chattering--they recognize JOHN DOE coming in.

Close shot: At a side door in broadcasting station. As the COLONEL and MIKE take their places.

Int. office in broadcasting station: Full shot: JOHN is led by BEANY into the office. They are immediately followed by several photographers.

BEANY
Here he is.

ANN
Hello, John. All set for the big night? Swell!

PHOTOGRAPHER
Turn around.

2ND PHOTOGRAPHER
One moment--hold it! Now stand still, Mr. Doe.

ANN
Okay, Beany, take them outside.

Two shot: JOHN and ANN.

ANN
Now, look, John. Here's the speech. It's in caps and double-spaced. You won't have any trouble reading it. Not nervous, are you?

JOHN
No.

ANN
Of course not. He wouldn't be.

JOHN
Who?

ANN
John Doe. The one in there.
(pointing to speech)

BEANY
Hey, don't let your knees rattle. It picks up on the mike!

ANN
Oh, Beany! You needn't be nervous, John. All you have to remember is to be sincere.

Wider shot: Man pokes his head in.

MAN
Pick up the phone, Miss Mitchell. It's for you.

ANN
(takes phone)
Hello? Yes, Mother. Oh, thank you, darling.

Full shot: While she speaks on the phone, MRS. BREWSTER barges in, accompanied by two other ladies.

MRS. BREWSTER
Oh, there he is, the poor, dear man! Oh, good luck to you, Mr. Doe. We want you to know that we're all for you. The girls all decided that you're not to jump off any roof a'tall. Oh, we'll stop it!

ANN completes the phone call--crosses to MRS. BREWSTER.

ANN
Sorry, ladies. Mr. Doe can't be bothered now. He's gotta make a speech out there, and--

While she gets them out--MIKE slips into the room.

Close shot: MIKE and JOHN.

MIKE
Have you got the speech I gave you?

JOHN
(taps breast pocket)
Yeah.

MIKE
Now, look. I'll give this money to the Colonel just as soon as you get started. We'll have a car waiting at the side entrance for you.

JOHN
Okay.

Full shot: ANN turns away from the door.

ANN
(to MIKE)
How'd you get in here?

MIKE
Huh? Oh, I just came in to wish him luck.

ANN
Come on, out. Out!
(turning to John)
Mother says good luck, too. John, when you read that speech, please, please believe every word of it. He's turned out to be a wonderful person, John.

JOHN
Who?

ANN
John Doe, the one in the speech.

JOHN
Oh. Yeah.

ANN
You know something? I've actually fallen in love with him.

Full shot: They are interrupted by the arrival of CONNELL. He is accompanied by several photographers--and a beautiful girl in a bathing suit. A banner across her front reads: "Miss Average Girl".

CONNELL
All right, there he is, sister. Now, come on--plenty of oomph!

The GIRL, all smiles, throws her arms around JOHN's shoulder--and strikes a languid pose. The flashlights go off.

ANN
What's the idea?

CONNELL
No, no, no. Now that's too much!

PHOTOGRAPHER
One moment, please.

ANN
This is no time for cheap publicity, Mr. Connell!

CONNELL
Listen. If that guy lays an egg. I want to get something out of it. I'm getting a Jane Doe ready!

ANN
(trying to get rid of them)
That's fine, honey. Now, get out!

PHOTOGRAPHER
All right. I need one more.

ANN
Go right ahead.

While there is this confusion, the COLONEL pushes in and stands in the doorway.

COLONEL
How're you doin'?

CONNELL
(calls to Beany outside)
All right, Beany- bring 'em in!

While CONNELL speaks, two MIDGETS push the COLONEL out of the way and enter the room. The COLONEL glances down--and nearly jumps out of his skin. BEANY follows them in.

COLONEL
Holy smoke! A half a heelot!

BEANY
There you are, Boss, just like you ordered. Symbols of the little people.

CONNELL
Okay. Get them up.

BEANY lifts them and places them, one on each of JOHN's arms. The flashlights go off.

ANN
This is ridiculous, Mr. Connell! Come on, give him a chance. The man's on the air!

While she speaks, she tries to shove the photographers out.

BOY MIDGET
(to girl midget)
Come on, Snooks--you better bail out.

GIRL MIDGET
(coquettishly)
Goodbye, Mr. Doe!

BEANY lifts her off--and ANN pushes them all out--just as the STAGE MANAGER reappears.

STAGE MANAGER
Better get ready. One minute to go!

Two shot: JOHN and ANN. ANN turns quickly to JOHN.

ANN
Wow! One minute to go, and the score is nothing to nothing! Now, please, John, you won't let me down, will you? Will you? 'Course you won't. If you'll just think of yourself as the real John Doe.
Listen. Everything in that speech are things a certain man believed in. He was my father, John. And when he talked, people listened. They'll listen to you, too.
Funny--you know what my mother said the other night? She said to look into your eyes--that I'd see Father there.

STAGE MANAGER
Hey--what do you say?

ANN
Okay! We're coming. Come on!

ANN
Now, listen, John. You're a pitcher. Now, get in there and pitch!
(kisses his cheek)
Good luck.

For a moment he just stares at her, under a spell. Then, turning, he exits. After a second of watching him, ANN follows.

STUDIO OFFICIAL
Give him room, let him through. Come on.

Int. broadcasting stage: Med. shot: Camera retreats in front of JOHN and the official, as they leave the office and proceed to the microphones. Everyone stares curiously at JOHN--whispering to each other.

Med. shot: Shooting through glass partition, toward control booth. We see the two men at the board. They glance nervously at their watches--then at the clock on the wall.

Close shot: Of ANN. She has taken a position at a table near the mike. Next to her sits CONNELL. ANN watches JOHN with intense interest.

The COLONEL has followed JOHN up to the microphone.

COLONEL
(to John)
Hey. Let's get out o' here. There's the door right there.

M.C.
Hey, what're you doing here?

COLONEL
That's what I'd like to know!

M.C.
Come on, out. Out.

JOHN
Say, he's a friend of mine.

ANN
(at John's elbow)
Never mind. Let him alone. He's all right. I'll be right over there pulling for you.

JOHN starts to follow ANN away from mike. ANN leads him back to mike again.

ANN
No, John--over here.

2ND M.C.
Stand by.

Med. shot: At door. The COLONEL surreptitiously tries the door, to see that it opens readily. Standing near him is BEANY and the others.

Med. shot: Group around SPENCER. They wait expectantly. Their eyes sparkling with excitement.

SPENCER
Phone the Chronicle. Tell 'em to start getting those extras out.

Med. shot: Toward control booth. The man with the earphones on has his hand up ready to give the signal. He listens a moment, then abruptly drops his hand.

Close-up: The man near the announcer throws his hand up as a signal to someone off scene.

Med. shot: An orchestra in a corner. The conductor waves his baton--and the orchestra blasts out a dramatic fanfare.

Close shot: ANNOUNCER and JOHN. ANNOUNCER holds his script up and the moment the music stops he speaks dramatically.

ANNOUNCER
(rapid-fire)
And good evening, ladies and gentlemen. This is Kenneth Frye, speaking for the New Bulletin. Tonight we give you something entirely new and different. Standing beside me is the young man who has declared publicly that on Christmas Eve he intends to commit suicide, giving as his reason--quote: "I protest against the state of civilization." End quote. Ladies and gentlemen, the New Bulletin takes pleasure in presenting the man who is fast becoming the most talked-of person in the whole country, JOHN DOE!

The man next to him waves his hand--there is an outburst of music.

A flash: Of ANN--she looks at JOHN intently.

Med. shot: Group around BEANY. They all applaud, except for MIKE and the COLONEL. MIKE, with his hand hanging down, nudges the COLONEL.

Close shot: Of their hands meeting and we see the envelope change hands. Camera pans up to the COLONEL's face which is twisted into a miserable grimace.

Close-up: Of JOHN. He glances around, uncertainly.

Close shot: Of MIKE and the COLONEL. MIKE elbows the COLONEL to throw his signal. The COLONEL looks toward JOHN and nods his head.

Close shot: Of JOHN. He catches the COLONEL'S signal and quickly his hand goes to his pocket. Just as he is about to bring it out, his hand pauses. He turns and looks at ANN.

Close-up: Of ANN. A warm, pleading look in her eyes.

Med. shot: Around JOHN. He is still staring at ANN, when the ANNOUNCER reaches over and nudges him--pointing to the mike. JOHN snaps out of it--turns his face to the mike--pushes the paper back in his pocket--and starts reading ANN'S speech.

JOHN
(reading speech)
Ladies and gentlemen: I am the man you all know as John Doe.
(clearing his throat)
I took that name because it seems to describe--because it seems to describe
(his voice unnatural)
the average man, and that's me.
(repeats, embarrassedly)
And that's me.

Med. shot: The COLONEL and MIKE. The COLONEL realizes JOHN is not going to make SPENCER'S speech, and his face breaks into a broad grin. He takes MIKE'S hand and slaps the envelope into his palm. Over the shot we hear JOHN'S voice.

JOHN'S VOICE
Well, it *was* me--before I said I was gonna jump off the City Hall roof at midnight on Christmas Eve. Now, I guess I'm not average any more. Now, I'm getting all sorts of attention, from big shots, too.

Med. shot: To include JOHN and ANN.

Med. shot: Around SPENCER, as MIKE enters to him and hands him envelope.

MIKE
(whispering)
We've been double-crossed!

SPENCER stares at the envelope, frothing at the mouth.

SPENCER
We have!?

Med. shot: Featuring JOHN and ANN.

JOHN
The Mayor and the Governor, for instance. They don't like those articles I've been writing.

Suddenly they are startled by SPENCER's voice.

SPENCER'S VOICE
You're an imposter, young fella! That's a pack of lies you're telling!

Quick flashes: Of reaction from audience, CONNELL and others.

SPENCER
Who wrote that speech for you?
(pointing accusing finger at JOHN)

CONNELL
Beany, get that guy!

Med. shot: Around SPENCER. It is as far as he gets. Several attendants, BEANY among them, have reached him and start throwing him out.

Cut to: Int. D. B. NORTON's study: Med. shot: D. B. and TED SHELDON are listening to JOHN's speech over the radio. D. B. is astonished at the disturbance in the program.

D. B.
(recognizing the voice)
That's Spencer!

Cut to: Int. broadcasting stage:

Close shot: Of ANNOUNCER.

M.C.
Ladies and gentlemen, the disturbance you just heard was caused by someone in the audience who tried to heckle Mr. Doe. The speech will continue.

Med. shot: Featuring JOHN and ANN.

JOHN
Well, people like the Governor
(laughing--ad libs)
People like the Governor and that fella there can--can stop worrying. I'm not gonna talk about them.

ANN smiles admiringly.

Close-up: Of JOHN. He is becoming strangely absorbed in what he is saying.

JOHN
I'm gonna talk about us, the average guys, the John Does. If anybody should ask you what the average John Doe is like, you couldn't tell him because he's a million and one things. He's Mr. Big and Mr. Small. He's simple and he's wise. He's inherently honest, but he's got a streak of larceny in his heart. He seldom walks up to a public telephone without shoving his finger into the slot to see if somebody left a nickel there.

Close-up: Of ANN. Her eyes are glued on JOHN.

JOHN'S VOICE
He's the man the ads are written for. He's the fella everybody sells things to. He's Joe Doakes,[8] the world's greatest stooge and the world's greatest strength.
(clearing throat)
Yes, sir. Yessir, we're a great family, the John Does. We're the meek who are, er, supposed to inherit the earth. You'll find us everywhere. We raise the crops, we dig the mines, work the factories, keep the books, fly the planes and drive the busses! And when a cop yells: "Stand back there, you!" He means us, the John Does!

Cut to: Int. D. B.'s study:

Med. shot: D. B. and TED listen near the radio. TED's eyes flash angrily.

TED
Well, what kind of a speech is that? Didn't you read it?

D. B. stops him with a gesture of his hand. He doesn't want to miss a word.

Cut to: Int. broadcasting stage:

Med. shot: Toward JOHN.

JOHN
We've existed since time began. We built the pyramids, we saw Christ crucified, pulled the oars for Roman emperors, sailed the boats for Columbus, retreated from Moscow with Napoleon and froze with Washington at Valley Forge!
(gasping)
Yes, sir. We've been in there dodging left hooks since before history began to walk! In our struggle for freedom we've hit the canvas many a time, but we always bounced back!

Med. shot--panning: Around audience--to get a variety of interested faces.

JOHN'S VOICE
Because we're the <u>people</u>--and we're tough!

Close-up: Of JOHN.

JOHN

They've started a lot of talk about free people going soft--that we can't take it. That's a lot of hooey! ... A free people can beat the world at anything, from war to tiddle-de-winks, if we all pull in the same direction!

Med. shot: To include radio announcer and other radio officials. Their interest centers on JOHN.

JOHN

I know a lot of you are saying "What can I do? I'm just a little punk. I don't count." Well, you're dead wrong! The little punks have always counted because in the long run the character of a country is the sum total of the character of its little punks.

Int. D. B.'s study. Med. Shot. D. B.'s expression of disturbance has vanished. It is now replaced by one of thoughtfulness and interest. He looks off toward the foyer, and impulsively goes in that direction.

Cut to:
Int. foyer.

Med. shot: D. B. crosses to a pantry door and pushes the swinging door open slightly.

Int. pantry: Med. shot: All we can see through the slightly open door is one side of the room. Clustered around the radio on a table are all the household help. They listen, fascinated.

Int. foyer: Closeup of D. B. His eyes begin to brighten with an idea. Meantime, over the foregoing shots, JOHN's voice has continued.

JOHN'S VOICE

But we've all got to get in there and pitch! We can't win the old ball game unless we have team work. And that's where every John Doe comes in! It's up to him to get together with his teammate!

Cut to: Int. broadcasting station:

Med. shot: Closeup: Of JOHN.

JOHN

And your teammates, my friends, is the guy next door to you. Your neighbor! He's a terribly important guy, that guy next door! You're gonna need him and he's gonna need you ... so look him up! If he's sick, call on him! If he's hungry, feed him! If he's out of a job, find him one! To most of you, your neighbor is a stranger, a guy with a barking dog, and a high fence around him.

Med. shot: Somewhere in audience.

JOHN'S VOICE
Now, you can't be a stranger to any guy that's on your own team. So tear down the fence that separates you, tear down the fence and you'll tear down a lot of hates and prejudices! Tear down all the fences in the country and you'll really have teamwork!

Med. shot: Around BEANY and the LUGS. They, too, are interested.

JOHN'S VOICE
I know a lot of you are saying to yourselves: "He's asking for a miracle to happen. He's expecting people to change all of a sudden." Well, you're wrong. It's no miracle. It's no miracle because I see it happen once every year. And so do you. At Christmas time! There's something swell about the spirit of Christmas, to see what it does to people, all kinds of people ...

Close-up: Of ANN. Her eyes go from JOHN to the audience--as she watches their reaction.

Full shot: Shooting toward audience over JOHN's shoulder.

JOHN
Now, why can't that spirit, that same warm Christmas spirit last the whole year round? Gosh, if it ever did, if each and every John Doe would make that spirit last three hundred and sixty-five days out of the year, we'd develop such a strength, we'd create such a tidal wave of good will, that no human force could stand against it.

Close-up: Of JOHN. He has become visibly affected by the speech himself.

JOHN
Yes, sir, my friends, the meek can only inherit the earth when the John Does start loving their neighbors. You'd better start right now. Don't wait till the game is called on account of darkness! Wake up, John Doe! You're the hope of the world!

He has finished--but does not move. He drops his head to conceal the moisture in his eyes.

Close-up: Of ANN. She, too, remains seated. Her moist eyes riveted on JOHN.

Med. long shot: Of Audience. There is no outburst of applause. All continue to stare forward, emotionally touched.

Med. shot: Of ANN. She runs over to John.

ANN
John! You were wonderful!

Med. shot: Of the audience. They too realize it is over--and gradually they rise and applaud him wildly, and the radio station rings with cheers.

Med. shot: JOHN and ANN. JOHN stares at ANN, then turns to COLONEL.

JOHN
(as he reaches COLONEL)
Let's get out of here.

They exit through the door at which the COLONEL has been on guard.

COLONEL
Now you're talking!

Med. shot: At side door. The COLONEL opens it, and a little crowd of autograph hounds wait for JOHN.

COLONEL
Gangway, you heelots!

They push their way to a taxi waiting at the curb.

Close-up: Of ANN. She stares at them leaving, follows and tries to stop them, but her efforts are unsuccessful.

Dissolve to: Ext. under a bridge: Med. shot: JOHN and the COLONEL are in a secluded spot. The lights of the city can be seen in the distance. The COLONEL is building a fire.

COLONEL
I knew you'd wake up sooner or later! Boy, am I glad we got out of that mess.

Close-up: Of JOHN. He reaches around and pulls his pitcher's glove out of his back pocket, and starts pounding his fist into it.

JOHN
I had that five thousand bucks sowed up! Could have been on my way to old Doc Brown!
(imitates Ann)
"You're a pitcher, John," she said, "Now go in there and pitch!
(self-beratingly)
What a sucker!

Wider shot: To include the COLONEL, who has quite a mound of twigs built, under which he lights a match.

COLONEL
Yeah, she's a heelot just like the rest of them. It's lucky you got away from her.

JOHN
What was I doin' up there makin' a speech, anyway? Me? Huh? Gee, the more I think about it the more I could ...

COLONEL
Tear down all the fences. Why, if you tore one picket off of your neighbor's fence he'd sue you!

JOHN
Five thousand bucks! I had it right in my hand!

Dissolve to: Int. D. B.'s study: Close-up: D. B. on telephone.

D. B.
What do you mean, he ran away? Well, go after him! Find him! That man is terrific!

Dissolve to: Ext. a box car (process). Close shot: Of JOHN and the COLONEL. They play a duet on their instruments.

Fade out:

Fade in: Ext. a small town street--day: Med. shot: As JOHN and the COLONEL come from around a corner. Camera pans with them as they enter "Dan's Beanery".

Int. DAN's Beanery: Full shot: They enter and flop down on stools. Half a dozen other customers are present.

Med. shot: Kids dancing to phonograph.

COLONEL
Jitterbugs.[9]

Close shot: JOHN and the COLONEL.

JOHN
Yeh. Say, how much money we got left?

COLONEL
Four bits.

JOHN
Better make it doughnuts, huh?

COLONEL
Yeh.

DAN
What'll it be, gents?

JOHN
Have you got a coupla steaks about that big and about that thick?
(measuring)

COLONEL
Er, yeh, with hash-brown potatoes and tomatoes and--and apple pie and ice cream and coffee--

DAN
And doughnuts! I know. Hey, Ma! Sinkers, a pair!

MA'S VOICE
Sinkers, a pair, coming up.

COLONEL
Glad he took the "T" out of that.

JOHN
(sees something off--nudges the Colonel)
Hey look!

Long shot: Shooting from their view through the store window. In the street outside, a delivery wagon is passing. On its side is a sign reading "JOIN THE JOHN DOE CLUB".

Int. DAN's beanery: Close-up: JOHN and the COLONEL.

COLONEL
Join the John Doe Club.

JOHN
John Doe Club?

Close shot: Of the WAITER standing near the coffee urn. From back of it he has taken a local paper--on the front page of which is JOHN's picture. The WAITER looks at it and then turns his head to JOHN.

Two shot: JOHN and the COLONEL. They turn and see the waiter watching them peculiarly.

COLONEL
Oh-oh.

Wider shot. As the WAITER approaches them.

WAITER
Are you John Doe?

JOHN lowers his head.

COLONEL
Who?

WAITER
(pointing to paper)
John Doe.

COLONEL
You need glasses, buddy.

WAITER
Well, he's the spittin' image of--

COLONEL
Yeah, but his name's Willoughby.

DAN
Oh!

JOHN
Long John Willoughby.
(takes glove out of pocket)
I'm a baseball player.

COLONEL
Sure.

DAN
(eyes brightening)
Oh, no. I'd know that voice anywhere. You can't kid me! You're John Doe! Hey, Ma! Ma! That's John Doe!

MA

John Doe?

DAN

Yeah. Sitting right there, big as life.

CUSTOMER

Who'd you say it was?

DAN

John Doe! The big guy there! Picture's in the paper!

JOHN gives the COLONEL the office and they hastily exit. Several customers, who had gathered around, now evince interest. DAN identifies JOHN as JOHN DOE, and the people follow JOHN out into the street. DAN hastily seizes the phone.

DAN

Hey, Operator? Dan's Beanery. Look. Call everybody in town. John Doe was just in my place. Yeh. He ordered doughnuts.

Long shot: Shooting out of window toward street. We see JOHN and the COLONEL as they hurry away, being followed by the crowd which is gradually growing larger ... as we see people crossing the street to get to them--

TOWNSPEOPLE

There he is!
John Doe!
There he is! Come on!
Gotta see John Doe!

Dissolve to: Ext. sidewalk: Med. shot: Millville City Hall. The sidewalk is crowded with people. Those near the entrance are trying to force their way in. MAYOR HAWKINS guards the door.

MAYOR HAWKINS

I know, you all voted for me and you're all anxious to see John Doe. We're all neighbors, but my office is packed like a sardine box.

GIRL

What does John Doe look like, Mr. Mayor.

MAYOR HAWKINS

Oh, he's one of those great big outdoor type of men. No, you can't see him.

MAYOR notices one member of the crowd particularly.

MAYOR HAWKINS

You didn't vote for me the last time. Shame on you--get off my front porch!

(turning)

Mr. Norton come yet? What's keeping him? He should of been here fifteen minutes ago. Oh, there he comes now. Now, everybody on your dignity. Don't do anything to disgrace us. This is a little town, but we gotta show off.

Wider shot: Of curb. From off-scene we hear the wail of sirens, and as the crowd on the sidewalk turn they see two motorcycle cops drive in, followed by a limousine.

Two shot: ANN and D. B.

ANN
Better let me talk to him.

D. B.
All right, but present it to him as a great cause for the common man.

ANN nods as they start toward building. Camera pans with them as the cops break through the curious mob.

Med. shot: MAYOR HAWKINS endeavors to assist them.

MAYOR HAWKINS
Ah, here he comes! Give him room down there! Give him room, folks! How do you do, Mr. Norton! I'm the Mayor--

COP
(to Mayor)
Come back here!

MAYOR HAWKINS
(to cop)
Let me go, you dern fool! I'm the Mayor! Mr. Norton! I'm Mayor Hawkins. Your office telephoned me to hold him.

Int. City Hall: Med. shot: As they walk toward MAYOR'S office.

D. B.
(to Mayor Hawkins)
Well, that's fine. How is he?

MAYOR
Oh, he's fine. He's right in my office there. You know, this is a great honor having John Doe here, and you too. Haven't had so much excitement since the old city hall burned down.
(chuckling)
People were so excited, they nearly tore his clothes off.
(turns to secretary)
Oh, Matilda darling, phone the newspapers. Tell them Mr. Norton is here. Step right inside, Mr. Norton--my office is very comfortable here, Mr. Norton. Just had it air-conditioned. Gangway, please. Make room for Mr. Norton. Gangway, gangway. Here he is, Mr. Norton, well taken care of. The neighbors are serving him a light lunch.

Int. MAYOR's office. Full shot: JOHN and the COLONEL are surrounded by a room full of people, including the SHERIFF in full uniform and several policemen. JOHN sits at the MAYOR'S desk, which is filled with edibles. D. B., ANN and the MAYOR enter. JOHN, upon seeing ANN, gets to his feet.

ANN
Hello, John.

JOHN
Hello.

D. B.
Mister Mayor, if you don't mind, we'd like to talk to him alone.

MAYOR
Why, certainly, certainly. All right, everybody, clear out.

They all start to shuffle out--the MAYOR excitedly egging them on.

MAYOR'S WIFE
Quit pushing.

MAYOR
Don't argue with me here. Wait till we get home.

WIFE
Don't you push me around like that! Even though I'm your wife, you can't push me around--

MAYOR
Ohhhh!

They all shuffle out, and D. B. shuts the door. JOHN watches him, doesn't like his proprietary manner.

JOHN
Look, Mr. Norton, I think you've got a lot of nerve having those people hold us here.

D. B.
There's nobody holding you here, Mr. Doe.
(laughing)
It's only natural that people--

JOHN
Well, if there's nobody holding us here, let's get going. Incidentally, my name isn't Doe. It's Willoughby.

ANN
(gets in front of him--pleads)
Look, John. Something terribly important's happened. They're forming John Doe Clubs. We know of eight already and they say that there's going--

JOHN
(interested despite himself)
John Doe Clubs? What for?

ANN
Uh-huh. To carry out the principles you talked about in your radio speech.

JOHN
(regains his former attitude)
I don't care what they're forming. I'm on my way and I don't like the idea of being stopped either.

ANN
Oh, but you don't know how big this thing is. You should see the thousands of telegrams we've received and what they're saying about you.

JOHN
Look, it started as a circulation stunt, didn't it?

ANN
Uh-huh ...

JOHN
Well, you got your circulation. Now, why don't you let me alone?

ANN
Oh, it started as a circulation stunt, but it isn't any more. Mr. Norton wants to get back of it and sponsor John Doe Clubs all over the country. He wants to send you on a lecture tour.

JOHN
Me?

ANN
Uh-huh.

D. B.
Why, certainly. With your ability to influence people, it might grow into a glorious movement.

JOHN
Say, let's get something straight here. I don't want any part of this thing. If you've got an idea I'm going around lecturing to people, why you're crazy! Baseball's my racket, and I'm sticking to it. Come on, Colonel, let's get out of here.

ANN
John!

The beaming COLONEL starts to follow him to the door. When they get there, the door suddenly flies open and a crowd of townspeople push their way in--with the MAYOR and the SHERIFF trying to hold them back.

MAYOR
Please, please! I just got rid of one crowd.

WOMAN
Oh, but please. Mr. Mayor, tell him the John Doe Club wants to talk to him.

Close-up: Of D. B. He gets an idea. These people might influence JOHN.

D. B.
Let them in, Mr. Mayor. Let them come in.

Full shot: As the MAYOR and the SHERIFF back away.

MAYOR
Okay, folks, but remember your manners. No stampeding. Walk slow, like you do when you come to pay your taxes.

Med. shot: Of the group. They shuffle forward grinning happily. Those in the rear rise on tiptoes for a better look. The men doff their hats as they come forward.

Med. shot: Of JOHN, the COLONEL, ANN and D. B. John glances around nervously. The COLONEL is worried.

Med. shot: Of the townspeople. They just stand there, awkwardly, some grinning sheepishly, others staring at JOHN. Finally someone nudges a young man in the foreground and whispers.

SOMEONE
Come on, Bert.

BERT
Okay. All right, give me a chance.

WOMAN
(making room for him)
Come right in.

Wider shot: As the group around JOHN wait expectantly.

BERT
(clearing throat)
My name's Bert Hansen, Mr. Doe, I'm the head soda jerker at Schwabacher's Drug Store.

Close shot: Of BERT--as he plunges into his story.

BERT
Well, sir, you see, me and my wife, we heard your broadcast, and we got quite a bang out of it, especially my wife.

Wider shot: To include JOHN and the others.

BERT
Kept me up half the night saying "That man's right, honey. The trouble with the world is--nobody gives a hoot about his neighbor. That's why everybody in town's sore and cranky at each other."

And I kept saying, "Well, that's fine, but how's a guy gonna go around loving the kind of neighbors we got? Old Sourpuss for instance!"
(laughing)
You see, Sourpuss Smithers is a guy who lives all alone next door to us. He's a cranky old man and runs a second-hand furniture store. We haven't spoken to him for years. I always figured he was an ornery old gent that hated the world cause he was always slamming his garage door and playing the radio so loud he kept half the neighbors up.
(laughing)

Close-up: Of BERT.

BERT
Well, anyway, the next morning I'm out watering the lawn and I look over and there's Sourpuss on the other side of the hedge straightening out a dent in his fender and, er, my wife yells to me out of the window. She says, "Go on. Speak to him, Bert." And I figured, well, heck, I can't lose anything--so I yelled over to him "Good morning, Mr. Smithers." He went right on pounding his fender, and was I burned! So I turned around to give my wife a dirty look and she said, "Louder, louder. He didn't hear you." So, in a voice you could of heard in the next county, I yelled. "Good morning, Mr. Smithers!"

Med. shot: Featuring JOHN and BERT. JOHN is very interested.

BERT
Well, sir, you coulda knocked me over with a feather. Old Sourpuss turned around surprised like, and he put on a big smile, came over and took my hand like an old lodge brother, and he said. "Good morning, Hansen. I've been wanting to talk to you for years, only I thought you didn't like me." And then he started chatting away like a happy little kid, and he got so excited his eyes begin waterin' up.

Med. shot: Of a group of neighbors. They smile sympathetically.

BERT'S VOICE
Well, Mr. Doe, before we got through, I found out Smithers is a swell egg, only he's pretty deaf, and that accounts for all the noises.

Wider shot: To include BERT, JOHN and others.

BERT
And he says it's a shame how little we know about our neighbors, and then he got an idea, and he said, "How's about inviting everybody some place where we can all get together and know each other a little better?" Well, I'm feeling so good by this time, I'm ripe for anything.

Close shot: Of ANN and D. B. They listen, amused and excited.

BERT
So Smithers goes around the neighborhood inviting everybody to a meeting at the school house and I tell everybody that comes in the store, including Mr. Schwabacher, my boss.
(laughing)
Oh, I'm talking too much.

Med. shot: JOHN and BERT.

BERT
Well, I'll be doggoned if over forty people don't show up. 'Course none of us knew what to do, but we sure got a kick out of seeing how glad everybody was just to say hello to one another.

BERT'S WIFE
Tell him about making Sourpuss chairman, honey.

BERT
Oh, yeah. We made Sourpuss chairman and decided to call ourselves The John Doe Club. And, say, incidentally, this is my wife. Come here, honey.

His WIFE comes forward and stands beside him.

BERT
This is my wife, Mr. Doe.

MRS. HANSEN nods her head shyly--and JOHN acknowledges the introduction by a half wave of his hand.

WIFE
How do you do, Mr. Doe ... Er, Sourpuss is here, too.

BERT
(turns around)
Oh, is he?

WIFE
(pointing)
Uh-huh.

Med. shot: Of a group around SOURPUSS. He is as described, except when he smiles, his whole face warms up. Those around him push him forward. At first he looks bewildered, then, understanding, he starts toward BERT, grinning sheepishly.

Med. shot: Around BERT--as SOURPUSS comes forward.

BERT
This is Sourpuss. Er, excuse me. Er, Mr. Smithers, Mr. Doe.

SOURPUSS
Th-that's all right. If you didn't call me Sourpuss, it wouldn't feel natural.
(laughing)

There are snickers from the background.

BERT
Well, anyway, I--I guess nearly everybody in the neighborhood came, except the DeLaneys. The Delaneys live in a big house with an iron fence around it and they always keep their blinds drawn, and we always figured that he was just an old miser that sat back counting his money, so why bother about inviting him? Until Grimes, the milkman spoke up and he said, "Say, you've got the Delaneys all wrong." And then he tells

us about how they cancelled their milk last week, and how, when he found a note in the bottle he got kinda curious like and he sorta peeked in under the blinds and found the house empty. "If you ask me," he says, "they're starving."

SOURPUSS
Old man Delaney has been bringing his furniture over to my place at night, one piece at a time, and selling it.

Close shot: Of JOHN. Profoundly impressed by this.

Wider shot: BERT clears his throat.

BERT
Yeah. And, well, sir, a half a dozen of us ran over there to fetch them and we got them to the meeting. What a reception they got. Why, everybody shook hands with them and made a fuss over them, and, well, finally, Mr. and Mrs. Delaney just sat right down and cried.

He smiles, embarrassed, and JOHN, as well as the others, clear their throats.

SOURPUSS
And then we started to find out about a lot of other people.

BERT
Yeah, sure. Er, you know Grubbel, for instance.

BERT'S WIFE
Grubbel's here. See?
(pointing)

BERT
Yeah. That's--that's him. Of course, you don't know Grubbel, but he's the man that everybody figured was the worst no-account in the neighborhood because he was living like a hermit and nobody'd have anything to do with him. Er, that is until Murphy, the postman told us the truth. "Why, Grubbel," he says, "he lives out of garbage cans because he won't take charity. Because it'd ruin his self-respect," he says.

BERT'S WIFE
Just like you said on the radio, Mr. Doe.

SOURPUSS
Well, sir, about a dozen families got together and gave Grubbel a job watering their lawns. Isn't that wonderful? And then we found jobs for six other people and they've all gone off relief!

BERT
Yeh. Er, and my boss, Mr. Schwabacker made a job in his warehouse for old man Delaney--

WIFE
And he gave you that five dollar raise.

BERT
Yeah! Wasn't that swell!
(laughing)

Med. shot: Around MAYOR HAWKINS. He steps forward.

MAYOR
Why, Bert, I feel slighted. I'd like to join but nobody asked me.

Med. shot: Around BERT and SOURPUSS.

SOURPUSS
Well, I'm sorry, Mayor, but we voted that no politicians could join.

BERT'S WIFE
Just the John Does of the neighborhood. Cause you know how politicians are.
(becomes embarrassed)

Close-up: Of the MAYOR--completely deflated.

SOURPUSS
Yeah ...

Med. shot: Around JOHN. As they smile, amused at the MAYOR's discomfiture.

Med. shot: Around BERT. He looks over at JOHN, hesitates a moment, and then speaks.

BERT
Well, er, the reason we wanted to tell you this, Mr. Doe, was to give you an idea what you started. And from where I'm sitting, I don't see any sense in your jumping off any building.

GROUP
No!

SOURPUSS
No!

BERT
Well, thank you for listening. Goodbye, Mr. Doe. You're a wonderful man and it strikes me you can be mighty useful walking around for a while.

Close-up: Of JOHN. Deeply touched. Shifts awkwardly, unable to say anything.

Med. shot: As D. B. and ANN watch his face to see the effect.

GROUP
Well, goodbye.

SOURPUSS
Goodbye Mr. Doe.

BERT has turned to go, and the rest follow suit. They all shuffle silently out.

Med. shot: Of an old couple who remain looking up at JOHN, as those around them leave. The old lady takes the old man's arm and starts toward JOHN. Camera pans with them until they reach him.

OLD LADY
I'm Mrs. Delaney, Mr. Doe ... and God bless you, my boy.
(she gently kisses his hand)

The two OLD PEOPLE leave.

Close up: Of JOHN. He swallows a lump in his throat. He watches the old people until they have left, then with a quick glance at his hand--and self-consciously in front of the others, stuffs his hand into his pocket.

Full shot: As they all watch him, without speaking. JOHN runs his hand through his hair, stealing a fleeting glance at the others, and grins awkwardly.

Close shot: Of D. B. as he signals to the MAYOR and the SHERIFF, who have remained, to leave.

Med. shot: Of the MAYOR and the SHERIFF, who receive the signal and discreetly exit.

Full shot: They wait for JOHN to speak, but JOHN begins walking around, profoundly thoughtful.

Close-up: Of the COLONEL watching him, concerned.

Two shot: Of D. B. and ANN. Their eyes glued on him, expectantly.

Full shot: JOHN still paces, disturbed by clashing emotions. He stops, glances at the door, a soft, thoughtful expression in his eyes. Then, as his thought shifts, he runs his left hand over his pitching arm.

JOHN
Gee, whiz--I'm all mixed up--I don't get it. Look, all those swell people think I'm gonna jump off a building or something.

He looks toward the door.

JOHN
I never had any such idea. Gosh! A fella'd have to be a mighty fine example himself to go around telling other people how to-- Say, look, what happened the other night was on account of Miss Mitchell, here. She wrote the stuff.

ANN walks over to JOHN.

Two shot: ANN and JOHN. She faces him, looking up into his face.

ANN
Don't you see what a wonderful thing this can be?
(softly)
But we need *you,* John.

Close-up: Of the COLONEL. He stares at JOHN, sees him weakening, and grimaces disgustedly.

Wider shot: The COLONEL watches JOHN as he continues to turn it over in his mind.

COLONEL
(suddenly)
You're hooked! I can see that right now.

They all look up, startled.

COLONEL
They got you. Well, I'm through.
(crosses to door--stops, turns)
For three years I've been trying to get you up to the Columbia River country. First, it was your glass arm. Then it was the radio. And now it's the John Doe clubs. Well, I ain't waiting another minute.

He opens the door and when he sees the townspeople still gathered outside, he yells to them.

COLONEL
Gangway, you heelots!

He pushes his way out.

JOHN
(calling)
Hey, Colonel! Wait a minute!

He starts after the COLONEL, but when he gets to the door, the townspeople surge toward him and block his way.

JOHN
Hey, Colonel!

CROWD
Oh, please, Mr. Doe--

Close-up: Of JOHN.

JOHN
(calling futilely)
Hey, Colonel!

He tries to peer over the heads of the townspeople who go on chattering. There is a trapped look on JOHN's face.

Two shot: D. B. and ANN. They exchange victorious glances:

Dissolve to: Int. office of headquarters. Close shot: Of large map of the U.S. over the top of which we read: "John Doe Clubs." There are a dozen pegs scattered over the map, indicating where the clubs are. We hear D. B.'s voice.

Camera draws back and we find D. B. talking to a group of men in front of him.

D. B.
I want you personally to go along with John Doe and Miss Mitchell and handle the press and the radio.

CHARLIE
(an experienced promoter)
Me?

D. B.
Yes. I don't want to take any chances. And Johnson?

JOHNSON
Yes. D. B.

D. B.
Your crew will do the mop up job. They'll follow John Doe into every town, see that the clubs are properly organized and the charters issued.

CHARLIE
Right.

D. B.
There are only eight flags up there now. I want to see that map covered before we get through!

Med. shot: D. B. is still speaking as camera moves down to the map again, which constantly remains a background for the montage following. As the montage proceeds, pegs begin to appear in abundance on the map.

A montage: Accompanied by a fanfare of music.

1. Flashes of banners reading:
"JOHN DOE COMING"--"JOHN DOE TONIGHT"
"GOODBYE JOHN DOE, CALL AGAIN"

2. Close-ups of JOHN speaking--superimposed over long shots of audiences of various types.

3. Flashes of ANN typing.

4. Flashes of sheets of paper being ripped out of a typewriter.

5. Flashes of JOHN on the radio with ANN by his side.

6. Flashes of people listening.

7. Flashes of people applauding.

8. Series of signs being nailed up: "JOHN DOE CLUB--BE A BETTER NEIGHOR."

9. Superimposed shots of JOHN and ANN riding in trains, planes and automobiles.

10. Against stock shots of these cities, the names zoom up to the foreground of Kansas City, Chicago, Buffalo, Washington, Baltimore, Philadelphia, New York.

11. Superimpose map over the above titles, showing the states they are in being covered with pegs.

12. A picture of JOHN DOE on front page of <u>Time</u> magazine, with a caption under it reading: "MAN OF THE HOUR."

13. Conference Room.

SPEAKER
This has been growing like wildfire! If they only made demands, but the John Does ask for nothing!

14. A man sits at a desk on which is a nameplate reading: "Relief Administrator."

MAN
People are going off relief! If this keeps up, I'll be out of a job!

15. Stock shot--of Capitol Hill.

16. Corner of a club smoking room. A group of legislators--some sit--some stand. The room is filled with smoke.

MAN
As soon as he gets strong enough, we'll find out what John Doe wants! Thirty every Thursday--sixty at sixty--who knows what!

17. Insert: Sign reading: DEMOCRATIC HEADQUARTERS. A man reports to the boss behind the desk.

MAN
I'm sorry, boss. they just won't let anybody talk politics to them. It's, it's crazy.

18. Insert: Sign reading: REPUBLICAN HEADQUARTERS. A man at a desk talks to several in front of him.

MAN
We've got to get to them! They represent millions of voters!

Dissolve to: Insert: Of Map. Nearly every state in the union have pegs in them, varying in volume. Camera pulls back and we find the map is on a stand near a door, the sign on which we see in reverse. It reads: "OFFICE OF JOHN DOE HEADQUARTERS."

Int. JOHN DOE headquarters. Med. shot: D. B. standing behind his desk, speaking to a group of people in front of him. We recognize the MAYOR, and the President of the Chamber of Commerce. Representatives of several other branches of the City Administration are also present. CONNELL sits near D. B.--scrutinizing him thoughtfully. On the other side of D. B. is TED SHELDON.

D. B.
I tell you, ladies and gentlemen, this thing has been nothing short of a prairie fire. We've received so many applications for charters to the John Doe Clubs we haven't been able to take care of them.

MAYOR LOVETT
I'd hate to have that many pins stuck in me!

Group laughs.

D. B.
This John Doe convention is a natural. It's gonna put our city on the map. Why, over twenty-four hundred John Doe clubs are sending delegates. Can you imagine that? You, Mr. Mayor, will be the official host. You will make the arrangements for decorating the city, parades and a reception for John Doe when he gets home! And--don't wear your high hat!

MAYOR LOVETT
(disappointed)
No high hat?

D. B.
No high hat. And from you, Connell, I want a special John Doe edition every day until the convention is over.
(dismissing them)
And now, if you will please just step into the outer office and look your prettiest because there are photographers there to take pictures of this committee.

They start to exit. The MAYOR is full of excitement.

MAYOR
Don't worry, D. B. Everything'll be taken care of!

D. B.
Good.

COMMITTEE WOMAN
Isn't it all too wonderful?

The group, chattering, exit into outer office.

PHOTOGRAPHER'S VOICE
(from the outer office)
Oh, Mr. Mayor, would you step right in the front row, please? Will you ladies get close to him? That's it!

Close up. Of CONNELL. To inter-cut with above speech. He has been watching D. B.--deeply disturbed about something.

Wider shot. All have left except CONNELL, TED, and D. B. CONNELL rises from his chair--with a deep sigh.

CONNELL
(shaking his head)
Well, I don't get it.

D. B.
Huh? Get what?

CONNELL
Look, D. B. I'm supposed to know my way around. This John Doe movement costs you a fortune. This convention's gonna cost plenty.

D. B.
(annoyed)
Well?

CONNELL
Well, I'm stuck with two and two--but I'm a sucker if I can make four out of it.
(cocking his head)
Where do _you_ come in?

D. B.
Why--uh--
(suddenly smiles)
Why, I'll have the satisfaction of knowing that my money has been spent for a worthy cause.

Close-up: Of CONNELL. He stares at D. B. a moment. He realizes he has been told to mind his own business.

Two shot: CONNELL picks up his hat.

CONNELL
I see. I'd better stick to running the paper, huh?

D. B.
I think maybe you'd better. And Connell--I'd like to have the John Doe contract, all the receipts for the money we have advanced him and the letter Miss Mitchell wrote, for which I gave her a thousand dollars.

CONNELL
Yes. Sure.

CONNELL leaves.

Dissolve to: Int. a hotel living room--night. Full shot: ANN's luggage is packed and ready to be taken out. She stands near a desk stuffing papers into a manuscript case. She seems lost in worried thought. The door opens as CHARLIE, high pressure exploitation man, enters.

CHARLIE
Well, we leave for the airport in half an hour. Is that Johnny-boy's room? I'd better hustle him up!

ANN
He'll be ready on time. He's packing now.

CHARLIE
Ah, good!
(crosses to Ann)
Did you see his picture on the cover of _Time_?

ANN
Yeah.

CHARLIE drops the magazine on the desk in front of her. ANN glances at it, unenthusiastically. CHARLIE goes to a table where there are several bottles of coca-cola and starts to pour himself a drink.

CHARLIE
I gotta give you credit, Annie-girl. I've handled a good many big promotions in my time ... everything from the world's fair to a channel swimmer, but this one has certainly got me spinning. And now a John Doe Convention! Wow! Say! If you could only get him to jump off the City Hall roof on Christmas Eve, I'd guarantee you half a million people there.

ANN
Charlie!

ANN is lost in troubled thought.

CHARLIE'S VOICE
Huh?

ANN
(nods toward door)
What do you make of him?

Two shot: CHARLIE and ANN.

CHARLIE
Who, Johnny-boy?

ANN nods.

CHARLIE
Well, I don't know what angle you want, but I'll give it to you quick. Number one, he's got great yokel appeal; but he's a nice guy. Number two, he's beginning to believe he really wrote that original suicide letter that you made up. Number three, he thinks that you're Joan of Arc or something!

Close-up: Of ANN. This is definitely troublesome to her.

ANN
(hoarsely)
Yeah, I know.

Wider shot: ANN walks away--pacing perturbedly.

CHARLIE
Number four, well, you know what number four is. He's nuts about you. Yeah, it's running out of his ears.

ANN runs her hand through her hair. Suddenly she wheels around to CHARLIE.

ANN
You left out number five. We're all heels, me especially.

She returns to her packing. CHARLIE watches her a second.

CHARLIE
Holy smoke!

They are interrupted by a knock on the door.

ANN
(calling)
Come in.

JOHN enters, carrying a suitcase.

JOHN
I'm all packed.

CHARLIE
(starts out)
Good. I'll go and get Beany-boy.

JOHN
(kidding him)
Okay, Charlie-boy!

CHARLIE
Huh?
(laughing)[10]

CHARLIE winks good-naturedly and exits. JOHN turns to ANN, who concentrates on her packing.

Med. shot: He looks at ANN with great interest, and walks toward her, camera panning with him. ANN feels him coming, but does not turn.

JOHN
(after a pause)
Can I help you pack?

ANN
No, thank you.

JOHN wanders over to a chair and sits on the edge--watching her.

Close-up: Of ANN. She is conscious of his eyes on her and fumbles with her packing. Finally she turns.

Close-up: Of JOHN. He stares at her, a warm smile on his face.

Close-up: Of ANN. She becomes self-conscious and resumes her packing.

Med. shot: JOHN.

JOHN
Do you care if I sit down out here?

ANN
No.

A broad smile appears on JOHN'S face.

JOHN
(laughing)
You know, I had a crazy dream last night. It was about you.

ANN
About me?

JOHN
(laughing)
Sure was crazy. I dreamt I was your father.

Close-up: Of ANN. The fact that he has seen himself in the image of her father disturbs her. She turns slowly.

Two shot: JOHN clears his throat nervously.

JOHN
There was, there was something I was trying to stop you from doing. So, er, so I got up out of bed and I walked right through the wall here, right straight into your room.
(laughing)
You know how dreams are.

ANN stares at him--fearful of the trend his dream is taking.

JOHN
And there you were in bed.
(quickly apologizing)
But you--you were a little girl. You know--
about ten.

He pauses and recalls the scene.

JOHN
And very pretty, too. So, I shook you, and
the moment you opened your eyes, you hopped out
of bed and started running like the devil, in
your nightgown.
You ran right out the window there. And you
ran out over the tops of buildings and roofs and
everything for miles, and I was chasing you.
(laughing)
And all the time you were running you kept growing bigger and bigger and bigger--and pretty
soon you were as big as you are now. You know--
grown up. And all the time I kept asking myself,
"What am I chasing her for?" And I didn't know.
(laughing)
Isn't that a hot one? Well, anyway, you ran
into some place, and then I ran in after you
and--and when I got there, there you were getting married.

Close-up: Of JOHN. He suddenly becomes aware he is treading on sensitive grounds.

JOHN
(awkwardly)
And the nightgown had changed into a beautiful
wedding gown. You sure looked pretty, too.
(laughing)
And then I knew what it was I was trying to stop
you from doing.

Close-up: Of ANN. She, too, begins to feel uncomfortable--not quite knowing how to handle it.

Two shot: JOHN glances at her.

JOHN
Dreams are sure crazy, aren't they?

ANN smiles, noncommittedly.

JOHN
Well, would you like to know who it was you were
marrying?

ANN
(forced lightness)
Well, a tall handsome Ubangi, I suppose.

JOHN
No, not that bad. It was a fella that sends you
flowers every day. Er, what's his name? Mr. Norton's nephew.

Close-up: Of ANN. She recognizes the significance in this.

ANN
(quietly)
Ted Sheldon.

JOHN
Yeah, that's the one.

ANN turns back to her packing.

Wider shot: JOHN starts to chuckle.

JOHN
But here's the funniest part of it all. I was the fella up there doing the marrying. You know, the Justice of the Peace or something ...

ANN
You were? I thought you were chasing me?

JOHN
Well, yes, I was. But I was your father then, see? But the real me, John Doe, er, that is, Long John Willoughby, I was the fellow up there with the book. You know what I mean?

ANN
(amused)
I guess so. Then what happened?

JOHN
Well, I took you across my knee and I started spanking you.

ANN turns and stares at him, eyes widening.

JOHN
(quickly explaining)
That is, I didn't do it.
(correcting himself)
I mean, I did do it, but it wasn't me. You see, I was your father then. Well, I laid you across my knee and I said: "Annie, I won't allow you to marry a man that's, that's just rich, or that has his secretary send you flowers. The man you marry has got to swim rivers for you! He's got to climb high mountains for you! He's got to slay dragons for you! He's got to perform wonderful deeds for you! Yes, sir!"

BEANY enters and stands back of him, listening.

JOHN
And all the time, er, the guy up there, you know, with the book, me, just stood there nodding his head and he said, "Go to it, Pop, whack her one for me, because that's just the way I feel about it, too."
So he says, "Come on down here and whack her yourself." So I came down and I whacked you a good one, see? And then he whacked one--and I whacked you another one, and we both started whacking you like ...

He demonstrates by slapping his knees, first with one hand and then with the other. Suddenly he becomes aware of BEANY and stops, embarrassed.

BEANY
(interrupting)
Well, if you're through whacking her, come on, let's get going.
(to bell boys)
Okay, fellows, right in here.
(to JOHN)
You go out the side entrance. There's a bunch of autograph seekers out front. We'll be down with the bags in a minute. Come on!
(speaking to boys)
Don't make a government project out of this!

The bell boys have lifted her luggage and all exit.

Close-up: Of JOHN. He has been left with his proposal unfinished.

Dissolve to: Int. airport lunchroom--night. Med. shot: Scene opens with BEANY entering airport lunchroom to end of counter at which CHARLIE is seated.

CHARLIE
How're you, Beany?

BEANY
When does our plane take off again.

CHARLIE
In a couple of minutes.

Camera moves down counter to pick up JOHN and ANN at table. They sit silently for a moment. We hear the strains of music from a "juke" box.

JOHN
(after a pause)
How many people do you think we've talked to already, outside the radio, I mean?

ANN
I don't know. About three hundred thousand.

JOHN
Three hundred thousand? What makes them do it, Ann? What makes them come and listen and, and get up their John Doe Clubs the way they do? I've been trying to figure it out.

ANN
(in an effort to disillusion him)
Look, John--what we're handing them are platitudes. Things they've heard a million times: "Love thy neighbor," "Clouds have silver linings," "Turn the other cheek." It's just a--

JOHN
(sincerely)
Yeah, I've heard them a million times, too, but--there you are. Maybe they're like me. Just beginning to get an idea what those things mean.

ANN is deeply concerned. She watches him, helplessly.

JOHN
(continuing)
You know, I never thought much about people before. They were always just somebody to fill up the bleachers. The only time I worried about them was if they--is when they didn't come in to see me pitch. You know, lately I've been watching them while I talked to them. I could see something in their faces. I could feel that they were hungry for something. Do you know what I mean?

ANN nods.

JOHN
Maybe that's why they came. Maybe they were just lonely and wanted somebody to say hello to. I know how they feel. I've been lonely and hungry for something practically all my life.

ANN forces a smile. The moment threatens to become awkward--until they are saved by the pilot's voice.

PILOT
All aboard, folks!

They suddenly snap out of their mood--and as they rise:

Fade out.

Fade in: Int. D. B.'s dining room. Full shot: As D. B., ANN and TED SHELDON enter and cross to table. ANN starts to sit and notices a fur coat flung over the back of the chair.

ANN
Oh, somebody else sitting there?

D. B.
No, no, no--that's your seat.

TED
And this is your coat.

ANN
Mine?

D. B.
A little token of appreciation.

Ann pauses a moment, glances toward D. B.--while TED throws the coat over her shoulders.

ANN
(glances into a mirror)
Oh! Oh, it's beautiful, D. B. Well--I don't quite know what to say ...

D. B.
Well, don't say anything at all. Just sit down.

Close-up: Of ANN. She sits down, picks up her serviette--and something she sees suddenly makes her look with surprise at D. B.

Camera pans down to a jewel box which had been under the serviette.

Camera pans back to ANN. She glances up at D. B. somewhat bewildered.

ANN
Oh!

D. B.
Go ahead, open it, open it.

ANN opens the box and holds up a lovely diamond bracelet. Her eyes dance.

ANN
Oh! Oh, it's lovely!

TED
And a new contract goes with it.

Wider shot: D. B. and TED exchange satisfied glances. ANN admires the bracelet on her wrist--and then turns to D. B., looks directly at him.

ANN
(shrewdly)
Well, come on, spring it! You've got something on your mind.

D. B. laughs.

ANN
Must be stupendous.

Wider shot: As D. B. roars with laughter.

D. B.
You know, that's what I like about her. Right to the point, like that! All right, practical Annie, here it is.

He leans forward. ANN waits. TED watches her face.

Two shot: ANN and D. B.

D. B.
Tomorrow night, before a crowd of fifteen thousand people, and talking over a nation-wide radio hook-up, John Doe will announce the formation of a third party.

ANN
(eyes widening)
A third party?

D. B.
Yes. The John Doe Party.

Wider shot: TED watches ANN, expectantly.

D. B.
Devoted entirely to the interests of all the John Does all over the country. Which practically means, ninety per cent of the voters. He will also announce the third party's candidate for the presidency. A man whom he, personally, recommends. A great humanitarian; the best friend the John Does have.

Ann
(in an awed whisper)
Mr. D. B. Norton!

D. B. verifies her guess by leaning back, a pleased grin on his face, his huge chest expanded.

D. B.
Yes.

Ann looks from one to the other, a little awed by the size of the project.

ANN
(on her breath)
Wow!

Dissolve to: Int. broadcasting booth--ball park--night. Med. shot: The place is a bee-hive of activity. Announcers walk about with "mikes" in their hands--all speaking at once--as they describe the scene below.

Close shot: Of N.B.C. ANNOUNCER

N.B.C. ANNOUNCER
And although the opening of the convention is hours off, the delegates are already pouring into the ball park by the droves, with lunch baskets, banners and petitions, asking John Doe not to jump off any roof ...

Camera pans over to KNOX MANNING.

KNOX MANNING
It is still a phenomenal movement. The John Does, or the hoi polloi as you've heard people call them, have been laughed at and ridiculed but here they are, gay and happy, having traveled thousands of miles, their expenses paid by their neighbors, to come here to pay homage to their hero, John Doe.

Camera pans over to JOHN B. HUGHES.

JOHN B. HUGHES
And in these days of wars and bombings, it's a hopeful sign that a simple idea like this can sweep the country, an idea based on friendliness, on giving and not taking, on helping your neighbor and asking nothing in return. And if a thing like this can happen, don't let any of our grumbling friends tell you that humanity is falling apart. This is John B. Hughes, signing off now and returning you to our main studio until nine o'clock when the convention will officially open.

Dissolve to: Int. ANN's living room. Med. shot: At Door. ANN's MOTHER opens it and JOHN stands on the threshold. He has a small box of flowers in his hand. Water drips from his hat.

MRS. MITCHELL
Oh, John. Come in.

JOHN
Say, I'm kinda--it's raining out a little--

MRS. MITCHELL
That's all right.

Wider shot: MRS. MITCHELL lays his hat down somewhere. John takes a few steps inside the room, not quite knowing what to do.

MRS. MITCHELL
(turning to him)
It's good to see you. Sit down.

JOHN
(mumbles)
Thanks.

He sits on the edge of a sofa, still clinging to the little box. Then holds box out awkwardly.

JOHN
(awkwardly)
It's for Ann

MRS. MITCHELL
(taking the box)
Oh, how nice! Thank you very much.

JOHN
Flowers.

MRS. MITCHELL
I'm terribly sorry she isn't here.

JOHN
She isn't?

MRS. MITCHELL
No, she just left. I'm surprised you didn't run into her. She went over to Mr. Norton's house.

JOHN
Oh!

MRS. MITCHELL
Did you want to see her about something important?

JOHN
Yeah. I, uh, well ... No. It'll wait.
(suddenly)
Say, he's a nice man, isn't he? Mr. Norton, I mean. He's, er, he's done an awful lot for the--

Close-up: Of MRS. MITCHELL. She watches him, amused.

JOHN
Say, my coat's pretty wet. I'm afraid I might have wet the couch a little.

Wider shot: JOHN is still struggling to find conversation.

JOHN
Well, I guess I'll see her at the convention later.

MRS. MITCHELL
Yes, of course. I'll see that she gets the flowers.

He rises and looks around for hat on the floor and back of the chair.

JOHN
Thanks. Good night, Mrs. Mitchell.

MRS. MITCHELL
(finds his hat and gives it to him)
Good night, John.

Close-up: Of JOHN. He starts away and suddenly stops, speculatively. He glances out of the corner of his eye toward MRS. MITCHELL.

JOHN
(going back to her)
Say, Mrs. Mitchell, I, er, I'm kinda glad Ann isn't here. You see, I was, I came over here hoping to see her alone and kinda hoping I wouldn't, too. You know what I mean? There was something I wanted to talk to her about. But, well, I--It'll wait, I guess. Good night.

Close-up: Of MRS. MITCHELL. She begins to sense what is on his mind, and her face becomes serious.

Close-up: Of JOHN. He smiles helplessly. Starts toward door.

MRS. MITCHELL'S VOICE
Good night, John.

Two shot: JOHN and MRS. MITCHELL. He stares at her a second.

JOHN
(suddenly)
Say, look, Mrs. Mitchell, have you ever been married?

(catches himself)
Oh, sure you have.
(grins sheepishly)
Gosh! That's pretty silly! I guess you must think I'm kinda batty!

JOHN shakes his head at his own stupidity.

JOHN
(can't get over it)
Well, I guess I'd better be going at that!

He bows again, and starts for the door. When he gets there, he is stopped by MRS. MITCHELL's voice.

MRS. MITCHELL'S VOICE
John. My husband said: "I love you. Will you marry me?"

JOHN
(whirls)
He did? What happened?

MRS. MITCHELL
I married him.

JOHN comes right back to her.

Two shot: JOHN and MRS. MITCHELL.

JOHN
(full of excitement)
Oh, yeah. That's what I mean. See? It was easy as all that, huh?

MRS. MITCHELL
Uh-huh.

JOHN
Yeah, yeah, but look, Mrs. Mitchell, you know I love Ann and it's gonna be awfully hard for me to say it because, well, you know, she's so wonderful, and, well, the best I ever was was a bush-league pitcher.

Close-up: Of JOHN.

JOHN
And you know, I think she's in love with another man, the one she made up. You know, the real John Doe. Well, that's pretty tough competition.

Two shot: JOHN and MRS. MITCHELL. She is terribly fond of JOHN and deeply sympathetic.

JOHN
I bet you he'd know how to say it all right. And me, I get up to it and around it and in back of it, but, but I never get right to it. Do you know what I mean? So the only chance I've got is, well, if somebody could kinda give her a warning sort of, sorta prepare her for the shock!

MRS. MITCHELL
You mean you'd like me to do it, huh?

JOHN
Well, I was thinking that--Yeah, you know, sort of break the ice.

Close-up of MOTHER. She doesn't know how she can, with her present strained relationship with ANN, but JOHN's sincerity touches her.

MOTHER
Of course I will, John.

Two shot: JOHN's face lights up, gratefully.

JOHN
Gee whiz! Thank you, Mrs. Mitchell.
(grabs her hand)
Gee, you're--uh--you're okay!

He exits from scene--but almost immediately he is back. He plants a kiss on her cheek and goes.

Cut to: Ext. sidewalk. Front of ANN's apartment. Med. Shot: An automobile stands at the curb, in front of which is BEANY. Also waiting, are four motorcycle policeman.

BEANY
(to the other men)
This John Doe meeting is gonna be one of the biggest things that ever happened.

As JOHN appears in the doorway of the apartment house, he pretends to throw a baseball at them.

BEANY
Why, they're coming from all over; trains, box cars, wagons--
(sees JOHN)
look out!

Med. shot: Reverse angle. As BEANY holds the door open for JOHN.

JOHN
Hello, bodyguards! Hey, had your dinner yet?

BODYGUARD
Not yet.

JOHN
Well, look. No. Go ahead and have your dinner. I'll--

He is about to enter the car when a voice from off-scene stops him.

CONNELL'S VOICE
Wait a minute, John.

Camera pans over to a taxicab which has just driven in. CONNELL hands the driver a bill and walks, rather unsteadily toward JOHN.

Med. shot: Around BEANY's car. CONNELL ambles into the scene.

JOHN
Hello, Mr. Connell.

CONNELL
Hiyah, John.
(broad wink)
John, I want to have a little talk with you.
(lurches--John holds him up)
What's the matter--are you falling? Come here.

Takes his arm to lead him off.

BEANY
(protesting)
Hey, Boss.

CONNELL
Oh, quiet, quiet, quiet.
(to John)
Say, tell me something did you read that speech you're gonna make tonight?

JOHN
No, I never read the speeches before I make them. I get more of a kick out of it that way.

CONNELL
(wisely)
Uh-huh. That's exactly what I thought. Beany, go on down to the office, tell Pop to give you the speech. There's a copy on my desk.

BEANY
(protesting)
Gee whiz, Boss, you know Mr. Norton told me not to leave him, not even for a minute.

CONNELL
(shooing him away)
Go on, go on, go on. And we'll be at Jim's Bar up the street.

He points in the general direction and again takes JOHN's arm. JOHN watches him, rather amused to see CONNELL off his milk diet, and allows himself to be led away.

Wipe to: Int. a barroom. Close shot: In a corner booth, JOHN and CONNELL sit, close together, drinks in front of them. JOHN's drink has remained untouched. CONNELL is just taking a long swig. From off-scene we hear the strains of an old-fashioned torch ballad, coming from an automatic piano.

CONNELL
(after a pause)
You're a nice guy, John. I like you. You're gentle. I like gentle people. Me? I'm hard--hard and tough.
(shakes his head--disparagingly)
I got no use for hard people. Gotta be gentle to suit me. Like you, for instance.

JOHN smiles, amused at him. CONNELL starts to light his cigarette, which is bent. He hold the match up, but it never reaches the tip of the bent cigarette. He puffs, satisfied.

CONNELL
Yep, I'm hard. But you want to know something? I've got a weakness. You'd never guess that, would you? Well, I have. Want to know what it is?

JOHN nods.

CONNELL
The Star Spangled Banner.
(looks directly at John)
Screwy, huh?
(turns back to his glass)
Well, maybe it is. But play the "Star Spangled Banner"--and I'm a sucker for it. It always gets me right here--
(thumps his diaphragm)
You know what I mean?

Close-up: Of JOHN. His face has become serious.

JOHN
Yeah.
(points to back of neck)
It gets me right back here.

Two shot: JOHN and CONNELL. CONNELL speculates about this with his head cocked.

CONNELL
Oh, back there, huh?
(shrugs, dismissing it)
Well, every man to his own taste.

JOHN smiles at him. CONNELL tries lighting his bent cigarette again--with the same result--while JOHN watches, amused.

CONNELL
You weren't old enough for the first world war, were you?

JOHN starts to answer, but CONNELL goes right on.

CONNELL
Course not. Must have been a kid.

He pours JOHN's drink into his own glass.

CONNELL
I was. I was just ripe. And rarin' to go.
(takes drink)
Know what my old man did when I joined up? He joined up too.

Close-up: Of JOHN. He finds himself intensely interested.

CONNELL'S VOICE
Got to be a sergeant.

Two shot: JOHN and CONNELL.

CONNELL
(as he raises his glass)
That's a kick for you. We were in the same outfit. Funny, huh?

Close-up: Of CONNELL. He lifts his glass to his lips, and without drinking, lowers it.

CONNELL
(voice lowers)
He was killed, John.

Close-up: Of JOHN. His face enveloped in an expression of sympathy.

Two shot: CONNELL stares down at the glass which he revolves between his palms.

CONNELL
I saw him get it. I was right there and saw it with my own eyes.

Without glancing at JOHN, he lifts the glass and drains it.

CONNELL
(turns to JOHN)
Me? I came out of it without a scratch. Except for my ulcers. Should be drinking milk.
(picks up his glass)
This stuff's poison.

As he holds up his glass, he realizes it is empty.

CONNELL
(yelling to bartender)
Hey, Tubby!

BARTENDER'S VOICE
Yes, Mr. Connell?

CONNELL
(indicates the empty glass)
Whadda you say?

TUBBY
All right.

Close shot: JOHN and CONNELL. CONNELL looks around guardedly, to make certain he is not overheard.

CONNELL
(confidentially)
Yessir. I'm a sucker for this country.
(gets a little sore about it)
I'm a sucker for the Star Spangled Banner--and I'm a sucker for this country.
(taps table with his middle finger)
I like what we got here! I like it!

(emphasizes each point)
A guy can say what he wants--and do what he wants--without having a bayonet shoved through his belly.

Med. shot: As he leans back and nods his head, satisfied he made his point.

CONNELL
Now, that's all right, isn't it?

JOHN
You betcha.

The BARTENDER comes in with drink and departs.

CONNELL
All right. And we don't want anybody coming around changing it, do we?

JOHN shakes his head.

JOHN
No, sir.

Two shot: JOHN and CONNELL.

CONNELL
No, sir. And when they do I get mad! I get b-boiling mad. And right now, John, I'm sizzling!

JOHN looks at him, puzzled.

CONNELL
I get mad for a lot of other guys besides myself--I get mad for a guy named Washington! And a guy named Jefferson--and Lincoln. Lighthouses, John! Lighthouses in a foggy world! You know what I mean?

JOHN
(huskily)
Yeah, you bet!

CONNELL takes a drink and looks at JOHN a moment before he speaks.

CONNELL
(leans on the table)
Listen, pal--this fifth column stuff's pretty rotten, isn't it?[11]

JOHN
Yeah. It certainly is.

CONNELL
And you'd feel like an awful sucker if you found yourself marching right in the middle of it, wouldn't you?

JOHN glances up sharply.

CONNELL
And you, of course you wouldn't know it because you're gentle. But that's what you're doing. You're mixed up with a skunk, my boy, a no-good, dangerous skunk!

JOHN'S resentment vanishes--and is replaced by puzzlement.

JOHN
Say, you're not talking about Mr. Norton, are you?

Two shot: JOHN and CONNELL.

CONNELL
(emphatically)
I'm not talking about his grandfather's pet poodle!

CONNELL again makes an effort to light his bent cigarette--and again is unsuccessful.

JOHN
You must be wrong, Mr. Connell, 'cause he's been marvelous about the John Doe Clubs.

CONNELL
(sarcastically)
Yeah?
(suddenly)
Say, you're sold on the John Doe idea, aren't you?

JOHN
Sure.

CONNELL
Sure. I don't blame you. So am I.

Close-up: Of CONNELL.

CONNELL
(sincerely)
It's a beautiful miracle. A miracle that could only happen right here in the good old U.S.A. And I think it's terrific! What do you think of that! Me! Hard-boiled Connell! I think it's plenty terrific!

Two shot: John is rather pleased to hear him say this.

CONNELL
All right! Now, supposing a certain unmentionable worm, whose initials are D. B., was trying to use that to shove his way into the White House. So he could put the screws on, so he could turn out the lights in those lighthouses. What would you say about that? Huh?

JOHN
Nobody's gonna do that, Mr. Connell. They can't use the John Doe Clubs for politics. That's the main idea.

CONNELL
Is that so? Then what's a big political boss like Hammett doing in town? And a labor leader like Bennett? And a lot of other big shots who are up at D. B.'s house right now? Wolves, John, wolves waiting to cut up the John Does!
(snorting)
Wait till you get a gander at that speech you're gonna make tonight!

JOHN
You're all wet. Miss Mitchell writes those speeches and nobody can make her write that kind of stuff.

CONNELL
(cynically)
They can't, huh?
(then barking)
Who do you think writes 'em? My Aunt Emma? I know she writes them.

Close-up: Of JOHN. His jaw stiffens, angrily.

CONNELL'S VOICE
And get a big bonus for doing them, too. A mink coat and a diamond bracelet.

JOHN glares at him, his rage mounting.

Close-up: Of CONNELL. Unaware of JOHN's wrath.

CONNELL
Don't write 'em? Why, that gold-grabbin' dame would double-cross her own mother for a handful of Chinese yen!

JOHN
(in an outraged outcry)
Shut up! If you weren't drunk I'd--

Simultaneously his hand comes in and grabs the startled CONNELL violently by his shirt front, lifting him out of his seat. Camera pulls back to include JOHN--who towers over CONNELL.

Wider shot: JOHN is still holding CONNELL, glaring down at him, enraged, when BEANY runs into the scene.

BEANY
(holding out the envelope)
Hey, Boss! Here's the speech, Boss.

Suddenly he sees what's happening, and stares open-mouthed.

BEANY
Hey!

Med. shot: As JOHN pushes CONNELL back into the seat, snatches the envelope from BEANY, and exits.

CONNELL
Go on and read it, John, and then start socking!

Wider shot: As JOHN exits from place. BEANY suddenly realizes he has gone--and chases after him.

BEANY
Hey, wait a minute, Mr. Doe!

CONNELL
... Tubby?

BEANY'S VOICE
Yes, sir?

CONNELL
Better bring me a glass of milk.

Close-up: Of CONNELL. He stares at his unlighted cigarette--grimaces unhappily.

CONNELL
(mumbling)
I'm smoking too much.

He grinds out the unlighted cigarette in the tray.

Dissolve to: Int. D. B.'s dining room. Close shot: Of D. B., who is at head of table, talking on phone.

D. B.
(into telephone)
... Yes, Charlie? You've got everything all set? Fine! Has John Doe been taken care of? Good! How many people do you think will be there?

A pleased expression comes over his face.

D. B.
Fifteen thousand? Oh my, that's fine. Now, listen, Charlie, as soon as John Doe stops talking about me, I want you to start that demonstration. And make it a big one, you understand?

As D. B. hangs up.

Wider shot: Including TED SHELDON.

TED
Don't worry about that, D. B. My boys are there. They'll take care of it.

D. B.
(into telephone)
What? yes, I'll be there fifteen minutes after I get your call.

Camera draws back as he speaks. We see that dinner has been concluded. His listeners, besides TED and ANN, are half a dozen distinguished looking men, some with cigars stuck in their mouths, others sip from champagne glasses. ANN sits to D. B.'s right.

Cut to: Int. foyer: Med. shot: At D. B.'s front door. A butler is opening the door for JOHN.

BUTLER
Why, Mr. Doe ...

JOHN
Where are they?

BUTLER
In the dining room, sir.

JOHN strides toward the dining room. Camera pans with JOHN, who is dripping wet, as he crosses the foyer until he comes within sight of the open door of the dining room. JOHN stops.

Cut back to: Int. D. B.'s dining room. Wider shot: D. B. addressing the group at the table.

D. B.
Well, gentlemen, I think we're about ready to throw that great big bombshell--

SOMEONE'S VOICE
Yeah, well it's about time.

D. B.
Even a conservative estimate shows that we can count on anywhere between ten and twenty million John Doe votes. Now, add to that the labor vote that Mr. Bennett will throw in ...

He indicates BENNETT who nods, importantly.

D. B.
... and the votes controlled by Mr. Hammett and the rest of you gentlemen in your territories--
(emphatically)
and nothing can stop us!

Close-up: Of ANN. She seems distressed. She apparently has been listening to things that have caused her considerable anxiety.

Wider shot: WESTON leans forward and speaks to D. B.

WESTON
As I said before, I'm with you--providing you can guarantee the John Doe vote.

D. B.
Don't worry about that.

BENNETT
You can count on me under one condition. Little Bennett's gotta be taken care of!

D. B.
Didn't I tell you that everybody in this room would be taken care? My agreement with you gentlemen stands!

BARRINGTON
I'm with you, D. B., but I still think it's a very daring thing we're attempting!

D. B.
These are daring times, Mr. Barrington. We're coming to a new order of things. There's been too much talk going on in this country.

SOMEONE'S VOICE
Exactly--

ANN glances up at D. B., a startled look in her eyes.

Close shot: D. B.'s audience beams with satisfaction as he continues.

D. B.
Too many concessions have been made! What the American people need is an iron hand!

WESTON
You're right!

BENNETT
That's true. You're quite right, D. B.!

D. B.
Discipline!

GROUP
Quite right! Exactly!

There are cries of: "Hear, hear!" and applause.

Close-up: Of ANN. She is completely seized by panic- and although she attempts applauding, it is feeble.

Med. shot: Shooting through open door toward dining room. Prominently in view is ANN, still lost in troubled thought. D. B. is still on his feet.

D. B.
And now--
(lifting champagne glass)
may I offer a little toast to Miss Ann Mitchell--the brilliant and beautiful lady who is responsible for all this!

The men rise.

GROUP
Miss Mitchell! Miss Mitchell!

ANN
Mr. Norton, I'd like to talk to you alone for a moment.

D. B.
Oh, oh.
(chortling)
Miss Mitchell has something to say to us.

GROUP
Well, that's fine. Speech! Speech!

Ann spots John.

D. B.
(spotting John)
Hello?

ANN
John! I'm so glad to see you. I--I was terribly worried.

JOHN
(showing her a copy of the speech)
Did you write this?

ANN
Yes, I did, John. But I--I had no idea what was going on.

JOHN
You didn't?

Close-up: Of JOHN. His mouths screws up bitterly.

JOHN
(quiet contempt)
That's a swell bracelet you're wearing.

He leaves her, abruptly.

Int. dining room: Full shot: JOHN enters and looks the men over appraisingly as he goes toward D. B. They all stare at him.

D. B.
John--
(concerned)
Why aren't you at the convention?

JOHN doesn't answer.

D. B.
Is there anything wrong?

JOHN
(after a pause)
Oh, no. Nothing's wrong. Everything's fine! So there's gonna be a new order of things, huh? Everybody's gonna cut himself a nice, fat slice of the John Does, eh?
(turns toward D. B.)
You forgot one detail, Mr. Big Shot--you forgot me, the prize stooge of the world. Why, if you or anybody else thinks he's gonna use the John Doe clubs for his own rotten purpose, he's gonna have to do it over my dead body!

D. B.
Now, hold on a minute, young man! Hold on! That's rather big talk! I started the John Doe clubs with my money and I'll decide whether or not they're being properly used!

JOHN
No you won't! You're through deciding anything!

D. B. cannot believe his ears.

JOHN

And what's more, I'm going down to that convention and I'm gonna tell those people exactly what you and all your fine-feathered friends here are trying to cook up for them!

He looks up at ANN--and starts tearing the speech in his hand.

JOHN

(strongly)

And I'll say it in my <u>own</u> words this time.

He flings the torn paper toward ANN--and starts out.

HAMMETT AND OTHERS

Stop him, somebody! He'll ruin us, D. B.!

Med. shot: At Door. As JOHN reaches it, TED steps up in front of him.

TED

(menacingly)

Wait a minute, young feller--my uncle wants to talk to you.

D. B. walks up to JOHN.

D. B.

Listen to me, my son! Before you lose your head completely, may I remind you that I picked you up out of the gutter and I can throw you right back there again! You've got a nerve accusing people of things! These gentlemen and I know what's the best for the John Does of America, regardless of what tramps like you think!

Get off that righteous horse of yours and come to your senses. <u>You're</u> the fake! We believe in what we're doing! You're the one that was paid the thirty pieces of silver! Have you forgotten that? Well, I haven't!

You're a fake, John Doe, and I can prove it! You're the big hero that's supposed to jump off tall buildings and things! Do you remember? What do you suppose your precious John Does will say when they find out that you never had any intention of doing it? That you were being paid to say so? You're lucky if they don't run you out of the country!

Why, with the newspapers and the radio stations that these gentlemen control, we can kill the John Doe movement deader than a doornail, and we'll do it, too, the moment you step out of line! Now, if you still want to go to that convention and shoot your trap off, you go ahead and do it!

Full shot: D. B. leaves JOHN and returns to his chair. JOHN stares at him, unbelievingly.

Close shot: Of JOHN.

JOHN
(after a pause)
Do you mean to tell me you'd try to kill the John Doe movement if you can't use it to get what you want?

D. B.'S VOICE
You bet your bottom dollar we would!

JOHN
(cynically)
Well, that certainly is a new low. I guess I've seen everything now.

Wider shot: As JOHN's lips curl up contemptuously and he steps up to the table.

JOHN
(throwing his hat on the table)
You sit there back of your big cigars and think of deliberately killing an idea that's made millions of people a little bit happier! An idea that's brought thousands of them here from all over the country, by bus and by freight, in jalopies and on foot--so they could pass on to each other their own simple little experiences.

Close-up: Of ANN. Her eyes light up happily.

JOHN'S VOICE
Why, look, I'm just a mug and I know it. But I'm beginning to understand a lot of things. Why, your type's old as history. If you can't lay your dirty fingers on a decent idea and twist it and squeeze it and stuff it into your own pocket, you slap it down! Like dogs, if you can't eat something, you bury it!

Close-up: Of JOHN. His voice is pleading.

JOHN
Why, this is the one worthwhile thing that's come along. People are finally finding out that the guy next door isn't a bad egg. That's simple, isn't it? And yet a thing like that's got a chance of spreading till it touches every last doggone human being in the world--and you talk about killing it!

Full shot: They listen to him--unmoved.

JOHN
Why, when this fire dies down, what's going to be left? More misery, more hunger and more hate. And what's to prevent that from starting all over again? Nobody knows the answer to that one, and certainly not you, with those slimy, bolloxed-up theories you've got! The John Doe idea may be the answer, though! It may be the one thing capable of saving this cockeyed world! Yet you sit back there on your fat hulks and tell me you'll kill it if you can't use it!

Well, you go ahead and try! You couldn't do it in a million years, with all your radio stations and all your power! Because it's bigger than whether I'm a fake! It's bigger than your ambitions! And it's bigger than all the bracelets and fur coats in the world!

Wider shot: ANN runs to JOHN.

ANN
(sincerely)
You bet it is, John!

JOHN starts to exit.

Med. shot: Shooting toward door.

JOHN
(turning to them)
And that's exactly what I'm going down there to tell those people!

As JOHN reaches door, TED SHELDON jumps in front of him.

Close shot:

TED
Wait a minute, you ungrateful rat! My Uncle's been too good to--

While he speaks, JOHN looks down at the fist clutching his shirt, and then, with a suddenness that startles TED, he steps aside and clips TED on the jaw. TED's knees buckle and he goes down. JOHN exits.

Wider shot: As several men rush to TED's assistance, D. B. does not move.

MAN
He's getting away!

ANN
John!

Ext. entrance to D. B.'s house: Med. shot: As JOHN hurries out. He goes by half a dozen members of TED SHELDON's motorcycle troops who wait around to escort D. B. to the convention.

Int. Dining room: Full shot: The room is full of commotion. ANN is running out of the room, going after JOHN. Several men bend over TED. D. B. glares toward door, his face hardening. HAMMETT is barking at him.

D. B. reaches under the table, lifts up two phones. Hands one to HAMMETT.

D. B.
Get the Bulletin!

He, himself, dials the other phone.

ANN
John!

BARRINGTON
I've always told you, D. B. you're playing with dynamite!

D. B.
(calling to men)
Don't let that girl get away!

The butler rushes out.

WESTON
Before he gets through tonight he'll ruin us all!

BENNETT
You've got to stop him, D. B.!

D. B.
I'll stop him! I'll stop him cold! Don't worry, I've been ready for this!

Cut to: Ext. D. B.'s entrance--at gate. Med. shot: As ANN runs alongside JOHN.

ANN
John! Oh, John, please listen to me! Please--I can explain everything, John. I didn't know what they were going to do! Let me go with you, John! John, please!

JOHN gets into taxi--slams door--ANN runs beside cab as it starts off.

JOHN
Go ahead, driver! Ball park!

ANN
John, please let me go with you! Please, John!

Several troopers grab ANN.

TROOPER
Mr. Norton wants to see you.

ANN
Oh!

As the men get a firmer grip on her and ANN fights to get loose: Cut to: Int. D. B.'s study: Med. shot: D. B. is on the phone. The others pace around, perturbedly. HAMMETT has the second phone in his hand.

D. B.
(into phone)
Listen to me, Mayor Lovett, you do as I say. I want them both arrested. You tell the police department to pick up Connell. I've got the girl here.

HAMMETT
(holds out phone)
I've got the <u>Bulletin</u>!

D. B.
(hotly)
I don't care what you charge them with! If you're worried, let them go in the morning, but keep them in jail over night!

He bangs up the receiver. Grabs another phone from HAMMETT.

D. B.
Hello, Bulletin? Put Pop Dwyer on.

Dissolve to: Ext. entrance to ball park: Med. shot: Over the entrance gate a huge banner reads:

WELCOME TO
JOHN DOE CONVENTION

People come from all directions and pour through the gates. Some carry umbrellas over their heads, others have their coat collars turned up. Women hold newspapers over their heads to protect their hats. It is a misty, drizzling rain.

Ext. ball park: Long shot: Shooting from ANNOUNCER's view down at the Speaker's platform which has been erected on "Home Plate." On it, in the rear, is a brass band. In front of it is a speaker's table, over which dangles the microphone of a public address system. Attached to the table are several microphones with names of broadcasting stations on them.

Med. shot: Shooting toward audience. They sing: "Oh, Susanna."

Med. shot: Toward people seated in grandstand. They join in the singing.

Another angle: Toward a third section. They also pick up the song.

Long shot: Taking in as many as possible. Everyone sings, and the volume has risen considerably.

Med. shot: Shooting down an aisle. A stream of people take up the song, as they march to their seats.

Med. shot: At entrance to Park. Crowds are coming in--and they, too, begin singing. They are also joined by the policemen posted at the gates.

Med. shot: A second entrance to Park. Another crowd is entering, also singing.

Med. shot: Of BERT and SOURPUSS in the foreground of a group on platform, all of whom sing. BERT has a large rolled-up scroll in his hand.

Close-up: Of the COLONEL. Sitting in a corner somewhere, looking around speculatively, with a stubborn mental reservation that they are still all heelots.

Several close shots: Of small groups--with their wet faces held high, singing lustily, eyes sparkling.

Long shot: Shooting from the platform down toward the audience. The song finally comes to a climax--and immediately, lusty cheering starts, as they see JOHN coming on platform.

Med. shot: Toward platform. JOHN goes to the microphone of the public address system.

MAN
Three cheers for John Doe!

JOHN
Listen, ladies and gentlemen!

Before he can go any further, the band strikes up the strain of "AMERICA" and immediately the large assembly begins singing it.

Close-up: Of JOHN. As his lips form the words. His expression is solemn.

Various shots: Of groups, singing.

Long shot: As people sing. Finally the song is ended, and an enthusiastic cheer is emitted by the crowd.

Med. shot: On platform. JOHN again steps toward the microphone and makes another effort to speak, but the CLERGYMAN places a detaining hand on his arm.

CLERGYMAN
Just a moment, John. We begin with a short prayer.

Longer shot: Shooting over the heads of the audience toward the platform in the background. Gradually the cheering subsides.

CLERGYMAN
(speaking into public address system)
Quiet, please. Ladies and gentlemen--let us have a moment of silent prayer for the John Does all over the world ... many of whom are homeless and hungry. Rise, please. Everybody rise.

The CLERGYMAN and JOHN, standing next to him, immediately bow their heads.

Long shot: Shooting toward audience. As far as the Camera eye can see, heads are bowed in prayer. The reflection on the wet umbrellas creates a strange and mystic light.

Several close shots: Of small groups--in silent prayer.

Close-up: Of the COLONEL. Rather grudgingly, he has his head lowered.

Close-up: Of JOHN. His eyes are shut--his face wreathed in an expression of compassion.

Med. shot: At press section. They, too, bow respectfully. The reporters are quiet for the first time.

Ext. street: Long shot: Directly in front of entrance to ball park. A stream of news trucks pull up, filled with newsboys--they immediately alight.

Ext. street: Med. shot: In front of another entrance. More trucks arrive--packed with newsboys.

Ext. street: Med. shot: Shooting toward entrance. As an army of newsboys, each carrying a stack of newspapers, run toward us yelling:

NEWSBOYS
Extry, extry! Read all about it!

Med. shot: Toward another entrance. Another swarm of newsboys dash in, also shouting.

NEWSBOYS
Extry! John Doe a fake!

Long shot: Of audience with their heads still bowed. Slowly, they begin turning around, puzzled, as from all directions and down every aisle, boys are running, waving papers in the air.

NEWSBOYS
(shouting)
Here you are! John Doe a fake! Read all about it! John Doe movement a racket!

Close shot: Of JOHN. He looks up, terror-stricken.

Med. shot: At press section. Great excitement prevails here.

ANNOUNCER (JOHN B. HUGHES)
Newsboys! Hundreds of yelling newsboys are swarming into the park like locusts! They're yelling, "John Doe's a fake! Fake!"

Med. shot: Of audience. As newsboys are distributing papers to the baffled people.

NEWSBOYS
Here you are! No charge! John Doe a fake!

Med. shot: Of a second group. Some already have papers and peer, unbelievingly, at the headlines. Others grab papers from newsboys' hands.

MAN
(reading)
"Federal investigation urged by Chamber of Commerce."

Med. shot: Speaker's platform. SOURPUSS and BERT, reading paper.

SOURPUSS
How could he be a fake?
(laughing)

BERT
It must be some kind of a gag.

SOURPUSS
A what?

BERT
A gag. A gag!

Ext.: Somewhere inside ball park: Long shot: We hear the shrieking of sirens and almost immediately a limousine, escorted by Sheldon's motorcycle troops, pulls up. Directly behind it is a string of cars.

Med. shot: The door of the limousine flies open and D. B. comes out. He immediately heads for the platform.

Camera pans over and we see troopers pouring out of the cars with TED SHELDON directing them.

TED
Come on, come on, step on it! Step on it! Step on it! You all know your places now, so let's get going! Wait for the signal!

Med. shot: DRUNK with a balloon. He holds balloon up to TED, getting in TED's way.

DRUNK
Hey, mister, will you autograph my balloon?

TED
Sure!
(and breaks balloon)

TROOPER
(pushing drunk aside)
Gangway!

Ext.: Park. Med. shot: At Speaker's platform. JOHN is in front of the microphone trying to make himself heard over thousands of voices, all speaking at once.

JOHN
Ladies and gentlemen! This is exactly what I came down here to tell you about tonight. Please, if you'll all just be quiet for a few minutes I can explain this whole thing to you. As you all know, this paper is published by a man by the name of D. B. Norton ...

Med. shot: Shooting towards audience. Down an aisle stalks D. B., his hand waving in the air.

D. B.
(shouting)
Don't listen to that man! He's a fake!

Camera pans with him as he hurries down the aisle to the platform--all eyes turned toward him.

Close-up: Of JOHN. As he stares at D. B. approaching, too flustered to know what to do.

Med. shot: Toward platform. As D. B. runs up the few steps and proceeds to the microphone, troopers clearing the way for him.

TROOPER
(drags John from mike)
Stand back!

D. B.
Wait a minute! Everybody wait a minute! Wait a minute, ladies and gentlemen! My name is D. B. Norton . . . you all know me! I accuse this man of being a faker! We've been taken for a lot of suckers! And I'm the biggest of the lot!

I spent a fortune backing this man in what I believed to be a sincere and worthy cause, just as you all did! And now I find out it's nothing but a cheap racket! Cooked up by him and two of my employees for the sole purpose of collecting dues from John Does all over the country!

JOHN breaks away from the troopers and gets to the mike.

JOHN
That's a lie!

D. B.
It's not a lie! Nickels and dimes! To stuff into their own pockets! You can read all about it in the newspapers there!

JOHN
That's a lie! Listen--don't believe what he says ...

D. B.
(overlapping above speech)
Let go of me! This man had no intention of jumping off of the top of a building! He was paid to say so!
(turning to John)
Do you deny that?

JOHN
That's got nothing to do with it!

D. B.
Were you paid for it--or weren't you?

JOHN
Yes! I was paid! But the--

D. B.
(over-lapping above speech)
And what about the suicide note? You didn't write that, either!

JOHN
What difference does that make?

D. B.
Did you write it--or didn't you?

JOHN
No, I didn't write it, but--

D. B.
Ah, you bet your life you didn't! You look in your papers, ladies and gentlemen, and you'll find Miss Mitchell's signed confession that she was the one that wrote it!

JOHN
Listen, folks, it's a fact that I didn't write the letter, but this whole thing started--

D. B.
There! You see? He admits it! You're a fake, John Doe! And for what you've done to all these good people--they ought to run you out of the country--and I hope they do it!

He leaves the platform--followed by his troopers.

Several shots: Of groups as they stare at JOHN, silent and stunned, waiting for him to speak.

Full shot: The whole park full of people wait in breathless anticipation. From somewhere in the distance we hear a single voice of a man.

VOICE
Speak up, John! We believe you!

Med. shot: Under the platform. We see several of D. B.'s troopers pulling at the cables of the public address system.

Close shot: Of JOHN. He speaks into the microphone.

JOHN
Please listen, folks! Now that he's through shooting off his face, I've got a couple of things to tell you about--

Close shot: Under the platform. One of the troopers disconnects the public address system by cutting the cable.

Close-up: Of JOHN. He realizes the loud speaker is dead, and looks around helplessly.

Med. shot: Somewhere in audience TED SHELDON directs troopers.

TED
Come on! The rest of you get in here and riot! Break this crowd up! Come on!

Med. shot: Of a group of John Does. They still stare uncertainly. Suddenly, the head of one of SHELDON's troopers appear--and cupping his hands over his mouth, he yells toward platform.

TROOPER
John Doe's a fake! Boo! Boooooo!

Long shot: From ANNOUNCER's view. Shooting toward audience. The crowd is all yelling at once now.

Med. shot:

ANNOUNCER
I'm sorry, folks, but we can't hear him any more. Something's gone wrong with the loudspeaker.

Med. shot: Of JOHN. Trying to talk over microphone.

JOHN
Say, they can't hear me! The thing's not working!

(shouts)
Ladies and gentlemen! Look--this thing's bigger than whether I'm a fake--
(turns to BERT)
Look, Bert, you believe me, don't you?

BERT
(cynically)
Sure, I believe you. Walking my legs off digging up five thousand signatures for a phoney!

Suddenly, nervously, he begins tearing up the petition in his hand.

BERT
Well, there you are, Mr. Doe!
(flinging crumpled petition at him)
Five thousand names asking you not to jump off any roof!

He turns to leave.

Close shot: Of SOURPUSS, who, heartbroken, stops BERT.

SOURPUSS
It makes no difference, Bert--the ideas's still good. We don't have to give up our club.

BERT
(harshly)
Yeah? Well, you can have it!

He exits.

Long shot: From ANNOUNCER's view. Crowd is yelling wildly.

ANNOUNCER
They're starting to throw things!

2ND ANNOUNCER
Somebody's going to get hurt!

Close-up: Of JOHN. He looks helplessly down at the hostile crowd.

Int. police station: Full shot: ANN and CONNELL are surrounded by several policemen. A sergeant sits at his desk, on which is a radio. ANN's face is haggard and desperate as she listens to the radio announcer.

ANNOUNCER
I'm afraid it'll be John Doe. Listen to that mob!

Unable to stand it any longer, ANN suddenly jumps out of her seat.

ANN
I've got to go to him!

OFFICER
Sorry, lady--I can't let you out.

ANN
(sobbing)
Oh, let me go! Let me go to him! Oh, please, please let me go! They're crucifying him! I can help him!

OFFICER
Sorry, sister. We got orders to hold you.

ANN
Orders from who? Can't they see it's a frameup?

She is still desperately struggling to get free--when her mother comes hurrying in.

MRS. MITCHELL
Ann, darling!

ANN
Oh, Mother! They won't let me go! They won't let me go!

The police release her and she throws herself into her mother's arms.

Ext.: Ball park. Close shot: Of JOHN. He still attempts to get himself heard.

JOHN
Listen, folks! You gotta listen to me, everybody!

Med. shot: Of a group of John Does.

A MAN
(yelling toward JOHN)
Back to the jungle, you hobo!

2ND MAN
(disgustedly)
Just another racket!

JOHN'S VOICE
Stick to your clubs!

MAN
(shouting)
We've been fed baloney so long we're getting used to it!

Close shot: Of JOHN. He disregards the missiles that fly around his head.

JOHN
(supplicatingly)
The idea is still good! Believe me, folks! ...

Ext.: Ball park. Med. long shot: Toward platform. The crowd pushes menacingly around the platform, with policemen struggling to control them. JOHN still stands there, pathetic and helpless. Missiles of all kinds fly into the scene. The members of the band are scrambling off the platform--as well as the others, until John is left alone.

Long shot: Shooting toward audience. They still boo and yell.

Med. shot: Of the COLONEL. Fearful for JOHN, he starts pushing his way through the crowd toward him.

Med. shot: Of a group of people. Suddenly a woman reaches into a lunch basket she carries and takes out a tomato.

WOMAN
(shouting)
You faker!

She reaches back to throw the tomato.

Close-up: Of JOHN. His voice is gone. His eyes are glassy. He is making one last effort to speak.

JOHN
(hoarsely)
Listen ... John Does ...
(weakly)
You're the hope of the world ...

As if in challenge to that statement, the tomato flies in and strikes him on the forehead. It seems to stun him. He remains motionless, staring before him with sightless eyes. The red smear of the tomato trickles down his face.

Med. shot: Of the COLONEL, amidst the crowd. He sees JOHN hit and winces. Then, setting his jaw, he pushes people violently aside, trying to reach JOHN.

Med. shot: On platform, JOHN stares futilely before him. The COLONEL reaches his side and glancing sympathetically up at his face, starts to lead him off the platform. A squadron of policemen also rush to his rescue and precede JOHN and the COLONEL.

Trucking shot: Down the aisle--as police disperse the crowd who boo and threaten JOHN from the sidelines.

Close shot: Of JOHN. He is oblivious of the jeering, shouting mob--and of the wet newspapers flung in his direction.

Med. shot: At dug-out exit--as the police finally manage to get him safely out of the park.

Med. shot: ANNOUNCER's booth.

JOHN B. HUGHES
The police finally manage to get him out of the park! If that boy isn't hurt, it'll be a miracle!

Int.: Police station. Med. shot: ANN and her mother sit on a bench. A policeman is in the background. ANN stares into space. Her mother has an arm around her.

ANNOUNCER'S VOICE
Ladies and gentlemen, this certainly looks like the end of the John Doe movement.

A policeman snaps the radio off.

CONNELL
(lifts glass of milk)
Well, boys, you can chalk up another one to the Pontius Pilates.

Two shot: ANN and her mother.

ANN
(sobbing)
I should have been there. I could have helped him.
(desolately)
He was so all alone!

Her MOTHER draws ANN consolingly to her, and lays her head on her breast.

Dissolve to:

Ext.: A highway. Med. shot: Of BERT's car on the way home.

Int.: Car. Close shot: BERT and SOURPUSS. They both look depressed. After a silence, SOURPUSS speaks.

SOURPUSS
(throatily)
A lot of us are going to be mighty ashamed of ourselves after tonight. We certainly didn't give that man much of a chance.

They lapse again into silence. BERT stares grimly at the road.

Dissolve to: Ext.: Clearing under the bridge. Close-up: Of JOHN. He sits on a rock, his head bent low, tears streaming shamelessly down his cheeks. Camera draws back and we find the COLONEL before the fire, boiling water in a small tin pan.

COLONEL'S VOICE
Have some more coffee, Long John?

JOHN
No, thanks, Colonel.

JOHN lifts his eyes skyward, stares profoundly, a curious expression over his face.

Dissolve to: A Montage. Long shot: Of JOHN, a lonely figure, walking dejectedly. As he walks, faces begin to appear one by one, to taunt him. Their accusing voices are heard.

WOMAN'S VOICE
Faker!

MAN'S VOICE
Racketeer!

2ND VOICE
Liar!

3RD VOICE
Cheat!

4TH VOICE
Imposter!

5TH VOICE
Why don't you jump!

GIRL'S VOICE
Christmas Eve at midnight!
(she laughs, sneeringly)

Dissolve to: Another shot: Of JOHN walking, his expression immobile. Over the shot appear several scenes through which JOHN has lived:

1. BERT shaking hands with him, saying:

BERT
You're a wonderful man, Mr. Doe.

2. MRS. DELANEY kissing his hand and saying:

MRS. DELANEY
May God bless you, my boy.

3. ANN in Broadcasting Station, kissing him:

ANN
Now, get in there and pitch!

4. D. B. issuing his tirade at JOHN:

D. B.
You're a fake, John Doe, and I can prove it! You're the big hero that's supposed to jump off tall buildings and things. You remember? What do you suppose your precious John Does will say when they find out that you never had any intention of doing it--that you were being paid to say so?

5. Again the girl who laughed appears:

GIRL
Christmas Eve at midnight?

And again she laughs sneeringly.

Dissolve to: Ext.: City Hall tower--night. Long shot: It is a picturesque scene of the City Hall outlined in silhouette against the sky. A peaceful mantle of snow silently descends upon it. Over the shot we hear the plaintive voices of children singing "Holy Night."

Dissolve to: Ext.: Outside of D. B.'s house: Med. shot: Outside D. B.'s Study--through window. A group of eight young carolers sing "Holy Night." It is a continuation of the music from previous scene.

Cut to: Int. D. B.'s study. Med. shot: In the dimly lit room, we see the lonely figure of D. B., as he stands near a window staring out, meditatively. The voices of the children singing Christmas carols are faintly heard.

Close-up: Of D. B. He peers into the night, enveloped by disturbing thoughts. After a moment, he takes out his watch and glances at it. Then, as if annoyed by his own apprehension, he shoves it violently back into his pocket.

Camera retreats in front of him as he crosses, determinedly, to a humidor, takes a cigar and shoves it into his mouth. Just as he is about to light it, he becomes aware of the singing, and cocks his head, listening.

Wider shot: As he drops the match and the unlighted cigar--and starts toward door. Just then the BUTLER comes through.

BUTLER
Merry Christmas, sir.

D. B.
Oh. Merry Christmas.

D. B. hands him a bill and nods toward the children. The BUTLER exits.

Close-up: Of D. B. Staring out into space moodily. We hear the voices of the children saying, "Thank you, sir! Merry Christmas!" D. B.'s mouth screws up, unhappily. It is far from a "merry" Christmas. It is a very lonely, conscience-stricken one.

Dissolve to: Int.: Police station. Med. shot: A SERGEANT sits in front of his desk. Opposite him is a POLICEMAN. Their rummy game has been interrupted by a phone call which the SERGEANT is now answering.

SERGEANT
Who? John Doe? Is that screwball still around?
(laughing)

POLICEMAN
(with disgust)
Aw, that dame's been callin' all day.

DESK SERGEANT
Sure, sure, I know. Yeah. At midnight, huh?
Okay, lady. We'll have the place surrounded
with nets.

He hangs up the phone--twirls his finger at his temple, shrugs--and reaches for a card.

Cut to: Int.: ANN's bedroom. Close shot: ANN is in bed. She looks wan. Her hand still rests on the phone.

Camera pulls back to reveal a doctor by her side and her mother at the foot of the bed. They watch her--concerned.

ANN
Oh--they're laughing at me!

Impulsively, ANN picks up the receiver and starts dialing again.

DOCTOR'S VOICE
You're a sick girl, Ann. You'd better take
it easy.

MRS. MITCHELL
Whom are you calling now? You called that number not ten minutes ago!

ANN
(into phone)
Hello. Mr. Connell? Have you seen him yet? Have you--

Cut to: Int: Corridor of City Hall. Med. shot: Toward a telephone booth. CONNELL speaks into the phone.

CONNELL
Now listen, Ann--he can't possibly get in without our seeing him. I'm watching the side door and the Colonel's out front, so stop worrying.

Int.: ANN's bedroom. Close shot:

ANN
Thank you.

She hangs up the receiver, despairingly. Then, suddenly, she jumps out of bed and runs to a clothes closet--grabbing a coat and scarf.

MRS. MITCHELL
Why, Ann! ...

DOCTOR
Ann, don't be foolish!

Dissolve to: Insert: The City Hall tower clock registers 11:45.

Cut to: Ext.: Highway. Med. shot: BERT's car driving in the snow.

Int.: Car. Full shot: BERT HANSEN drives. In the car with him are his wife, SOURPUSS and several others.

BERT
(complainingly)
If this isn't the craziest, the battiest, the looniest wild goose chase I ever heard of?

MRS. HANSEN
Oh, shut up, Bert. Sourpuss is right.

BERT
Yeah? Well, if he is, I'm a banana split!

SOURPUSS
That man is gonna be on that roof. Don't ask me how I know. I just know. And you know it as well as I do.

BERT
Sure, sure. I'd like to believe in fairy tales, but a guy that's a fake isn't gonna jump off any roof.

MRS. HANSEN
I don't think he was any fake--not with that face. And, anyway, what he stood for wasn't a fake.

D. B.
I hope nobody finds out we've been here.

They all start to exit, when suddenly D. B. stops. He puts his hand out, and they all stop to listen. They hear footsteps, and back into the shadows.

Med. shot: Shooting toward stairs. JOHN appears around the bend and mounts the last few steps.

Med. shot: Of the huddled group. They watch breathlessly. In the darkness, their eyes dominate the scene.

Med. shot: Over their shoulders. As JOHN, expressionless, his cigarette in his hand, crosses to the parapet, and looks out. He takes a puff of his cigarette and exhales the smoke.

Med. shot: Of the huddled group. The MAYOR is for stepping forward, but D. B. with an extended hand stops him, indicating for them to wait and see what happens.

Close-up: Of JOHN. He takes the envelope out of his pocket and examines it.

Close shot: Of the group. Their eyes glued on him tensely.

Close shot: Of JOHN. He stares at the envelope.

Insert: Of envelope. On it is written: "TO JOHN DOES EVERYWHERE".

Close-up: Of JOHN. He replaces the envelope in his pocket.

Int.: Tower. Close shot: The group. Their eyes riveted on JOHN. They feel the moment has come. Several of them glance toward D. B.

Wider shot: To include them all, and JOHN. He drops his cigarette on the ground, and bending over, crushes it with his foot. Just as he straightens out again, D. B. speaks.

D. B.
(restrained voice)
I wouldn't do that if I were you, John.

Close-up: Of JOHN. As he turns sharply, startled. He stares blankly at the five people.

Med. shot: Of the group. They move slightly forward and stop.

D. B.
It'll do you no good.

Close-up: Of JOHN. He continues to stare at them, strangely.

Wider shot: To include them all.

D. B.
The Mayor has policemen downstairs with instructions to remove all marks of identification you may have on your person. You'll be buried in Potter's Field[12] and you will have accomplished nothing.

Close shot: Of JOHN. After a moment, he speaks.

JOHN
(in a sepulchral voice)
I've taken care of that. I've already mailed a copy of this letter to Mr. Connell.

Med. shot: Of the group. Amazed that he thought of this. They feel themselves helpless. D. B. tries taking an authoritative tone.

D. B.
(his throat is dry)
John, why don't you forget this foolishness?

He steps forward as he speaks.

JOHN
(quickly--threateningly)
Stop right where you are, Mr. Norton, if you don't want to go overboard with me.

Close-up: Of JOHN's face. His eyes have a wild, maniacal look in them.

Close-up: Of D. B. He stares into JOHN's eyes and a terrified expression covers his face.

Wider shot: As D. B. instinctively backs up.

JOHN
(throatily)
I'm glad you gentlemen are here. You've killed the John Doe movement, all right, but you're going to see it born all over again. Now, take a good look, Mr. Norton.

Int.: Landing to tower. Med. shot: As ANN practically has to pull herself up to the last step. Her face is wet from fever and exhaustion.

ANN
(an outcry)
John!

Int.: Tower. Full shot: As everyone, startled by the outcry, turns. ANN staggers into scene.

ANN
(crying)
John!

She rushes and throws her arms around him.

ANN
(muffled sobs)
Oh, John, darling. No! No!

Close shot: JOHN and ANN. He stares down at her, blankly. ANN clutches him, her head buried in his shoulder.

ANN
(muffled sobs)
I won't let you. I love you, darling.

Med. shot: Of the group. They remain motionless, watching.

Close shot: JOHN and ANN. She emits wracking sobs, then lifts her eyes up to him.

ANN
(in a desperate plea)
John. Please, John, listen to me. We'll start all over again, just you and I. It isn't too late. The John Doe movement isn't dead yet.

Suddenly she becomes conscious of the others present, and she turns her head.

Camera pans over to what she sees. The group of men watching, silently.

Camera pans back to ANN. Her eyes widen slowly. She looks from them to JOHN and back again, and her face takes on an excited, breathless look, as the reason for their being there becomes comprehensible to her.

ANN
(excitedly)
See, John! It isn't dead, or they wouldn't be here! It's alive in them. They kept it alive. By being afraid of it. That's why they came up here.

Close shot: ANN and JOHN. He continues to stand with his hands at his sides, looking at her, while she clings to him desperately. While she speaks, he turns his face from her and stares at the men.

ANN
Oh, darling. Sure, it should have been killed before. It was dishonest.

Close-up: Of JOHN. He is staring strangely at the group of men--as slowly, gradually, the curtain is being lifted from his clouded brain.

ANN'S VOICE
But we can start clean now. Just you and I. It'll grow again, John. It'll grow big. And it'll be strong, because it'll be honest!

Close-up: Of ANN. Her strength is fast ebbing away. She clings to JOHN more tenaciously.

ANN
(last bit of effort)
Oh, darling, if it's worth dying for, it's worth living for. Oh, please, John ...

She looks up at his face, seeking some sign of his relenting--but she finds none.

Close-up: Of ANN, who still clinging to him, lays her cheek on his chest--and lifts her eyes heavenward.

ANN
(a murmured prayer)
Oh, please, God--help me!

Flash: Of the men--as they stare transfixed, waiting breathlessly.

Med. shot: At entrance. BERT, SOURPUSS and others appear--having run up the stairs breathlessly. Their eyes are filled with apprehension. CONNELL and the COLONEL are with them. When they see the scene before them, they stop, awed.

Close-up: Of ANN. Suddenly she stares before her--as a divine inspiration comes to her. Her eyes light up with a wide, ecstatic fire.

Two shot: ANN and JOHN. ANN turns and glances up at JOHN's face.

ANN
(tensely)
John!

She takes his face in her two hands and turns it to her.

ANN
John, look at me. You want to be honest, don't you? Well, you don't have to die to keep the John Doe idea alive! Someone already died for that once! The first John Doe. And He's kept that idea alive for nearly two thousand years.

Close shot: BERT, his WIFE and SOURPUSS. The cynical expression on BERT's face begins to soften.

ANN'S VOICE
(with sincere conviction)
It was He who kept it alive in <u>them</u>--and He'll go on keeping it alive for ever and always! For every John Doe movement these men kill, a new one will be born!

Two shot: ANN and JOHN. JOHN remains grimly unmoved. ANN continues.

ANN
(ecstatically)
That's why those bells are ringing, John! They're calling to us--not to give up--but to keep on fighting! To keep on pitching! Oh, don't you see, darling? This is no time to give up!

Several flashes: To intercut with ANN's speech--one of BERT; his WIFE; CONNELL; D. B.

Med. shot: Toward ANN and JOHN. ANN's strength is slowly waning.

ANN
You and I, John, we can--
(suddenly)
No, John, if you die, I want to die, too!
(weakly)
Oh, I love you so--

Her strength leaves her--and as her eyelids slowly shut, she collapses limply in his arms.

Med. shot: Of BERT's group, as they react to this. BERT stares, profoundly moved.

Med. shot: JOHN and ANN--as he stares bewildered, at ANN at his feet. Mechanically, he reaches down and lifts her in his arms.

BERT'S VOICE

Mr. Doe ...

JOHN vaguely becomes aware of BERT's presence and glances toward him.

Med. shot: BERT, his WIFE and SOURPUSS.

BERT

(his voice choked--haltingly)

You don't have to--Why, we're with you, Mr. Doe. We just lost our heads and acted like a mob. Why, we ...

BERT'S WIFE

(jumping in)

What Bert's trying to say is--well--we need you, Mr. Doe. There were a lot of us didn't believe what that man said.

Close-up: Of JOHN--as he listens to her, expressionless.

WIFE'S VOICE

We were going to start up our John Doe Club again whether we saw you or not.

Med. shot: BERT, his WIFE and SOURPUSS.

WIFE

Weren't we, Bert?

BERT nods.

WIFE

And there were a lot of others that were going to do the same thing. Why, Mr. Sourpuss even got a letter from his cousin in Toledo, and . . .

SOURPUSS

(joining--eagerly)

Yeah, I got it right here, Mr. Doe!

Close-up: Of JOHN. The bewildered look in his eyes has vanished. It is now replaced by an expression of softness and understanding.

WIFE'S VOICE

(choked)

Only--only it'll be a lot easier with you. Please--please come with us, Mr. Doe!

JOHN remains standing, thoughtful.

Med. shot: Of BERT's group. They all look supplicatingly at him.

Close-up: Of JOHN. He stares at BERT's group and, shifting his gaze, looks at D. B. and his crowd. Then, turning back to BERT, his eyes light up and something of a warm smile appears on his face.

Full shot: As JOHN, having decided on his course, starts forward with ANN in his arms. The church bells chime loud and victoriously.

Med. shot: Around BERT. Their eyes brighten ecstatically as JOHN walks toward them. They all speak at once.

BERT'S GROUP
(ad-lib)
Mr. Doe!
She'll be all right!
We've got a car downstairs ...

They follow JOHN out, chattering excitedly. Only CONNELL and the COLONEL remain.

COLONEL
Long John!

Close up. Of CONNELL. He glares at D. B. defiantly.

Close-up: Of D. B. awe-stricken by the scene he has witnessed.

Med. shot: CONNELL and the COLONEL.

CONNELL
(to D. B.--defiantly)
There you are, Norton! The people! Try and lick that! Come on, Colonel.

They exit, arm in arm, as the music swells--suggesting emergence from darkness and confusion to light and understanding.

Fade out.

Notes

1. "Lavender and old lace" is a Riskinism for "old hat" or old-fashioned.

2. "A stick" is a printer's composing stick; a stickful is the amount of type a stick might hold.

3. The Ladies' Auxiliary and the Junior Auxiliary were well-known terms for organizations of civic-minded ladies, often from the upper classes. Riskin deprecatingly refers to the similarly inclined Junior Leaguers in *Platinum Blonde.*

4. A "wing" is the arm a baseball pitcher throws with, especially in 1920s and 1930s parlance.

5. The "bush leagues" are the minor leagues of professional baseball.

6. A "doohickey" is any unidentified gadget or trinket.

7. The "Community Chest" is a voluntary charitable federation, succeeding World War I "War Chest" organizations, based primarily in U.S. cities and spearheaded by civil leadership of financiers, industrialists, and merchants.

8. Joe Doakes was another synonym for John Doe. Both had British derivations. John Doe was used for legal purposes as the name of any anonymous plaintiff, versus defendant Richard Roe, in any court case.

9. A "jitterbug" was a fan of jitterbug, jazz, or swing music.

10. This long dialogue sequence between Willoughby and Ann Mitchell, about her father and his dream, which extends into the airport lunchroom sequence, is missing in video prints of *Meet John Doe*. It may have been edited out after initial engagements.

11. A "fifth column" in 1941, when *Meet John Doe* was released, was a term with sinister implications for the audience. This is as close as Riskin came to identifying D. B. Norton as a Hitlerite demagogue in league with corrupt labor leaders, politicians, and media magnates—all of whom are represented at Norton's mansion meeting before the mass rally of John Does. "What the American people need is an iron hand!" exclaims Norton on that occasion.

The origins of the phrase were politically charged. "The term was first used in the Spanish Civil War, 1939, when a general of Franco's announced that he had four columns marching on Madrid and a fifth column (spies, propagandists, saboteurs) already within its walls" (from Joseph T. Shipley, *The Dictionary of Word Origins*, Littlefield, Adams and Co., 1967).

12. "Potter's Field" is "a name given (after Matt. xxvii.7) to a piece of ground used as a burial place for the poor and for strangers" (from *Oxford English Dictionary*, Clarendon Press, 1989).